The Evolution of Economic Thought

THIRD EDITION

The Evolution of Economic Thought THIRD EDITION

Jacob Oser
Utica College of Syracuse University

William C. Blanchfield
Utica College of Syracuse University

Harcourt Brace Jovanovich, Inc.

NEW YORK   CHICAGO   SAN FRANCISCO   ATLANTA

Library of Congress Catalog Card Number: 74-29371

ISBN: 0-15-525002-7

PRINTED IN THE UNITED STATES OF AMERICA

Preface

The study of the history of economic thought continues to grow as new ideas, new problems, and new values call for a reconsideration of basic issues and a reappraisal of older economists' theories.

In the third edition of *The Evolution of Economic Thought* we have added three major economists: Milton Friedman, Paul A. Samuelson, and Kenneth Arrow. To keep the book from becoming overpopulated as a result of these additions, we have dropped four less influential economists: Herman H. Gossen, A. Augustin Cournot, Francis A. Walker, and W. W. Rostow. Thus the book now deals with seventy-one economists instead of the seventy-two dealt with in the second edition.

In this edition we place greater emphasis on the interrelations among economists. We have enlarged upon the similarities and conflicts between Wilhelm Roscher and Gustav Schmoller; John A. Hobson, John Maynard Keynes, and Thorstein Veblen; Gustav Schmoller and Friedrich List; Karl Marx and Charles Darwin; Henry George and Alfred Marshall; Henry George and Friedrich Engels.

Also new to this edition are a discussion of Veblen's analysis of monopolistic competition, developed a whole generation before Edward Chamberlin's and Joan Robinson's presentations of the subject, and a section on the role American economists played in the early 1930s in anticipating the ideas of Keynes. We stress post-Keynesian economics and raise questions about the efficacy of the Keynesian prescriptions for economic stability. Finally, in view of the greater awareness today of the need for equal rights for women, we have added a section on John and Harriet Mill's study of the subjection of women.

The extensive quotations from original sources in this book are designed to give readers a first-hand acquaintance with the flavor and substance of history's major economic works and perhaps to whet their appetites so that they will turn to the original works for further reading.

As always, we welcome evaluations and suggestions from both teachers and students. An exchange of ideas and a challenge to traditional thinking offer the best hope for intellectual excellence.

JACOB OSER
WILLIAM C. BLANCHFIELD

Contents

List of Tables and Figures

Tables

Figures

1

Introduction

Our story of the evolution of economic thought will begin in the six-teenth century with mercantilism. Economic problems and economic thinking about them can of course be traced back to antiquity. But to discuss the economic ideas of the middle ages, the ancient Greeks, Romans, Egyptians, and those to be found in the Bible would make this book too long. Moreover, A.D. 1500 is a natural dividing line be-tween two epochs with vastly different economic characteristics. We can find a truly enormous range of economic conditions from A.D. 1500 back to 3000 B.C., when people began to record their history in picture language. But the whole epoch generally had these common characteristics: there was little trade, and most goods were produced for consumption in the community that produced them without first being sent to market; money and credit were therefore not widely used, although they existed in ancient times; strong national states and integrated national economies had not yet developed; and sys-tematic economic theorizing had not yet evolved to any considerable extent, nor had any schools of thought been formed.

During the period since 1500 we can also find highly divergent economic conditions from one time to another and from one place to another. Yet the general characteristics of this epoch differentiate it from the earlier period. Trade was expanding rapidly, with the great geographical explorations both resulting from this process and accel-erating it; the money economy increasingly superseded the natural or self-sufficient economy; national states and unified national econo-mies became a dominant force; and economic schools arose, repre-

senting unified and systematic bodies of thought and policy formation.

Finally, we shall be concerned with economic thinking only since
1500 because it deals with problems that are nearest to us in time,
because it is most relevant to current ideas, and because it conforms
to the modern trend toward the coherent organization of knowledge.

Economic thought is woven into the complex fabric of society, and
we should not wrench it out of its social context. It must be analyzed
and judged by the standards of the society out of which it grew, although this does not preclude our using the wisdom of hindsight to
judge it in relation to its time.

In economics, social relationships and institutions are probably as
important as individual efforts and accomplishments. That is why it
is worthwhile to examine society as a whole when looking at a set of
economic ideas. We can thereby better explain why certain theories
were brought forth, why they achieved some measure of popularity
or success, and why they declined and sometimes disappeared.

The Five Major Questions

As each important school of economic thought is introduced, five
major questions about it will be considered. This method will provide perspective on the school and the social background that produced it. Such a concise summary at the outset will help clarify the
main points as we study the ideas of the leading economists. The
study of the economists will illustrate the characteristics of the
schools with which they have been linked, and quotations from
their writings will indicate the flavor of their thinking.

What Was the Social Background of the School?

Here we will look at the social background that nurtured a system of
thought. The assumption is that economic theory developed in response to changes in the environment that drew attention to new
problems. Since ideas have historically grown out of contemporary
problems and issues, some knowledge of the times is essential if we
are to understand why people thought and acted the way they did. It
is true, of course, that many systems of thought exist simultaneously
in the heads of many individuals. People can spin out a wide multiplicity of ideas, ranging from the most sensible to the wildly fantastic—or so they seem to contemporaries. Ideas irrelevant to society
at the time they are presented wither and die, whereas those that are
useful and effective in answering at least some questions and in solv-

ing some problems are disseminated and popularized, thereby making their authors famous. An Adam Smith contributed much to economic thinking, but can anyone doubt that, had he never lived, the same ideas would have been forthcoming from someone else? Perhaps they would have come somewhat later. Perhaps they would not have been expressed so well or so clearly. Then thinking people would have stumbled about a bit more before they found themselves on the path that he so clearly laid out.

Smith made a great contribution precisely because his ideas answered the requirements of his time. If, for example, the theory of comparative advantage in international trade had been discovered in the feudal epoch, it would have been without significance in a world of local self-sufficiency with a minimum of trade. The dispute over the corn laws in England in the early 1800's brought forth the theory of rent. Had Keynes published *The General Theory of Employment, Interest and Money* in 1926 instead of in 1936, it probably would have attracted far less attention than it did. Clearly the social milieu in which ideas grow is important.

This point was well made by Wesley C. Mitchell, who wrote:

> Economists are prone to think their work is the outcome of a play of free intelligence over logically formulated problems. They may acknowledge that their ideas have been influenced by their reading and the teaching which they were wise enough to choose, but they seldom realize that their free intelligence has been molded by the circumstances in which they have grown up; that their minds are social products; that they cannot in any serious sense transcend their environment.
>
> To realize all this about themselves is important if students are to become properly self-critical; that is, if they are to realize the limits to which their vision is subject. But it is exceedingly difficult for a mind which has been shaped by a given environment not to take that environment as a matter of course, or to see that it is itself the product of transitory conditions and so subject to a variety of limitations. It is far easier to see such things in reference to other minds, and particularly in reference to minds which have been shaped by environments quite different from theirs.[1]

Many other economists, however, would disagree with—or would at least qualify—the idea that environmental forces are significant in shaping economic theory. Professor George J. Stigler may be allowed to speak for them:

[1] Wesley C. Mitchell, *Types of Economic Theory*, ed. by Joseph Dorfman, Vol. I (New York, 1967), pp. 36–37.

Every major development in economic theory in the last hundred years, I believe, could have come much earlier if appropriate environmental conditions were all that were needed. Even Keynes's *General Theory* could have found an evident empirical basis in the post-Napoleonic period or the 1870's or the 1890's. Perhaps this amounts only to saying— what is surely true and almost tautological—that the elements of an economic system which economists believe to be basic have been present for a long time. The nature of economic systems has changed relatively little since Smith's time.

Thus I assign a minor, and even an accidental, role to the contemporary economic environment in the development of economic theory since it has become a professional discipline. Even where the original environmental stimulus to a particular analytical development is fairly clear, as in Ricardo's theory of rent, the profession soon appropriates the problem and reformulates it in a manner that becomes increasingly remote from current events, until finally its origin bears no recognizable relationship to its nature or uses.[2]

What Was the Essence of the School?

Here we will make broad generalizations about the ideas of successive economic schools. The strength of such a procedure is that we can get at the heart of the matter very concisely. The weakness is that there will be exceptions that we cannot take up in detail. A succinct summary presents patterns of uniformity in the ideas of an epoch, but the exceptions may contain the seeds of ideas that will triumph in the future. Thus we will argue that mercantilists favored the accumulation of gold and silver; yet there were some among them that took an antibullionist position. They were overwhelmed and scarcely heard at first, but ultimately their ideas were vindicated. Similarly, the classical school believed in free foreign trade; yet Malthus, a classical economist, was a protectionist.

What Groups of People Did the School Serve or Seek to Serve?

If we assume that economic theory seeks answers to questions, it is important to know what questions are asked and who asks them. Questions that are dominant in the thoughts of one group may be insignificant to another. Theologians in the middle ages, for example, were very much concerned about the morality of charging interest for money lent out. With the passage of time this problem seemed less important. The merchant capitalists in their heyday asked, "How can a country best accumulate gold and silver?" The classical

[2] George J. Stigler, *Essays in the History of Economics* (Chicago, 1965), p. 23.

economists were more concerned with, "How can we increase production?" The Socialists wanted to know, "How can we best improve the condition of the working classes?" A system of ideas must fit the needs of all of society, or it must at least be acceptable to a powerful group that will try to defend, develop, and popularize it.

Most economic theorists assume that the self-interest of the individual is dominant and guides the economic process. Yet individual self-interest does not result in the chaotic condition of individuals going their own way in opposition to the rest of society, for individuals are guided by market, social, political, and ethical forces to cooperate with other people in organizing a reasonable working relationship with society. Moreover, they coalesce into groups because of social pressures, common interests and ideas, and natural gregariousness. Thus there are religious, political, aesthetic, social, economic, and other groups, each of which presents a unified outlook and program in its sphere of special interest. We are concerned here with groups of people who develop common economic ideas based partly on self-interest and partly on other considerations that help shape their concept of how an economy should be organized and in what direction it should move. We shall try to identify the groups that supported each school of thought and the groups to which each school appealed for support, successfully or unsuccessfully.

How Was the School Valid, Useful, or Correct in Its Time?

Here we have to find our way between two opposing dangers. One is the erroneous idea that thinkers of the past were wrong, naive, ignorant, or foolish—that we, being much wiser, have discovered the final truth. Thus, J. B. Say, writing over a hundred and fifty years ago, asked: "What useful purpose can be served by the study of absurd opinions and doctrines that have long ago been exploded and deserved to be? It is mere useless pedantry to attempt to revive them. The more perfect a science becomes the shorter becomes its history."

We reject this view, popular as it has been since Say expressed it. It applies more to the physical than to the social sciences. Because the physical universe has not changed perceptibly during recent centuries, the laws under which it operates have not changed much either. Since our scientific knowledge has grown, we have come closer to the truth. Nevertheless the history of physical science is meaningful. But society *has* changed, and with those changes we must expect new theories to explain it. A plausible theory or policy in the seventeenth century would be questionable three hundred years later.

The other extreme is to find every dominant idea of the past right, just, and good in its time. The possible validity of economic ideas must of course be related to their time and place, but they may have been wrong or unreasonable even when first presented. This critical approach may well be applied to current thinking also. When John Maynard Keynes implied that pyramid-building in ancient Egypt was a counterdepression measure, he was wrong, for he confused two different societies; public works in Egypt did not arise for the same reasons as ours. The writer who recently stated that mercantilists followed a full employment policy suffered from a similar confusion; mercantilists were primarily concerned, not with avoiding unemployment, but rather with pushing more and more men, women, and children into workshops. Concepts that are serviceable today may have been inapplicable in earlier times, and they may become inappropriate in the future; ideas that are widely accepted today may be erroneous or inappropriate, but they persist because of the difficulty of changing people's minds.

How Did the School Outlive Its Usefulness?

Ideas that were once useful can outlive their usefulness as social conditions change. The evolutionary approach to economic thinking recognizes that society is changing continually. As new problems arise new analyses become appropriate.

These five questions will be used as guides for presenting the historical background, the content, and the relevance of economic schools.

The Interrelationships of Economic Ideas

There has been a significant degree of continuity in economic thinking over the centuries. The founders of a new type of theory may draw upon the ideas of their predecessors and develop them further; or they may react in opposition to earlier ideas that stimulate their own thinking in new directions. These relations among different schools of thought are depicted graphically on pages 494–95.

It is remarkable that modern ideas can bear a certain similarity to long-abandoned and long-repudiated concepts of past epochs. For example, the mercantilists of the sixteenth to the eighteenth centuries were certain that the national economy could not be safely left to run itself. One of their major concerns as a goal of government regulation was how to promote the increased wealth of the nation; that is, they were concentrating on economic development. The mercantilist doctrines and policies were driven from the stage of history by Adam Smith and the classical school. But in modern times we have come back to the idea that the economy cannot be permitted to run itself under laissez-faire conditions. In addition, governments must exert themselves to promote economic development.

This is not to say that history moves in circles, and that we are back to where we were more than two hundred years ago. Conditions have changed completely since mercantilist times. The characteristics of the governments then and now are very different; the reasons for intervening in the economy have changed drastically; and the effects on different groups of people are not what they once were. The common people, for example, benefit very much more from government intervention today than they did before 1776.

History moves in spirals rather than in circles. Our theories and policies frequently do return to similar theories and policies of an earlier epoch; but they are on different planes under very different conditions. The differences are as significant as the similarities, and both are worth examining closely. This we try to do in the following chapters.

Bibliography

BLAUG, MARK, *Economic Theory in Retrospect*, 2d ed. Homewood, Ill.: Irwin, 1968.

MEEK, RONALD L., *Economics and Ideology and Other Essays: Studies in the Development of Economic Thought.* London: Chapman and Hall, 1967.

MITCHELL, WESLEY C., *Types of Economic Theory*, ed. by Joseph Dorfman. 2 vols. New York: Kelley, 1967, 1969.

ROGIN, LEO, *The Meaning and Validity of Economic Theory.* New York: Harper, 1956.

SCHUMPETER, JOSEPH A., *History of Economic Analysis.* New York: Oxford University Press, 1954.

SPENGLER, JOSEPH J. and WILLIAM R. ALLEN, eds., *Essays in Economic Thought: Aristotle to Marshall.* Chicago: Rand McNally, 1960.

SPIEGEL, HENRY WILLIAM, ed., *The Development of Economic Thought: Great Economists in Perspective.* New York: Wiley, 1952.

STARK, W., *The History of Economics in Its Relation to Social Development.* London: Routledge & Kegan Paul, 1944.

TAYLOR, OVERTON H., *A History of Economic Thought.* New York: McGraw-Hill, 1960.

2

The Mercantilist School

The type of economic doctrine known as mercantilism appeared between the middle ages and the period of the triumph of laissez faire. It can be dated roughly from 1500 to 1776, although the dates vary in different countries and regions.

Overview of Mercantilism

The Social Background of the School

The self-sufficiency of the feudal community slowly gave way to the new system of merchant capitalism. Cities, which had been growing gradually during the middle ages, became increasingly important. Trade flourished both within each country and between countries, and the use of money expanded. The discovery of gold in the Western Hemisphere facilitated the growing volume of commerce and stimulated theorizing about the precious metals. Great geographical discoveries, based in part on the development of navigation, were extending the sphere of commerce. Production was small-scale, but more and more the merchant stood between the producer and the consumer. Although they remained contemptible tradesmen in the eyes of the landed aristocracy, the merchant capitalists were becoming key figures in the world of business.

National states were rising, and the most powerful of them were acquiring colonies and spheres of influence. Economic rivalries between nations were intensified. A body of doctrine was required to supersede feudal concepts, to promote nationalism, to give new dignity and importance to the merchant, and to justify a policy of economic and military expansion.

The Essence of the Mercantilist School

The main principles of this school can be summarized as follows:

1. Mercantilists regarded gold and silver as the most desirable form of wealth. Some mercantilists even believed that the precious metals were the only type of wealth worth pursuing. All of them valued bullion as the means by which power and riches could be achieved. A surplus of exports from a country was therefore necessary if payments were to be received in hard money. Even if one's country were at war, goods would be exported to the enemy if they were paid for in gold.

Mercantilist writers in Austria, a silver-producing country, estimated that if mining silver exactly paid for its cost of production, the enterprise was as profitable to the state as a 100 per cent profit would be to a private person. If the silver sold for one-half its cost of production, the profit was 50 per cent, but in either case only the state could undertake the mining.

2. Mercantilists promoted nationalism. Of course all countries could not simultaneously enjoy a surplus of exports. Therefore one's own country should promote exports and accumulate wealth at the expense of its neighbors. Only a powerful nation could capture and hold colonies, dominate trade routes, win wars against rivals, and engage successfully in economic warfare. According to this static concept of economic life, there was a fixed quantity of economic resources in the world; one country could increase its resources only at the expense of another. The French essayist Michel de Montaigne wrote in 1580: "The profit of one man is the damage of another. . . . No man profiteth but by the loss of others."

Mercantilistic nationalism of course meant militarism. Strong navies and merchant fleets were an absolute requirement. Because fisheries were "nurseries for seamen," the mercantilists imposed "political Lent" on England in 1549. People were forbidden by law to eat meat on certain days of the week in order to ensure a domestic market for fish. This enactment was vigorously maintained for about a century, and it did not disappear from the statute book until the nineteenth century.

3. Mercantilists advocated the import of raw materials without tariffs if they could not be produced at home, protection for manufactured goods and raw materials that could be produced at home, and the restriction of the outward movement of raw materials. This emphasis

on exports, this reluctance to import, has been called "the fear of goods." The interests of the merchant took precedence over those of the consumer. Prices would be kept high and gold would accumulate. In 1615 Antoine de Montchrétien, the French playwright and economist, wrote the first book using the term "political economy"; in it he said: "He who wishes for good order in the arts and maintenance of their standing, must never decrease profits through abundance. The brightness of the lamp is dimmed if it be too plentifully filled with oil."

An act passed in 1565–66 during Queen Elizabeth's reign forbade the export of live sheep. The penalties for violating this law were the confiscation of property, a year in prison, and the cutting off of the left hand. The death penalty was prescribed for a second offense. The export of raw wool was prohibited and the same penalties were applied in a law enacted during the reign of Charles II (1660–85).

4. The merchant capitalists believed in dominating and exploiting colonies and in monopolizing colonial trade for their own benefit. They wanted to keep the colonies eternally dependent on and subservient to the mother country. If any benefits from the home country's economic growth and military power spilled over to the colonies, this was an accidental by-product of the policy of exploitation.

The English Navigation Acts of 1651 and 1660 were good examples of this policy. Goods imported into Great Britain and the colonies had to move in English ships, which included colonial ships, or in ships of the country where the goods originated. Certain colonial products had to be sold only to England, and others had to be landed in England before being shipped to foreign countries. Foreign imports into the colonies were restricted or prohibited. Colonial manufacturing was curbed or in some cases outlawed, so that dependent territories would remain suppliers of raw materials and importers of English manufactured goods.

5. To promote their business interests, mercantilists believed in free trade within a country; that is, they were opposed to internal taxes, tolls, and other restrictions on the movement of goods. However, they did not favor free internal trade in the sense of allowing anybody to engage in whatever trade he wished. On the contrary, mercantilists preferred monopoly grants and exclusive trading privileges whenever they could acquire them.

Tolls and taxes could throttle business enterprise. On the Elbe River in 1685 a shipment of sixty planks from Saxony to Hamburg required the payment of fifty-four planks at toll stations, and only six arrived at the destination. But at least with payments in kind, the total tolls had to be less than 100 per cent. If cash had been paid, the charges could have added up to much more than the original value of the goods.

6. Mercantilism favored a strong central government to enforce the regulation of business. The government granted monopoly privileges to companies engaged in foreign trade. Free entry into business at home was restricted in order to limit competition. Agriculture, mining, and industry were promoted with subsidies as well as tariffs. Methods of production and quality of goods were closely regulated so that a country would not get a bad name for its products in foreign markets, which would hamper exports. In other words, mercantilists did not trust the judgment and honesty of the individual merchant, and their common interest required that poor workmanship and shoddy materials be prohibited by the government.

A strong central government was therefore required to ensure uniform national regulation. Strong national governments were also necessary to achieve the goals discussed above: nationalism, protectionism, colonialism, and internal trade unhampered by tolls and excessive taxes.

7. Although mercantilism promoted wealth for the nation, it did not encourage wealth for the majority of its population. In fact, the mercantilists favored a large, hard-working population that would provide cheap labor and an abundance of soldiers and sailors ready to fight for the glory of the nation and the enrichment of their masters. Idleness and begging by able-bodied people were dealt with mercilessly, and thievery was severely punished. During the reign of Henry VIII in Great Britain (1509–47), seventy-two hundred thieves were hanged. In 1536 it was decreed that "sturdy vagabonds" should have their ears cut off, and death was the penalty for the third offense of vagabondage. In 1547 those who refused to work were condemned to be the slaves of whoever denounced them. A law passed in Queen Elizabeth's reign in 1572 decreed that unlicensed beggars of fourteen years or older were to be flogged and branded unless someone were willing to employ them; for a second offense they were to be executed unless someone would take them into service; for a third offense they were to be considered as felons and executed without mercy.

Bernard de Mandeville (1670?–1733), the Dutch philosopher, satirist, and medical doctor who settled in London, wrote:

In a free Nation where Slaves are not allow'd of, the surest Wealth consists in a Multitude of laborious Poor. . . . As they ought to be kept from starving, so they should receive nothing worth saving. . . . It is the Interest of all rich Nations, that the greatest part of the Poor should almost never be idle, and yet continually spend what they get. . . . The Poor should be kept strictly to Work, and that it was Prudence to relieve their wants, but Folly to cure them. . . . To make the Society happy and People easy under the meanest Circumstances, it is requisite that great Numbers of them should be Ignorant as well as Poor.

William Temple, in his *Essay on Trade and Commerce,* published in 1770, gave thoughtful consideration to full employment for children:

When these children are four years old, they shall be sent to the country workhouse and there taught to read two hours a day and be kept fully employed the rest of their time in any of the manufactures of the house which best suits their age, strength and capacity. If it be objected that at these early years, they cannot be made useful, I reply that at four years of age there are sturdy employments in which children can earn their living; but besides, there is considerable use in their being, somehow or other, constantly employed at least twelve hours in a day, whether they earn their living or not; for by these means, we hope that the rising generation will be so habituated to constant employment that it would at length prove agreeable and entertaining to them.[1]

What Groups of People Did the Mercantilist School Serve or Seek to Serve?

Obviously this doctrine served the merchant capitalists, and also the kings and their immediate followers. But it especially served those interests that were most powerful and entrenched and that had the most favored monopolies and privileges. In England, for example, the wool interests saw to it that importing printed calicoes was prohibited. In 1721 the use of printed calicoes was outlawed, but exports were allowed. It was not until 1774 that the domestic consumption of such cloth was permitted. In the late 1600's the law required the dead to be buried in woolen shrouds even though religious traditions required linens.

In France mercantilism had a stronger feudal flavor, and the entrenched monopolistic interests were even more successful in getting the government to intervene on their behalf. From 1686 to 1759 the production, import, and use of printed calicoes were prohibited. In armed conflicts and executions arising from the enforcement of these measures, it is estimated that sixteen thousand people died, and many more were sent to the galley ships.

[1] Edgar S. Furniss, *The Position of the Laborer in a System of Nationalism* (Boston, 1920), pp. 114–15.

A host of government officials, inspectors, judges, and enforcement officers also gained from mercantilist regulations. The French government (but not the English) received significant revenue from fines, concessions, and monopoly privileges sold to businessmen. Officials kept a percentage of the fines levied against violators of the many government regulations.

How Was the Mercantilist School Valid, Useful, or Correct in Its Time?

The arguments for bullionism, although exaggerated, made some sense in a period of transition between the predominantly self-sufficient economy of the middle ages and the money and credit economy of modern times. The rapid growth of commerce required more money in circulation, and banking was insufficiently developed to produce it. Wars were fought on a pay-as-you-go basis, and bullion provided a reserve that could be used to hire soldiers and pay for their upkeep, build ships, buy allies, and bribe enemies.

British trade with the Baltic region and the East Indies required international liquidity by way of precious metals. Great Britain produced little that could have been exported to these areas, and the latter would not accept sterling exchange because of the underdeveloped international money market. The British colonies were therefore tapped to yield silver and gold that could be used in payment for Baltic and East Indian wares. Before the development of international finance and multilateral trade, bullion was of major significance in making international payments.

Mercantilists were also aware that an influx of precious metals made tax collection easier. They knew that prices would rise, or at least would not fall, if the quantity of money increased as trade expanded. Not only was the volume of output expanding, but the self-sufficient household was being drawn into the market economy. More money was therefore needed to maintain the same volume of output. Mercantilists were aware of the quantity theory of money, but they usually overlooked the significance of the velocity of circulation.

Mercantilists understood that an increased quantity of money would lower the rate of interest, thereby promoting business. They also made a lasting contribution by overcoming the medieval ethical and religious scruples about usury.

Mercantilism permanently influenced prevailing attitudes toward the businessman. The medieval aristocracy had classed the man of business as a contemptible second-class citizen who was immersed in the muck of business and money. The mercantilists gave respectability and importance to the businessman, arguing that he enriched not only himself but also the kingdom and the king. The landed aristocrats were eventually allowed to participate in business ventures without losing their status and dignity. Ultimately they gave their children in marriage to the offspring of business families, thereby merging aristocratic lineages with great commercial fortunes.

Mercantilism made a lasting impact by promoting nationalism, a force that is very much alive today. Central government regulation was necessary when uniform weights, measures, coinage, and laws had to be imposed on local authorities; when production and trade had not yet developed enough to permit reliance on competition to give the consumer a wide choice of goods; when the risks of trade were high, and monopoly privileges may have been necessary to induce more risk-taking than would otherwise have occurred.

The privileged chartered companies, ancestors of the modern corporation, were promoted under mercantilism. They helped transform the economic organization of Europe, bringing in new goods, providing outlets for manufactured goods, and furnishing incentives to the growth of capital investment. By colonizing abroad they expanded the market economy.

Mercantilism made a permanent contribution by expanding the internal market, promoting the free movement of goods unhampered by tolls, establishing uniform laws and taxes, and protecting people and goods in transit within and between countries.

How Did Mercantilism Outlive Its Usefulness?

The growth of domestic and international banking overcame the need to rely so heavily on bullion and coin. The further expansion of the market economy revealed that real estate, factories, machinery, inventories of goods, and money in checking accounts were more important items of wealth than gold and silver; and the industrial revolution replaced the merchant capitalist with the industrial entrepreneur as the key figure. Economic growth permitted society to rely on competitive forces and laissez faire rather than on promoting and regulating monopolies. The phenomenal progress made in science and technology enabled people to see that a country could become richer not only by impoverishing its neighbors but also by mastering the forces of nature more efficiently, investing more capital, and making labor more effective. It was also found that all countries could enrich themselves simultaneously. When progress was slow, world resources, output, and wealth seemed fixed, and attempts were made to redistribute wealth, as the mercantilists did, in favor of themselves. But when progress was rapid, new hopes were aroused for a great increase of wealth without conflicting interests upsetting world peace.

Even if the regulations protecting the quality of goods were once necessary, they ultimately became a barrier to progress. The rules published in France from 1666 to 1730 on textiles alone were printed in seven huge volumes. The dyeing manual, alleged to be the best set of instructions on dyeing technique at the time, contained 317 articles. These regulations prevented inferior methods from being used, but they also seriously impeded experimentation and development.

Mercantilist regulations to promote a large population, hard work, and low wages were no longer required by the late 1700's. After workers had been dispossessed from their tools and denied access to the land, laws to keep their wages down became unnecessary. During the industrial revolution, high birth rates and reduced death rates increased the population. Farmers, handicraftsmen, women, and children were driven into the factories by economic necessity, without government intervention.

The doctrines of mercantilism have not completely outlived their usefulness or disappeared from the current scene; there are ideas and policies extant today that resemble the ideas of two hundred and fifty years ago. Four examples will be cited here. First, during the 1960's there was great concern in the United States over the loss of gold because of the deficit in our international balance of payments. This concern was legitimate to the extent that it reflected not a blind love of gold but a condition that had sooner or later to be corrected. Second, nationalism in the new nations is an attempt to overcome the tribalism and local loyalties that impede economic development. Third, protectionism in these new nations can be defended as a precondition for industrialization. Fourth, developing countries frequently offer monopoly grants to encourage new investment. It seems reasonable to hold that if prospective entrepreneurs want monopoly concessions before they invest, then such monopoly grants are a prerequisite to growth. But it is important to realize that although these ideas and policies resemble mercantilist doctrines, they are being applied today in different circumstances, for different reasons, and in the context of social policies different from those of the mercantilist era.

Mun

Thomas Mun (1571–1641), the son of a dealer in textiles, acquired wealth and reputation while he was a merchant in the Italian and the Near Eastern trade. After he was elected a director of the East India Company, he became involved in a controversy over that company's policy of exporting gold and published a tract in its defense. In 1621 Mun published *A Discourse of Trade from England unto the East Indies,* in which he argued that as long as total exports exceeded total imports, the drain of specie from a country in any one branch of trade did not matter.

Around 1630 Mun wrote his famous exposition of mercantilist doctrine in *England's Treasure by Forraign Trade,* published posthumously by his son in 1664. The title of Chapter 2 of this work posed a key problem: "The means to enrich the Kingdom, and to encrease our Treasure." And how was the kingdom enriched? According to Mun, the answer lay neither in production nor in the accumulation of capital, but in a surplus of exports. Of course one must produce in order to export, but production is subservient to the grand design— the accumulation of gold. The first page of the two-page chapter on this issue reads as follows:

> Although a Kingdom may be enriched by gifts received, or by purchase taken from some other Nations, yet these are things uncertain and of small consideration when they happen. The ordinary means therefore to encrease our wealth and treasure is by *Forraign Trade,* wherein wee must ever observe this rule; to sell more to strangers yearly than wee consume of theirs in value. For suppose that when this Kingdom is plentifully served with the Cloth, Lead, Tinn, Iron, Fish and other native commodities, we doe yearly export the overplus to forraign Countries to the value of twenty two hundred thousand pounds; by which means we are enabled beyond the Seas to buy and bring in forraign wares for our use and Consumptions, to the value of twenty hundred thousand pounds; By this order duly kept in our trading, we may rest assured that the Kingdom shall be enriched yearly two hundred thousand pounds, which must be brought to us in so much Treasure; because that part of our stock which is not returned to us in wares must necessarily be brought home in treasure.

Mun argued that although England was rich, it could be still richer if it used waste land to grow hemp, flax, lumber, tobacco, and other things "which now we fetch from strangers to our great impoverishing." Exports should be carried in English ships to gain insurance and freight charges.

In defending the East India Company's export of gold to pay for goods, Mun argued for multilateral rather than bilateral trade:

> In some Countrys we sell our commodities and bring away their wares, or part in mony; in other Countreys we sell our goods and take their mony, because they have little or no wares that fits our turns: again in some places we have need of their commodities, but they have little use of ours: so they take our mony which we get in other Countreys: And thus by a course of traffick (which changeth according to the accurrents of time) the particular members do accommodate each other, and all accomplish the whole body of the trade.

Mun was looking at England's overall balance of trade rather than at its separate account with each foreign country. In addition, he thought that increasing imports would increase England's stock of precious metals if the wares were exported to some other country at a profit. Therefore the export of gold should be allowed to pay for the import of goods, which would in turn increase the total volume of goods exported.

> Why should we then doubt that our monys sent out in trade, must not necessarily come back again in treasure; together with the great gains which it may procure. . . . If we only behold the actions of the husbandman in the seed-time when he casteth away much good corn into the ground, we will rather accompt him a mad man than a husbandman: but when we consider his labours in the harvest which is the end of his endeavours, we find the worth and plentiful encrease of his actions.

But Mun's emphasis was on purchase and sale at a profit rather than on the processing of imported raw materials into manufactured goods, although the latter was mentioned in the case of textiles.

This emphasis on importing treasure led to the strange conclusion that trade at home could not enrich a country: "We may exchange either amongst our selves, or with strangers; if amongst our selves, the Commonwealth cannot be enriched thereby; for the gain of one subject is the loss of another. And if we exchange with strangers, then our profits is the gain of the Commonwealth."

In looking at the total balance of payments, Mun was astute enough to include invisible items. Over the centuries to the present day the major emphasis has usually been on the import and export of goods. Writing almost three and a half centuries ago, Mun listed the invisible items that should be included in an overall balance if it is to show whether "we prosper or decline in this great and weighty business." He included in the balance of payments the freight charges for shipping goods; ships lost at sea; insurance; money paid out in supporting foreign wars; international payment of bribes and funds for espionage "the receipt whereof notwithstanding is plain Treachery"; expenses of travelers; gifts to foreigners and ambassadors; interest on money; smuggling to evade tariffs; and contributions to religious orders that secretly send the money abroad. On this last point Mun added, "If this mischief cannot be prevented, yet it must be esteemed [estimated] and set down as a cleer loss to the Kingdome."

Malynes

Gerard Malynes (died 1641) was born in Antwerp of English parents. He returned to England and became a merchant in foreign trade. Not being very successful in this occupation, he spent a short term in a debtor's prison. He also served as the English commissioner of trade in Belgium, a government advisor on trade matters, an assay master of the mint, and a commissioner of mint affairs.

In *Lex Mercatoria: Or, The Ancient Law-Merchant,* published in 1622 and reissued in 1686, Malynes observed that trade was considered too low for the aristocracy yet too important for incompetents. He cited a long list of savants "and divers other Doctors and learned of the civil Law" who needed to deal with merchants.

> And hereunto they add a declaration of such as may trade; and by the contrary thereof, is to be understood who may not trade, *viz.* Clergymen, Noblemen, Gentlemen, Souldiers, Counsellors at the Laws both Ecclesiasticall and Temporal, publick Officers and Magistrates, frantick persons and mad-men, Youths under years, Orphans, Lunaticks and Fools, all these are exempted to be Merchants.

But Malynes sprang to the defense of merchants:

> For the maintenance of Traffick and Commerce is so pleasant, amiable and acceptable unto all Princes and Potentates, that Kings have been and at this day are of the Society of Merchants: And many times, notwithstanding their particular differences and quarrels, they do nevertheless agree in this course of Trade, because Riches is the bright Star, whose height Traffick takes to direct it self by, whereby Kingdoms and Common-weals do flourish; Merchants being the means and instruments to perform the same, to the Glory, Illustration, and benefit of their Monarchies and States. Questionless therefore the State of a Merchant is of great dignity, and to be cherished; for by them Countries are discovered, familiarity between Nations is procured, and politick experience is attained.

The regulation of goods to assure good quality was defended by Malynes in a section of *Lex Mercatoria* headed "Benefits which will arise by the true making of Clothes in England, according to the Statute made in the fourth year of His Majesties raign of Great Britain":

> The Cloth being truly made, will be more vendible beyond the Seas, where many complaints are daily made of the false making thereof; . . . hereby traffick will increase for the general good of the Realm, and his Majesties Custom will be duly payed, according to the said Statute, and all will tend to the glory of God, and honour of the King, in all Equity and Justice to be observed in all well-Govrened Commonweals.

Whereas most mercantilists wanted a large population that would work hard for low wages, Malynes had an almost Malthusian fear of overpopulation:

> For unless the three Impostumes of the World, namely Wars, Famine, and Pestilence, do purge that great Body, all Kingdoms and Countreys become very populous, and Men can hardly live in quiet, or without danger. Merchants therefore seeking to discover new Countreys, are much to be commended and cherished.

The mercantilist idea that more money in a country would raise prices and thereby stimulate good business was developed by Malynes as follows:

> Plenty of Mony maketh generally all things dear, and scarcity of Mony maketh generally things good cheap: Whereas particularly Commodities are also dear or good cheap, according to plenty or scarcity of the Commodities themselves, and the use of them. Mony then (as the blood in the body) constraineth the Soul which infuseth life: for if Mony be wanting, Traffique doth decrease, although Commodities be abundant and good cheap: And on the contrary, If Monies be plentiful Commerce increaseth, although Commodities be scarce, and the price thereof is thereby more advanced.

Davenant

Charles Davenant (1656–1714), the son of poet and dramatist Sir William Davenant, spent much of his life in various government posts having to do with taxes, imports, and exports. He was also a member of Parliament.

Davenant has been called an enlightened mercantilist, an eclectic who tried to blend the old and the new, a man who foreshadowed more of the argument of laissez faire than any other influential mercantilist. So he was. But an examination of his writings indicates that in some respects he was an orthodox mercantilist.

He developed the following bullionist argument in *An Essay on the East-India Trade* (1696):

> I have often wonder'd upon what Grounds the Parliament proceeded in the Act for Burying in Woollen: It Occasions indeed a Consumption of Wooll, but such a Consumption, as produces no advantage to the Kingdom. For were it not plainly better, that this Wooll made into Cloth, were Exported, paid for, and worn by the Living abroad, than laid in the Earth here at home. And were it not better, That the Common People (who make up the Bulk and are the great Consumers) should be bury'd in an old Sheet, fit for nothing else, as formerly, than in so much new Wooll, which is thereby utterly lost. . . . For it is the Interest of all Trading Nations whatsoever, that their Home-Consumption should be little, of a Cheap and Foreign Growth, and that their own Manufactures should be sold at the highest Markets, and spent Abroad; since by what is Consum'd at Home, one loseth only what another gets, and the Nation in General is not at all the Richer; but all Foreign Consumption is a clear and certain Profit.

In *An Essay on the Probable Means of Making the People Gainers in the Balance of Trade* (1699) Davenant argued that a kingdom can reap the benefit of the entire value of an exported product if it is made from domestic raw materials. If raw materials are imported and the product exported, then the net profit is the difference between the two values.

In *Discourses on the Publick Revenues, and on the Trade of England* (1698) Davenant expressed a preference for wars fought within a country rather than abroad:

> A Foreign War must needs drein a Kingdom of its Treasure. . . . *France,* from the time of *Charles* IX to the Reign of *Harry* IV, had a continual Civil War in its Bowels, and was often ravag'd by Armies from *Spain* and *Germany;* but this War exporting no Treasure, did not Impoverish the Kingdom.

In the same work Davenant called for government regulation of business because merchants were not to be trusted:

> There is hardly a Society of Merchants, that would not have it thought the whole Prosperity of the Kingdom depends upon their single Traffick. So that at any time, when they come to be Consulted, their Answers are dark and partial; and when they deliberate themselves in Assemblies, 'tis generally with a byass, and a secret Eye to their own Advantage. . . . And 'tis now to be apprehended, That they who stand pos-

sess'd of the ready Cash, when they discover the Necessities of other People, will, in all likelihood, prompted by their Avarice, make a use of it very destructive to their Fellow-Subjects, and to the King's Affairs, if not prevented by the Care and Wisdom of the State.

Davenant was enlightened enough to say that the wealth of a country is what it produces, not its gold or silver. Trade governs money rather than the other way around. Wealth invested in ships, buildings, manufactures, furniture, apparel, and so forth, constitutes riches as much as coins and bullion do. He favored a surplus of exports because he believed that when the quantity of money increases, interest rates fall, land values rise, and taxes increase. But too much gold and silver can be detrimental, as it was in Spain, where affluence caused neglect of the arts and manufactures. Davenant defended both the Navigation Acts and multilateral trade. In other words, he maintained that whenever possible a nation should enforce bilateralism between itself and its colonies, excluding foreigners from trading there, but that multilateral trade is desirable among equals.

Colbert

Jean Baptiste Colbert (1619–83) represents the heart and soul of mercantilism, which is called Colbertism in France. He was the French Minister of Finance from 1661 to 1683 under Louis XIV. In spite of his modest origin (he came from a family of dry-goods merchants) he rose to a position of great power, often by unscrupulous means. Matching his unbounded ambition was a tremendous capacity for work and attention to the most minute details of his office.

Colbert was a bullionist who believed that the strength of a state depends on its finances, its finances rest on its collection of taxes, and tax revenues in turn are greatest if money is abundant. He favored expanded exports, reduced imports, and laws preventing the outflow of bullion from the country.

As an arch-nationalist and militarist, Colbert held that there are four professions that are useful for great purposes: "Agriculture, trade, war on land, and that on sea." Colonies are desirable as markets for French goods and as sources of raw materials, and a big navy and merchant marine are essential. He felt that one nation can become richer only at the expense of another, because the volume of trade, the number of ships engaged in commerce, and the production of manufactured goods are all relatively fixed. Commerce is therefore a continual and bitter war among nations for economic advantage.

Colbert did his best to facilitate internal trade. He tried to give France a uniform system of weights and measures but was rebuffed by feudal localism and tradition and the vested interests of the church and the nobility. He unsuccessfully opposed tolls on the movement of goods, internal customs barriers, and excessive local taxes. He subsidized the construction of the Canal of Languedoc, which joined the Atlantic and the Mediterranean. By enforcing the feudal system of compulsory labor of peasants on the roads, the *corvée,* he made himself thoroughly hated; but fifteen thousand miles of roads were surfaced.

Government regulation of business, which had a strong feudal flavor in France, was an important feature of Colbert's policies. Reflecting the prevailing feudal contempt for businessmen, Colbert considered them a shortsighted, selfish, grasping lot who sacrifice the national interests to their own profit. The quality of goods and methods of production were thus closely regulated to attain uniformity, protect the consumer, and earn a good name for French goods in foreign markets. Monopoly privileges and subsidies were offered for new industries, especially those that were difficult and expensive to establish. But the system could be abused, and some monopolies were granted to raise money for the state or to endow favorite courtiers.

Despite his contempt for men of business, Colbert had laws passed that permitted aristocrats to participate in commerce without losing their status and privileges. An edict of 1669 declared: "We desire that a gentleman shall have the right to participate in a company and take a share in merchant vessels, so long as he does not sell at retail."

Colbert favored a large, hard-working, poorly paid population. No child, he thought, was too young to enter industry, and the state should enforce child labor. He remarked in 1665 that "experience has always certainly shown that idleness in the first years of a child's life is the real source of all the disorders in later life." In a decree of 1668 he commanded that all the inhabitants of Auxerre send their children into the lace industry at the age of six, or pay a penalty of thirty *sous* per child.

Colbert regarded monks, nuns, lawyers, and officials as unproductive idlers, and he tried to reduce their number. Attempts were made to curb religious feelings and limit religious institutions. He canceled seventeen holy days, leaving only twenty-four (in addition to Sundays) when work ceased.

In an edict of 1666, people were exempted from taxes for a number of years if they married early. Every father of ten living children was also exempted from taxes. (Interestingly enough, sons who died in the armed forces were counted as living, but priests, nuns, and monks were not counted.) This law was revoked in 1683 because of widespread fraud.

It remained for the French Revolution of 1789 to abolish feudal rights, internal tolls and tariffs, special privileges, and local power. The practice of openly selling offices was discontinued, taxes were equalized, and weights and measures were standardized on the basis of the metric system. These steps opened the way for great advances in French commerce, industry, and agriculture.

Petty

Sir William Petty (1623–87) was a mercantilist who offered some new ideas that foreshadowed classical economics.

Before he was sixteen he had mastered Latin, Greek, French, mathematics, astronomy, and navigation. The son of a poor clothier, he achieved great wealth, fame, and honor. This is an example of the upward mobility that was slowly becoming possible in seventeenth century Britain. During his busy life he was a sailor, a physician, a professor of anatomy, an inventor, a surveyor, a member of Parliament, a promoter of iron and copper works, an experimental shipbuilder, an author, a statistician, and a large landowner.

We shall discuss first his mercantilist views and then those of his ideas that anticipated Adam Smith's.

Petty's Mercantilist Views

In *A Treatise of Taxes and Contributions* (1662) Petty was concerned with "this supernumerary 100" unemployed out of a thousand people for whom there was food enough in the nation; he complained that they starved, begged, or stole. For the last the penalty was sometimes hanging or exile. But he was opposed to these remedies: "I think 'tis plain, they ought neither to be starved, nor hanged, nor given away." Indigent people should be employed working on roads, making rivers navigable, planting trees, building bridges, mining, and manufacturing. But true mercantilist that he was, Petty added: "Now as to the work of these supernumeraries, let it be without expence of Foreign Commodities, and then 'tis no matter if it be employed to build a useless Pyramid upon *Salisbury Plain*, bring the Stones at *Stonehenge* to *Tower-Hill*, or the like." He was a harbinger of Keynes's theory that in both ancient and modern times building pyramids was an antidote to unemployment!

How would these public works be paid for? By taxes. Since people were concerned with their relative incomes as compared with their neighbors', a proportional tax would not matter so long as the money was spent within the country:

> Let the Tax be never so great, if it be proportionable unto all, then no man suffers the loss of any Riches by it. For men (as we said but now) if the Estates of them all were either halfed or doubled, would in both cases remain equally rich. For they would each man have his former state, dignity and degree; and moreover, the Money leavied not going out of the Nation, the same also would remain as rich in comparison of any other Nation.

Petty favored a large population because he recognized increasing returns to governing, which would reduce unit costs of governing a larger population; but he failed to see decreasing returns to labor in farming: "Fewness of people, is real poverty; and a Nation wherein are Eight millions of people, are more than twice as rich as the same scope of Land wherein are but Four; For the same Governours which are the great charge, may serve near as well, for the greater, as the lesser number."

In *A Treatise of Taxes and Contributions* Petty expressed his enthusiasm for the mercantilist version of "full employment." The argument in favor of a poll tax was succinct: "It seems to be a spur unto all men, to set their Children to some profitable employment upon their very first capacity, out of the proceed whereof, to pay each childe his own Poll-money."

He also was against hanging thieves, but hardly from humanitarian motives:

> Why should not insolvent Thieves be rather punished with slavery then death? so as being slaves they may be forced to as much labour, and as cheap fare, as nature will endure, and thereby become as two men added to the Commonwealth, and not as one taken away from it; for if *England* be under-peopled (suppose by half) I say that next to the bringing in of as many more as now are, is the making these that are, to do double the work which now they do; that is, to make some slaves.

In his analysis of foreign trade Petty expressed views ahead of his time. He favored freer foreign trade, partly to circumvent smuggling. But he wanted imported consumer goods taxed so that they "may be made somewhat dearer then the same things grown or made at home, if the same be feasible." Imports of raw materials and tools ought to be "gently dealt with"—only lightly taxed. He opposed laws prohibiting the export of money, but in *Political Arithmetick* he deplored the money paid to foreigners for shipping, the money paid to Hollanders for their fishing trade "practised upon our Seas," and the money spent on imported commodities that could be manufactured in England.

Petty as a Forerunner of Classical Economics

Petty was a pioneer statistician. In the preface of *Political Arithmetick*, written from 1672 to 1676 and first published in 1690, he stated: "Instead of using only comparative and superlative Words, and intellectual Arguments, I have taken the course . . . to express my self in Terms of *Number, Weight, or Measure.*" He made some rash calculations. For example, he wanted to know the number of people in Ireland in 1641, before the rebellion against Cromwell's England had been crushed. Since one-third more oxen, sheep, butter, and beef were exported in 1664 than in 1641, he concluded that there were one-third more people in 1641 than in 1664! But this lapse does not detract from the fact that he was a founder of the science of statistics.

In the same work he pointed out the economies of division of labor. He also noted that "there is much more to be gained by Manufacture than Husbandry, and by Merchandize than Manufacture." This is mercantilist thinking, but he placed more emphasis on manufacturing than did most of his contemporaries.

In *Verbum Sapienti*, probably written in 1667 and first published in 1691, Petty de-emphasized the importance of the quantity of money. He recognized that the velocity of circulation, as well as the quantity, is important. If payments are made weekly rather than quarterly, less money will do the same work. He even suggested that there might be too much money as well as too little. "For Money is but the Fat of the Body-politick, whereof too much doth as often hinder its agility as too little makes it sick." He recommended the sale of surplus gold abroad to prevent harm at home.

In *A Treatise of Taxes and Contributions* Petty arrived at a primitive theory of rent:

> Suppose a man could with his own hands plant a certain scope of Land with Corn, that is, could Digg, or Plough, Harrow, Weed, Reap, Carry home, Thresh, and Winnow so much as the Husbandry of this Land requires; and had withal Seed wherewith to sowe the same. I say, that when this man hath subducted his seed out of the proceed of his Harvest, and also, what himself hath both eaten and given to others in exchange for Clothes, and other Natural necessaries; that the remainder of Corn is the natural and true Rent of the Land for that year.

This analysis of rent as the surplus from land was a real advance in economic thinking. But Petty did not separate the return to capital from the return to land—an error easy to commit in the 1600's, when capital investments in tools and fertilizer were insignificant. Nor did he show rent to be a differential return arising at the extensive and intensive margins of cultivation. But he did realize that land near a market yielded a higher rent because the cost of transporting the produce was lower.

Petty's reflections on capital remind one of Böhm-Bawerk's later theory. In *The Political Anatomy of Ireland,* written in 1672 and first published in 1691, Petty wrote:

> We must make a Par and Equation between Art and Simple Labour; for if by such Simple Labour I could dig and prepare for Seed a hundred Acres in a thousand days; suppose then, I spend a hundred days in studying a more compendious way, and in contriving Tools for the same purpose; but in all that hundred days dig nothing, but in the remaining nine hundred days I dig two hundred Acres of Ground; then I say, that the said Art which cost but one hundred days Invention is worth one Mans labour for ever, because the new Art, and one Man, perform'd as much as two Men could have done without it.

Very unmercantilist was Petty's emphasis on production rather than on exchange.

Petty developed a labor theory of value, saying that labor is the father and land the mother of wealth. In *A Treatise of Taxes and Contributions* he said that the value of a bushel of corn will be equal to that of an ounce of silver if the labor necessary to produce each is the same.

Petty's groping for a theory of value that determines price initiated a new line of reasoning. His ideas were to be extended and improved by economists who followed.

Bibliography

COLE, CHARLES W., *Colbert and a Century of French Mercantilism.* 2 vols. New York: Columbia University Press, 1939.

DAVENANT, CHARLES, *Discourses on the Publick Revenues, and on the Trade of England.* 1698.

FURNISS, EDGAR S., *The Position of the Laborer in a System of Nationalism.* Boston: Houghton Mifflin, 1920.

HECKSCHER, ELI F., *Mercantilism,* 2d ed. 2 vols. London: Allen and Unwin, 1955.

JOHNSON, E. A. J., *Predecessors of Adam Smith.* New York: Prentice-Hall, 1937.

MALYNES, GERARD, *Lex Mercatoria: Or, The Ancient Law-Merchant.* 1686. [Written in 1622.]

MUN, THOMAS, *England's Treasure by Forraign Trade.* New York: Macmillan, 1895. [Written c. 1630.]

PETTY, WILLIAM, *Economic Writings,* ed. by Charles H. Hull. 2 vols. Cambridge, Eng.: The University Press, 1899.

VINER, JACOB, *Studies in the Theory of International Trade.* New York: Harper, 1937.

3

The Physiocratic School

The physiocrats appeared in France toward the end of the mercantilist epoch. The beginning of this school can be dated at 1756, when Quesnay published his first article on economics in the *Grande Encyclopédie*. The school may be said to have ended in 1776 with the downfall of Turgot from his high office and the publication of Smith's *Wealth of Nations*. But the influence of the physiocrats lasted well beyond the two decades during which they led the world in economic thinking.

Overview of the Physiocrats

The Social Background of the School

Physiocracy was a reaction to mercantilism and to the feudal characteristics of the old regime in France, yet it could not completely escape the medieval concepts that pervaded French society.

The minute government regulation of production, even specifying the required threads per inch of cloth, may once have promoted good order and high quality, but it certainly imprisoned production in a strait jacket that did not allow for experimentation, improvement of production methods, or changing consumer tastes. A corrupt and extravagant government made equitable enforcement of the rules impossible. The growth of business enterprise and increasing competition made such rules unnecessary.

French industry was retarded in its development by the local authorities who imposed internal tolls, taxes, and tariffs, thereby impeding the movement of goods. French agriculture was burdened by the conditions enforced by the landowning nobility. Peasants were subject to taxes on land and cn the profits of farming while the nobility and the clergy were exempt from such taxes. Taxes varied from year to year, depending on the whim of the collector and the wealth of the peasants. Incentives to accumulate wealth and expand investments were thereby seriously impaired. Peasants had to pay dues to the lord when they inherited a holding or when they transferred it through sale. They had to do business with and pay heavy charges to the lord's millers, bakers, and winepressers. The nobles had the right to hunt game across the cultivated fields of their peasants, and game laws prohibited weeding and hoeing if young partridges would be disturbed by this. The hated feudal *corvée*, revived by Colbert and perpetuated after him, forced the peasants and their draft animals to work without pay on the public roads, largely for the benefit of others.

For centuries the French government and the authorities in the towns had subjected the grain trade to a bewildering maze of regulations. Even the little freedom allowed to other kinds of trade was denied to the grain trade. The export of grain from France was prohibited—a typically feudal law that was more concerned with maintaining adequate supplies than with good business and high prices. But exceptions were granted in years of plenty. Special permits to individuals might be issued indicating the quantity and kind of grain to be exported, and frequently its destination. Within the kingdom grain and flour could not be moved from one province to another without permission. To receive a license to sell grain between provinces one had to submit all details of the enterprise to an inspector; after the grain had been transported, a certificate had to be produced showing that the consignment had actually reached the prescribed destination. Within each province grain was subject to further restriction. Laws specified where grain was to be sold and what the price should be. In times of shortage, marketing was compulsory to prevent hoarding. Tolls as well as regulations impeded the grain trade, so that in one area surpluses might glut the warehouses while a few miles away people starved.

The guilds, which arose during the medieval period, persisted longer in France than in England. Their character changed as national authorization and regulation of guilds replaced the authority of towns or feudal lords. But until 1789 guilds impeded the free entry of labor into certain occupations, restricted and regulated output, fixed prices, and opposed competition from other towns and from abroad. Guild jurisdictional quarrels and litigation dragged on for generations and centuries at great cost in time and money. The annual cost of legal battles to the Paris guilds during the middle 1700's was eight hundred thousand to one million livres. Goose-roasters and poulterers quarreled for half a century until the latter were finally restricted to the sale of uncooked game. The successful roasters then turned on the cooks, who had won a triumph over the sauce-makers. A three-hundred-year litigation between the secondhand-clothes dealers and the tailors in Paris had not been resolved by 1789, when the Revolution swept the guilds aside and destroyed them.

It was through this corrupt and decayed society that physiocratic ideas swept like a fresh breeze.

The Essence of the Physiocratic School

The concepts of the physiocratic school may be summarized as follows:

1. The physiocrats developed the idea of natural order. According to this belief human societies were subject to laws of nature such as those that govern the physical world. It was therefore necessary that all human activities be brought into harmony with these laws of nature. The object of all scientific study was to discover the laws to which all the phenomena of the universe were subject. In the economic sphere the chief natural right of people was to enjoy the fruits of their own labor, provided that such enjoyment was consistent with the rights of others. Governments, it followed, should never extend their interference in economic affairs beyond the minimum absolutely essential to protect life and property and to maintain freedom of contract.

2. The physiocrats were opposed to almost all feudal, mercantilist, and government restrictions. Vincent de Gournay (1712–59), an inspector of the quality of products as guaranteed by trademarks, is credited with uttering the famous phrase "laissez faire, laissez passer." In effect this means freedom of business enterprise at home and free trade abroad. Gournay was not the only high functionary of the mercantilist system who became an adherent of laissez faire as a result of his experiences.

3. The physiocrats thought that industry, trade, and the professions were useful but sterile, simply reproducing the value consumed in the form of raw materials and subsistence for the workers. Only agriculture (and possibly mining) was productive, for it produced a surplus, a net product above the costs of production.

4. They thought that since only agriculture produced a surplus, which went to the landowners, only the landowners should be taxed. All taxes imposed on others would be passed on to them anyway. A direct tax was preferable to indirect taxes, which increased as they were passed along to others.

5. They opposed the consumption of luxury goods as being a barrier to the accumulation of capital.

6. They looked at the economy as a whole and analyzed the circular flow of wealth.

What Groups of People Did the Physiocratic School Serve or Seek to Serve?

The peasants stood to gain from the ideas of the physiocrats if all the onerous obligations to the landowners could be shaken off; but if the physiocrats had had their way, the peasants would have become wage laborers on large farms. Businessmen would be better off if all restrictions on production and the movement of goods were removed. By advocating the doctrine of laissez faire the physiocrats were promoting industry, even though this was not their intention. With their emphasis on agriculture they were interested in encouraging freer internal grain trade and in stimulating the export of farm products and the import of manufactured goods.

The physiocrats especially favored capitalistic farms employing wage labor and advanced techniques. These progressive farms could be found mostly in northern France. Big producers with surpluses for sale would be helped by the physiocratic emphasis on agricultural development and free internal trade in grain. The tax on the surplus produced in agriculture would have lowered land values and hurt the landowning nobility instead of the current or prospective farm entrepreneurs who paid rent. The nobility and clergy were exempt from the multiplicity of taxes that burdened the commoner landowners, but a single tax applicable to all land in production would have helped these nontitled owners.

The physiocrats tried to placate the nobility by genuinely defending their right to own land and receive rent. Unlike Henry George (see Chapter 18), who later wanted to abolish private landownership by taxing away all economic rent, the physiocrats thought that a tax taking one-third of the economic surplus would be sufficient. This, they believed, would not redistribute wealth from the rich to the poor, because the landowners paid all taxes in any case; rather, converting the taxes from an indirect to a direct basis would lower the overall burden. In their view the nobility would be aided if their program were enacted; but this belief was erroneous, for it was based on their faulty analysis that all taxable surpluses could come only from the land.

How Was the Physiocratic School Valid, Useful, or Correct in Its Time?

Before the industrial revolution, industry was in a sense sterile because of the extremely low productivity of a handicraft economy. This was especially true of France during the last decades of the *ancien régime*. Production of luxury items for conspicuous consumption in a miserably poor country could not help but appear "sterile." Farming, however, sometimes produced bountiful harvests in spite of the primitive methods of cultivation. Agriculture often provided the surpluses that could be saved and reinvested to initiate a rising rate of economic growth and industrial development not only in France but also in the United States, Germany, Japan, Russia, and other countries.

In promoting laissez faire, the physiocrats were opposing obstacles to capitalistic economic development. They unwittingly promoted the French Revolution, which swept away the numerous obstacles to progress. By emphasizing the productivity of agriculture, they were getting away from the older concept that only commerce produces and augments wealth; the physiocrats emphasized production rather than exchange as a source of wealth. They also favored direct taxes rather than the indirect taxes that pervaded and corroded French society of their time. They argued for capital accumulation through reduced consumption by the wealthy. By looking at society as a whole and analyzing the laws that governed the circulation of wealth and goods, they founded economics as a science.

How Did Physiocratic Doctrine Outlive Its Usefulness?

This school was always wrong, however, to consider industry and trade as sterile; the more industry and trade developed in France, the more conspicuously incorrect the physiocratic analysis became. This fault led to another error—the belief that only landowners should be taxed because only land could yield a surplus. Wealthy industrialists could smile as they endorsed the doctrine that they should not be made to pay taxes because they added nothing to wealth. This anomaly inspired Voltaire to write a lively satire, *The Man with Forty Crowns;* in it the wealthy financier who escapes taxation taunts the poor farmer who pays taxes for both, although his income is only forty crowns.

The physiocrats extolled the capitalistic farmer as the key figure in French economic development, but here they were wrong on two counts. First, the industrialist became the most important in the economic growth of the country, while the relative importance of agriculture declined. Second, the small peasant farmer rather than the large farm entrepreneur became typical in France. Had the land remained in the hands of the nobility, a tax on land ownership would have curbed wasteful luxury consumption. But when the small peasants got the land after the Revolution, they would have borne the bulk of the tax burden.

There was something in the physiocratic doctrine for almost everybody to object to. The tax farmers [1] and the financiers could take exception to the attacks directed against them. The manufacturers and merchants disapproved of their callings being described as sterile, and, more important, they were threatened by the agitation for terminating their exclusive privileges. The guilds rejected physiocratic demands for their abolition; the landowners of course disapproved of the single tax on land rent; and the common people rightly feared that the doctrine of the "just price" would make their bread dearer. It was not surprising, therefore, that the physiocratic regime under Louis XVI was ousted after being in office less than two years.

Physiocracy did not entirely disappear by 1776; some of its ideas have lived on to the present day. The principle that only land should be taxed was justified by David Ricardo's theory of rent, although Ricardo did not advocate this idea. John Stuart Mill did propose that future increases in rent be taxed by the state taking all capital gains from increases in the price of land. Henry George, writing more than a hundred years after the physiocrats, proposed that all economic rents be confiscated. The doctrines of the physiocrats live on where some governments, either nationally or locally, tax land but not people's improvements on the land; these governments may also tax away increases in land rents. Finally, the modern physiocrats are those who glorify agriculture, who claim that it is more important than any other type of economic activity, that it is the "backbone of the nation," and that farming is somehow cleaner, healthier, and more virtuous than other occupations.

---

[1] Persons who had bought a "franchise" allowing them to collect for themselves as much in taxes as they could squeeze from the inhabitants of a given area. They paid a fixed annual fee to the government at the beginning of each tax year, and they kept everything they collected above that.

Quesnay

François Quesnay (1694–1774) was the founder and leader of the physiocratic school. He was the son of a landed proprietor. Trained to be a physician, he made a fortune through his skill in medicine and surgery. He rose to be the court physician of Louis XV and Madame de Pompadour. In 1750 he met Gournay and soon became more interested in economics than in medicine. He and his school hoped to transform the king into an "enlightened despot" as the instrument of peaceful reform. In an encyclopedia article in 1757 Quesnay noted that small farms were incapable of using the most productive methods; he favored large farms managed by "entrepreneurs," thereby anticipating the large agricultural enterprises of our time.

To Quesnay society was analogous to the physical organism. The circulation of wealth and goods in the economy was like the circulation of blood in the body. The term "physiocracy" was derived from the Greek, meaning the rule of nature. Fundamental to physiocratic theory was the belief that laws made by people should be in harmony with natural laws.

The dauphin of France once bemoaned to Quesnay the difficulties of the office of king (which he was not destined to live to assume). "I do not see," said Quesnay, "that it is so troublesome." "What then," asked the dauphin, "would you do if you were king?" Said Quesnay, "Nothing." Asked who would govern, Quesnay replied cryptically, "The Law." He meant natural law.

His famous *Tableau Economique,* constructed for the king of France in 1758 and revised in 1766, depicted the circular flow of goods and money in an ideal freely competitive economy. This was the first systematic analysis of the flow of wealth on what later came to be called a macroeconomic basis. Economists such as Smith, Marx, and Keynes, who favored the description of economic activities in terms of large aggregates, paid tribute to Quesnay for originating this approach. Neoclassical economists, on the other hand, who prefer the microeconomic approach of describing activities in terms of individuals, have tended to belittle him.

A simplified account of Quesnay's *Tableau Economique* is presented in Figure 1. Quesnay assumed that the land is owned by landlords but is cultivated by tenant farmers, who are therefore the only really productive class. The product that the tenant farmers create has to satisfy not only their own needs but also the needs of the landowners (including the king, the church, the public servants,

Figure 1 Quesnay's *Tableau Economique*

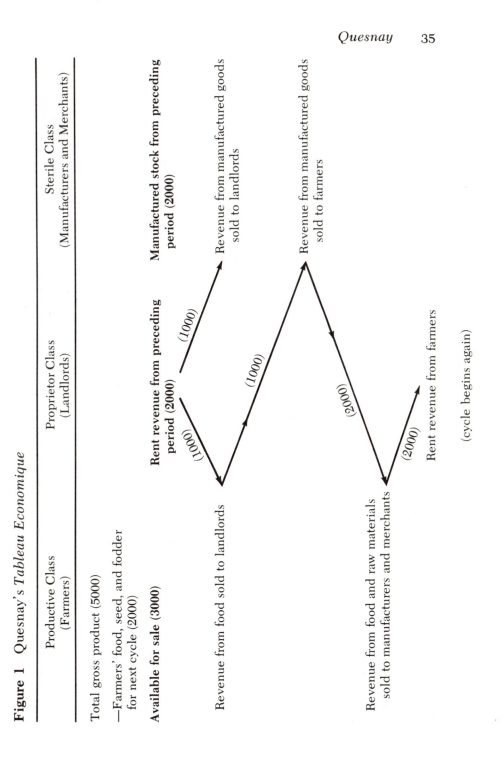

Productive Class (Farmers)	Proprietor Class (Landlords)	Sterile Class (Manufacturers and Merchants)

Total gross product (5000)

—Farmers' food, seed, and fodder for next cycle (2000)

Available for sale (3000)

Rent revenue from preceding period (2000)

Manufactured stock from preceding period (2000)

Revenue from food sold to landlords

(1000)

(1000)

Revenue from manufactured goods sold to landlords

(1000)

(1000)

Revenue from manufactured goods sold to farmers

(2000)

Revenue from food and raw materials sold to manufacturers and merchants

(2000)

Rent revenue from farmers

(cycle begins again)

and others who depend on the income of the landowners). In addition, the output of the farmers provides for the needs of the sterile class (manufacturers and merchants). The *Tableau* shows how the net product circulates among the three classes and how it is reproduced each year.

The farmers start with an annual gross product of 5000 million livres. Of this, 2000 million livres are immediately deducted as necessary expenses of production to provide food, seed, and fodder for the farmers themselves. The landlords start with 2000 million livres in rent paid by the farmers during the preceding cycle. The manufacturers and merchants start with 2000 million livres' worth of goods manufactured during the preceding cycle.

The landlord class uses its 2000 million livres to buy 1000 million in food from the farmers and 1000 million in manufactured goods from the sterile class. The farmers use the 1000 million revenue received from the landlords to buy that amount of manufactured goods from the sterile class. This group has now sold its stock of manufactured goods for 2000 million livres, which it uses to buy food (1000 million) and raw materials (1000 million) from the farmers. At the end of the cycle the farmers have 2000 million livres in food, seed, and fodder, which they will use to produce 5000 million livres' worth of farm products in the next year; the landlords have food, manufactured goods, and a claim for 2000 million in rent from the farmers' next harvest; and the sterile class has 2000 million livres' worth of food and raw materials, which it will use to produce 2000 million livres' worth of manufactured goods.

Apparently the manufacturing class is left with no manufactured goods for its own consumption. Ronald L. Meek has a solution to this problem—a solution that he says is implied in the physiocratic writings.[2] The number of people in the sterile class is one-half that in the productive class, and therefore their total personal consumption must be one-half that of the productive class. The productive class consumes 1000 million livres' worth of food and 1000 million livres' worth of manufactured goods. The sterile class must therefore consume 500 million livres' worth of each. Since it possesses 1000 million livres' worth of food, it can export half of it to pay for imported manufactured goods.

Quesnay's *Tableau Economique* foreshadowed national income analysis and laid the foundation for statistical work to describe an

---

[2] Ronald L. Meek, *The Economics of Physiocracy* (Cambridge, Mass., 1963), pp. 282–83.

economy. Quesnay himself tried to estimate the values of annual output and other aggregates. The table also explicitly conveyed the concept of equilibrium within the economy as a whole, for if one of the interdependent variables changed, others would also change.

It was odd that Quesnay called nonagricultural production sterile yet did not question the right of the proprietors of the soil to receive rent. It is nature that produces the surplus, he said, and not the worker. The landowners therefore have a right to the surplus product, which goes with the title to the land. Because their class makes the original capital investment in land to make it productive, they are entitled to the surplus product. Yet Quesnay's proposal (later taken up by Henry George) to tax only landowners was in effect an attack on their interests.

Quesnay argued that "an excess of luxury in the way of decoration may quickly ruin with magnificence an opulent Nation." He preferred spending on raw materials. This was the language of economic growth at a time when the aristocracy was wasteful in its consumption and industry was far less important than agriculture and mining as a means to accumulate wealth for further investment.

The medieval flavor of Quesnay's thinking was apparent in his glorification of agriculture and in his belief that the government should fix the rate of interest, although Turgot and Du Pont opposed usury laws. Quesnay also favored the "just price," but he relied on a free market rather than on regulation by authority to achieve it.

Turgot

Anne Robert Jacques Turgot (1727–81) was born of a noble family of Normandy that for several generations had furnished the state with able administrative officials. As a younger son he was educated for the church, but after receiving his theological degree he decided instead to enter the judicial and administrative service. He rose in the ranks of government service until he became the finance minister of France in 1774; this had been Colbert's office a hundred years earlier. In less than two years in office he introduced antifeudal and antimercantilist measures in keeping with physiocratic ideas. Freedom of internal grain trade was ordered, and guilds and privileged trading corporations were abolished. He ended the oppressive *corvée*—the twelve or fifteen days of unpaid labor required of the peasants yearly to maintain roads, bridges, and canals; in its place he enacted a tax that all landowners had to pay. He cut government spending drastically. The credit of the government was so improved that he was able to borrow a huge sum from the Dutch at four per cent instead of the previous seven to twelve per cent. Annual government interest payments were reduced by almost two-thirds. Turgot advocated a tax on the nobility, freedom of all people to choose their occupations without restriction, universal education, religious liberty, and the creation of a central bank such as Napoleon was to create in 1800.

When Turgot was accused of pushing his reforms too quickly, he replied, "What would you have me do? The needs of the people are enormous, and in my family we die of gout at fifty." He came to power at 47, lost power at 49, and died at 54, having suffered terribly from gout.

Turgot's edicts and plans aroused the most determined opposition from all kinds of people. The nobility hated him because he wanted to levy all taxes upon the land. The clergy distrusted him as an unbeliever who not only rarely went to Mass but urged religious liberty! The financiers resented his getting loans abroad at lower rates of interest than they charged. The members of the king's entourage were angered by his opposition to their extravagance, their sinecures, and their pensions. The tax farmers who paid lump sums to the government for the right to collect as much taxes as they could were infuriated because he wanted to replace them with government tax collectors. The rich and entrenched bourgeoisie objected to his interference with their monopolies. He was dismissed by Louis XVI because of the protests of the court, Marie Antoinette, and the other powerful people who were losing privileges because of his enlightened policies. His reforms were canceled at once, not to be reintroduced until the French Revolution of 1789. In fact, Turgot's downfall made the French Revolution inevitable, for it proved that the old regime could not reform itself.

Turgot, like other physiocrats, believed in an enlightened absolutism, and he looked to the king to carry through all reforms. He opposed the interference of parliaments in legislation. A plan that he submitted to the king would have allowed only land proprietors to form the electorate. The elected parliament would have had no legislative powers but would have administered taxation, education, and poor relief. Obviously Turgot and the other physiocrats had their roots in the old feudalistic regime of France, and they were reformers rather than revolutionaries. But the reactionary French regime could not tolerate their reforms.

In *Reflections on the Formation and the Distribution of Riches*, written in 1766, Turgot developed a theory of wages in which he held that competition among workers lowers the wage to the minimum subsistence level—an early statement of what was later called the "iron law of wages." Only farmers produce a surplus, which is used to feed and provide raw materials for all society.

> He [the husbandman] is, therefore, the sole source of the riches, which, by their circulation, animate all the labors of the society; because he is the only one whose labor produces over and above the wages of the labor. . . . It is the earth which is always the first and only source of all wealth; it is that which as the result of cultivation produces all the revenue.

Turgot, using the term *entrepreneur*,[3] said that the rich capitalist tenant farmers are most capable of efficient farming because they have the capital to invest in the soil. They receive profits and the return of their investment with interest. Entrepreneurs reinvest most of their profits and savings, but not so the landlords:

> It is even generally true that, although the proprietors have a greater superfluity, they save less because as they have more leisure, they have more desires and more passions; they regard themselves as more assured of their fortunes; they think more about enjoying it agreeably than about increasing it: luxury is their inheritance.

In a letter to David Hume written in 1767 Turgot stated that taxes imposed on other groups were passed on to the landowner. A tax on wage earners would not be passed on unless wages were above the minimum subsistence level, but this was a temporary deviation. Wages at the minimum subsistence level could not be lowered by taxes because workers had to earn enough to survive. A direct tax on the landowners was therefore preferable to indirect taxes, which were passed on to them. This inevitable incidence of taxes was also best for economic development, as implied above, because the landlords wasted their share of the revenue.

Turgot was a persistent advocate of economy in government. In a letter to Hume in 1766 he wrote:

> You also know as well as I do what is the great end of all governments on earth: submission and money. The object is, as they say, to pluck the bird without making it squeal; now it is the proprietors who are squealing, and one has always preferred to attack them indirectly, because then they notice the harm only when the thing has become an accepted fact.

[3] Before him, Quesnay used the term in his encyclopedia article on "Grain," 1757. Richard Cantillon wrote about the entrepreneur before 1734.

Turgot's greatest contribution in the realm of economic theory was in correctly presenting the law of diminishing returns. This appeared in his *Observations sur un Mémoire de M. de Saint-Péravy,* written about 1767. It can never be imagined, he said, that a doubling of expenditure in agriculture will double the product.

> The earth's fertility resembles a spring that is being pressed downwards by the addition of successive weights. If the weight is small and the spring not very flexible, the first attempts will leave no results. But when the weight is enough to overcome the first resistance then it will give to the pressure. After yielding a certain amount it will again begin to resist the extra force put upon it, and weights that formerly would have caused a depression of an inch or more will now scarcely move it by a hair's breadth. And so the effect of additional weights will gradually diminish.

It is curious that Adam Smith, who knew Turgot and his work, did not apply the law of diminishing returns to agriculture. The doctrine was later used in the analysis of rent by Ricardo, Malthus, and Edward West; but none of them recognized, as Turgot did, that when successive units of variable factors of production are added to land (the fixed factor), there may be increasing returns at first.

Du Pont de Nemours

Pierre Samuel du Pont de Nemours (1739–1817) became an intimate disciple of Quesnay, Turgot, and others of the physiocratic school. He served as inspector general of manufactures under Turgot, and he fell with Turgot's fall in 1776. He met Jefferson while the latter was Minister to the Court of Louis XVI on the eve of the French Revolution, and they remained good friends until Du Pont's death. Like Jefferson, Du Pont rooted his faith in the soil, and he sought the regeneration of humankind through the elimination of artificial economic and intellectual restrictions.

Du Pont advocated free trade in his *Exportation et Importation des Grains* (1764). The name for this school was taken from his book, *La Physiocratie* (1767). He served as editor, journalist, secretary, biographer, and friend of the school and its leaders.

Du Pont helped negotiate the treaty with England that recognized American independence in 1783. He also drew up the conditions of the treaty of commerce signed by England and France in 1786. He supported the French Revolution and was elected president of the revolutionary constituent assembly in 1790. As a moderate he favored the establishment of liberty without ending the monarchy. This antagonized the radicals, and he went into hiding. He was found, arrested, and imprisoned during the Reign of Terror, and only the death of Robespierre saved him from the guillotine.

In 1797 Du Pont's house was sacked by a mob, and two years later he emigrated to the United States. Jefferson asked him to design a system of national education, which was published in 1800. He returned to France, where he lived and held high offices from 1802 to 1815. Then he went again to the United States. He died near Wilmington, Delaware, where his son, Eleuthère Irénée du Pont de Nemours, had founded a small gunpowder mill in 1802.

Bibliography

BEER, MAX, *An Inquiry into Physiocracy.* London: Allen and Unwin, 1939.

HIGGS, HENRY, *The Physiocrats.* New York: Langland Press, 1952. [Originally published in 1897.]

MEEK, RONALD L., *The Economics of Physiocracy.* Cambridge, Mass.: Harvard University Press, 1963.

TURGOT, ANNE ROBERT JACQUES, *Reflections on the Formation and the Distribution of Riches.* New York: Macmillan, 1898. [Originally published in 1766.]

WARE, NORMAN J., "The Physiocrats: A Study in Economic Rationalization." *American Economic Review*, XXI, No. 4 (December 1931), 607–19.

4

The Classical School:
Forerunners

The beginning of the classical school can be dated at 1776, when Adam Smith's great book was published. It ended in 1871, when both W. Stanley Jevons and Carl Menger published works expounding what was later called neoclassical theory. There were, of course, advanced thinkers before Smith, including the physiocrats, who influenced his thinking. But this in no way detracts from the tremendous contribution he made.

Overview of the Classical School

The Social Background of the School

In the seventeenth century England was behind Holland in commerce and behind France in manufacturing production. But by the middle of the eighteenth century England was supreme in commerce as well as in industry. Both classical political economy and the industrial revolution developed first in England. Smith and his contemporaries, living during the early stages of the industrial revolution, could not adequately identify the significance of this phenomenon and the direction its development would take; such wisdom is usually displayed through hindsight. But they were aware of the substantial growth of manufacturing, trade, inventions, and the division of labor. This growth of industry led to increased emphasis on the industrial aspect of economic life in current thinking.

By 1776 England, as the most efficient and powerful country in the world, could afford free trade without fear of foreign competition. As

English entrepreneurs became stronger, they no longer had to rely on government subsidies, monopoly privileges, and tariff protection. And with entrepreneurs becoming numerous enough to make monopoly agreements difficult to achieve and enforce, competition could be depended upon to establish moderate prices and ensure products of good quality. Many mercantilist practices were breaking down under the upsurge of business activity, which spread in every direction.

The world of business and industry required a free, mobile, poorly paid, hard-working labor force. Before the final triumph of classical political economy, national and local governments had regulated labor and working conditions. Sometimes labor was protected, but more frequently employers were favored. Wages in England had been regulated by local justices of the peace for centuries, with wage ceilings usually being imposed. This practice died out by 1762, however, for wages could be kept low enough merely through the workings of a free-market economy. Enclosures drove tenant farmers and even many small owners off the land, and wage earners lost their right of access to the village pastures and woodlands where they could once graze a cow or a pig and gather fuel. Handicraftsmen lost their independence as the putting-out system of the merchant, and later the factory system, turned them into wage laborers. A high birth rate and a falling death rate increased the population, and child laborers and bankrupt Irish peasants who came to England also augmented the labor force. Government steps to keep wages down were therefore no longer necessary, and laissez faire became the gospel of the businessman. Now it was the workers' turn to try, unsuccessfully, to invoke government regulation to establish minimum wages.

In eighteenth-century England one could still find vestiges of the feudal-agrarian paternalism that included some concern for the welfare of the poor. But it was giving way to the harsh, impersonal relations of early industrialism. Taxes on the landowners provided funds for poor relief, paid through local government. Parishes tried to unload their poor on the parishes from which the indigents had originally come. Even preventive expulsion—removal of the poor to their home parishes if they might some day need relief—was practiced. Dying people or women in labor were rushed to their places of birth by officials who wished the present or future financial burdens to fall elsewhere. Preventive expulsion, which impeded the mobility of the population, was abolished in 1795; after that only people actually on relief could be sent back to their original parishes. And in 1834 the poor laws were made so harsh that many people preferred to starve quietly at home rather than undergo the indignities of poor relief and workhouses.

The Speenhamland Law of 1795 provided that the poor should have a minimum income irrespective of their earnings. The family income was linked to the price of bread, and if earnings were below the prescribed level, allowances from taxes would be used to make up the difference. This system prevailed in most of the rural areas and in some manufacturing districts. When the Speenhamland system was ended in 1834, a competitive labor market was fully established in England.

The Essence of the Classical School

Classical doctrine is frequently called economic liberalism. Its bases are personal liberty, private property, individual initiative, and individual control of enterprise, all resting on the laissez faire doctrine. The term "liberalism" should be considered in its historical context: Classical ideas were liberal in contrast to feudal and mercantilist restrictions on choice of occupation, land transfers, trade, and so forth. But we would hardly call a person liberal today if he or she advocated an unmodified laissez faire program.

The major features of this body of thought may be summarized briefly as follows:

1. The first principle of the classical school was laissez faire. That government is best which governs least. The forces of the free, competitive market guide production, exchange, and distribution. The economy was held to be self-adjusting and tending toward full employment without government intervention.

2. The classicists, with the important exception of Ricardo, emphasized the existence of a harmony of interests. By seeking his or her own interests, each individual serves the best interests of society.

3. The classicists emphasized the importance of all economic activities, especially industry. The mercantilists had said that wealth was derived from commerce; the physiocrats had seen in agriculture the source of all wealth. The classical school added industry to commerce and agriculture and regarded all three as productive.

4. The classical school made tremendous contributions by providing a method of analyzing the economy and the economic laws that operate within it.

5. Classical economists sought to promote maximum economic growth and development. The basis for this was their belief in the individual's innate desire to accumulate wealth as an end in itself. Hard work and limited consumption were the means to increase

one's capital. The drive for unlimited acquisition was justified by the claim that it was rooted in human nature.

6. The classicists looked at the economy as a whole—the macro-economic approach.

What Groups of People Did the Classical School Serve or Seek to Serve?

The classical school most directly served businessmen. It gave them respectability in a world that offered the greatest honors to the land-owning nobility and the gentry. Businessmen, especially indus-trialists, achieved a new status and dignity as the promoters of the nation's wealth, and entrepreneurs were assured that by seeking profit they were serving society. These doctrines ultimately led to more material benefits, for they helped create the political, social, and economic climate that promoted industry, trade, and profit.

In the long run classical economics served all society because the application of its theories promoted capital accumulation and eco-nomic growth. Historically speaking, we can apply the harmony-of-interests doctrine to classical theories. Somebody had to pay the heavy costs of industrialization; in Great Britain it was the wage earners who bore the heaviest share of the costs through long hours of hard work at low pay. But ultimately economic progress enabled them to improve their own position, and in this sense classical eco-nomics served them too. Although their slice of the total pie was rel-atively small, the growth of the pie benefited succeeding generations of workers along with all other groups.

How Was the Classical School Valid, Useful, or Correct in Its Time?

The classical doctrine was a rationalization of practices engaged in by enterprising men because they were profitable. It justified the overthrow of mercantilist restrictions, which had outlived their use-fulness. Competition was a rising phenomenon, and reliance upon it as the great regulator of the economy was a tenable viewpoint. Gov-ernments were notoriously wasteful and corrupt, and under the cir-cumstances, the less government intervention the better. By helping to remove the remnants of the feudal system, classical economics promoted business enterprise. For example, when feudal land laws were abolished and land could serve as security for credit, land-owners were able to raise large sums for investment in agriculture or industry.

When industrialization was beginning, society's greatest need was to concentrate resources on the maximum possible expansion of production. The elevation of the private sector over the public sector served this end admirably. Since consumers were generally poor and investment opportunities were seemingly unlimited, capitalists had every incentive to reinvest most of their profits. The outcome was a rapid expansion of output. But any growth of the public sector would have required increased taxation, thereby diverting resources from private capital formation.

Classical economics and the businessmen who endorsed it enlarged the market not only by achieving freer international trade but by promoting an urban labor force. Subsistence farmers would consume much of their own product while buying little in the market; urban laborers of the late 1700's, by contrast, might be compelled to reduce their total consumption to a level below that of the subsistence farmers, but the laborers would still buy much more in the market. The food supply was absorbed into the monetary sector of the economy, and the merchant and processor came between the farmer and the consumer.

The classical economists gave the best analysis of the economic world up to their time, far surpassing the analyses of the mercantilists and the physiocrats. They laid the foundation of modern economics as a science, and the generations that followed built upon their insights and achievements. Their emphasis on the division of labor, the gains from international trade, and economic development are still basically compatible with the goals that modern societies have set for themselves.

How Did the Classical School Outlive Its Usefulness?

The doctrine of laissez faire succumbed as business fluctuations shook capitalistic society to its core and as competition gave way to changing market structures characterized by quasi-monopoly, oligopoly, regulated industries, and so forth. The harmony-of-interests theory could no longer be defended when the concentration of wealth produced great disparity in bargaining power among individuals. Classical economists were frequently opposed to humane poor laws and factory acts, especially those that regulated the conditions of adult labor. The government was increasingly called upon to ameliorate social conditions and to regulate conflicting interests. Even where competition survived, it was not always deemed to be an efficient enough regulator of economic activities. Health laws, for instance, became more necessary with the growth of cities; in 1800 a small farmer's infected milk supply might sicken a few neighbors, whereas a century later contaminated milk could produce a massive epidemic. Obviously competition in the milk industry does not preclude strict government regulation.

Laissez faire was carried to absurd extremes by the advocates of classical economics. To cite but one example, the London *Economist* of July 13, 1850, criticized the "sanitary movement," which urged that the government require a pure water supply and proper sewage disposal. Even after sewage lines were built, owners of houses were not required at first to hook up to them. The *Economist* declared that poor housing and high urban death rates

> spring from two causes, both of which will be aggravated by these new laws. The first is the poverty of the masses, which, if possible, will be increased by the taxation inflicted by the new laws. The second is that the people have never been allowed to take care of themselves. They have always been treated as serfs or children, and they have to a great extent become in respect to those objects which the government has undertaken to perform for them, imbecile. . . . There is a worse evil than typhus or cholera or impure water, and that is mental imbecility.

It is doubtful that the classical economists were correct in assuming that the acquisitive spirit is a natural human inclination. People throughout the world in all epochs have not always thought and acted like eighteenth-century Englishmen. Some people in some periods of history have not been strongly driven to "better themselves." Beyond making a living, they have had sources of satisfaction other than growing rich.

Classical economists committed the error of thinking that what applied to contemporary England was valid everywhere for all time. When they predicted, for example, that rents would rise and the rate of profit would fall, they were belittling future technological change. Their enthusiastic endorsement of free trade was good for England, but it could have harmed underdeveloped countries then, as it might well do now. The classicists viewed economic laws as immutable, not to be tampered with or thwarted. They and their followers could not understand that economic laws, which are generalizations about tendencies, can be curbed, overcome, or redirected—that people can control economic life. Economic laws that are valid under laissez faire may become inoperative in a regulated economy; the classical school, however, did not admit that this was possible or desirable, for theirs was a static analysis.

The philosophy of natural law, so basic to classical economics, is no longer believed to be valid. We do not hold that natural laws will guide the economic system and the actions of people. Therefore the philosophical foundation for laissez faire has crumbled.

Classical economics was especially deficient in its analysis of demand, interest, and the role of money in a private enterprise system. Finally, classical economics with its labor theory of value led to socialist doctrines; it was therefore condemned as a pernicious theory by the defenders of private enterprise.

North

Sir Dudley North (1641–91), living during the height of the mercantilist period, struck hard at the heart of mercantilist doctrine. He was a wealthy merchant in the Turkish trade. Later he became commissioner of customs and then a treasury official. North has been called the world's first prominent free-trader.

His brief tract, *Discourses upon Trade,* was his only published work, appearing anonymously in 1691. Such caution was understandable in a merchant and high government official of a prominent family who did not conform to prevailing ideas. Decades later his brother hinted that the publication was deliberately suppressed. When Ricardo read a reprinted edition, he wrote: "I had no idea that any one entertained such correct opinions, as are expressed in this publication, at so early a period."

North emphasized that trade is not a one-sided benefit to whichever country realizes a surplus of exports, but rather an act of mutual advantage to both sides. Its object is not to accumulate specie but to exchange surpluses. A division of labor and international trade would promote wealth even if there were no gold and silver in existence:

> Trade is nothing else but a Commutation of Superfluities; for instance: I give of mine, what I can spare, for somewhat of yours, which I want, and you can spare. . . . He who is most diligent, and raiseth most Fruits, or maketh most of Manufactory, will abound most in what others make, or raise; and consequently be free from Want, and enjoy most Conveniences, which is truly to be Rich, altho' there were no such thing as Gold, Silver, or the like amongst them.

North repudiated the concept that wealth should be measured by a country's stock of precious metals. His emphasis was on business enterprise and accumulation. Here he struck at the theory rather than the practice of the mercantilists. But, understandably for his time, he did not include manufacturing in his list of productive activities.

Even taking its original meaning of "making by hand," manufacturing was relatively unimportant in the seventeenth century.

> No Man is richer for having his Estate all in Money, Plate, etc. lying by him, but on the contrary, he is for that reason the poorer. That man is richest, whose Estate is in a growing condition, either in Land at Farm, Money at Interest, or Goods in Trade: If any man, out of an humour, should turn all his Estate into Money, and keep it dead, he would soon be sensible of Poverty growing upon him, whilst he is eating out of the quick stock.
>
> But to examine the matter closer, what do these People want, who cry out for Money? I will begin with the Beggar; he wants, and importunes for Money: What would he do with it if he had it? buy Bread, etc. Then in truth it is not Money, but Bread, and other Necessaries for Life that he wants. Well then, the Farmer complains, for the want of Money; surely it is not for the Beggar's Reason, to sustain Life, or pay Debts; but he thinks that were more Money in the Country, he should have a Price for his Goods. Then it seems Money is not his want, but a Price for his Corn, and Cattel, which he would sell, but cannot.

The profound truth of the last paragraph has not been mastered by most people even today. If money is considered a measure of value, we want all the money we can get (if the effort of acquiring it is not too great). But if money is considered merely a means of payment, we want it only to part with it, except for working balances.

North observed that commerce among nations distributes the money supply according to the needs of trade:

> For it hath been observed, that where no Mints were, Trade hath not wanted a full supply of Money; because if it be wanted, the Coyn of other Princes will become currant, as in *Ireland,* and the *Plantations.*
> . . . Then let not the care of Specifick Money torment us so much; for a People that are rich cannot want it, and if they make none, they will be supplied with the Coyn of other Nations.

North argued for laissez faire and a harmony of interests in trading, both within each country and internationally. This was bold theorizing in an age of rampant nationalism.

> Now it may appear strange to hear it said, That the whole World as to Trade is but as one Nation or People, and therein Nations are as Persons. That the loss of a Trade with one Nation, is not that only, separately considered, but so much of the Trade of the World rescinded and lost, for all is combined together. That there can be no Trade unprofitable to the Publick; for if any prove so, men leave it off; and whereever the Traders thrive, the Publick, of which they are a part, thrives also. That to force Men to deal in any prescrib'd manner, may profit such as

happen to serve them; but the Publick gains not, because it is taking from one Subject, to give to another. . . . That Money is a Merchandize, whereof there may be a glut as well as a scarcity, and that even to an Inconvenience. That a People cannot want Money to serve the ordinary dealing, and more than enough they will not have. . . . In short, That all favour to one Trade or Interest against another, is an Abuse, and cuts so much of Profit from the Publick.

Although North believed that free trade would help both the traders and the country, he did not profess a crude harmony-of-interests doctrine. Indeed he saw that many special interests were profiting at the expense of the public by using the power of government to acquire special privileges. His idea that the authorities therefore should not support narrow private interests was quite contrary to mercantilist doctrine.

> Whenever Men consult for the Publick Good, as for the advancement of Trade, wherein all are concerned, they usually esteem the immediate Interest of their own to be the common Measure of Good and Evil. And there are many, who to gain a little in their own Trades, care not how much others suffer; and each Man strives, that all others may be forc'd, in their dealings, to act subserviently for his Profit, but under the covert of the Publick.
>   So Clothiers would have men be forc'd to buy their Manufacture; and I may mention such as sell Wool, they would have men forc'd to buy of them at an high Price, though the Clothier loseth. . . . And in general all those who are lazy, and do not, or are not active enough, and cannot look out, to vent the Product of their Estates, or to Trade with it themselves, would have all Traders forc'd by Laws, to bring home to them sufficient Prizes, whether they gain or lose by it.

North disagreed with the mercantilist concept that war and conquest enrich a country: "Money Exported in Trade is an increase to the Wealth of the Nation; but spent in War, and Payments abroad, is so much Impoverishment." By "payments abroad" he probably meant payments made without receiving an equivalent in return, as in the case of military subsidies to allies. Of what virtue is such an export of money if equivalent imports do not follow? These are antimercantilist views of the strongest kind, which many people would not endorse wholeheartedly even today.

Cantillon

Richard Cantillon (1680?–1734) was born in Ireland. He spent many years in Paris, becoming a wealthy banker and a successful speculator in stocks and foreign currencies. In 1734 he was robbed and murdered and his house was set afire, probably by a cook he had dismissed ten days earlier. His only book, *Essai sur la Nature du Commerce en Général*, was written between 1730 and 1734 and published in French in 1755. It may have been translated by Cantillon himself from his English manuscript, which was never found.

Cantillon developed a theory of value and price. His emphasis on the role of land and labor, on supply and demand, and on the fluctuations of price around intrinsic value make him a direct forerunner of classical economics.

> The Villagers come to Town on Market-Days to sell their produce and to buy the things they need. Prices are fixed by the proportion between the produce exposed for sale and the money offered for it. . . . When the price has been settled between a few the others follow without difficulty and so the Market-price of the day is determined. . . .
>
> The Price or intrinsic value of a thing is the measure of the quantity of Land and of Labour entering into its production, having regard to the fertility or produce of the Land and to the quality of the Labour.
>
> But it often happens that many things which have actually this intrinsic value are not sold in the Market according to that value: that will depend on the Humours and Fancies of men and on their consumption. . . .
>
> If the Farmers in a State sow more corn than usual, much more than is needed for the year's consumption, the real and intrinsic value of the corn will correspond to the Land and Labour which enter into its production; but as there is too great an abundance of it and there are more sellers than buyers the Market Price of the Corn will necessarily fall below the intrinsic price or Value. If on the contrary the Farmers sow less corn than is needed for consumption there will be more buyers than sellers and the Market Price of corn will rise above its intrinsic value.
>
> There is never a variation in intrinsic values, but the impossibility of proportioning the production of merchandise and produce in a State to their consumption causes a daily variation, and a perpetual ebb and flow in Market Prices.

Cantillon recognized the importance of the velocity of circulation of money, with a faster circulation requiring a smaller quantity of money:

> But it usually happens in States where money is scarcer that there is more Barter than in those where Money is plentiful, and circulation is more prompt and less sluggish than in those where Money is not so scarce. Thus it is always necessary in estimating the amount of money in circulation to take into account the rapidity of its circulation.

Cantillon used the term "entrepreneur" and emphasized the role of this figure in economic life. This was quite an innovation, because for a long time economists had theorized that the only factors of production were land, labor, and capital. Businessmen, Cantillon said, commit themselves to definite payments in expectation of uncertain receipts; this risk-taking is remunerated by profit, which competition tends to reduce to the normal value of the entrepreneurs' services. He analyzed interest as a reward for the risk taken in lending, based on profits that the entrepreneurs can make by borrowing and investing. Bankers, he pointed out, create credit, for if a hundred thousand ounces of gold are deposited with them, as much as ninety thousand can be lent out; such loans will not, of course, diminish the original demand deposit.

With one foot in the mercantilist camp, Cantillon opted for a surplus of exports as being good for business. But he did not believe that gold and silver mined at home would serve the same purpose. His emphasis was on the production of goods and their sale abroad, so that business would flourish. But he believed that an export surplus could not be maintained indefinitely; a self-balancing mechanism would wipe it out. His analysis of the equilibrium of forces that prevents a perpetual export surplus and his emphasis on the sale of goods rather than on the accumulation of gold came close to classical thinking.

Cantillon held that the discovery and exploitation of rich mines of gold and silver would raise domestic prices, rents, and wages. These increased costs would in turn promote imports to the detriment of domestic workers and manufacturers for money would flow out of the country. "The great circulation of Money, which was general at the beginning, ceases: poverty and misery follow and the labour of the Mines appears to be only to the advantage of those employed upon them and the Foreigners who profit thereby." That was what happened in Spain, he said.

But if the increase in money comes from a surplus of exports of goods, it enriches merchants and entrepreneurs and gives employment to workers. However, as money flows into the country and business prospers, consumption and prices rise, spending on imported luxury items grows, and the export surplus dwindles. The state begins to lose some branches of its profitable trade, and workmen leave the country.

This will gradually impoverish the State and cause it to pass from great power into great weakness. When a State has arrived at the highest point of wealth (I assume always that the comparative wealth of States consists principally in the respective quantities of money which they possess) it will inevitably fall into poverty by the ordinary course of things. The too great abundance of money, which so long as it lasts forms the power of States, throws them back imperceptibly but naturally into poverty. Thus it would seem that when a State expands by trade and the abundance of money raises the price of Land and Labour, the Prince or the Legislator ought to withdraw money from circulation.

No reliance on natural law or the automatic re-establishment of equilibrium!

Cantillon was mercantilistic—and probably realistic—in his emphasis on the uses of money in warfare:

If of two Princes who war upon each other for the Sovereignty or Conquest of a State one have much money and the other little money but many estates which may be worth twice as much as all the money of his enemy, the first will be better able to attach to himself Generals and Officers by gifts of money than the second will be by giving twice the value in lands and estates. Grants of Land are subject to challenge and revocation and cannot be relied upon so well as the money which is received. With money munitions of war and food are bought even from the enemies of the State. Money can be given without witnesses for secret service. Lands, Produce, Merchandise would not serve for these purposes, not even jewels or diamonds, because they are easily recognised.

This hardheaded businessman regretted that both nobles and monks lived in luxury and idleness. But nobles are a great ornament to the country, he pointed out, and during wartime they will at least use their retinues and horses for victory, "while the Monks are, as people say, neither useful nor ornamental in peace or war on this side of heaven." Furthermore, he said, in Catholic countries there are too many holy days, "which diminish the labour of the People by about an eighth part of the year."

Cantillon anticipated Malthus' views on population by saying that "Men multiply like Mice in a barn if they have unlimited Means of Subsistence."

A thread of physiocratic thought can also be detected in Cantillon. Writing a generation before Quesnay constructed his *Tableau Economique*, Cantillon stated:

Cash is therefore necessary, not only for the Rent of the Landlord, . . . but also for the City merchandise consumed in the Country. . . . The circulation of this money takes place when the Landlords spend in detail in the City the rents which the Farmers have paid them in lump sums, and when the Entrepreneurs of the Cities, Butchers, Bakers, Brewers, etc. collect little by little this same money to buy from the Farmers in lump sums Cattle, Wheat, Barley, etc.

Hume

David Hume (1711–76) was born in Scotland twelve years before his fellow countryman and friend Adam Smith. He entered the University of Edinburgh at the age of twelve and left at fifteen without taking a degree. Later, eminent as a philosopher, Hume was twice refused a chair in Philosophy at Edinburgh because of his skeptical spirit and unorthodox thinking. In fact Adam Smith was once nearly expelled from Oxford University because a copy of Hume's *A Treatise of Human Nature* was found in his rooms.

Hume spent his life as a tutor to a marquis and as a minor government official. Upon retirement he returned to his inherited estate, where he wrote prolifically. His fame as a historian derived from his multivolume *History of England,* which went through numerous editions; his reputation as an economist was established by his economic essays in *Political Discourses,* published in 1752. Of all the forerunners of classical economics, Hume came closest to the ideas of Smith. Had he written a complete and systematic treatise on economics, he would have ranked near the top as one of the founders of the science.

Hume's greatest contribution as an economist was in presenting what has since been called the price specie-flow mechanism. The mercantilists wanted to promote a surplus of exports in order to accumulate specie. In the somber view of Cantillon, this tactic was self-defeating, because if more specie were available, prices would go up and imports would increase. But to pay for the imports, money would be shipped abroad, leaving poverty and bankruptcy behind; therefore the government should prevent an excess of money. The physiocrats were basically unconcerned with foreign trade, except that they wished to permit the free flow of grain abroad. But Hume, who like Cantillon accepted the quantity theory of money, analyzed the mechanism of international equilibrium that would operate without government intervention. Laissez faire could prevail with happy results. In his essay "Of the Balance of Trade" (1752) Hume wrote:

Suppose four-fifths of all the money in GREAT BRITAIN to be annihilated in one night, and the nation reduced to the same condition, with regard to specie, as in the reigns of the HARRYS and EDWARDS, what would be the consequence? Must not the price of all labour and commodities sink in proportion, and everything be sold as cheap as they were in those ages? What nation could then dispute with us in any foreign market, or pretend to navigate or to sell manufactures at the same price, which to us would afford sufficient profit? In how little time, therefore, must this bring back the money which we had lost, and raise us to the level of all the neighbouring nations? Where, after we have arrived, we immediately lose the advantage of the cheapness of labour and commodities; and the farther flowing in of money is stopped by our fulness and repletion.

Again, suppose, that all the money of GREAT BRITAIN were multiplied fivefold in a night, must not the contrary effect follow? Must not all labour and commodities rise to such an exorbitant height, that no neighbouring nations could afford to buy from us; while their commodities, on the other hand, became comparatively so cheap, that, in spite of all the laws which could be formed, they would be run in upon us, and our money flow out; till we fall to a level with foreigners, and lose that great superiority of riches, which had laid us under such disadvantages?

The price specie-flow mechanism was the first force that Hume described as leading toward international equilibrium. This mechanism no longer works very well, of course, because now that the full gold standard has been abandoned everywhere, the quantity of money no longer depends on the flow of gold. Nor are prices flexible downward as they once were. Another objection to Hume's optimism in this analysis is that it ignores the relations between debtors and creditors within a country. The macroeconomic approach sometimes overlooks important problems within a particular sector of the economy.

Hume was aware of a second factor in promoting equilibrium in international trade—a factor that precedes price changes and gold movements. When exchange rates fluctuate between the gold points, an imbalance of trade tends to correct itself. In a footnote to "Of the Balance of Trade" Hume wrote:

There is another cause, though more limited in its operation, which checks the wrong balance of trade, to every particular nation to which the kingdom trades. When we import more goods than we export, the exchange turns against us, and this becomes a new encouragement to export; as much as the charge of carriage and insurance of the money which becomes due would amount to. For the exchange can never rise but a little higher than that sum.

An increase of imports, Hume emphasized, would stimulate exports. He was aware of the concept of elasticity of demand, saying that if duties on wine are lowered, the government will collect more revenue. But he did not realize that with an inelastic demand for a country's products abroad, a surplus of imports that would cause a price drop at home would not stimulate exports enough to produce equilibrium.

In "Of the Jealousy of Trade" (1758) Hume disputed the mercantilist concept that trading states are rivals, with one gaining only at the expense of the other:

> In opposition to this narrow and malignant opinion, I will venture to assert, that the encrease of riches and commerce in any one nation, instead of hurting, commonly promotes the riches and commerce of all its neighbours; and that a state can scarcely carry its trade and industry very far, where all the surrounding states are buried in ignorance, sloth, and barbarism.

He perhaps exaggerated the international harmony of interest, but this was a healthy antidote to the suspicion and the economic warfare of the eighteenth century.

Hume was egalitarian, for he assumed a diminishing marginal utility of added units of wealth. In his essay "Of Commerce" he wrote:

> A too great disproportion [of income] among the citizens weakens any state. Every person, if possible, ought to enjoy the fruits of his labour, in a full possession of all the necessaries, and many of the conveniences of life. No one can doubt, but such an equality is most suitable to human nature, and diminishes much less from the *happiness* of the rich than it adds to that of the poor.

This interesting use of the idea of happiness foreshadowed the Benthamite philosophy that later played so large a role in economics.

Although he was not opposed to luxury spending based on individual preferences, in "Of the Refinement in the Arts" Hume rejected the idea (later proposed by Malthus) that luxury was beneficial because it created work. Said Hume: "The same care and toil that raise a dish of peas at Christmas, would give bread to a whole family during six months."

He also anticipated Malthus in "Of the Populousness of Ancient Nations": "Almost every man who thinks he can maintain a family will have one; and the human species, at this rate of propagation, would more than double every generation."

In a letter to Lord Kames in 1758 Hume displayed an optimism about underdeveloped countries that in the main has not been justified during the more than two hundred years since then. He pointed to the advantages that rich nations enjoy: extensive commerce, great capital, developed industry, skilled labor, and so forth. Will these advantages persist and increase? No, they must check themselves, he said. Provisions and labor become dearer. The poorer countries can then compete successfully in the coarser manufactures, and later in the more elaborate ones. Then laissez faire and the international harmony of interests will reign supreme in the best of all possible worlds.

Hume's idea of an international equilibrium that would narrow the gap between rich and poor countries has failed more often than it has succeeded. His concept is challenged by the idea of a widening gap between rich and poor under laissez faire because of cumulative growth and cumulative stagnation. Rich countries attract capital and talent, which the poor countries cannot do so successfully. Wealth leads to improvements in health and education, increased social overhead capital, larger markets, and other benefits that in turn result in the expansion of wealth and income. Poverty, in contrast, leads to conditions that perpetuate poverty. Therefore Hume's optimism about poor countries catching up with the rich has been unwarranted in most instances. His optimism was justified only when a country boasted a peculiar set of favorable conditions that enabled it to close the gap, or when governments, in defiance of laissez faire doctrines, used all their powers to promote economic development.

In a letter to Turgot in 1766, Hume opposed the physiocratic idea that all taxes must fall on the landowner. If laborers got more than the minimum needed for subsistence, they might pay the taxes instead of passing them along to someone else. Labor, he pointed out, is dearer in Switzerland, where there are no taxes, than it is in France, where there are many. There are almost no taxes in the English colonies, yet labor is three times dearer there than in any European country. Wages of labor depend, he said, on the supply of and demand for labor—not on taxes. When a tax is laid on consumption, the immediate consequence is that people consume less or work more; the tax is not simply passed on to the landowner.

Hume and Adam Smith were good friends. When the latter published *The Theory of Moral Sentiments*, Hume wrote a letter complimenting him with sardonic humor:

> I proceed to tell you the melancholy news that your book has been very unfortunate, for the public seem disposed to applaud it extremely. It was looked for by the foolish people with some impatience; and the mob of literati are beginning already to be very loud in its praises. . . . Millar [the publisher] exults and brags that two-thirds of the edition are already sold, and that he is now sure of success. You see what a son of the earth that is, to value books only by the profit they bring him. In that view, I believe, it may prove a very good book.[1]

[1] John Rae, *Life of Adam Smith*. London: Macmillan, 1895, pp. 143–44.

Hume displayed insight into rent theory in a letter to Smith. On April 1, 1776, having read Smith's *Wealth of Nations,* he wrote:

> I am much pleas'd with your Performance. . . . If you were here at my Fireside, I should dispute some of your Principles. I cannot think, that the Rent of Farms makes any part of the Price of the Produce, but that the Price is determined altogether by the Quantity and the Demand. . . . But these and a hundred other Points are fit only to be discussed in Conversation; which, till you tell me the contrary, I shall still flatter myself with soon. I hope it will be soon: For I am in a very bad state of Health and cannot afford a long Delay.

Less than five months later Hume was dead, but Smith had visited him during the last days of his illness.

Bibliography

CANTILLON, RICHARD, *Essai sur la Nature du Commerce en Général,* ed. by Henry Higgs and printed in French and English. London: Macmillan, 1931. [Originally published in 1755.]

NORTH, DUDLEY, *Discourses upon Trade,* ed. by Jacob H. Hollander. Baltimore, Md.: Johns Hopkins Press, 1907. [Originally published in 1691.]

POLANYI, KARL, *The Great Transformation.* New York: Rinehart, 1944.

ROTWEIN, EUGENE, *David Hume: Writings on Economics.* Madison, Wis.: University of Wisconsin Press, 1955.

5

The Classical School:
Adam Smith

Adam Smith (1723–90), the kindly, brilliant founder of the classical school, was born in the seaport and manufacturing town of Kirkaldy, Scotland. His father, comptroller of the customs in the town, died before his son was born. Margaret Douglas Smith provided a home for her son until her death in 1784 in her ninetieth year.

Young Smith attended Glasgow College at fourteen years of age, and later he studied moral and political science and languages at Balliol College, Oxford. He then returned to his mother's home to continue independent studies for two years. After that he moved to Edinburgh, where he gave lectures on rhetoric and literature. He was elected professor of logic at Glasgow College in 1751, and in the following year he was given the chair of moral philosophy, which he held for nearly twelve years. In 1759 he published *The Theory of Moral Sentiments*, after which his lectures concentrated less on ethical doctrines and more on jurisprudence and political economy.

Smith resigned his professorship to become the tutor of the stepson of Charles Townsend, chancellor of the exchequer, who later came to prominence in America on the issue of the colonial tea tax. Smith spent more than two years with his charge in France, where he established close personal friendships with the physiocrats, including Quesnay and Turgot. He praised the physiocratic system "with all its imperfections" as "perhaps the nearest approximation to the truth that has yet been published upon the subject of Political Economy." The physiocrats' attack on mercantilism and their proposals to remove tariff barriers won his admiration. From these thinkers he drew the theme of wealth as "the consumable goods annually reproduced by the labour of society," the doctrine of productive labor, and the concept of the circular process of production and distribution. He had planned to dedicate his *Wealth of Nations* to Quesnay, had the latter lived till the book was completed. After returning to Scotland Smith retired on the three-hundred-pounds-per-year pension that his tutorship paid him for the rest of his life.

In 1776 Smith published his monumental work, which he had begun in France: *An Inquiry into the Nature and Causes of the Wealth of Nations.* Its fame was immediate and Smith's reputation was established forever. During his lifetime the book went through five editions.

Smith spent the two years after the publication of his book in London, where he mingled with the leading intellectuals of the day. Then, on being appointed commissioner of customs in Scotland, he went to live in Edinburgh with his mother. It is believed that much of his income was spent secretly on charities. He was always happy to receive his friends at dinner, even without the formality of an invitation, and his Sunday suppers were long celebrated in Edinburgh. Among the honors bestowed on him was his election as lord rector of Glasgow College. Shortly before he died in 1790, most of his manuscripts were destroyed according to his wish and without explanation.

The Theory of Moral Sentiments

We shall discuss this book here because it contains much of interest to us today yet is seldom read, because its ideas are different in some ways from those in *Wealth of Nations,* and because it is the only other book published by the great founder of modern economics.

The Theory of Moral Sentiments went through six editions during Smith's lifetime, the last in the final year of his life, so it cannot be said that this book represented his earlier ideas and *Wealth of Nations* his later thought. The books stand side by side, presenting different facets of his thinking.

The book opens with a chapter called "Of Sympathy." Sympathy, said Smith, overcomes even selfishness. Sympathy interests us in the fortune of others and renders their happiness necessary to us. This is true in spite of the fact that we derive nothing from another's happiness except the pleasure of seeing it. Grief and joy in others arouse similar emotions in ourselves. If we place ourselves in another person's position, our imaginations can evoke sympathy for a situation of which the other person is unaware. Persons who go mad may laugh and sing and be entirely insensible of any misery. Thus the anguish we feel in observing such persons comes not from their suffering, but from our awareness of their situation through our own powers of reason and judgment. This is sympathy. We sympathize even with the dead, because we imagine our own living souls in their inanimate bodies and then conceive what our emotions would be under such circumstances. The dread of death poisons our happiness but restrains the injustice of humankind; this dread afflicts and mortifies the individual, but it guards and protects society.

There are, according to Smith, unsocial and social passions. Examples of the former are hatred and resentment. With regard to such passions, our sympathy is divided between the person who feels them and the person who is the object of them, for the interests of these two individuals are contradictory. The social passions are generosity, humanity, kindness, compassion, and mutual friendship and esteem. These please indifferent spectators on almost every occasion, for their sympathy with the person who feels these passions coincides exactly with their concern for the person who is the object of them. We always have the strongest sympathy for the benevolent passions, for they appear in every respect agreeable to us.

Because people are disposed to sympathize more with our joy than with our sorrow, we parade our riches and conceal our poverty. Much of the toil and bustle of this world is undertaken not to supply our necessities but to gratify our vanity. We want to be observed, to be attended to, to be noticed with sympathy and approbation. The rich glory in their riches because they draw upon them the attention of the world; the poor are ashamed of their poverty, which leaves them in obscurity.

> This disposition to admire, and almost to worship, the rich and the powerful, and to despise, or, at least, to neglect, persons of poor and mean condition, though necessary both to establish and to maintain the distinction of ranks and the order of society, is, at the same time, the great and most universal cause of the corruption of our moral sentiments. That wealth and greatness are often regarded with the respect and admiration which are due only to wisdom and virtue; and that the contempt, of which vice and folly are the only proper objects, is often most unjustly bestowed upon poverty and weakness, has been the complaint of moralists in all ages. . . .
>
> We frequently see the respectful attentions of the world more strongly directed towards the rich and the great, than towards the wise and the virtuous. We see frequently the vices and follies of the powerful much

less despised than the poverty and weakness of the innocent. To deserve, to acquire, and to enjoy the respect and admiration of mankind, are the great objects of ambition and emulation. Two different roads are presented to us, equally leading to the attainment of this so much desired object; the one, by the study of wisdom and the practice of virtue; the other, by the acquisition of wealth and greatness. . . .

In equal degrees of merit there is scarce any man who does not respect more the rich and the great than the poor and the humble. With most men the presumption and vanity of the former are much more admired than the real and solid merit of the latter. . . . To attain to this envied situation, the candidates for fortune too frequently abandon the paths of virtue; for unhappily, the road which leads to the one and that which leads to the other, lie sometimes in very opposite directions. But the ambitious man flatters himself that, in the splendid situation to which he advances, he will have so many means of commanding the respect and admiration of mankind, and will be enabled to act with such superior propriety and grace, that the lustre of his future conduct will entirely cover, or efface, the foulness of the steps by which he arrived at that elevation. [Part I, Sec. 3, Ch. 3]

People, said Smith, can exist only in society; they are exposed to mutual injuries, and they need one another's assistance. When the necessary assistance is reciprocally offered out of love, gratitude, friendship, and esteem, the society flourishes and is happy. Even if mutual love and affection are absent, however, the society may continue to exist because of its utility, though it will be less happy and agreeable. But it cannot exist among those who are at all times ready to hurt and injure one another. If robbers and murderers want to form a viable society, they must at least abstain from robbing and murdering one another.

Beneficence, therefore, is less essential to the existence of society than justice. Society may subsist, though not in the most comfortable state, without beneficence; but the prevalence of injustice must utterly destroy it. [Part II, Sec. 2, Ch. 3]

Smith considered the disturbing problem of our own selfishness and how it could be curbed and controlled:

To the selfish and original passions of human nature, the loss or gain of a very small interest of our own appears to be of vastly more importance, excites a much more passionate joy or sorrow, a much more ardent desire or aversion, than the greatest concern of another with whom we have no particular connection. His interests, as long as they are surveyed from his station, can never be put into the balance with our own, can never restrain us from doing whatever may tend to promote our own, how ruinous soever to him. Before we can make any proper comparison of those opposite interests, we must change our position. We must view them, neither from our own place nor yet from his, neither with our own eyes nor yet with his, but from the place and with the eyes of a third person, who has no particular connection with either, and who judges with impartiality between us. Here, too, habit and experience have taught us to do this so easily and so readily, that we are scarce sensible that we do it; and it requires, in this case, too, some degree of reflection, and even of philosophy, to convince us, how little interest we should take in the greatest concerns of our neighbour, how little we should be affected by whatever relates to him, if the sense of propriety and justice did not correct the otherwise natural inequality of our sentiments.

Let us suppose that the great empire of China, with all its myriads of inhabitants, was suddenly swallowed up by an earthquake, and let us consider how a man of humanity in Europe, who had no sort of connection with that part of the world, would be affected upon receiving intelligence of this dreadful calamity. He would, I imagine, first of all express very strongly his sorrow for the misfortune of that unhappy people, he would make many melancholy reflections upon the precariousness of human life, and the vanity of all the labours of man, which could thus be annihilated in a moment. He would, too, perhaps, if he was a man of speculation, enter into many reasonings concerning the effects which this disaster might produce upon the commerce of Europe, and the trade and business of the world in general. And when all this fine philosophy was over, when all these humane sentiments had been once fairly expressed, he would pursue his business or his pleasure, take his repose or his diversion, with the same ease and tranquillity as if no such accident had happened. The most frivolous disaster which could befall himself would occasion a more real disturbance. If he was to lose his little finger to-morrow, he would not sleep to-night; but, provided he never saw them, he will snore with the most profound security over the ruin of a hundred millions of his brethren, and the destruction of that immense multitude seems plainly an object less interesting to him than this paltry misfortune of his own. To prevent, therefore, this paltry misfortune to himself, would a man of humanity be willing to sacrifice the lives of a hundred millions of his brethren, provided he had never seen them? Human nature startles with horror at the thought, and the world, in its greatest depravity and corruption, never produced such a villain as could be capable of entertaining it. But what makes this difference? When our passive feelings are almost always so sordid and so selfish, how comes it that our active principles should often be so generous and so noble? When we are always so much more deeply affected by whatever concerns ourselves than by whatever concerns other men; what is it which prompts the generous upon all occasions, and the mean upon many, to sacrifice their own interests to the greater interests of others? It is not the soft power of humanity, it is not that feeble spark of benevolence which Nature has lighted up in the human heart, that is thus capable of counteracting the strongest impulses of self-love. It is a stronger power, a more forcible motive, which exerts itself upon such occasions. It is reason, principle, conscience, the inhabitant of the breast, the man within, the great judge and arbiter of our conduct. . . .

When the happiness or misery of others depends in any respect upon our conduct, we dare not, as self-love might suggest to us, prefer the interest of one to that of many. The man within immediately calls to us, that we value ourselves too much and other people too little, and that, by doing so, we render ourselves the proper object of the contempt and indignation of our brethren. . . .

One individual must never prefer himself so much even to any other individual as to hurt or injure that other in order to benefit himself, though the benefit to the one should be much greater than the hurt or injury to the other. The poor man must neither defraud nor steal from the rich, though the acquisition might be much more beneficial to the one than the loss could be hurtful to the other. The man within immediately calls to him in this case, too, that he is no better than his neighbour, and that by his unjust preference, he renders himself the proper object of the contempt and indignation of mankind, as well as of the punishment which that contempt and indignation must naturally dispose them to inflict, for having thus violated one of those sacred rules, upon the tolerable observation of which depend the whole security and peace of human society. There is no commonly honest man who does not more dread the inward disgrace of such an action, the indelible stain which it would for ever stamp upon his own mind, than the greatest external calamity which, without any fault of his own, could possibly befall him; and who does not inwardly feel the truth of that great stoical maxim, that for one man to deprive another unjustly of any thing, or unjustly to promote his own advantage by the loss or disadvantage of another, is more contrary to nature than death, than poverty, than pain, than all the misfortunes which can affect him, either in his body, or in his external circumstances. [Part III, Ch. 3]

Our moral faculties, said Smith, prescribe rules of conduct to be regarded as the commands and laws of the Deity. If we violate God's rules, we will be punished by the torments of inward shame and self-condemnation. If we obey His wishes, we will be rewarded with tranquillity of mind, contentment, and self-satisfaction. Thus God promotes the happiness of human beings. The rich must share their income with the poor who serve them, and therefore God's work is good.

The produce of the soil maintains at all times nearly that number of inhabitants which it is capable of maintaining. The rich only select from the heap what is most precious and agreeable. They consume little more than the poor; and in spite of their natural selfishness and rapacity, though they mean only their own conveniency, though the sole end which they propose from the labours of all the thousands whom they employ be the gratification of their own vain and insatiable desires, they divide with the poor the produce of all their improvements. They are led by an invisible hand to make nearly the same distribution of the necessaries of life which would have been made had the earth been divided into equal portions among all its inhabitants; and thus, without intending it, without knowing it, advance the interest of the society, and afford means to the multiplication of the species. When Providence divided the earth among a few lordly masters, it neither forgot nor abandoned those who seemed to have been left out in the partition. These last, too, enjoy their share of all that it produces. In what constitutes the real happiness of human life, they are in no respect inferior to those who would seem so much above them. In ease of body and peace of mind, all the different ranks of life are nearly upon a level, and the beggar, who suns himself by the side of the highway, possesses that security which kings are fighting for. [Part IV, Ch. 1]

In *The Theory of Moral Sentiments* Smith discussed the ethical forces that bind people together in a workable society; in *Wealth of Nations* he assumed the existence of a just society and showed how the individual is guided and limited by economic forces. (In the later book, however, Smith did sometimes overemphasize economic interests and motivations at the expense of morals and ethics. He believed, for example, that the Quakers freed their slaves not because their compassion was so great but because the economic loss resulting from this action was minimal: "The late resolution of the Quakers in Pennsylvania to set at liberty all their negro slaves, may satisfy us that their number cannot be very great. Had they made any considerable part of their property, such a resolution could never have been agreed to." [Bk. III, Ch. 2])

In *The Theory of Moral Sentiments* sympathy and benevolence overcame selfishness; in *Wealth of Nations* competition curbs selfishness. In the first book the natural order is guided by a benevolent God; in the second book God is excluded, leaving Smith free to find defects in the order of nature without casting reflections on the workmanship of its Author. Smith believed that prudence in managing one's own affairs is related to justice toward others—that is, justice toward others is the best policy in one's efforts to rise in the world. He agreed with his friend Benjamin Franklin that "honesty is the best policy." Both books reconcile the individual with the social interest through the principle of the invisible hand, or natural harmony, and the principle of natural liberty of the individual, or the right to justice.

Wealth of Nations

The Division of Labor

The first chapter of *Wealth of Nations* is titled "Of the Division of Labour," a phrase not familiar in Smith's time. The first sentence reads as follows. "The greatest improvement in the productive powers of labour, and the greater part of the skill, dexterity, and judgment with which it is any where directed, or applied, seem to have been the effects of the division of labour." [1]

Smith, clearly impressed with the division of labor, gave a graphic description of it in a pin factory:

> To take an example, therefore, from a very trifling manufacture; but one in which the division of labour has been very often taken notice of, the trade of the pin-maker; a workman not educated to this business (which the division of labour has rendered a distinct trade), nor acquainted with the use of the machinery employed in it (to the invention of which the same division of labour has probably given occasion), could scarce, perhaps, with his utmost industry, make one pin in a day, and certainly could not make twenty. But in the way in which this business is now carried on, not only the whole work is a peculiar trade, but it is divided into a number of branches, of which the greater part are likewise peculiar trades. One man draws out the wire, another straights it, a third cuts it, a fourth points it, a fifth grinds it at the top for receiving the head; to make the head requires two or three distinct operations; to put it on, is a peculiar business, to whiten the pins is another; it is even a trade by itself to put them into the paper; and the important business of making a pin is, in this manner, divided into about eighteen distinct operations, which, in some manufactories, are all performed by distinct hands, though in others the same man will sometimes perform two or three of them. I have seen a small manufactory of this kind where ten men only were employed, and where some of them consequently performed two or three distinct operations. But though they were very poor, and therefore but indifferently accommodated with the necessary machinery, they could, when they exerted themselves, make among them about twelve pounds of pins in a day. There are in a pound upwards of four thousand pins of a middling size. Those ten persons, therefore, could make among them upwards of forty-eight thousand pins in a day. Each person, therefore, making a tenth part of forty-eight thousand pins, might be consid-

[1] All references in the rest of this chapter are to Adam Smith, *The Wealth of Nations*, ed. by Edwin Cannan (New York, Modern Library edition, 1937). [Originally published in 1776.] Reprinted with permission of Random House, Inc.

ered as making four thousand eight hundred pins in a day. But if they had all wrought separately and independently, and without any of them having been educated to this peculiar business, they certainly could not each of them have made twenty, perhaps not one pin in a day. [Bk. I, Ch. 1]

This division of labor, said Smith, increases the quantity of work produced for three reasons. First, each worker develops increased dexterity in performing one simple task over and over. Second, time is saved if the worker need not go from one kind of work to another. Third, machinery can be invented to increase productivity once tasks have been simplified and routinized through the division of labor.

But there is a darker side to the division of labor. While it increases human productivity, it stultifies the mind and warps the personality:

In the progress of the division of labour, the employment of the far greater part of those who live by labour, that is, of the great body of the people, comes to be confined to a few very simple operations, frequently to one or two. But the understandings of the greater part of men are necessarily formed by their ordinary employments. The man whose whole life is spent in performing a few simple operations, of which the effects too are, perhaps, always the same, or very nearly the same, has no occasion to exert his understanding, or to exercise his invention in finding out expedients for removing difficulties which never occur. He naturally loses, therefore, the habit of such exertion, and generally becomes as stupid and ignorant as it is possible for a human creature to become. The torpor of his mind renders him, not only incapable of relishing or bearing a part in any rational conversation, but of conceiving any generous, noble, or tender sentiment, and consequently of forming any just judgment concerning many even of the ordinary duties of private life. Of the great and extensive interests of his country he is altogether incapable of judging; and unless very particular pains have been taken to render him otherwise, he is equally incapable of defending his country in war. The uniformity of his stationary life naturally corrupts the courage of his mind, and makes him regard with abhorrence the irregular, uncertain, and adventurous life of a soldier. It corrupts even the activity of his body, and renders him incapable of exerting his strength with vigour and perseverance, in any other employment than that to which he has been bred. His dexterity at his own particular trade seems, in this manner, to be acquired at the expence of his intellectual, social, and martial virtues. But in every improved and civilized society this is the state into which the labouring poor, that is, the great body of the people, must necessarily fall, unless government takes some pains to prevent it. [Bk. V, Ch. 1, Part 3]

As a step in this direction, said Smith, the government should promote the education of the common people through free and possibly compulsory parish schools.

Laissez Faire and the Harmony of Interests

Smith was the great advocate of laissez faire—nonintervention by government in business. According to him, governments are wasteful, corrupt, inefficient, and the grantors of special privileges to the detriment of society as a whole. Individuals, if left to pursue their own interests, will serve society even though this is not their intention. Smith applied the free-enterprise doctrine to both domestic and international affairs, and he devoted a fourth of *Wealth of Nations* to a devastating attack on mercantilism.

Smith's defense of laissez faire, the harmony of interests, and free foreign trade can best be summarized in his own colorful language: "It is not from the benevolence of the butcher, the brewer, or the baker, that we expect our dinner, but from their regard to their own interest." [Bk. I, Ch. 2]

Every individual necessarily labours to render the annual revenue of the society as great as he can. He generally, indeed, neither intends to promote the public interest, nor knows how much he is promoting it. By preferring the support of domestic to that of foreign industry, he intends only his own security; and by directing that industry in such a manner as its produce may be of the greatest value, he intends only his own gain, and he is in this, as in many other cases, led by an invisible hand to promote an end which was no part of his intention. Nor is it always the worse for the society that it was no part of it. By pursuing his own interest he frequently promotes that of the society more effectually than when he really intends to promote it. I have never known much good done by those who affected to trade for the public good. It is an affectation, indeed, not very common among merchants, and very few words need be employed in dissuading them from it.

What is the species of domestic industry which his capital can employ, and of which the produce is likely to be of the greatest value, every individual, it is evident, can, in his local situation, judge much better than any statesman or lawgiver can do for him. The statesman, who should attempt to direct private people in what manner they ought to employ their capitals, would not only load himself with a most unnecessary attention, but assume an authority which could safely be trusted, not only to no single person, but to no council or senate whatever, and which would nowhere be so dangerous as in the hands of a man who had folly and presumption enough to fancy himself fit to exercise it.

To give the monopoly of the home market to the produce of domestic industry, in any particular art or manufacture, is in some measure to direct private people in what manner they ought to employ their capitals, and must, in almost all cases, be either a useless or a hurtful regulation. If the produce of domestic can be brought there as cheap as that of foreign industry, the regulation is evidently useless. If it cannot, it must generally be hurtful. It is the maxim of every prudent master of a family, never to attempt to make at home what it will cost him more to make than to buy. The taylor does not attempt to make his own shoes, but buys them of the shoemaker. The shoemaker does not attempt to make his own clothes, but employs a taylor. The farmer attempts to make neither the one nor the other, but employs those different artificers. All of them find it for their interest to employ their whole industry in a way in which they have some advantage over their neighbours, and to purchase with a part of its produce, or what is the same thing, with the price of a part of it, whatever else they have occasion for.

What is prudence in the conduct of every private family, can scarce be folly in that of a great kingdom. If a foreign country can supply us with a commodity cheaper than we ourselves can make it, better buy it of them with some part of the produce of our own industry, employed in a way in which we have some advantage. [Bk. IV, Ch. 2]

Elsewhere Smith speaks about how foreign trade can promote greater division of labor by overcoming the narrowness of the home market. Exports also remove surplus products for which there is no demand at home and bring back products for which there is a demand.

Smith's distrust even of England's government was unequivocal. Yet we should remember that the regime he was criticizing was probably one of the more honest and efficient ones in the world at that time.

But though the profusion of government must, undoubtedly, have retarded the progress of England towards wealth and improvement, it has not been able to stop it. The annual produce of its land and labour is, undoubtedly, much greater at present than it was either at the restoration or at the revolution. The capital, therefore, annually employed in cultivating this land, and in maintaining this labour, must likewise be much greater. In the midst of all the exactions of government, this capital has been silently and gradually accumulated by the private frugality and good conduct of individuals, by their universal, continual, and uninterrupted effort to better their own condition. It is this effort, protected by law and allowed by liberty to exert itself in the manner that is most advantageous, which has maintained the progress of England towards opulence and improvement in almost all former times, and which, it is to be hoped, will do so in all future times. England, however, as it has never been blessed with a very parsimonious government, so parsimony has at no time been the characteristic virtue of its inhabitants. It is the highest impertinence and presumption, therefore, in kings and ministers, to pretend to watch over the economy of private people, and to restrain their expence, either by sumptuary laws, or by prohibiting the importation of foreign luxuries. They are themselves always, and without any exception, the greatest spendthrifts in the society. Let them look well after their own expence, and they may safely trust private people with theirs. If their own extravagance does not ruin the state, that of their subjects never will. [Bk. II, Ch. 3]

Contrary to the mercantilist belief that each nation enriches itself at the expense of its neighbors, Smith believed in an international harmony of interests:

The wealth of a neighbouring nation, however, though dangerous in war and politics, is certainly advantageous in trade. In a state of hostility it may enable our enemies to maintain fleets and armies superior to our own; but in a state of peace and commerce it must likewise enable them to exchange with us to a greater value, and to afford a better market, either for the immediate produce of our own industry, or for whatever is purchased with that produce. As a rich man is likely to be a better customer to the industrious people in his neighborhood, than a poor, so is likewise a rich nation. [Bk. IV, Ch. 3]

Smith was suspicious of businessmen, who were ready and willing to sacrifice everyone else's interests to promote their own. How, then, could they be trusted to foster the general welfare? Competition was the answer. They could not unscrupulously enrich themselves at the expense of the rest of society, even though they usually tried; for extraordinary profits would only attract new competitors who would wipe out their excessive gains. "People of the same trade seldom meet together, even for merriment and diversion, but the conversation ends in a conspiracy against the public, or in some contrivance to raise prices." [Bk. I, Ch. 10]

The prejudices of some political writers against shopkeepers and tradesmen, are altogether without foundation. So far is it from being necessary, either to tax them, or to restrict their numbers, that they can never be multiplied so as to hurt the publick, though they may so as to hurt one another. The quantity of grocery goods, for example, which can be sold in a particular town, is limited by the demand of that town and its neighbourhood. The capital, therefore, which can be employed in the grocery trade cannot exceed what is sufficient to purchase that quantity. If this capital is divided between two different grocers, their competition will tend to make both of them sell cheaper, than if it were in the hands of one only; and if it were divided among twenty, their competition would be just so much the greater, and the chance of their combining together, in order to raise the price, just so much the less. Their competition might perhaps ruin some of themselves; but to take care of this is the business of the parties concerned, and it may safely be trusted to their discretion. It can never hurt either the consumer, or the producer; on the contrary, it must tend to make the retailers both sell cheaper and buy dearer, than if the whole trade was monopolized by one or two persons. [Bk. II, Ch. 5]

Smith always attacked government intervention on behalf of the narrow special interests of businessmen. In condemning bounties on exports he defended consumers in opposition to businessmen in language that might be applied to United States farm and export policies:

Whatever extension of the foreign market can be occasioned by the bounty, must, in every particular year, be altogether at the expence of the home market; as every bushel of corn which is exported by means of the bounty, and which would not have been exported without the bounty, would have remained in the home market to increase the consumption, and to lower the price of that commodity. The corn bounty, it is to be observed, as well as every other bounty upon exportation, imposes two different taxes upon the people; first, the tax which they are obliged to contribute, in order to pay the bounty; and secondly, the tax which arises from the advanced price of the commodity in the home market, and which, as the whole body of the people are purchasers of corn, must, in this particular commodity, be paid by the whole body of the people. In this particular commodity, therefore, this second tax is by much the heaviest of the two. [Bk. IV, Ch. 5]

If Smith relied on laissez faire to promote competition and the general welfare, what, in his view, should be the role of the state? He saw three major functions of government: First, to protect society from foreign attack. Second, to establish the administration of justice within the country. Third, to erect and maintain the public works and institutions that private entrepreneurs cannot undertake profitably. At scattered points throughout his book Smith favored a variety of state interventions that fit into the above three categories or that enlarge the scope of acceptable government action. He thought the law should enforce the performance of contracts. Control over the issue of paper money by bankers is necessary even though it might be considered a violation of natural liberty. Legal control over interest rates is acceptable; but the rate should be somewhat (though not much) above the lowest market rate to promote sound projects rather than frivolous, wasteful, and speculative ones, which high interest rates might permit. Laws ensuring the security of the agricultural tenant are good because they promote improvements and investments in the land. Smith approved of patents and copyrights of limited duration. He even favored two kinds of protectionist tariffs: (1) those that protect a domestic industry essential to the defense of the country and (2) those that equalize the tax burden on a particular domestic industry by imposing a tariff on imports of that good. Otherwise, free trade is in order. But if free trade is to be introduced after a long period of protectionism, it should be done gradually in order to avoid suddenly throwing many people out of work and entrepreneurs into bankruptcy. Among the public works that a government should support are those that promote commerce and education, including bridges, canals, roads, harbors, post offices, coinage, schools, and churches.

To finance these government activities Smith recommended taxation. His four famous maxims for good taxes are as follows: (1) Taxes should be proportional to the revenue enjoyed under the protection of the state. This was a drastic departure from the regressive taxes prevalent at the time. (2) Taxes should be predictable and uniform as to the time of payment, the manner of payment, and the amount to be paid. (3) Taxes should be levied at the time and in the manner most convenient to the contributor. (4) Taxes should be collected at minimum cost to the government.

The Economic Laws of a Free-Enterprise Society

VALUE.   According to Smith, there are two kinds of value.

> The word VALUE, it is to be observed, has two different meanings, and sometimes expresses the utility of some particular object, and sometimes the power of purchasing other goods which the possession of that object conveys. The one may be called "value in use;" the other, "value in exchange." The things which have the greatest value in use have frequently little or no value in exchange; and on the contrary, those which have the greatest value in exchange have frequently little or no value in use. Nothing is more useful than water: but it will purchase scarce any thing; scarce any thing can be had in exchange for it. A diamond, on the contrary, has scarce any value in use; but a very great quantity of other goods may frequently be had in exchange for it. [Bk. I, Ch. 4]

There would be no point, then, in comparing the magnitudes of different use values. But exchange value, the power that the possession of a commodity provides to purchase other goods, has been one of the central problems of economics since the market economy developed.

What determines the exchange value, or simply "value," of a commodity? What it really costs, not simply in terms of money but also in terms of "the toil and trouble of acquiring it." Here is one of the important links between the classical and the marginalist schools. Work is irksome and will be avoided as much as possible. Wealth enables a person to avoid toil and trouble by imposing them on other people. Therefore, according to Smith, the value of any commodity to the person who possesses it, if he wishes to exchange it for other commodities, "is equal to the quantity of labour which it enables him to purchase or command. Labour, therefore, is the real measure of the exchangeable value of all commodities." But there are different qualities of labor, and allowance has to be made for the difficulty of the task and the skill and ingenuity with which the labor is applied. The "higgling and bargaining of the market" adjusts these differences.

The labor theory of value immediately presents a contradiction. Imagine two commodities made from labor of equal skill. Suppose we add up all the time required to make each commodity, including the labor necessary to produce the raw materials and the labor required to make capital goods used in its production. Let us assume that each commodity takes two hours to produce. But commodity A—say, growing potatoes with a hoe where good land is abundant—requires virtually no capital to produce. Commodity B—cotton yarn—is produced only with intricate and expensive machinery. If a pound of cotton yarn and ten pounds of potatoes, each containing two hours of labor, could be exchanged for each other in the market, which would people produce? Potatoes, of course, because they could avoid investing large amounts of capital, and they would get the same return for their labor. This dilemma, of which Smith was aware, will come up later when Ricardo's and Marx's labor theories of value are discussed.

Smith realized that the growth of capital would vitiate a simple labor theory of value. He therefore believed that only "in that early and rude state of society which precedes both the accumulation of stock and the appropriation of land" do commodities exchange in proportion to the quantities of labor required to produce them. If among a nation of hunters, he said, it usually takes twice the labor to kill a beaver as to kill a deer, one beaver will exchange for two deer.

In a society where capital investments become important, said Smith, goods will normally be exchanged for other goods, for money, or for labor at a figure high enough to cover both wages and profits of the entrepreneur. Moreover, profits will depend on the whole value of the capital advanced by the employer. After the land of a country becomes private property, rent also must be paid. Prices of commodities therefore cover wages, profit, and rent. The real value of commodities can no longer be measured by the labor contained in them. They can, however, be measured by "the quantity of labour which they can, each of them, purchase or command." The quantity of labor that a commodity can buy exceeds the quantity of labor embodied in its production by the total profits and rents.

Demand, according to Smith, does not influence the value of commodities; only the cost of production—made up of wages, profit, and rent—determines value in the long run. This is a reasonable proposition if we base it on Smith's implicit assumption that production will expand or shrink at constant cost per unit of output. However, if we assume either increasing or decreasing costs, Smith's principle becomes untenable. If the demand for products rises, and if as the industry expands it will produce the goods at higher costs, then the increased demand will cause a long-run rise in price. If rising output results in falling costs per unit, then an increased demand will be followed by a falling long-run price.

MARKET PRICE. There are ordinary, or average, rates of wages, profit, and rent in every society or neighborhood. Smith called these the natural rates of wages, profit, and rent. When a commodity is sold for its natural price, there will be exactly enough revenue to pay the natural rates of wages, profit, and rent. The natural price is a long-run price, which is the lowest price at which entrepreneurs would *continue* to sell their goods. In a desperate situation they would sell goods more cheaply, but this would not continue. They could always go out of business or enter another line of production.

The actual price at which any commodity is sold is called its market price. It may be above, below, or exactly the same as its natural price. The market price depends on the aberrations of short-run supply and demand and it will tend to fluctuate around the natural price. If it is above the natural price, more goods will come to market, depressing the price. If it is below the natural price, some productive factors will be withdrawn, the quantity supplied will fall, and the market price will rise toward the natural price. That is, short-run supply and demand are not fundamental determinants of price, but they cause market-price fluctuations around the natural price or value of commodities.

WAGES.   Smith saw a conflict of interest between workers and their masters as each side tried to combine to influence wages:

> It is not, however, difficult to foresee which of the two parties must, upon all ordinary occasions, have the advantage in the dispute, and force the other into a compliance with their terms. The masters, being fewer in number, can combine much more easily; and the law, besides, authorises, or at least does not prohibit their combinations, while it prohibits those of the workmen. We have no acts of parliament against combining to lower the price of work; but many against combining to raise it. In all such disputes the masters can hold out much longer. A landlord, a farmer, a master manufacturer, or merchant, though they did not employ a single workman, could generally live a year or two upon the stocks which they have already acquired. Many workmen could not subsist a week, few could subsist a month, and scarce any a year without employment. In the long-run the workman may be as necessary to his master as his master is to him, but the necessity is not so immediate. [Bk. I, Ch. 8]

The minimum rate of wages must be that which will enable a worker with a family to survive and perpetuate the labor supply. But when the demand for labor is high, wages will rise above this minimum. The rate of increase of national wealth determines the demand for labor and the laborer's wage. Hence Smith's emphasis on capital accumulation and economic growth. This produces the best conditions for the majority of people. If the wealth of a country were great but stationary, population would multiply beyond the employment opportunities, and wages would be at the minimum subsistence level; but where rapid expansion occurs, wages rise. Smith applauded this development, thereby opposing the low-wage doctrine of mercantilism.

> Is this improvement in the circumstances of the lower ranks of the people to be regarded as an advantage or as an inconveniency to the society? The answer seems at first sign abundantly plain. Servants, labourers and workmen of different kinds, make up the far greater part of every great political society. But what improves the circumstances of the greater part can never be regarded as an inconveniency to the whole. No society can surely be flourishing and happy, of which the far greater part of the members are poor and miserable. It is but equity, besides, that they who feed, cloath, and lodge the whole body of the people, should have such a share of the produce of their own labour as to be themselves tolerably well fed, cloathed and lodged. [Bk. I, Ch. 8]

When more workers are employed, wages rise, marriages are encouraged, and more children survive. The increased demand for labor thereby generates an increased supply. But when there is an oversupply of labor, wages fall and the marriage rate and the survival rate of children decline. High wages, however, increase the health and strength of the workers, animating them to do their best work because they give hope for an improved life.

Smith assumed a society with perfect liberty, a society in which all were free to choose and change their occupations. Under these assumed conditions the advantages and disadvantages of every type of employment would be equal or would tend toward equality. Actual wage rates for different jobs would vary according to five factors:

1. *The agreeableness of the occupation.* Smith argued that the harder, the dirtier, the more disagreeable, and the more dangerous the work, the higher the wages paid. William S. Jevons, one of the founders of the marginalist school, agreed with this; he held that all other factors being equal, wages vary directly with the disutility of labor. By contrast, John Stuart Mill, the last of the great classical economists, suspected that wages vary inversely with the disutility of effort—that the hardest, dirtiest jobs are generally the worst paid.

2. *The cost of acquiring the necessary skills and knowledge.* Smith developed an idea that has only recently become significant in analyses of economic development and how to promote it. He pointed out that an expensive machine has to yield a return that covers both its initial cost and profits on the investment. Similarly, he said, people's income must pay for the cost of their education and training and still provide a rate of return on that investment. Recently there has been a renewed emphasis on the importance of education and on the fact that investments in education seem to pay a higher rate of return than investments in capital goods.

3. *The regularity of employment.* Smith held that the less regular the employment, the higher the wage. This theory presupposes that other factors, especially the bargaining power of the workers, are equal. Thus the argument would not hold for agricultural workers in the United States, who suffer from both the lowest wage rates and the highest level of seasonal unemployment.

4. *The trust and responsibility given to those employed.* Therefore, said Smith, goldsmiths, jewelers, physicians, and attorneys should get higher pay than others.

5. *The probability or improbability of success*—the degree of risk-taking—in the occupation. The person who trains as a shoemaker is surer of success than the person who trains as a lawyer, and therefore the latter should receive a premium for running a greater risk of failure.

PROFIT. Every investment, said Smith, is exposed to the risk of loss, so the lowest rate of profit must be high enough to compensate for such losses and still leave a surplus for the entrepreneur. The gross profit includes compensation for loss and the surplus. Net or clear profit is the surplus alone, the net revenue of the businessman.

In countries that are advancing rapidly in wealth, competition among businessmen lowers profit. The forces that raise wages thereby lower profit. The low rate of profit may compensate for high wage rates in the sale of commodities; thus thriving countries may sell goods as cheaply as their less fortunate neighbors, among whom wage rates may be lower.

Classical economists generally did not handle interest as a separate distributive share; it was treated simply as a deduction from profit. The lowest rate of interest must be a little higher than the losses that sometimes occur through lending. The interest that the borrower can afford to pay is in proportion to the net or clear profit only, and the rate must generally be lower than the rate of profit in order to induce borrowing. As profits rise, more money is sought by borrowers and interest rates rise, and conversely.

RENT. "As soon as the land of any country has all become private property, the landlords, like all other men, love to reap where they never sowed." [Bk. I, Ch. 6] Here Smith was not criticizing or condemning landlords; he was merely reporting the truth as he saw it.

Rent is the price paid for the use of land. It is the highest price the tenant can afford to pay after deducting wages, the wear and tear of capital, average profits, and other expenses of production. The rent of land "is naturally a monopoly price." In this Smith was of course in error. With the many owners of land and with even more actual or potential users, land is not ordinarily rented under monopoly conditions.

Rent is a surplus that varies with the fertility and the location of the land. High prices yield high rents, and low prices low rents. Yet Smith had said earlier that the rent of land enters into the price of the product. It was this statement that David Hume had criticized (see p. 58). However, the two statements are not necessarily inconsistent. When Smith said that high rents were the effect rather than the cause of high prices, he was looking at changes in rents and prices, at causes and effects. But in the statement that Hume criticized, Smith was discussing the components of the price of commodities in general. When commodities are sold, the revenue received must cover wages, profit, and rent. Where else could rent come from? It is correct to say that rent is a component of prices in general and that prices break down into distributive shares that include rent. It is also correct to say that rental payments do not influence the level of prices; instead, the level of prices influences rents. It is only the marginal part of the supply of farm produce that contains no rent in its price. This Smith failed to see. (These matters were developed more fully about forty years later by Ricardo.)

If rent is a surplus above the return necessary for the worker and the entrepreneur, Smith said, then the more productive the land, the greater the surplus and therefore the greater the rent. If we discovered a plant that was much more productive than wheat, production of foodstuffs would rise and rents on land producing it would rise. Smith's conclusion is wrong, of course, if population and demand are assumed to be constant. He failed to measure the surplus from the marginal land in use. He was also wrong in believing that the price of minerals is regulated by the richest mines.

Smith anticipated Henry George by advocating a tax on rent. It would not raise the rent of houses, nor would it discourage any sort of industry. It would fall on the landowners alone, who, said Smith, always act as monopolists and charge the highest possible rents.

An adequate theory of rent came to be based on the law of diminishing returns, but Smith had only a rudimentary understanding of this law. He did apply it to fishing, but not to agriculture.

> As population increases, as the annual produce of the land and labour of the country grows greater and greater, there come to be more buyers of fish. . . . But it will generally be impossible to supply the great and extended market without employing a quantity of labour greater than in proportion to what had been requisite for supplying the narrow and confined one. A market which, from requiring only one thousand, comes to require annually ten thousand ton of fish, can seldom be supplied without employing more than ten times the quantity of labour which had before been sufficient to supply it. The fish must generally be sought for at a greater distance, larger vessels must be employed, and more expensive machinery of every kind made use of. The real price of this commodity, therefore, naturally rises in the progress of improvement. It has accordingly done so, I believe, more or less in every country. [Bk. I, Ch. 11, Part 3]

The theories that analyze how wages, profit, and rent are determined constitute a theory of income distribution. Smith's was a systematic and comprehensive theory of distribution, based in part on the theory of the physiocrats, but far superior to it.

THE ROLE OF MONEY AND DEBT. Smith established the classical tradition of de-emphasizing the importance of money. Money is vital as a means of payment, to be sure, for without it business would be shackled with a barter system. But money itself does not add to the revenue of society. It facilitates the circulation of goods, but it is the production of the latter that makes up the revenue. Although the gold and silver coins that circulate are a valuable part of the capital of the country, they are dead stock, producing nothing.

Here Smith developed the idea that was the opposite of mercantilist doctrine. Paper money in place of gold and silver would do equally well and require much less effort to produce. Gold and silver are like a highway that enables goods to be brought to market without being itself productive. Banking, he said, would save the labor of producing gold by providing paper money, just as a highway through the air would save land that might be used for other things. As long as paper money were redeemable in gold, a small reserve of metal would do.

The mercantilists argued that consumable commodities are soon destroyed, whereas gold and silver are more durable. Would we therefore reckon, asked Smith, that the exchange of English hardware for French wines is disadvantageous? We could augment our supply of pots and pans to an incredible degree, but we need only a limited supply of utensils. So it is with coin. We require only a certain amount to circulate goods, and an excess is unnecessary and will be exported rather than left idle at home. Smith's refutation of the mercantilistic overemphasis on gold, however, ignored the special qualities of this metal. By being a universally acceptable medium of exchange, it can, unlike pots and pans, be spent in any direction.

Smith deplored the growth of public debt and the taxes it required. The view among some Keynesians that an internally held debt does not matter because we owe it to ourselves was voiced in Smith's time. He answered in the following terms:

> In the payment of the interest of the public debt, it has been said, it is the right hand which pays the left. The money does not go out of the country. It is only a part of the revenue of one set of the inhabitants which is transferred to another; and the nation is not a farthing the poorer. This apology is founded altogether in the sophistry of the mercantile system. [Bk. V, Ch. 3]

Smith was afraid that heavy taxes would induce merchants and manufacturers to invest their capital abroad to the detriment of the home country. Writing before the development of recurring business cycles, he was not concerned with government spending to counteract a depression. Assuming full employment, government debt and interest charges represented resources that might have been used productively by private individuals if government had not diverted them to its own purposes. With militaristic, corrupt, and wasteful governments far removed from the people and partial to special interests, such a diversion of resources would not serve society.

Smith gloomily forecast that growing debts would in the long run probably ruin all the great nations of Europe. The British debt that troubled him so was £129 million in 1775.

Economic Development

Smith looked at the economy as a whole and emphasized growth and development. Machinery and the division of labor increase the production of wealth. The division of labor increases productivity, and the emphasis lies there rather than on trade and accumulating treasure. Trade is significant because it permits labor specialization, which is limited by the extent of the market. Widening markets therefore increase productivity.

Smith discovered the great truth that the division of labor makes possible the introduction of machinery to increase peoples' productivity. When a man made a complete pair of shoes himself there could be no single machine to do his work, for it was too complicated. But when shoemaking was broken down into a series of simple operations, tools and machines could be invented to replace hand labor. However, writing as he did before the factory system became dominant, Smith failed to emphasize sufficiently the changes in technology that would improve the productivity of labor so tremendously. His emphasis was on the improved dexterity that resulted from a division of labor rather than on mechanization as both a result and a cause of division of labor.

Although the division of labor increases productivity, how would the workers fare under conditions of economic growth? Later classical economists assumed that the workers tend to receive the minimum of subsistence and therefore have nothing to gain from economic development. This was not Smith's view, for he thought that those who live by wages would benefit most, not from *great* national wealth, but rather from *increasing wealth:*

> It deserves to be remarked, perhaps, that it is in the progressive state, while the society is advancing to the further acquisition, rather than when it has acquired its full complement of riches, that the condition of the labouring poor, of the great body of the people, seems to be the hap-

piest and the most comfortable. It is hard in the stationary, and miserable in the declining state. The progressive state is in reality the cheerful and the hearty state to all the different orders of the society. The stationary is dull; the declining melancholy. [Bk. I, Ch. 8]

As capital accumulates more rapidly than population increases, competition among the capitalists tends to lower profits. Economists after Smith returned to this idea of a falling rate of profit, but with different analyses to explain the theory.

As society progresses, the real rents of land rise for two reasons. First, with every improvement in cultivation, the surplus rises, and the surplus goes to the landlords. Second, as improvements in industry occur, the real price of manufactured goods falls. The landlords are then able to exchange their share of the farm products for an increasing quantity of manufactured goods.

Therefore, concluded Smith, the interests of landlords and workers coincide with the general interest of society. These two groups progress together as society progresses. But the interests of businessmen who live by profit are opposed to those of society as a whole, for they thrive when competition is limited and profits are high, whereas the rest of society gains from increased competition and reduced profits.

Smith distinguished between productive labor, which adds value to a product, and unproductive labor, which does not. Productive employment stores up labor in a salable commodity. Unproductive labor is that invested in offering services. Unproductive laborers include kings, soldiers, churchmen, lawyers, doctors, men and women of letters, players, buffoons, musicians, opera singers, dancers, and so forth. Among the productive workers are "artificers, manufacturers and merchants."

To us it seems odd that Smith would say that the person who gives a public piano recital is unproductive, but that the one who prints the tickets is productive. To Smith it would have seemed strange that we, in our national income accounting, say that payments to servants, military personnel, advertisers, and public officials are additions to national income. He would have considered such expenditures as deductions. But to understand Smith, we should look at the problem through his approach to capital accumulation and economic growth. In fact, he called Chapter 3 of Book II "Of the Accumulation of Capital, or of Productive and Unproductive Labour." According to Smith, material goods can be accumulated and are therefore a potential means of increasing wealth. Even consumer goods produced today can be used to support workers in the future, thereby enabling them to work and produce more goods. But services are of the moment only; they vanish in the simultaneous acts of production and consumption, and they cannot be accumulated. From this point of view they are unproductive, although in many cases they are useful.

In refuting the physiocratic concept of productive and sterile labor, Smith seems to have caught his toe in the physiocratic trap. In opposing their doctrine he argued that merchants, artificers, and manufacturers are not sterile or barren, even if they only reproduce annually the value of their own consumption. "We should not call a marriage barren or unproductive, though it produced only a son and a daughter, to replace the father and mother." But a marriage that results in three children is more productive than one that produces two. "So the labour of farmers and country labourers is certainly more productive than that of merchants, artificers and manufacturers." This is so because in agriculture, livestock and nature labor beside people to add to value. Ricardo objected to this argument, pointing out that even in manufacturing the assistance of nature is considerable. The powers of wind and water, the pressure of the atmosphere and the elasticity of steam, the heating of metals, dyeing, and fermentation all rely on the gratuitous assistance of nature.

Smith, writing at a time when investment and production were burgeoning, pinned his hopes on widening markets, increasing accumulation of capital, and continuous progress. Business cycles, overproduction, unemployment, and redundant capital still lay in the future. The harmony of interests prevailed, with a free and competitive market forcing each individual to serve society while he served himself. No wonder Smith is called an optimist.

Bibliography

RAE, JOHN, *Life of Adam Smith.* London: Macmillan, 1895.

SMITH, ADAM, *An Inquiry into the Nature and Causes of the Wealth of Nations,* ed. by Edwin Cannan. New York: Random House, Modern Library edition, 1937. [Originally published in 1776.]

————, *The Theory of Moral Sentiments.* London: Henry G. Bohn, 1853. [Originally published in 1759.]

6

The Classical School:
David Ricardo

Although Smith was the founder of the classical school, David Ricardo (1772–1823) was the leading figure in further developing the ideas of that school. Ricardo demonstrated the possibilities of the abstract method and gave economics its later form by emphasizing the distribution of income. Around Ricardo rallied an ardent band of disciples who enthusiastically disseminated his doctrines. His followers changed and amended his theories, moving toward neoclassical positions.

Ricardo, the third of seventeen children, was born of Dutch Jews who had migrated to England. He was trained for his father's stock-brokerage business, which he entered at fourteen. At twenty-one he married a Quaker woman and left the Jewish faith to become a Unitarian. Because of this his father disowned him, but there was a later reconciliation. Young Ricardo entered the stock market on his own, with funds advanced by bankers who knew and trusted him. In a few years he was richer than his father, and at forty-three he retired from business with a considerable accumulation of wealth though he looked after his business interests for the rest of his life. At fifty-one he died from an ear infection leaving about £725,000, two-thirds of it in landed estates and mortgages.

Ricardo's principles for making money on the stock exchange may be at least as interesting to many as his abstract economic theorizing. He was quoted as saying that he had made all his money by observing that people generally exaggerated the importance of events. If there was reason for a small advance in stocks, he bought because of the certainty that an unreasonable advance would be profitable to him. When stocks were falling, he sold in the conviction that alarm and panic would produce a decline not warranted by circumstances. Ricardo also explained his financial success by his being contented with small profits, never holding commodities or securities too long when small profits could be had quickly. He had his eye on every new road, bank, or other joint-stock enterprise, and when he deemed the prospect of success to be fair he bought shares. With new undertakings, he claimed, shares soon rose above their long-run price, and he sold quickly in order to invest elsewhere. His high reputation as a judicious speculator led others to buy when he bought. "In this state of things, it must be manifest that I may often have created that very demand which enabled me to dispose of the article purchased, with a small profit, only a very short time afterward."

As a man of firm convictions and high principles, Ricardo frequently advocated policies that conflicted with his own personal interests. He argued against the excessive gains of the Bank of England although he was a stockholder of that institution. He defended the cause of investors in British government bonds when he had ceased to be an investor himself. Even after he had become a large landowner, he put forward theories that, according to his critics, would ruin the landlords. Parliamentary reform, which he supported with enthusiasm, would have deprived him of the seat he had bought representing an Irish constituency that he had never lived in or even visited. He advocated a levy on capital to liquidate the national debt although he was one of the richest people in England. Other reforms that he favored included voting by secret ballot; legalizing the right to discuss religious opinions freely; reducing the number of offenses subject to capital punishment; the abolition of flogging as a court punishment; and the ending of discriminatory laws against Roman Catholics. Only after Ricardo's death was an act passed (in 1829) that gave Catholics the right to sit in Parliament and to hold some public offices.

Ricardo, without any formal schooling beyond the age of fourteen, turned to the systematic study of political economy rather late in life. During his spare time in his youth, he worked rather diligently at physical science and mathematics. Then at twenty-seven he came across Smith's *Wealth of Nations,* and it was this happy accident that fixed his attention on economics. His first "published work"—a letter to a newspaper on currency problems—did not appear until ten years later. Within the next decade, however, he had completed his major contributions. Writing was difficult and painful for Ricardo despite his keen, analytical mind. "Oh that I were capable of writing a book!" he wrote to his friend James Mill. And Mill urged him on: "For as you are already the best *thinker* on political economy, I am resolved you shall also be the best writer." Mill read and criticized Ricardo's writing, always driving him to produce when Ricardo felt that writing was impossible for him.

Ricardo was an outstanding example of a deductive thinker—for better or for worse. He made sweeping generalizations, frequently based on premises which he failed to state or changed without notice. He called these generalizations economic laws, and he considered the operation of laws as valid in economics as in physics. For example, there were laws that regulated the distribution of precious metals throughout the world, laws that governed the international exchange of goods, laws that regulated the distribution of income, and so on. Although Ricardo was very well acquainted with the facts of business and economic life through his personal experience, he did not use the inductive method; he did not reason from the part to the whole, from particulars to the general, from facts to theories. Instead, he enunciated sweeping laws and then sometimes drew upon facts to illustrate their operation. Yet the theoretical questions that interested Ricardo had a significant bearing on the practical problems of both his own and later times.

Ricardo changed the emphasis of economic analysis from production to distribution. Smith had inquired into the nature and causes of the wealth of nations; in the very first page of *Wealth of Nations* he stated that the well-being of a nation depends on its total production and the number of people who must share it. Smith's emphasis on production and the division of labor had been appropriate in a time when the productivity of society was low; the industrial revolution in Great Britain had barely begun, and it was almost imperceptible even to an astute observer like Smith. By Ricardo's time, productivity had increased remarkably, and distribution seemed to have become the major problem. The opening paragraph of Ricardo's *On the Principles of Political Economy and Taxation* pinpointed as the key problem the division of the produce of the earth among three classes: landowners, capitalists, and laborers.

Ricardo emphasized the division of income rather than the growth of income partly because of his economic pessimism and partly because the momentous debate of his day concerned the corn laws (to be discussed later in this chapter). To Ricardo, Smith's optimism about a constantly improving world was erroneous. Population was expanding with amazing rapidity during the industrial revolution;

the increase in Great Britain was 8 per cent between 1700 and 1750, 60 per cent between 1750 and 1800, and 98 per cent between 1800 and 1850. Population pressure, thought Ricardo, would force people to till poorer soil and to work the better soil more intensively. Improved technology would not completely counteract this tendency. Therefore average output per worker or per pound sterling invested in agriculture would tend to fall, and this would impoverish the world in the long run. To Ricardo the central problem seemed to be the question of how and why a certain pattern of distribution of limited output developed among ever-growing numbers of people.

The Bullion Controversy

In 1797, in the midst of more than two decades of warfare between England and France, a panic and a run on gold dangerously depleted the Bank of England reserves. The government suspended cash payments, and England found itself on an irredeemable paper standard. The price of gold gradually rose from its mint parity of £3.17s.10½d. per ounce to a market price of £5.10s. in 1813. A general price inflation was the result. Instead of gold being brought to the mint, it was sold privately in the domestic or foreign markets. The worrisome questions were, Why is the market price of gold rising? and, How can it be stopped?

Because Ricardo had transactions with the Bank of England involving great sums of money, he began to reflect and write on these problems. He charged that the Bank was overissuing currency because it was no longer checked by the requirement to pay in gold on demand. Printing and lending bank notes was a profitable operation but hardly conducive to stable prices for gold or commodities. It was analogous to clipping coins.

The remedy Ricardo called for was a return to the gold standard. Then, if the price of gold in the market rose, currency would be exchanged for gold at the Bank at the mint price. Every overissue of bank notes would be automatically canceled by the flow of paper back to the Bank. The restoration of the gold standard would curb inflation.

The directors of the Bank of England and their friends argued that the market price of gold rose because of its scarcity; gold, not paper, changed value. If the gold standard were restored, every gold guinea would leave the country.

Ricardo replied that there was evidence that it was paper, not gold, that changed value. An ounce of gold would buy as many commodities as it had previously. But the paper that gold represented at the mint price would buy far less, because inflation of prices was in terms of paper money. As for gold leaving the country, it was already doing so except for that held in the coffers of the Bank. The gold standard could be restored safely if the Bank reduced its note circulation first. To eliminate the cost of coinage and to economize on gold that would otherwise circulate as coins Ricardo proposed a gold bullion standard. The Bank should buy and sell gold bullion rather than coin on demand, with at least twenty ounces as the minimum transaction.

Ricardo's plan was adopted by Parliament in 1819, when the Bank was ordered to resume gold payments in ingots of sixty ounces. In 1821 a law was passed requiring payment in coin. The gold standard served for over a century thereafter, except during major wars and financial crises.

Value and Price

Ricardo was concerned with relative values, not with absolute value. That is, he wanted to discover the basis for ratios of exchange between commodities. Utility, he said, is not the measure of exchangeable value, although it is absolutely essential to it. Possessing utility, commodities derive their exchangeable value from two sources: from their scarcity and from the quantity of labor required to obtain them. Commodities whose value is determined by their scarcity alone are nonreproducible, such as rare works of art, scarce books, and coins. But most commodities are reproducible, and Ricardo assumed that they are produced without restraint under conditions of competition.

Ricardo was unconditionally committed to a labor theory of value. Unlike Smith, who applied the labor theory solely to primitive societies, Ricardo linked it to capitalistic society as well. The exchange value of a commodity depends on the labor time necessary to produce it. The labor time includes not only the work done in making the commodity itself but also the work embodied in the raw materials and capital goods used up in the process of production.

This simple form of the labor theory of value would be logical (although not necessarily correct) only under two conditions: if all industries had the same ratios of capital to labor and if the capital investments in all industries had the same durability. Since these conditions do not exist, however, if all commodities sold at their value as measured by labor time, the consequences would be unequal rates of return in different industries. Both Smith and Ricardo were aware of this dilemma, and we can best illustrate the problem by using the example Ricardo gave in the third edition of his book *On the Principles of Political Economy and Taxation,* published in 1821 (first edition 1817). [Vol. I, pp. 33–34] [1]

Suppose a farmer employs a hundred workers for a year to grow grain, and a cotton manufacturer employs a hundred workers for a year to make a machine to produce yarn. The machine will have the same value as the grain. Now assume that during the second year the farmer again employs a hundred workers, and the cotton manufacturer uses a hundred workers to work the machine to produce the yarn. If we disregard the wear and tear of the machine, we see that the hundred workers growing grain during the second year will produce commodities of less value than the hundred workers spinning yarn, because the latter use capital and the former do not. If wage rates were £50 per year per worker and profits were 10 per cent, the value of the grain produced each year and the value of the machine would each be £5,500. The yarn produced during the second year would be worth £6,050, because 10 per cent would have to be earned on the investment in the machine. Otherwise such capital investments would not pay. Here, then, are two capitalists employing the same quantity of labor in the production of their commodities, and yet the goods they produce differ in value because of the different quantities of fixed capital used by each.

Two additional difficulties bring into question the validity of the labor theory of value: First, how are profits explained if all value is derived from labor time? Second, how are rents explained?

Rent will be discussed in the next section, but we can point out here that according to Ricardian theory, rent payments do not influence the prices of goods. On the contrary, the prices of goods are one of the elements that determine rent. No rent is paid on marginal land, and the rate of profit on marginal land governs the rate of profit in the whole economy. Rent results from the extra productivity on the better-than-marginal land, and it does not influence prices.

If all goods sell at their value as measured by labor time, the explanation of profit would be a thorny problem only if we were concerned with *absolute* value. Marx was concerned with this problem. Ricardo, however, dealt only with *relative* values, as we said at the beginning of this section. Regardless of whether profits rose or fell,

---

[1] All references in this chapter are to Piero Sraffa, ed., *The Works and Correspondence of David Ricardo,* 10 vols. (Cambridge, Eng., 1951–55). Reprinted with permission of Cambridge University Press.

they would not influence the relative values of goods. If a pair of shoes embodying five hours of labor exchanges for a dress also made with five hours of labor, a rise in wages and a decline in profits or vice versa will not affect the one-to-one ratio of exchange. Labor does not have to get the whole product simply because labor time is the measure of value. There is no hint of exploitation in Ricardo's analysis; in fact, he defended the institution of private property. It was Marx who later drew revolutionary implications from Ricardo's labor theory of value.

We remain, then, with the problem of different industries using fixed capital and labor in different ratios. Ricardo simply stated that this cause of variation in the value of commodities is slight in its effect. Much more important in determining the value of a commodity is the labor time required to produce it. A commodity will sell at more than its labor-time value if more capital than average is tied up in its production; conversely, a commodity will sell at less than its labor-time value if less-than-average capital is invested in its production.

Labor, in Ricardo's view, is the foundation of the value of commodities, but market prices deviate from value or natural price because of accidental or temporary fluctuations of supply and demand. If the market price rises above the natural price, profits rise, and more capital is used to produce the commodity. If the market price falls, capital flows out of the industry. The actions of individuals seeking maximum advantage tend to equalize the rates of profit and to keep market prices proportional to values. The short-run price depends on supply and demand, but long-run values depend on the costs of production, and the relative costs of production of two commodities are nearly proportional to the total quantity of labor required for the entire production process.

> However abundant the demand it can never permanently raise the price of a commodity above the expence of its production, including in that expence the profits of the producers. It seems natural therefore to seek for the cause of the variation of permanent price in the expences of production. Diminish these and the commodity must finally fall, increase them and it must as certainly rise. What has this to do with demand? [Vol. VII, pp. 250–51]

This is an interesting contrast to the demand theory later introduced by the marginalist economists. The latter were concerned primarily with short-run fluctuations in market prices; demand is important in that context. Ricardo and the other classical economists were concerned mainly with the long-run prices around which market prices fluctuate; cost of production is the main consideration in the long run. Put another way, Ricardo's concern was to explain why potatoes sell for an average of $40 a ton and steel for $150 a ton. The marginalists were more concerned with why the price of potatoes was $39 yesterday and $41 today.

Ricardo agreed with Smith that riches, or wealth, represent "the necessaries, conveniences, and amusements of human life." Value differs from riches in that it depends not on abundance but on the relative difficulty of production. If a certain number of people increase their production of stockings from a thousand pair to two thousand, riches increase but the value produced remains the same. If water becomes scarce and one person monopolizes it, that person's riches increase, for the increased value of water supports the purchase of a larger quantity of goods. But the rest of society loses what this person gained, and total wealth does not increase.

> Because it has been said, that abundance may be prejudicial to the interests of the producers, it has been objected that the new doctrine on this subject is, that the bounty of Providence may become a curse to a country; but this is essentially changing the proposition. No one has said that abundance is injurious to a country, but that it frequently is so to the producers of the abundant commodity. [Vol. IV, p. 221]

Wages and Profits

Labor, said Ricardo, like all other things that are bought and sold, has its natural price and its market price. The natural price of labor is that price which enables workers to subsist and to perpetuate themselves without a change in their numbers. The natural price of labor depends on the price of the necessities of life required by the laborers and their families. If the cost of necessities rises, money wages will rise so that the workers can continue to buy just enough to survive and perpetuate the labor force. If the cost of living falls, wages fall. The market price of labor depends on supply and demand, but as with commodities, the market price tends to fluctuate around the natural price.

In the long run, both the natural price of labor and money wages tend to rise, said Ricardo, because of the increased difficulty and cost of producing food for growing numbers of people—factors that lead to higher food costs. Improvements in agriculture and imports of food partly counteract this tendency by lowering the cost of living, but the forces raising the cost of living remain predominant. Ultimately, therefore, money wages must rise in order to meet the increasing costs of food.

Ricardo's idea that in the long run the worker only gets a minimum subsistence wage came to be known as "the iron law of wages." When the market price of labor rises above the natural price, a worker can rear a large and healthy family. As population increases, wages fall to their natural price and even below. When the market price of labor is below the natural price, misery reduces the working population and wage rates rise. The long-run tendency is therefore for workers to receive the subsistence minimum. This grim analysis was modified by two potential countervailing forces. First, in an industrializing society with expanding capital investments, wages may remain above the subsistence minimum for an indefinite period because the demand for labor is growing. Second, the natural price of labor—that subsistence minimum—varies at different times in the same country. It also differs substantially from country to country according to the habits and customs of the people and what they consider to be the minimum acceptable subsistence.

Ricardo argued that the rates of profit in different fields of enterprise within a country tend to become equalized. Entrepreneurs seek the maximum rate of profit, after allowing for the advantages or disadvantages that one business offers as compared with another. Price movements influence rates of profit that in turn direct the flow of capital. The moneyed class in particular can quickly shift funds to the most profitable business. The free, competitive market and the actions of individuals tend to produce rates of profit that are equal or equally advantageous, on balance, for all types of businesses.

Ricardo, concentrating on the division of national income rather than on its growth, emphasized that profits and wages vary inversely. Thus one increases only at the expense of the other. Why, we may ask, must higher wages come out of profits instead of being passed on in higher prices? The answer lies in the equation of exchange and in the international balance of payments. If prices rise, more money will be required to sell a given quantity of goods. Where will the money come from? Instead of gold flowing in from abroad, gold will leave the country because prices abroad would be lower than at home. With a shrinking money supply, prices cannot rise. Therefore employers themselves must bear the higher money costs of production, and wage increases come out of profits. Conversely, if wages fall, prices will not fall. If they do, gold will flow into the country, and prices will rise again. Therefore a fall in wages will result in a rise in profits.

In the third edition of *On the Principles of Political Economy and Taxation* Ricardo inserted a new chapter called "On Machinery." This was an interesting addition because it represented a complete change of mind on Ricardo's part, to the consternation of his followers and friends. In it he raised the possibility of technological unemployment, which further accentuated the conflict of interests between workers and capitalists.

Ricardo claimed that he had erred in supporting the view that the introduction of machinery would help all three major classes. Their money incomes, he once thought, would remain the same while their real incomes would rise, because goods could be produced more cheaply with machinery. Even labor would gain because the same labor would be demanded as before mechanization, and therefore money wages would not fall. Even if the number of workers in one industry became excessive, capital would shift to some other industry and increase employment there. The only inconvenience would be the temporary maladjustment that occurs when capital and labor move from one employment to another.

Ricardo's revised argument, however, stated that the introduction of machinery would benefit the landlord and the capitalist, as he had believed in the past, but would frequently be very injurious to labor. If more capital were invested in machinery, less would be available to pay wages. In other words, capital is scarce, and the portion that is diverted to machinery represents a deduction from that allocated to wages.

Ricardo used the following example to illustrate his idea. Suppose a capitalist invests £20,000 to carry on a joint business as farmer and manufacturer of necessities. £7000 of this capital is invested in fixed capital such as buildings and implements, and £13,000 goes for wages. Profits are 10 per cent, or £2000 per year. Each year the enterprise produces food and manufactured goods worth £13,000, which the capitalist sells to the workers. They pay for these with the wages they have received. By the end of the year the workers produce £15,000 worth of consumer goods. £13,000 in goods replaces what the workers had consumed, and £2000 in goods are available for the capitalist to consume.

Suppose now that the capitalist decides to employ half the workers in constructing a machine and the other half in producing consumer goods as usual. During that year, as before, £13,000 are paid in wages, and goods are sold amounting to that value that were in stock from the previous year. But during the year the machine was being built, the workers produced only half as much consumer goods as in previous years. The machine is worth £7500, and the consumer goods

£7500. The capitalist still has £20,000 invested, but now £14,500 is in fixed capital and only £5500 is available for wages (instead of £13,000), with an equal value of consumer goods (£5500) available for the workers to buy. Thus £7500 worth of labor becomes superfluous.

The reduced quantity of labor that the capitalist can employ must, with the assistance of the machine and after deductions for its repairs, produce a value equal to £7500; it must replace the circulating capital with a profit of £2000 on the whole capital. The net income of the capitalist is not diminished, but the gross income is reduced from £15,000 to £7500; this, of course, does not concern the capitalist. The support of a population depends on total output, however, and not on net output or profit. There will follow a reduced demand for labor, population will become redundant, and the laboring classes will suffer distress and poverty. "The opinion entertained by the labouring class, that the employment of machinery is frequently detrimental to their interests, is not founded on prejudice and error, but is conformable to the correct principles of political economy." [Vol. I, p. 392]

Ricardo thought that the long-run effect of the introduction of machinery might be more favorable than the short-run effect. Even if the money profit of the capitalist remains the same after an increased investment in machinery, more can be saved as the cost of producing consumer goods falls. Thus the capitalist can invest more, ultimately reemploying the redundant population. Technological unemployment is therefore likely to be only a short-run problem for the workers, but a very real one nonetheless.

In any case, said Ricardo, government should never discourage the use of machinery. The capitalist who is not permitted to receive the greatest possible profit from the use of machinery at home will invest capital abroad. The demand for labor will be reduced if machinery is introduced at home, but it will disappear altogether to the extent that the capital is invested abroad. In addition, since new machinery lowers the cost of producing goods, a country can remain competitive with foreign countries that are permitting new and better machines to be used.

Rent and the Law of Diminishing Returns

The theory of rent was developed separately by four writers and presented in pamphlets, all published during February of 1815. Malthus was the first to appear in print with his theory, followed by Edward West, Ricardo, and Robert Torrens. This coincidence is an interesting example of how a pressing contemporary issue can call forth a theory developed independently by different people. Ricardo modestly stated that Malthus and West deserved most of the credit.

Rent was a pertinent subject in England because tenant farming was widespread. The impending parliamentary debate in 1815 on the corn laws—tariffs on grain imports—was the immediate issue that sparked the development of rent theory. As the Napoleonic Wars drew to a close, farmers and landlords feared that grain would pour into Great Britain at ruinously low prices. The landowners, who dominated Parliament, clamored for higher protection in the name of the general welfare. The business interests, on the other hand, spoke against higher tariffs on grain imports and argued for repeal of the existing corn laws. They found support in Ricardo's economics: If wages tend toward the minimum subsistence level, then lower prices on grain and on bread would keep wages low, thus reducing the businessman's production costs and allowing British goods to compete more effectively in foreign markets. In addition, the manufacturers were aware that the more grain Great Britain imported, the more manufactured goods businessmen could export. They were perfectly willing to sacrifice the interests of the landlords in order to benefit themselves.

This conflict generated the theory of rent. Although Ricardo was not the sole originator of this theory, he developed it most clearly and completely. He also integrated rent theory with the theory of wages and profits and with economic change. Ricardo was the first to hypothesize a marginal principle in economic theory. Ricardo's theory of rent is therefore seminal in the rise of the marginalist school.

"Rent," said Ricardo, "is that portion of the produce of the earth, which is paid to the landlord for the use of the original and indestructible powers of the soil." He modified this definition by including as rent the return on long-run capital investments that are amalgamated with the land and increase its productivity.

No one pays rent in a newly settled country in which fertile soil is abundant. But

> when in the progress of society, land of the second degree of fertility is taken into cultivation, rent immediately commences on that of the first quality, and the amount of that rent will depend on the difference in the quality of these two portions of land.
>
> When land of the third quality is taken into cultivation, rent immediately commences on the second, and it is regulated as before, by the difference in their productive powers. At the same time, the rent of the first

quality will rise, for that must always be above the rent of the second, by the difference between the produce which they yield with a given quantity of capital and labour. With every step in the progress of population, which shall oblige a country to have recourse to land of a worse quality, to enable it to raise its supply of food, rent, on all the more fertile lands, will rise. [Vol. I, p. 70]

The produce from marginal land will bring in enough revenue to cover all the expenses of production plus the average rate of profit on the investment in labor and capital. The value of farm produce depends on the labor required per unit of output on the least productive land in use. The better land produces a surplus that is taken by the landowner as rent. This explains rent measured at the extensive margin of cultivation.

Rent also arises from the intensive cultivation of land because of the law of diminishing returns. If successive units of labor and capital are added to a piece of land while technology remains constant, each added unit of investment will add less to the output than previous units. If this were not so, food for the entire world could be grown in a flower pot. The last unit of labor and capital must pay for itself and provide an average rate of profit as well. Earlier units yield a surplus return, which is rent.

Table 1 illustrates Ricardo's theory of rent by showing how rent is measured from the extensive margin of cultivation. We have five grades of land—A to E. Investing $10 per acre gives us the greatest return from A, because it is the best land, and E is the worst. If wheat were under 50¢ per bushel, none would be produced. At 50¢ it pays to invest $10 per acre on land A, because the yield covers all

Table 1   Rent Measured from the Extensive Margin of Cultivation

| PRICE OF WHEAT PER BUSHEL | RENT DERIVED FROM EACH GRADE OF LAND | | | | |
	A	B	C	D	E
	Input: $10 *Yield: 20* *bu./acre*	*Input: $10* *Yield: 15* *bu./acre*	*Input: $10* *Yield: 10* *bu./acre*	*Input: $10* *Yield: 5* *bu./acre*	*Input: $10* *Yield: 4* *bu./acre*
$ .50	0*				
.66⅔	$ 3.33	0*			
1.00	10.00	$ 5.00	0*		
2.00	30.00	20.00	$10.00	0*	
2.50	40.00	27.50	15.00	$2.50	0*

* Price level at which $10 input is made.

labor and capital costs, including the average rate of profit. But there would be no rent. If wheat rises to 66⅔¢ it pays to invest $10 per acre on land B. The wheat produced on A would also sell for 66⅔¢, and the return on A would be $13.33. Since a $10 return is considered reasonable by tenants, competition among them causes them to bid $3.33 per acre for the right to farm A, and the landlord receives this sum in the form of economic rent. If wheat rises to $1 per bushel, C becomes the no-rent marginal land, B yields rent of $5 per acre, and A $10. If wheat rises to $2, land D will be worked, and the rent on A, B, and C will be $30, $20, and $10.

Table 2 analyzes rent at the intensive margin of cultivation, where the revenue received from the marginal output has to be compared with the cost of producing that extra output, just as it was at the extensive margin. The principle of diminishing returns shows that on each grade of land, as an extra $10 is invested, the increase in output is less than for the previous $10. On grade A land, it does not pay to invest $20 unless wheat rises to 66⅔¢ per bushel. At this price the marginal output of 15 bushels justifies the second $10 input. The first $10 input, however, then brings in revenue of $13.33, of which $3.33 is rent. If wheat rises to $1 per bushel, the input of the third $10 is justified by the marginal productivity of 10 bushels, which bring in $10 revenue. Rent is then $15 per acre. If wheat rises to $2 per bushel, it pays to invest $40 per acre on grade A land, because marginal productivity is 5 bushels, and rent is $60.

Table 2   Rent Measured from the Intensive Margin of Cultivation

PRICE OF WHEAT PER BUSHEL	LAND GRADE A			
	Input	Output	Marginal output	Rent
$ .50	$10	20		0
.66⅔	20	35	15	$ 3.33
1.00	30	45	10	15.00
2.00	40	50	5	60.00
2.50	50	54	4	85.00

	LAND GRADE B				LAND GRADE C			
	Input	Output	Marginal output	Rent	Input	Output	Marginal output	Rent
.66⅔	$10	15		0				
1.00	20	25	10	$ 5.00	$10	10		0
2.00	30	30	5	30.00	20	15	5	$10.00
2.50	40	34	4	45.00	30	19	4	17.50

If wheat were $2.50 per bushel, it would pay to invest $50 on Grade A land, $40 on B, and $30 on C; the total investment would be $120. The total yield would be 107 bushels, which would sell for $267.50, yielding a total rent of $147.50 on 3 acres, one of each grade of land.

It is obvious that every increase in the price of wheat, whether through tariffs on imports of grain or through population growth, raises rent. Every fall in the price of grain, whether through lowered tariffs or technological improvements or reduced population, lowers rents. Therefore, said Ricardo, if we are to be consistent, we should prohibit improvements in cultivation if we tax imports of grain.

Ricardo was also aware that rent can originate through differences in location. If lands of equal fertility are situated at varying distances from the market, the farthest land worked must pay the normal returns to labor and capital. The more favorably located land will yield extra returns because of smaller transport costs, and these returns constitute rent.

Rent is both a differential return and a surplus above costs. Ricardo argued that rent is price-determined but not price determining—that is, rents are high because the prices of farm products are high, but high prices cannot be explained by high rents. This viewpoint is based on the law of diminishing returns and the assumptions that the supply of the best land is limited and that land has no alternative uses.

The average rate of profit at any time is determined by the rate of profit on marginal land. No rent is paid on this land, and the total product is divided between the farmer-employers and the laborers. If wages rise, profits will fall, and vice versa. If the rate of profit in industry is higher than in farming marginal land, capital will flow from agriculture to industry, and a better grade of land will become the new marginal land. If agriculture is more profitable than industry, capital will flow toward agriculture, and the next worse grade of land will become the marginal land worked.

As stated in the previous section, Ricardo saw a conflict of interests between workers and capitalists. An even more basic conflict exists, he said, between landlords and the rest of society. As population increases, the increased demand for food will raise its price. Poorer land will be brought into cultivation, and better land will be worked more intensively. Rents will therefore rise. Wages will also rise to give the workers their minimum of subsistence, and thus profits will fall. "All classes, therefore, except the landlords, will be injured by the increase in the price of corn."

Improvements in agriculture and imports of cheap grain partially counteract the tendency toward rising rents and falling profits. Therefore Ricardo opposed the corn laws. By repealing the tariffs and other restrictions on the import of grain, society's interests would be promoted at the expense of the landlords. Ricardo was nevertheless pessimistic about the long-run trend.

Adam Smith thought the rate of profit would fall because of growing competition among entrepreneurs, and he welcomed this development. Ricardo thought that the rate of profit would fall because of the increasing difficulty of growing food for an expanding population, and this he deplored. Falling profits, he thought, would curb the accumulation and investment of capital, and ultimately the stationary state would prevail. This state would be reached when new investment ceased, when population could no longer expand because the limits of food production had been reached, and when every available surplus had been appropriated as rent.

Obviously this diagnosis of capitalism's fate was erroneous. The stationary state has seldom appeared under capitalism, nor when appearing has it remained stationary for long. Improvements in farming have more than kept pace with the growth of population in advanced countries, so that the percentage of the labor force in agriculture has tended to decline. Rents have not absorbed an increasing percentage of the national income. Agriculture, an ever-declining sector almost everywhere, cannot govern the rate of profit in the whole economy. It could do so only if Ricardo's implicit assumptions were correct: perfect competition, complete mobility of the factors of production within a country, and unchanging technology in agriculture. Ricardo was unaware that the proportionate increase in rents and prices for urban land would by far exceed the increases for farm land.

Ricardo drew the following conclusion from his analysis: A tax on rent would affect rent only. It would fall wholly on landlords and could not be shifted to any other people. The landlords could not raise rents to pay for the tax, because marginal land would pay no rent and therefore no tax. The tax on rent would leave undisturbed the difference in productivity between marginal and better land. The tax would not raise the price of farm produce, nor would it discourage the cultivation of land. This was the analysis that led to Henry George's idea of a single tax, a tax that took all the economic rent. This was not Ricardo's idea of justice.

Accused of considering landlords the enemies of society, Ricardo denied the allegation. "High rent and low profits, for they invariably accompany each other, ought never to be the subject of complaint, if they are the effect of the natural course of things." [Vol. IV, p. 21]

Ricardo thought that laissez faire was the ideal policy not only in foreign trade but in domestic affairs. Wages should not be regulated, nor should poor relief be given to the indigent:

> Like all other contracts, wages should be left to the fair and free competition of the market, and should never be controlled by the interference of the legislature.
>
> The clear and direct tendency of the poor laws, is in direct opposition to those obvious principles: it is not, as the legislature benevolently intended, to amend the condition of the poor, but to deteriorate the condition of both poor and rich; instead of making the poor rich, they are calculated to make the rich poor. [Vol. I, pp. 105–06]

Ricardo overemphasized the role of diminishing returns. This law is correct only if other factors, including the level of technology, are kept constant. Historically, improvements in agriculture have resulted in increasing returns per unit of labor in the most advanced, progressive countries. Nor was Ricardo correct in emphasizing that landlords as a whole are never interested in increased productivity in agriculture. Land that cannot support the people who work on it cannot be tilled. Improvements permit poorer land to be worked, thereby increasing the surplus available for rent. Only if improvements in agriculture are not accompanied by an increased demand for farm products does rent fall.

Ricardo's idea of opposing interests—this germ of the concept of class conflict—was not forgiven by adherents of the later neoclassical school. The idea of labor as the source of all value led to the socialist concept that the worker deserved the whole product, to which Marx added the doctrine of class struggle.

The Theory of Comparative Cost

Smith advocated foreign trade without impediments in order to widen markets and remove surpluses; trade was based on differences in absolute costs—everybody buying in the cheapest market. Ricardo made a brilliant and lasting contribution to economic thought by developing the theory of comparative cost. If one country is more efficient than another in producing all commodities, trade between the two nevertheless will be of mutual advantage. The more efficient country should export those commodities whose comparative cost is lowest, and it should import those whose comparative cost is highest. This is the basis for Ricardo's free-trade policy for manufactured goods. As we saw above, the significance of free trade in agricultural products was to keep down the cost of food, wages, and rent, thereby keeping profits high and promoting investment. But the actual trade in farm produce would also be based on comparative cost.

Using Ricardo's example, Portugal can produce a certain quantity of wine with 80 man-years of labor, and cloth with 90 man-years. England can produce the wine with 120 man-years, and the cloth with 100. Portugal requires one-third less labor than England to produce wine, and one-tenth less labor for cloth. Portugal should therefore export wine and import cloth. By producing and exporting wine, Portugal will obtain cloth for 80 man-years of labor which otherwise would cost it 90. England, by producing and exporting cloth, will get wine for 100 man-years of labor which otherwise would cost it 120.

Ricardo explicitly assumed that capital and labor did not flow between countries. Otherwise both wine and cloth would be made in Portugal. He implicitly assumed constant costs rather than increasing costs as output expanded. Otherwise specialization would not be carried on to its fullest extent.

Suppose, said Ricardo, England improved its manufacture of wine, so that it still paid to ship cloth from England to Portugal, but it was no longer profitable to ship wine in the opposite direction. The Portuguese importer would have to pay more for the pound sterling bought in England to pay for the cloth. This might cut off imports entirely. But if the premium on British currency were less than the profit from importing cloth, gold or silver would flow to England in payment for cloth. The declining money supply in Portugal would cause falling prices there, and the rising money supply in England would cause rising prices in that country. This would bring about a new equilibrium in foreign trade. Here is Hume's price specie-flow mechanism once again.

Ricardo has been criticized for basing his theory of comparative cost on the labor theory of value and for implicitly assuming a full-employment economy. If there were unemployment in Portugal, would it not pay it to produce wine and cloth both for its own use and for export to England? Actually Ricardo's labor theory of value is not crucial to his international trade theory. It is possible to compare money costs of domestic and foreign goods based on foreign exchange rates. If both Portuguese cloth and wine were cheaper in Portugal than the British goods that might be imported, no imports could be sold if cost were the only consideration. Exchange rates would fluctuate, however, to the point where British cloth in Portugal would become cheaper than domestic cloth. The theory of comparative cost actually does help to explain international trade, although the problems are more complicated than in Ricardo's simplified model. Furthermore, Ricardo did not attempt to explain what determines the ratios of exchange between commodities traded internationally, although his theory did define the limits within which the ratios could fluctuate.

We shall illustrate Ricardo's theory of comparative cost with two examples. The first example shows how the basic principle can be applied to intranational as well as international trade; it also illustrates the limits of the ratios of exchange of goods and the possible gains from trade.

Suppose New York state can produce a pair of shoes with 4 hours of labor and a bushel of apples with 1 hour; the state of Washington can produce a pair of shoes with 12 hours of labor and a bushel of apples with 2 hours. New York has an absolute advantage in both shoes and apples and a comparative advantage in shoes. The reason is that New York is three times as productive as Washington in producing shoes, but only twice as productive in producing apples. Washington has a comparative advantage in producing apples.

We assume that production can be expanded or reduced at constant cost per unit of output, that differences in cost between the two states persist, and that transport costs are zero. New York should be willing to sell 1 pair of shoes for 4 or more bushels of apples; Washington should be willing to offer 6 or fewer bushels of apples for a pair of shoes. Therefore the limits of exchange are 4-to-6 bushels of apples for 1 pair of shoes.

Assume that the final terms of trade are 5 bushels of apples for 1 pair of shoes. What does each side gain from trade? If New York devotes 20 hours to producing its own shoes and apples, it can have 4 pairs of shoes and 4 bushels of apples. Through specialization and trade, however, it can produce 5 pairs of shoes in 20 hours, keep 4 pairs, and exchange 1 pair for 5 bushels of apples. Its gain is 1 bushel of apples.

Washington can produce 1 pair of shoes and 4 bushels of apples in 20 hours. Or, alternatively, it can produce 10 bushels of apples, keep 5, and exchange 5 for 1 pair of shoes. Its gain is also a bushel of apples.

The second example shows how Ricardo's principle can be stated in terms of different currencies instead of in terms of labor cost; it illustrates one possible path toward international equilibrium. Suppose Great Britain can produce steel for £40 per ton and cotton yarn for £60 per ton; the United States produces steel for $100 per ton and yarn for $200 per ton. If the British pound exchanges for $4, then both steel and yarn will be cheaper in the United States than in Britain. We will refuse to buy British steel, which would cost us $160 compared with out domestic cost of $100, or British yarn, which would cost us $240 instead of our own $200. Again assuming no transport costs, Great Britain can buy our steel for £25 compared to its own cost of £40, and it can buy our yarn for £50 compared to its own domestic cost of £60.

If we assume a two-country, two-commodity model, the British will wish to acquire dollars to buy our goods, but we will not wish to buy pounds because we do not want British goods. The price of the dollar will rise, and the price of the pound will fall. If the pound now goes to $3, we will find that yarn is cheaper in Britain than at home. Britain finds that steel is cheaper in the United States than at home, but yarn is more expensive abroad. Therefore it is of mutual benefit for Britain to produce yarn for both countries and for the United States to produce steel for both.

We shall end this chapter with Ricardo's powerful plea for laissez faire in foreign trade, based on his concept of a harmony of interests in international affairs, although not in domestic matters.

> Under a system of perfectly free commerce, each country naturally devotes its capital and labour to such employments as are most beneficial to each. This pursuit of individual advantage is admirably connected with the universal good of the whole. By stimulating industry, by rewarding ingenuity, and by using most efficaciously the peculiar powers bestowed by nature, it distributes labour most effectively and most economically: while, by increasing the general mass of productions, it diffuses general benefit, and binds together by one common tie of interest and intercourse, the universal society of nations throughout the civilized world. It is this principle which determines that wine shall be made in France and Portugal, that corn shall be grown in America and Poland, and that hardware and other goods shall be manufactured in England. [Vol. I, pp. 133–34]

Bibliography

BLAUG, MARK, *Ricardian Economics.* New Haven, Conn.: Yale University Press, 1958.

MALTHUS, THOMAS, *An Inquiry into the Nature and Progress of Rent,* 1815, ed. by Jacob H. Hollander. Baltimore, Md.: Johns Hopkins Press, 1903.

RICARDO, DAVID, *Works and Correspondence,* ed. by Piero Sraffa. 10 vols. Cambridge, Eng.: The University Press, 1951–55.

WEST, EDWARD, *On the Application of Capital to Land,* 1815, ed. by Jacob H. Hollander. Baltimore, Md.: Johns Hopkins Press, 1903.

7

The Classical School:
Thomas Robert Malthus

Thomas Robert Malthus (1766–1834) was a curate, a writer, and a professor of history and political economy in the East India College in England. *An Essay on the Principle of Population,* which first appeared in 1798, established his enduring fame; it went through six editions during twenty-eight years. He also published *Principles of Political Economy* in 1820.

Malthus and Ricardo enjoyed a warm, close friendship in spite of the fact that they disagreed about almost every aspect of political economy except Malthus' analysis of population. Through frequent personal visits and through correspondence beginning in June 1811, they subjected each other's views to merciless scrutiny. Neither ever persuaded the other, as Ricardo observed in his last letter to Malthus, written August 31, 1823, eleven days before Ricardo's unexpected death. "And now my dear Malthus I have done. Like other disputants after much discussion we each retain our own opinions. These discussions however never influence our friendship; I should not like you more than I do if you agreed in opinion with me."

The two outstanding contributions of Malthus were his theories of population and of market gluts. While he fits into the classical tradition, Malthus is sufficiently at variance with some basic classical principles to merit a separate analysis of the background and significance of his ideas. The five questions we use in analyzing each school will therefore be applied to him.

Overview of Malthusian Theories

The Social Background of Malthusian Theories

By 1798 many of the evil effects of the industrial revolution were showing themselves. Unemployment, poverty, and disease were already problems that called for remedial treatment. Tax rates for poor relief were burdensome to property owners. The ferment of the French Revolution radiated outward to infect the poorer classes in other countries; the reaction of the British propertied classes was to deny any responsibility for widespread poverty. The landlords were under attack as people who loved to reap where they had not sown, as Adam Smith had phrased it. Their political power was challenged by the rising merchant and industrial capitalists and their followers.

The immediate cause of Malthus' pessimistic outlook on the human prospect was his father's optimistic belief in the perfectibility of people and society. The faith of his father was based on the works of Godwin and Condorcet. Young Malthus assumed the task of demolishing their philosophies.

William Godwin (1756–1836), father-in-law of the poet Shelley, was a minister, novelist, and political philosopher who turned anarchist and atheist and whose doctrines resembled those of the French revolutionaries. He published his influential book, *An Enquiry Concerning Political Justice and Its Influence on General Virtue and Happiness*, in 1793. This work was among the first to formulate the philosophy of anarchism. Godwin was an extreme individualist who opposed not only all coercive action by the state but also collective action by the citizens. He relied entirely on the voluntary good will and sense of justice of the individual person guided by the ultimate rule of reason. According to Godwin the human race is perfectible through a continuous advance toward higher rationality and increased well-being. Since a person's character depends on the social environment instead of being immutable and determined by heredity, a more perfect society will produce more perfect people. The major obstacles to progress, he said, are private property, economic and political inequality, and the coercive state. On population, his view was that when the limit of population is reached, humanity will refuse to propagate itself further to the point of overpopulation. Godwin regretted that his optimism helped to evoke what he thought was the evil genius of Malthusian pessimism about overpopulation and the hopelessness of the human condition.

The Marquis de Condorcet (1743–94) was an eminent French mathematician of an aristocratic family who was elected to the Academy of Science at twenty-six and to the French Academy at thirty-nine. He was a skeptic in religion, a democrat in politics, a physiocrat in economics, and a pacifist. Among his friends were Turgot, Voltaire, Thomas Paine, Thomas Jefferson, Benjamin Franklin, and Adam Smith. After the outbreak of the French Revolution, which he greeted with enthusiasm, he and Paine founded the journal *Le Républicain.*

Condorcet favored universal suffrage for men and women. He vigorously opposed the provisions of the French Constitution in 1791 that established property qualifications for voting and election to office. The fierce party strife of the Revolution left him isolated, and his arrest was ordered in 1793. Friends hid him for nine months, after which he deliberately left his refuge in order not to endanger further the woman who sheltered him. After several days of wandering in disguise, he was arrested as a suspect and imprisoned; the morning after his arrest he was found dead from either exposure or suicide by poison.

While in hiding, Condorcet wrote his most important work, *Sketch of the Intellectual Progress of Mankind.* In spite of his persecution by the Revolution he had welcomed so ardently, his theme was the idea of social progress based on three fundamental principles: (1) equality among nations, (2) equality of individuals within a nation, and (3) the perfectibility of humankind. Ultimately the equality of nations would abolish war "as the greatest of plagues and as the greatest of crimes," he wrote. A permanent league of nations would maintain peace and the independence of every nation. The equality of individuals would be won when differences in wealth, inheritance, and education were wiped out. He favored the wide distribution of property, social security, and universal free education for men and women. He believed that the natural order tends toward economic equality, but that existing laws and institutions encouraged inequalities. Equality would overcome the social evils of the day and lead to perfection. The only inequalities that should be permitted, he thought, are those based on natural abilities. Population would increase as a result of these beneficent reforms, but the food supply would increase even more rapidly. If the problem of subsistence could eventually no longer be solved in this way, Condorcet favored birth control to limit the growth of population.

These were the ideas against which young Malthus rebelled. The vices and misery that plague society are due, he said, not to evil human institutions, but to the fecundity of the human race. The abolition of war Condorcet dreamed of would merely remove one of the essential remedies for overpopulation. The Frenchman's welfare programs would vitiate a second factor limiting population—hunger. Godwin's equalitarian, communistic society would mean more food for the masses and therefore a more massive growth of population. Godwin and Condorcet seemed to stand for all the excesses of the French Revolution, whereas Malthus' voice appealed to conservatives as a sane and able defense of the status quo.

The Essence of the Malthusian Population Theory

In the first edition of *An Essay on the Principle of Population* Malthus presented his "law of population." Population when unchecked increases geometrically; subsistence increases at best only arithmetically. That is, every twenty-five years population tends to increase at the rate of one, two, four, eight, sixteen, thirty-two, and so forth, while the rate of increase for subsistence is at best only one, two, three, four, five, six. He pointed to America (the India or China of his day with respect to rate of population growth) for proof of his propositions.

It has been stated frequently that in 1798 Malthus was a rash young man, overenthusiastic and too extreme in presenting his theory; in his more mature writing he is supposed to have relinquished the idea of mathematical ratios. Let us look therefore at *A Summary View of the Principle of Population*, which appeared in 1830. This work was published even later than the last edition of *An Essay on the Principle of Population*. In *A Summary View*, published thirty-two years after the first edition of the *Essay* and four years before his death, Malthus wrote:

> It may be safely asserted, therefore, that population, when unchecked, increases in a geometrical progression of such a nature as to double itself every twenty-five years. . . . If, setting out from a tolerably well peopled country such as England, France, Italy, or Germany, we were to suppose that, by great attention to agriculture, its produce could be permanently increased every twenty-five years by a quantity equal to that which it at present produces, it would be allowing a rate of increase decidedly beyond any probability of realization. . . . Yet this would be an arithmetical progression, and would fall short, beyond all comparison, of the natural increases of population in a geometrical progression.

Malthus identified certain preventive checks to population growth—those that reduced the birth rate. The preventive check Malthus approved was moral restraint. People who could not afford children should either postpone marriage or never marry; conduct before marriage should be strictly moral. The preventive check Malthus disapproved of was vice. This included prostitution and birth control, both of which reduced the birth rate. During his lifetime the English reformer Francis Place and others were popularizing birth control. In the appendix to the fifth edition of his *Essay* in 1817, Malthus wrote:

> Indeed I should always particularly reprobate any artificial and unnatural modes of checking population, both on account of their immorality and their tendency to remove a necessary stimulus to industry. If it were possible for each married couple to limit by a wish the number of their children, there is certainly reason to fear that the indolence of the human race would be very greatly increased; and that neither the population of individual countries, nor of the whole earth, would ever reach its natural and proper extent.

While opposing the preventive check to population that could work, he endorsed moral restraint, the check that would not work. His concern over the indolence of the human race might lead one to think that he was more interested in maintaining a large, hard-working, poorly paid population than he was in establishing really effective measures for limiting human reproduction.

Malthus also recognized certain positive checks to population—those that increased the death rate. These were famine, misery, plague, and war. They were elevated to the position of natural phenomena or laws, necessary evils required to limit the population. These positive checks represented punishments for people who had not practiced moral restraint. If the positive checks could somehow be overcome, people would face starvation as a rapidly growing population pressed upon a food supply that at best would grow slowly. In the sixth edition of his *Essay* Malthus pictured the positive checks to population as follows:

> It is an evident truth that, whatever may be the rate of increase in the means of subsistence, the increase of population must be limited by it, at least after the food has once been divided into the smallest shares that will support life. All the children born, beyond what would be required to keep up the population to this level, must necessarily perish, unless room be made for them by the deaths of grown persons. . . . To act consistently therefore, we should facilitate, instead of foolishly and vainly endeavouring to impede, the operations of nature in producing this mortality; and if we dread the too frequent visitation of the horrid form of famine, we should sedulously encourage the other forms of destruction, which we compel nature to use. Instead of recommending cleanliness to the poor, we should encourage contrary habits. In our towns we should

make the streets narrower, crowd more people into the houses, and court the return of the plague. In the country, we should build our villages near stagnant pools, and particularly encourage settlements in all marshy and unwholesome situations. But above all, we should reprobate specific remedies for ravaging diseases; and those benevolent, but much mistaken men, who have thought they were doing a service to mankind by projecting schemes for the total extirpation of particular disorders. If by these and similar means the annual mortality were increased . . . we might probably every one of us marry at the age of puberty, and yet few be absolutely starved. [Bk. IV, Ch. 5]

According to Malthus, then, poverty and misery are the natural punishment for the "lower classes," which have failed to restrain their multiplication. From this view followed his highly significant policy conclusion: There must be no government relief for the poor. To give them aid would cause more children to survive, thereby ultimately worsening the problem of hunger. This is the way he phrased it in the second edition of his *Essay* in 1803:

A man who is born into a world already possessed, if he cannot get subsistence from his parents on whom he has a just demand, and if the society do not want his labour, has no claim of *right* to the smallest portion of food, and, in fact, has no business to be where he is. At nature's mighty feast there is no vacant cover for him. She tells him to be gone, and will quickly execute her own orders, if he do not work upon the compassion of some of her guests. If these guests get up and make room for him, other intruders immediately appear demanding the same favour. . . . The order and harmony of the feast is disturbed, the plenty that before reigned is changed into scarcity.

Malthus withdrew that statement from later editions of the *Essay*, but he offered a specific proposal concerning the poor laws in the sixth edition:

I have reflected much on the subject of the poor-laws, and hope therefore that I shall be excused in venturing to suggest a mode of their gradual abolition. . . . We are bound in justice and honour formally to disclaim the *right* of the poor to support.
    To this end, I should propose a regulation to be made, declaring that no child born from any marriage, taking place after the expiration of a year from the date of the law, and no illegitimate child born two years from the same date, should ever be entitled to parish assistance. . . .
    With regard to illegitimate children, after proper notice had been given, they should not be allowed to have any claim to parish assistance, but be left entirely to the support of private charity. If the parents desert their child, they ought to be made answerable for the crime. The infant

is, comparatively speaking, of little value to society, as others will immediately supply its place. [Bk. IV, Ch. 8]

Some of Malthus' ideas were adopted in the "scientifically" harsh Poor Law Amendment of 1834. The law abolished all relief for able-bodied people outside workhouses. A man applying for relief had to pawn all his possessions and then enter a workhouse before assistance was granted; his wife and children either entered a workhouse or were sent to work in the cotton mills. In either case the family was broken up and treated harshly in order to discourage its becoming a public charge. The workhouse was invested with a social stigma, and entering it was made psychological and moral torture. The law aimed at making public assistance so unbearable that most people would rather starve quietly than submit to its indignities. This system was to be the basis of English poor-law policy until early in the twentieth century. Malthus, who died four months after the Poor Law Amendment was passed, must have regarded it as a vindication of his idea that there is not room enough at nature's feast for everybody. No wonder Thomas Carlyle, after reading Malthus, called political economy the "dismal science"!

While Ricardo endorsed the population theory of Malthus, he was not so dogmatic. A true apostle of economic growth, he wrote in *On the Principles of Political Economy and Taxation:*

> It has been calculated, that under favourable circumstances population may be doubled in twenty-five years; but under the same favourable circumstances, the whole capital of a country might possibly be doubled in a shorter period. In that case, wages during the whole period would have a tendency to rise, because the demand for labour would increase still faster than the supply. [Ch. 5]

In a lighter vein Ricardo wrote in a letter:

> Now that I am a grandfather I should be puzzled, even with the assistance of Mr. Malthus, and Major Torrens, to calculate the accelerated ratio at which my progeny is increasing. I am sure that it is neither arithmetical nor geometrical. I have some notion of consulting with Mr. Owen on the best plan of establishing one of his villages for me and my descendants, admitting only in addition a sufficient number of families to prevent the necessity of celibacy.

Malthus, who married at thirty-nine, had three children but no grandchildren. Ricardo, married at twenty-one, had eight children and twenty-five grandchildren. Had this progression continued, England would have been overrun with Ricardos!

The Essence of the Malthusian Theory of Gluts

In Book II of his *Principles of Political Economy* Malthus developed his theory of the inadequacy of effective demand to maintain full employment. There is an unlimited human desire for goods. But if the individual who wishes to buy has nothing to sell that others want, goods will remain unsold. If people have only their labor to sell, the employer will not hire them unless they produce a value greater than that which they receive; that is, the employer must be able to make a profit. Since the workers cannot buy back the total output, others must. The profit cannot be turned over to the workers because in a free-enterprise, private-property economy, production and employment cease if profits disappear.

Full employment can be maintained only if investment is high enough to absorb the surplus. Spending on capital goods stimulates production and employment about as much as spending on consumption goods does. But, said Malthus, the consumption by workers employed in productive labor can never alone furnish a sufficient motive to the accumulation and employment of capital. And if landlords and capitalists agree to be parsimonious in order to add to their capital, goods will remain unsold.

Who will consume the surplus? Workers cannot, or profits would disappear. Capitalists have the power to consume their profits, but it is not their habit to do so. The great object of their lives is to amass a fortune, and they are too busy in the countinghouse to consume it all.

> There must therefore be a considerable class of persons who have both the will and power to consume more material wealth than they produce, or the mercantile classes could not continue profitably to produce so much more than they consume. In this class the landlords no doubt stand pre-eminent; but if they were not assisted by the great mass of individuals engaged in personal services, whom they maintain, their own consumption would of itself be insufficient to keep up and increase the value of the produce, and enable the increase of its quantity more than to counterbalance the fall of its price. Nor could the capitalists in that case continue with effect the same habits of savings. [Bk. II, Ch. 1, Sec. 9]

Spending by landlords is the best way to overcome stagnation: Since rent is a differential surplus, its expenditure adds to effective demand without adding to the cost of production. Other forms of income—wages, interest, and profit—increase purchasing power but also raise costs of production, and costs must be kept down if a country is to maintain its competitive position in world markets.

Malthus did not agree with Ricardo's contention that if food is dearer, money wages must rise, and therefore costs of production rise.

While Malthus favored unproductive consumption by landlords, including the hiring of large numbers of menial servants, he opposed excessive unproductive consumption financed by the government. Statesmen, soldiers, sailors, and those who live from interest on the national debt necessitate higher taxes, which might stop the increase of wealth. Society should consider private property sacred, and it should not allow the redistribution of wealth through excessive taxation. Nor is a growing government debt desirable, for the inflation it promotes will hurt the receivers of fixed incomes.

War, wrote Malthus in *Principles of Political Economy*, offers another stimulus that can eliminate gluts in highly productive economies:

> England and America . . . suffered the least by the war, or rather were enriched by it, and they are now suffering the most by the peace. It is certainly a very unfortunate circumstance that any period should ever have occurred in which peace should appear to have been, in so marked a manner, connected with distress. [Bk. II, Ch. 1, Sec. 10]

He defended the corn laws, which would continue to enrich landlords and thereby promote unproductive consumption. For times of acute distress he recommended government spending on public works:

> It is also of importance to know that, in our endeavours to assist the working classes in a period like the present, it is desirable to employ them in those kinds of labour, the results of which do not come for sale into the market, such as roads and public works. The objection to employing a large sum in this way, raised by taxes, would not be its tendency to diminish the capital employed in productive labour; because this, to a certain extent, is exactly what is wanted; but it might, perhaps, have the effect of concealing too much the failure of the national demand for labour, and prevent the population from gradually accommodating itself to a reduced demand. This however might be, in a considerable degree, corrected by the wages given. [Bk. II, Ch. 1, Sec. 10]

Ricardo's answer to Malthus was based on his refusal to admit the possibility of chronic unemployment:

> A body of unproductive labourers are just as necessary and as useful with a view to future production, as a fire, which should consume in the manufacturers warehouse the goods which those unproductive labourers would otherwise consume. . . . In what way can a man's consuming my

produce, without making me any return whatever, enable me to make a fortune? I should think my fortune would be more likely to be made, if the consumer of my produce returned me an equivalent value.[1]

What Groups of People Did Malthusian Doctrines Serve or Seek to Serve?

Malthus' population theory served the wealthy by absolving them from any responsibility for poverty and its alleviation; the poor had only themselves to blame for their condition. He opposed the poor laws, which if abolished would have effectively reduced taxes on property at a time when property ownership was concentrated among relatively few people. His defense of the corn laws and unproductive consumption promoted the interests of the landlords, a group that had long been dominant but was rapidly losing its political power and social prestige. It was with some amazement that he wrote in his *Principles of Political Economy:* "It is somewhat singular that Mr. Ricardo, a considerable receiver of rents, should have so much underrated their national importance; while I, who never received, nor expect to receive any, should probably be accused of overrating their importance." [Bk. I, Ch. 3, Sec. 9]

How Were Malthusian Doctrines Valid, Useful, or Correct in Their Time?

They were useful insofar as they served the wealthy, the property owners, and the landlords. The theory of gluts showed the earliest awareness of the problem of unemployment. Malthus argued strongly that the economic system is not self-adjusting. His population theory was understandable when rising birth rates and falling death rates were causing phenomenal increases in population. Widespread poverty required an explanation, and Malthus developed what appeared to be a plausible theory to explain it.

Yet the theory of gluts was less useful in 1820 than it is today. In the nineteenth century capitalism was expanding rapidly, and investment was booming both in England and overseas. Depressions were milder and affected fewer people in the early decades of the century than later on. Only in recent decades has the problem of unemployment awakened new interest in Malthus.

[1] Piero Sraffa, ed., *The Works and Correspondence of David Ricardo*, Vol. II (Cambridge, Eng., 1951), pp. 421–22.

How Did the Malthusian Doctrines Outlive Their Usefulness?

The theory of population was based on the law of diminishing returns, which Malthus treated as a historically valid principle. As population grew over the years, more workers would be required to grow more food, and the average and marginal yield per worker would decline. But this law is valid only under static conditions, with technology remaining unchanged. In fact, fewer workers in agriculture grow more food than ever. Malthusian pessimism resulted from underestimating the possibilities of increasing agricultural production. Nor did Malthus foresee sharply reduced birth rates in those societies where urbanization, education, and rising standards of living became important.

Malthus and his theory of population are still useful to those who wish to attribute poverty and war to excessive and indiscriminate breeding among the world's impoverished people. Human beings have not yet been persuaded that war, far from being a cure for overpopulation and poverty, is one of the greatest causes of poverty ever devised.

While the Malthusian theory of gluts was the first attempt to explain unemployment, it was not a theory of business cycles. It dealt with the tendency toward chronic depression because of underconsumption but not with the ups and downs of business activity. In the huge military budgets of today the concept of unproductive consumption can be observed. But modern societies have tried to alleviate the problem of gluts by moderate redistribution of income, which Malthus opposed. The many fiscal and monetary controls that can reduce the amplitude of fluctuations were unknown in his day. The history of industrial society has shown his theory of gluts to have been a brilliant insight into a major problem of a capitalistic economy. But he used it to defend agriculture against the advance of industrialization. His was a backward-looking bias, justifying the big landlords—the heroes of a bygone era.

Bibliography

ERLICH, PAUL R. and ANNE H., *Population, Resources, Environment.* San Francisco: W. H. Freeman, 1970.

GODWIN, WILLIAM, *An Enquiry Concerning Political Justice and Its Influence on General Virtue and Happiness.* 2 vols. New York: Knopf, 1926. [Originally published in 1793.]

MALTHUS, THOMAS, *An Essay on the Principle of Population.* London: 1798.
——, *Principles of Political Economy.* New York: Kelley, 1951. [Originally published in 1820.]
OSBORN, FAIRFIELD, *Our Plundered Planet.* Boston: Little, Brown, 1948.
OSER, JACOB, *Must Men Starve? The Malthusian Controversy.* London: Cape, 1956; New York: Abelard-Schuman, 1957.
SCHAPIRO, J. SALWYN, *Condorcet and the Rise of Liberalism.* New York: Harcourt Brace Jovanovich, 1934.
SMITH, KENNETH, *The Malthusian Controversy.* London: Routledge and Kegan Paul, 1951.
TYDINGS, JOSEPH D., *Born to Starve.* New York: William Morrow, 1970.
VOGT, WILLIAM, *Road to Survival.* New York: Sloane, 1948.

8

The Classical School:
Bentham, Say, Senior,
and Mill

Bentham

The life span of Jeremy Bentham (1748–1832) overlapped the publication of David Hume's economic essays, Adam Smith's *Wealth of Nations*, the works of David Ricardo and Thomas Robert Malthus, and the early writings of John Stuart Mill. Not only was Bentham an enthusiastic adherent of the classical school, but he made some original contributions to its philosophy and economics. Bentham boasted, "I was the spiritual father of [James] Mill, and Mill was the spiritual father of Ricardo: so that Ricardo was my spiritual grandson."

Bentham, a precocious child, read history and studied Latin at four. He matriculated at Queen's College, Oxford, at twelve and took his degree at fifteen. After that he studied law as his father wished. But he soon deserted the legal profession for a scholarly life, relying on his indulgent and admiring father for support. Bentham gathered around him a circle of congenial friends and ardent disciples who promoted his ideas, but most of his prolific writings were not published until well over a century after his death.

In accordance with his wishes, Bentham's body was dissected in the interests of science. He left his entire estate to the University of London with the stipulation that his remains be present at all meetings of its Board. His skeleton, stuffed and dressed, is seated in a chair, with cane in gloved hand. The head of the body is wax, but his actual head, preserved in the manner of South American head-hunters, rests between his feet.

The central and most controversial theme of Bentham's thought has been called utilitarianism, or the principle of the greatest happiness. The underlying philosophy, which goes back to the Greeks of antiquity, is that of hedonism: All individuals seek their own greatest happiness. Utilitarianism superimposed on hedonism the ethical doctrine that conduct should be directed toward promoting the greatest happiness of the greatest number of people. The extremely individualistic outlook of hedonism was moderated by utilitarianism, which at least recognized that organized society has a role to play. If an individual pursues only individual pleasure, will this course necessarily promote the general happiness? Not necessarily, thought Bentham. Society, however, has its own methods of compelling individuals to promote the general happiness. The rule of law establishes political sanctions to punish individuals who in their own pursuit of pleasure harm others excessively. Moral or social sanctions also exist, of which ostracism is an example. Even theological sanctions, such as fear of punishment in the hereafter, would help reconcile the individualistic self-interest of hedonism with the utilitarian principle of the greatest happiness for the greatest number of people.

Using utilitarianism as his foundation, Bentham developed a systematic set of philosophical and economic doctrines pointing toward reform. We can let Bentham speak for himself on the principle of utility, as he did in the first chapter of *An Introduction to the Principles of Morals and Legislation,* first printed in 1780:

> Nature has placed mankind under the governance of two sovereign masters, *pain* and *pleasure.* It is for them alone to point out what we ought to do, as well as to determine what we shall do. On the one hand the standard of right and wrong, on the other the chain of causes and effects, are fastened to their throne. They govern us in all we do, in all we say, in all we think: every effort we can make to throw off our subjection, will serve but to demonstrate and confirm it. In words a man may pretend to abjure their empire: but in reality he will remain subject to it all the while. The *principle of utility* recognises this subjection, and assumes it for the foundation of that system, the object of which is to rear the fabric of felicity by the hands of reason and of law. . . .
>
> By the principle of utility is meant that principle which approves or disapproves of every action whatsoever, according to the tendency which it appears to have to augment or diminish the happiness of the party whose interest is in question: or, what is the same thing in other words, to promote or to oppose that happiness. I say of every action whatsoever; and therefore not only of every action of a private individual, but of every measure of government.
>
> By utility is meant that property in any object, whereby it tends to

produce benefit, advantage, pleasure, good, or happiness, . . . or . . . to prevent the happening of mischief, pain, evil, or unhappiness to the party whose interest is considered: if that party be the community in general, then the happiness of the community: if a particular individual, then the happiness of that individual.

. . . The community is a fictitious body, composed of the individual persons who are considered as constituting as it were its *members.* The interest of the community then is, what?—the sum of the interests of the several members who compose it.

It is in vain to talk of the interest of the community, without understanding what is the interest of the individual. A thing is said to promote the interest . . . of an individual, when it tends to add to the sum total of his pleasures: or, what comes to the same thing, to diminish the sum total of his pains.

An action then may be said to be conformable to the principle of utility . . . when the tendency it has to augment the happiness of the community is greater than any it has to diminish it.

A measure of government . . . may be said to be conformable to or dictated by the principle of utility, when in like manner the tendency which it has to augment the happiness of the community is greater than any which it has to diminish it.

Two conclusions can be drawn about Bentham's doctrines. On the one hand, in their time these doctrines promoted progress, reform, wider democracy, and the amelioration of social conditions. On the other hand, they led to insoluble contradictions and confusions; his doctrines could not provide a firm basis for a system of economics, philosophy, or aesthetics.

First, on the positive side: Bentham lived and wrote at a time when common people, the "labouring poor," had no voice and no vote in the management of social and political affairs. They were expected to be subservient, docile, and hard-working. Their toil and sacrifices enhanced the power of the nation, the glory of its rulers, the wealth of the industrial and commercial moneyed class, and the indolent ease of the aristocrats. Yet here was a philosopher who said that people are people regardless of their social position. Thus, if something adds to a commoner's pleasure more than it detracts from the pleasure of an aristocrat, it is commendable; if government intervention enhances the happiness of a community more than it diminishes it, the intervention is justified.

Bentham emphasized that legislators ought to augment the total happiness of the community. Instead of people serving the state, the state should serve the people. He concluded that most existing state controls and regulations were harmful, and his slogan for government was "Be quiet." But he did not worship laissez faire as a principle to be accepted blindly. If special reasons exist, the government ought to intervene. For example, he thought the state should monopolize the issue of paper money, thereby saving interest on its borrowing. It should also operate life and annuity insurance and tax inheritances, monopolies, and so forth. Where people's interests are not naturally harmonious, the state should establish an artificial harmony of interests that promotes the greatest happiness of the greatest number.

The utilitarian philosophers hoped to make morals an exact science. In their view, if only pleasure and pain could be measured quantitatively and compared among different individuals, every law and every act could be judged by balancing the total pleasure produced against the total pain. Money, Bentham concluded, is the instrument that measures the quantity of pleasure or pain. "Those who are not satisfied with the accuracy of this instrument must find out some other that shall be more accurate, or bid adieu to politics and morals." [1]

In *The Philosophy of Economic Science* Bentham argued that wealth is a measure of happiness, but that wealth has diminishing marginal utility as it increases:

> Of two persons having unequal fortunes, he who has most wealth must by a legislator be regarded as having most happiness. But the quantity of happiness will not go on increasing in anything near the same proportion as the quantity of wealth:—ten thousand times the quantity of wealth will not bring with it ten thousand times the quantity of happiness. It will even be matter of doubt, whether ten thousand times the wealth will in general bring with it twice the happiness. The effect of wealth in the production of happiness goes on diminishing, as the quantity by which the wealth of one man exceeds that of another goes on increasing: in other words, the quantity of happiness produced by a particle of wealth (each particle being of the same magnitude) will be less and less at every particle; the second will produce less than the first, the third than the second, and so on.[2]

Here Bentham introduced the idea of the marginal utility of money, just as Ricardo introduced the concept of marginal productivity in his theory of rent.

Bentham's argument for egalitarianism was one the welfare economists later wrestled with. If you take income from the hundred-

---

[1] W. Stark, *Jeremy Bentham's Economic Writings*, Vol. I (New York, 1952), p. 117.
[2] *Ibid.*, p. 113.

thousand-pounds-per-year person and give it to the ten-pounds-per-year person, said Bentham, more happiness will be gained by the poor person than will be lost by the wealthy one. But he was not radical enough to suggest that the theory be put into practice. By marshaling new arguments against the redistribution of income, he was able to repudiate the conclusions of his own theory. Equalizing incomes, he thought, would destroy happiness by alarming the rich and depriving them of a feeling of security, by taking away their enjoyment of the fruits of their work and by destroying all inducement to labor. When security and equality are in opposition, said Bentham, equality should give way.

Bentham's devotion to the greatest good for the greatest number led him to study and advocate many democratic reforms. He defended universal male suffrage, equal electoral districts, annual parliaments, and the secret ballot. He opposed the monarchy and the House of Lords, arguing that only in a democracy do the interests of the governors and the governed become identical. At a time when there was little enthusiasm for education, Bentham urged a system of national education, even for pauper children. Frugality Banks, he suggested, should be organized to stimulate saving by the poor. Public works should provide jobs for unemployed workers during slack times. He endorsed free trade, competition, and legal reforms. He designed an elaborate plan for a model prison that would reform criminals rather than punish them. No wonder Bentham and his circle, including James and John Stuart Mill and Ricardo, were called "philosophic radicals."

Despite its positive aspects, however, Bentham's economics is not altogether satisfactory. Since Bentham's goal was to measure pleasure and pain quantitatively, he had to assume that people are rational in calculating their own interests, that individuals are the best judges of what most effectively promotes their own well-being. One doubts the complete validity of this assumption. Bentham sought an exact quantitative measure of utility, but the difficulty of this task was compounded by introducing the concept of the diminishing marginal utility of wealth. It is difficult enough to compare precisely the increase in happiness of two people who begin at the same income and receive equal increases in wealth, but it is even more difficult when the two people start at different levels of wealth and income. Further, Bentham's outlook was steeped in a tradition of individualism. But collective activity was increasingly required to pursue society's goals of increasing the production of goods and services and distributing them in a satisfactory manner.

The idea that "the interest of the community . . . is . . . the sum of the interests of the several members who compose it" is not necessarily true. Each individual may be uninterested in conservation if the cost is greater than the present value of the expected future income resulting from conservation measures. But society may favor conservation because it thinks in terms of the needs of future generations or because it wants a make-work scheme during depressions. Again, each individual might prefer not to pay taxes to promote flood control, but it is in the interest of society to tax itself for such a purpose. Each manufacturer might gain by being the only one to lower wages, but if all were to do so they might sell fewer goods. Illustrations of Bentham's "fallacy of composition" can be multiplied endlessly.

More specifically, it was a utilitarian fallacy to claim that the total happiness of a society is the sum of all the individual happiness. In modern terms, each individual may be very happy on acquiring a car; but the total is less than the sum of individual happiness if we suffer from traffic jams, pollution, fuel shortages, and an increased chance of accidents. Again, each individual is happy to take a trip to Yellowstone National Park; but when a million individuals go there, the total happiness is not a million times each individual's joy.

Utilitarianism is also deficient as a philosophy. Bentham, abjuring all value judgments on the quality of pleasure, stated that the "quantity of pleasure being equal, push-pin is as good as poetry." He playfully described the difference between prose and poetry: *"Prose* is where all the lines but the last go on to the margin—poetry is where some of them fall short of it." If, in a recent decade, Mickey Spillane's detective stories gave more joy to more people than Shakespeare's dramas, Bentham would say that Spillane's contribution to humanity during that time was greater. Yet qualitative measures of happiness may be more significant than quantitative ones. Shakespeare explored all aspects of life; he portrayed characters in a comprehensive manner and showed how they change under the force of changing circumstances. He can be reread with pleasure, and each reading can increase one's understanding of people and how they act and react in different circumstances. By reading Spillane, on the other hand, we can easily form the wrong ideas about how blondes behave!

Contrary to utilitarian belief, understanding the world may be preferable to enjoying it. Being of service to humanity may be a higher aim than selfishly seeking one's own happiness, although this idea may sound quaintly old-fashioned today. The utilitarian would say: "If you feel so strongly about serving humanity, this gives you the greatest personal pleasure and conforms to our principle of happiness." This line of reasoning reduces hedonism to empty tautology. Even if you risk your life rescuing a drowning child you must be doing it for your own pleasure at being a hero. But if we say that serving society is preferable to pursuing one's own narrow self-interest, we contradict the utilitarian, for a preference scale ranks happiness qualitatively, not quantitatively. Our value judgments in aesthetics and our philosophy of the good life aim at more than happiness. As John Stuart Mill said, "It is better to be a human being dissatisfied than a pig satisfied; better to be Socrates dissatisfied than a fool satisfied." Or as George Bernard Shaw said, "Happiness is not the object of life: life has no object: it is an end in itself: and courage consists in the readiness to sacrifice happiness for an intenser quality of life."

There are widely held explanations of human behavior that dispute the hedonistic view that people are motivated solely by the desire to maximize pleasure and minimize pain. Early experimental psychologists, for example, studied the association of stimulus and response in the learning process. The behaviorists added the idea of the conditioned reflex. Freudian psychiatry claimed that the fundamental driving force governing human behavior is the conflict between opposing forces deep within the personality. Students of cultural anthropology pointed out that in one way or another, society imposes on the individual its system of ideas, patterns of behavior, and way of living. These ideas all challenge the pleasure-pain principle as the guiding force of human behavior.

Bentham's utilitarianism has also been challenged by rival ethical systems. The idea that every society and every government should promote the greatest happiness for the greatest number of people has been denied by many. Plato taught that pleasure is subordinate in value to knowledge and that it should be a by-product of effective achievement. The Stoics favored disciplining the sensual appetites of the body, for they considered passion and desire morbid conditions of the soul. Various religions preached resignation to the inescapable sufferings of this world as the key to the good and worthy life, mortification and self-denial as the means of overcoming impulses to sin, or the performance of Christian duty as the way to salvation. Thomas Hobbes (1588–1679) held that humans have a fundamentally depraved nature that drives them toward war, strife, and the selfish appropriation of all that they can lay their hands on; therefore a strong and absolute government is required to keep them in check. John Locke (1632–1704), who did not think every good was a moral good, found in people a social bent and sense of obligation that would bind where no constraint of law existed. Modern fascists glorify the strong state as the supreme good, and Communists place the advancement of class interests above the individual quest for happiness. Advocates of all these ethical systems, which represent alternatives to utilitarianism, would claim that they too seek the greatest happiness of the greatest number of people. Nevertheless Benthamism depicted the greatest-happiness principle as the most immediate force directing behavior; the other systems would approach this goal indirectly, either in this world or in the next, either in the present or in some vague and undefined future.

Bentham's concept of human nature became the foundation for the economic systems of Ricardo, Mill, and the early marginalists, especially William Stanley Jevons. Underlying the marginalist theory of demand was the concept of marginal utility, which assumed that each person would compare the intensity of satisfactions received from a great variety of goods. People were considered to be perfectly rational and carefully calculating. Labor was believed to be painful. To achieve maximum happiness, one would work just up to the point at which the marginal utility of one's earnings was equal to the marginal disutility of one's labor. The entrepreneurs, in determining volume of output, would always try to maximize their income or minimize their losses. Later marginalists have argued, however, that their analysis does not depend on the extreme form of utilitarianism that Bentham presented. Economic theory should take other motives and other behavior patterns into account.

Say

Jean Baptiste Say (1767–1832) was a Frenchman who popularized Adam Smith on the continent. His major work, *Traité d'Economie Politique (A Treatise on Political Economy)*, was published in 1803. Say's career was temporarily blocked because Napoleon was displeased with his extreme laissez faire views. Some time after Napoleon's defeat at Waterloo, Say became a professor of political economy, after having spent years as a businessman.

Say opposed the labor theory of value of the classical school, replacing it with supply and demand, which in turn are regulated by cost of production and utility. He added a fourth factor of production—the entrepreneur—to land, labor, and capital. But his chief claim to fame rests on his theory that general overproduction is impossible. This doctrine came to be known as Say's Law of Markets. In his *Treatise* he wrote:

Should a tradesman say, "I do not want other products for my woollens, I want money," . . . he may be told, . . . "You say, you only want money; I say, you want other commodities, and not money. For what, in point of fact, do you want the money? Is it not for the purchase of raw materials or stock for your trade, or of victuals for your support? Wherefore, it is products that you want, and not money." [Ch. 15]

Here Say added a cheerful footnote:

Even when money is obtained with a view to hoard or bury it, the ultimate object is always to employ it in a purchase of some kind. The heir of the lucky finder uses it in that way, if the miser do not: for money, as money, has no other use than to buy with.

Apparently a possible lag of a whole generation between the receipt of money and its expenditure was not at all disturbing to him.

Say continued his exposition:

It is worth while to remark, that a product is no sooner created, than it, from that instant, affords a market for other products to the full extent of its own value. When the producer has put the finishing hand to his product, he is most anxious to sell it immediately, lest its value should vanish in his hands. Nor is he less anxious to dispose of the money he may get for it; for the value of money is also perishable. But the only way of getting rid of money is in the purchase of some product or other. Thus, the mere circumstance of the creation of one product immediately opens a vent for other products. . . .

But it may be asked, if this be so, how does it happen, that there is at times so great a glut of commodities in the market, and so much difficulty in finding a vent for them? Why cannot one of these superabundant commodities be exchanged for another? I answer, that the glut of a particular commodity arises from its having outrun the total demand for it in one of two ways; either because it has been produced in excessive abundance, or because the produce of other commodities has fallen short.

Though refuted by Sismondi and Marx, Say's law continued to dominate economic thinking until Keynes relegated it to a position of minor importance. Uncritical acceptance of Say's Law of Markets appears to have delayed the study of business cycles for many decades.

Although Say was wrong in assuming that the economy always tends toward full-employment equilibrium, there was a certain long-run validity to his doctrine. Underdeveloped economies are characterized by low income payments to people and low output. As an economy grows, it simultaneously generates an increased supply of goods and increased payments to the factors of production, which in turn generate an increased demand for goods. Similarly, in international trade, as a country produces more it can export more, and it can therefore afford to import more. Both in domestic and in foreign trade, "supply creates its own demand" in the long run. This principle does not hold true, however, for short-run business fluctuations in a laissez faire economy. Even though payments to factors of production would be enough to buy all the goods produced, there is no guarantee that these income payments will be entirely spent by those who receive them.

Senior

Nassau William Senior (1790–1864) was the oldest son of a country clergyman who had ten children. In 1825 he became the first professor of political economy at Oxford. The government appointed him a member of several royal commissions that investigated important social problems. In his economic thinking Senior departed significantly from classical economics and moved toward the neoclassical position that triumphed after 1870.

Senior wished to separate the science of political economy from all value judgments, all policy pronouncements, and all efforts to promote welfare. According to him, the economist should concern himself with wealth, not happiness.

> But his conclusions, whatever be their generality and their truth, do not authorize him in adding a single syllable of advice. That privilege belongs to the writer or the statesman who has considered all the causes which may promote or impede the general welfare of those whom he addresses, not to the theorist who has considered only one, though among the most important, of those causes. The business of a Political Economist is neither to recommend nor to dissuade, but to state general principles.[3]

The exchange value of goods, according to Senior, depends on demand and supply. Underlying demand is the concept of the diminishing marginal utility of goods as more units are acquired. Supply depends on cost of production. But cost is subjective—the sum of sacrifices required in order to use nature's agents to produce useful goods. The costs of production are the labor of the workers and the abstinence of the capitalists. "Abstinence" is the term Senior contributed to the lexicon of political economy.

[3] Nassau William Senior, *An Outline of the Science of Political Economy* (New York, 1951), p. 3. [Originally published in 1836.]

But although Human Labour, and the Agency of Nature, independently of that of man, are the primary Productive Powers, they require the concurrence of a Third Productive Principle to give them complete efficiency. . . . To the Third Principle, or Instrument of Production, without which the two others are inefficient, we shall give the name of *Abstinence:* a term by which we express the conduct of a person who either abstains from the unproductive use of what he can command, or designedly prefers the production of remote to that of immediate results. . . . *By the word Abstinence, we wish to express that agent, distinct from labour and the agency of nature, the concurrence of which is necessary to the existence of Capital, and which stands in the same relation to Profit as Labour does to Wages.*[4]

Senior's use of the term abstinence implied a value judgment about the sacrifices undertaken by the capitalist in postponing (or foregoing forever) the consumption of his wealth. Marx and the German state socialist Ferdinand Lassalle made great sport of this concept. The latter wrote scornfully of the abstinence of a Baron Rothschild and the profligate wastefulness of the English laborer who squandered all his income of a few shillings a week on consumption. Alfred Marshall later redesignated the function of saving as *waiting*—that is, postponing consumption. This term was both less colorful and less controversial than "abstinence"; it did not imply any suffering or sacrifice by the rich while they were accumulating wealth.

The socialist critics who ridiculed the concept of the irksomeness of saving overlooked one crucial point: As the idea of the *margin*— that is, the point of change at which decisions are made—finally matured, the sacrifice of foregoing consumption was measured only at the margin; the sacrifice was not intended to represent the total supply of saving. It is likely that a millionaire could save ten thousand dollars with far less agonized tightening of the belt than a poor man would undergo to save a dollar. Let us consider, however, that portion of the saving that is made at the borderline of uncertainty— the point at which one decides whether to save an extra sum or spend it on consumption. At that margin the sacrifice of postponing consumption may well be large enough to require remuneration in the form of interest to compensate for the sacrifice. The widest discrepancy exists, *on the average*, between the sacrifice of a rich person who saves a dollar and that of a poor person who does; but the discrepancy is narrowed considerably if we consider the sacrifice of saving a *marginal* dollar in the two cases.

Senior disagreed with Adam Smith, who thought that the pro-

[4] *Ibid.*, pp. 58–59.

ducers of services are all unproductive. Lawyers, doctors, and teachers, Senior said, are productive because they promote the increase of wealth. Where a soldier must protect the husbandman, both are productive. Suppose a thousand men are constantly employed in forging bars and bolts to keep out thieves; if a hundred of them can achieve the same purpose by becoming watchmen instead, is wealth diminished by this conversion from "productive" to "unproductive" workers? To Senior the proper distinction was not between productive and unproductive labor, but rather between productive and unproductive consumption. The latter category includes consumption of lace, embroidery, jewelry, tobacco, gin, and beer, all of which diminish the mass of commodities without adding to the workers' capacities to produce.

Senior served on the Poor Law Commission appointed in 1832. He wrote the bulk of the report resulting in the harsh Poor Law Amendment Act of 1834, which sought to discourage applications for relief by people physically able to work. The Act established the principle that the living conditions of those receiving relief should be worse than those of the poorest-paid employed laborers. These poor laws were in force for seventy years. The prevailing view was that the able-bodied poor were lazy or improvident rather than being victims of the social conditions that impoverished them. The whip of starvation was to be placed securely in the hands of employers and government officials.

As a passionate champion of laissez faire, freedom (as he saw it), and mobility of labor, Senior was unequivocally opposed to the trade union movement. Among his proposals were prohibition of all conspiracies and restraints of trade by labor; severe punishment for all solicitations to form unions; prohibition of and severe punishment for all picketing; confiscation of funds owned by unions; and compensation from public funds for people who were injured in resisting unions.

In 1837 Senior published a pamphlet opposing the English Factory Acts, which at the time limited the working day to twelve hours in factories where children were employed. While he endorsed the principle of regulating child labor, he opposed laws limiting the hours of adults. In calculating the economic effect of a shorter working day, Senior made no allowance for reduced outlays for raw materials, heating, lighting, depreciation, and so forth. He also ignored the probability of increased output per hour with a reduced working day. His confused and erroneous reasoning led to the conclusion that all profit was derived from the last hour of work. If the working day were shortened by more than an hour, capitalists would actually lose money, and England would be ruined in competition with foreign producers. His major concern was to attack the "ten-hours agitation" of his time.

Senior did not heed his own prescription that economists should never offer a single syllable of advice. In his long career in public life, he never explained whether his recommendations were offered with all the weight of his economic theories behind them or not.

Mill

John Stuart Mill (1806–73) was the last great economist of the classical school, undoubtedly the greatest since Ricardo, who died in 1823. He made some significant original contributions and he systematized and popularized the whole body of economic thought of his predecessors. The classical school was already in decline during Mill's mature years. He himself departed from some of the key concepts built into the classical structure by Smith and Ricardo. Before his death neoclassical economics had appeared on the scene, ultimately to displace its classical forebears. Mill's great *Principles of Political Economy,* first published in 1848 and reprinted in the United States as late as 1920, was the leading textbook in the field, at least until the publication of Alfred Marshall's *Principles of Economics* in 1890. The popularity of Mill's book for so long seems to be due to two causes: It was well written to begin with, and there is an academic cultural lag that permits books to linger on in the classroom even after they are antiquated.

Mill reported his amazing upbringing in his *Autobiography,* published shortly after his death. His father, James Mill, was the man who urged Ricardo to write, publish, and sit in Parliament; he popularized Bentham's ideas and helped found the group known as philosophic radicals, which pushed for political reforms in Great Britain. A strict disciplinarian, James Mill himself supervised the education of John, the oldest of his nine children. The elder Mill was strongly committed to the idea that all people were born alike, with little or no significant variation in their innate genetic potential for learning. Any child could be molded into what mistakenly appeared to be a genius. Therefore John was to be raised to carry on the great work of his predecessors in utilitarian economics and politics. The boy began to learn Greek at three, but as he wrote apologetically, "I learnt no Latin until my eighth year." By then he was reading the Greek philosophers in the original but not always understanding them. At eleven he read the proofs of his father's *History of India* and was greatly impressed. He mastered algebra and elementary geometry and began studying differential calculus by the time he was twelve; he had by then written a history of the Roman government—which was not published. He then began to study logic, and at thirteen he began the study of political economy. Between the ages of fifteen and eighteen Mill edited and published five volumes of Bentham's manuscripts. At nineteen he was publishing original scholarly articles, and at twenty he had a well-earned nervous breakdown.

John Stuart Mill wrote in his *Autobiography* that his father made him read and give verbal accounts of books in which he had no interest. He was permitted few toys or children's books, he was not allowed to take holidays or associate much with other boys lest the habit of work be broken and a taste for idleness acquired. "But my father, in all his teaching, demanded of me not only the utmost that I could do, but much that I could by no possibility have done." No wonder Mill wrote of his father that "the element which was chiefly deficient in his moral relation to his children was that of tenderness."

The boy was taught that he was quite ordinary and that any special abilities he had were due to the special advantages of being James Mill's son. Therefore late in life John Stuart Mill could write in his *Autobiography:*

> What I could do, could assuredly be done by any boy or girl of average capacity and healthy physical constitution. . . . If I thought anything about myself, it was that I was rather backward in my studies, since I always found myself so, in comparison with what my father expected from me.

It was when John was fourteen and about to leave home for a long absence that his father broke the news to him that he had been taught much more than the average educated youth his age. But, his father continued, this advantage should not go to his head:

> He wound up by saying, that whatever I knew more than others, could not be ascribed to any merit in me, but to the very unusual advantage which had befallen to my lot, of having a father who was able to teach me, and willing to give the necessary trouble and time; that it was no matter of praise to me, if I knew more than those who had not had a similar advantage, but the deepest disgrace to me if I did not.

The son was more modest than the father!

Mill met Mrs. Harriet Taylor (1807–58) when he was twenty-four years old, and there followed a warm friendship and association between them; they even took vacations together on the continent and in the English countryside. Twenty years later, after Mr. Taylor died, they were married. Mill attributed to Mrs. Taylor his humanitarianism, his hope for and faith in human progress, his love of liberty, and his passionate defense of the rights of women. He tried to persuade the world that his whole intellectual development (other than his technical competence in economics) was due to Mrs. Taylor. He called his writings both before and after their marriage the joint product of their minds, claiming that her share constantly increased as the years advanced; it did not matter which of them held the pen.

The views of Harriet and John Mill on the subjection of women are interesting. Before they were married in 1851, John wrote a statement repudiating the law that gave him legal power and control over the person, property, and freedom of action of his wife independent of her own wishes. He pledged that he would never use those powers and that his wife would retain the same absolute freedom of action and freedom to dispose of herself and her property as if no marriage had taken place.

In the essay "Enfranchisement of Women," first published in 1851, the Mills were enthusiastic over the powerful political movement for women's rights developing in the United States. This, they said, was not a pleading by male writers and orators *for* women, but it was a movement being pushed *by* women. The Declaration of Independence should apply to women as well as to men, to blacks as well as to whites. In England the gap between the stated freedoms and actual practice was as bad as in the United States.

> It is an axiom of English freedom that taxation and representation should be coextensive. Even under the laws which give the wife's property to the husband, there are many unmarried women who pay taxes. It is one of the fundamental doctrines of the British Constitution, that all persons should be tried by their peers: yet women, whenever tried, are tried by male judges and a male jury. . . . We are firmly convinced that the division of mankind into two castes, one born to rule over the other, is in this case, as in all cases, an unqualified mischief; a source of perversion and demoralization, both to the favoured class and to those at whose expense they are favoured.[5]

In the same essay the authors deplored the exclusion of women from certain fields that are considered to be "unfeminine"; they repudiated the idea that the "proper sphere" of women is not politics or publicity, but private and domestic life. They denied the right of

[5] John Stuart Mill, *Dissertations and Discussions*, Vol. II, "Enfranchisement of Women" (London, 1859), pp. 418–19.

any people to decide for others what is and what is not their "proper sphere."

> Let every occupation be open to all, without favour or discouragement to any, and employments will fall into the hands of those men or women who are found by experience to be most capable of worthily exercising them. There need be no fear that women will take out of the hands of men any occupation which men perform better than they. Each individual will prove his or her capacities, in the only way in which capacities can be proved—by trial; and the world will have the benefit of the best faculties of all its inhabitants. But to interfere beforehand by an arbitrary limit, and declare that whatever be the genius, talent, energy, or force of mind of an individual of a certain sex or class, those faculties shall not be exerted, or shall be exerted only in some few of the many modes in which others are permitted to use theirs, is not only an injustice to the individual, and a detriment to society, which loses what it can ill spare, but is also the most effectual mode of providing that, in the sex or class so fettered, the qualities which are not permitted to be exercised shall not exist.[6]

The Mills argued that equal rights for women would also benefit men. They opposed the views of "the moderate reformers" who would maintain the old bad principles and only mitigate their consequences.

> These say, that women should be, not slaves, nor servants, but companions; and educated for that office (they do not say that men should be educated to be the companions of women). But since uncultivated women are not suitable companions for cultivated men, and a man who feels interest in things above and beyond the family circle wishes that his companion should sympathize with him in that interest; they therefore say, let women improve their understanding and taste, acquire general knowledge, cultivate poetry, art, even coquet with science, and some stretch their liberality so far as to say, inform themselves on politics; not as pursuits, but sufficiently to feel an interest in the subjects, and to be capable of holding a conversation on them with the husband, or at least of understanding and imbibing his wisdom. Very agreeable to him, no doubt, but unfortunately the reverse of improving. It is from having intellectual communion only with those to whom they can lay down the law, that so few men continue to advance in wisdom beyond the first stages. The most eminent men cease to improve, if they associate only with disciples. When they have overtopped those who immediately surround them, if they wish for further growth, they must seek for others of their own stature to consort with. The mental companionship

[6] *Ibid.*, p. 423.

which is improving, is communion between active minds, not mere contact between an active mind and a passive.[7]

In *The Subjection of Women* (published in 1869), Mill pursued further the idea that equal rights for women would also benefit men. Think what it is to a boy, he said, to grow up believing that without any merit or exertion of his own, although he may be empty and ignorant, by the mere fact of being born a male he is superior to every woman on earth. This perverts the whole manner of existence of the man. His feeling is similar to that of a hereditary king who thinks that he is excellent above all others by being born a king. The relation between husband and wife is very like that between lord and vassal. "However the vassal's character may have been affected, for better and for worse, by his subordination, who can help seeing that the lord's was affected greatly for the worse?"

We shall now turn to Mill's contributions in the field of economics.

Mill, raised in the Benthamite tradition, finally rejected the latter's narrow and dogmatic utilitarianism, for he regarded as too limited Bentham's view that human beings are motivated in their conduct by nothing more than self-love and the desire for self-gratification. He charged Bentham with neglecting the human search for perfection, honor, and other ends entirely for their own sakes. Mill did not abandon the utilitarian ideas but modified them. He was concerned, for example, with the quality of enjoyment as well as the quantity.

Mill's *Principles of Political Economy with Some of Their Applications to Social Philosophy* is divided into five books: "Production," "Distribution," "Exchange," "Influence of the Progress of Society on Production and Distribution," and "Of the Influence of Government."

In the first book he analyzed the three productive factors—land, labor, and capital. Wealth is defined as including all useful things that possess exchange value; only material objects are included because only they can be accumulated. Productive labor includes only those kinds of exertion that produce utilities embodied in material objects. But labor that yields a material product only indirectly is also held to be productive. Thus educators and government officials are productive because their services create the conditions required for the output of material goods. Unproductive labor is that which does not terminate in the creation of material wealth. For example, labor that ends in immediate enjoyment without any increase of the accumulated stock or permanent means of enjoyment is unproduc-

[7] *Ibid.*, pp. 437–38.

tive; saving a friend's life is unproductive unless the friend is a productive laborer of greater production than consumption; and missionaries or clergymen are unproductive unless they teach the arts of civilization in addition to religious doctrines. Unproductive labor may nevertheless be useful.

Capital, the result of saving, is the accumulated stock of the produce of labor, and its aggregate amount limits the extent of industry. Every increase of capital is capable of giving additional employment to labor without limit. This tendency eliminates the need for unproductive expenditure by the rich to give employment to the poor. Mill assumed that everything saved through the abstinence of the capitalist would be invested. If capitalists spent less on luxury consumption and more on investment, the demand for labor would rise. If population increased, the increased demand for necessities by wage earners would offset the decreased demand for luxuries by capitalists. If population did not increase in proportion to the growth of capital, wages would rise and luxury consumption by workers would supplant luxury consumption by their employers. This is the optimistic world of full employment. "Thus the limit of wealth is never deficiency of consumers, but of producers and productive power. Every addition to capital gives to labour either additional employment, or additional remuneration; enriches either the country, or the labouring class." [Bk. 1, Ch. 5]

What are the obstacles to increasing production? Lack of labor is not one of them, said Mill, for population could increase geometrically. That it does not is due to impulses superior to mere animal instincts. People do not propagate like swine but are restrained by prudence from multiplying beyond the means of subsistence. Population is limited by fear of want rather than by want itself.

The increase of capital depends on two things—the surplus product after the necessities are supplied to all engaged in production and the disposition to save. The greater the profit that can be made from capital, the stronger the motive for its accumulation. The inclination to save also varies from person to person and from country to country.

The limited extent of land and its limited productiveness are the real barriers to the increase of production. Mill recognized increasing returns to scale in industry; that is, within certain limits, the larger the enterprise, the more efficient it becomes. He thought that agriculture exhibits decreasing returns to scale. But he applied the law of diminishing returns only to agriculture. That is, if the supply of land is constant, adding labor will not add to the product in the same proportion. Mill did not concern himself with whether the same proposition would be true in industry if capital were kept constant. The reason for his differentiating between the two is obvious: The supply of capital can be increased easily, whereas land cannot.

Population must therefore be restrained, not because of inequality of property, but because of the niggardliness of nature. An unjust distribution of wealth does not even aggravate the evil of overpopulation but, at most, causes it to be felt somewhat earlier.

In Book II, "Distribution," Mill began with his famous, far-reaching pronouncement:

> The laws and conditions of the production of wealth, partake of the character of physical truths. There is nothing optional or arbitrary in them. . . . It is not so with the Distribution of Wealth. That is a matter of human institution solely. The things once there, mankind, individually or collectively, can do with them as they like.

Mill did not see that production and distribution are interrelated and that interference with one involves interference with the other. The "things" are not there as a mass of goods already produced. They appear as a continuous flow that can be reduced or completely interrupted if the distribution is unfavorable to the maintenance of production. Though both his propositions are exaggerations, they allowed Mill to raise the prospect of a greater role for government in economic affairs. It can be said to Mill's credit that he abandoned Ricardo's idea of inexorable "laws of distribution," with man helpless beneath them. He flung a challenge at the classical school's belief in the universality and permanence of natural law.

Mill immediately entered into a discussion of communism. The judgment expressed in the fifth edition of his book follows:

> If, therefore, the choice were to be made between Communism with all its chances, and the present state of society with all its sufferings and injustices; . . . all the difficulties, great or small, of Communism, would be but as dust in the balance. But to make the comparison applicable, we must compare Communism at its best, with the régime of individual property, not as it is, but as it might be made. The principle of private property has never yet had a fair trial in any country.

Mill called himself a socialist, but this seemed to be an exaggeration and misuse of the concept. He criticized society and hoped to improve it, and he flirted occasionally with utopian socialism (a set of beliefs that had developed and spread throughout Europe half a century earlier, to be discussed in the following chapter). He was, however, basically committed to a private-enterprise profit-oriented economic system. Even when he advocated cooperative societies, as he did in the following quote, he thought they would operate within the capitalist system instead of destroying it. From his *Autobiography* we can see that he was hoping for change through a reformation of the human character.

> We [Mill and Mrs. Taylor] saw clearly that to render any such social transformation either possible or desirable, an equivalent change of character must take place both in the uncultivated herd who now compose the labouring masses, and in the immense majority of their employers. Both these classes must learn by practice to labour and combine for generous, or at all events for public and social purposes, and not, as hitherto, solely for narrowly interested ones. . . . The deep-rooted selfishness which forms the general character of the existing state of society, is *so* deeply rooted, only because the whole course of existing institutions tends to foster it. . . . We regarded all existing institutions and social arrangements as being . . . merely provisional, and we welcomed with the greatest pleasure and interest all socialistic experiments by select individuals (such as the Co-operative Societies).

Mill continued his discussion of distribution in Book II of *Principles of Political Economy* by defending limitations on inheritance. He favored a broader diffusion of property, with a reduction of very large heritable fortunes.

Mill, like Senior, Malthus, Ricardo, James Mill, and Smith before him, accepted what has been called the wages-fund theory. Wages, he said, depend mainly upon the demand for labor and its supply. The demand for labor depends on that part of the capital set aside for the payment of wages. The supply of labor depends on the number of people seeking work. Under the rule of competition, wages cannot be affected by anything but the relative amounts of capital and population. Wage rates cannot rise except by an increase of the aggregate funds employed in hiring laborers or by a diminution in the number of workers for hire. Nor can wage rates fall except by a diminution of the funds devoted to paying labor or by an increase in the number of laborers to be paid. The wages-fund theory therefore presupposes a unitary elasticity of demand for labor; no matter what the wage rate, the same sum is expended for labor.

It follows then, according to Mill, that government cannot fix a minimum wage above the equilibrium level; with a wages fund of a fixed size some workers have to become unemployed. To remedy this condition the government can increase the size of the wages fund by instituting forced saving through taxation, using the proceeds to overcome the unemployment created by minimum-wage laws. Then there is no restraining influence on the procreation of the poor. "But no one has a right to bring creatures into life, to be supported by other people."

The wages-fund doctrine provided a basis for opposing unionism, although Mill did not use it for this purpose as others did. Workers cannot raise their incomes through collective action. If one group raises its wage rate, wages must fall elsewhere. Mill, passionately devoted to liberty, argued that workers should have the right to combine to raise their wages even though he considered unions seldom effectual, and when effectual, seldom desirable.

The wages-fund concept was erroneous because there is no predetermined proportion of capital that must go to labor. Capital can be shifted from one employment to another, and more or less can be spent on labor. The idea of a fund arose because the harvest of one season was used to provide subsistence for labor for the following year. But after a business gets under way wages are paid not from an advance fund of capital but from a flow of income to the enterprise that the worker helps generate. The relative sizes of the rivulets into which the income stream is subdivided can be altered within certain limits.

Mill finally repudiated the wages-fund doctrine in a book review he published in *Fortnightly Review* in 1869. He recognized that economic conditions allow a considerable range in the wage rate; therefore unions may raise wages to a certain extent. The price of labor, he said, is not determined by the size of a given wages fund; instead the labor price determines the size of the fund. If the employer must pay more for labor, the employer's income will be reduced. The real limit to the rise in wages comes at the point at which the employer would be ruined financially or driven to abandon the business if wages were increased further.

Profit, said Mill, resolves itself into three parts: interest, insurance, and the wages of superintendence. These are the rewards for abstinence, risk, and exertion implied in the employment of capital. Allowing for differences in risk, attractiveness of different employments, and natural or artificial monopolies, the rate of profit in all spheres of employment tends toward equality.

In "Exchange," Mill confidently stated the following:

> Happily there is nothing in the laws of Value which remains for the present or any future writer to clear up; the theory of the subject is complete: the only difficulty to be overcome is that of so stating it as to solve by anticipation the chief perplexities which occur in applying it. [Bk. III, Ch. 1]

Price expresses the value of a thing in relation to money; the value of a commodity is measured by its general power to purchase other commodities. There can be a general rise of prices but not a general rise of values, for in relative terms all things cannot rise simultaneously.

The value of a commodity cannot rise higher than its estimated use value to the buyer. Effectual demand—desire plus purchasing power—is therefore one determinant of value. But different quantities are demanded at different values. If demand depends partly on value and value depends on demand, is this not a contradiction? asked Mill. He resolved it by introducing the concept of a demand schedule. Demand means the quantity demanded; the quantity varies according to the value. The interaction of demand and supply results in a market value.

Mill had a definite understanding of supply and demand schedules, elasticity of supply and demand, and their influence on prices. These were significant concepts on which Alfred Marshall built further in his elaboration of marginalist principles. With respect to elasticity of supply, Mill classified goods into three categories. The first is "of things absolutely limited in quantity, such as ancient sculptures or pictures." We would call this a perfectly inelastic supply. The value of such goods, said Mill, is regulated by demand and supply, with demand being most important. The second category of goods is a perfectly elastic supply, and Mill said that the majority of all things bought and sold fit into this category. Production can be expanded without limit at constant cost per unit of output, and the values of such commodities depend on supply, or costs of production. The third category of goods—a relatively elastic supply—falls between two extremes: As Mill put it, "Only a limited quantity can be produced at a given cost; if more is wanted, it must be produced at a greater cost." This is especially the case with agricultural and mineral products, which have several costs of production. Their value depends on "the cost necessary for producing and bringing to market the most costly portion of the supply required," or, as we would say, the marginal cost.

The above analysis applies to the values of commodities in the long run. In the short run, prices fluctuate around values according to the relationship of supply and demand; prices rise as the demand rises and fall as the supply rises.

Mill's concept of elasticity of demand follows:

Let us suppose that the demand at some particular time exceeds the supply, that is, there are persons ready to buy, at the market value, a greater quantity than is offered for sale. Competition takes place on the side of the buyers, and the value rises: but how much? In the ratio (some may suppose) of the deficiency: if the demand exceeds the supply by one-third, the value rises one-third. By no means: for when the value has risen one-third, the demand may still exceed the supply; there may, even at that higher value, be a greater quantity wanted than is to be had; and the competition of buyers may still continue. If the article is a necessary of life, which, rather than resign, people are willing to pay for at any price, a deficiency of one-third may raise the price to double, triple, or quadruple. Or, on the contrary, the competition may cease before the value has risen in even the proportion of the deficiency. A rise, short of one-third, may place the article beyond the means, or beyond the inclinations, of purchasers to the full amount. At what point, then, will the rise be arrested? At the point, whatever it be, which equalizes the demand and the supply. [Bk. III, Ch. 2]

Mill accepted Ricardo's Law of Rent and Say's Law of Markets. To Ricardo's endorsement of free international trade based on the Law of Comparative Cost, Mill added the Law of International Values, one of his important original contributions to economic analysis. Here again the elasticity of demand for goods entered into his theory.

Ricardo's international trade doctrine is incomplete; although it shows how nations gain by trade, it fails to tell how the gain is divided among the trading countries. Mill showed that the actual barter terms of trade depend not only on domestic costs but also on the pattern of demand. The terms of international exchange depend on the strength and elasticity of demand for each product in the foreign country.

Suppose ten yards of cloth made in England cost as much as fifteen yards of linen at home but as much as twenty yards of linen in Germany. If there were no transport costs, the limits of the terms of trade between the two countries would be ten yards of cloth for between fifteen and twenty yards of linen.

Now suppose Germany increases the efficiency of producing linen, so that it produces thirty yards with the same effort that formerly produced twenty. How will these gains be divided between the two countries? If ten yards of cloth formerly exchanged for seventeen yards of linen, will they now exchange for twenty-five and a half yards? This would hold only if the elasticity of demand for linen in England were unitary, so that it would spend the same portion of its income on linen as before. But if the demand for linen in England were elastic (greater than one), England would buy up linen before its price fell to reflect the full amount of its reduced cost of production; the ratio of exchange might settle at ten yards of cloth for twenty-one of linen, and Germany would get most of the benefits of its increased efficiency in producing linen. If, however, the English demand for linen were inelastic, the price would have to fall considerably to induce England to buy the increased output Germany could produce with the same effort. Germany would have to offer more than twenty-five and a half yards of linen for ten yards of cloth, and most of the gains would go to England. Mill implicitly assumed that under any given technological conditions, output could be changed without altering unit costs of production.

The first three books of his *Principles*, said Mill, cover the economic laws of a stationary and unchanging society in equilibrium, which he called Statics. In the final two books he added a theory of motion, of progressive changes and ultimate tendencies—Dynamics. In Book IV, "Influence of the Progress of Society on Production and Distribution," Mill forecast increasing production and population, continuing growth of man's mastery over nature, increasing security of person and property, and a growing role for corporations. Improvements in industrial production would be offset by diminishing returns in agriculture and mining as the population continued to grow.

Mill, like Smith and Ricardo, thought that the rate of profit would continue to fall. He agreed with Ricardo that a falling rate of profit was inevitable because of the increased cost of producing food for a growing population.

> The economical progress of a society constituted of landlords, capitalists, and labourers, tends to the progressive enrichment of the landlord class; while the cost of the labourer's subsistence tends on the whole to increase, and profits to fall. Agricultural improvements are a counteracting force to the two last effects; but the first, though a case is conceivable in which it would be temporarily checked, is ultimately in a high degree promoted by those improvements; and the increase of population tends to transfer all the benefits derived from agricultural improvements to the landlords alone. [Bk. IV, Ch. 3]

But Mill was more optimistic than his predecessors in showing why a falling rate of profit would be acceptable, thereby pointing to a more hopeful future.

> There is at every time and place some particular rate of profit, which is the lowest that will induce the people of that country and time to accumulate savings, and to employ those savings productively. This minimum rate of profit varies according to circumstances. It depends on two elements. One is, the strength of the effective desire of accumulation; the comparative estimate made by the people of that place and era, of fu-

ture interests when weighed against present. This element chiefly affects the inclination to save. The other element, which affects not so much the willingness to save as the disposition to employ savings productively, is the degree of security of capital engaged in industrial operations. [Bk. IV, Ch. 4]

Social progress, Mill wrote, would tend to diminish the minimum acceptable rate of profit. More security, less destruction by war, reduced private and public violence, improvements in education and justice—all these would reduce the risks of investment and thereby reduce the minimum necessary rate of profit. In addition, people would tend to show more forethought and self-control in sacrificing present indulgences for future goals. This too would promote accumulation at lower rates of profit. Reduced risks and increased providence would lower profits and interest in Mill's happy world of the future.

The growth of capital would not cause a glut on the market, for Say's Law of Markets would keep the economy operating at full employment; but the rate of profit would decline. This tendency would be counterbalanced, however, by the waste and destruction of capital values during crises, improvements in production, the inflow of cheap commodities from abroad, and the outflow of capital into colonies and foreign countries.

The final result of progress, Mill thought, would be a stationary state. But why, he wondered, must we have a rapid rate of progress? Why not settle for a large output and a more equitable distribution of wealth?

> I cannot, therefore, regard the stationary state of capital and wealth with the unaffected aversion so generally manifested towards it by political economists of the old school. I am inclined to believe that it would be, on the whole, a very considerable improvement on our present condition. I confess I am not charmed with the ideal of life held out by those who think that the normal state of human beings is that of struggling to get on; that the trampling, crushing, elbowing, and treading on each other's heels, which form the existing type of social life, are the most desirable lot of human kind, or anything but the disagreeable symptoms of one of the phases of industrial progress. . . . It is only in the backward countries of the world that increased production is still an important object: in those more advanced, what is economically needed is a better distribution, of which one indispensable means is a stricter restraint on population. [Bk. IV, Ch. 6].

As the working classes increased their intelligence, education, and love of independence, their good sense would grow correspondingly. Their habits of conduct would then lead to a population that would diminish in relation to capital and employment. Profit-sharing business and cooperative enterprises, operating within a competitive milieu, would further ameliorate conditions. This is preferable, Mill argued, to full-blown socialism, which by deprecating competition would promote monopoly.

In "On the Influence of Government" Mill defended laissez faire and then introduced enough exceptions to smother the idea.

> In all the more advanced communities, the great majority of things are worse done by the intervention of government, than the individuals most interested in the matter would do them, or cause them to be done, if left to themselves. The grounds of this truth are expressed with tolerable exactness in the popular dictum, that people understand their own business and their own interests better, and care for them more, than the government does, or can be expected to do. [Bk. V, Ch. 11]

Mill then pointed out that individuals operating in a market economy are not necessarily the best judges of how much education society should provide. Child labor should be regulated. Natural monopolies such as gas and water companies should be operated by municipal authorities, or their rates should be regulated by the state. Where individuals are good judges of their own interests, the government may act to give effect to that judgment; for example, if the workers would gain from reducing the working day from ten hours to nine, government action might be required to win this concession. If people are to receive charitable aid, it is desirable that such help come from public authorities rather than from casual and uncertain private charity. Legislators should supervise and regulate colonization schemes—this from a man who was employed all his working life by the East India Company, which controlled British trade and colonization in India from 1600 to 1858. Government should also do those things that serve the general interests of all people but are not profitable to individuals, such as undertaking geographic or scientific exploration. Finally,

> in the particular circumstances of a given age or nation, there is scarcely anything, really important to the general interest, which it may not be desirable, or even necessary, that the government should take upon itself, not because private individuals cannot effectually perform it, but because they will not. At some times and places there will be no roads, docks, harbours, canals, works of irrigation, hospitals, schools, colleges, printing presses, unless the government establishes them. [Bk. V, Ch. 11]

John Stuart Mill must appear prominently in any intellectual history. His importance was not limited to his being the last great economist of the classical school, the greatest of the orthodox economists during the two generations between Ricardo and Marshall. His first important book, *System of Logic* (1843), established him as a leading logician. The essays he published, including "On Liberty" (1859), "Considerations on Representative Government" (1861), and "The Subjection of Women" (1869), showed him to be an outstanding political scientist, social philosopher, and champion of the democratic way of life. He looms large as a man of courage and honesty in his trenchant criticisms of the status quo, his support of reforms that were radical in his day, and his repudiation of the wages-fund doctrine. Cynics may scorn his belief in progress through the development of our intellectual and moral faculties, but it cannot be denied that he had a noble vision of the perfectibility of humanity. Mill's warmth, his humanitarianism, and his empathy for the poor and lowly are unusual for a leading theoretician in a science some people consider too coldly objective and even dismal.

We take leave of John Stuart Mill to turn to the socialists, who were less compromising in their ideas.

Bibliography

BENTHAM, JEREMY, *An Introduction to the Principles of Morals and Legislation.* New York: Hafner, 1948. [Originally published in 1780.]

———, *The Collected Works of Jeremy Bentham*, ed. by J. H. Burns. Vols. I and II, *The Correspondence of Jeremy Bentham*. London: University of London, The Athlone Press, 1968.

BOWLEY, MARIAN, *Nassau Senior and Classical Economics.* New York: Kelley, 1949.

HALÉVY, ELIE, *The Growth of Philosophic Radicalism*, tr. by Mary Morris, 2d ed. London: Faber and Faber, 1934.

HAYEK, F. A., *John Stuart Mill and Harriet Taylor, Their Friendship and Subsequent Marriage.* Chicago: The University of Chicago Press, 1951.

MACK, M. P., *Jeremy Bentham: An Odyssey of Ideas.* New York: Columbia University Press, 1963.

MILL, JOHN STUART, *Autobiography.* London: 1873.

———, *Dissertations and Discussions.* 2 vols. London: 1859.

———, *Essays on Some Unsettled Questions of Political Economy.* London: The London School of Economics and Political Science, 1948. [Originally published in 1844.]

———, *Principles of Political Economy*, 7th ed. London: 1871. [Originally published in 1848.]

———, *Utilitarianism.* London: 1861.

ROSSI, ALICE S., ed., *John Stuart Mill and Harriet Taylor Mill, Essays on Sex Equality.* Chicago: The University of Chicago Press, 1970.

SAY, JEAN BAPTISTE, *A Treatise on Political Economy,* tr. by C. R. Prinsep. 2 vols. Boston: Wells and Lilly, 1821. [Originally published in 1803.]

SENIOR, NASSAU W., *An Outline of the Science of Political Economy.* New York: Kelley, 1951. [Originally published in 1836.]

——, *Industrial Efficiency and Social Economy,* ed. by S. Leon Levy. 2 vols. New York: Holt, 1928. [Written 1847–52.]

STARK, W., *Jeremy Bentham's Economic Writings.* 3 vols. New York: Franklin, 1952–54.

9

The Rise of Socialist
Ideologies

Hints of socialistic ideas can be found in antiquity, but the concepts we are considering are quite recent, arising in the early 1800's. Although socialists disagree violently among themselves, three strands of thought characterize them. First, they all repudiate the idea of laissez faire and a harmony of interests among different classes. Second, they advocate collective action and public ownership of enterprise to ameliorate conditions for the masses; public ownership can be undertaken by the central government, local governments, or cooperative enterprises. Third, they all optimistically believe in the perfectibility of people; with the proper environment, human nobility will shine in all its glory.

Overview of Socialism

The Social Background of Socialism

The industrial revolution did not lead to the millennium. Instead, the security of the old agricultural-village-handicraft economy was shattered; the new industrialism brought large factories, with the workers living crowded around them in noisome and pestilential slums where vice, crime, disease, hunger, and misery were a way of life. Industrial accidents brought scant or no compensation for the families of the maimed and the killed. There were no political rights for wage earners, and unions were proscribed. Every ill wind that reduced production and employment compounded the misery of the proletariat, and every new triumph of industrialization threw tens of thousands of impoverished handicraft workers onto the labor market. The poverty of the masses seemed increasingly oppressive as great fortunes multiplied. As George Crabbe wrote in *The Village* in 1783:

> Where Plenty smiles, alas! she smiles for few,
> And those who taste not, yet behold her store,
> Are as the slaves that dig the golden ore,
> The wealth around them makes them doubly poor.

No wonder that a century after the beginning of the industrial revolution in England John Stuart Mill believed that "hitherto it is questionable if all the mechanical inventions yet made have lightened the day's toil of any human being. They have enabled a greater population to live the same life of drudgery and imprisonment, and an increased number of manufacturers and others to make fortunes."

The rise of Marxian socialism was given additional force by the failure of the utopian socialists to persuade capitalists to join in humanitarian movements.

The Essence of Socialism

Here we shall define the various forms of socialism and of capitalism, which socialism sought to replace.

Capitalism has as its essential characteristics private ownership of capital and land and the predominance of the profit motive as a guiding force in a market system. In free-enterprise, laissez faire capitalism, competition rather than monopoly or oligopoly prevails, and there is a minimum of government regulation; prices freely formed in the market guide production and distribution. But capitalism can also be controlled or regulated: in business this can be done either by government or by monopolistic organization, and in the labor market, through unions. Such an economy might be called *private* enterprise rather than *free* enterprise. But it is still capitalism.

State capitalism means that a government in a capitalist milieu owns and operates industries for maximum profit or minimum loss, as a private entrepreneur would. The state is the entrepreneur, operating an island of public enterprise in the surrounding sea of private enterprise. When Bismarck had the state take over the railways in Germany, he was a state capitalist, not a socialist. When the New York City government took over the bankrupt and obsolete private subway systems (at a price that caused the stock of the subways to rise on the exchanges), that too was an example of state capitalism.

State socialism occurs when a government, existing in a capitalistic framework, undertakes to own and operate sectors of the economy for overall social objectives rather than for profit. Examples in the United States would be the federal social security system, the Tennessee Valley Authority, and the publicly owned canals. Historically, the state socialists were those who considered the state an impartial power that could be influenced to favor the working class if the vote were extended and the workers educated and organized. Then the state would take over enterprises and become the employer; or it could foster and subsidize cooperatives. Louis Blanc, to be discussed later, was a state socialist. So was Ferdinand Lassalle, who is alleged to have made a secret agreement to support Bismarck's expansionist policies in return for an extension of the vote to wage earners. Lassalle urged the organization of cooperative producers' associations under the benevolent guidance of the state, with the government using its public credit to raise the necessary capital.

The present British economic system, according to these definitions, is mixed—predominantly capitalist, but including elements of state capitalism and state socialism. In the United States the admixture of state capitalism and state socialism is smaller; in India, larger.

Utopian socialism dates from about 1800, with Henri Comte de Saint-Simon, Charles Fourier, and Robert Owen as the founders. They developed their ideas at a time when the industrial workers were still weak and unorganized, demoralized by the rapid changes of the industrial revolution, deprived of the franchise, and not yet aware of their latent power. The utopian socialists regarded the competitive capitalist market economy as unjust and irrational. They worked out concepts of perfect social arrangements and then appealed to the whole world to adopt them. They preached universal brotherly love rather than class struggle and looked to the capitalists to cooperate with and even finance their schemes. Imaginary model cooperative communities were elaborated, and some were actually tried, usually unsuccessfully.

Christian socialism developed in England and Germany after 1848, with Charles Kingsley a leading advocate of this doctrine in England. It arose after the defeat of radical movements in both countries. The workers were offered the solace of religion to assuage their pain and to give them hope. The Bible was to form the manual of the statesman, the employer, and the worker; God's order was mutual love and fellowship. Property owned by the rich was to be held in trust for the benefit of everybody. This movement, repudiating violence and class struggle, advocated sanitary reform, education, factory legislation, and cooperatives.

Anarchism, with Pierre-Joseph Proudhon one of its early propo-
nents, held that all forms of government are coercive and should be
abolished. As Mikhail Bakunin (1814–76) said, "The State is the root
of the evil." Anarchists did not advocate a society without order, but
rather that society's order arise out of self-governing groups through
voluntary or associative effort. Human nature, they contended, is essentially good if not corrupted by the state and its institutions. Private property should be replaced by collective ownership of capital
by cooperating groups. Anarchists envisioned communities engaging
in production and carrying on trade with other communities, with associations of producers controlling agricultural, industrial, and even
intellectual and artistic production. Associations of consumers were
expected to coordinate housing, lighting, health, food, and sanitation.
For specific purposes, still wider groups might embrace a whole
country, or possibly several countries. Mutual understanding, cooperation, and complete liberty would characterize anarchist society.
Individual initiative would be encouraged, and every tendency to
uniformity and centralized authority would be effectively checked.
Although the methods for achieving their goals differed, the ideal
community of the anarchists resembled that of other socialists.

Marxian socialism resuscitated Ricardo's labor theory of value and
added to it a theory of exploitation of the wage earners by the capitalists. This type of socialism is based on the materialist conception of
history: In every historical epoch, the prevailing method of production and exchange and the social organization following from it form
the basis for legal, political, cultural, and intellectual superstruc-
tures. As each social system develops its productive forces, the relations of production become a barrier to further progress. Then the
system has to be changed—revolutionized—so that new productive
relations among people will permit the higher development of the
forces of production. The mechanism for overthrowing old societies
is the class struggle.

Karl Marx and Friedrich Engels claimed that they were doing for
history what Charles Darwin's theory of evolution had done for biology. They saw society as evolving through six stages. In the earliest
stage, which they called primitive communism, there were no antagonistic classes, no exploitation, and no class struggles. Land was held
in common ownership, and people cooperated in group activity in
wresting a meager living from nature. The efficiency of production
was very low, so low that workers could not produce much of a
surplus beyond the subsistence of themselves and their dependents.
Slavery and exploitation were therefore impossible, because that

requires the toilers to produce more than they must consume in order to survive. The society of the American Indians before the Europeans came would be an example of primitive communism.

Gradually the efficiency of production rose to the level where the workers could produce more than their own subsistence. Then slavery became profitable, and exploitation and class conflicts arose. Here Marx and Engels meant the slavery of antiquity, such as that among the Hebrews, Egyptians, Greeks, and Romans; they did not mean the slavery of the United States, which was an anachronism existing within a capitalist society. Slavery permitted a higher development of the productive forces of society, but eventually it became a barrier to further progress. Slaves were not the most highly motivated workers, and slave rebellions shook society and tore it apart. Eventually the system was overthrown and replaced by feudalism, a higher stage in the evolution of social systems.

Feudalism is unique, said Marx and Engels, because the exploitation of the serf is most clearly visible. Under slavery the slaves appear to get nothing for their labor, even though they do receive subsistence. Under capitalism the workers appear to be paid for all the hours they work, even though the capitalist actually appropriates part of their labor time without payment. But in the feudal system serfs may work three days per week on the land assigned to them, but must work three days on their lord's land. This is obvious exploitation. The serf has more incentive to work well than the slave had, and feudalism brings a higher development of the productive forces of society. But the system finally limits further progress, and it is overthrown and superseded by capitalism.

While Marx and Engels hated capitalism with passion, they paid tribute to the great increases in productivity and production that it unleashed. But capitalism faced class struggles and contradictions that inevitably would lead to its being overthrown and replaced by socialism. They viewed the state as an instrument of force used by one class against another. The capitalist state oppresses the workers. The working class, in overthrowing the bourgeois state, will establish its own dictatorship of the proletariat to destroy the bourgeoisie as a class.

Under socialism, private property in consumer goods is permitted, but the capital and land are publicly owned by the central government, local authorities, or cooperatives promoted and regulated by the state. Production is planned, as is the rate of investment, with the profit motive and the free market eliminated as guiding forces for the economy.

Communism is the next higher stage of society, according to Marxism. The socialist slogan is "From each according to his ability, to each according to his work." Under communism the slogan is "From each according to his ability, to each according to his need." This presupposes a superabundance of goods, the elimination of money payments based on work performed, and a devotion to society as selfless as a person's loyalty to his family is at present. The state will wither away when antagonistic classes disappear, and government over people will be replaced by administration over things, such as large railway systems and coal-iron-machinery complexes.

The so-called Communist countries today have actually established socialism or are in the process of establishing it. Communism exists nowhere at present except in small cooperative communities, usually motivated by a common religious or other crusading fervor. Here people work together, pool their earnings, and draw from the common fund the things they need.

Revisionism, with Eduard Bernstein a leading advocate, followed the rise of Marxism in Germany. In England the Fabian socialists were revisionists, but unlike the German left-wing movement they had never adhered to Marxism to any significant degree. Revisionism abjured the class struggle, denied that the state is a class institution, and pinned its hopes on education, electioneering, and gaining control of government through the ballot. The government was to regulate monopolies, control factory working conditions, take over some public utilities, and gradually extend its ownership of capital. Because the revisionists, especially the Fabian branch, favored municipal ownership of public utilities, revisionism has sometimes been called "gas and water socialism."

Syndicalism was promoted and popularized in labor circles in the Latin countries of Europe by Georges Sorel (1847–1922). Syndicalists were antiparliamentarian and antimilitarist. They believed that socialism deteriorates into bourgeois beliefs when it engages in political and parliamentary activity. If represented in parliament, the movement will degenerate into opportunism in order to gain political influence. What the workers require is one big union that will not play the bourgeois game of seeking social reform and the amelioration of conditions. The union must not dabble in strike and insurance funds, union contracts, union treasuries, or piecemeal reform. Strikes must be fomented to stir up the revolutionary consciousness and militancy of workers; sabotage frequently must be used as a weapon in the class struggle. Eventually the general strike of the one big union will overthrow capitalism; each industry will then be organized as an autonomous unit managed by the workers, and these units will be combined in a federation that will become the administrative center. The syndicalists expected coercive government to disappear.

Syndicalism differed from anarchism in that the former relied exclusively on revolutionary unionism and the general strike for the overthrow of government. But both favored the abolition of private property and the extinction of political government. The Industrial Workers of the World (nicknamed "the Wobblies"), organized in the United States in 1905, was an example of a syndicalist union.

Guild socialism's major advocate was G. D. H. Cole (1889–1959), a professor of economics at Oxford University. This type of socialism remained primarily a British movement, one of gradualism and reform, which reached its height around the time of World War I. The guild socialists accepted the state as a necessary institution for the expression of the general interests of citizens as consumers. The actual management of industries was to be entrusted to the employees (the producers), organized in their industrial guilds, rather than to the government. But the government was to develop overall economic policy on behalf of the whole community, not merely for the workers. Every worker would be a partner in the enterprise for which he or she worked; this was the essence of the "industrial democracy" that guild socialists favored. The nation would no longer be divided into opposing camps of capital and labor; instead, it would be divided into producers and consumers, with each having its national association—the guild and the government. Thus producers and consumers would form a partnership of equals.

What Groups of People Did Socialism Serve or Seek to Serve?

The more moderate groups (utopian, Christian, and guild socialists) claimed to represent everybody's interests, with primary emphasis on the needs and interests of the workers. They did serve the workers by arousing the conscience of society and inspiring middle-class reformers, thereby promoting reform legislation. To the extent that they diverted workers from organizing unions and political parties to promote their own interests, they also served the employers and landowners. Christian socialism arose at a time when socialist doctrines were gaining ground among the workers. Its adherents felt that the radical movement must be Christianized or Christianity would lose its appeal.

The more extreme socialist groups (Marxists, anarchists, and syndicalists) proclaimed class warfare against the rich; they aimed at promoting the interests of the working class. Through vigorous trade union activity, parliamentary pressure, or the threat of revolts, their agitating and organizing helped win concessions from the capitalists.

How Was Socialism Valid, Useful, or Correct in Its Time?

Workers had legitimate grievances against laissez faire capitalism as it developed in its early decades. In the early 1800's utopian socialism expressed the disturbed conscience of humanity. Marxian socialism offered an involved theoretical dissection of contemporary society that exposed and perhaps exaggerated all its evils. But like other socialist criticisms it had a certain validity in its time. The two problems of poverty and recurring business depressions had not been faced squarely by those speaking for the status quo, and the socialists performed a real service by concentrating their fire on these unsolved problems. Marx also correctly predicted the growth of monopoly. He contributed an evolutionary approach to the study of society and social problems, strengthening the idea that social institutions grow and change historically in response to changes in their environment. His theory of economic development was impressive at the time. His ideas won considerable popularity in Europe, where class lines were clearly drawn and the working class was at the bottom of the social and economic ladder—a position in which the dominant classes fully intended to keep it.

Socialism played a historically useful role by promoting factory acts, sanitary reforms, cooperative associations, unions, pensions, workmen's compensation laws, and so on.

How Did Socialist Doctrines Outlive Their Usefulness?

They have not, in a sense. One-third of the world's people live under regimes basically guided by Marxian economics. Perhaps another third of the people either live under governments that are guided considerably by socialist aspirations (as in India, Tanzania, Sweden) or form large socialist minorities in nonsocialist milieus (as in Japan, Italy, France).

The socialist groups that sought reforms have outlived their usefulness to the extent that nonsocialist groups have instituted the changes they advocated. Today's social programs and labor's present status would have been considered revolutionary in the Great Britain and United States of 1850. Yet by now the socialists' minimal demands have been more than fulfilled, and this has been accomplished peacefully. For a variety of reasons the capitalists undertook reforms, and they were able to do so without giving up their property. First, as the workers grew stronger the capitalists feared that if a little were not given, much more would be taken. Second, as the system grew richer it could afford to offer more. Third, middle-class reformers worked for the amelioration of conditions. And finally, capitalists as a group could give up what one capitalist could not, for fear of weakening his competitive position.

Revolutionary socialism made a number of remarkably accurate predictions, but enough of its forecasts were incorrect to vitiate its role and function. Marx extrapolated into the future the trends of the past. He believed that the absolute impoverishment of the working class would continue, meaning that the standard of living would continue to fall. It is difficult to see how the terrible conditions of the wage earners even in mid-nineteenth-century Britain, which Marx pictured so well by quoting from official government reports, could have become much worse. He had a better case for predicting the relative impoverishment of the workers: Marx claimed that if workers' incomes rise, the capitalists' incomes will rise even faster. There is a sound basis for this belief, for it is well known that the second million dollars is much easier to acquire than the first. But Marx did not foresee that unions, political action, and government intervention could curb this tendency.

Marx also predicted the disintegration and decline of the middle class. The upper echelons would merge with the bourgeoisie, while the lower strata would be ground down into the ranks of the proletariat. This would lead to a polarization of the population into two opposing classes. Marx's typical middle-class man was the small businessman who owned his own capital. The belief that small business would be overcome in competition with big business was a brilliant economic forecast. But Marx did not foresee that a new middle class would arise—self-employed professional people, salaried scientists, engineers, teachers, salesmen, advertisers, administrators, and so forth.

The hard-bitten, grasping capitalists, according to Marx, would exploit labor to the utmost of their ability, thereby driving the workers into revolutionary activity. This tendency was not due to any inherent meanness or other defect of the capitalist mentality; it was an inexorable law of the social system. In the competition among capitalists the generous or easy-going or incompetent employer would go under. The state, which acted as the executive committee of the bourgeoisie as a whole, would guarantee those conditions that would perpetuate wage slavery. Marx did not believe the state could be influenced to ameliorate conditions. Nor did he understand that the interests of the capitalist class as a whole do not necessarily coincide with those of each individual within it. Thus, it may be in the interest of a single employer to cut wages; but if all were to cut wages, their market for goods would be reduced. Therefore the class as a whole can live with minimum wage laws. Again, a capitalist may resist to the utmost the granting of pensions. But when all employers have to grant them under identical terms, the burden is not so great as when only one must sacrifice a competitive position by incurring such a cost. Unions frequently negotiate pensions, with the employer paying the difference between the federal social security pension and the negotiated benefit; in such situations, employers frequently join their employees in pressing for larger government pensions to reduce their own payments. Such class collaboration is very un-Marxian.

Marx predicted a falling rate of profit and ever-worsening crises, which would make the capitalist system untenable. While he recognized certain counteracting tendencies to the falling rate of profit, he underestimated their importance. And he did not foresee massive government intervention in the economy to reduce the severity of fluctuations.

Marx erred in expecting revolutions to occur first in the most advanced industrial countries and to take place in many countries simultaneously or in rapid succession. He and Engels underestimated the force of nationalism when they ended *The Communist Manifesto* (1848) with "The proletarians have nothing to lose but their chains. They have a world to win. Workingmen of all countries, unite!" The tentacles of imperialism, Marx believed, would not be disengaged from the colonies except with fire and sword; yet we have seen political freedom obtained with only moderate violence by India, the Gold Coast, French Guinea, and other colonies. Capitalism has not demonstrated the bull-headed obstinacy assumed by Marx and has indicated a greater ability to adjust to new circumstances than he thought possible.

There is much doubt concerning the validity of the Marxian scheme of the evolution of social systems through the six stages. Not all societies have proceeded consecutively through primitive communism, slavery, feudalism, and capitalism. Sometimes stages have been skipped, sometimes the progression was thwarted and interrupted, sometimes societies reverted from a later to an earlier stage. Older modes of production may persist for centuries along with the newer modes within the same society. One can accept the idea of continual change, continual evolution, without the inevitable progression of social systems that early Marxism expounded.

Many socialists of various persuasions have been disappointed with the way the system developed in Soviet Russia. The reorganization of society, they had hoped, would bring about a new flowering of freedom, increased collective activity for the common good, better standards of morality and justice, greater security for the individual, and a cultural renaissance. During the Stalin dictatorship these dreams turned to gall and wormwood for millions who had dreamed of a socialist utopia. Even with the post-Stalin thaw in the Soviet Union, one wonders how much room there is for independent thinking and for dissent from orthodoxy when the state is the dominant employer. One wonders whether the state as an instrument of force has thwarted the growth of democracy and individuality. And one cannot help wondering if the all-powerful state will ever wither away.

The socialist principle of "From each according to his ability, to each according to his work" is difficult to apply equitably. It is feasible within a particular trade that lends itself to a piece-rate system: If one worker sews twice as many buttonholes as another, she will get twice the pay. But how much more productive is a factory superintendent than a tool-and-die-maker? How many times more money should a poet get than a worker on an automated assembly line? In the Soviet Union, income payments are quite arbitrary, helping to create a group of loyal, highly paid intellectuals and administrators, and an impoverished mass of unskilled workers. The inequality of incomes among a Russian factory's employees is probably as great as among those in an American factory, if we consider the incomes of factory employees only from the superintendent level on down.

Socialism presents formidable problems not only in the sphere of income distribution but in the allocation of productive resources as well. How much should go for consumption goods, and how much for investment? Which consumption goods should be produced, and how many of each? What are the alternatives if the only supplier of a certain good offers shoddy wares? How can the masses of people make their voices heard and their wishes known to the top government planners who make decisions that vitally affect the humblest individual in the farthest corner of the land? The socialist regimes and their populations are beset with stupendous problems that their leading theoreticians of the past and present have not solved successfully.

Saint-Simon

Henri Comte de Saint-Simon (1760–1825) came from an impoverished family of the nobility. He fought on the colonial side in the
American Revolution as a regular officer, distinguishing himself in
the battle at Yorktown. During the early stages of the French Revolution he renounced his title. At the height of the Revolution he became a big speculator in the nationalized land of the Church and of
the *émigrés*, buying on credit and later paying in rapidly depreciating
assignats. He served a term in prison but was released after the fall
of Robespierre. Later he abandoned the role of financier to become a
philosopher and prophet. With reckless extravagance he entertained
and subsidized promising young scientists, artists, and scholars, but
this prodigality soon left him penniless, and he lived for several
years at the home of a former servant. Upon the death of his mother,
Saint-Simon surrendered his rights of inheritance in return for a
small pension from his family. In 1823, being in a desperate financial
position, he fired seven pistol bullets at his head but miraculously
survived with only the loss of an eye.

Saint-Simon, a utopian socialist, developed his ideas before the political movement of the working class in France had taken shape. He
therefore made no appeal to the workers to struggle against their employers. Regarding idleness as a sin, he made a religion of work and
industry. This is an interesting contrast to our own theories that it is
natural to want to avoid work because it is irksome or painful. Saint-
Simon alarmed the rich, for he made production, not property, the
basis for his new society. The line he drew separated producers from
nonproducers.

An industrial parliament, he wrote, should consist of three
chambers—invention, review, and execution. The first chamber,
composed of artists and engineers, would plan public works. The
second chamber, run by scientists, would examine the projects and
control education. The third chamber, consisting of the leaders of industry, would carry out the projects and control the budget. This was
one of the earliest proposals for a centrally planned economy governed by an educated elite.

Saint-Simon rejected the fundamental assumption of the classical
economists that the interests of the individual automatically coincide
with the general interest. He insisted that a new ethic was required
to restrain the antisocial egoism of the rich and to prevent an anar-
chic uprising of the poor. Humanitarian concern for the working
class was a dominant theme in his later writings.

Saint-Simon's attack on idlers led his followers to oppose the laws of inheritance and to urge the collective ownership of property. After his death, his disciples organized a school that became almost a religion. The Saint-Simonian enthusiasm for large-scale industry helped inspire big banks, railways, highways, the Suez Canal, and huge industrial undertakings.

A few selections from Saint-Simon's works will illustrate his ideas.[1]

The sole aim of our thoughts and our exertions must be the kind of organization most favourable to industry—industry understood in the widest sense, including every kind of useful activity, theoretical as well as practical, intellectual as well as manual. . . . Our desire is that men should henceforth do consciously, and with better directed and more useful effort, what they have hitherto done unconsciously, slowly, indecisively and too ineffectively. . . . Now, in my opinion, the time has come when the general revolution common to all civilized peoples in every land will come about. Governments will no longer order men about; their functions will be limited to ensuring that useful work will not be hindered. They will no longer have more than a small amount of power or money, for these functions will not require much. The money required for useful undertakings on a small or large scale will be supplied by voluntary subscription, and the subscribers will themselves supervise the spending and administration of their own money.

Suppose that France suddenly lost fifty of her best physicists, chemists, physiologists, mathematicians, poets, painters, . . . engineers, . . . bankers, . . . business men, . . . farmers, . . . miners, . . . metalworkers, . . . ; making in all the three thousand leading scientists, artists, and artisans of France.

These men are the Frenchmen who are the most essential producers, those who make the most important products, those who direct the enterprises most useful to the nation, those who contribute to its achievements in the sciences, fine arts and professions. They are in the most real sense the flower of French society; they are, above all Frenchmen, the most useful to their country, contribute most to its glory, increasing its civilization and prosperity. The nation would become a lifeless corpse as soon as it lost them. . . . It would require at least a generation for France to repair this misfortune. . . .

Let us pass on to another assumption. Suppose that France preserves all the men of genius that she possesses in the sciences, fine arts and professions, but has the misfortune to lose in the same day Monsieur the King's brother [and other members of the royal household]. . . . Suppose that France loses at the same time all the great officers of the royal

[1] F. M. H. Markham, ed., *Henri Comte de Saint-Simon, Selected Writings* (Oxford, Eng., 1952), pp. 70–74, 77–80. Reprinted with permission of Basil Blackwell.

household, all the ministers (with or without portfolio), all the councillors of state, all the chief magistrates, marshals, cardinals, archbishops, bishops, vicars-general, and canons, all the prefects and subprefects, all the civil servants, and judges, and, in addition, ten thousand of the richest proprietors who live in the style of nobles.

This mischance would certainly distress the French, because they are kindhearted, and could not see with indifference the sudden disappearance of such a large number of their compatriots. But this loss of thirty thousand individuals, considered to be the most important in the State, would only grieve them for purely sentimental reasons and would result in no political evil for the State.

In the first place, it would be very easy to fill the vacancies which would be made available. There are plenty of Frenchmen who could fill the function of the King's brother as well as can Monsieur. . . . The ante-chambers of the palace are full of courtiers ready to take the place of the great household officials. . . . As for the ten thousand aristocratic landowners, their heirs could need no apprenticeship to do the honours of their drawingrooms as well as they.

The prosperity of France can only exist through the effects of the progress of the sciences, fine arts and professions. The Princes, the great household officials, the Bishops, Marshals of France, prefects and idle landowners contribute nothing directly to the progress of the sciences, fine arts and professions. Far from contributing they only hinder, since they strive to prolong the supremacy existing to this day of conjectural ideas over positive science. They inevitably harm the prosperity of the nation by depriving, as they do, the scientists, artists, and artisans of the high esteem to which they are properly entitled. They are harmful because they expend their wealth in a way which is of no direct use to the sciences, fine arts, and professions: they are harmful because they are a charge on the national taxation, to the amount of three or four hundred millions under the heading of appointments, pensions, gifts, compensations, for the upkeep of their activities which are useless to the nation. . . . Society is a world which is upside down. The nation holds as a fundamental principle that the poor should be generous to the rich, and that therefore the poorer classes should daily deprive themselves of necessities in order to increase the superfluous luxury of the rich.

Saint-Simon was arrested and tried for this heresy in 1819, but he was acquitted.

The richest and most powerful men have an interest in the growth of equality, since the means of satisfying their wants increases in the same proportion as the levelling of the individuals composing the community. . . . Scientists, artists and industrialists, and the heads of industrial concerns are the men who possess the most eminent, varied, and most positively useful ability, for the guidance of men's minds at the present time. . . . They . . . are the men who should be entrusted with administrative power. . . .

The community has often been compared to a pyramid. I admit that the nation should be composed as a pyramid; I am profoundly convinced that the national pyramid should be crowned by the monarchy, but I assert that from the base of the pyramid to its summit the layers should be composed of more and more precious materials. If we consider the present pyramid, it appears that the base is made of granite, that up to a certain height the layers are composed of valuable materials, but that the upper part, supporting a magnificent diamond, is composed of nothing but plaster and gilt.

The base of the present national pyramid consists of workers in their routine occupations; the first layers above this base are the leaders of industrial enterprises, the scientists who improve the methods of manufacture and widen their application, the artists who give the stamp of good taste to all their products. The upper layers, which I assert to be composed of nothing but plaster, which is easily recognizable despite the gilding, are the courtiers, the mass of nobles whether of ancient or recent creation, the idle rich, the governing class from the prime minister to the humblest clerk. The monarchy is the magnificent diamond which crowns the pyramid.

Here are revolutionary implications indeed! Despite these extreme statements, Saint-Simon missed being a socialist in one respect: He did not advocate the appropriation of private property, though some of his disciples did.

Fourier

Charles Fourier (1772–1837) was an eccentric utopian socialist who slowly acquired a large and devoted following late in life and posthumously. He was by no means a revolutionary, and his appeals were usually addressed to the wealthy or to the king. The son of a middle-class merchant family that lost most of its possessions during the French Revolution, he was a clerk in various cloth houses and other businesses. A poor laborer all his life, he had to acquire his education in spare moments in library reading rooms.

Fourier was a critic of capitalism. Unlike Saint-Simon, he disliked large-scale production, mechanization, and centralization in all forms. Competition, he thought, multiplies waste in selling, and businessmen withhold or destroy commodities to raise their prices. Commerce to him was pernicious and corrupt, and he laid bare the material and moral poverty of the bourgeois world. He denounced a society that "accords its high protection to the agents of famine and pestilence." And he criticized the "progress of financiering, systems of extortion, indirect bankruptcy, anticipations of revenue, art of devouring the future." Under "progress of the mercantile spirit" he included "consideration accorded to commercial plundering and knavery. Stock-jobbing raised to a power which scoffs at law, encroaches upon all the fruits of industry, shares in the authority of governments, and propagates everywhere the frenzy of gambling in the public funds." [2]

Fourier's solution to social problems was to organize cooperative communities called *phalansteries,* or *phalanxes.* His love of order, symmetry, and precision drove him to draw elaborate plans for these communities, down to the most insignificant details. Each association would combine three hundred families—eighteen hundred people—on nine square miles of land. Everybody would live in a palacelike dwelling three stories high, which he described minutely. Agricultural and handicraft production would predominate, and the output of wealth would increase tenfold over that of chaotic private industry. One large granary would be more economical to build and easier to guard against fire than three hundred small ones. People's living together in honor and comfort would eliminate theft and the expense of guarding against it. Collective work would improve climatic conditions, and fewer clothes would be required. The economies of a common kitchen and apartments rather than separate dwellings were carefully calculated. The *phalanx* would solve the major problem, which was not the inequality of wealth, but its insufficiency.

Who would do the "dirty work" in this utopian colony? The children. Children love dirt, and they love to organize into gangs. Instead of thwarting these natural tendencies, they should be directed into useful social functions, such as doing the most disagreeable work. Meanwhile children should learn a variety of trades, so that as adults they will not be overspecialized and limited to a single task.

Fourier advocated complete equality between the sexes. He asserted that if a woman is confined to housekeeping, that interferes with the proper development of her natural talents.

After the minimum of subsistence was provided for each member of a *phalanx,* regardless of his or her own contribution to the enterprise, the surplus would be divided five-twelfths to labor, four-twelfths to capital, and three-twelfths to talent and skill. Therefore an appeal could be made to capitalists to finance such a project on the basis of earning a satisfactory return on their investment. In fact Fourier announced to the world that he would be at home every day

[2] Julia Franklin, tr., *Selections from the Works of Fourier* (London, 1901), pp. 93–94.

at noon to await a capitalist who would underwrite an association. For the rest of his life he waited in vain, although many *phalanxes* were started throughout the world by his followers.

In the United States the movement was popularized before the Civil War by Albert Brisbane, Horace Greeley, George Ripley, and others. Of the forty Fourierist *phalanxes* organized in this country, all of which failed, the best known were the North American Phalanx, located near Red Bank, New Jersey, which lasted from 1843 to 1856, and Brook Farm, which was organized in 1841 near Boston. Among the members and interested visitors at Brook Farm were Charles A. Dana, Nathaniel Hawthorne, Ralph Waldo Emerson, Amos Bronson Alcott, Margaret Fuller, Theodore Parker, Orestes Bronson, and William Henry Channing. A disastrous fire in 1846 ended this experiment.

Perhaps the closest approach at present to Fourier's *phalanxes* can be seen in the communes of China, although they have gone far beyond his *phalanxes* in enforcing centralized control and planning and in promoting large-scale enterprise.

Fourier showed much originality, and his ideas have remained influential, even though he is seldom credited with having reconnoitered new and uncharted ground. Cooperative living was central to his thinking as the way to change the environment in order to generate an entirely new and noble type of person. The *phalanxes* would provide cradle-to-grave, or womb-to-tomb, social security. For the early stages of his ideal society he advocated "guaranteeism"—the assurance that every person would be given a minimum of subsistence, security, and comfort. The idea that gangs of children should do the dirty work prefigured the system of assigning workers to tasks according to their aptitudes; this is an interesting way of solving one of the problems of resource allocation in a nonprice society. Fourier objected to overspecialization, warning that routine assembly-line work warps and thwarts the individual, although it greatly expands output. The Fourierist *phalanxes*, though ultimately failures, influenced the labor movement at the time and inspired much thought on how to eliminate the wastes of private enterprise and promote a better economic system. The cooperative movement is in part a living monument to Fourier.

Sismondi

Simonde de Sismondi (1773–1842) was a Swiss economist and historian of French descent. He and his family took refuge in England during the revolutionary disturbances of 1793–94. On their return to

Switzerland they sold most of their property and bought a small farm in Italy, which they worked themselves. Sismondi later returned to Geneva, where he wrote many scholarly works, among them a six-teen-volume *History of the Italian Republics of the Middle Ages* and a twenty-nine-volume *History of the French.*

Sismondi was among the first to launch a direct attack on classical economics, although he had been an ardent follower of Adam Smith in his earlier years. While he was never a socialist in the modern sense, he helped pave the way for socialist thought. In 1819, after viewing the appalling conditions in England following his absence of twenty-four years, he published *New Principles of Political Econ-omy.* In this book he stated that unrestricted capitalist enterprise, far from yielding the results that Smith and Say expected of it, was bound to lead to widespread misery and unemployment. His criti-cism of Say's Law of Markets and his denial that a free-enterprise economy tends toward full employment were stated fairly early in the rise of modern industrial society; John Stuart Mill a half century later and the neoclassical economists more than a century later were still proclaiming the impossibility of general gluts. Sismondi, raising the possibility of overproduction and crises, was one of the early con-tributors to business-cycle theory. He thought that when wages are at the subsistence level, more capital funds become available for in-vestment in machines. The output of manufactured goods is thereby increased, while the demand for consumption goods is reduced. The consequence is that the system can be maintained only by periodic crises that liquidate a large part of the capital overinvested in large-scale industry. Bankers, by extending credit, worsen the problem of overproduction and crises. As the concentration of wealth narrows the home market more and more, industry is increasingly compelled to open up foreign markets, which necessarily results in nationalistic wars. Sismondi thus explicitly formulated the charge that economic imperialism is inherent in capitalism.

Only state intervention would ensure the worker a living wage and a minimum of social security. Sismondi denied that the largest possi-ble aggregate production necessarily coincides with the greatest hap-piness of the people. A smaller output, well distributed, would be preferable. In the general interest, therefore, the state should enact laws regulating distribution. Small-scale family farming, as opposed to tenant farming, would promote a good distribution of income. He also urged small-scale production in the towns to avoid producing more than could be sold. Agriculture should be promoted at the ex-pense of urbanization. He favored inheritance taxes; curbing new in-

ventions by discontinuing patent rights so that "the zeal for such discoveries will grow cold"; compelling employers to provide security
for their workers in old age, illness, and unemployment; cooperation
and solidarity between workers and employers; and profit sharing.

Sismondi was concerned not merely with excessive and poorly distributed production but also with insufficient production, which he
believed reflects the conflict between the individual and the social
interest. The peasant, he thought, tries to increase his or her gross
product, while large landowners are concerned only with net revenue.
Suppose, he said, a well-cultivated piece of land produces a total output
of 1000 shillings, of which 100 go to the proprietor as rent. If the land
were let out as pasture, it would yield 110 shillings rent. The proprietor
would therefore dismiss the tenants in order to gain 10 shillings, while
the nation would lose 890 shillings.

Sismondi was the first to apply the term "proletary" to the wage laborer. The term had originally referred to the men in the Roman
republic who had nothing, who paid no taxes, and who could contribute only their offspring—the "proles"—to the country.

Sismondi offered a relatively modern prescription for curing a glut
in a particular industry:

> The government ought, in fact, to come to the assistance of men, and not
> of industry; it ought to save its citizens, and not business. Far from mak-
> ing advances to the master manufacturer, to encourage him to manufac-
> ture to a loss, it ought largely to contribute funds to take the operatives
> from an employment which increases the embarrassment of all their
> fellow citizens. It ought to employ them in those public works whose
> products do not bear upon the markets, and do not increase the general
> glut. Public edifices, town-halls, markets, public walks, are native
> wealth, though not of a kind that can be bought and sold. . . .
>
> But in assisting the workmen in any depressed industrial business by
> public works, government must adhere principally to the following
> rules:—not to compete with an existing business, and thus bring fresh
> disturbances into the markets; not to make of those works which it
> orders and pays for a permanent occupation, to which will be attached a
> new class of day-labourers—*proletarii*—but to make them perceive how
> long it will last, and where it will end, that they may not marry in this
> precarious state. . . .
>
> On whatever side we look, the same lesson meets us everywhere, *pro-
> tect the poor,* and ought to be the most important study of the legislator
> and of the government. . . . Protect the poor, that they may keep . . .
> that share of the income of the community which their labour ought to
> secure to them; protect the poor, for they want support, that they may
> have some leisure, some intellectual development, in order to advance

in virtue; protect the poor, for the greatest danger to law, public peace and stability, is the belief of the poor that they are oppressed, and their hatred of government; protect the poor, if you wish industry to flourish, for the poor are the most important of consumers.[3]

Sismondi was less a socialist than a social critic and a dissenter from classical theory. His strong interest in the business cycle and his humanitarian views set him apart from the orthodox economists of his day and inspired the socialists, but he made no fundamental attack on the institution of private property.

Owen

Robert Owen (1771–1858) was the most spectacular and most famous of the utopian socialists. The son of a Welsh ironmonger and saddler, he attended school for only a few years. At nine he went to work in a neighboring store as a shopboy; later he was employed in dry-goods stores in London. At eighteen he borrowed a hundred pounds and set up a partnership with a mechanic who could build the newly invented textile machinery. When his partner left him, Owen set himself up in business, using the machines he had on hand. He was successful, but a better opportunity came his way; while still under twenty, he became manager of one of the largest and best-equipped spinning mills in Lancashire, with five hundred workers under him. Owen was the first spinner in Britain to use American sea-island cotton. His employer offered him a partnership, but instead he started a new company for the manufacture of yarn. Again highly successful, at twenty-eight he bought the New Lanark Mills in Scotland from David Dale, whose daughter he married soon afterward. Owen's spinning mills became the largest and best equipped in Scotland.

By examining Owen's ideas, we can see what led him to become a factory reformer, pioneer socialist, advocate of cooperatives, trade union leader, founder of utopian communities, and theorist in the field of education. His central thesis was that human nature is molded for better or worse by the environment. Human beings cannot form their own characters; they are without exception formed for them. Since character is made by circumstances, people are not responsible for their actions, and they should be molded into goodness instead of being punished for being bad. All Owen's theories, dreams, and programs, like Fourier's, were based on the belief that

---

[3] Simonde de Sismondi, *Political Economy and the Philosophy of Government* (London, 1847), pp. 220, 221, 223. [Originally published from 1826 to 1837.]

providing better conditions would produce better people. One should try to serve the community and thereby achieve one's own highest happiness. This concept reversed classical economics and Benthamite thinking, which held that self-interest will serve society.

In an essay published in 1813, Owen wrote:

> Any general character, from the best to the worst, from the most ignorant to the most enlightened, may be given to any community, even to the world at large, by the application of proper means; which means are to a great extent at the command and under the control of those who have influence in the affairs of men. . . .
>
> The happiness of self, clearly understood and uniformly practised . . . can only be attained by conduct that must promote the happiness of the community. . . .
>
> These plans must be devised to train children from their earliest infancy in good habits of every description (which will of course prevent them from acquiring those of falsehood and deception). They must afterwards be rationally educated, and their labour be usefully directed. Such habits and education will impress them with an active and ardent desire to promote the happiness of every individual, and that without the shadow of exception for sect, or party, or country, or climate. They will also ensure, with the fewest possible exceptions, health, strength, and vigour of body; for the happiness of man can be erected only on the foundations of health of body and peace of mind.[4]

Owen proceeded to convert the New Lanark Mills into a model community, a show place inspected by distinguished visitors from all over the world. On arriving there, he found five hundred pauper children living in the factory boarding house, serving seven- to nine-year apprenticeships. They started working at the age of six, and their working day, summer and winter, was twelve hours, six days a week. There was also a factory village to house the families of workers, who lived in poverty, crime, debt, sickness, and misery. Yet David Dale, the former owner, was far more humanitarian than most employers.

Owen introduced his reforms at New Lanark to prove that character could thereby be reshaped for the better. He discontinued the use of pauper children. Youngsters were not admitted into the factory until they were ten, and free schooling was available to them between the ages of five and ten. For preschool children he founded an infant school, or nursery, the first in Britain. He wanted children to grow up happily in a healthy environment. Comfortable houses were

---

[4] Robert Owen, *A New View of Society and Other Writings* (London, 1927), pp. 16, 17, 20.

built for the families who worked at New Lanark. Food, fuel, and clothing were sold to the workers at cost. The working day was reduced to ten and a half hours, and wages were high. He paid his employees during slack times and sickness, gave them old age insurance, and provided adult educational and recreational facilities. Fines and punishments, so characteristic of the time, were abolished. Owen reformed his employees, who worshipped him, and still he made good profits. But his partners objected to such extravagance. Twice he had to buy out his partners and acquire new ones. His third and last partnership, formed in 1814, included Jeremy Bentham. The partners agreed to limit their dividends to 5 per cent on invested capital and to use all surplus revenue in the interests of the employees. Owen withdrew from his business in 1829 because of friction with some of his partners. In severing relations with one of his partners he said, "All the world is queer save thee and me, and even thou art a little queer."

This great textile manufacturer shocked the world when he denounced all established religions because they taught that people were responsible for their evil ways instead of attributing evil to bad environment. He preached social rather than moral reformation. Even he himself was a mere product of forces over which he had no control:

> Causes, over which I could have no control, removed in my early days the bandage which covered my mental sight. If I have been enabled to discover this blindness with which my fellow-men are afflicted, to trace their wanderings from the path which they were most anxious to find, and at the same time to perceive that relief could not be administered to them by any premature disclosure of their unhappy state, it is not from any merit of mine; nor can I claim any personal consideration whatever for having been myself relieved from this unhappy situation. But, beholding such truly pitiable objects around me, and witnessing the misery which they hourly experienced from falling into the dangers and evils by which, in these paths, they were on every side surrounded,— could I remain an idle spectator? . . .
>
> No! The causes which fashioned me in the womb,—the circumstances by which I was surrounded from my birth, and over which I had no influence whatever, formed me with far other faculties, habits, and sentiments. These gave me a mind that could not rest satisfied without trying every possible expedient to relieve my fellow-men from their wretched situation, and formed it of such a texture that obstacles of the most formidable nature served but to increase my ardour, and to fix within me a settled determination, either to overcome them, or to die in the attempt.[5]

[5] *Ibid.*, p. 108.

Owen always did things for the people instead of relying on their own initiative to get them done. He pleaded with his fellow manufacturers to follow his example. Why not care for your living machines as well as your inanimate ones? he asked. If you help the workers, he said, you will increase your own happiness and intellectual enjoyment. He appealed to the government to enact factory legislation and was mainly responsible for the Factory Act of 1819, although he denounced it as being far weaker than he wished. During the slump following the end of the Napoleonic Wars, Owen urged the government to employ the poor in "villages of cooperation," modeled after his own establishment at New Lanark. Having failed to persuade either capitalists or government to follow his example, he himself promoted a model cooperative community to show the way. In 1825 he established the New Harmony colony on thirty thousand acres in Indiana, which he bought from the Rappites, a sect that did not have much of a future, since its followers practiced celibacy. His type of organization, Owen thought, would sweep away capitalism and the competitive system. While Fourier had allowed profit on the capital invested in utopian colonies, Owen favored only a fixed rate of interest until the owners of capital voluntarily gave it up, as he believed they would. Within three years the colony failed and Owen had lost four-fifths of his $250,000 fortune. Other villages of cooperation, established later in Great Britain, also failed.

Owen now found himself at the head of a growing army of working-class disciples. The modification of the British anti-union laws in 1825 was followed by considerable growth of trade unionism. Workers also promoted cooperatives as the forerunners of Owen's "villages of cooperation." Owen placed himself at the head of both movements. In 1832 he founded the National Equitable Labour Exchange as a market where products could be exchanged on the basis of notes representing labor time. His hope was to eliminate money and profit, twin social evils, by bringing producers and consumers into direct contact with one another. Although this experiment failed in two years, his followers founded the Rochdale Pioneers' Co-operative Society in 1844. This was the beginning of a highly successful consumers' cooperative movement in Great Britain, inspired by Owen but a far cry from the producers' cooperatives he had hoped would replace capitalism.

Disappointment in the Reform Act of 1832, which left the workers voteless, led to an upsurge of unionism and later to the Chartist movement. Owen plunged into union activity in 1833 by promoting the Grand National Consolidated Trades Union, which soon recruited half a million members. Hasty strikes and bitter lockouts followed. There was internal dissension, with Owen opposing militant action, conflict, and strikes. He suddenly ordered the union dissolved in 1834, after six farm laborers were sentenced to deportation to Australia for seven years because they had administered secret oaths in organizing farm laborers in their district. But many of the constituent trade unions in the Grand National reorganized themselves as separate societies, living on to become the nuclei of the modern British union movement.

Owen had a significant impact on socialism as well as on cooperation and unionism. The word "socialism" in the modern sense was first used in the Owenite *Co-operative Magazine* in 1827 to designate the followers of Owen's cooperative doctrines. It was formed from the word "social" as opposed to "individual," applied to the ownership of capital. His sharp criticisms of capitalism and his dream of collective action to organize cooperative communities based on large-scale industry inspired a whole generation of socialists. He retained his devotion to social reform to the end of his life, at which time he also turned to spiritualism, which he used as an additional weapon to advance his many causes.

Owen had four sons, all of whom became United States citizens. The oldest, Robert Dale Owen (1801–77), sat in Congress, drafted a bill founding the Smithsonian Institution, represented the United States as ambassador to Italy, and advocated birth control, emancipation for the slaves, women's rights, and free public education.

Blanc

Louis Blanc (1811–82), commonly regarded as a founder of state socialism, was a French social reformer, journalist, and historian who came from a royalist family. His grandfather, a prosperous merchant, was guillotined during the first French Revolution, and the family was impoverished after Napoleon fell. The publication of his *Organisation du Travail* (*Organization of Work*) in 1839 brought him fame and a position of leadership in the socialist movement. In the revolution of 1848 he was elected to the provisional government that overthrew the monarchy, the first avowed socialist to be elected to public office anywhere. Under pressure of Blanc and his followers over the issue of the right to work, the government organized national workshops to give work to the unemployed. This make-work scheme, consisting mostly of common labor on public works, was deliberately mismanaged by Blanc's political enemies. To disperse the national workshops, the government gave the men employed in them the alternative of entering the army or leaving Paris for the provinces. The Paris workers threw up barricades in revolt, but the army blasted them with artillery. In four days of fighting at the end of June 1848, sixteen thousand people were killed on both sides, according to the British ambassador. Blanc had to flee to England, but he returned to France in 1870. He was elected to the National Assembly, where he ended his days as a mild social reformer.

In Blanc's view universal suffrage would transform the state into an instrument of progress and welfare. Uncompromising in his attacks on capitalism and competition, which he said would ruin both the laboring class and the bourgeoisie, he was opposed to the doctrine of class war. He condemned even trade unionism, for he saw in strikes the futility of unprepared, isolated action. The solidarity of the entire community would promote state economic planning for full employment, the development of welfare services, government capital for getting national workshops started, and workers' cooperatives financed and promoted by the government. The state should become the "banker of the poor" by establishing a publicly owned bank to distribute credit to cooperatives. Capitalists could join the associations, receiving a fixed rate of interest for their capital, as guaranteed by the state. He believed that producers' associations aided by the state would attract the best workers and drive the capitalists out of business through superior competitive efficiency. Capitalism would simply fade away.

Blanc's attitude toward the state was expressed succinctly in his little book *A Catechism of Socialism* (1849):

> Q.—How are we to pass from the present order of things to that which you contemplate?
> A.—By the intervention of Government.
> Q.—What is the Government or State?
> A.—It is a body of upright and distinguished men, chosen by their equals to guide us all on our way to liberty. . . .
> Q.—Does not the word Government or State imply an idea of tyranny?
> A.—Yes; wherever power is something distinct from the people.

In his *Organization of Work* Blanc wrote:

> Who would be blind enough not to see that under the reign of free competition the continuous decline of wages necessarily becomes a general law with no exception whatsoever? . . . The population increases steadily; command the mothers of the poor to be sterile and blaspheme God who made them fruitful; for if you do not command it, the space will be too small for all strugglers. A machine is invented; demand it to be

broken and fling an anathema against science! Because if you do not do it, one thousand workmen, whom the new machine displaces in the workshops will knock at the door of the next one and will force down the wages of their fellow-workers. A systematic lowering of wages resulting in the elimination of a certain number of laborers is the inevitable effect of free competition. . . .

The government ought to be considered as the supreme regulator of production and endowed for this duty with great power. This task would consist of fighting competition and of finally overcoming it. The government ought to float a loan with the proceeds of which it should erect *social workshops* in the most important branches of national industry. . . . It would use competition as a weapon, not to destroy private industries without consideration, which would be to its own interest to avoid, but to guide them imperceptibly into the new system. Soon, indeed, workmen and capitalists would crowd to every industrial sphere where social workshops are opened, on account of the privileges they offer to their members. . . . Everybody, irrespective of position, rank or fortune, is interested in the creation of a new social order.[6]

Blanc's foremost contribution was to popularize the socialist ideas that arose before he appeared on the scene. He rejected the self-contained and diversified Owenite and Fourierist communities that were to undertake cooperative consumption as well as production. Instead, he favored cooperative producers' societies in each trade, with the workers operating their specialized workshops and selling their products to the rest of society. Because the large-scale enterprise he envisaged required large capital investments, Blanc, unlike other advocates of cooperation, looked to the government to supply the initial capital.

Kingsley

Charles Kingsley (1819–75) was a clergyman, poet, novelist, and reformer. He was a chaplain to Queen Victoria, professor of modern history at Cambridge, and canon of Westminster. Early in his career he and the other Christian socialists wanted to "socialize the Christian and Christianise the socialist." Kingsley was swept along by the Chartist movement when he went to London during the turbulent times of 1848. He shocked and angered the aristocrats when he announced at a public meeting, "I am a Chartist!" while the workers cheered.

Why was this vehement declaration so shocking to the respectable

---

[6] Louis Blanc, *Organization of Work*, tr. by Maria P. Dickoré (Cincinnati, Ohio, 1911), pp. 16, 51–53, 59. [Originally published in 1839.]

and the powerful? The Chartists had six demands: equal electoral districts; universal suffrage for both men and women; voting by secret ballot; parliaments elected annually; no property qualifications for serving in the House of Commons; and payment to members of parliament. By 1928 these demands—except for annual parliaments —were all enacted into law. What, then, was all the excitement about in 1848? First, reforms are dangerous when they are wrested from the rulers by mass agitation and action; they are much safer when handed down from above. Revolutionary movements are unlikely to stop at the reforms they originally demand, and small victories simply spur them on. Second, large numbers of Chartists were striking and rioting, undertaking military training, and preparing for possible insurrection. Third, Chartists were threatening to elect a people's parliament to meet at Birmingham with half a million workers to protect it. No wonder Kingsley's declaration was shocking to many.

In 1848 the Christian socialists issued a weekly journal called *Politics for the People*. Kingsley wrote a series of "Letters to Chartists" over the signature "Parson Lot." His second letter included a passionate defense of the poor:

My friends,—If I was severe on some of you in my last letter, believe me, it is not because I do not feel for you. There are great allowances to be made for most of you. If you have followed a very different 'Reformer's Guide' from mine, it is mainly the fault of us parsons: we have never told you that the true Reformer's Guide, the true poor man's book, the true 'God's Voice against Tyrants, Idlers, and Humbugs,' was the Bible. Ay, you may sneer, but so it is; it is our fault, our great fault, that you should sneer—sneer at the very news which ought to be your glory and your strength. It is our fault. We have used the Bible as if it was a mere special constable's handbook—an opium-dose for keeping beasts of burden patient while they were being overloaded—a mere book to keep the poor in order. We have told you that the powers that be were ordained of God, without telling you who ordained the impotences and imbecilities that be, alas, sometimes! We have told you that the Bible preached to you patience, while we have not told you that it promised you freedom. We have told you that the Bible preached the rights of property and the duties of labour, when (God knows!) for once that it does that, it preaches ten times over the *duties of property* and the *rights of labour*. We have found plenty of texts to rebuke the sins of the poor, and very few to rebuke the sins of the rich. You say that we have not preached to you; really I think we have preached to you a great deal more than your fair share. For, for one wholesome rating that we have given the rich, we have given you a thousand. I have been as bad as any one, but I am sick of it.

It is interesting to compare Kingsley's religion-and-opium state-ment with that of Marx. In 1844 Marx wrote an essay called "Con-tribution to the Critique of Hegel's Philosophy of Right." In it he dealt sympathetically with people's dependence on religion:

> *Religious* distress is at the same time the *expression* of real distress and the *protest* against real distress. Religion is the sigh of the op-pressed creature, the heart of a heartless world, just as it is the spirit of a spiritless situation. It is the *opium* of the people.
>
> The abolition of religion as the *illusory* happiness of the people is required for their *real* happiness. The demand to give up the illusions about its condition is the *demand to give up a condition which needs illusions*.

In his third letter Kingsley was more moderate and more typically Christian socialist:

> My friends,—and when I say friends, I speak honestly, and from the bot-tom of my heart, for you and I are, after all, I believe, longing for the same thing—*to see all humbug, idleness, injustice swept out of Eng-land;* only I think you are going, if not the wrong road, yet certainly neither the shortest, the safest, nor the wisest road, to gain the good end.
>
> My friends, I have to tell you that in the Bible you will find what you long for, promised more fairly than any man in these days promised it you; that in that book you will find what you want to say, said for you; you will find how much of what you want to see done, God wants to see done. Let me try if I cannot prove my words somewhat.
>
> What are the things which you demand most earnestly? Is not one of them, that no man shall enjoy wages without doing work?
>
> The Bible says, at once, that *"he that will not work, neither shall he eat";* and as the Bible speaks to rich as well as poor, so is that speech meant for the idle rich as well as for the idle poor. . . .
>
> I entreat you, I adjure you, to *trust the Bible,* to trust my samples from it, and *to read it honestly for yourselves,* and see if it be not the true *Radical Reformer's Guide*—God's everlasting witness against oppres-sion, and cruelty, and idleness.

Elsewhere Kingsley wrote: "God will only reform society on con-dition of our reforming every man his own self—while the devil is quite ready to help us to mend the laws and the parliament, earth and heaven, without ever starting such an impertinent and 'personal' request."

Kingsley repudiated mass meetings, physical violence, union strikes, and hatred of the rich by the poor. The rich were ignorant, not hostile. His doctrines included love, religion, cooperative associ-ations, sanitary reforms, and education. After a few years he abandoned his intense activities on behalf of Christian socialism, except for his continuing interest in the sanitary movement.

Proudhon

Pierre-Joseph Proudhon (1809–65) promoted anarchism as a mass movement. He was fiercely proud of his humble origins. His father, a poor cooper and brewer, and his mother, formerly a farm maid, tried to promote his education as best they could, in spite of extreme poverty. As a young man he became a printer and proofreader; he also experienced his share of unemployment and underwent imprisonment for his writing.

Liberty of the individual and justice were the goals Proudhon proclaimed. In his view the ideal system is anarchism, which means not disorder, but the absence of a master, a sovereign. As he wrote in *What Is Property?* (1840):

> In a given society, the authority of man over man is inversely proportional to the stage of intellectual development which that society has reached. . . . As man seeks justice in equality, so society seeks order in anarchy. . . . Every question of domestic politics must be decided by departmental statistics; every question of foreign politics is an affair of international statistics. The science of government rightly belongs to one of the sections of the Academy of Sciences, whose permanent secretary is necessarily prime minister; and since every citizen may address a memoir to the Academy, every citizen is a legislator. But, as the opinion of no one is of any value until its truth has been proven, no one can substitute his will for reason—nobody is king.[7]

In 1851 Proudhon attacked government in the following manner:

> Experience, in fact, shows that everywhere and always the Government, however much it may have been for the people at its origin, has placed itself on the side of the richest and most educated class against the more numerous and poorer class; it has little by little become narrow and exclusive; and, instead of maintaining liberty and equality among all, it works persistently to destroy them, by virtue of its natural inclination towards privilege. . . . We may conclude without fear that the revolutionary formula cannot be *Direct Legislation,* nor *Direct Government,* nor *Simplified Government,* that it is NO GOVERNMENT. Neither monarchy, nor aristocracy, nor even democracy itself in so far as it may imply any government at all, even though acting in the name of the people, and calling itself the people. No authority, no government, not even

---

[7] Pierre-Joseph Proudhon, *What Is Property?* tr. by Benjamin R. Tucker (London, no date), pp. 264–65. [Originally published in 1840.]

popular, that is the Revolution. . . . Governing the people will always be swindling the people. It is always man giving orders to man, the fiction which makes an end of liberty.[8]

"What is property?" asked Proudhon. "Property is theft." By "property" he really meant large property that permitted its owner to live without working by exacting rent, interest, and profit from the producers. He favored small-property ownership of dwellings, land, tools, and the products of labor by the laborer. According to him, large industries should be owned by associations of workers, with society controlling the associations so that they charge a just price, as near as possible to cost. Proudhon basically disliked large-scale machinery because he felt it to be incompatible with his small producers' commonwealth. He favored equality of incomes despite inequality of abilities, strength, talents, and output:

> Let Homer sing his verse. I listen to this sublime genius in comparison with whom I, a simple herdsman, a humble farmer, am as nothing. What, indeed,—if product is to be compared with product,—are my cheeses and my beans in the presence of his "Iliad"? But, if Homer wishes to take from me all that I possess, and make me his slave in return for his inimitable poem, I will give up the pleasure of his lays and dismiss him. I can do without his "Iliad," and wait, if necessary, for the "Aeneid." Homer cannot live twenty-four hours without my products. Let him accept, then, the little that I have to offer; and then his muse may instruct, encourage and console me.[9]

To promote individual freedom and equity in exchange, Proudhon proposed that the gold standard be abolished. Credit, he said, is to an economy what blood is to an animal, but the "bankocracy" has monopolized it. Only bank paper redeemable in merchandise and services should circulate, and French citizens should have the right to establish banks as they do retail shops. He urged that a Bank of Exchange be organized with a thousand subscribers. The amount of paper it would issue would be proportional to the gross output of these subscribers, and the paper would be negotiable only among themselves. As additional people joined, the circulation of bills would grow. Eventually all France would be under one system. Inflation could never occur because the amount of paper issued would be proportionate to the delivery of products. The banks would buy goods from members at between 50 and 100 per cent of the cost of

---

[8] Pierre-Joseph Proudhon, *General Idea of the Revolution in the Nineteenth Century*, tr. by John B. Robinson (London, 1923), pp. 108, 126. [Originally published in 1851.]
[9] Proudhon, *What Is Property?* pp. 142–43.

production. This transaction would really be a loan on goods for a limited time, for the producer could sell the goods, pay back the loan, and keep the excess revenue. Or, after the loan matured, the bank would sell the consignment at public auction and pay the original seller the excess of the selling price over the loan after deducting a small commission. Thus interest, a tribute representing exploitation, would be abolished. Every worker or group of workers could get free credit with which to buy capital goods, and the class structure of society would disappear. Property and labor would be reunited.

Proudhon actually succeeded in organizing a People's Bank in Paris in 1849. The basic capital of the bank was to be fifteen million francs, issued in five-franc shares of non-interest-bearing stock. Many thousands of shares were subscribed, but Proudhon's arrest and trial ended the bank before it could get under way.

Proudhon, the philosophical anarchist, appears to have been the mildest sort of reformer; yet the ideas he planted came to fruition among his more militant intellectual descendants.

Bibliography

BEER, MAX, *A History of British Socialism*, 2d ed. London: Allen and Unwin, 1940.

BLANC, LOUIS, *Organization of Work*, tr. by Maria P. Dickoré. Cincinnati, Ohio: University of Cincinnati Press, 1911. [Originally published in 1839.]

COLE, G. D. H., *The Case for Industrial Partnership*. London: Macmillan, 1957.

————, *A History of Socialist Thought*. 6 vols. New York: St. Martin's, 1953–58.

COLE, MARGARET, *Robert Owen of New Lanark*. London: Batchworth Press, 1953.

FOURIER, CHARLES, *Selections from the Works of Fourier*, tr. by Julia Franklin. London: Swan Sonnenschein, 1901.

————, *Theory of Social Organization*. New York: Somerby, 1876. [Written in 1822.]

HARVEY, ROWLAND HILL, *Robert Owen, Social Idealist*. Berkeley, Calif.: University of California Press, 1949.

JOHNSON, OAKLEY C., *Robert Owen in the United States*. New York: Humanities Press, 1970.

KINGSLEY, CHARLES, *Works*, ed. by Mrs. Charles Kingsley. Vol. VII, *Letters and Memories*. Philadelphia: Morris, 1899.

LICHTHEIM, GEORGE, *The Origins of Socialism*. New York: Praeger, 1969.

LOUBÈRE, LEO A., *Louis Blanc*. Evanston, Ill.: Northwestern University Press, 1961.

MANUEL, FRANK E., *The New World of Henri Saint-Simon*. Cambridge, Mass.: Harvard University Press, 1956.

MARRIOTT, J. A. R., *The French Revolution of 1848 in Its Economic Aspect*. Vol. I, *Louis Blanc's* Organisation du Travail. Oxford, Eng.: Clarendon, 1913.

OWEN ROBERT, *A New View of Society and Other Writings*. London: Dent, 1927. [Written 1813–21.]

———, *Politics for the People*. London: John W. Parker, 1848.

POPE-HENNESSEY, UNA, *Canon Charles Kingsley*. London: Chatto and Windus, 1948.

PROUDHON, PIERRE-JOSEPH, *General Idea of the Revolution in the Nineteenth Century*, tr. by John B. Robinson. London: Freedom Press, 1923. [Originally published in 1851.]

———, *Solution of the Social Problem*, ed. by Henry Cohen. New York: Vanguard, 1927.

———, *What Is Property?* tr. by Benjamin R. Tucker. London: Reeves, no date. [Originally published in 1840.]

RAVEN, CHARLES E., *Christian Socialism, 1848–1854*. London: Macmillan, 1920.

RIASANOVSKY, NICHOLAS V., *The Teaching of Charles Fourier*. Berkeley: University of California Press, 1969.

RITTER, ALAN, *The Political Thought of Pierre-Joseph Proudhon*. Princeton: Princeton University Press, 1969.

SAINT-SIMON, HENRI COMTE DE, *Selected Writings*, ed. by F. M. H. Markham. Oxford, Eng.: Blackwell, 1952.

SISMONDI, SIMONDE DE, *Political Economy and the Philosophy of Government*. London: Chapman, 1847. [Originally published 1826–37.]

WILSON, WILLIAM E., *The Angel and the Serpent: The Story of New Harmony*. Bloomington, Ind.: Indiana University Press, 1964.

WOODCOCK, GEORGE, *Pierre-Joseph Proudhon*. London: Routledge and Kegan Paul, 1956.

10

Marxism and Revisionism

Marxism

Karl Heinrich Marx (1818–83) and Friedrich Engels (1820–95) were the founders and leading theoreticians of Marxian, or "scientific," socialism. They also organized and actively led a revolutionary movement they thought would overturn the citadels of capitalism during their lifetimes. In this they were disappointed, but they never despaired of ultimate triumph. Their movement grew in strength, and they lived to see one revolution of the type they advocated—the Paris Commune, which lasted ten weeks in 1871.

Marx was born in Prussia in a Jewish family that converted to Protestantism during his childhood. He studied law, history, and philosophy at the universities of Bonn, Berlin, and Jena, and he received the degree of doctor of philosophy at twenty-three. Two years later he married Jenny von Westphalen, the daughter of a baron who occupied a high government office. She was a most devoted companion to Marx through all the vicissitudes of his career.

University positions were closed to Marx because of his radicalism. He turned to journalism, was exiled from Germany, studied French socialism and English political economy in Paris, was exiled from France at the request of the Prussian government, and finally settled in London. Except for brief visits to the Continent, he lived the rest of his life in England. Marx spent days and years in the reading room of the British Museum exploring "the confounded ramifications of Political Economy." Tormented by illness, extreme poverty, and the death of several of his children in infancy, he continued to study, write, and organize. He wrote many articles for the *New York Tribune*, whose payments helped him subsist. He organized and led the International Working Men's Association, the "First International," which lasted from 1864 to 1876. In 1867 he published the first volume of his magnum opus, *Capital*. After Marx's death, Engels edited his manuscripts and also published Volumes II and III of this work. After Engels died, the remaining manuscripts were left to the leading Marxian of the time, Karl Kautsky, who published another three volumes under the title *Theories of Surplus Value*.

Friedrich Engels, close friend, coworker, and financial supporter of Marx, was the son of a prosperous German cotton manufacturer. He pursued a dual career: From 1842 until his retirement in 1869 he looked after the family manufacturing interests in Manchester, England; at the same time he was a scholar, writer, and revolutionist. During a brief visit to Paris in 1844 he met Marx (whom he had known in 1842), and they remained lifelong friends and collaborators. Together the two young men wrote the *Manifesto of the Communist Party* in 1848. Engels once wrote that he was happy to play second fiddle to Marx, and Marx replied to Engels, "You know I am always slow to grasp things, and that I always follow in your footsteps."

The Labor Theory of Value

Marx sought "to lay bare the economic law of motion of modern society." His starting point was the analysis of commodities in capitalist society. A commodity must be capable of satisfying human wants, whether "they spring from the stomach or from fancy." This commodity may satisfy these wants directly, as means of subsistence, or indirectly, as means of production. Use values constitute the substance of all wealth. Marx did not try to measure use values quantitatively, nor did he consider diminishing utilities with increasing quantities of a commodity. He would therefore have said that a large wheat crop represents greater utility, and therefore greater wealth, than a small wheat crop, even though it might have no greater exchange value.

In addition to use value, or utility, a commodity has exchange value, commonly abbreviated as value. What determines the value of a commodity? The socially necessary labor time embodied in it, considering normal conditions of production and the average skill and intensity of labor at the time. The socially necessary labor time includes the direct labor in producing the commodity as well as the labor embodied in the machinery and raw materials that are used up and the value transferred to the commodity during the process of production.

Suppose the average labor time contained in a pair of shoes is ten hours. This average determines the value of the shoes. If a worker is incompetent or lazy and takes twenty hours to produce a pair of shoes, its value is still only ten hours. Suppose a worker or an employer leads the field in technological improvement and efficiency, and a pair of shoes is produced with five hours of labor. Its value is nevertheless ten hours, the average labor cost for society as a whole.

A product's value is measured in units of simple average labor. Skilled work counts as multiple units of unskilled average labor. Thus an engineer's hour of productive effort might contribute as much value to a commodity as five hours of simple labor. The equalization of labor time of different skills to one common denominator of unskilled labor occurs in the marketplace.

The market also determines prices that are based on the underlying labor cost. One commodity, such as gold, becomes the universal equivalent that reflects all values. One coat will exchange for two ounces of gold because both require the same amount of socially necessary labor time in their production. If two ounces of gold are coined into two monetary pounds, then one coat will sell for two pounds. Temporary fluctuations of supply and demand will cause prices to deviate from true values, sometimes rising above value and sometimes falling below. The continual oscillation of prices allows them to compensate each other and reduce themselves to average prices that reflect the values of commodities.

Marx's labor theory of value differed from Ricardo's in holding that labor time determines the *absolute* value of goods, for Ricardo believed that the *relative* values of different goods are proportional to the labor time embodied in each. Marx's labor theory opened the door to a theory of exploitation by assuming that all value is created by labor; thus the owner of capital goods has no legitimate claim to any of the product.

In Volume I of *Capital* Marx analyzed the capitalist process as a whole, thrusting aside certain complications that become apparent when the details of an economic system are examined. In Volume III he considered the problem that troubled Ricardo: If labor is the sole source of value, the industry that employs much socially necessary labor (variable capital) and little constant capital (machinery, raw materials) will produce greater value than the one that uses much constant capital and little labor. Therefore the former industry is likely to be more profitable than the latter.

A hypothetical example will illustrate Marx's dilemma. Let's take an industry that produces hand-carved wooden animals. Someone works one hour to make a knife (constant capital), and a carver works ninety-nine hours using the knife to make the final product; by that time the knife is worn out and discarded. The value of the product is a hundred hours of socially necessary labor—ninety-nine hours of direct labor and one hour of labor embodied in the tool and transferred to the value of the product as the tool is worn out.

Now imagine another industry—one that spins cotton into yarn. Suppose it uses a machine (constant capital) that took nine hundred and fifty hours to construct and will last ten years. This means that with every year of the machine's use, ninety-five hours of socially necessary labor are transferred from the machine to the product. In addition, suppose a year's output of yarn is produced by the machine with only five hours of direct labor, because one worker can attend to many machines if they work automatically. The value of the product is then a hundred hours of socially necessary labor.

Which industry is likely to show a higher rate of profit? The hand-carved animal industry of course, because it can produce goods of a value equal to that of the yarn industry's goods, but with a much smaller investment of capital. Yet this theoretical conclusion contradicts what Ricardo and Marx knew from their own observation—that mechanized industries, using much capital and little labor, have at least as high a rate of profit as industries using little capital and much labor.

Marx argued that permanent variations of the profit rates for different industries are untenable where competitive conditions prevail. Capital will flow out of industries in which investments in constant capital are large in relation to investments in labor. Prices of goods produced by these industries will therefore rise above their values, and the average rate of profit on the total investment will be earned. Conversely, capital will flow into industries in which rates of profit are above the average because the ratio of constant capital to labor is low. The selling prices of goods produced in such industries will be below their values. In the above example, yarn will sell above its value, and hand-carved animals will sell below their value. Marx called these selling prices "prices of production," which he defined as the cost of production plus the average rate of profit on the total capital invested. According to him, the labor theory of value holds for the capitalist system as a whole, but individual commodities will sell at prices above or below their values in order to equalize rates of profit for the whole economy. Only when a given industry's ratio of capital to labor is the same as for the whole economy will that industry's product sell at its value.

The Theory of Exploitation

Marx assumed in Volume I of *Capital* that all commodities sell at their value. How, then, does the capitalist receive a profit? By purchasing the one commodity that can create a value greater than its own—labor power. Here we must distinguish carefully between Marx's concepts of labor power and labor time. Labor power refers to a person's ability to work; labor time is the actual process and duration of work. Labor power is a commodity, bought and sold in the market; labor time is the ingredient that gives all commodities, including labor power, their value. The value of labor power is determined by the socially necessary labor time required to produce the necessities of life the individual workers and their families consume. If these necessities could be produced in four hours per day, the value of the commodity labor power would be four hours per day, even if the labor time worked per day were eight hours. If the productivity of labor power doubled, so that the articles of subsistence could be produced in two hours per day, the value of labor power would fall 50 per cent, from four hours of labor time to two hours; but the value produced by a day's labor of the same duration as previously would still be eight hours. If the productivity of labor were so low that the worker had to consume goods equivalent in value to his own output, the value of a day's labor power would be a day's labor time. Then there would be no profit, no surplus, no exploitation, and no capitalism. According to Marx, only when the worker can produce more than he must consume in order to survive and to replenish the labor force through reproduction can exploitation arise. The employer pays the worker the full value of his labor power, but the daily pay equals only part of the worker's daily output and therefore only part of the value he creates. The labor time the worker spends during the workday creates a larger sum of values than the value of his own labor power, the cost of subsistence.

Marx illustrated these ideas with a numerical example. Suppose that six hours of socially necessary labor time are embodied in the commodities a worker and her family must consume each day. Then half the labor of a twelve-hour workday (then customary) forms the value of a day's labor power. If half a day's average socially necessary labor time is also required to produce the gold contained in three shillings, then three shillings represents the value of a day's labor power. If this is the wage rate, the worker receives the full value of the one commodity she sells—labor power. (In this illustration the value imparted to a commodity by an hour of labor can also be represented by half a shilling; that is, an hour of labor will produce a quantity of gold designated as half a shilling because a worker can produce gold worth six shillings in a twelve-hour workday.)

The capitalists employ the laborer, whom they supply with the required machinery and raw materials. Suppose that in six hours of labor the worker converts ten pounds of cotton into ten pounds of yarn. Assume that the wear and tear of the spindles amounts to four hours of labor or two shillings during the half-day of labor. To explain this assumption, suppose that all the spindles one worker operates will wear out after ten days of working. Assume also that eighty hours were required to manufacture the spindles. These eighty hours are part of the socially necessary labor time required to manufacture the yarn. As the spindles wear out, their value reappears in the yarn. In half a day, the worker uses up one-twentieth of the value of the spindles and transfers it to the yarn; this is four hours of labor time.

On the money side, assume that all the spindles a worker uses cost forty shillings. Since they will last ten days, two shillings will be transferred to the value of the yarn during each half-day of use.

Thus we assume that the wear and tear of the spindles amounts to four hours of labor or two shillings, and the cotton used up has a value of twenty hours of labor or ten shillings. The total value of the yarn produced in six hours is thirty hours of labor: six for the labor power, twenty for the cotton, and four for the used-up value of the spindles. The total money cost of production is fifteen shillings: three for the labor power, ten for the cotton, and two for the used-up value of the spindles. If profit does not arise from buying cheaply and selling dearly and if all commodities sell at their value, then the yarn must sell for fifteen shillings.

> Our capitalist stares in astonishment. The value of the product is exactly equal to the value of the capital advanced. . . . [He] exclaims: "Oh! but I advanced my money for the express purpose of making more money." The way to Hell is paved with good intentions, and he might just as easily have intended to make money, without producing at all. He threatens all sorts of things. He won't be caught napping again. In future he will buy the commodities in the market, instead of manufacturing them himself. But if all his brother capitalists were to do the same, where would

he find his commodities in the market? And his money he cannot eat. He tries persuasion. "Consider my abstinence; I might have played ducks and drakes with the fifteen shillings; but instead of that I consumed it productively, and made yarn with it." Very well, and by way of reward he is now in possession of good yarn instead of a bad conscience. . . . Our friend, up to this time so purse-proud, suddenly assumes the modest demeanour of his own workman, and exclaims: "Have I myself not worked? Have I not performed the labour of superintendence and of overlooking the spinner? And does not this labour, too, create value?" His overlooker and his manager try to hide their smiles. Meanwhile, after a hearty laugh, he re-assumes his usual mien. Though he chanted to us the whole creed of the economists, in reality, he says, he would not give a brass farthing for it. He leaves this and all such like subterfuges and juggling tricks to the professors of political economy, who are paid for it. He himself is a practical man; and though he does not always consider what he says outside his business, yet in business he knows what he is about.[1]

The answer to the riddle that Marx posed about the source of profit lies in the fact that the worker is required to work another six hours without being paid for it. The ten pounds of yarn produced in the second half-day of work are also worth fifteen shillings, but they cost the capitalist only twelve—hence the capitalist makes three shillings' profit, or surplus value. It does not matter that part of the industrial capitalist's profit is turned over to the banker in the form of interest, part to the landlord in the form of ground rent, and part to the merchant capitalist in the form of mercantile profits. All property income arises from the exploitation of labor in the productive process.

Within capitalism, said Marx, all labor appears to be paid labor, but this is an illusion. Under slavery an opposite error was made: All labor appeared to be unpaid, although the owner's provision of subsistence for the slave represented partial payment. Only under feudalism was exploitation obvious, when the serfs worked part of the time for themselves and part for their overlord.

The part of the capital invested in machinery and raw materials Marx called constant capital (c). The value of this capital is transferred to the final product without any increase. The capital that goes for wages, for the purchase of labor power, is variable capital (v). It produces a value greater than its own. The extra value it produces, which the capitalist takes without compensating the worker who produced it, is surplus value (s). The rate of surplus value, or the rate of exploitation, is the ratio of the surplus value to the variable capital,

[1] Karl Marx, *Capital*, Vol. I (Chicago, 1906), pp. 212–15. [Originally published in 1867.]

or the ratio of total profit to wages, or the ratio of unpaid labor time to paid labor time, or s/v. The rate of profit is the ratio of surplus value to the total capital invested, or $s/(c+v)$.

In Marx's hypothetical example above, the rate of surplus value was 100 per cent. If the working day had been extended to fifteen hours, it would have been 150 per cent. If it had been reduced to nine hours, the rate of exploitation would have been 50 per cent. What is the proper length of the working day?

> The capitalist maintains his rights as a purchaser when he tries to make the working day as long as possible, and to make, whenever possible, two working days out of one. On the other hand, the peculiar nature of the commodity sold implies a limit to its consumption by the purchaser, and the labourer maintains his right as seller when he wishes to reduce the working day to one of definite normal duration. There is here, therefore, an antinomy, right against right, both equally bearing the seal of the law of exchanges. Between equal rights force decides. Hence is it that in the history of capitalist production, the determination of what is a working day, presents itself as the result of a struggle, a struggle between collective capital, *i.e.*, the class of capitalists, and collective labour, *i.e.*, the working class.[2]

Even if the working day were not lengthened, surplus value could be increased by increasing the efficiency of production and thus reducing the value of the worker's labor power. If the worker's necessities could be produced in a shorter time, a larger share of the new value would go to the capitalist. Suppose the working day were shortened from twelve hours to ten; but instead of being divided into six hours of paid labor for the worker and six hours for the capitalist, it was divided into four for the worker and six for the capitalist. The rate of exploitation would rise from 100 to 150 per cent.

Marx's labor theory of value and the theory of exploitation were his explanation of class conflict between workers and capitalists. There are other possible explanations of the clash of interests, so that one does not have to accept these theories to become an opponent of the private-enterprise system. One might argue, for example, that the capitalists are no longer essential to an advanced society, or that they demand too much for their services, or that they could make the same contribution while being hired employees of the state. Radical arguments such as these do not stand or fall on the validity of Marx's labor theory of value.

[2] *Ibid.*, Vol. III (1909), p. 190.

The Falling Rate of Profit

If value and profit are produced only by labor, should not the capitalist invest more in labor power and less in machinery? Why the drive toward more and more efficiency through mechanization and invention? There are two reasons. First, one capitalist who leads in promoting efficient production through the use of more and better machines will receive extra profits; the employer who lags behind the trends in a particular industry will go under. Second, the greater the efficiency of production, the lower the value of labor power and the more profit produced per working day.

The increasing proportion of constant to variable capital means that there is a long-run tendency for the rate of profit to fall, even though the amount of profit rises as the labor force grows. Marx thought that this law demonstrated that capitalist production faced internal barriers to its own indefinite expansion. As machinery displaces labor, an "industrial reserve army" of unemployed is created that further impoverishes the proletariat by forcing wages downward. Larger capital investments for each individual establishment lead to "a growing concentration of capital (accompanied by a growing number of capitalists, though not to the same extent)."

Marx perceived certain countervailing forces to the falling rate of profit that make it a long-run tendency rather than an inexorable and invariable law. First, the intensity of exploitation can be increased by forcing the workers to speed up or by lengthening the working day. Second, wages may be cut below their value. Third, the constant capital can be cheapened. The ratio of constant capital to labor is a *value* relationship, and as machinery and raw materials become cheaper, the fall of the rate of profit is retarded. Fourth, growing overpopulation in relation to available jobs and increasing unemployment is conducive to setting up new industries that use much labor and little capital. The high rates of profit in such industries enter into the average rate of profit for the system as a whole. Fifth, foreign trade raises the rate of profit by cheapening the elements of both constant capital and the necessities of life. In addition, capital invested in colonies yields higher rates of profit because the ratio of constant capital to variable capital is lower and because the exploitation of colonial peoples is more intense than the exploitation of wage labor at home. Sixth, the rate of exploitation is increased by reducing the value of labor power through increased efficiency of production.

The falling rate of profit is but one of the insoluble problems of capitalism, according to the Marxian analysis. We shall now examine the overall trends and consequences of capital accumulation.

Capitalist Accumulation and Crises

Marx attacked Say's Law of Markets, saying that it applied only to simple commodity production. Self-employed small artisans, seeking to acquire use values, produce commodities in order to exchange them for others they wish to consume. The weaver produces linen, sells it, and uses the money to buy a Bible. The process can be represented by *C-M-C*, with the linen and the Bible representing commodities of equal exchange values and different use values. Money is simply the medium of exchange.

But even under simple commodity production the possibility of crisis exists:

> Nothing can be more childish than the dogma, that because every sale is a purchase, and every purchase a sale, therefore the circulation of commodities necessarily implies an equilibrium of sales and purchases. If this means that the number of actual sales is equal to the number of purchases, it is mere tautology. . . . No one can sell unless some one else purchases. But no one is forthwith bound to purchase, because he has just sold. Circulation bursts through all restrictions as to time, place, and individuals, imposed by direct barter, and this it effects by splitting up, into the antithesis of a sale and a purchase, the direct identity that in barter does exist between the alienation of one's own and the acquisition of some other man's product. . . . If the interval in time between . . . the sale and the purchase becomes too pronounced, the intimate connexion between them, their oneness, asserts itself by producing—a crisis.[3]

Under large-scale capitalist production the process of exchange becomes *M-C-M*, buying in order to sell, instead of selling in order to buy as in handicraft production. Money is changed into commodities such as labor power, raw materials, and machinery. The products are then sold for money. This process does not make sense, however, if the two *M*'s are equal. Therefore the correct representation of the capitalist process is *M-C-M'*, where *M'* is larger than *M* by the amount of surplus value squeezed out of the productive workers. This is the process of expanding investment. "Accumulate, accumulate! That is Moses and the prophets!"

One result of this trend, said Marx, is the concentration of capital in few hands.

---

[3] *Ibid.*, Vol. I, pp. 127–28.

Capital grows in one place to a huge mass in a single hand, because it has in another place been lost by many. . . . The battle of competition is fought by cheapening of commodities. The cheapness of commodities depends, *caeteris paribus,* on the productiveness of labour, and this again on the scale of production. Therefore, the larger capitals beat the smaller. It will further be remembered that, with the development of the capitalist mode of production, there is an increase in the minimum amount of individual capital necessary to carry on a business under its normal conditions. The smaller capitals, therefore, crowd into spheres of production which Modern Industry has only sporadically or incompletely got hold of. Here competition rages in direct proportion to the number, and in inverse proportion to the magnitudes, of the antagonistic capitals. It always ends in the ruin of many small capitalists, whose capitals partly pass into the hand of their conquerors, partly vanish. Apart from this, with capitalist production an altogether new force comes into play—the credit system.

In its beginnings, the credit system sneaks in as a modest helper of accumulation and draws by invisible threads the money resources scattered all over the surface of society into the hands of individual or associated capitalists. But soon it becomes a new and formidable weapon in the competitive struggle, and finally it transforms itself into an immense social mechanism for the centralisation of capitals.[4]

The increase of labor-saving machinery and the growth of big business lead to both absolute and relative impoverishment of the workers. The tendency toward absolute impoverishment means that the standard of living of workers will fall. Relative impoverishment means that even if standards of living remain stationary or rise somewhat, the percentage share the workers receive of the new value they produce will decline; workers will grow poorer relative to the capitalists. With the growing "misery, oppression, slavery, degradation, exploitation" of the workers, their will to revolt also grows. "The knell of capitalist private property sounds. The expropriators are expropriated."

As early as 1848 Marx and Engels described capitalist crises:

Modern bourgeois society with its relations of production, of exchange and of property, a society that has conjured up such gigantic means of production and of exchange, is like the sorcerer who is no longer able to control the powers of the nether world whom he has called up by his spells. For many a decade past the history of industry and commerce is but the history of the revolt of modern productive forces against modern conditions of production, against the property relations that are the conditions for the existence of the bourgeoisie and of its rule. It is enough to

---

[4] *Ibid.,* pp. 686–87.

mention the commercial crises that by their periodical return put the existence of the entire bourgeois society on trial, each time more threateningly. In these crises a great part not only of the existing products, but also of the previously created productive forces, are periodically destroyed. In these crises there breaks out an epidemic that, in all earlier epochs, would have seemed an absurdity—the epidemic of over-production. . . . And how does the bourgeoisie get over these crises? On the one hand by enforced destruction of a mass of productive forces; on the other, by the conquest of new markets, and by the more thorough exploitation of the old ones. That is to say, by paving the way for more extensive and more destructive crises, and by diminishing the means whereby crises are prevented.[5]

Later, in analyzing the causes of crises, Marx held that the accumulation of capital leads to overproduction relative to "needs with capacity to pay." That is, cumulative technological developments and increasing productivity of labor lead to expanded production, but the market expands more slowly because of the limited purchasing power of the workers. Periodic crises occur because supply exceeds demand, and thus the profitability of production temporarily disappears. The workers *cannot* buy the flood of consumer goods that follows a period of rapid capital investment, and the capitalists *will* not. A related problem caused by growing productivity in a limited market is the falling rate of profit for the capitalists.

If accumulation proceeds rapidly enough, the demand for laborers may exceed the supply, and therefore wages may rise. If "the stimulus of gain is blunted," the rate of accumulation is lessened and the price of labor falls as the economy goes into a slump. Crises are therefore inevitable, and rising wages "leave intact the foundations of the capitalistic system."

The system recovers from each crisis, however, even though the way is paved for more severe crises in the future. How does it recover? Some capital values are destroyed because the monetary value of fixed capital assets collapses in a depression; some factories close; prices of commodities fall; credit contracts; and wages fall. The fall in prices and the competitive struggle give every capitalist an impulse to raise profits "by means of new machines, new and improved working methods, new combinations." The depreciation of the value of constant capital tends to raise the rate of profit. "The present stagnation of production would have prepared an expansion of production later on, within capitalistic limits."

[5] Karl Marx and Friedrich Engels, *Manifesto of the Communist Party* (New York, 1948), pp. 14–15. [Originally published in 1848.]

After the death of Engels in 1895, revisionism—an offshoot of Marxist orthodoxy—won favor among many socialists throughout the world. We shall now consider the two most significant European revisionist movements, in England and Germany, as well as the most recent revisionist groundswell, in China.

Fabian Revisionism: The Webbs

It may seem odd to classify the Fabians, who never claimed to be followers of Marx, as revisionists. They preferred to base themselves on Bentham, Ricardo, Mill, and Jevons, yet their thinking and their program influenced Marxian groups almost everywhere, especially in England and Germany.

The British Fabian Society, organized in 1884, a year after Marx's death in London, was named after Quintus Fabius Maximus. This Roman general, surnamed Cunctator (the Delayer), took all steps against his enemy, Hannibal, except to fight him on the battlefield. Though never very large, the society was most influential in the British Labor Party, in government circles, and among intellectuals. It attracted such luminaries as George Bernard Shaw, Sidney Webb, Beatrice Webb, Graham Wallas, H. G. Wells, John Galsworthy, Bertrand Russell, R. H. Tawney, and Harold Laski.

The Fabians undertook prodigious research and educational activities. They favored trade unionism, factory acts, extension of the ballot, tax reform, consumers' cooperatives, government regulation of industry, social legislation, and the nationalization of key industries. Repudiating the doctrines of class struggle and revolution, they worked to introduce significant reforms by influencing government leaders, forming alliances with liberal groups, and promoting the Labor Party. They hoped that ultimately an enlightened electorate would, in the name of social justice, slowly and peacefully socialize the basic means of production, turning the management of industry over to local, regional, and national agencies.

In international affairs the Fabians were imperialists who supported the British government in the Boer War and in World War I. In *Fabianism and the Empire,* written by George Bernard Shaw and revised and published in 1900 by the Fabian Society as its official position, imperialism was explicitly endorsed. Great Britain, the society argued, should become the nucleus of one of the future world empires rather than stupidly lose its colonies and be reduced to a tiny pair of islands in the North Sea. A great power must govern in the interests of civilization as a whole.

Sidney Webb (1859–1947), the son of lower-middle-class parents, became a government clerk several years after completing his college education at sixteen and was later admitted to the bar. He possessed a very orderly mind, a prodigious memory, a passion for social justice, and unusual skill in persuading people in high places to promote his program of social reform. Public administration was far more interesting to him than economic and social theory. Webb served in Parliament and as a cabinet minister in successive Labor governments. His wife Beatrice (1858–1943) was the daughter of a big financier and railway magnate. Her interest in social problems was intensified during a month's visit with her Lancashire cousins, who were impoverished factory workers. Beatrice's independent income enabled Sidney to leave the civil service after they were married, and together they formed a brilliant research team, which she called "the firm of Webb."

The Webbs founded the London School of Economics and Political Science (now a part of the University of London). They also helped organize the influential weekly *New Statesman*. This indefatigable pair published forty-five books, in addition to numerous pamphlets, articles, and essays. For their books on trade unionism, they ransacked the archives of important unions throughout Great Britain. In their research on local government, they examined the records of hundreds of villages and towns and attended meetings of local government bodies. To see how a sweatshop industry looked from the inside, Beatrice Webb learned tailoring and obtained employment as a "plain trouser hand."

The Webbs believed that consumers' cooperatives and unions would ultimately replace capitalism with the "Cooperative Commonwealth." They had no faith in producers' cooperatives, such as agricultural credit banks and creameries, for they believed that such organizations seek to increase profits and are therefore a part of the capitalist system. These producers' cooperatives exclude their own employees from membership. When agricultural cooperatives unite with capitalist combinations in monopolizing the distributive trades, they become a public menace. Producers in different industries (and even within a single industry) have diverse interests, but consumers are united. Farm organizations should sell to consumers' cooperatives, and the latter should compete with municipalities and national government organizations in manufacturing.

As a result of the disillusionment that followed World War I, the Webbs came forth with a sharp indictment of capitalism in *The Decay of Capitalist Civilization* (1923). Following the Great Depression, they published in 1935 a eulogy of the Soviet Russian system in their two-volume work *Soviet Communism: A New Civilization?*

German Revisionism: Bernstein

The German Social Democratic Party was the largest Marxist party in the world before World War I. Its vigor would be expected in the homeland of the two founders of "scientific socialism," particularly since German laborers lived under even worse conditions than the French or British. Surprisingly, however, the German party's dogmatic enthusiasm for Marx's doctrines turned increasingly to revisionism.

The leading advocate of this new and moderate approach to socialism was Eduard Bernstein (1850–1932), a political exile from Germany from 1881 to 1901 because of Bismarck's Anti-Socialist Laws. During this period he lived in Switzerland, where he was coeditor of the *Sozialdemokrat* (the organ of the party smuggled into Germany in large numbers). When that country expelled him in 1888, he went to London, where he was associated with Engels in his last years and with the Fabians, whose approach to politics appealed to him. After returning to Germany, he served in the Reichstag for eighteen years.

Beginning in 1896, a year after Engels' death, Bernstein began urging the revision and modernization of Marxism. He argued that social conditions had not sharpened class conflicts as Marx and Engels had predicted in *The Manifesto of the Communist Party* in 1848. Instead, Bernstein said, the common interest had increasingly gained ascendancy over the private interest. The severity of crises had diminished, and the middle classes had not disintegrated and disappeared. Concentration of capital had not occurred in all branches of production; instead, shareholdings were being diffused among increasing numbers of people. In all technically advanced countries the privileges of the capitalists were yielding to democratic institutions. Working-class organizations were growing stronger. Factory acts, democracy in local government, trade unions and cooperatives freed from legal restrictions, humane labor conditions in work undertaken by public authorities—all these characterized the new evolutionary approach toward the amelioration of capitalism. Bernstein denied the Marxian concept that socialism is the necessary outcome of an objective historical process. Instead he recommended socialism as the goal of civilized mankind, free to mold its future to conform to higher ethical and moral standards.

Bernstein repudiated the anti-imperialism and working-class internationalism of the Marxists.

But has social democracy, as the party of the working classes and of peace, an interest in the maintenance of the fighting power? From many points of view it is very tempting to answer the question in the negative, especially if one starts from the sentence in the *Communist Manifesto:* "The proletarian has no fatherland." This sentence might, in a degree, perhaps, apply to the worker of the 'forties without political rights, shut out of public life. To-day in spite of the enormous increase in the intercourse between nations it has already forfeited a great part of its truth and will always forfeit more, the more the worker, by the influence of socialism, moves from being a proletarian to a citizen. The workman who has equal rights as a voter for state and local councils, and who thereby is a fellow owner of the common property of the nation, whose children the community educates, whose health it protects, whom it secures against injury, has a fatherland without ceasing on that account to be a citizen of the world. . . .

Just as little as it is to be wished that any other of the great civilised nations should lose its independence, just as little can it be a matter of indifference to German social democracy whether the German nation, which has indeed carried out, and is carrying out, its honourable share in the civilising work of the world, should be repressed in the council of the nations.

. . . The Imperial Government will think ten times before venturing on a war which has social democracy as its determined opponent. . . . But . . . where really important national interests are at stake, internationalism can be no reason for a weak yielding to the pretensions of foreign interested parties. . . .

If we take into account the fact that Germany now imports yearly a considerable amount of colonial produce, we must also say to ourselves that the time may come when it will be desirable to draw at least a part of these products from our own colonies. . . . If it is not reprehensible to enjoy the produce of tropical plantations, it cannot be so to cultivate such plantations ourselves. . . . Only a conditional right of savages to the land occupied by them can be recognised. The higher civilisation can ultimately claim a higher right.[6]

Bernstein's views were voted down at Social Democratic Party congresses in 1899 and 1901. Yet in practice the party became increasingly revisionist. It supported the fatherland in World War I and voted for military appropriations in the Reichstag. Bernstein himself voted for war credits twice in 1914, abstained twice in 1915, and finally voted against additional funds for the military.

[6] Eduard Bernstein, *Evolutionary Socialism*, tr. by Edith C. Harvey (New York, 1909), pp. 169–71, 178–79.

Eduard Bernstein died at eighty-two, six weeks before Hitler became chancellor. But his ideas lived on and triumphed once again in West Germany. In November 1959 the German Social Democratic Party voted officially to bury its Marxist past: It renounced class struggle, extended a friendly hand to organized religion, endorsed private property of capital goods, favored parliamentary democracy, and opted for "free competition in a free economy." The old socialist demand for the socialization of industry was replaced by the principle that "effective public controls" must prevent "misuse of the economy by the powerful." National defense was declared to be the duty of every citizen.

Chinese Revisionism: Maoism

Several key doctrines of Marx and Engels have been revised by Mao Tse-tung (born 1893), Chairman of the Chinese Communist Party. In contrast to the rightist revisionism of the German Social Democrats, however, Chinese revisionism is more radical than its predecessors in several important respects. The path Chinese Marxism has taken helps to explain the protracted and bitter ideological and political conflict between China and Soviet Russia.

The first aspect of Chinese revisionism concerns the questions of who will make the revolution and where. Marx and his followers thought that the socialist revolutions would occur in the advanced industrial countries of Western Europe, led by the urban working class. Even when the revolution occurred in Russia in 1917, Lenin and other Marxists regarded it as a prelude to revolution in Germany and other countries of Central and Western Europe. Marx and Engels did recognize that the center of revolutionary activity was shifting to Russia, but their principal hope remained with the proletariat of the highly industrialized countries. In China the Communist movement was originally led by the urban industrial workers, but it was crushed mercilessly in 1927. It was then that Mao Tse-tung shifted his ground, escaping to the rural hinterland and drawing support for his guerrilla revolutionary movement from the peasantry. This departure from Marx's idea has been developed even further since then. Mao argued that the rich urban and industrial countries offer poor immediate prospects for revolution; the possibilities for revolution are far better in the poor agricultural countries. After winning power in these rural countries, the Communists can then beleaguer the urbanized countries of Western Europe and North America.

The official pronouncements of Chinese Marxism illustrate the idea that revolutions will draw their basic thrust from the peasantry of the agricultural countries. Marshal Lin Piao, then the Minister of National Defense and now dead and in disgrace, wrote in 1965:

> The October Revolution [in Russia] began with armed uprisings in the cities and then spread to the countryside, while the Chinese revolution won nationwide victory through the encirclement of the cities from the rural areas and the final capture of the cities. . . .
>
> Many countries and peoples in Asia, Africa, and Latin America are now being subjected to aggression and enslavement on a serious scale by the imperialists headed by the United States and their lackeys. The basic political and economic conditions in many of these countries have many similarities to those that prevailed in old China. As in China, the peasant question is extremely important in these regions. The peasants constitute the main force of the national-democratic revolution against the imperialists and their lackeys. In committing aggression against these countries, the imperialists usually begin by seizing the big cities and the main lines of communication, but they are unable to bring the vast countryside completely under their control. The countryside, and the countryside alone, can provide the broad areas in which the revolutionaries can maneuver freely. . . .
>
> Taking the entire globe, if North America and Western Europe can be called "the cities of the world," then Asia, Africa, and Latin America constitute "the rural areas of the world." Since World War II, the proletarian revolutionary movement has for various reasons been temporarily held back in the North American and West European capitalist countries, while the people's revolutionary movement in Asia, Africa, and Latin America has been growing vigorously.[7]

This reliance on the peasantry as the main revolutionary force has an important consequence: Agricultural development has been promoted as vigorously as industrial development. This is called "walking on two legs" and is in sharp contrast to the practice in most other underdeveloped countries. City populations have been stabilized, and the migration from the countryside to the cities is regulated and curbed. City people are frequently sent to the hinterland to work. Small-scale industry is scattered throughout the rural areas. This serves to encourage local initiative and self-sufficiency, upgrade human skills and living standards in the poorer rural regions, reduce transport costs, limit the growth of cities, and improve the national defense position.

[7] K. H. Fan, ed., *The Chinese Cultural Revolution: Selected Documents* (New York, 1968), pp. 92, 95–96. Reprinted by permission of Monthly Review Press. Copyright © 1968 by Monthly Review Press.

The second element of Chinese revisionism involves the question of how the Communists will gain power. Can it be accomplished peacefully and democratically, or must it result from armed conflict? Marx and Engels made scattered references to the possibility of taking power peacefully under ideally democratic regimes. But the major thrust of their analysis was that the revolution would have to result from armed uprisings. "Force," said Marx, "is the midwife of every old society pregnant with a new one." This is what Mao Tse-tung believed, apparently without exception. "Political power," he said, "grows out of the barrel of a gun." He also said: "The seizure of power by armed force, the settlement of the issue by war, is the central task and the highest form of revolution. This Marxist-Leninist principle of revolution holds good universally, for China and for all other countries." [8]

This Chinese doctrine does not revise Marxism so much as it revises Soviet Russian revisionism. The Russian leaders seem to have turned away from the idea of armed uprisings to achieve socialism, and they rely almost totally on parliamentary procedures. This revised doctrine can be seen in their condemnation of the student uprisings and student-worker unity in the general strike in France in mid-1968. It can also be seen in their refusal to support armed guerrilla uprisings in Latin America. Judging from their lack of response to current revolutionary movements, the Soviet Marxists apparently expect peaceful transitions to socialism in the presently nonsocialist countries, and this expectation has aroused the ire and scorn of the Chinese Marxists.[9]

The third aspect of Chinese revisionism concerns problems that arise after the Marxists take power. Mao Tse-tung deplored what has happened in Soviet Russia, in China, and in other countries where the Communists have triumphed: A new elite has emerged, a new bureaucracy of planners, administrators, party officials, scientists, engineers, educators, and intellectuals of all kinds. They are paid far

[8] *Ibid.*, pp. 92–93.
[9] We have not discussed Soviet Russian revisionism because, although the Soviet leaders have shown a pragmatic revisionism in their politics, their economics is apparently in tune with the spirit of Marx and Engels. As indicated above, Soviet Russia is less revolutionary than it once was, perhaps because its leaders wish to protect its economy and its people from nuclear destruction. By proclaiming the possibility of socialism in one country during the 1920's, Stalin departed from Marxian doctrine, as he and his successors have done in suppressing freedom. In economic measures, however, Soviet Russia seems to be adhering to the basic Marxian precepts. Of course, since Marx and Engels wrote rather little about the socialist society that still lay in the future, it is hard to know whether Soviet Russia is drastically revising Marxian economics. The Chinese, however, are clearly doing so.

more than the rank-and-file toilers, the workers and peasants. Their children have great advantages over poor people's children in acquiring education and the best positions and incomes. Instead of being fired with revolutionary enthusiasm to serve the people, Mao argued, the bureaucrats are concerned with the personal advantages they can derive from the economic system. This corruption has been extended to the poorer segments of the population, where material incentives such as piece-rate wages and profit considerations corrupt the revolutionary zeal of the workers and peasants.

Mao Tse-tung instigated and supported the Proletarian Cultural Revolution to reverse what he considered a pernicious revisionist and capitalist trend. He sought to perpetuate and widen the spirit of self-sacrifice and public service that motivated the army and the people during the decades of revolutionary struggle that culminated in Communist victory on the mainland in 1949. He called for a continuing class struggle against those who would allow individual self-interest to remain a major force in society.

Official documents of the Chinese Cultural Revolution, which began in mid-1966, illustrate the idea that a continuous struggle is necessary to oppose selfishness, revisionism, and the resurgence of capitalism.

> Chairman Mao Tse-tung has taught us that classes and class struggle continue to exist in socialist society. . . .
>
> Long before our nationwide victory, Chairman Mao Tse-tung had warned us: "After the enemies with guns have been wiped out, there will still be enemies without guns; they are bound to struggle desperately against us; we must never regard these enemies lightly. If we do not now raise and understand the problem in this way, we shall commit very grave mistakes."
>
> Invariably capitalism is restored either by violent means or by "peaceful evolution" or by a combination of both. U.S. imperialism and the other class enemies at home and abroad not only try to overthrow us by violence, but also attempt to conquer us by "peaceful evolution" by the use of "sugar-coated bullets." In a hundred and one ways, they are spreading reactionary political and ideological viruses and the bourgeois way of life in an attempt to corrupt and demoralize the Communists, the proletariat, and the other revolutionary people, hoping that some weak-minded persons in our ranks degenerate into bourgeois elements and that socialism gradually regresses to capitalism. . . .
>
> We, the Red Guards, while seizing power from the handful of persons in the Party who are in authority and taking the capitalist road, must at the same time carry out the struggle of seizing power in our own minds, to seize the power of "self-interest," to rebel against it and to defeat it!

. . . To defeat "self-interest," it is necessary to follow the teachings of Chairman Mao, to integrate ourselves with the workers and peasants and . . . thoroughly to remold our world outlook and foster the concept of wholeheartedly serving the workers, peasants, and soldiers. . . .

Economism and material incentives are outright counterrevolutionary revisionist wares. The masses of people who are armed with Mao Tse-tung's thought firmly reject such rubbish. They fully understand that the great Proletarian Cultural Revolution aims precisely to destroy what is bourgeois and establish what is proletarian, to eradicate self-interest and foster devotion to the public interest, to transform people to the core of their being, to revolutionize people's thinking, so as to eliminate the source of revisionism and consolidate and develop the socialist system.[10]

This campaign against elitism and self-interest and in favor of serving the people is a continuing one. It can be seen in the unique policies that the Chinese Communists have seized upon and pushed vigorously. The pay differentials for different grades and skills of labor are very much narrower than they are in Soviet Russia, the United States, and all other countries. Common manual labor is glorified, and the upper echelons of society must participate in it. High school graduates must work somewhere for a minimum of two years before they will be accepted at a university. Both students and faculties of the universities are expected to spend part of each year in a factory or an agricultural commune, either as workers or as observers sent there to study problems and bring back reports. Even factory managers will spend one day a week in such physical labor as sweeping the floors. These measures are meant to promote the unity of all the people, give dignity to all kinds of manual labor, and foster an unselfish devotion to society.

To prove their doctrinal purity, Marxists typically love to cite chapter and verse from their prophets, Marx and Engels, and the bibles they wrote. We may therefore ask whether Mao Tse-tung has really revised Marxism itself in this case or whether he has corrected Russian revisionism. We can find one answer in Marx's *Critique of the Gotha Program,* a work written in response to the program adopted by the German socialists at a congress held in Gotha, Germany, in 1875. Marx described what he thought would be the first, or socialist, stage of society after the proletarian revolution, before the higher stage of communism was achieved. Because the socialist stage emerges from capitalist society, it is "economically, morally and intellectually still stamped with the birthmarks of the old society from

[10] Fan, ed., *The Chinese Cultural Revolution: Selected Documents,* pp. 35, 117, 194–95, 228–29.

whose womb it emerges." Individual producers will receive from society payment in proportion to what they each contribute. In other words, material incentives are necessary as long as the people's nature is deformed by the ideology of capitalism. However, "in a higher phase of communist society, . . . the narrow horizon of bourgeois right [can] be fully left behind and society [can] inscribe on its banners: from each according to his ability, to each according to his needs!"

Apparently Mao Tse-tung departed from the original doctrine of Marxism. He sought to hasten the process of perfecting the human character by doing away with material incentives before China could produce an abundance of consumer goods that would supposedly make material incentives irrelevant. It would be an amazing feat if he succeeded in this objective for a majority of the population.

We can test Mao Tse-tung's doctrine of a continuing class struggle after the revolution against what Engels wrote:

> *The proletariat seizes the state power, and transforms the means of production in the first instance into state property.* But in doing this, it puts an end to itself as the proletariat, it puts an end to all class differences and class antagonisms, it puts an end also to the state as the state. . . . As soon as there is no longer any class of society to be held in subjection; as soon as, along with class domination and the struggle for individual existence based on the former anarchy of production, the collisions and excesses arising from these have also been abolished, there is nothing more to be repressed which would make a special repressive force, a state, necessary. The first act in which the state really comes forward as the representative of society as a whole—the taking possession of the means of production in the name of society—is at the same time its last independent act as a state. The interference of the state power in social relations becomes superfluous in one sphere after another, and then ceases of itself. The government of persons is replaced by the administration of things and the direction of the processes of production. The state is not "abolished," *it withers away.*[11]

Perhaps Engels believed that the class struggle would end and the state begin to wither away immediately after the revolution because the revolution would be worldwide instead of succeeding in only one or a few countries. Or it may be argued that Engels was writing about a process that would take fifty or a hundred years or more to complete. But apparently Mao Tse-tung's doctrine of a continuing class struggle after the revolution represents a major revision of the

[11] Friedrich Engels, *Herr Eugen Dühring's Revolution in Science* (New York, 1939), pp. 306–07. [Originally published in 1878.]

ideas of Marx and Engels. This of course says nothing about who is correct, and perhaps neither is correct. Much more time and many controversies will pass before these issues are finally settled, if they ever are.

Bibliography

BARAN, PAUL A., and PAUL M. SWEEZY, *Monopoly Capital*. New York: Monthly Review Press, 1966.

BARNETT, A. DOAK, *China after Mao*. Princeton, N. J.: Princeton University Press, 1967.

BERNSTEIN, EDUARD, *Evolutionary Socialism*, tr. by Edith C. Harvey. New York: Huebsch, 1909.

CHRISTMAN, HENRY M., ed., *The American Journalism of Marx & Engels*. New York: The New American Library, 1966.

COLE, G. D. H., *The Meaning of Marxism*. London: Gollancz, 1948.

COLE, MARGARET, *The Story of Fabian Socialism*. London: Heinemann, 1961.

FAN, K. H., ed., *The Chinese Cultural Revolution: Selected Documents*. New York: Monthly Review Press, 1968.

FREEDMAN, ROBERT, ed., *Marx on Economics*. New York: Harcourt Brace Jovanovich, Inc., 1961.

GAY, PETER, *The Dilemma of Democratic Socialism*. New York: Columbia University Press, 1952.

GRIFFITH, WILLIAM E., *The Sino-Soviet Rift*. Cambridge, Mass.: The M.I.T. Press, 1964.

MANDEL, ERNEST, *Marxist Economic Theory*, tr. by Brian Pearce, 2 vols. New York: Monthly Review Press, 1970.

MARX, KARL, *Capital*, tr. by Samuel Moore, Edward Aveling, and Ernest Untermann. 3 vols. Chicago: Kerr, 1906–09. [Originally published 1867–95.]

————, *Theories of Surplus Value*, tr. by G. A. Bonner and Emile Burns. London: Lawrence and Wishart, 1951. [Originally published 1905–10.]

————, *Value, Price and Profit*, ed. by Eleanor Marx Aveling. New York: International Publishers, 1935. [Originally delivered as a speech in 1865.]

————, *Wage-Labour and Capital*. New York: International Publishers, 1933. [Originally published in 1849.]

MARX, KARL, and FRIEDRICH ENGELS, *Manifesto of the Communist Party*. New York: International Publishers, 1948. [Originally published in 1848.]

MCBRIAR, A. M., *Fabian Socialism and English Politics*. Cambridge, Eng.: The University Press, 1962.

PEASE, EDWARD R., *The History of the Fabian Society*. London: Fifield, 1916.

SCHRAM, STUART, *Mao Tse-tung*. Baltimore, Md.: Penguin Books, Inc., 1966.

SCHURMANN, FRANZ, *Ideology and Organization in Communist China.* Berkeley and Los Angeles, Calif.: University of California Press, 1966.

SEMMEL, BERNARD, *Imperialism and Social Reform.* Cambridge, Mass.: Harvard University Press, 1960.

SHERMAN, HOWARD, *Radical Political Economy. Capitalism and Socialism from a Marxist-Humanist Perspective.* New York: Basic Books, 1972.

SWEEZY, PAUL M., *The Theory of Capitalist Development.* New York: Oxford University Press, 1942.

WEBB, BEATRICE, *Our Partnership.* London: Longmans, Green, 1948.

WEBB, SIDNEY and BEATRICE, *The Decay of Capitalist Civilization.* New York: Harcourt Brace Jovanovich, Inc., 1923.

11

The German Historical School

In this chapter we shall consider the German historical school,[1] which arose in the 1840's with major publications by Friedrich List and Wilhelm Roscher. It ended by World War I, when Gustav Schmoller died. By then some of its ideas had been absorbed by economists in general, and the school had ceased to exist as a school.

Overview of the German Historical School

The Social Background of the School

The peace treaty after the Napoleonic Wars left Germany divided into thirty-nine separate states, most of them monarchical, almost all of them undemocratic. The victorious Great Powers of Europe manipulated Germany to promote their own ulterior purposes. Austria wanted to keep Germany weak and divided; Britain wished to see a strong Prussia to thwart a future resurgent France; Russia wanted for itself the parts of Poland not yet seized by Germany or Austria.

The German struggle against Napoleon had aroused patriotic and nationalistic emotions. Many Germans demanded unification and constitutional reforms, but the quest for national unity was frustrated for about half a century. The aspirations toward democracy remained unrealized for over a century and then were achieved only briefly

[1] This chapter has benefited substantially from Jack C. Myles's unpublished doctoral thesis at Princeton University, "German Historicism and American Economics," 1956.

under the most adverse conditions—under the stigma of losing World War I.

In 1815 the Holy Alliance of Prussia, Austria, and Russia was organized as a means of defeating revolution wherever it might threaten. Minor revolutionary outbursts in Germany from 1830 to 1832 were repressed, and the major upheavals of 1848 were crushed by Prussian and Austrian troops.

Prussia, the largest, richest, most militaristic, and most powerful state in Germany, dominated the country. Foreign countries wooed Prussia as a powerful ally. Foreign and native conservatives saw in Prussia a bulwark against democracy and socialism. Native nationalists relied on Prussia to forge a unified Germany. Prussians dominated the German government and armed forces. A series of successful wars further strengthened nationalism under Prussian hegemony. Advanced social legislation, enacted by Bismarck, expressed the paternalism of the monarchy and evoked loyalty and patriotism among the German workers. Bismarck bragged that in Germany the kings made the revolutions.

Since certain key economic institutions of nineteenth-century Germany differed substantially from those of Britain, the same economic ideology could not apply to both countries. Mercantilist regulations persisted in Germany at least until the formation of the Empire in 1871, long after they had disappeared from the British scene. Competition and freedom of enterprise, which the classicists took for granted in their economic analyses, were severely restricted in Germany. Because of the large bureaucracy that administered and regulated manifold phases of German economic life, the science of public administration was highly developed. British theories were obviously inapplicable to the German situation. The historical school defended and rationalized the German way of life by questioning the historical relevance of the classical economic doctrines from Britain.

The Germany that gave birth to the historical school was divided, weak, and primarily agricultural. Nationalism, patriotism, militarism, paternalism, devotion to duty, hard work, and massive government intervention all combined to change the pattern and promote industrial growth. Because Germany of the mid-nineteenth century was far behind England in the development of industry, it required government assistance in order to catch up.

The Essence of the German Historical School

There were four principles that were basic in the thinking of the German historical school:

1. The historical school applied an evolutionary approach to its

study of society. It concentrated on cumulative development and growth. An analogy was sometimes drawn to Darwin's evolutionism in biology: The social organism is born, develops and grows, and finally decays and dies. Society is constantly changing. Therefore what is relevant economic doctrine for one country at a particular time may be inappropriate for another country or another age. This relativistic approach was especially useful in attacking classical economics as being suitable for England but not for Germany.

2. The historical school was nationalistic, whereas classical economics was individualistic and cosmopolitan. If the social organism is the center of study, if it is the force for dynamic movement, then society and the state rather than the individual occupy the center of the stage. In Germany it was the state that fostered industry, transportation, and economic growth. In the process of defending a unified economy it was easy to develop an ardent nationalistic glorification of the state. The historical school gave great prominence to the need for state intervention in economic affairs and emphasized that the community has interests of its own that are quite distinct from those of the individual.

3. The economists of the historical school emphasized the importance of studying the economy historically, as part of an integrated whole. Because economic and other social phenomena are interdependent, political economy cannot be treated adequately except in combination with other branches of social science. The historical school criticized the abstract, deductive, static, unrealistic, unhistorical qualities of classical and marginalist methodology. They undertook massive inductive studies, using primary source material and studying changing social institutions. The school claimed that its historical method allowed it to study *all* the forces of an economic phenomenon, *all* the facets of economic behavior, not merely their economic logic. Some of the historical economists became opposed to theorizing altogether, denying that there are any valid economic laws, with one exception: They believed that patterns of development are discernible in history and can be generalized into "laws of development."

4. The historical economists were reformers, although conservative. Political economy, they said, has important ethical tasks. It must not merely analyze motives that prompt economic activity but must weigh and compare the moral merit. It must determine a standard of the proper production and distribution of wealth so that the demands of justice and morality are satisfied. The historical economists thought the German state should be entrusted with the amelioration of conditions for "the common man." This would strengthen loyalty to

the state while it safeguarded the health, well-being, and efficiency of the factory workers. Reforms, they hoped, would also divert the working class from socialistic ideology. The advocates of moderate social changes were dubbed "Socialists of the Chair," a reference to the academic positions they held.

What Groups Did the German Historical School Serve or Seek to Serve?

First, the members of the German historical school served themselves. They enjoyed close and friendly relations with government officials and rose to dominant positions in academic life. In fact the German government controlled most universities, and Schmoller, known as the "professor maker," controlled most academic appointments in Germany through his influence at the Prussian Ministry of Education. His students and followers were placed in academic posts, whereas the German adherents of the Austrian marginalist school were excluded from university positions.

This school also served the German imperial government well by defending its role in a nationalistic state.

The historical economists served the dominant business, financial, and landowning groups by promoting moderate reforms that frustrated the drive for a more radical democratization of society. Instead of the poor and lowly fighting and winning their own battles for improvements, concessions were handed down to them by a paternalistic state. As a result, servility, nationalism, and loyalty to the regime were more widespread in Germany than anywhere else.

How Was the German Historical School Valid, Useful, or Correct in Its Time?

The evolutionary approach to society and to economic thought provided a necessary antidote to the static thinking of the classical and marginalist schools. How else could one attempt to explain Great Britain's adherence to laissez faire in the nineteenth century and its considerable departure from it in the twentieth? If certain economic principles are appropriate everywhere for all time, why are many underdeveloped countries refusing to rely exclusively on free enterprise to build their economies? Some, devoted to a never-changing world, say that departures from once-reliable doctrines represent colossal errors. But obviously we must familiarize ourselves with changing history and changing environments, with economic and social evolution, in order to understand the present world. For this task, inductive factual studies are required. New theories and new ideas ~~must be evoked if we are to understand new situations. This~~ realization was the lasting contribution of the German historical school.

Through its nationalism and glorification of the state, this school promoted German unification and economic growth.

The historical economists were the leaders in the attack on laissez faire. This theme was the trend of the future. They were astute enough to know that unrestricted free enterprise does not necessarily produce the best possible results for society as a whole. And they were right in their belief that reform can be a substitute for worse upheavals, which might occur if the class struggle is allowed to develop and sharpen.

How Did the German Historical School Outlive Its Usefulness?

The task of the German historical school was completed when economists of various persuasions agreed that historical empirical studies are required to explain the present, to test old theories, and to develop new ones. The limitations of the historical school were pointed out by John Neville Keynes (the father of John Maynard Keynes), an eminent economist who accepted both the historical inductive method and the abstract deductive method but favored the latter. He argued that if society is constantly changing and if new situations call for new analyses, then past experience has only limited relevance:

> It is still more important to observe that just because of the evolution of industrial systems, and the shifting character of economic conditions, upon which the historical school of economics so much insist, the study of the past is rendered the less serviceable for the solution of present-day problems. Upon many of these problems extremely little light is thrown by economic history that relates to an earlier period than the nineteenth century. How indeed can generalizations based upon one set of circumstances be safely applied to quite another set of circumstances? Not only may the problems calling for solution be novel in their character; there may even arise new industrial classes. With what classes in the fourteenth century, for example, are we to compare the modern factory operative and the modern capitalist employer? If, therefore, for no other reason than that institutions and habits and conditions change, another method of investigation than the historical must for very much of our economic work be essential. Political economy can never become a specifically historical science.[2]

[2] John Neville Keynes, *The Scope and Method of Political Economy*, 4th ed. (London, 1917), p. 327. [Originally published in 1890.]

Today the historical inductive method has become generally accepted as complementary to the abstract deductive approach; changing times and methodological controversies have forced the two into an uneasy but tolerably placid marriage.

The usefulness of the German historical school was also diminished, paradoxically, by its success in promoting the economic growth and power of Germany. Germany has surpassed Great Britain, and it no longer needs protection and paternalism as it once did. Since World War II there is more laissez faire in Germany than in Britain. The historical school's analyses of its country's situation have become antiquated through the process of change, which the school itself recognized in economic affairs. The tools of historical analysis, however, are as applicable in Germany today as they were in the past.

Finally, the German nationalism advocated by the historical economists overreached itself as it evolved into a frenzied militarism. Academic people are likely to be rather shamefaced about chauvinism—except in time of war. During the century ending in 1914, the hope was rising that the world could win peace, international cooperation, and universal harmony. The German historical economists struck a strident note of nationalism that jarred these internationalist sentiments of good will. Their ideas seemed to lead logically to the holocaust of World War I. Theirs was the more realistic tone in a world of hatred and conflict, but they offered little hope and few dreams of good will to which people could cling.

List

Friedrich List (1789–1846), a forerunner of the historical school, was inclined neither toward formal study in school nor toward his father's occupation as a tanner. He became a government clerk and by 1816 had risen to the post of ministerial undersecretary. A year later he accepted a professorship in administration and politics at the University of Tübingen, but his dissident political views caused his dismissal in 1819. He then became active in promoting a strong political and commercial union of the German states. In 1819 List presented a petition for a customs union to the Federal Assembly on behalf of an association of merchants and manufacturers that he had organized.

> Thirty-eight customs boundaries cripple inland trade, and produce much the same effect as ligatures which prevent the free circulation of the blood. The merchant trading between Hamburg and Austria, or Berlin and Switzerland must traverse ten states, must learn ten customs-

tariffs, must pay ten successive transit dues. Any one who is so unfortunate as to live on the boundary-line between three or four states spends his days among hostile tax-gatherers and custom-house officials; he is a man without a country.[3]

Elected to his state legislature in 1820, List advocated other administrative and financial reforms that were considered very radical in his day. He favored doing away with tolls on roads, tithes, state ownership of industries, feudal property taxes and limitations on productive land use, and excise duties. He advocated trial by jury, a reduction in the number of civil service officers, and a single direct income tax to meet the expenses of government. These views were regarded as treasonable, and he served eight months in prison, after which he was deported. From 1825 to 1832 List lived in the United States, where he became a farmer, a journalist, and a business promoter, making and losing a fortune in coal mining. His protectionist ideas gained much more popularity in the United States than in Germany.

After his return to Germany List became an ardent advocate of a railway network for Germany. The railway lines later built in Germany were to follow closely his sketch in a pamphlet published in 1833. His efforts to create a German customs union were realized in the establishment of the *Zollverein* in 1834. The plans he presented for a German postal system and a national patent law were realized more than twenty years after his death. Ill health, financial difficulties, and despair over the delay in German unification darkened his later days, however, and he committed suicide in 1846.

In the introduction to his famous work, *National System of Political Economy,* List referred to himself in the third person:

> The author will begin, as theory does not begin, by interrogating History, and deducing from it his fundamental principles. . . . For greater clearness, we give here a cursory view of the principal results of his researches and meditations: The association of individuals for the prosecution of a common end, is the most efficacious mode towards ensuring the happiness of individuals. Alone, and separated from his fellow-creatures, man is feeble and destitute. The greater the number of those who are united, the more perfect is the association, and the greater and the more perfect is the result, which is the moral and material welfare of individuals. The highest association of individuals now realized, is that of the state, the nation; and the highest imaginable, is that of the whole human race. . . .

[3] Margaret E. Hirst, *Life of Friedrich List and Selections from His Writings* (London, 1909), p. 139.

A nation may by war be deprived of its independence, its wealth, its liberty, its constitution, its laws, of its own special features, of that degree of culture and national well-being to which it may have attained; it may be wholly enslaved. Nations are thus the victims of each other, and selfish policy is continually disturbing and delaying the economical development of nations. To preserve, to develop, and to improve itself as a nation is consequently, at present, and ever must be, the principal object of a nation's efforts. . . .

In the economical development of nations, it is necessary to distinguish the following principal stages: the savage state, the pastoral state, the agricultural state, the agricultural and manufacturing state, and finally, the agricultural, manufacturing, and commercial state. . . . A nation that greatly values its independence and its safety, must make a vigorous effort to elevate itself as fast as possible, from an inferior to a higher state of civilization, uniting and perfecting as quickly as possible, its own agriculture, manufactures, navigation, and commerce. . . . The elevation of an agricultural people to the condition of countries at once agricultural, manufacturing, and commercial, can only be accomplished under the law of free trade, when the various nations engaged at the time in manufacturing industry shall be in the same degree of progress and civilization; when they shall place no obstacle in the way of the economical development of each other, and not impede their respective progress by war or adverse commercial legislation.

But some of them, favored by circumstances, having distanced others in manufactures, commerce, and navigation, and having early perceived that this advanced state was the surest mode of acquiring and keeping political supremacy, have adopted and still persevere in a policy so well adapted to give them the monopoly of manufactures, of industry and of commerce, and to impede the progress of less advanced nations or those in a lower degree of culture. . . . The anterior progress of certain nations, foreign commercial legislation and war have compelled inferior countries to look for special means of effecting their transition from the agricultural to the manufacturing stage of industry, and as far as practicable, by a system of duties, to restrain their trade with more advanced nations aiming at manufacturing monopoly. . . .

Experience teaches us, it is true, that the wind carries with it the seeds of one country to another, and that desert places have thus been changed into heavy forests. But would it be wise for the proprietor of waste land to wait for the wind to perform this office of planting and transformation during the lapse of centuries? Is it folly in him to force nature by planting his uncultivated lands, that he may attain his object in a score of years? . . .

The doctrine of Adam Smith in regard to international commerce, is but a continuation of that of the physiocrats. Like the latter, it disregards nationality; it excludes almost entirely politics and government; it supposes the existence of perpetual peace and universal association; it depreciates the advantages of national manufacturing industry, as well as the means of acquiring it; it demands absolute free trade.[4]

List advocated free trade within Germany, while championing a high tariff against imports of manufactured goods to protect infant domestic industries. He opposed protection for agriculture because this was an old, mature industry and because manufacturing required cheap food for labor and cheap raw materials. Besides, the development of large-scale industry through protection would enlarge the home market for agriculture. List severely condemned Adam Smith and classical economics for claiming universality for doctrines that were well suited for England but inappropriate for underdeveloped countries. Heavy emphasis was placed on what history teaches us, and the importance of the state was stressed. List popularized the idea of stages of economic growth and urged that the government actively assist a people who wished to pass from a lower to a higher stage against the competition of more advanced nations. Only after a country reached industrial maturity could it revert to free trade.

List denied Smith's harmony of interests between the individual and society, arguing that the immediate private interests of certain members of the community do not necessarily lead to the highest good of the whole. A nation may suffer, for example, from an absence of manufacturing industry, but some people may flourish in selling foreign manufactures. One person may grow rich by extreme parsimony, but if a whole nation follows that person's example, there will be no consumption and no support of industry. National unity, which is the result of past development, is necessary to the individual, whose interests should be subordinated to the preservation of this unity.

List thought that only in the temperate zone would manufacturing develop, for only this climate could foster the appropriate intellectual and physical efforts. The tropics should remain on a free-trade basis and continue to supply tropical products in exchange for manufactured goods. He saw this as the true foundation for the international division of labor and world trade. A country of the torrid zone would make a fatal mistake, he said, if it tried to become a manufacturing country. Nature did not invite it to that vocation. Tropical countries will therefore sink into dependence on those of the temperate zone. But competition among the manufacturing nations will provide manufactured goods at low prices, and it will also prevent

[4] Friedrich List, *National System of Political Economy*, tr. by G. A. Matile (Philadelphia, Pa., 1856), pp. 70–73, 181, 420. [Originally published in 1841.]

any one nation from taking advantage, through its superiority, of the weaker nations of the torrid zone.

Military preparations, wars, and war debts, said List, may in certain cases immensely increase the productive powers of a country. He pointed to England as an example. War expanded its productive power so much that the increased values it received annually far exceeded the interest on its enlarged war debts. Spending money on supplying its armies meant shipping goods to the theater of war, which ruined foreign manufacturers and assured England's industrial supremacy.

Roscher

Wilhelm Roscher (1817–94) was one of the founders of the "older historical school." This group wanted to supplement classical theory, whereas the younger school wanted to supersede it entirely with historical studies and policy considerations. Roscher became professor of political economy at Göttingen and later at Leipzig. Roscher's five-volume textbook, *Economic Science*, took forty years to complete (1854–94) and was widely used in the German schools for a long time. The first volume reached thirteen editions by 1878, when it was translated into English as *Principles of Political Economy*. While Roscher repudiated the classical economics he had learned in his youth, he still built upon those ideas. This was the basis for the "younger historical school's" condemning the older forerunners. Schmoller held that Roscher and his associates had criticized classical economics and its methods effectively; but when it came to reconstructing economics, they had themselves lapsed into the methods that they had formerly condemned.

Roscher's ideas on the role of the state and on historical method follow:

By the science of national, or Political Economy, we understand the science which has to do with the laws of the development of the economy of a nation, or with its economic national life. . . . National life, like all life, is a whole, the various phenomena of which are most intimately connected with one another. Hence it is, that to understand one side of it scientifically, it is necessary to know all its sides. But, especially, is it necessary to fix one's attention on the following seven: language, religion, art, science, law, the state and economy. . . .

If, by the public economy of a nation, we understand economic legislation and the governmental guidance or direction of the economy of private persons, the science of public economy becomes, so far as its form is concerned, a branch of political science, while as to its matter, its subject is almost coincident with that of Political Economy. . . . Just as clear, is the close connection between politics and Political Economy, in the case of the science of finance, or of the science of governmental house-keeping, otherwise the administration of public affairs. . . . As the physiologist cannot understand the action of the human body, without understanding that of the head; so we would not be able to grasp the organic whole of national economy, if we were to leave the state, the greatest economy of all, the one which uninterruptedly and irresistibly acts on all others, out of consideration. . . .

The thorough application of this [the historical] method will do away with a great number of controversies on important questions. Men are as far removed from being devils as from being angels. We meet with few who are only guided by ideal motives, but with few, also, who hearken only to the voice of egotism, and care for nothing but themselves. It may, therefore, be assumed, that any view current on certain tangible interests which concern man very nearly, and which has been shared by great parties and even by whole peoples for generations, is not based only on ignorance or a perverse love of wrong. The error consists more frequently in applying measures wholesome and even absolutely necessary under certain circumstances, to circumstances entirely different. And here, a thorough insight into the conditions of the measure suffices to compose the differences between the two parties. Once the natural laws of Political Economy are sufficiently known and recognized, all that is needed, in any given instance, is more exact and reliable statistics of the fact involved, to reconcile all party controversies on questions of the politics of public economy, so far, at least, as these controversies arise from a difference of opinion. It may be that science may never attain to this, in consequence of the new problems which are ever arising and demanding a solution. It may be, too, that in the greater number of party controversies, the opposed purposes of the parties play a more important part even than the opposed views. Be this as it may, it is necessary, especially in an age as deeply agitated as our own, when every good citizen is in duty bound to ally himself to party, that every honest party-man should seek to secure, amid the ocean of ephemeral opinions, a firm island of scientific truth, as universally recognized as truth as are the principles of mathematical physics by physicians [physicists?] of the most various schools.[5]

Roscher added that the historical method does away with feelings of self-sufficiency, and that higher civilizations will not look down with contempt on lower ones. Societies are continually evolving from immature to mature forms, which may be considered the most

[5] Wilhelm Roscher, *Principles of Political Economy,* tr. by John J. Lalor, Vol. I (New York, 1878), pp. 87–88, 91–92, 112–13. [Originally published in 1854.]

perfect. These mature societies, however, eventually decline and decay.

Roscher showed his affinity for economic theory by including a simplified version of English classical price theory in his *Principles of Political Economy*. Instead of disdaining abstract theory, he sought to discover its historical basis. He asserted that the study of contemporary facts and opinions was an essential adjunct to the classical deductive method.

Schmoller

Gustav Schmoller (1838–1917), the leading figure of the "younger historical school," was a professor of political science at Halle, Strasbourg, and Berlin. He taught many generations of students and administrative officials and wielded great influence in academic and government circles. In addition to his work as a professor, he was an active member of the Academy of Sciences, and also of the House of Lords of the Prussian Diet. He was one of the founders and a major leader of the *Verein für Sozialpolitik* (Association for Social Policy). This organization advocated social legislation and helped promote the idea of greater government activity in social and economic affairs.

The task of accumulating historical and descriptive factual materials was one that Schmoller considered should come prior to, and was far more important than, deductive theorizing. He and his followers always protested against the separate study of a small segment of economic phenomena based on the assumption that everything else remains unchanged. They held that we lose the essence of economic processes as soon as we isolate and fragment them. Schmoller wanted to develop economics exclusively on the basis of historical monographs. In fact Schmoller was so antagonistic to deductive economists that he declared publicly that members of the "abstract" school were unfit to teach in a German university.

Schmoller engaged in a famous controversy with Carl Menger, founder of the abstract Austrian marginalist school, as to which was more fruitful—inductive or deductive analysis. This debate was named the *Methodenstreit*, or the "Battle of Methods." In 1883, when the method of historicism was nearing high tide, Menger published a book on methodology that defended theoretical analysis and rated Schmoller's school as merely secondary in importance. Schmoller reviewed the book unfavorably in his *Jahrbuch*, and Menger replied in an angry pamphlet called *Errors of Historicism*, in which he wrote: "The historians have stepped upon the territory of our science like foreign conquerors, in order to force upon us their language and their customs, their terminology and their methods, and to fight intolerantly every branch of enquiry which does not correspond with their special method." [6] When Schmoller received a copy of Menger's pamphlet for review in his *Jahrbuch,* he printed an announcement that he was unable to review it because he had returned it immediately to the author. Schmoller also printed the insulting letter to Menger that he had included with the pamphlet.

This controversy aroused bitter feelings and resulted in many publications on both sides. In the end the *Methodenstreit* seemed to resolve itself into the belief that both inductive and deductive methods are important and that they supplement each other: Historical research and a set of analytic tools to handle the accumulated materials are both necessary.

Schmoller's emphasis on historical research was repeated in his book *Political Economy and Its Method,* published in 1894.

> The historical sciences provide empirical material and data which transform the scholar from a mere beggar into a rich man as far as knowledge of reality is concerned. And it is this historical-empirical material which, like all good observation and description, serves to illustrate and verify theoretical conclusions, to demonstrate the limitations of the validity of certain truths, and, more than anything else, to obtain inductively new truths. This applies particularly to the more complicated fields of political economy, in which it is possible to advance only on the basis of historical investigations. For example, purely abstract deductions are without value as regards the effects of machinery on wages and the influence of the production of precious metals on the value of money. This is even truer with respect to the evolution of economic institutions and theories, and the problem of economic progress in general. . . . To consult history belongs to the most appropriate methods of political economy. The most prominent opponent of the historical school, Karl Menger, admits that the most important economic institutions such as property, money, and credit have both an individual nature and a historical side to their existence; consequently "he who knows the essence of these phenomena only in one phase of their existence does not know them at all." If this is true with respect to money and credit it is even truer with respect to the family economy, the division of labor, the formation of social classes, different forms of business organization, the phenomena of the market and other institutions of trade, guilds, freedom of domestic trade, patterns of rural life and indeed, of all typical patterns and specific arrangements which are known as economic institutions and which, after

[6] Quoted in Keynes, *The Scope and Method of Political Economy,* p. 324.

having crystallized into law, tend to dominate either permanently or for centuries the economic process.[7]

Schmoller believed that ethical value judgments were to be encouraged. Justice in the economic system was to be realized through a paternalistic policy of social reform furthered by the state and all social groups. The guiding principle of social reform, he said, was a more equitable distribution of income. Social science was to be the guide for the attainment of the objectives of social policy.

What are economic institutions but a product of human feelings and thought, of human actions, human customs and human laws? . . .

If in the economic order we could recognize only the ruling of blind forces, of selfish interests, natural masses and mechanical processes, it would be a constant battle, a chaotic anarchy. . . . No, harmony does not exist *per se;* selfish impulses combat each other, natural masses tend to destroy each other, the mechanical action of natural forces interferes relentlessly still to-day; the struggle for existence is to-day still carried on in the struggle of competition. . . . While struggle and strife never cease they do not preserve the same character throughout the course of history. The struggle which ended in annihilation, in subjugation, turns into a peaceful contest which is decided by an umpire. The forms of dependence grow milder and more human. Class government grows more moderate. Every brutal strength, every undue assertion of superior force is made punishable by law. Demand and supply, as they confront each other in the different systems of custom and law, are quite different in their results. . . .

There is no worse delusion than that of the older English economists that there are a number of simple and natural legal and economic institutions which have always been as they are and will always remain so; that all progress of civilization and wealth is simply an individual or technical one; that this is simply a question of increased production or consumption which will and can be accomplished on the basis of the same legal institutions. This faith in the stability of economic institutions was the result of the naive overweening confidence of the older economists in the omnipotence of the individual and of the individual life. Socialism then has perhaps over-estimated the significance of social institutions. Historical economics and the modern philosophy of law have given them their due position by showing us that the great epochs of economic progress are primarily connected with the reform of social institutions.[8]

[7] Contemporary Civilization Staff of Columbia College, *Introduction to Contemporary Civilization in the West: A Source Book,* Vol. II (New York, 1946), pp. 520–21. Reprinted with permission of Columbia University Press.

[8] Gustav Schmoller, *Idea of Justice in Political Economy* (Philadelphia, Pa., no date), pp. 22, 26, 27, 37.

Schmoller accused the older historical school of attempting to apply the lessons of history too quickly. He called for much more historical study in order to establish an empirical basis for national economic theory. Yet despite the innumerable massive historical studies he and his disciples published, they failed to produce an economic theory, and their major contribution lay in the area of economic history.

Late in life Schmoller changed his views on protectionism. In his younger years he had been an ardent advocate of free trade. By 1901 he favored a protective tariff for Germany, and he hailed Alexander Hamilton and Friedrich List as his teachers. He denied that the new era of protectionism had arisen because economists and statesmen had been unable to understand the beautiful arguments for free trade. He justified tariffs on the basis of List's "infant industry" argument, but he went further than that. Protectionism, he said, arose from the natural instinct of people. In addition, he felt that tariffs were international weapons that might benefit a country if used skillfully.

Weber

Max Weber (1864–1920) established himself in Berlin's legal profession. After publishing several scholarly works, he became a professor of political economy and sociology at Freiburg, and later at Heidelberg and Munich. He considered himself an intellectual descendant of Schmoller.

Weber aroused a lively controversy that has persisted through the years over the relationship between Protestantism and the rise of capitalism. He rejected the Marxian idea that religious doctrines are merely ideological manifestations of particular economic conditions. Ideas for Weber were at least in part autonomous entities with the power to influence social changes. It seemed to him that capitalism was a result rather than a cause of the Reformation. He believed that Calvinist theology in particular contained certain elements exceedingly conducive to rationalized, individualistic economic activity undertaken for profit. Speaking of Protestantism, Weber wrote:

> The religious valuation of restless, continuous, systematic work in a worldly calling, as the highest means to asceticism, and at the same time the surest and most evident proof of rebirth and genuine faith, must have been the most powerful conceivable lever for the expansion of that attitude toward life which we have here called the spirit of capitalism. When the limitation of consumption is combined with this release of ac-

quisitive activity, the inevitable practical result is obvious: accumulation of capital through ascetic compulsion to save. The restraints which were imposed upon the consumption of wealth naturally served to increase it by making possible the productive investment of capital.[9]

R. H. Tawney and others have disputed Weber's analysis. Religion of course has influenced people's outlook on society, but economic and social changes have acted powerfully on religion. Weber, it has been said, emphasized the first point but touched upon the second point only in passing. The rise of business enterprise induced the middle class to do away with Catholicism, which condemned usury, suspected economic motives, and took a dim view of private fortunes. Besides, as the largest feudal landowner, the Catholic Church sought to perpetuate such feudal institutions as the just price, primogeniture, entail, and mortmain. Because the Reformation struck a powerful blow at authority, it loosened the hold of tradition on people's minds. Because it called into question ideas that had long held sway, it strengthened the temper of rationalism. It is true, Tawney argued, that Calvinism offered new sanctification to economic activities and the accumulation of wealth, but economic changes such as the great geographic discoveries and the expansion of commerce were ultimately responsible for the transformation of the Christian ethic from the sixteenth century onward. Both Calvinism and the spirit of capitalism, he said, were produced by the profound change in economic organization and social structure.

Several historical facts seem to support Tawney's thesis. First, contrary to Weber's paradigm, Luther's Protestant doctrines were surrounded by a feudal aura, while on the other side of the coin, Catholicism was adaptable to the new world of business enterprise. Early capitalist manifestations were discernible in the late medieval cities in Catholic Italy and in Catholic France before the Revolution; the adaptation of Catholicism was apparently hastened by the threat of the Reformation. Second, a notably powerful motive for the revolt against Rome, especially among people who had no interest in business enterprise, was the prospect of plundering wealthy Church organizations. Third, peasants with grievances against their feudal overlords were swept into the Protestant movement. And, finally, the rising nationalist spirit in many countries conflicted with the Catholic internationalism centered in Rome.

In the complex interrelations of Protestantism and the rise of capi-

---

[9] Max Weber, *The Protestant Ethic and the Spirit of Capitalism,* tr. by Talcott Parsons (London, 1930), p. 172. [Originally published in 1904–05.]

talism, it is difficult to disentangle cause from effect. Did Protestantism produce capitalism, as Weber said? Or did rising capitalism produce Protestantism as a more suitable credo for its business activities, as his opponents believe? Or is there some truth in both positions?

Sombart

Werner Sombart (1863–1941), a German economic historian, was the son of a prosperous farmer who was elected to the Reichstag and settled in Berlin. The younger Sombart studied in Pisa and Berlin and taught at the universities of Breslau and Berlin. His encyclopedic researches into the origins and evolution of capitalism revealed the intellectual influence of Marx as well as that of the German historical school, especially Schmoller. As a student at the University of Berlin, Sombart absorbed from Schmoller a nationalistic outlook, a hostility to classical economics, and an antipathy toward liberal individualism. Although the German historical school may be said to have ended by World War I, Sombart carried on the school's methodology and perspectives beyond that time. As a critic of the capitalistic form of economic organization, Sombart started his adult life as a socialist; he ended it as a Nazi.

Sombart sought to explain the rise and growth of capitalism. The foundations of this revolutionary system of economic organization, he wrote, rest on the business enterpriser, the modern state, and the machine process. The enterpriser, a new type of person, has assumed the direction of economic activities. Because a few people were smitten with a passion for making money, society has been changed completely. This process has also depended on certain historical accidents, such as the discovery of great gold deposits and the existence of virgin resources awaiting exploitation. Sombart questioned Weber's thesis that puritanism had a large share in forming the capitalistic spirit of businessmen. Instead, he stated that "those parts of the Puritan dogma which appear to be of real importance for the formation of the spirit of capitalism are borrowed from the realm of ideas of the Jewish religion." It was the Jews who gave capitalism its impersonal, rational, and materialistic qualities. But, said Sombart, puritanism did help discipline the workers to the new way of life. In order to overcome the great difficulties of adapting workers to the technical and disciplinary requirements of capitalism, the workers had to be inspired with the desire to get ahead in the world through capitalistic ideals. The desire for gain, instead of being an inborn trait of human nature, had to be deliberately inculcated in order that capitalism might flourish.

It is interesting to note that Sombart assigned to the Jews a decisive role in the development not only of capitalism but of socialism. Early in his life, when he leaned toward Marxism and was critical of capitalism, Sombart emphasized the role of the Jews in the development of capitalism. After World War I, when he developed a strong antipathy toward Marxian socialism, he found that socialism was strongly influenced by Jewish thought.

Sombart divided capitalism into three stages of development: early capitalism, which dated from about 1400 to 1760; high capitalism, which lasted from 1760 to 1914; and late capitalism, from 1914 on. The phenomenon of capitalism, he said, must be studied as a part of cultural history. The appearance and growth of capitalism brought about not only technological changes but economic, political, military, psychological, religious, and intellectual changes, which dissolved the medieval social order.

The period of high capitalism, according to Sombart, marked the ascendancy and the decline of the system. The decline was marked by unmistakable symptoms: Business leaders became fat, rich, and complacent; they lost the spirit of adventure. Risk-taking became subordinate to a policy of caution and routine business methods. Economic life was increasingly stabilized and regulated by the state. The scope for aggressive and energetic enterprise was decreased by cartels and other monopolistic arrangements. The decline of the rate of population growth and the narrowing of investment opportunities further increased capitalism's difficulties. By 1914, when the period of late capitalism set in, these decadent tendencies had become quite pronounced.

Sombart predicted the eventual rise of a new economic organization. He expected capitalism to endure indefinitely, but to continue to change in the future as it had changed in the past. Public control and conscious planning for satisfying needs rather than for making money would increasingly come to the fore. Small craftsmen, shopkeepers, and farmers would continue to survive along with capitalistic enterprises, cooperatives, and public regulation. The farmers would grow in importance with the continued growth of world population.

By 1933 Sombart had become a full-fledged supporter of the Nazi philosophy. Germany under Hitler, he thought, was the new, dynamic system that would overcome capitalist decadence. He glorified German racism and nationalism as welcome alternatives to the debilitated society that had been vanquished.

> The results of the economic age show, first of all, that in public life there is in fact but one basis and one measure of success, that of wealth in money; and only one order of rank, that of money or income. . . . An intellectual person obtains neither standing nor approval in society until he has a large income. . . . Wealth has become an object of admiration, whereas earlier—at least in the case of private persons—it was rather an object of contempt or scorn unless its bearers were possessed of other values, such as culture or noble lineage. . . .
>
> "Comfortism," the name I have given to this practical materialism, which means the deviation of the direction of human life toward amenity-values, brings the whole body of people to decay. . . . The necessity, touched upon above, of filling the void created in the materialistic soul after each enjoyment by a new enjoyment, has led to the chase in which modern man spends his life. The capitalistic economic system was here the pacemaker in so far as it urged, in accordance with its nature, the acceleration of the tempo, so that the future would be continually anticipated by the present. . . .
>
> With every new generation there is a new-born capacity to be bearers of culture, which is lost only through racial degeneracy—a danger which wise precaution can prevent. . . .
>
> For us there is only one aim—Germany. For the sake of Germany's greatness, power and glory, we will gladly sacrifice every "theory" and every "principle," whether it bears a liberal or any other stamp. . . .
>
> If, finally, we are to understand that our own [artistic and literary] creations should be influenced by foreigners, this kind of relation would constitute a great danger to German culture which really has no need of such inspiration from without.[10]

As a devotee of Hitler, he of course glorified the role of the state. He therefore loved Lassalle's defense of the state, and quoted him sympathetically:

> Ferdinand Lassalle, . . . in the time of the bleakest Manchester period, under the spell of his teacher, Fichte, represented the idea of the state in eloquent words, when he explained: "The state is this unity of individuals in a moral whole, a unity which increases a millionfold the power of all individuals who are included within this union. . . . The purpose of the state is, therefore, to bring the human being to a positive development and a progressive development; in other words, to bring

[10] Werner Sombart, *A New Social Philosophy*, tr. by Karl F. Geiser (Princeton, N.J., 1937), pp. 22–23, 34, 147, 152, 187.

human determination, that is, the culture of which the human race is capable, into actual being.

"However wide a gulf separates you and me from one another, my lords!"—thus he apostrophized his judges at the conclusion of his famous defense before the Supreme Court—"opposed to this dissolution of everything moral, we stand hand in hand! The ancient vestal fire of all civilization, the State, I will defend with you against those modern barbarians" [of the Manchester school].[11]

Sombart, like other members of the German historical school, neglected value and distribution theory in favor of history. He believed that the "laws" of capitalism, like all economic laws, are neither final nor universal; they are valid only for capitalism. In describing the evolution of capitalism, he tried to explain economic behavior in a type of theory, but not a conventional type. According to Wesley C. Mitchell, Sombart's chief weakness as a scientific inquirer was that he did not restudy and enrich his preconceptions as he gathered and assimilated his data. His greatest strength, however, was that his encyclopedic studies and the frequently provocative conclusions he drew from them stimulated further research.

Bibliography

HIRST, MARGARET E., *Life of Friedrich List and Selections from His Writings.* London: Smith, Elder, 1909.

LIST, FRIEDRICH, *National System of Political Economy,* tr. by G. A. Matile. Philadelphia, Pa.: Lippincott, 1856. [Originally published in 1841.]

MYLES, JACK C., "German Historicism and American Economics." Unpublished doctoral thesis at Princeton University, 1956.

ROSCHER, WILHELM, *Principles of Political Economy,* tr. by John J. Lalor. 2 vols. New York: Holt, 1878. [Originally published in 1854.]

SCHMOLLER, GUSTAV, *Idea of Justice in Political Economy.* Philadelphia, Pa.: American Academy of Political and Social Science, No. 113, no date.

SOMBART, WERNER, *The Jews and Modern Capitalism,* tr. by M. Epstein. Glencoe, Ill.: Free Press, 1951. [Originally published in 1911.]

———, *Der Moderne Kapitalismus.* 3 vols. Munich and Leipzig: Duncker & Humblot, 1916–28.

———, *A New Social Philosophy,* tr. by Karl F. Geiser. Princeton, N.J.: Princeton University Press, 1937.

———, *Socialism and the Social Movement,* tr. by M. Epstein. New York: Dutton, 1909.

TAWNEY, R. H., *Religion and the Rise of Capitalism.* New York: Harcourt Brace Jovanovich, Inc., 1926.

[11] *Ibid.,* p. 160.

WEBER, MAX, *The Protestant Ethic and the Spirit of Capitalism,* tr. by Talcott Parsons. London: Allen and Unwin, 1930. [Originally published in 1904–05.]

————, *The Theory of Social and Economic Organization,* tr. by A. M. Henderson and Talcott Parsons. New York: Oxford University Press, 1947. [Originally published in 1921.]

12

The Rise of the Marginalist
School: Jevons

The marginalist school developed in several countries and through the efforts of different people working independently of each other at first. Among the pioneers were Herman Heinrich Gossen in Germany, Carl Menger in Austria, Léon Walras at Lausanne, Switzerland, and W. Stanley Jevons and Alfred Marshall in England. Here is another interesting case of new ideas arising almost simultaneously in different places and from different people, after enough dissatisfaction had developed over old doctrines to create a strong feeling that new ones were needed.

By the 1870's, about one hundred years after Adam Smith, marginalism was well on its way to displacing classical economics. Marginalism reigned supreme in Western economic thought until it was suddenly challenged by the Keynesian onslaught in 1936. Since then both types of economic analysis have continued to flourish side by side in a symbiotic relationship. Marginalism, having adapted itself to new ideas and new situations, has changed considerably from its earliest form. It is still the dominant school in microeconomic, or partial, analysis. Almost every elementary college textbook uses marginal economics to analyze the single firm and its behavior, the individual in his or her productive and consumptive activities, the market for a single product, and the formation of individual prices. In this sense marginalism has remained triumphant for a hundred years. It had to move aside, however, to allow Keynesian economics the macroeconomic sphere—the analysis of the economy as a whole, including general price movements, levels of business activity, and the role of government.

Overview of the Marginalist School

The Social Background of the School

Serious social problems remained unsolved even a hundred years after the beginning of the industrial revolution. Poverty was widespread, although productivity was increasing magnificently. The extremely uneven distribution of wealth and income created much dissatisfaction even while average levels of living were rising. Business fluctuations affected many people adversely; individuals could no longer depend exclusively on their own initiative and ability to overcome conditions that were thrust upon them. Farmers and farm laborers had their difficulties; many drifted to the cities, attracted by the carrot of better opportunities and driven by the club of rural poverty. Industrial accidents often brought serious hardships to workers and their families before adequate workmen's compensation laws were enacted. Long hours of labor, dangerous and unhealthy working conditions, the preponderant economic power of employers in bargaining with workers, usury, the rise of monopolistic business, insecurity in old age—these and many other problems caused people to seek solutions beyond the narrow confines of classical economic thinking.

The trend of the nineteenth century in Europe was to develop three lines of attack on pressing social problems, and all three flouted classical economic precepts. Movements arose to promote socialism, trade unionism, and government action to ameliorate conditions by regulating the economy, eliminating abuses, and redistributing income. The marginalist economists opposed all three trends. They theorized with seemingly Olympian impartiality and concluded that this was the best of all possible worlds. The marginalists defended laissez faire, deplored government intervention, denounced socialism, and sought to discourage labor unionism as either ineffective or pernicious.

To the leading early marginalists, classical economic theory was especially pernicious because it seemed to conclude that economic rent was an unearned income and because it was based on a labor theory of value. The first idea was seized and expanded by Henry George, the second by Karl Marx. If classical economics could be made to say what its creators never intended—namely, that rent was immoral and labor created all values—then the science of wealth was ripe for a thoroughgoing revision.

The Essence of the Marginalist School

The basic ideas of marginalism can be condensed into ten major principles. They are listed briefly below and amplified later in the discussion of six leading marginalist economists.

1. This school concentrated on the *margin*—the point of change where decisions are made—to explain economic phenomena. They extended to all of economic theory the marginal principle that Ricardo developed in his theory of rent.

2. The marginalist approach was microeconomic rather than macroeconomic, and in it the individual takes over the center of the stage. Instead of considering the aggregate economy, the marginalists considered individual decision-making, market conditions and prices for a single type of goods, the output of a single firm, and so forth.

3. The method of this school was abstract and deductive, as was the method of the classical school.

4. The marginalist analysis focused on an economic system based on pure competition (with occasional consideration of pure monopoly at the other extreme). In this world of small, individualistic, independent entrepreneurs there are many buyers, many sellers, homogeneous products, uniform prices, and no advertising. No one person or firm has enough economic power to influence market prices perceptibly. Individuals can adapt their own actions to demand, supply, and price as worked out in the market through the interactions of thousands of people. Each person is such a tiny operator in the huge market anthill that no one notices her or his presence or absence.

5. Demand became the primary force in price determination. The classical school had emphasized cost of production (supply) as the sole determinant of value. The early marginalists swung to the opposite extreme and emphasized demand to the virtual exclusion of supply. Alfred Marshall synthesized both supply and demand into what may be called neoclassical economics, which is basically marginalism with a judicious recognition of the surviving contributions of the classical school.

6. Economics became subjective and psychological. According to the marginalists demand depends on marginal utility, which is a psychic phenomenon. Costs of production include the sacrifices and irksomeness of working, managing a business, and saving money to form a capital fund.

7. The marginalists believed that economic forces generally tend

toward equilibrium, toward a balancing of opposing forces. Whenever disturbances cause dislocations, new movements toward equilibrium occur.

8. Marginalist theory developed partly to deprecate Ricardo's rent theory. The uncomfortable idea had gotten around that rent is an unearned income and an unnecessary payment in order to ensure the use of land. Marginalist theory generally merged land with capital goods (produced by human labor), coupling the reward to the landowner with interest theory.

9. The marginalists assumed that people are rational in balancing pleasures and pains, in measuring marginal utilities of different goods, and in balancing present against future needs. They also assumed that rational behavior is normal and typical and that random abnormalities will cancel each other out. Their approach was hedonistic, for they assumed that the dominant drives are to maximize pleasure and minimize pain.

10. The marginalists continued the classical school's defense of laissez faire as the most desirable policy. There should be no interference with natural economic laws if maximum social benefits are to be realized.

What Groups of People Did the Marginalist School Serve or Seek to Serve?

Marginalism, the economics of conservatism, favored all those whose interests committed them to the status quo, who resisted the currents of change. This type of theory favored employers (even though most of them did not really understand it) by opposing unions and by attributing unemployment to wages that were inflexible on the downward side. Marginalism defended landowners against Ricardian rent theory. This school favored the wealthy, who generally were opposed to government intervention that might tend to redistribute income.

How Was the Marginalist School Valid, Useful, or Correct in Its Time?

The marginalist school developed new and powerful tools of analysis, especially geometrical diagrams and mathematical techniques. Economics became a more exact science, thanks to the marginalists. Conditions of demand were given importance as one set of determinants for prices of both final goods and factors of production. The school emphasized the forces that shape individual decisions; this was valid in a world where such decisions were significant in determining the course of economic activities. Fundamental assumptions underlying economic analysis, lurking in the background of classical thinking, were explicitly stated by the marginalists. The methodological controversies they aroused finally led to a separation of objective and verifiable principles that are based on stated assumptions and principles that depend on value judgments and philosophical outlook.

The method of partial analysis can be justified on the ground that it enables us to investigate complex phenomena by taking one step at a time. We allow one variable at a time to change, assuming that everything else remains constant. The problems of our immensely complicated society with its countless variables can thereby be simplified and penetrated in an orderly and systematic manner. As we introduce successive variables, we approach more realistic situations. Assuming that everything remains unchanged except the one factor we allow to vary is a technique used all the time. If you say, "I am going to the movies tonight," you are implicitly making hundreds of assumptions about other circumstances not changing unexpectedly. For example, you are assuming that you will not break a leg or die of a heart attack during the day; that the theater will not burn down; that a flood or an earthquake will not cut off the highway to town; that something more interesting will not come along before evening.

There is a certain virtue in not neglecting the individual economic unit or the small sectors of the economy; the microeconomic approach of marginalism complements the macroeconomic approach, which may overlook many problems by viewing the economy as a whole. As examples we cite the following: (1) Certain groups of people may become increasingly impoverished, although average real per capita income for the nation may be rising. (2) The business cycle is of prime importance to the profitability of a big steel corporation; but to a small grocer, the business cycle is far less important than the opening of a supermarket across the street. (3) Aggregate analysis tells us that investments in education pay higher returns than investments in capital; yet a banker is justified in not lending an individual money to go to college unless the government guarantees the loan. Clearly the microeconomic approach of marginalism has validity if the macroeconomic view is not neglected.

How Did the Marginalist School Outlive Its Usefulness?

In a sense the marginalist school did not outlive its usefulness; it still dominates the field in Western countries along with the Keynesian school, and both share the international field with socialism. However, marginalism as it remained from 1870 to 1930 had to be modified considerably before it could continue as a viable set of ideas. Nevertheless some of the weaknesses that permeated its structure still persist.

The microeconomic approach, while it has its uses, introduced the famous fallacy of composition that leads to erroneous conclusions. The fallacy is the belief that what is true for one is necessarily true for all, or that what is true for part of a situation is necessarily true for the whole situation. If you were to get to work two hours early, you would find a parking place for your automobile; but if everybody were to get there early, would everybody solve their parking problems? If one employer were to cut wages, he could expand his market by selling more goods at lower prices. The decline in purchasing power among his own employees would not affect him, as they would normally buy only a negligible portion of his output, if any. However, if all employers were to cut wages, they might find their markets shrinking rather than expanding. Yet the eminent marginalist economist Lionel Robbins could write as late as 1934 that wage reductions were one of the prerequisites for overcoming the Great Depression:

> In the United States the word went forth that consumers' purchasing power must at all costs be maintained. President Hoover pledged the leaders of big industry to make no reduction of wage rates. Until the summer of 1930 no serious reduction of wage rates took place. At the same time special efforts were made to maintain rates of dividends for shareholders. In Germany, too, throughout 1930 wage rates were well maintained. Now this policy was the reverse of what was needed. . . .
>
> The very fact, therefore, that there was unemployment on this scale is a proof that, in some parts of the labour market, the rates charged were too high. . . . Wage rates in Great Britain were more or less constant from 1924 onwards. All that happened was that, in the face of a tendency to a decline in the demand for labour, wage rates were not lowered.[1]

The assumption of pure competition was a reasonable abstraction looking backward from the 1870's. But it was too unrealistic to be useful as competition declined after the 1870's. In large sectors of the economy today pure competition does not exist.

The subjective, psychological, individualistic equilibrium approach to economic analysis has several serious weaknesses. One is revealed by the opening paragraph in the chapter of Alfred Mar-

[1] Lionel Robbins, *The Great Depression* (New York, 1935), pp. 69, 82, 83.

shall's *Principles of Economics* headed "Temporary Equilibrium of Demand and Supply":

> The simplest case of balance or equilibrium between desire and effort is found when a person satisfies one of his wants by his own direct work. When a boy picks blackberries for his own eating, the action of picking is probably itself pleasurable for a while; and for some time longer the pleasure of eating is more than enough to repay the trouble of picking. But after he has eaten a good deal, the desire for more diminishes; while the task of picking begins to cause weariness, which may indeed be a feeling of monotony rather than of fatigue. Equilibrium is reached when at last his eagerness to play and his disinclination for the work of picking counterbalance the desire for eating. The satisfaction which he can get from picking fruit has arrived at its *maximum:* for up to that time every fresh picking has added more to his pleasure than it has taken away; and after that time any further picking would take away from his pleasure more than it would add.[2]

In practice, however, how often are people able to adjust their work schedules to the exact point of their own individual equilibriums? In a footnote 197 pages later, Marshall admitted that a person might have to work a standard day even though the disutility of the last hour of labor might be greater than the utility of the earnings from that hour. "But such cases are rare," he added.

In fact, however, historical and institutional factors are more important in determining the length of the working day than is the equilibrium of the individual. More significant than Marshall's berry-picking boy was the post-World-War-II case of the Seventh Day Adventist who for religious reasons refused to work overtime on Saturday in a shoe plant. Obviously the marginal utility of her earnings for the week was far less than the marginal disutility of her work on the seventh day of the week. Yet the arbitrator in her case agreed to her dismissal because she violated the union-management contract. In 1973 a major conflict between the auto workers' union and the auto companies was over compulsory overtime. The workers objected to being compelled to work extra hours even at much higher wage rates. The discipline of the factory time clock, worked out through collective agreements, is more relevant to the length of the working day than the whims of the employee acting in isolated contemplation of her maximum welfare—and the fact that she can always quit her job

---

[2] Alfred Marshall, *Principles of Economics*, 8th ed. (London, 1920), p. 331. [Originally published in 1890.] Reprinted with permission of Macmillan & Co. Ltd., The Macmillan Company of Canada Limited, and The Macmillan Company.

is scant consolation. Yet individualism remained triumphant in economic theory despite a world of growing collective action.

The early marginalists held that a laissez faire regime produced the best possible results. Economic laws seemed to them natural laws that must not be tampered with. At a time when government intervention was growing, they generally denied its desirability because they supposed the economy to be self-regulating, served unwittingly by individuals who sought to serve themselves. They believed that what was good for General Motors was good for the country. This was exactly what the classical economists believed. But, one might ask, how does an individual or a group promote the social interest when output is restricted and prices raised? The classical economists relied on competition to curb the selfish interests of the individual, and in their day competition was widespread enough to produce reasonably good results. That is, no General Motors then existed. But with the decline of competition, laissez faire became increasingly untenable. Recognition of these monopolistic trends, however, would have undermined faith in individualism.

The marginalists assumed a positive time preference, which means that people prefer present to future spending. A rate of interest is therefore required to induce people to postpone consumption, for interest is the reward for abstinence or waiting. This concept assumes that rational people are in this case irrational, for they underestimate their future needs and therefore refuse to save unless they receive a monetary inducement. Moreover, this theory overlooks the drive toward the accumulation of wealth as a means to power and prestige. The marginalist theory of saving might have some applicability in a world of small business and small savers, but it is less relevant when the bulk of the saving is done through corporate decisions, the expansion of bank credit, and government taxation. The rate of interest rather than the level of income is made the prime reason for saving. If interest is the reward for the sacrifice of waiting, there should be no persistent problem of unemployment. As soon as unemployment appears, the rate of interest falls; but owners of wealth then increase their spending for consumer goods, for they refuse to abstain from spending if they will receive a lower rate of return in interest. A rise in consumption spending should therefore offset any drop in investment. But this is not what happens.

The neglect of rent theory by the marginalists makes sense from the individual viewpoint. To the person who buys land and machinery there is no significant theoretical difference between them. To the person who pays rent the payment is necessary to win the land away from competing uses. Land here is a part of the cost of production, and the selling price must cover that cost. It is only from the total social viewpoint that land is sufficiently different from other means of production to merit separate treatment. The total supply of land, unlike that of goods produced by people, is almost completely inelastic, even though the supply of land for any one use is quite elastic. From society's viewpoint land has no alternate uses and therefore rent is not a necessary payment. Rent does not enter into cost of production; high rents are a consequence of high prices, not a cause. Rent is an unearned income from society's viewpoint because land costs society nothing. To the individual who bought the land, however, it represents a very real cost. In condemning Ricardian rent theory the marginalists generally failed to consider the alternative point of view on which that analysis was based. By predicating a stationary state they assumed that the supply of capital was also fixed; the differences between land and capital were thereby obliterated.

The marginalist analysis originally was static, timeless, and unhistorical. There were few attempts at inductive verification of theories; in fact, hypotheses were framed in ways that excluded testing. Business cycles were generally ignored in the firm conviction that Say was right when he said that supply creates its own demand and therefore full employment is normal. The school failed to explain economic growth, and its theory was inadequate for underdeveloped countries. The marginalists tried unsuccessfully to stem the tide of social change that threatened to engulf their concepts. Finally, floundering helplessly during the Great Depression of the 1930's, they merged forces with the Keynesians and salvaged something from the wreckage.

Jevons

William Stanley Jevons (1835–82) spent five years of his youth in Australia as an assayer at the mint. There he earned enough to return to England to continue his studies. He was disappointed and bitter when he failed to win a prize in political economy at University College, London, and attributed this failure to the prejudice of his professor against the new ideas he was developing. Jevons published several books on logic and became professor of logic, political economy, and philosophy, first in Manchester and later at University College, London. He invented a logic machine, exhibited before the Royal Society in 1870, that could yield a conclusion mechanically from any given set of premises. Jevons was also famous as a historian of science, and he made outstanding contributions to the development of index numbers. At forty-seven, this active and versatile man drowned while swimming.

Jevons called Ricardo "that able but wrong-headed man" who "shunted the car of Economic science on to a wrong line." Mill, he felt, pushed the car further toward confusion. Malthus and Senior were much more to Jevons' taste.

On the first page of *The Theory of Political Economy* Jevons stated, "Repeated reflection and inquiry have led me to the somewhat novel opinion, that *value depends entirely upon utility.*" In dismissing the labor theory of value, he did agree that labor often indirectly determines value by varying the utility of the commodity through an increase or limitation of the supply. Elsewhere in the same work Jevons formulated his theory of value this way:

> Cost of production determines supply;
> Supply determines final degree of utility;
> Final degree of utility determines value.[3]

Why, therefore, does not cost of production determine value? Jevons, in refuting the labor theory of value, argued that labor cannot be the regulator of value because labor itself is of unequal value; it differs infinitely in quality and efficiency. "I hold labour to be *essentially variable,* so that *its value must be determined by the value of the produce, not the value of the produce by that of the labour.*" [4] Labor itself is a subjective, psychological cost, a "painful exertion." The problem of economics is "to satisfy our wants with the least possible sum of labour." His own formulation should have led him to concede, however, that cost of production also plays a significant role in determining value.

The keystone of the whole theory of exchange, said Jevons, lies in this proposition: "The ratio of exchange of any two commodities will be the reciprocal of the ratio of the final degrees of utility of the quantities of commodity available for consumption after the exchange is completed." [5] Suppose, Jevons explained, one trader possesses only corn and another only beef. Exchange will increase total utility but will cease when, at the margin, a pound of beef has as much utility as ten pounds of corn and exchanges for ten pounds of corn. But if the trader who possesses corn considers ten pounds of

[3] William Stanley Jevons, *The Theory of Political Economy*, 4th ed. (London, 1911), p. 165. [Originally published in 1871.]
[4] *Ibid.*, p. 166.
[5] *Ibid.*, p. 95.

corn less useful than one pound of beef, that person will desire to carry the exchange further. The trader who possesses beef, on finding one pound of beef less useful than ten pounds of corn, will also desire to continue the exchange. Exchange will thus go on until each party has obtained all possible benefit and loss of utility would result if more were exchanged. In other words, Jevons' proposition amounts to this: If a pound of steak costs ten times as much as an ice cream cone, each person will consume both up to the point at which the steak has ten times the marginal utility of the ice cream cone.

Jevons presented graphically the equilibrium between the pain of work and the pleasure of earnings. (See Figure 2) The line *OX* represents the potential working day. The height of points above the line *OX* denotes pleasure and the depths below it pain. At the beginning of the working day labor is usually more irksome than later in the

Figure 2   Jevons' Equilibrium Between the Pain of Work and the Pleasure of Earnings

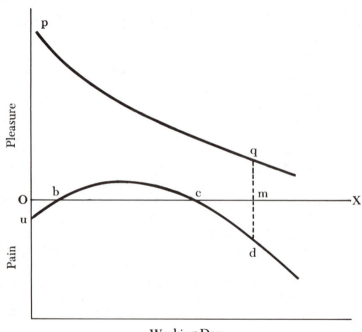

Working Day

SOURCE: William Stanley Jevons, *The Theory of Political Economy*, 4th ed. (London, Macmillan, 1911), p. 173.

day when one adjusts to it. Thus there is neither pleasure nor pain at *b* and *c*, and there is actual pleasure from working between those two points. Beyond *c*, however, the pain of additional work increases.

The utility of the product (it would have been more appropriate to call it "the utility of the earnings") is shown by the line *pq*. Its downward slope reflects the law of diminishing marginal utility. At *m*, where *qm* equals *dm*, the pleasure gained is exactly equal to the pain of the labor endured. The laborer will cease working at point *m*. Jevons did indicate that "it is not always possible to graduate the work to the worker's liking."

Jevons rejected any attempt to compare intensity of pleasures among different people. Even for one person, total utilities cannot be compared. But a person can compare his or her utilities and disutilities at the margin itself:

> The whole amount of pleasure that a man gains by a day's labour hardly enters into the question; it is when a man is doubtful whether to increase his hours of labour or not, that we discover an equality between the pain of that extension and the pleasure of the increase of possessions derived from it.[6]

Yet later in the same work Jevons did compare marginal utilities among different people. By extending the principle of diminishing marginal utility to money, he gave a theoretical justification for the welfare economists' argument that redistributing income from the rich to the poor might increase total happiness. Jevons himself, however, did not draw this conclusion from his theory.

> What, for instance, is the utility of one penny to a poor family earning fifty pounds a year? . . . Its utility is equal to the utility of the quantity of bread, tea, sugar, or other articles which they could purchase with it, this utility depending upon the extent to which they were already provided with those articles. To a family possessing one thousand pounds a year, the utility of a penny may be measured in an exactly similar manner; but it will be much less, because their want of any given commodity will be satiated or satisfied to a much greater extent, so that the urgency of need for a pennyworth more of any article is much reduced. . . . In Economics we regard only commercial transactions, and no equalisation of wealth from charitable motives is considered. . . . So far as is consistent with the inequality of wealth in every community, all commodities are distributed by exchange so as to produce the maximum of benefit.[7]

[6] *Ibid.*, pp. 13–14.
[7] *Ibid.*, pp. 140–41.

Jevons' law of diminishing marginal utility solved the paradox of water and diamonds that puzzled some of the classical economists. Adam Smith believed that utility had nothing to do with the *magnitude* of exchange value because water was more useful than diamonds but diamonds were more valuable than water. The principle of diminishing marginal utility reveals that while the total utility of water is greater than the total utility of diamonds, the marginal utility of diamonds is far greater than the marginal utility of water. We would rather have all the water in the world and no diamonds than the other way around; but we would rather have an additional diamond than an extra unit of water.

Jevons used his theory of the diminishing marginal utility of money to show that gambling does not pay and insurance does. Assuming that there is no pleasure attached to gambling except in winning, the money we may lose has a higher marginal utility than an equal amount of money we may gain. In the case of insurance, the small sums we pay out for premiums have less utility, dollar for dollar, than the large sums we may lose without insurance coverage.

Jevons did not fully develop a general theory of distribution based on marginal productivity. Nor did he adequately explain the law of diminishing returns on which such a theory of distribution could be built. Yet he hit on the rudiments of both ideas, as Figure 3 shows. Successive units of capital investments, he said, are less productive than preceding units. Hence the tendency toward a falling rate of profit. The rate of interest tends toward uniformity at any one time. Distances along the line OX in Figure 3 represent quantities of capital employing a fixed number of laborers in any industry. The area under the curve pq denotes the whole product of labor and capital. With capital On, the total product is measured by the area between the vertical lines OY and qn. A small increase of capital at that point will add qn to the product, which is all the entrepreneur can pay for that portion of the capital. With uniform interest rates, the total interest on capital will be On times qn, or the area of the rectangle $Onqr$. The remainder of the product, $rqpY$, will belong to the workers. Were capital available, say Om, its rate of interest would be pm, total interest would be $Omps$, and only spY would remain for labor. Interest, he said, is one of three components of profit, the other two being wages of superintendence and insurance against risk.

Jevons accepted Ricardian rent theory, which is based on a marginal analysis. He did not apply a similar approach to labor. To Jevons wages were a residual after other claims were met. "The wages of a working man are ultimately coincident with what he pro-

Figure 3   Jevons' Determination of Interest Rates Through Diminishing Returns to Capital

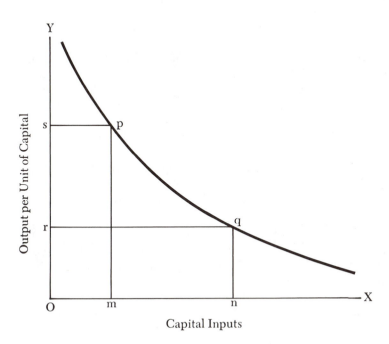

SOURCE: William Stanley Jevons, *The Theory of Political Economy*, 4th ed. (London, Macmillan, 1911), p. 258.

duces, after the deduction of rent, taxes, and the interest of capital." It was John Bates Clark who ultimately formulated the best exposition of the law of diminishing returns and the marginal productivity theory of distribution.

The problem of business cycles attracted Jevons' attention. He believed that the sun-spot cycle influences the weather, which in turn affects the size of crops. Large crops occur when sun spots are at a minimum, and the resulting low prices of agricultural products stimulate the economy. The effects may manifest themselves internationally; a large crop and cheap food in India will leave the wage earner surplus income for clothing, thereby promoting prosperity for the cotton mills of Manchester.

Jevons favored free public museums, concerts, libraries, and education. He believed that child labor should be restricted by law, and that health and safety conditions in factories should be regulated. He approved of trade unions as benefit, or friendly, societies, for their insurance functions keep men off public relief. But unions should leave the rate of wages to the operation of natural laws. If they obtain wage increases, it is at the expense of other workers or from the population in general through higher prices. "The supposed conflict of labour with capital is a delusion. The real conflict is between producers and consumers." Profit-sharing is preferable to union efforts to raise wages, and workers should save to improve their lot.

Jevons opposed regulating the hours of labor of adult males. He advocated excluding mothers with children below school age from factories and workshops for the sake of their children. But he deplored free hospitals and medical charities of all kinds because they "nourish in the poorest classes a contented sense of dependence on the richer classes for those ordinary requirements of life which they ought to be led to provide for themselves." He opposed government conservation measures to check the waste of coal because such modes of interference "break the principles of industrial freedom, to the recognition of which, since the time of Adam Smith, we attribute so much of our success."

Jevons supported a cautious extension of legislation to improve public sanitation but was undecided about whether imprisonment for debt should be abolished. Moderate government regulation of railways won his approval. In his view, consumption taxes, such as the match tax, are most desirable because they do not affect industry adversely; besides, all people above the rank of actual paupers should contribute to the state in proportion to their incomes. Believing that people are essentially hedonistic, Jevons advocated the greatest-happiness principle. No laws, no customs, no rights of property, he said, are so sacred that they must remain if it can be proven that they stand in the way of the greatest happiness. But, he asked, how can we prove that a certain change will increase the sum of happiness? Without conclusive evidence, "the present social arrangements have the considerable presumption in their favour that they can at least exist, and they can be tolerated."

Bibliography

JEVONS, WILLIAM STANLEY, *Investigations in Currency and Finance*, 2d ed. London: Macmillan, 1909. [Originally published in 1884.]

———, *Methods of Social Reform*. London: Macmillan, 1883.

———, *The State in Relation to Labour*. London: Macmillan, 1882.

———, *The Theory of Political Economy*, 4th ed. London: Macmillan, 1911. [Originally published in 1871.]

13

The Marginalist School:
The Austrians and Clark

Menger

Carl Menger (1840–1921), a professor at the University of Vienna, published his path-breaking treatise on marginalist economics in 1871, the same year that Jevons' major book appeared. His long-range goal was to produce a systematic work on economics and a comprehensive treatise on the character and methods of the social sciences in general. His interests and the scope of his projects continued to expand, and in 1903 he resigned his professorship in order to devote himself entirely to his work. Yet during the last three decades of his long life Menger published very little because he was never satisfied with his writing. At his death he left voluminous fragmentary and disordered manuscripts.

Menger's exposition of diminishing marginal utility and the balancing of marginal utilities included a table reproduced here as Table 3. The most important item of consumption is food, and the first unit of food consumed is assumed to have a utility of ten, as shown in Column I. If a second unit of food were consumed in the same day, its utility would be nine. With ten units of food available, the last unit would give a satisfaction of one. An eleventh unit of food would add nothing to total satisfaction.

Tobacco, less urgently needed, is shown in Column V. The first unit consumed gives a satisfaction of only six, and beyond six units increased consumption does not increase satisfaction. If an individual obtained four units of food, the individual's utility per unit would

Table 3 Menger's Concept of Diminishing Marginal Utility

Unit consumed	*Degree of Marginal Satisfaction*									
	I (FOOD)	II	III	IV	V (TOBACCO)	VI	VII	VIII	IX	X
1st	10	9	8	7	6	5	4	3	2	1
2nd	9	8	7	6	5	4	3	2	1	0
3rd	8	7	6	5	4	3	2	1	0	
4th	7	6	5	4	3	2	1	0		
5th	6	5	4	3	2	1	0			
6th	5	4	3	2	1	0				
7th	4	3	2	1	0					
8th	3	2	1	0						
9th	2	1	0							
10th	1	0								
11th	0									

SOURCE: Carl Menger, *Principles of Economics*, tr. and ed. by James Dingwall and Bert F. Hoselitz (Glencoe, Ill., Free Press, 1950), p. 127. Reprinted with permission of The Macmillan Company. Copyright 1950 by The Free Press, a Corporation.

fall from ten through seven. He or she would then find that a fifth unit of food would afford the same satisfaction (six) as the first unit of tobacco. However, if one could afford to buy only three units, one would buy two of food and one of the commodity represented in Column II. An implicit assumption of Menger's table is that each unit of each commodity represents the same expenditure of money or effort or sacrifice. Otherwise, if a unit of tobacco could be obtained with ten cents or five minutes of work whereas a unit of food required twenty cents or ten minutes of work, the first unit of tobacco would be more desirable than even the first unit of food.

The other columns of the table represent the marginal utilities of different commodities (or classes of commodities) consumed by a single individual. The successive figures down each column represent successive additions to total satisfaction resulting from increased consumption of the designated commodity.

Another implicit assumption of Menger's table is that the economizing individual is able to rank satisfactions not only ordinally but cardinally as well. Ordinal ranking allows one to say that the first dime spent on food in any one day gives more satisfaction than either the second dime spent on food or the first dime spent on anything else represented in the table; it is a relative statement indicating merely that one item is more or less valuable than others. With cardinal values, one may say that the first dime spent on food gives exactly twice as much satisfaction as either the sixth dime spent on food or the second dime spent on tobacco. The validity of such precise comparisons is of course highly questionable.

Menger drew an interesting conclusion from his table. Suppose an individual could afford only seven units of food. That individual would then satisfy only those needs for food that ranged in importance from ten through four, and the other needs, ranging in importance from three to one, would remain unsatisfied. What would be the usefulness to him or her of seven units of food? Jevons would add the marginal utilities of each unit from the first through the seventh, and the answer would be forty-nine. Menger's answer would be twenty-eight—the marginal utility of the last unit (four) times the number of units (seven). Why? Because all units are alike, and thus each has the same utility as the marginal unit. If a woman had only one unit of food per day, her state of semistarvation would attribute high utility to that unit. But if she had seven units, no one unit of food would give her more satisfaction than the marginal unit would.

Menger thereby identified exchange value with *total* utility, unlike Jevons, who equated exchange value with marginal utility. Jevons would have said that in Table 3, Column I, ten units of food have greater total utility than five units, but the tenth unit has a smaller marginal utility than the fifth unit; similarly, a large wheat crop offers more total utility than a small wheat crop, even if the larger one sells for less money. According to Menger, five units of food offer more satisfaction for the individual ($5 \times 6 = 30$) than ten units ($10 \times 1 = 10$); thus a small wheat crop may be *more* satisfying to consumers than a large one, if the smaller one sells for more money, because the marginal utility of the larger crop is so low.

The measure of value, said Menger, is entirely subjective. Therefore a commodity can have great value to one individual, little value to another, and no value at all to a third, depending on the differences in the requirements of the three individuals and the amounts available to each. Hence, not only the nature of value but the measure of value is subjective. Value has nothing to do with cost of production.

> The value an economizing individual attributes to a good is equal to the importance of the particular satisfaction that depends on his command of the good. There is no necessary and direct connection between the value of a good and whether, or in what quantities, labor and other goods of higher order were applied to its production. A non-economic

good (a quantity of timber in a virgin forest, for example) does not attain value for men if large quantities of labor or other economic goods were applied to its production. Whether a diamond was found accidentally or was obtained from a diamond pit with the employment of a thousand days of labor is completely irrelevant for its value. In general, no one in practical life asks for the history of the origin of a good in estimating its value, but considers solely the services that the good will render him and which he would have to forgo if he did not have it at his command. Goods on which much labor has been expended often have no value, while others, on which little or no labor was expended, have a very high value. Goods on which much labor was expended and others on which little or no labor was expended are often of equal value to economizing men. The quantities of labor or of other means of production applied to its production cannot, therefore, be the determining factor in the value of a good.[1]

The basis of the exchange of goods, said Menger, is the difference in relative subjective valuations of the same goods by different individuals. He denied Smith's dictum that exchange is due to the propensity of people to truck, barter, and exchange one thing for another—that trading is an end in itself because it is pleasurable. Menger argued instead that trading is undertaken to increase the satisfactions enjoyed by the traders. If a farmer has more grain than he needs and a winegrower has more wine than he needs, it will be of mutual advantage for them to trade. Even if each farmer could use all the goods he produced, the marginal utility of grain is low for the first farmer and high for the second, whereas the marginal utility of wine is low for the second and high for the first. Trade therefore increases the total utility for both farmers. "The principle that leads men to exchange is the same principle that guides them in their economic activity as a whole; it is the endeavor to ensure the fullest possible satisfaction of their needs."

Menger originated the idea of imputation in pricing factors of production. The marginalists emphasized the importance of consumer demand, especially in its subjective psychological aspects, in determining price. The concepts of marginal and total utility refer to consumer wants; therefore they apply only to consumer goods and services. What governs the prices of goods used in production, such as machinery, raw materials, land, and so on? Menger, in his theory of imputation, held that such goods also yield satisfactions to con-

[1] Carl Menger, *Principles of Economics*, tr. and ed. by James Dingwall and Bert F. Hoselitz (Glencoe, Ill., 1950), pp. 146–47. [Originally published in 1871.] Reprinted with permission of The Macmillan Company. Copyright 1950 by The Free Press, a Corporation.

sumers, though only indirectly, by helping to produce things that do satisfy consumer wants directly. The consumer's marginal utility for a piece of iron is governed by the marginal utility of the final product that is made from that iron—say, a thimble; the iron has usefulness imputed to it by the usefulness of the thimble. The principle of marginal utility is thereby extended to the whole area of production and distribution. The rent received by landowners, for example, is governed by the utility of the products grown on that land. The factors, or agents, of production are assigned use values that govern their exchange values. The present value of the means of production is equal to the prospective value (based on marginal utility) of the consumer goods they will produce, with two deductions: First, a margin has to be subtracted "for the value of the services of capital" (interest); second, there must be a reward for entrepreneurial activity (profit).

This doctrine of imputation was an attack on the labor and real-cost theories of value. Menger said that it is a most egregious and fundamental error to argue that goods attain value for us because goods that have value to us were employed in their production. This false doctrine, he said, cannot explain the value of the services of land, the value of labor services, or the value of the services of capital. On the contrary, the value of goods used in production must without exception be determined by the prospective value of the consumer goods they help produce. Menger denied that the price of common labor is determined by the cost of minimum subsistence for the laborer and his family. The prices of labor services, like the prices of all other goods, are governed by their value. And their values are governed "by the magnitude of importance of the satisfactions that would have to remain unsatisfied if we were unable to command the labor services."

In considering the problem of monopoly Menger suggested several important concepts that others later developed more fully.

> The monopolist is not completely unrestricted in influencing the course of economic events. As we have seen, if the monopolist wishes to sell a particular quantity of the monopolized good, he cannot fix the price at will. And if he fixes the price, he cannot, at the same time, determine the quantity that will be sold at the price he has set. He cannot, therefore, sell large quantities of the monopolized good and at the same time cause the price to settle at as high a level as it would have reached if he had marketed smaller quantities. Nor can he set the price at a certain level and at the same time sell as large a quantity as he could sell at lower prices. But what does give him an exceptional position in eco-

nomic life is the fact that he has, in any given instance, a choice between determining the quantity of a monopolized good to be traded or its price. He makes this choice by himself and without regard to other economizing individuals, considering only his economic advantage. . . .

A monopolist will therefore raise his price, within the limits between which exchange operations have economic character, if he anticipates a greater economic gain from selling small quantities of the monopolized good for a high price. He will lower his price if he finds it more to his advantage to market larger quantities of the monopolized good at a lower price. . . . Under some circumstances, he may even have occasion to abandon part of the quantity of the monopolized good at his disposal to destruction instead of bringing it to market, or, with the same result, to leave unused or to destroy part of the corresponding means of production of the monopolized good. . . .

It would be entirely erroneous to assume that the price of a monopolized good always, or even usually, rises or falls in an *exactly* inverse proportion to the quantities marketed by the monopolist, or that a similar proportionality exists between the price set by the monopolist and the quantity of the monopolized good that can be sold. If, for example, the monopolist brings 2,000 instead of 1,000 units of the monopolized good to market, the price of one unit will not necessarily fall from six florins, for example, to three florins. On the contrary, depending upon the economic situation, it may in one case fall only to five florins, for example, but in another to as little as two florins.[2]

Menger indicated that the monopolist would price products at the level that would give the maximum profit.

The theoretical system of this pioneer marginalist was based on a more extreme individualism than that of his disciple Wieser, to whom we now turn.

Wieser

Friedrich von Wieser (1851–1926) was born into a distinguished aristocratic family in Vienna whose sons usually entered the public service. He studied law at the University of Vienna, and after graduation he came across a copy of Menger's book on economics and was captivated by it. After studying economics in German universities, Wieser was appointed, with Menger's help, to a professorship of economics at the German University of Prague. He later taught at the University of Vienna, and he also held high posts in the Austrian government, serving at one time as minister of commerce. It was he

[2] *Ibid.*, pp. 211–13.

who introduced the term *marginal utility,* although others developed the concept before him, without giving it the label that stuck.

Wieser, true to the marginalist doctrine, said that there is no "objective" exchange value, for "its roots are bedded in the subjective estimates of individuals, grouped to determine the result." We might well ask if the marginal price offer really reflects the marginal utility for a good: A well-fed millionaire offers ten dollars for a steak dinner for which a starving beggar will not pay more than fifty cents. But which has the greater marginal utility for the dinner? Wieser was fully aware of this kind of problem.

> In order, however, properly to appraise the service of exchange value in economic life, it must be remembered that it does not contain exactly the same elements as does value in use in the self-contained economy. The latter simply depends upon utility: the former is besides dependent upon purchasing power. . . . Value in use measures utility; exchange value measures a combination of utility and purchasing power.[3]

Therefore, said Wieser, diamonds and gold are exceptionally high-priced because they are luxuries, valued and paid for according to the purchasing power of the richest classes. Coarser foodstuffs and iron are low in price because they are common goods, whose prices depend primarily on the purchasing power and the valuation of the poor.

> Production is ordered not only according to simple want, but also according to wealth. Instead of things which would have the greatest utility, those things are produced for which the most will be paid. The greater the differences in wealth, the more striking will be the anomalies of production. It will furnish luxuries for the wanton and the glutton, while it is deaf to the wants of the miserable and the poor. It is therefore the distribution of wealth which decides how production is set to work, and induces consumption of the most uneconomic kind.[4]

Wieser then introduced the concept of natural value as the product of the quantity of goods times their marginal utility.

> In natural value goods are estimated simply according to their marginal utility; in exchange value, according to a combination of marginal utility and purchasing power. In the former, luxuries are estimated far lower, and necessaries, comparatively, much higher than in the latter. Exchange value, even when considered as perfect, is, if we may so call it, a

[3] Friedrich von Wieser, *Natural Value,* tr. by Christian A. Malloch (London, 1893), p. 57. [Originally published in 1889.]
[4] *Ibid.,* p. 58.

caricature of natural value; it disturbs its economic symmetry, magnifying the small and reducing the great.[5]

From this distinction Wieser drew a conclusion that was more typically Germanic than marginalist: There is room for limited government intervention in the economy whenever exchange value and natural value diverge too much.

> People look for something better from a government. This does not, however, in the least involve that the form of undertaking for profit be entirely rejected. It may be retained, but, with the endeavour to obtain the highest business return, must be conjoined, in some way or other, the endeavour to serve the interests of the public. In particular, where any considerable want is concerned while the power to pay is wanting, the service must be undertaken at limited prices,—that is to say, valuation according to exchange value must be replaced by valuation according to natural value. Thus emerges the "public enterprise." [6]

Wieser held that the utility of each unit of the same type of goods equals the marginal utility of the last unit, for any one unit can be considered the marginal unit. In situations in which needs remain the same and supply increases, the marginal utility must fall; this is Wieser's law of supply. His law of demand is shown when needs increase and supply remains the same, thereby increasing the marginal utility. Wieser agreed with Menger that the total utility of a good is its marginal utility times the number of units available. This produces "the paradox of value." Each additional quantity of goods brings with it a diminished increment of utility and therefore a diminished increment of value. Value, and therefore utility, is zero when we have no goods or when goods become superabundant. At some point, marginal utility times the units of goods gives a declining total. Although Wieser did not spell it out, this occurs where demand becomes inelastic. Do we therefore find a larger supply of goods less useful than a smaller supply where the demand is inelastic, because it will sell for a smaller sum of money? Should we convert superfluity into want, and want into a greater want, in order to create and increase value? No, Wieser replied. The highest principle of all economy is utility. Where value and utility conflict, utility must conquer. He was confident, however, that human economies move almost entirely in the range where increasing supplies of goods increase both exchange value and total utilities; that is, demands are elastic. "In most things we are so far from having a superfluity that

[5] *Ibid.*, p. 62.
[6] *Ibid.*, p. 225.

almost every multiplication of goods shows a corresponding increase in the total value," and "value is the form in which utility is calculated." Free competition prevents entrepreneurs from restricting output to raise prices, and any one producer's supply will not lower prices significantly. If monopolies restrict output in order to raise prices, then government must take over, "but such cases are too few to call for the socialist organization of society." All we need is for the free economic order of society to be "supplemented by suitable interference on the part of governments."

> The assumptions of the simple economy are so framed as to demand the domination of the general interest. A paradox that arises in the opposition between personal power and social interest is therefore excluded. Yet even in the simple economy there are such glaring cases of this sort that the semblance of paradox is apt to arise. This mystery is most easily solved if we presuppose the extreme case in which a method of production makes possible an increase of stocks to the point of superabundance. Let us assume, for example, that by driving an artesian well or opening up a copious mountain spring it is possible to provide a town with pure water in superabundant quantities. If the principle of marginal utility were strictly adhered to, such an enterprise would never be started; a superabundant stock of free goods has a marginal utility of zero. But will such a consideration deter the public from incurring expenses for such an enterprise? Surely not. The undertaking guarantees the greatest possible benefit. The public will realize this benefit irrespective of the fact that the utility which results cannot be computed. It will be seen that the computation according to marginal utility does not simplify matters in this case, as it usually does in others. Rather it leads one astray. Hence the more complicated computation of total benefit will be resorted to.
>
> This is precisely the state of affairs where we examine all other cases of apparent paradox. Whenever the increase of the supply, computed at the marginal utility, leads to a lower numerical expression, the reckoning by marginal utility ceases to simplify and the plan of production must be drafted on the basis of total utility.
>
> Marginal utility may be used as a basis for calculations where the larger stock still gives a larger product. It is inapplicable when the product is smaller. Cases of the first kind are altogether too general; the latter are exceptional.[7]

That is, private enterprise serves society only when the demand for each firm's output is elastic. And demand will always be elastic under competitive conditions.

[7] Friedrich von Wieser, *Social Economics*, tr. by A. Ford Hinrichs (New York, 1927), p. 128. [Originally published in 1914.]

Wieser is famous for the doctrine that came to be called the opportunity-cost principle, or the alternative-cost principle. This concept turned cost of production into a subjective psychological cost. The entrepreneur who produces something for a market gives up the opportunity to produce and sell alternative commodities:

> Whenever the business man speaks of incurring costs, he has in mind the quantity of productive means required to achieve a certain end; but the associated idea of a sacrifice which his efforts demand is also aroused. In what does this sacrifice consist? What, for example, is the cost to the producer of devoting certain quantities of iron from his supply to the manufacture of some specific product? The sacrifice consists in the exclusion or limitation of possibilities by which other products might have been turned out, had the material not been devoted to one particular product. Our definition in an earlier connection made clear that cost-productive-means are productive agents which are widely scattered and have manifold uses. As such they promise a profitable yield in many directions. But the realization of one of these necessarily involves a loss of all the others. It is this sacrifice that is predicated in the concept of costs: the costs of production or the quantities of cost-productive-means required for a given product and thus withheld from other uses. . . . The business man, comparing the profits of one product with its cost, compares in truth two masses of utility.[8]

It is generally agreed that the opportunity-cost principle has wide applicability in economic affairs. Producing more automobiles may mean producing fewer houses. If school attendance increases in a full-employment economy, the labor pool is diminished and output may fall in the near future. Building a school may require giving up a hospital or giving up certain consumer or investment goods. Buying a pound of tobacco may mean sacrificing two visits to the cinema. Opportunity costs are involved when the small entrepreneur considers her implicit wage, interest, and rent costs, for she could earn these factor incomes in other employments. It is doubtful, however, that this principle contributes and explains anything fundamental about value and market price, for it seems to offer a chain of circular reasoning.

Wieser was ready and willing to rely much more on the government than were the English marginalists. He said that the private economy could take care of the wants of an individual but that the public economy should provide for the common or collective wants. The state has to defend the people against foreign enemies, provide internal security, and enforce the laws. It has to provide goods and

[8] *Ibid.*, pp. 99–100.

services whose production costs something but that have to be made available to the public free of charge, such as streets and highways. Many undertakings are necessary but give promise of profit only in the distant future, such as some railways; therefore the state has to provide them because no private individual would. Wieser strikes a modern note in his justification of government intervention to promote economic development:

> What hidden wealth may not slumber in a land favoured by nature but uncultivated, its existence suspected, even known, but out of reach owing to the general backward condition of industry, of wealth, of education, of credit, of law, or of peace! And, although, in such a case, there is as yet no secure foundation for private enterprise, what government would not regard it as a duty itself to come forward and take hold, not only in the way of general administration, but by economic undertakings which train and ripen human faculty though they may give no direct return? Sometimes only the want is there, crying urgently for satisfaction, while those who feel it have no power to pay for its satisfaction; in this case no private undertaker can do anything, and the state must step in to mitigate an evil which might grow to be a great public ill. Many other similar circumstances might be added, all acting in the same direction; that is to say, excluding private enterprise by reason of their unprofitableness, but demanding the activity of the state on account of the importance of the goods concerned.[9]

Böhm-Bawerk

Eugen von Böhm-Bawerk (1851–1914) was the third member of the triumvirate (along with Menger and Wieser) who founded and promoted the Austrian marginalist school. He was a professor of political economy at the University of Vienna and served in the Austrian government as minister of finance. He was married to Wieser's sister.

Böhm-Bawerk's major contribution to economic theory was his analysis of the element of time—not time in relation to systematic changes in the economy or in relation to economic growth, but time as a significant element in the normal course of economic affairs, influencing all values, prices, and incomes.

How Böhm-Bawerk used the concept of time may be seen in his famous agio (premium) theory of interest. His theory of interest has three bases, of which the first two are subjective. First, goods are appreciated more highly in the present than in the future. "We systematically underestimate future wants, and the goods which are to sat-

---

[9] Friedrich von Wieser, *Natural Value*, pp. 224–25.

isfy them." This is a failure of perspective, the only irrationality that Böhm-Bawerk introduced into his "economic man." People underestimate future needs because they have defective imaginations, because they have limited will power and cannot resist present extravagances even when they are aware of future needs, and because they know that life is short and uncertain and therefore they feel it is better to live it up today than to plan for the future. The second basis for interest, also subjective, derives from the idea that we are prepared to pay interest for present rather than future goods because we expect to be better off in the future. So far interest is based on consumption. The third basis for interest involves production. The process of production is lengthened, or becomes more roundabout, when more and more capital goods are produced and used to turn out final products. To fish more successfully, one builds a boat; this lengthens the process of production, and the physical product (that is, the number of fish caught) is greater than if all the time were spent fishing instead of building the boat. Until Böhm-Bawerk's time, the length of the production period was regarded as a technological datum and therefore constant. Böhm-Bawerk turned it into a variable.

From this followed the explanation of interest. It is an agio, or premium, placed on the value and price of present consumer goods. Workers and landowners receive the present value of their productive services. The increments in value, which are due to the more highly productive methods made possible by the passage of time, remain in the hands of the entrepreneur. From the entrepreneur interest flows to the capitalist who made funds available for roundabout, or capital-using, production. Therefore workers and landowners do receive the value of the product of their services, but the value is discounted to the present time.

In brief, interest *can* be paid by the entrepreneur, because the more roundabout the process of production, the more productive and efficient it becomes. Interest *must* be paid because people prefer present to future consumption.

Böhm-Bawerk agreed with the other two leaders of the Austrian marginalist school that the total utility of a good is its marginal utility times the number of units. He also agreed with them that the value of means of production depends on the value of the final goods produced, which in turn depends on the marginal utility of the final goods. The value of the final product is greater than the value of the services that produce it by the amount of interest over the period of time that elapses.

Böhm-Bawerk, like the marginalists generally, accepted Say's analysis that the economy normally tends toward full employment. He rebutted criticism of his belief that if all members of a community simultaneously save one-quarter of their incomes, production will not fall:

> The fault in the reasoning [of his critic] is indeed not far to seek. It is that one of the premises, the one which asserts that a curtailment of "consumption for immediate enjoyment" must involve also a curtailment of production, is erroneous. The truth is that a curtailment of consumption involves, not a curtailment of production generally, but only, through the action of the law of supply and demand, a curtailment in certain branches. . . . There will not, however, be a smaller production of goods generally, because the lessened output of goods ready for immediate consumption may and will be offset by an increased production of "intermediate" or capital goods.[10]

Böhm-Bawerk then quoted his critic as saying that the production of capital goods is called forth and guided only by the demand for consumer goods; if the demand for consumer goods is reduced by one-quarter, why will more capital goods than formerly be demanded and produced? This is his reply:

> The man who saves curtails his demand for *present* consumption goods but by no means his desire for pleasure-affording goods generally. This is a proposition which, under a slightly different title, has already been repeatedly and, I believe, conclusively discussed in our science both by the older writers and in contemporary literature. Economists are to-day completely agreed, I think, that the "abstinence" connected with saving is no true abstinence, that is, no final renunciation of pleasure-affording goods, but . . . a mere "waiting." The person who saves is not willing to hand over his savings without return, but requires that they be given back at some future time, usually indeed with interest, either to himself or to his heirs. Through saving not a single particle of the demand for goods is extinguished outright, but, as J. B. Say showed in a masterly way more than one hundred years ago . . . , the demand for goods, the wish for means of enjoyment is, under whatever circumstances men are found, insatiable. A person may have enough or even too much of a particular kind of goods at a particular time, but not of goods in general nor for all time. This doctrine applies particularly to saving. For the principal motive of those who save is precisely to provide for their own futures or for the futures of their heirs. This means nothing else than that they wish to secure and make certain their command over the means to

[10] This and the next quotation are from Eugen von Böhm-Bawerk, "The Function of Saving," *Annals of the American Academy of Political and Social Science*, Publication No. 304 (May 1901), pp. 62–64.

the satisfaction of their future needs, that is over consumption of goods at a future time. In other words, those who save curtail their demand for consumption goods in the present merely to increase proportionately their demand for consumption goods in the future.

Böhm-Bawerk's emphasis on the productivity of capital, his defense of interest, and his support of Say's Law of Markets were probably partly a reaction to the growing influence of Marxism in his time. In 1896 he produced a famous criticism of Marx, which was published in English translation as *Karl Marx and the Close of His System.*

Clark

John Bates Clark (1847–1938) won a worldwide reputation and represented America's great contribution to marginalist economics. He was born in Rhode Island, studied at Amherst and in Germany, and taught at Carleton, Smith, Amherst, Johns Hopkins, and Columbia. Thorstein Veblen was Clark's student at Carleton College, and his later fame was a source of great pride to Clark. The latter was undisturbed by the fact that much of Veblen's fame rested on criticisms of the kind of economic theory Clark had developed.

About 1880 Clark seems to have thought out independently the concept of marginal utility and its influence on exchange value; apparently he had not read Jevons. He not only invented the term "marginal productivity" but he presented the clearest and best analysis up to his time of the marginal productivity theory of distribution. His theory was based on the law of diminishing returns, which Clark applied to all factors of production.

In the opening paragraph of the preface to his most important book, *The Distribution of Wealth,* Clark summarized his analysis of distribution and his conclusions:

It is the purpose of this work to show that the distribution of the income of society is controlled by a natural law, and that this law, if it worked without friction, would give to every agent of production the amount of wealth which that agent creates. However wages may be adjusted by bargains freely made between individual men, the rates of pay that result from such transactions tend, it is here claimed, to equal that part of the product of industry which is traceable to the labor itself; and however interest may be adjusted by similarly free bargaining, it naturally tends to equal the fractional product that is separately traceable to capital. At the point in the economic system where titles to property originate,—where labor and capital come into possession of the amounts that the state afterwards treats as their own,—the social procedure is true to the principle on which the right of property rests. So far as it is not obstructed, it assigns to every one what he has specifically produced.[11]

Clark's theory of distribution was based on the law of diminishing returns, which he first presented in a paper at the third annual meeting of the American Economic Association in 1888. This law, originally applied to agriculture, states in modern terms that as more of any variable factor of production is added to the fixed factors, the output increases less than proportionally after a given level. In essence this law means that factors of production are not perfect substitutes for one another. The underlying assumption is that all other things, especially technology, remain unchanged, while one factor is varied. Thus, if capital, land, and entrepreneurship are kept constant while labor is added, the average output per worker will ultimately fall even though total output continues to increase. Similarly, if capital is added while the other factors remain fixed, the average return per unit of capital will eventually fall.

Clark stated the law as follows:

> The last tool adds less to man's efficiency than do earlier tools. If capital be used in increasing quantity by a fixed working force, it is subject to a law of diminishing productivity. . . . The diminishing productivity of labor, when it is used in connection with a fixed amount of capital, is a universal phenomenon. . . . This action of the general law . . . becomes the basis of a theory of distribution.[12]

Clark's marginal productivity theory of distribution under pure competition is illustrated in Figure 4. In Figure 4-a, line BC represents the marginal productivity of labor and is therefore a demand curve for labor. Diminishing returns to labor are represented by the downward slope of BC. The quantity and quality of capital are assumed to be constant. The first laborer will produce AB output. But even if a second laborer is just as efficient as the first, he or she will add less to the output than the first, because when a given quantity of capital is shared by two workers, each has less than a lone worker with the same quantity. Each additional worker adds less to total output than the worker added before. If AD workers are employed, the last worker produces an output of DC, and that is the worker's wage. If this wage were higher than DC, the capitalist would hire fewer workers. If this wage were lower than DC, more workers would be

[11] John Bates Clark, *The Distribution of Wealth: A Theory of Wages, Interest and Profits* (New York, 1899), p. v.
[12] *Ibid.*, pp. 48–50.

Figure 4   Clark's Marginal Productivity Theory of Distribution

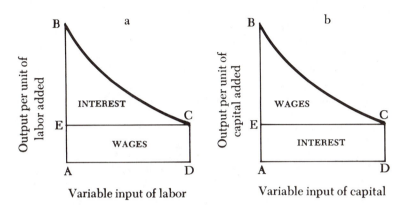

SOURCE: John Bates Clark, *The Distribution of Wealth: A Theory of Wages, Interest and Profits* (New York, Macmillan, 1899), p. 201.

hired. Equilibrium occurs when the marginal productivity of the variable factor is equal to the cost, or the earnings, of the factor. Clark's model assumes that all workers are alike in their ability to produce, so they all get a wage of *DC,* and total wages are the number of workers times the wage, represented by the area *AECD.* Since total output is *ABCD,* the surplus of *EBC* accrues to capital as interest.

In Figure 4–b we hold the quantity of labor constant and vary the supply of capital used in production. Line *BC* represents the marginal productivity of capital and is therefore a demand curve for capital. At equilibrium each unit of capital gets as its reward the marginal output of capital, which is *DC.* Total interest is *AECD,* and *EBC* is the residue that goes to labor. If the supply of capital were greater, other things being equal, the marginal productivity of capital and the rate of interest would be lower. If the supply of capital were smaller, the marginal productivity of capital and the rate of interest would be higher.

Clark considered land and capital one factor of production, and therefore he merged rent, which land receives, with interest. Clark recognized that his theory of distribution was a generalization of Ricardo's theory of rent.

Ground rent we shall study as the earnings of one kind of capital-goods—as merely a part of interest. We are now able to see that wages and interest, though they are determined by the law of final productivity, are also capable of being measured exactly as ground rent has been measured. That is to say, the Ricardian formula, which describes what is earned by a piece of land, may be used to describe what is earned by the whole fund of social capital: all interest may be made to take the form of a differential gain, or a surplus. Again, the Ricardian formula may be employed to describe the earnings of the whole force of social labor; for wages, in their entirety, are a differential gain. It is one of the most striking of economic facts that the income of all labor, on the one hand, and that of all capital, on the other, should be thus entirely akin to ground rent. They are the two generic rents, if by that term we mean differential products; and the earnings of land constitute a fraction of one of them.[13]

What about profit? "Profit has no place in such static conditions," said Clark. In a perfectly competitive society, profits tend to disappear at both ends of the productive process. "By bidding against each other in selling goods, employers make the prices smaller; and by bidding against each other in hiring labor and capital, they make wages and interest larger." In a no-profit economy goods sell at cost of production. The businessman receives wages for whatever labor he performs and interest for any capital he furnishes.

It is possible, said Clark, for profits to exist temporarily as the economy moves toward equilibrium. Profits are then a residual. In Figure 4, if wages and interest do not exhaust the total output, the residual income is pure profit claimed by the entrepreneur. In Figure 4–b, *AECD* is interest, as directly determined, and *EBC* is the remainder, which is left in the entrepreneur's hands for the payment of wages. What the entrepreneur must pay to the workers is *AECD* of Figure 4–a. If that is less than *EBC* of Figure 4–b, there is a residuum, or profit, for the entrepreneur. "Static conditions, however, exclude such a profit by making these two areas equal."

Because marginal productivity theory is concerned with the demand for factors of production, it says little about supply. Alfred Marshall emphasized supply of as well as demand for productive inputs, thereby showing how equilibrium in factor markets results in a price for each factor of production. Marginal productivity of a factor alone cannot determine its rate of reward unless the supply of a productive factor is assumed to be fixed in the short run. Let us take labor. If we define its supply in terms of total hours worked rather than number of workers, then supply is not fixed even in the short run. It is therefore apparent that while Clark's theory of distribution was far superior to that of Jevons and the Austrians, it required considerable improvement by Alfred Marshall.

[13] *Ibid.*, p. 191.

Clark claimed that his theory was static, best suited to be a purely analytical instrument. (Since his time "static" seems to have become a term of opprobrium in economics.) He assumed that all changes cease. Toward what level will prices, wages, and interest tend if labor and capital remain fixed in quantity, improvements in methods of production cease, and wants of consumers never change? We study static laws separately in order to understand what goes on in a dynamic society, he said. The truth that the world is dynamic does not invalidate the conclusions of a static theory, for static laws are nevertheless real laws that reassert themselves after every dynamic change in the economy. Clark did not develop any dynamic (historical) theories. He relied almost exclusively on what is now known as the method of comparative statics, for he compared different stationary equilibria.

In the real world, said Clark, a legal monopoly may secure a permanent profit for an entrepreneur. Labor and capital are thus prevented from moving into the favored industry, despite the pull of natural economic forces. This condition, however, is not a true static state. Like a body of tranquil water, a static state has perfect fluidity but no flow; factors of production have perfect mobility but no motion. A monopoly represents an obstruction that prevents the working out of static economic laws.

Capital is productive, and therefore interest exists. "Paying interest is buying the product of capital, as paying wages is buying the product of labor." Interest furnishes a motive for abstinence. The motive for accumulating productive wealth is the desire for permanent income. Abstinence leads to new capital goods, but no additional abstinence is required to maintain the existing capital stock. Accumulation, said Clark, is a part of economic dynamics. In the real world capital increases faster than the supply of labor, and thus its rate of earnings, interest, declines.

Capital goods are employed in the order of their productivity, so far as people judge productivity correctly. The rudest hatchet will enormously increase people's power to get firewood, but better tools developed later will increase productivity by a smaller percentage.

> As accumulation proceeds, there are always made costlier machines, representing more capital; and the product that comes from using them is a smaller fraction of their cost. The straightening of the curves in railroads is one of the ways in which capital may find investment. This may cost as much as the first making of the corresponding parts of the road themselves; but it does not liberate as much labor, in proportion to its cost, as did the building of the old and crooked road. . . . Every-

where do the forms of the capital show differences in earning power; and the owners choose first the most productive forms, and later the less productive. To this fact is due the present low rate of interest. We are utilizing the opportunities for investment that stand late in the series and are low in the scale of productivity.[14]

Most marginalists agree on the tendency for the rate of interest (or profit) to fall.

Clark's overall conclusion was that the division of the social income into wages, interest, and profit is in principle equitable. Society is not at liberty to violate the "fixed laws of distribution." If all people receive all they create, the different classes of people who combine their forces in industry have no grievances against one another. Private property is ethically justified because it is based on an ethical distribution of income.

In 1896 Clark was quite sanguine about business monopolies.[15] Their high prices attract new competitors, and their large profits are reinvested and thereby promote progress. The financial toll extracted from the public by the trusts works arithmetically. Progress, however, works geometrically through accumulation and reinvestment, which forever multiplies the fruitfulness of industry. As giant trusts invade one another's fields, they are driven to be efficient, and large firms are inherently more efficient than small ones.

In 1907, however, in his book *Essentials of Economic Theory,* dealing with what he called economic dynamics, Clark became gloomy about the trust problem. Trusts are a product of economic dynamics. Fierce and costly strife among trusts induces them to take the final step in organization, thus bringing competition to an end. Goods become scarcer and more costly.

> No description could exaggerate the evil which is in store for a society given hopelessly over to a régime of private monopoly. Under this comprehensive name we shall group the most important of the agencies which not merely resist, but positively vitiate, the action of natural economic law. Monopoly checks progress in production and infuses into distribution an element of robbery. It perverts the forces which tend to secure to individuals all that they produce. It makes prices and wages abnormal and distorts the form of the industrial mechanism. . . . Prices do not conform to the standards of cost, wages do not conform to the standard of final productivity of labor, and interest does not conform to the marginal product of capital. The system of industrial groups and sub-

[14] *Ibid.,* pp. 185–86.
[15] John Bates Clark, "The Theory of Economic Progress," *Economic Studies,* American Economic Association, Vol. I, No. 1 (April 1896), pp. 11–15.

groups is thrown out of balance by putting too much labor and capital at certain points and too little at others. Profits become, not altogether a temporary premium for improvement,—the reward for giving to humanity a dynamic impulse,—but partly the spoils of men whose influence is hostile to progress.[16]

Clark favored government regulation of monopolies to preserve competition. In effect, he urged that we ride roughshod over laissez faire to gain the goal of that doctrine—namely, a system activated by the vivifying power of competition.

Clark was optimistic over the outcome of economic dynamics if monopolies could be curbed. He saw five trends helping to promote industrial progress: (1) Population is increasing. (2) Capital is accumulating. (3) Technical processes of industry are improving. (4) Modes of organizing labor and capital are becoming more efficient. (5) Human wants are being multiplied and refined. Population is increasing less rapidly than capital, and therefore most of the benefits of progress will accrue to the wage-earning classes. Clark's conclusion was that economic harmony, based on competition, should and will prevail.

Bibliography

BÖHM-BAWERK, EUGEN VON, *The Positive Theory of Capital*, tr. by William Smart. London: Macmillan, 1891. [Originally published in 1888.]

CLARK, JOHN BATES, *The Distribution of Wealth: A Theory of Wages, Interest and Profits*. New York: Macmillan, 1899.

———, *Essentials of Economic Theory*. New York: Macmillan, 1907.

MENGER, CARL, *Principles of Economics*, tr. and ed. by James Dingwall and Bert F. Hoselitz. Glencoe, Ill.: Free Press, 1950. [Originally published in 1871.]

STIGLER, GEORGE J., *Production and Distribution Theories*. New York: Macmillan, 1941.

WIESER, FRIEDRICH VON, *Natural Value*, tr. by Christian A. Malloch. London: Macmillan, 1893. [Originally published in 1889.]

———, *Social Economics*, tr. by A. Ford Hinrichs. New York: Adelphi, 1927. [Originally published in 1914.]

[16] John Bates Clark, *Essentials of Economic Theory* (New York, 1907), pp. 375, 377.

14

The Marginalist School:
Alfred Marshall

Alfred Marshall (1842–1924), the greatest figure in the marginalist school, was the son of a cashier in the Bank of England. His father was a rather tyrannical gentleman, author of a tract called *Man's Rights and Woman's Duties.* He overworked Alfred at his studies, made him promise never to play chess because it was a waste of time, and tried to banish mathematics from the boy's life since it was irrelevant to the ministry, which the father had picked for his son's career. Young Marshall, however, rejected a scholarship at Oxford that would have led to the church, rejected the ministry, and rejected the study of "dead languages." Instead, he devoted himself to mathematics, physics, and later to economics at Cambridge. He was aided by a well-to-do uncle, for his father was too poor to pay for his tuition when he gave up the Oxford scholarship.

Marshall was a hypochondriac about his health and hypercritical about his writing. He threw much of what he wrote into the wastebasket, and in fact many of his major ideas were worked out a decade or more before they appeared in 1890 in the first edition of his *Principles of Economics.* In successive editions of that work he introduced so many qualifications, exceptions, and hesitations into his system that he weakened the clear and definite principles on which many people love to lean. Marshall criticized Jevons for rushing into print before he was ready. He himself kept portions of his book *Industry and Trade* (1919) in printed proofs for fifteen years before publication. Because he was slow to publish his work, his ideas seemed commonplace by the time they appeared. Yet he was the most influential economic theorist of his day and undoubtedly the greatest of his generation. As early as 1888 it was being said that half the economic chairs in the United Kingdom were occupied by his former students.

Marshall was the founder of modern diagrammatic economics—the bane of beginning students—which really helped elucidate certain fundamental principles. Although he was an expert mathematician, he was skeptical of the value of mathematics in economic analysis. He was also the great synthesizer, seeking to combine the best of classical economics with marginalist thinking; hence the name "neo-classical" is sometimes used synonymously with marginalist. Many of his footnotes and appendices offer hints of ideas he was aware of, but which were later worked out in greater detail by others.

Marshall defined his subject as follows: "Political Economy or Economics is a study of mankind in the ordinary business of life; it examines that part of individual and social action which is most closely connected with the attainment and with the use of the material requisites of wellbeing." [1]

Economists, he said, like other scientists, collect, arrange, interpret, and draw inferences from facts. They seek knowledge of the interdependence of economic phenomena, of cause-and-effect relationships. Every cause tends to produce a definite result if nothing occurs to hinder it. Economics is not a body of concrete truth, but an engine for the discovery of concrete truth.

We seek to discover economic laws. Any law is a general proposition, or statement of tendencies, more or less certain, more or less definite. Social laws are statements of social tendencies. Economic laws, or statements of economic tendencies, are those social laws that relate to human conduct in which the strength of the major motives can be measured by a financial price. Economics is less exact than other sciences, but progress is being made toward greater precision.

The implications of Marshall's approach and definitions are interesting. Economic laws are not natural laws that are necessarily beneficent. It is not imperative, though it may be desirable, that they be allowed to work themselves out without any restraining hand. It is not true that "we cannot repeal the law of supply and demand," as is frequently said by the uninformed. Economic laws are not like political laws, which may be broken only at the risk of suffering a penalty. The relationships among supply, demand, and price tend to

---

[1] Alfred Marshall, *Principles of Economics*, 8th ed. (London, 1920), p. 1. [Originally published in 1890.] Reprinted with permission of Macmillan & Co. Ltd., The Macmillan Company of Canada Limited, and The Macmillan Company.

produce certain results if they are allowed to work themselves out by themselves, but society can influence the outcome if it so desires. During wars, for example, the state can thwart the tendency for prices to rise by establishing price controls. This does not violate any sacrosanct law. Marshall was far less rigid than most marginalists, and his thinking left room for cautious reform, for modest departures from laissez faire.

Marshall had little to say about business cycles, partly because of his microeconomic approach. The narrower the sector we consider, the less important the cycle, as we discussed in Chapter 12 (p. 224). Marshall and others who dealt with individuals and small representative firms found it easy to ignore fluctuations. Only aggregative economics grapples with such problems.

Marginal Utility and Demand

According to Marshall, demand is based on the law of diminishing marginal utility. "The marginal utility of a thing to anyone diminishes with every increase in the amount of it he already has." Marshall introduced two important qualifications at this point. First, he was concerned with a moment in time, which was too short an interval to consider any changes in character and tastes of a given person. With the passage of time one's tastes can change, so that, for example, the more good music one hears, the stronger one's taste for it is likely to become. Again, the virtue of cleanliness and the vice of drunkenness both grow on what they feed upon. These are not exceptions to the law of diminishing marginal utility, for we exclude such long-run changes by concerning ourselves with a moment in time when dynamic changes are imperceptible.

Marshall's second qualification concerns consumer goods that are "indivisible." "A small quantity of a commodity may be insufficient to meet a certain special want; and then there will be a more than proportionate increase of pleasure when the consumer gets enough of it to enable him to attain the desired end." Marshall cited the case of wallpapering a room. If twelve pieces of wallpaper are required to cover the walls, securing all twelve pieces will yield disproportionately much more pleasure than securing only ten pieces and thus being unable to finish the job. Or, in modern terms, securing the fourth tire for an automobile will yield far more satisfaction than the first three tires together.

There is, said Marshall, one general law of demand: "The greater the amount to be sold, the smaller must be the price at which it is offered in order that it may find purchasers; or, in other words, the amount demanded increases with a fall in price, and diminishes with a rise in price."

Demand is based not only on the law of diminishing marginal utility but on the balancing of marginal utilities. In a money economy, each line of expenditure will be pushed to the point at which the marginal utility of a shilling's worth of goods will be the same as in any other direction of spending. Each person will attain this result "by constantly watching to see whether there is anything on which he is spending so much that he would gain by taking a little away from that line of expenditure and putting it on some other line." Thus the clerk who is in doubt as to whether to ride to town or to walk and have some extra little indulgence for lunch is weighing the marginal utilities of two different types of expenditures.

The subjective psychological approach of the Marshallian system dealt with pleasures and pains, desires and aspirations, incentives to action. How can we measure such intangibles? With money. Other marginalists said that the strength of a person's motives determines the amount of his money payments. Marshall, however, turned the relationship around so as to measure motivation according to the financial scale of payments. Other marginalists would say that if shoes are twice as useful to you as a hat, you are willing to pay $10 for shoes and $5 for a hat. Marshall would say that because you pay twice as much for shoes as for a hat, we can conclude that the shoes are twice as useful to you. The precise money measurement of motives in business life makes economics the most exact of the social sciences, just as the chemist's fine balance has made chemistry more exact than most physical sciences. This measuring device of economics, rough and imperfect as it is, is the best device we have to gauge man's psychological drives as expressed in the marketplace.

We cannot directly compare the amounts of pleasure that two people derive from smoking. Nor can we compare the degrees of pleasure one person gets from smoking at two different times. However, if we find a man in doubt as to whether to spend a few cents on a cigar or on a cup of tea or on riding home instead of walking, we may say that he expects equal pleasure from them. Money measures utility at the margin.

> If then we wish to compare even physical gratifications, we must do it not directly, but indirectly by the incentives which they afford to action. If the desires to secure either of two pleasures will induce people in similar circumstances each to do just an hour's extra work, or will induce men in the same rank of life and with the same means each to pay a

shilling for it; we then may say that those pleasures are equal for our purposes, because the desires for them are equally strong incentives to action for persons under similar conditions.[2]

Two people with equal incomes will not necessarily derive equal benefit from their use. Take one pound from each of them, and the intensities of the satisfaction given up may not be nearly equal. But when many people are involved, the idiosyncrasies of individuals tend to counterbalance one another. Then we can say that the money people of equal incomes give to obtain a benefit or avoid an injury is a good measure of the extent of the benefit or injury.

An increment of money, like an additional unit of goods, has greater marginal utility to a poor person than to a rich person, because the poor person has less money to begin with. How, then, can we generalize about progress, happiness, and the effects of taxation if wealth and income have such wide differences of marginal utility for people in different income groups? Here again the answer lies in large numbers. If we take whole cross sections of the income groups of society, money becomes an acceptable measuring rod:

> By far the greater number of the events with which economics deals affect in about equal proportions all the different classes of society; so that if the money measures of the happiness caused by two events are equal, it is reasonable and in accordance with common usage to regard the amounts of the happiness in the two cases as equivalent. And, further, as money is likely to be turned to the higher uses of life in about equal proportions, by any two large groups of people taken without special bias from any two parts of the western world, there is even some *prima facie* probability that equal additions to their material resources will make about equal additions to the fulness of life, and the true progress of the human race.[3]

Let us measure the strength of motives by means of money, said Marshall. Let us ascertain how much money a particular group is willing to pay as the price of something it desires or how much money must be offered to induce a group to undergo a certain effort or abstinence it dislikes.

The idea that money has diminishing marginal utility was taken over by Marshall's student and successor at Cambridge University, A. C. Pigou. Pigou's conclusion was that if a poor person enjoys a higher marginal utility for money than a rich person, total utility will be increased if incomes are more equally distributed. This basic concept of welfare economics will be discussed further in Chapter 21.

[2] *Ibid.*, pp. 15–16.
[3] *Ibid.*, p. 20.

Marshall, unlike the Austrian marginalists, asserted that the total utility of a good is the sum of the successive marginal utilities of each added unit. Therefore the price a person pays for a thing never exceeds—and seldom equals—that which he or she would be willing to pay rather than go without the desired object. Only at the margin will price generally come up to a person's willingness to pay. Thus the total satisfaction a person gets from purchasing successive units of a good exceeds the sacrifices involved in paying for the good. This surplus of satisfaction Marshall called consumer's surplus.

Marshall used tea to illustrate this idea. Suppose a man would buy one pound of tea annually if the price were twenty shillings. At fourteen shillings he would buy two pounds, at ten shillings three pounds, at six shillings four pounds, at four shillings five pounds, and at three shillings six pounds. If the price is actually two shillings, he buys seven pounds of tea annually. He gets all seven pounds at two shillings each, even though the first pound gives him twenty shillings' worth of satisfaction. His consumer's surplus is eighteen shillings on the first pound, twelve shillings on the second, and so on, for a total of forty-five shillings. The consumer's surplus increases significantly in a productive social environment that lowers the price of goods by producing them more efficiently. As an individual reaches equilibrium at a lower point on his demand curve (since he will buy more goods as they become cheaper), his consumer's surplus growth. Referring again to the "paradox of value," Marshall would have said that a large wheat crop is more useful than a small one. If we pay less for the larger crop, our consumer's surplus is larger.

The idea of consumer's surplus is more applicable to Marshall's partial equilibrium analysis than it would be to aggregative problems. His selection of tea as an illustration is especially appropriate because the amount spent on tea is only a very small part of a person's total outlay for consumer goods. The price of tea is made to vary while all other prices are kept constant. If we consider total consumption spending, the theory is inadequate because we would be counting the consumer's surplus over and over again, and we would come up with too large a figure. Surely if you had to, you would give half your income for food, or half for shelter, and of course half for clothing if the alternative were to have absolutely none; and why not half for drugs and doctors, if your life depended on them? It could be argued that from the viewpoint of a person's total consumption spending, the consumer's surplus is approximately equal to his current saving. If he now saves 10 per cent of his income, he might save nothing if prices rose much higher. Therefore he gets goods now for which he will be willing and able to pay only 10 per cent more, no matter how crucial they are to his survival. If he has a good credit rating or if he has accumulated wealth from past saving, he can pay more than an additional 10 per cent for the goods he wants, and his consumer's surplus will exceed his current saving. The concept of consumer's surplus is not so useful in macroeconomics as it is in Marshall's microeconomic analysis.

Marshall was far superior to his predecessors in handling elasticity of demand. He analyzed the subject verbally, diagrammatically, and mathematically. The only universal law pertaining to a person's desire for a commodity, Marshall said, is that, other things being equal, it diminishes with every increase in his supply of that commodity. It follows, therefore, that the lower the price, the more he will buy; the higher the price, the less he will buy. That is why the demand curve slopes downward to the right. Elasticity of demand tell us whether the diminution of desire is slow or rapid as the quantity increases. It relates the percentage drop in price to the percentage increase in quantity demanded, which of course is based on the diminishing marginal utility of the good. The numerical coefficient of the elasticity of demand is the percentage change in quantity divided by the percentage change in price.

The principle of elasticity of demand is useful for a wide range of economic problems and policies. Governments, for example, tax commodities with inelastic demands (cigarettes) rather than those with elastic demands (canned peaches). Monopolistic prices are likely to be set at higher levels where demand is inelastic (such as on antibiotics rather than on cola soft drinks). Restrictions of agricultural output result in greater gross revenue to farmers if the demand for the product is inelastic (as for wheat) and smaller revenue if the demand is elastic (as for strawberries).

Supply and Market Prices

Supply is governed by cost of production. Marshall conceived of supply as a curve rather than a point—a whole series of quantities that would be forthcoming at a whole series of prices. Cost of production is measured in terms of money, but behind the financial costs lie the psychological sacrifices—the irksomeness of working and the sacrifice of putting off consumption. For the latter Marshall used the term "waiting" rather than "abstinence." Assuming that the efficiency of production depends solely upon the exertions of the workers, the supply curve will slope upward and to the right; the higher the price, the larger the quantity supplied.

What determines market price? The cost of production of the supply, said the classical economists, meaning objective labor-time cost and the sacrifice of abstinence. Demand, said the early marginalists. Both supply and demand, said Marshall, the great synthesizer. Behind supply lie both financial and subjective costs. Behind demand lie utility and diminishing marginal utility.

> We might as reasonably dispute whether it is the upper or the under blade of a pair of scissors that cuts a piece of paper, as whether value is governed by utility or cost of production. It is true that when one blade is held still, and the cutting is effected by moving the other, we may say with careless brevity that the cutting is done by the second; but the statement is not strictly accurate, and is to be excused only so long as it claims to be merely a popular and not a strictly scientific account of what happens.[4]

Here Marshall introduced the time element into economic analysis. As a general rule, he said, the shorter the period, the greater the influence of demand on value. The longer the period, the more important the influence of cost of production on value. The reason is that the influence of cost of production takes longer to work itself out than does the influence of changes in demand. Market value is influenced by passing events, but in long periods these irregular causes neutralize one another.

For purposes of exposition, Marshall divided time into the immediate present, the short run, and the long run. Market prices refer to the present, with no time allowed for adaptation of supply to changes of demand. The corresponding market period—which may be as short as one day—is defined as that period during which the supply cannot be increased in response to a suddenly increased demand. Nor can supply be decreased immediately in response to a decline of demand, because it takes time for production to be curtailed and inventories reduced. If there were a run on shoes in a city, the messages to increase production and shipments would be flashed back to the distributors and the manufacturers. Shoes would not arrive in the retail stores, however, until a lapse of perhaps a day or two.

If a good is perishable, and if we assume that the seller is trying to maximize her profits or minimize her losses, the market supply curve is a vertical straight line. She would rather sell her fresh fish for one cent a pound than let it spoil. If the good is not perish-

[4] *Ibid.*, p. 348.

able, the sellers have reservation prices below which they will not
sell. Some sellers, however, will sell at prices well below cost of
production, perhaps because they have pressing bills to pay. The
market supply curve therefore slopes upward and to the right until it
encompasses the total quantity on the market. Then it becomes vertical, for no matter how high the market price, by definition no
greater supply can be forthcoming during the market period. Therefore demand is the most important determinant of market price. The
market supply curve is not based on cost of production, for the costs
have already been incurred and are not necessarily recoverable.

Marshall illustrated the determination of equilibrium competitive
market price with both table and chart; his table is reproduced here
as Table 4. Given a grain market, as illustrated in the table, the
amount each farmer or other seller offers for sale at any price is governed by his or her own immediate need for money and estimate of
future prices. Assuming equality of bargaining power between sellers
and buyers, the "higgling and bargaining" of the market will result in a
price close to thirty-six shillings. This price can therefore be called the
true equilibrium price, because if it were fixed at the beginning and
adhered to throughout, it would exactly equate the quantities demanded and supplied.

Marshall, with his usual cautious qualifications, analyzed those
conditions that would produce a market price above or below thirty-
six shillings (illustrated in Table 4). "We tacitly assumed that the
sum which purchasers were willing to pay, and which sellers were
willing to take, for the seven hundredth quarter would not be affected by the question whether the earlier bargains had been made
at a high or a low rate." Some sellers, however, may have been
willing to sell at thirty-six shillings because they were in urgent
need of cash. If they sold some grain at a higher price, the diminish-

Table 4   Marshall's Determination of Equilibrium Competitive
Market Price

Price	Amount holders are willing to sell	Amount buyers are willing to buy
37s.	1000 quarters	600 quarters
36s.	700 quarters	700 quarters
35s.	600 quarters	900 quarters

SOURCE: Alfred Marshall, *Principles of Economics,* 8th ed. (London, Macmillan, 1920),
p. 333. Reprinted with permission of Macmillan & Co. Ltd., The Macmillan Company
of Canada Limited, and The Macmillan Company.

ing marginal utility of ready cash could make them less willing to sell all they might have if the price had been thirty-six shillings from the beginning of the market day. In this case the sellers, beginning with a bargaining advantage, might retain a price higher than thirty-six shillings at the day's end. Conversely, suppose the market opened to the disadvantage of the sellers and they sold some grain very cheaply. The marginal utility of money would remain high for them, and they would go on selling more grain than the table indicates at a price below thirty-six shillings. The market would then close at a price below thirty-six shillings.

Marshall, the humanitarian, drew the following conclusion from this analysis:

> The exceptions are rare and unimportant in markets for commodities; but in markets for labour they are frequent and important. When a workman is in fear of hunger, his need of money (its marginal utility to him) is very great; and, if at starting, he gets the worst of the bargaining, and is employed at low wages, it remains great, and he may go on selling his labour at a low rate. That is all the more probable because, while the advantage in bargaining is likely to be pretty well distributed between the two sides of a market for commodities, it is more often on the side of the buyers than on that of the sellers in a market for labour. Another difference between a labour market and a market for commodities arises from the fact that each seller of labour has only one unit of labour to dispose of. These are two among many facts, in which we shall find, as we go on, the explanation of much of that instinctive objection which the working classes have felt to the habit of some economists, particularly those of the employer class, of treating labour simply as a commodity and regarding the labour market as like every other market; whereas in fact the differences between the two cases, though not fundamental from the point of view of theory, are yet clearly marked, and in practice often very important.[5]

To analyze the short-run period, Marshall divided costs into two types, which he called prime and supplementary costs and which we now call variable and constant costs. Variable costs, such as those for labor and raw materials, can change over the short run with a changing scale of output. Constant costs are fixed, or overhead, costs such as depreciation of the plant and top executives' salaries; they cannot be changed in the short run. In fact, the short run is defined as that period during which the variable inputs can be increased or decreased, but the fixed plant cannot be changed. In the short run all variable costs must be covered, but some of the fixed costs may not

[5] *Ibid.*, pp. 335–36.

be. For example, a railroad will continue to be operated in the short run even if part of the fixed investment is never recovered. Its losses would be greater if it went out of business, for the scrap value of a railroad is rather small. In the short run, demand and supply are both important in determining price, and the supply curve is based on variable costs.

In the long-run period, all costs are variable, and they must all be covered if the firm is to continue in business. If price rises above total cost of production, more capital will enter the industry, typically through new firms. If price falls below cost of production, capital will withdraw, probably by the exit of firms. In the long run, therefore, cost of production is the most important determinant of price and value, and it determines the location of the supply curve. In a stationary state, with monetary aberrations ruled out, cost of production would govern price and value. In a changing world, however, with adaptations to change that are imperfect and gradual, both demand and supply are important.

An increase in the amount demanded generally raises the short-period supply price. As more workers are added to a plant of a fixed size, the principle of diminishing returns to labor asserts itself. Perhaps less efficient workers are hired. In the long run, however, more factories can be built and more workers can be attracted to the industry and trained. Supply can then be increased without a rise in price or perhaps with even a decrease in price if there are certain economies in large-scale production.

Marshall defined long-run normal price as one which in the long run would exactly balance supply and demand and which would be equal to long-run total cost of production. The normal price changes with every change in the efficiency of production. Market prices tend to fluctuate around normal prices, but it is only by accident that they are ever equal. There are very gradual or secular movements of normal price caused by the gradual growth of knowledge, population, and capital and the changing conditions of demand and supply from one generation to another.

Marshall's masterly handling of the element of time was one of his many significant contributions to economic thinking.

Marshall presented the idea of producer's surplus, which is analogous to the concept of consumer's surplus discussed above; both are illustrated in Figure 5. Producer's surplus exists both for the worker (who gets a worker's surplus) and for the owner of accumulated wealth (who gets a saver's surplus). The supply curve in Figure 5

Figure 5   Consumer's and Producer's Surplus

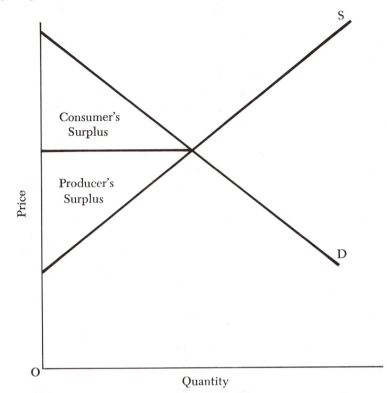

represents the cost of producing a good, which means the money cost; but behind that is the undesirability of working and the sacrifice of putting off consumption by saving. The worker finds additional hours of labor each day more and more irksome. His rate of remuneration has to be high enough to induce him to work that last hour. Although the earlier hours do not represent as great a sacrifice, he gets the same rate of wages for all his hours of work. He thereby derives a worker's surplus from all but his last hour of labor.

The supply curve of Figure 5 can also represent the saver's surplus. As discussed below, some saving would occur at very low or zero rates of interest. But postponing consumption basically represents a sacrifice according to Marshall, and the rate of interest has to be high enough to call forth the marginal supply of saving. As all savings receive the same rate of interest, some savers are receiving more than their sacrifice calls for. This is the saver's surplus.

Distribution

The distribution of income in a laissez faire economy is determined by the pricing of factors of production. Businessmen, said Marshall, must constantly compare the relative efficiency of every agent of production they employ. They must also consider the possibilities of substituting one agent for another. Horse power replaces hand power, and steam power replaces horse power. At the margin of indifference between two substitutable factors of production, their prices must be proportionate to their efficiency, or their cost must be proportionate to the money value they add to the total product. The most striking advantage of economic freedom is manifest when a businessman experiments at his own risk to find the combination of factor inputs that will yield the lowest costs in producing the output. Entrepreneurs must estimate how much net addition to the value of their total product will be contributed by an extra unit of any one factor of production. They will employ each agent up to that margin at which its net product would no longer exceed the price they would have to pay for it. Marshall based this analysis on the diminishing returns that result from the "disproportionate use of any agent of production."

Let us take labor as an example. Wages, said Marshall, are not determined by the marginal productivity of labor. Marginal productivity is the basis for the demand for labor, which is a derived demand depending on the demand by consumers for the final products. Wages, like the return to any factor of production, depend on both demand and supply. If the supply of labor increases, other things remaining constant, the marginal productivity of labor will fall, and wages will fall. If the supply of labor is reduced, the marginal productivity of labor will rise, and wages will rise. Marginal productivity by itself, therefore, does not determine wages, because varying the number of workers will produce many possible marginal productivities. It is correct, however, to say that wages measure and are equal to marginal productivity with a given supply of labor. For each employer the wage rate is fixed, so he varies the number of workers employed in order to reach equilibrium employment in his business—that level at which wages equal the marginal productivity of labor.

Another distributive share to be considered is interest. A rise in the rate of interest diminishes the use of machinery, for the businessman avoids the use of all machines whose net annual surplus is less than the rate of interest. Lower interest rates increase capital investments. The demand for the loan of capital is the aggregate of the demands of all individuals in all trades. As with final commodities, the higher the price, the less capital demanded; the lower the price, the more capital demanded. This relationship is based on diminishing marginal productivity as the quantity of a factor increases, just as the demand for consumer goods is based on diminishing marginal utility as the quantity increases.

The diminishing marginal productivity of capital as more units are acquired constitutes the demand for capital, with prices recorded in terms of rates of interest. The demand curve for capital therefore slopes down and to the right. The supply of capital is determined by saving, which depends mainly on the rate of interest. It might seem like circular reasoning to say that the supply of saving depends on the rate of interest and the rate of interest depends on the supply of saving. But Marshall spoke of supply as being a whole series of quantities that would be offered at different prices, just as he spoke of demand as a series of quantities that would be taken at different prices. With saving, as with other factors of production, the price (in this case the rate of interest) settles at the point of intersection of the demand and the supply curves.

The main motive for saving is the willingness of people to postpone consumption from the present in hopes of gaining greater reward in the future.

> Human nature being what it is, we are justified in speaking of the interest on capital as the reward of the sacrifice involved in the waiting for the enjoyment of material resources, because few people would save much without reward; just as we speak of wages as the reward of labour, because few people would work hard without reward.
>
> The sacrifice of present pleasure for the sake of future, has been called *abstinence* by economists. But this term has been misunderstood: for the greatest accumulators of wealth are very rich persons, some of whom live in luxury, and certainly do not practise abstinence in that sense of the term in which it is convertible with abstemiousness. What economists meant was that, when a person abstained from consuming anything which he had the power of consuming, with the purpose of increasing his resources in the future, his abstinence from that particular act of consumption increased the accumulation of wealth. Since, however, the term is liable to be misunderstood, we may with advantage avoid its use, and say that the accumulation of wealth is generally the result of a postponement of enjoyment, or of a *waiting* for it.[6]

[6] *Ibid.*, pp. 232–33.

Marshall recognized that other motives for saving might also be important. He mentioned family affection, force of habit, miserliness, magnitude of the income, and prudence in wishing to provide for the future. Some saving might therefore occur even if interest were zero or negative. If a man wanted a certain annuity for his old age, he might save less at a high rate of interest than at a low rate. But these are all exceptional cases. A fall in the interest rate will generally induce people to consume a little more in the present, and a rise will induce them to consume a little less. Thus interest tends toward an equilibrium level that equalizes the aggregate demand for capital in a market with the aggregate supply forthcoming at that rate.

According to Marshall, normal profits include interest, the earnings of management, and the supply price of business organization. Interest has already been discussed. The earnings of management are a payment for a specialized form of labor. Profits, the supply price of business organization, are a reward to entrepreneurship, that fourth factor of production that was added to those of the classical school—land, labor, and capital.

Marshall incorporated Ricardian rent theory into his system:

> The amount of . . . rent is itself governed by the fertility of land, the price of the produce, and the position of the margin: it is the excess of the value of the total returns which capital and labour applied to land do obtain, over those which they would have obtained under circumstances as unfavourable as those on the margin of cultivation. . . . The cost of production on the margin of the profitable application of capital and labour is that to which the price of the whole produce tends, under the control of the general conditions of demand and supply: it does not govern price, but it focusses the causes which do govern price.[7]

For the individual producer, said Marshall, land is merely a particular form of capital. There is not much difference between land and buildings; both are subject to diminishing returns as their owner tries to force more and more from them. For society as a whole, however, the supply of land is permanent and fixed. If one person has land, there is less for others to have. In contrast, if one were to invest in improvements of land or in buildings on it, he would not appreciably curtail the opportunities of others to invest capital in similar improvements.

In the short run, Marshall wrote, land and manufactured capital goods are similar because the supplies of both are fixed. Therefore the return to old capital investments is something akin to rent, and

---

[7] *Ibid.*, pp. 427–28.

Marshall called it quasi-rent. Interest is the earnings on "free," or "floating," capital or on new investments of capital; quasi-rent is the earnings on old capital investments in the short run. Even if part of the economic rent of land is taxed away, landowners will continue to rent out land, assuming that they wish to maximize their returns instead of withdrawing the land from use in a fit of pique. Similarly, a tax on part of the earnings on fixed capital will not interfere with production *in the short run,* because it is better to lose part of one's normal profits than to lose everything except scrap value. This analysis assumes that the capital is specialized and has no alternative uses. In the long run, of course, quasi-rent disappears, for a normal return to the fixed capital investment is essential if the investment is to be renewed and the business perpetuated.

This is another way of saying that only variable costs influence prices in the short run. Prices in turn determine the earnings of the fixed investment. In the long run, however, both variable costs and normal returns on the fixed investment must be covered, and they both affect price.

> To sum up the whole in a comprehensive, if difficult, statement:—Every agent of production, land, machinery, skilled labour, unskilled labour, etc., tends to be applied in production as far as it profitably can be. If employers, and other business men, think that they can get a better result by using a little more of any one agent they will do so. They estimate the net product (that is the net increase of the money value of their total output after allowing for incidental expenses) that will be got by a little more outlay in this direction, or a little more outlay in that; and if they can gain by shifting a little of their outlay from one direction to another, they will do so.
>
> Thus then the uses of each agent of production are governed by the general conditions of demand in relation to supply: that is, on the one hand, by the urgency of all the uses to which the agent can be put, taken together with the means at the command of those who need it; and, on the other hand, by the available stocks of it. And equality is maintained between its values for each use by the constant tendency to shift it from uses, in which its services are of less value to others in which they are of greater value, in accordance with the principle of substitution.[8]

Increasing and Decreasing Cost Industries

A key analytic device for Marshall was his concept of the "representative firm," which for him was the typical nineteenth-century small sole proprietorship.

[8] *Ibid.*, pp. 521–22.

We may read a lesson from the young trees of the forest as they struggle upwards through the benumbing shade of their older rivals. Many succumb on the way, and a few only survive; those few become stronger with every year, they get a larger share of light and air with every increase of their height, and at last in their turn they tower above their neighbours, and seem as though they would grow on for ever, and for ever become stronger as they grow. But they do not. One tree will last longer in full vigour and attain a greater size than another; but sooner or later age tells on them all. Though the taller ones have a better access to light and air than their rivals, they gradually lose vitality; and one after another they give place to others, which, though less material strength, have on their side the vigour of youth.

And as with the growth of trees, so was it with the growth of businesses as a general rule before the great recent development of vast joint-stock companies, which often stagnate, but do not readily die. Now that rule is far from universal, but it still holds in many industries and trades. Nature still presses on the private business by limiting the length of the life of its original founders, and by limiting even more narrowly that part of their lives in which their faculties retain full vigour. And so, after a while, the guidance of the business falls into the hands of people with less energy and less creative genius, if not with less active interest in its prosperity. If it is turned into a joint-stock company, it may retain the advantages of division of labour, of specialized skill and machinery: it may even increase them by a further increase of its capital; and under favourable conditions it may secure a permanent and prominent place in the work of production. But it is likely to have lost so much of its elasticity and progressive force, that the advantages are no longer exclusively on its side in its competition with younger and smaller rivals.

When therefore we are considering the broad results which the growth of wealth and population exert on the economies of production, the general character of our conclusions is not very much affected by the facts that many of these economies depend directly on the size of the individual establishments engaged in the production, and that in almost every trade there is a constant rise and fall of large businesses, at any one moment some firms being in the ascending phase and others in the descending. For in times of average prosperity decay in one direction is sure to be more than balanced by growth in another.[9]

Marshall's representative firm served at least three major purposes in his analysis. First, in speaking of the normal cost of producing a commodity, he referred to the expenses of a representative producer who is neither the most efficient nor the least efficient in the industry. Second, this analytic device showed that an industry can be in long-period equilibrium even though some firms are growing and

[9] *Ibid.*, pp. 315–17.

others declining; they simply neutralize each other. Third, even though the representative firm does not inherently increase its efficiency, it can experience falling costs of production as the industry expanded.

Marshall thought that an increased volume of production in an industry will generally increase the size and therefore the internal economies possessed by a representative firm; it will always increase the external economies to which the firm has access. Therefore, he said, the cost of production in terms of labor and sacrifice will fall if the volume of output of an industry expands.

Internal economies depend on the efficiencies introduced by an individual firm. As the firm grows larger, it can enjoy more specialization and mass production, using more and better machines to lower the cost of production. Buying and selling also become more economical as a firm's size increases. Larger firms can secure credit on easier terms, and they can utilize high-grade managerial ability more effectively.

External economies are external to the firm; they depend on the general development of the industry. To use our own example: The first automobile plant located in Detroit is far less efficient than the fiftieth plant, even if technology remains constant. The first entrepreneur has to train his labor force. He may draw steel from Pittsburgh, rubber tires from New Orleans, and glass from southern California. The fiftieth plant draws its labor from a pool of skilled workers who are already trained and living in the area. Suppliers build plants nearby to serve the expanding automotive industry, so steel, rubber tires, and glass are at hand; these supplies become cheaper both because transport costs are reduced and because they are mass produced in industries that expand to meet the growing needs of the automobile industry. Perhaps, in addition, railroad, highway, and water transportation facilities are expanded as the volume of traffic between Detroit and the rest of the country expands. These are typical external economies that a growing industry experiences.

Another external economy arises when, for example, a coal mine requires less water to be pumped from its shafts as the number of mines operating in the neighborhood increases. As water is removed from each mine, the underground water level is lowered for all, thereby reducing the pumping costs for everybody.

External economies are available to all firms in an industry. However, if internal economies grow with the size of the firm, how can competition be maintained? If the larger the firm grows the more efficient it becomes, will this not lead to monopoly? Marshall's concept of the representative firm provided the answer. The decline and death of the entrepreneur will lead to the decline and death of his firm. Businesses, Marshall thought, will typically not last long enough to realize all the benefits of an ever-increasing scale of production. New entrepreneurs will elbow their way into the business arena and renew the process of increasing the size and efficiency of their firms.

Marshall used the law of diminishing returns to argue that agriculture is subject to diminishing returns in the long run. An increase in the capital and labor applied in the cultivation of a fixed supply of land will cause a less-than-proportionate increase in the product, unless agricultural improvements counteract this tendency. Marshall felt certain that the latter force is the weaker. Eventually, increased applications of capital and labor to land will result in diminishing increments of extra produce. The principle of diminishing returns should, of course, be applied to every factor of production, assuming that the others are kept constant. Marshall did not develop this idea except in passing while discussing other matters. When he did discuss it, he treated it as a historic law. One should not, however, assume that the law implies change, for it has validity only in a static, timeless world, with technology in particular remaining constant. Nonetheless, the law of diminishing returns remains valid and useful.

Marshall used increasing and diminishing returns in industry in another sense: If all factors of production used in an industry expand, will the cost per unit of output rise or fall? (We now call this decreasing and increasing returns to scale.) He thought that we generally have increasing returns in industry; as labor and capital expand, organization and efficiency improve. Only when we rely heavily on nature, as in agriculture, do we have diminishing returns. Where the actions of the laws of increasing and diminishing returns are balanced we have the law of constant returns: Expanded output is obtained through a proportionate expansion of both labor and the sacrifice of waiting. With enlarged output of blankets, for example, the increasing cost of wool due to the need to bring poorer land into use to obtain this extra wool may be exactly counterbalanced by the growing efficiency of manufacturing blankets, and we will have constant returns. In most manufacturing, Marshall thought, the cost of raw materials counts for little, and the law of increasing returns is almost unopposed.

Marshall drew an optimistic conclusion from this analysis. Although there may be disadvantages resulting from a rapid growth of population, the final outcome is likely to be favorable. The collective efficiency of a people can be expected to increase more than proportionally to their increased numbers.

If an industry obeys the law of constant returns, an increased demand for its product will in the long run not affect the price. If it is an industry with diminishing returns, an increase in demand will raise the product's price; more will be produced, but not so much more as would be produced if it obeyed the law of constant returns. If the industry follows the law of increasing returns, increased demand will ultimately cause the price to fall, and more will be produced than if it were an industry of constant returns.

This analysis led Marshall to some interesting policy conclusions. An industry of increasing returns, especially in a new country, will produce more cheaply if it expands under tariff protection—the "infant industry" argument. The difficulty, he said, is that power politics may wrench this policy from its proper uses. He did recommend that industries of diminishing returns have their products taxed. By restricting their output in this way, their unit costs of production exclusive of the tax will fall. The revenue received should be used to subsidize the industries of increasing returns. As their output expands, their unit costs and selling prices fall. The consumers will thereby benefit from such taxes and subsidies.

The implication of this argument is that competitive prices and laissez faire do not necessarily result in maximum satisfaction to the community. Marshall was very much aware of this. If producers are very much poorer than consumers, he said, restricting supply and raising prices will increase aggregate satisfaction; conversely, if consumers are poorer than producers, expanding production and selling commodities at a loss will increase total satisfaction. Again, if an individual spends income in such a way as to increase the demand for the services of the poor and thereby increase their incomes, something more is added to the total happiness than if an equal amount were added to the incomes of the rich. If a person spends income on things that obey the law of diminishing returns, those things become more expensive for the neighbors, thereby lowering their real incomes.

> These conclusions, it will be observed, do not by themselves afford a valid ground for government interference. But they show that much remains to be done, by a careful collection of the statistics of demand and supply, and a scientific interpretation of their results, in order to discover what are the limits of the work that society can with advantage do

towards turning the economic actions of individuals into those channels in which they will add the most to the sum total of happiness.[10]

When Marshall died in 1924 John Maynard Keynes proclaimed him the "greatest economist in the world for a hundred years," but one cannot help wondering if Keynes would have subscribed to his earlier judgment in later years. Few would doubt, however, that Marshall was the most influential economic theorist of his day. Most economists would include him, with Adam Smith, David Ricardo, and John Stuart Mill, as one of the four greatest figures of the classical and marginalist schools during the last two hundred years.

Bibliography

MARSHALL, ALFRED, *Industry and Trade*, 4th ed. New York: Kelley, 1970 [Originally published in 1919.]

———, *Money, Credit and Commerce*. London: Macmillan, 1923.

———, *Principles of Economics*, 8th ed. London: Macmillan, 1920. [Originally published in 1890.]

PIGOU, A. C., ed., *Memorials of Alfred Marshall*. New York: Kelley, 1956. [Originally published in 1925.]

[10] *Ibid.*, p. 475.

15

The Marginalist School:
Monetary Economics

There is no separate school of monetary economics as such, and some economic schools emphasize monetary phenomena more than others. The classical and Marxist schools and the early marginalists, for example, regarded money merely as a veil that had to be pulled aside to examine the real world; they felt that money and prices were subordinate to the more basic factors. Others, such as the later marginalists and Mitchell and Keynes, combined monetary analysis with their study of fundamental economic processes. Money in economic theory was destined to increase in importance over the years with the growth of banking, credit, and fluctuations in the economic cycle as well as the increasingly important monetary policies of the central banks and governments.

The four monetary economists discussed in this chapter are all in the neoclassical, or marginalist, tradition. Their contribution to economic theory was twofold. First, they explored an area that had been neglected but was now growing in importance, and that therefore required emphasis. Second, they helped integrate monetary analysis into general economic theory. It is important to note, however, that they may have exaggerated the role of money; it is easy to overcompensate for past shortcomings by allowing the pendulum to swing too far in the opposite direction.

The monetary economists of the marginal school differed noticeably from the nonmonetary theorists in the same school because the monetary theorists had to deal with aggregative analysis, such as total demand, total income, total saving and investment. A bifurcation within the school ensued. The nonmonetary branch looked at the individual person's or firm's real sacrifices, income, consumption, saving, and investment. The monetary branch aggregated these categories for the whole economy, emphasizing monetary factors instead of real factors. It remained for Keynes to fully synthesize monetary and nonmonetary economics, although credit is due Wicksell as an important forerunner of Keynes.

Wicksell

John Gustav Knut Wicksell (1851–1926) was born in Stockholm of a middle-class family. After studying mathematics, languages, literature, and philosophy as an undergraduate at the University of Uppsala, he took advanced degrees in mathematics and physics there. He was elected president of the student body at the university and became increasingly active in the philosophical, political, and literary debates and activities of student circles. As a popular lecturer and pamphleteer he explored such social questions as the population problem, birth control, emigration, alcoholism and its causes, prostitution, the future of marriage, the right to universal suffrage, and the need for direct progressive income taxes. He was both a scholar and a social reformer, a combination that in his day was often considered incompatible.

Wicksell's interest in social problems and reform led him to a study of economics. From 1885 to 1890 he studied at universities in England, France, Germany, and Austria. His most memorable experience in the study of economic theory was his discovery in a Berlin bookshop of Böhm-Bawerk's book on capital theory soon after its publication in 1888; the book had a profound influence on his own economic thinking.

Wicksell obtained a modest government subsidy in 1896 to begin his monetary studies in Berlin. Otherwise, his small irregular income depended on journalism and popular lecturing on social questions, as well as on occasional private tutoring and high school teaching. He received his first small academic appointment in 1896 and a professorship in 1901 at fifty. In 1909 Wicksell served a brief prison term for making ironical remarks on church doctrine.

Wicksell made several major contributions to economic thinking: (1) an analysis of the role of interest rates in achieving an equilibrium of prices or in generating cumulative inflationary or deflationary movements; (2) recognition of the potential contribution of the government and the central bank in retarding or promoting price stability; and (3) the modern aggregate supply-demand or savings-investment approach to monetary phenomena that was one of the sources for Keynesian economics. Keynes himself complimented Wicksell as an important precursor of his own ideas. Wicksell's objective was to synthesize monetary theory, business-cycle theory, public finance, and price theory into one system.

To Wicksell, monetary theory turned on one main question: Why do prices rise or fall? To answer the question, he turned to an analysis of interest rates. The money rate of interest, he said, depends on supply and demand for real capital that is not yet invested. The supply of capital flows from those who postpone consuming part of their income and thereby accumulate wealth. The demand for capital depends on the profits that can be realized from its use, or its marginal productivity.

> The rate of interest at which *the demand for loan capital and the supply of savings* exactly agree, and which more or less corresponds to the expected yield on the newly created capital, will then be the normal or natural real rate. It is essentially variable. If the prospects of the employment of capital become more promising, demand will increase and will at first exceed supply; interest rates will then rise and stimulate further saving at the same time as the demand from entrepreneurs contracts until a new equilibrium is reached at a slightly higher rate of interest. And at the same time equilibrium must *ipso facto* obtain—broadly speaking, and if it is not disturbed by other causes—in the market for goods and services, so that wages and prices will remain unchanged. The *sum* of money incomes will then usually exceed the money value of the consumption goods actually produced, but the excess of income—i.e. what is annually saved and invested in production—will not produce any demand for present goods but only for labour and land for future production.[1]

The above applies only to credit between individuals. Banks, however, complicate matters, for unlike private persons, they are not restricted in their lending to their own funds or even to the funds placed at their disposal by savers. Because banks create credit they can extend loans even at very low rates of interest. If they lend money at materially lower rates than the normal or natural rate as defined in the quotation above, saving will be discouraged, and the demand for consumption goods and services will rise. Simultaneously entrepreneurs will seek more capital investments because of

[1] Knut Wicksell, *Lectures on Political Economy*, Vol. II, tr. by E. Classen (London, 1935), p. 193. [Originally published in 1906.] Reprinted with permission of Routledge & Kegan Paul Ltd.

the greater net profits to be realized as the cost of borrowing money falls. As investment increases, more income accrues to workers, land-owners, the owners of raw materials, and so forth. The prices of consumption goods therefore begin to rise. Juxtaposed with this increased demand for both consumption and investment goods, however, is an unchanged or even diminished supply of goods as saving diminishes, assuming that we start at a position of full employment. Anticipations of price increases will cause prices to rise even more. Equilibrium is disturbed, and a cumulative upward price movement begins. The fundamental cause is a bank or market rate of interest below the normal or natural rate that would bring into balance real saving and real investment at constant prices. The natural rate of interest is that rate that is equal to the marginal productivity of capital. Prices will rise without limit so long as the natural rate of interest exceeds the bank rate.

Conversely, prices will fall if the bank rate of interest is above the natural or normal rate. Only when the two rates of interest are equal will the banking and credit system be neutral and prices stable.

Wicksell's analysis of interest rates and his predilection for reform led him to emphasize the role of government and the central bank in promoting stability. He was perhaps the first to advocate stabilizing wholesale prices by controlling discount and interest rates, in his book *Interest and Prices*, published in 1898.

The principal cause of cyclical fluctuations, he said, is the fact that technological and commerical progress has not maintained the same rate of advance as the increase in needs, especially of an expanding population. With rising demand, people seek to exploit the situation by increasing investment; but it takes time to increase the volume of output through new discoveries, inventions, and other improvements. The rush to convert large masses of liquid capital into fixed capital produces a boom. If, however, the technical improvements are already in operation and no new ones promise a profit in excess of the margin of risk, depression occurs.

We have, then, the real cause of business fluctuations, which Wicksell did not pursue in great depth, and the monetary cause, which is the discrepancy between the market rate of interest and the natural rate. To eliminate this latter cause we need a rate of interest on loans that neither raises nor lowers commodity prices because it is equal to the natural rate of interest—that is, the rate that would be determined by supply and demand if money did not exist and all lending were in the form of real capital goods. The natural rate of interest itself, however, is not fixed. It fluctuates with all the real causes of fluctuations in the economy, such as the efficiency of production, the supply of fixed and liquid capital, the supply of labor and land, and so on. An exact coincidence of the market and natural rates of interest is therefore unlikely, unless bankers do something about it.

This does not mean that the banks ought actually to *ascertain* the natural rate before fixing their own rates of interest. That would, of course, be impracticable, and would also be quite unnecessary. For the current level of commodity prices provides a reliable test of the agreement or diversion of the two rates. The procedure should rather be simply as follows: *So long as prices remain unaltered the banks' rate of interest is to remain unaltered. If prices rise, the rate of interest is to be raised; and if prices fall, the rate of interest is to be lowered; and the rate of interest is henceforth to be maintained at its new level until a further movement of prices calls for a further change in one direction or the other.*

The more promptly these changes are undertaken the smaller is the possibility of considerable fluctuations of the general level of prices; and the smaller and less frequent will have to be the changes in the rates of interest. If prices are kept fairly stable the rate of interest will merely have to keep step with such rise or fall in the natural rate as is inevitable.

In my opinion, the main cause of the instability of prices resides in the inability or failure of the banks to follow this rule. . . .

The objection that a further reduction in rates of interest cannot be to the advantage of the banks may possibly in itself be perfectly correct. A fall in rates of interest may diminish the banks' margin of profit more than it is likely to increase the extent of their business. I should like then in all humility to call attention to the fact that the banks' prime duty is not to earn a great deal of money but to provide the public with a medium of exchange—and to provide this medium in *adequate measure*, to aim at stability of prices. In any case, their obligations to society are enormously more important than their private obligations, and if they are ultimately unable to fulfil their obligations to society along the lines of private enterprise—which I very much doubt—then they would provide a worthy activity for the State.[2]

Wicksell feared that the growing production and stock of gold would inflate currency, thus causing interest rates to fall and prices to rise. Therefore the free coinage of gold should be suspended, and the world should pass over to an international paper standard. Such a standard is usually regarded as a means of meeting a growing scar-

[2] Knut Wicksell, *Interest and Prices*, tr. by R. F. Kahn (London, 1936), pp. 189–90. [Originally published in 1898.] Reprinted with permission of Macmillan & Co. Ltd. (London).

city of gold, but it can just as well be used to correct an overabundance.

> In any case, such a prospect need not, on closer investigation, provide cause for consternation. On the contrary, once it had come into being it would perhaps be the present system which would sound like a fairy tale, with its rather senseless and purposeless sending hither and thither of crates of gold, with its digging up of stores of treasure and burying them again in the recesses of the earth. The introduction of such a scheme offers no difficulty, at any rate on the theoretical side. Neither a central bureau nor international notes would be necessary. Each country would have its own system of notes (and small change). These would have to be redeemable at par by every central bank, but would be allowed to circulate only inside the one country. It would then be the simple duty of each credit institution to regulate its rate of interest, both relatively to, and in unison with, other countries, so as both to maintain in equilibrium the international balance of payments and to stabilise the general level of world prices. In short, the regulation of prices would constitute the prime purpose of bank rate, which would no longer be subject to the caprices of the production and consumption of gold or of the demand for the circulation of coins. It would be perfectly free to move, governed only by the deliberate aims of the banks.[3]

Wicksell recognized the inadequacy of the purely competitive model in retail markets, thus anticipating by several decades the theory of monopolistic or imperfect competition proposed by Edward H. Chamberlin and Joan Robinson in the early 1930's (discussed in the following chapter). It is remarkable that thirty-two years passed between Wicksell's statement of the problem and its further systematic development, but the idea of pure competition was central to marginalist thinking, and its revision required overwhelming evidence of monopolistic tendencies in the economy.

In 1901 Wicksell wrote that retailers usually have a fixed circle of customers, and this fact enables them to have fixed rather than fluctuating prices. While retail prices do respond to changes in wholesale prices, they do so only after a time lag and in modified form.

> Practically every retailer possesses, within his immediate circle, what we may call an actual sales *monopoly*, even if, as we shall soon see, it is based only on the ignorance and lack of organization of the buyers. He cannot, of course, like a true monopolist, raise prices at will—only in places remote from trade centres can a considerable local rise in prices occur—but if he maintains the same prices and qualities as his competitors, he can almost always count upon his immediate neighbourhood for

[3] *Ibid.*, pp. 193–94.

customers. The result is not infrequently an *excess of retailers,* apparently for the convenience, but really *to the injury, of the consumers.* If, for example, two shops of the same kind are situated at different ends of the same street, it would be natural that their respective markets would meet in the middle of the street. Now if a new shop of the same kind is opened in the middle of the street each of the others will, sooner or later, lose some of its customers to the new shop, since the people living round the middle of the street believe that if they get the same goods at the same price they are saving time and trouble by making their purchases at the nearest shop. In this, however, they are mistaken, for the original shops which have now lost some of their customers without being able to reduce their overhead expenses to a corresponding degree, will gradually be compelled to raise their prices—and the same applies to the new competitors who have been obliged from the beginning to content themselves with a smaller turnover. . . . The correct remedy, unless one of the competitors (such as a great store) manages to overshadow all the others, is clearly the formation of some form of organization among buyers. But so long as such an association does not exist— and between persons in different positions in life and without more intimate bonds it is extremely difficult to establish—the anomaly must remain that competition may sometimes raise prices instead of always lowering them, as one would expect.[4]

Wicksell indicated that with a complete monopoly the volume of sales is artificially restricted to the point that yields maximum profits. Every rise in price reduces the quantity of goods demanded. "But so long as the falling off in demand is less than proportionate to the increased profit per unit of the commodity resulting from the higher price, the total net profit . . . will increase." Conversely, when the decrease in sales is more than proportionate to the increased profit per unit, further price increases are disadvantageous. It is important to note, said Wicksell, that fixed, or overhead, costs have no influence whatever in determining the most profitable monopoly price; only variable costs are to be considered.

In discussing the aggregate savings-investment problem, Wicksell analyzed the theory of forced saving. This was not a new idea. Bentham had presented this doctrine, which he called "forced frugality," in his *Manual of Political Economy,* written by 1804 but published in 1843. In analyzing the role of government in increasing capital, Bentham spoke of taxes and paper money as being forced frugality. Creating paper money, he said, is a kind of indirect taxation, for it acts as an income tax on those people with fixed incomes.

[4] Knut Wicksell, *Lectures on Political Economy,* Vol. I, tr. by E. Classen (London, 1934), pp. 87–88. [Originally published in 1901.]

John Stuart Mill in "On Profits, and Interest" in his *Essays on Some Unsettled Questions of Political Economy*, written in 1829 or 1830, stated that if bankers depreciate the currency, it operates to a certain extent as a forced accumulation. Léon Walras clearly stated the theory of forced saving in 1879, probably inspiring Wicksell and through him all the later German authors who dealt with the problem.

Wicksell hypothesized a case in which a new enterprise was financed through a bank loan—pure credit creation—without a corresponding accumulation of real capital. Assuming full employment at the outset, more land and labor would be employed in producing capital goods than if there were no credit creation to finance a new enterprise, leaving less available for turning out consumer goods. Nevertheless the demand for articles of consumption would increase rather than diminish, for entrepreneurs would bid up the prices of land and labor as they expanded investment. With the resulting rise in prices, entrepreneurs would acquire fewer capital goods than they originally contemplated based on the size of the loans they negotiated. At the same time consumption would be restricted as prices rose. This enforced restriction would in fact constitute the real accumulation of capital that must be achieved if capital investment is to increase. "The *real saving* which is necessary for the period of investment to be increased is in fact *enforced*—at exactly the right moment—on consumers as a whole."

Wicksell took from the marginalist and classical schools the idea that the normal tendency of the economy is to reach equilibrium at full employment; what is not spent on consumption is normally devoted to investment. Depressions are primarily monetary phenomena and only secondarily imbalances in real factors caused by changes in a dynamic economy. It remained for Keynes to deal more adequately with the problems of unemployment. Wicksell's historical significance lies in his combining general and monetary theory and in his developing a theory of the cumulative process of expansion and contraction of business activity.

Fisher

Irving Fisher (1867–1947) of Yale, a mathematician turned economist, was a man of many projects. In addition to his vast written output in economics he published several highly successful mathematical textbooks. Having suffered from tuberculosis as a young man, he turned to diet and health fads and cultivated these interests all his

life, writing several popular books on how to be healthy and live
long. He advocated eugenics and joined the antiliquor and anti-
tobacco crusades. Long before World War I he proposed a league of
nations to preserve peace. He invented many mechanical gadgets,
one of which was the visible card-index system that could be
mounted on a rotary stand; eventually Fisher received about a million dollars for this, his only commercially successful invention. The
fortune he and his wife possessed, which grew to about nine million
dollars in the stock market, was lost in the crash of 1929.

Fisher restated and amplified the old quantity theory of money
based on the equation of exchange. The key question he asked was,
What determines the purchasing power of money—or its reciprocal,
the level of prices? Fisher saw five determinants: (1) the volume of
currency in circulation, (2) its velocity of circulation, (3) the volume
of bank deposits subject to check, (4) its velocity, and (5) the volume
of trade. Monetary economics, the branch that handles these five
regulators of purchasing power, is an exact science, Fisher said, capable of precise formulation, demonstration, and statistical verification.

Fisher's equation of exchange was stated as

$$MV + M'V' = PT$$

where M is the quantity of currency, V is its velocity of circulation,
M' is the quantity of demand deposits, V' is its velocity of circulation, P is the average level of prices, and T is the quantity of goods
and services sold, with each unit being counted each time it is sold
or resold.

Prices vary directly with the quantity of money (M and M') and
the velocity of circulation (V and V') and vary inversely with the
volume of trade (T). The first of these three relations is the most important, said Fisher; it constitutes the "quantity theory of money."

Fisher assumed that M', the volume of demand deposits, tends to
hold a fixed relation to M, the quantity of currency in circulation; that
is, deposits are normally a relatively fixed definite multiple of currency. There are two reasons for this: First, bank reserves are kept in
fixed definite ratio to bank deposits. Second, individuals, firms, and
corporations maintain fairly stable ratios between their cash transactions and their check transactions, as well as between their currency
and deposit balances. If the ratio between M and M' is temporarily
disturbed, certain factors automatically come into play to restore it.
Individuals will deposit surplus cash, or they will cash surplus deposits. Transition periods of rising or falling prices will also disturb
the relation between M and M' but only temporarily. As long as the

normal relation holds in the long run, the existence of bank deposits magnifies but does not distort the effect on the level of prices produced by the quantity of currency in circulation.

To propound a cause-and-effect relationship between the quantity of currency and the price level, Fisher also had to assume that the velocity of circulation and the volume of trade are constant. He recognized that both fluctuate over the business cycle, but they always tend to return to an equilibrium level. The tendency toward stability in T also depends on full-employment equilibrium, for with considerable unemployment an increase in M might very well increase T instead of P. The volume of trade also grows in the long run with the change in population, efficiency of production, and so on. Yet in the short run, with a fully employed economy, the quantity of currency in circulation normally determines the price level.

> We come back to the conclusion that the velocity of circulation either of money or deposits is independent of the quantity of money or of deposits. No reason has been, or, so far as is apparent, can be assigned, to show why the velocity of circulation of money, or deposits, should be different, when the quantity of money, or deposits, is great, from what it is when the quantity is small.
>
> There still remains one seeming way of escape from the conclusion that the sole effect of an increase in the quantity of money in circulation will be to increase prices. It may be claimed—in fact it has been claimed—that such an increase results in an increased volume of trade. We now proceed to show that (except during transition periods) the volume of trade, like the velocity of circulation of money, is independent of the quantity of money. An inflation of the currency cannot increase the product of farms and factories, nor the speed of freight trains or ships. The stream of business depends on natural resources and technical conditions, not on the quantity of money. The whole machinery of production, transportation, and sale is a matter of physical capacities and technique, none of which depend on the quantity of money. . . . We conclude, therefore, that a change in the quantity of money will not appreciably affect the quantities of goods sold for money.
>
> Since, then, a doubling in the quantity of money: (1) will normally double deposits subject to check in the same ratio, and (2) will not appreciably affect either the velocity of circulation of money or of deposits or the volume of trade, it follows necessarily and mathematically that the level of prices must double. . . .
>
> We may now restate, then, in what causal sense the quantity theory is true. It is true in the sense that one of *the normal effects of an increase in the quantity of money is an exactly proportional increase in the general level of prices.*[5]

[5] Irving Fisher, *The Purchasing Power of Money* (New York, 1911), pp. 154–57.

If the quantity theory of money is valid, we have a way to stabilize the overall price level and thereby stabilize the economy: Control the quantity of currency in circulation. This might be achieved with irredeemable paper money, but Fisher took a dim view of that solution before the Great Depression of the 1930's. Paper money not redeemable in gold tends to arouse public distrust, be too easily overissued by the monetary authorities, provoke speculation, and align debtors in a campaign for inflation. The plan he advocated would make paper money redeemable on demand, not in any required weight or coin of gold, but in a quantity of gold that would represent constant purchasing power. The purchasing power of the dollar would therefore remain constant. The more gold in a dollar, the more a dollar would buy and the lower prices would be, and vice versa.

According to Fisher's plan, we would first abandon gold coins and use only gold certificates—paper money redeemable in gold bullion. The government would vary the quantity of gold bullion it would give or take for a paper dollar; that is, it would vary the price of gold in order to maintain stability in the general price level. If the price index rose 1 per cent, thereby indicating that the purchasing power of the dollar was too low, the weight of the gold dollar would be increased by 1 per cent. If the price index fell 1 per cent below par, the weight of the gold dollar would be reduced by 1 per cent. If this weight change does not fully correct the undesirable price change, further changes in the same direction would be called for.

If a flood of gold poured into our circulation from domestic or foreign sources, redundant gold certificates would cause a price rise, according to the quantity theory of money. Decreasing the price of gold would reduce the supply of gold certificates for two reasons: First, the deposit of gold with the government would be discouraged. Second, people would exchange their paper money for gold. The currency in circulation would thereby be reduced and prices would be forced downward. If, alternatively, gold were being exported, prices would fall as the money in circulation was reduced. Raising the price of gold would reverse the outflow and thereby restore the previous price level.

> The plan would put a stop, once for all, to a terrible evil which for centuries has vexed the world, the evil of upsetting monetary contracts and understandings. All contracts, at present, though nominally carried out, are really tampered with as truly as though false weights and measures were used for delivering coal or grain.[6]

[6] Irving Fisher, *Stabilizing the Dollar* (New York, 1920), p. 108.

Fisher, like most monetarists, believed that price fluctuations caused rather than resulted from business fluctuations; therefore stabilizing prices by controlling the quantity of money would eliminate the business cycle. In an article published in 1925 he concluded that "changes in price level almost completely explain fluctuations in trade, for the period 1915–23."

> If I were to choose a physical analogue it would be not the swing of a clock pendulum but the swaying of the trees or their branches. If, in the woods, we pull a twig and let it snap back, we set up a swaying movement back and forth. That is a real cycle, but if there is no further disturbance, the swaying soon ceases and the twig becomes motionless again. . . .
>
> Another objection to the theory of cyclical regularity in business is that it overlooks 'friction.' The twig, once deflected and then left to itself, soon stops swaying. So also a rocking chair, left to itself, will soon stop rocking; so also will a pendulum in a clock which has run down. Friction brings them to rest. To keep them going some outside force must be applied. So, in business we must assume that the effect of any initial disturbance would soon wear off, after a very few oscillations of rapidly diminishing amplitude. The resultant business cycle would speedily cease altogether if dependent only on its own reactions. To keep it up there must be applied some outside force. But, unless the outside force happens also to be cyclical and unless, in addition, the rhythm of said force or forces happens to be exactly synchronous with the business pendulum itself, these outside forces will not perpetuate, but obfuscate, the cycle, like the wind blowing on the trees. We cannot imagine anything analogous to the 'escapement' in a clock which so nicely times the outside force as to keep up the natural swing of the pendulum.
>
> I, therefore, have no faith whatever in 'the' business cycle. I do not doubt that, after any disturbance in one direction or the other, business tends to swing back to normal (and a very little beyond) just as does the tree.[7]

After the crash of 1929 Fisher saw in the growth of debts the greatest cause of deflation and depression. Excessive debts lead to liquidation, with the dumping of goods on the market. Falling prices of goods lead to further pressure for liquidation of debts. Fisher came to believe that fluctuations in demand deposits are the greatest cause of business fluctuations. In other words, he lost faith in the stable

---

[7] Irving Fisher, "Our Unstable Dollar and the So-Called Business Cycle," *Journal of the American Statistical Association*, Vol. XX, New Series, No. 149 (June 1925), pp. 192–93.

relationship between currency and demand deposits. He also implicitly accepted a criticism of his earlier stabilization plan—that checking accounts as means of payment are so vast compared to the gold reserves behind them that small changes in the price of gold have little effect on the average price level.

Fisher's solution was to require 100 per cent reserves behind demand deposits, thereby divorcing the process of creating and destroying money from the business of banking. First, a government currency commission would offer to buy liquid bank assets (up to 100 per cent of the bank's checking deposits) for currency or lend to banks currency on those assets as security. Then all checkbook money would have actual currency behind it. Thereafter all demand deposits would have to be backed 100 per cent by currency reserves. In other words, demand deposits would literally be deposits, consisting of cash held in trust for the depositor. Banks could lend out only their own money or money put into savings accounts. This would eliminate runs on banks, bank failures, much of the government debt, and most bank earnings. Banks would have to levy service charges on deposits to compensate themselves for their loss of earnings when their power to create credit was destroyed. The biggest benefit of Fisher's policy would be the elimination of great monetary inflations and deflations, thereby mitigating economic booms and depressions.

To stabilize the purchasing power of the dollar, the currency commission would be required to buy securities when the index was below the official par and to sell when it was above. This now familiar mechanism of open-market operations of the Federal Reserve System would be a substitute for gold price variations that Fisher had advocated earlier. The country had already departed from the gold standard when he began advocating this "100 per cent money" plan, and he did not favor returning to it.

It is apparent that Fisher did not think that business cycles were inherent in the economy. He regarded their causes as almost entirely monetary, and argued that their cure would be effected by stabilizing prices. As late as 1936, Fisher wrote:

> As explanations of the so-called business cycle, or cycles, when these are really serious, I doubt the adequacy of over-production, under-consumption, over-capacity, price-dislocation, mal-adjustment between agricultural and industrial prices, over-confidence, over-investment, over-saving, over-spending.

I venture the opinion, subject to correction on submission of future evidence, that, in the really great booms and depressions of the past, each of the above-named factors has played a subordinate role as compared with two dominant factors, namely (1) *over-indebtedness* (especially in the form of bank loans), to start with, and (2) *deflation* (or appreciation of the dollar), following soon after; also that, where any of the other factors do become conspicuous, they are often merely effects or symptoms of these two.

Though quite ready to change my opinion, I have, at present, a strong conviction that these two economic maladies, which may be called the "debt disease" and the "dollar disease" are, in the great booms and depressions, more important causes than all others put together.[8]

Fisher did outstanding work in mathematical economics, statistics, and index numbers. He was a pioneer in developing the new field of econometrics, which made statistical methods a part of economic theory and no longer a mere adjunct to it. He was honored for his contributions by being elected president of the American Economic Association, the American Statistical Association, and the Econometric Society.

Hawtrey

Ralph George Hawtrey (born 1879) was a British treasury official who found time to write many books about monetary economics. His main concern was business fluctuations, which he attributed largely to the instability of credit. There might be other causes of fluctuations, he admitted, but they are minor and can be controlled by monetary devices.

The key figure in Hawtrey's scheme is not the producer but the wholesale merchant or trader, and the key factor is the rate of interest. If the banks apply credit restrictions, the direct effect on production in agriculture, mining, and manufacturing is likely to be small. The producers' profit depends on output, and they cannot reduce working capital below a certain level without curtailing output. If producers rely on temporary borrowing, the interest charge, even at a high rate, will be a minor item among their costs.

Wholesalers, by contrast, are very sensitive to the rate of interest. They borrow money to hold inventories, and because their markup is quite small, interest charges are an important component of their costs. Higher interest charges will increase the cost of carrying goods, and

[8] Irving Fisher, *100% Money*, 2d ed. (New York, 1936), pp. 120–21.

they will have to reduce their inventories. Lower interest rates thus make it easier to carry large stocks of goods. Merchants take the initiative in production by increasing or decreasing orders. Their borrowing operations are influenced not only by the terms on which their banker is willing to lend but by the level of demand and the prospects of price movements in the market as well. If they expect prices to rise, they will wish to increase inventories to make an extra profit. In doing this, they must consider the interest charge for the additional money they must borrow, because the extra charge for interest is certain, whereas the rise in prices is speculative.

Why do business fluctuations occur? Because of the inherent instability of credit working through the merchants to upset the rest of the economy in cumulative departures from an unstable equilibrium.

If the banks increase their lending, there will ensue a release of cash and an enlargement of the consumers' income and outlay [on consumption and investment goods]. The increase in the consumers' outlay means increased demand for goods in general, and the traders find their stocks of finished products diminishing. There result further orders to producers; a further increase in productive activity, in consumers' income and outlay, and in demand; a further depletion of stocks. Increased activity means increased demand, and increased demand means increased activity. A vicious circle is set up, a *cumulative* expansion of productive activity.

Productive activity cannot grow without limit. As the cumulative process carries one industry after another to the limit of productive capacity, producers begin to quote higher and higher prices. The vicious circle is not broken, but the cumulative growth of activity makes way for a cumulative rise of prices. The vicious circle of inflation is set up.

Once an expansion of demand has been definitely *started*, it will proceed by its own momentum. No further encouragement from the banks to borrowers is required.

A similar principle applies to a contraction of demand. Suppose that the banks take steps to reduce their lending. There will ensue an absorption of cash and a compression of the consumers' income and outlay [on consumption and investment goods]. Demand falls off, traders' stocks of finished products accumulate, orders to producers are cut down. Decreased activity means decreased demand, and decreased demand means decreased activity.

The vicious circle of depression is the counterpart of the vicious circle of activity, except that it does not encounter any definite limit such as productive capacity interposes in the way of increasing activity. But the decline in activity is certain to be accompanied by a fall in wholesale prices, for producers will make price concessions, each of them endeavouring to get as big a share as possible of the limited amount of demand, in order to keep his plant at work. Here we see the vicious circle of deflation.[9]

The central bank can regulate credit and thereby promote stability. Sometimes it merely has to modify a tendency to expansion or contraction; at other times it must reverse the tendency. Because the existing tendency possesses a certain momentum, significant force is required to reverse it. The greatest danger is that action will be too late and success therefore more doubtful. If, for example, a vicious circle of inflation has taken hold, there may be such pressure to borrow that only a flat refusal to lend can counteract it. The central bank would thereby abrogate its function as the lender of last resort. Similarly, a depression may cause such pessimism among traders that they cannot be induced to borrow.

Hawtrey recommended several remedies for curbing the instability of credit and the ensuing instability of economic activity: central bank open-market operations, changes in the rediscount rate, and variations in the reserve requirements of commercial banks. If national income is to be kept steady, then both credit and currency must be allowed to vary. Raising interest rates and restricting bank reserves can curb an inflation, for such policies can always be pushed to the point where they become effective. But the converse is not necessarily true. Cheap money and greater bank reserves may not stimulate a revival. When the demand for goods is low, wholesalers seek to reduce their inventories by cutting their purchases to a level below their sales. But if sales fall off more quickly than they expect, the goods in stock will not diminish as much as the wholesalers intend; in fact, stocks may actually increase. In such a situation wholesalers cannot be induced to borrow even at very low rates of interest in order to build up the goods on hand. The outcome is what Hawtrey called a complete credit deadlock, with economic stagnation and deep depression, as in the early 1930's.

A deadlock is a rare occurrence, but unfortunately in the nineteen-thirties it came to plague the world, and raised problems which threatened the fabric of civilisation with destruction.[10]

Hawtrey seemed to lose some of his earlier faith in the effectiveness of lowering interest rates to stimulate a revival.

[9] R. G. Hawtrey, *The Art of Central Banking* (London, 1932), pp. 167–68. Reprinted with permission of Longmans, Green & Co. Limited.
[10] Ralph George Hawtrey, *Capital and Employment,* 2d ed. (London, 1952), p. 79.

That there are limits to the possibility of evoking an expansion of general demand by reducing the bank rate we have already shown. The reduction of the rate is to be regarded rather as the lifting of a check upon movement than as giving a positive stimulus. Cheap money is *one* of the conditions of revival, but may not be enough by itself.[11]

The correct solution, Hawtrey decided, lies in proper action during the previous boom. Early action must be taken to stop excessive monetary expansion. When the bank rate is raised sufficiently, the boom is reversed. After the reversal occurs the bank rate must be reduced rapidly in order to avoid a cumulative and vicious deflation:

> When we assume that the high bank rate has done its work, that means that it has successfully overcome the vicious circle of expansion and started the vicious circle of deflation. In order to break the latter, it is essential to infuse into the traders a sufficiently concentrated tendency to increase their purchases. At a time when their purchases are still adapted to the restrictive tendencies of a high bank rate, a *sudden* transition to a low bank rate will have this effect. If the transition is delayed and spread over a longer interval, its power at any one time may be insufficient, and the vicious circle of deflation will go on gathering impetus till it becomes irresistible.
>
> Possible though it is to stop this by taking prompt measures to relax credit in time, far better would it be to regulate credit at all times in such a way that neither of the two vicious circles ever gets a serious hold. In quiet conditions credit responds easily to moderate upward and downward movements of bank rate. If these movements were always initiated *in time*, the conditions need never be other than quiet in a monetary sense.[12]

After the Great Depression of the 1930's Hawtrey was more willing to endorse public works expenditures than he had been earlier. If a credit deadlock develops, he said, direct government expenditures may be the only effective way to keep consumption and investment spending from decreasing further. Public works take a long time to get under way, and therefore their effectiveness is limited; yet some benefit may be expected from such deficit spending.

Hawtrey's concept of the merchant as the crucial figure in economic life may have been more appropriate for England than elsewhere, because England was then the leader in world trade. Its declining position in world trade makes this view less tenable today. Hawtrey's uncritical faith in the efficacy of open-market operations made him quite popular in the United States during the 1920's, for

[11] *Ibid.*, p. 112.
[12] *Ibid.*, p. 113.

the idea then prevailed that the Federal Reserve System could stabilize the economy with that device. Hawtrey's early emphasis on the importance of inventories has received increasing recognition in the United States in recent decades. Fluctuations in stocks of goods have been identified as one of the key factors in the short three- to three-and-a-half-year cycle.

Friedman

Milton Friedman (born 1912) is the leading monetarist of recent decades. His undergraduate work was completed at Rutgers University and his graduate degrees were received from the University of Chicago and Columbia University. He has spent most of his professional life as Professor of Economics at the University of Chicago, where he is the major figure of the "Chicago school" of laissez-faire economics and public policies.

Friedman believes "that inflation is always and everywhere a monetary phenomenon, produced in the first instance by an unduly rapid growth in the quantity of money." [13] Since the Second World War, the stock of money has been permitted to rise too fast, thereby generating inflation. The only effective way, he asserted, to stop inflation is to restrain the rate of growth of the quantity of money. He counts in the money supply the currency outside of banks, and all demand and time deposits in commercial banks; time deposits of savings banks are excluded. The money supply should be allowed to increase by 3 to 5 per cent each year, with the expansion kept at a rate uniform when considered monthly or even weekly. Such a policy is not a panacea, but it could make a major contribution toward economic stability and the avoidance of both inflation and deflation.

Friedman also advocates a system of 100 per cent reserve banking. For every dollar of deposits, banks would be required to hold a dollar of currency or its equivalent. Banks would become warehouses for money. They would accept deposits payable on demand or transferable by check. For every dollar of deposit liabilities, the banker would hold a dollar of Federal Reserve notes or Federal Reserve deposits. The banks could lend out only the capital of their owners, or the capital they could raise by selling stocks or bonds to the public; they would thereby lose the power to create or destroy

[13] Milton Friedman, *Dollars and Deficits* (Englewood Cliffs, 1968), p. 18.

money. The essence of this plan, Friedman said, is to make all money, whether currency or deposits, a direct liability of the government.

The transition to 100 per cent reserves need not disrupt the economy. The Federal Reserve banks could increase reserves in a series of steps by buying government bonds in the open market. The increases in required reserves would therefore avoid any reduction in the stock of money in the system. Reserve money created in this way would take the form of increased Federal Reserve deposits held by the banks to meet the increased reserve requirements.

If we consider the government bonds that banks hold, says Friedman, we are already halfway to 100 per cent reserves. Under his scheme government securities held by banks would be converted into deposits at Federal Reserve banks—a mere bookkeeping operation. Commercial banks' reserves with Federal Reserve banks plus cash in their vaults plus government securities they own add up to about half their demand and time deposits. The remaining required reserves under the 100 per cent plan would be created by the Federal Reserve banks' purchases of government securities held by the public other than commercial banks, and by the banks' sale of their own stocks and bonds to the public. Banks would get their income primarily by imposing service charges and collecting interest on their reserve deposits. The Federal Reserve banks could pay this interest from their earnings on the government securities they hold.

Friedman has admitted that there is no proof that fluctuations in the stock of money over the business cycle were the cause of business fluctuations; but he strongly believes that this was the case. He wrote about his simple rule that the money supply should expand by 3 to 5 per cent per year: "It is nearly inconceivable that the monetary authorities would now permit the money stock to decline by one-third, as it did from 1929–33, or even by nearly 4% in 10 months, as it did in 1937." [14]

Friedman denies that a private-enterprise, laissez-faire economy is subject to serious tendencies toward instability. In this matter his ideas are opposed to those of Wesley Clair Mitchell of the institutionalist school, discussed in Chapter 20. Friedman believes that the 1929–33 crash and depression need not have occurred and the Federal Reserve authorities bear the major responsibility for that unprecedented debacle. The people responsible for monetary policy should

[14] Milton Friedman, *A Program for Monetary Stability* (New York, 1960), p. 94.

not have permitted the stock of money to decline as it did; they should have provided more liquidity to the banking system.

Friedman attributed the decline in business activity to the shrinkage in the supply of money. But might not the cause-and-effect relation run in the other direction? A decline in consumption and investment spending and in income could cause a shrinkage in currency in circulation and demand deposits. Perhaps fiscal policy is fully as important as monetary policy in avoiding depressions, in spite of Friedman's denials. There is no doubt that monetary policy can be a powerful tool in stabilization policy, but to neglect all the other factors that can cause or offset fluctuations is a serious weakness of his analysis. It fits well with his predilection for laissez faire.

Underlying Friedman's analysis is his political view that the government should stay out of economic affairs as much as possible. His economic analysis thus runs parallel with his political preference, that of laissez-faire government.

Bibliography

FISHER, IRVING, *The Money Illusion.* New York: Adelphi, 1928.

———, *The Nature of Capital and Income.* New York: Macmillan, 1906.

———, *100% Money,* 2d ed. New York: Adelphi, 1936.

———, *The Purchasing Power of Money.* New York: Macmillan, 1911.

———, *Stabilizing the Dollar.* New York: Macmillan, 1920.

FISHER, IRVING NORTON, *A Bibliography of the Writings of Irving Fisher.* New Haven, Conn.: Yale University Library, 1961.

———, *My Father: Irving Fisher.* New York: Comet, 1956.

FRIEDMAN, MILTON, *Dollars and Deficits.* Englewood Cliffs: Prentice-Hall, 1968.

———, *Essays in Positive Economics.* Chicago: The University of Chicago Press, 1953.

———, *A Program for Monetary Stability.* New York: Fordham University Press, 1960.

——— and ANNA J. SCHWARTZ, *A Monetary History of the United States, 1867–1960.* New York: National Bureau of Economic Research, 1963.

GORLUND, TORSTEN, *The Life of Knut Wicksell,* tr. by Nancy Adler. Stockholm: Almqvist and Wiksell, 1958.

HAWTREY, RALPH GEORGE, *The Art of Central Banking.* London: Longmans, Green, 1932.

———, *Capital and Employment,* 2d ed. London: Longmans, Green, 1952.

———, *Currency and Credit.* London: Longmans, Green, 1919.

SAULNIER, RAYMOND J., *Contemporary Monetary Theory.* New York: Columbia University Press, 1938.

UHR, CARL G., *Economic Doctrines of Knut Wicksell.* Berkeley, Calif.: University of California Press, 1960.

WICKSELL, KNUT, *Interest and Prices,* tr. by R. F. Kahn. London: Macmillan, 1936. [Originally published in 1898.]

————, *Lectures on Political Economy,* tr. by E. Classen. 2 vols. London: Routledge, 1934–35. [Originally published in 1901 and 1906.]

16

The Marginalist School:
The Departure from Pure
Competition

Theories concerned with monopoly and with monopolistic or imperfect competition are well within the scope and tradition of the marginalist, or neoclassical, school. Although these theories were not fully developed until the early 1930's, they have far deeper roots. These new ideas arose because the theory of pure competition was becoming increasingly untenable. Pure competition applied most fully to agriculture, but even there the theory was becoming less suitable to modern conditions than it had been in earlier times. Where only a few buyers offer to purchase farm products in a local market, as with tobacco, meat, grain, and milk, pure competition no longer reigns. In addition, government intervention in agriculture has made the conventional analysis of price formation irrelevant to the real world, even if it is a useful mental exercise and a valid model under certain assumed conditions.

The neoclassical theory of pure competition has become even less relevant to modern industrial production and trade than to agriculture. The theory presupposes many buyers and sellers all dealing with a perfectly homogeneous product so that no individual has a perceptible influence in the market; buyers are therefore completely indifferent as to which seller they patronize. In such a world every seller can dispose of any quantity of goods at the going market price, and no advertising, no brand names, and no salesmanship are required. A rather abstract world!

The methodology of monopolistic and imperfect competition theories discussed in this chapter shows all the characteristics of the neoclassical school. This methodology deals with marginalism and the microeconomic approach in an abstract, deductive, and subjective manner, and its economics assumes a rational, static, unchanging world that always tends toward equilibrium. Nothing in these theories explains fluctuations, growth, and change as a dynamic process.

By showing how monopolies can raise prices above the competitive equilibrium level to yield a permanent monopoly profit, the theories concerning departure from pure competition were influential in creating a greater willingness among economists to accept more vigorous government antitrust policies and government regulation of the profits of public utility monopolies. The theories thus provided the theoretical rationale for government objectives that had been enacted almost half a century earlier. The hope persisted that vigorous government action to encourage competition would reverse the trend toward big business that dated back to the 1870's in the United States and even earlier in England. The supposed blessings of pure competition that some economists still hope to achieve represent a reaction to monopoly and an exercise in futility. We cannot win back a world that resembles pure competition, and even if we could, it would not be a world of great stability, growth and efficiency. In fact, pure competition as a goal has been largely replaced by "workable competition," which represents a compromise between pure competition and oligopoly.

From these additions to neoclassical theory we learn that under monopolistic competition, even in the absence of the power to realize a monopoly profit, prices are likely to be higher and output lower than under pure competition. What can be done about it? Even the modifications of marginal theory cannot solve this problem, though they offer a better explanation of the world than does the theory of pure competition. The new theories struck a blow at the widespread idea that a free-enterprise system results in an optimum allocation of productive resources. Because of the downward-sloping demand curve facing each entrepreneur we are doomed to have too many gasoline stations and grocery stores that operate at less than the most efficient output.

It is remarkable that the new ideas were fully developed independently and almost simultaneously by Edward Chamberlin in the United States, Joan Robinson in England, and Heinrich von Stackelberg in Germany. Von Stackelberg's analysis led him to abandon all hope for economic order except as provided by the state. If the economic world disintegrates into a wasteful struggle of monopolies without an integrating force, then the force of the state must be called upon to impose order. No wonder Von Stackelberg wholeheartedly embraced Fascism.

The theory of monopoly goes back to Augustin Cournot in 1838, almost a hundred years before the neoclassical works on monopolistic competition were published. After Cournot others criticized the theory of pure competition, but the great contribution of Chamberlin and Robinson was in exploring the whole range of situations that lie between pure competition and pure monopoly.

Sraffa

Piero Sraffa (born 1898), an Italian who migrated to England, studied under Marshall, taught at Cambridge University, and was the editor of the definitive edition of Ricardo's collected works and correspondence. When France fell under the German blitzkrieg in 1940, he was interned by the British as an enemy alien. Keynes denounced the "fatheads" who were mistreating distinguished refugee scholars and wrote, "If there are any Nazi sympathizers still at large in this country, we should look in the War Office and our Secret Service, not in the internment camps."

In the December 1926 issue of the *Economic Journal*, Sraffa published an article whose influence was seminal in generating a critique of the theory of pure competition. Sraffa pointed out that unit costs of production may very well fall as a firm increases its scale of production. Unit costs may decrease because of internal economies as the firm expands output or because overhead charges are distributed over a larger number of units produced. These falling unit costs are incompatible with pure competition. If the firm grows more efficient as its size increases, there will be fewer firms and less competition. Thus it is necessary to abandon the path of free competition and turn toward monopoly. Sraffa offers us a well-defined theory, but it is important to remember that both pure competition and monopoly are extreme cases. In industries where competitive conditions appear to prevail, two forces frequently break up the unity of markets: First, a single producer can affect market prices by varying the quantity of goods he puts on the market; second, each producer may engage in normal production under circumstances of individual decreasing costs. Both conditions are more akin to monopoly situations than to pure competition and both derive from the fact that the producer faces a demand curve that slopes downward instead of being horizontal. Under pure competition, if a producer can sell all he produces at the going market price, he will continue to expand production as long as his cost per unit of output is below his selling price. But if he must lower his price in order to sell a greater quantity, he may curtail output even though a greater volume of production would lower the average cost per unit. In other words, the old theory predicted that costs increase as you produce more; Sraffa held that prices decrease if you try to sell more.

Everyday experience shows that a very large number of undertakings—and the majority of those which produce manufactured consumers' goods—work under conditions of individual diminishing costs. Almost any producer of such goods, if he could rely upon the market in which he sells his products being prepared to take any quantity of them from him at the current price, without any trouble on his part except that of producing them, would extend his business enormously. It is not easy, in times of normal activity, to find an undertaking which systematically restricts its own production to an amount less than that which it could sell at the current price, and which is at the same time prevented by competition from exceeding that price. Business men, who regard themselves as being subject to competitive conditions, would consider absurd the assertion that the limit to their production is to be found in the internal conditions of production in their firm, which do not permit of the production of a greater quantity without an increase in cost. The chief obstacle against which they have to contend when they want gradually to increase their production does not lie in the cost of production—which, indeed, generally favours them in that direction—but in the difficulty of selling the larger quantity of goods without reducing the price, or without having to face increased marketing expenses. This necessity of reducing prices in order to sell a larger quantity of one's own product is only an aspect of the usual descending demand curve, with the difference that instead of concerning the whole of a commodity, whatever its origin, it relates only to the goods produced by a particular firm; and the marketing expenses necessary for the extension of its market are merely costly efforts (in the form of advertising, commercial travellers, facilities to customers, etc.) to increase the willingness of the market to buy from it—that is, to raise that demand curve artificially.[1]

In general, each producer enjoys special advantages in his own protected segment of the total market. He would not lose all his business if he raised his price, and he would not take away all his rivals' business if he lowered his price. Therefore he enjoys certain monop-

---

[1] Piero Sraffa, "The Laws of Returns Under Competitive Conditions," *Economic Journal*, Vol. XXXVI, No. 144 (December 1926), p. 543. Reprinted with permission of the Royal Economic Society.

oly elements even in a market that appears competitive, and the demand curve he faces slopes down and to the right.

> We are led to ascribe the correct measure of importance to the chief obstacle which hinders the free play of competition, even where this appears to predominate, and which at the same time renders a stable equilibrium possible even when the supply curve for the products of each individual firm is descending—that is, the absence of indifference on the part of the buyers of goods as between the different producers. The causes of the preference shown by any group of buyers for a particular firm are of the most diverse nature, and may range from long custom, personal acquaintance, confidence in the quality of the product, proximity, knowledge of particular requirements and the possibility of obtaining credit, to the reputation of a trade-mark, or sign, or a name with high traditions, or to such special features of modelling or design in the product as—without constituting it a distinct commodity intended for the satisfaction of particular needs—have for their principal purpose that of distinguishing it from the products of other firms. What these and the many other possible reasons for preference have in common is that they are expressed in a willingness (which may frequently be dictated by necessity) on the part of the group of buyers who constitute a firm's clientele to pay, if necessary, something extra in order to obtain the goods from a particular firm rather than from any other.
>
> When each of the firms producing a commodity is in such a position the general market for the commodity is subdivided into a series of distinct markets. Any firm which endeavours to extend beyond its own market by invading those of its competitors must incur heavy marketing expenses in order to surmount the barriers by which they are surrounded; but, on the other hand, within its own market and under the protection of its own barrier each enjoys a privileged position whereby it obtains advantages which—if not in extent, at least in their nature—are equal to those enjoyed by the ordinary monopolist.[2]

In a stable industry, said Sraffa, a firm can lower its price and thereby increase its sales and profits to the detriment of competing firms. If a firm raises prices, however, profits are increased without injuring competition; in fact, rival firms gain from the rise in prices because they are then free to raise their own prices. The second method of raising profits is therefore more acceptable to businessmen than the first, because the profits are regarded as more stable if they do not arouse retaliation by competitors.

Sraffa's widely read and discussed article touched off an outburst of thinking and writing about the shortcomings of then current economic theory.

[2] *Ibid.*, pp. 544–45.

Chamberlin

Edward Hastings Chamberlin (1899–1967), a Harvard professor, published *The Theory of Monopolistic Competition* in 1933. (It had been submitted in an earlier version in 1927 as his doctoral thesis at Harvard.) His book fused the previously separate theories of monopoly and competition, and it sought to explain the wide range of market situations that are neither purely competitive nor totally monopolistic. Chamberlin held that most market prices are actually determined by both monopolistic and competitive elements.

A key concept of the theory of monopolistic competition is that the firm's demand curve slopes downward, and therefore the marginal revenue curve must lie below the demand, or average revenue, curve. Chamberlin was among the first of many theorists in the late 1920's and early 1930's who discovered and applied the idea of marginal revenue, defined as the addition to total gross revenue as a result of selling an additional unit of output. Under pure competition, with each firm able to sell all it produces at the going market price, the marginal revenue is equal to price, and both the marginal revenue curve and the demand curve are horizontal lines. Thus, if a farmer can sell all her wheat at $2 a bushel, every additional bushel she sells adds $2 to her gross revenue.

The situation is quite different in markets in which pure competition does not prevail. With a downward-sloping demand curve, the marginal revenue curve will slope downward more steeply. For example, if an entrepreneur can sell one pair of shoes per day if he prices it at $20, two pairs at $18, and three pairs at $16, in each case except the first the marginal revenue is less than the price. The marginal revenue is a full $20 for the first pair, but only $16 for the second pair. This can be calculated in two ways: First, total revenue goes from $20 to $36, an increase of $16. Second, the additional pair of shoes sells for $18, but the price of the first pair had to be reduced $2 in order to sell a second pair. Similarly, the marginal revenue derived from selling the third pair of shoes is $12.

Marginal cost is defined as the addition to total cost as a result of producing one more unit of output. As the firm expands its output toward the most efficient level, average unit costs fall and marginal costs lie below average costs. As the firm expands output beyond the most efficient level, average costs rise and marginal costs lie above average costs. Therefore the marginal cost curve crosses the average cost curve at its lowest point.

The equilibrium output for each firm is determined by the intersection of the marginal cost and the marginal revenue curves. As long as the addition to total revenue exceeds the addition to total costs as the result of producing one more unit, it pays to expand production. If, on the other hand, marginal cost is rising and it exceeds marginal revenue, it pays to reduce output. Maximum profits or minimum losses occur only at the output where marginal cost and marginal revenue are equal. This single law applies to both pure competition and monopoly, as well as to the range of situations in between.

Only where a firm enjoys significant monopoly powers will its price exceed average unit costs even in the long run; it will receive monopoly profits. But where many firms operate under monopolistic competition, free entry into the industry will cause monopoly profits to disappear in the long run. As more firms offer to sell goods that are close (although imperfect) substitutes for each other, each producer can sell fewer goods at each price than formerly. Long-run equilibrium will occur when each seller's demand curve is tangent to the average cost curve. Similarly, if too many firms enter the industry, losses will occur until some firms leave, and the demand curve for each remaining firm will rise to a position of tangency with the average cost curve. These ideas are illustrated graphically in Figure 6, based on Chamberlin's presentation. The firm's average cost curve includes the average rate of profit required to keep the business operating in the long run. Goods can therefore be sold at average cost and still show a profit in the accounting sense. Marginal cost is derived from average cost. The firm's demand curve D slopes downward because the firm can increase its sales by lowering its price; if it raises its price, sales will decline. Even customers who are devoted to a particular seller or to her product's brand name will accept close substitutes if her price becomes too high.

The marginal revenue curve MR intersects the marginal cost curve at the point determining that for maximum profit the output will be OB units, the price will be BN per unit, and the extra profit per unit will be SN. Total extra profit will be the extra profit per unit times the number of units produced, as represented by the area $LSNM$.

If the enterprise enjoys long-run monopoly power—as for example, if it can exclude new firms from entering the industry—this situation will represent the long-run equilibrium for the kind of costs and demand depicted in Figure 6. The extra profit is monopoly profit. If other firms are free to enter the industry, however, they will do so in order to participate in the extra rate of return. The demand curve will fall to D' in the long run, OA units will be produced selling for AR per unit, and all extra profits will disappear.

Figure 6   Equilibrium Under Monopolistic Competition

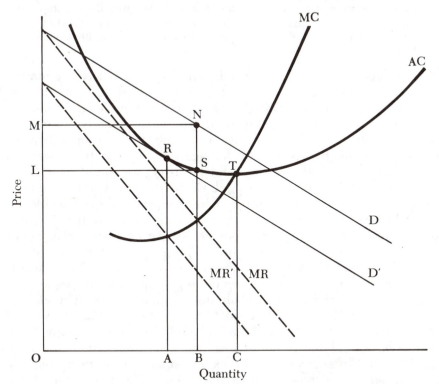

For a firm producing in a market of pure competition, the demand curve and the marginal revenue curve would be horizontal and identical. In the long run *OC* units would be produced, and the price per unit would be *CT*. Hence Chamberlin's significant conclusion:

> The price is inevitably higher and the scale of production inevitably smaller under monopolistic competition than under pure competition. . . .
>
> The common result of this assemblage of factors is excess productive capacity, for which there is no automatic corrective. Such excess capacity may develop, of course, under pure competition, owing to miscalculation on the part of producers, or to sudden fluctuations in demand or cost conditions. But it is the peculiarity of monopolistic competition that it may develop over long periods *with impunity,* prices always covering costs, and may, in fact, become permanent and normal through a failure of price competition to function. The surplus capacity is never cast off, and the result is high prices and waste. The theory affords an explanation of such wastes in the economic system—wastes which are usually referred to as "wastes of competition." In fact, they could never

occur under pure competition, and it is for this reason that the theory of pure competition is and must be silent about them, introducing them, if at all, as "qualifications," rather than as parts of the theory. They are wastes of monopoly—of the monopoly elements in monopolistic competition.[3]

Many economists, following Chamberlin's lead, have reiterated that pure competition would result in a larger output, more efficient production, and lower selling prices than occur under monopolistic competition, or monopoly. But these economists usually fail to state their implicit assumption that cost curves are the same in each situation—an unrealistic assumption for many industries. If we were to have pure competition in the steel industry, we might have thousands of small firms producing steel. Each "steel mill" might be little larger than a blacksmith's forge, and the price of steel would be much higher than it is at present, even with a few producers enjoying considerable monopolistic power. All we can say is that under pure competition each producer in the long run will tend to produce at the minimum point of his own average cost curve. If we depart from pure competition, output tends to decrease and prices tend to rise because of the downward-sloping demand curve. Therefore a firm's output will generally be smaller and its prices higher than if it were operating under conditions of pure competition. There is no doubt, however, that a modern steel mill is more efficient than a blacksmith's forge. The cost curves of a small firm in pure competition lie far above those of giant firms. Therefore pure competition would not necessarily give us the greatest volume of output and the lowest prices. The nostalgia for the bygone world of small business seems both futile and erroneous.

Robinson

Joan Robinson (born 1903), professor of economics at Cambridge University, was a student of Alfred Marshall. Her book, *The Economics of Imperfect Competition*, was published a few months after Chamberlin's and covers substantially the same ground. Since its appearance in 1933 Robinson has expanded her activities and has made important contributions in Keynesian economics, economic development, and international trade. She has also offered a significant critique of Marxist economics, though her position has been that of a friendly critic.

---

[3] Edward H. Chamberlin, *The Theory of Monopolistic Competition*, 5th ed. (Cambridge, 1946), pp. 88, 109. Reprinted with permission of Harvard University Press.

To the concept of monopoly Robinson added the concept of monopsony, the position of a single buyer in the market. When there are a large number of buyers of a commodity, their aggregate demand curve slopes down and to the right, for it is based on marginal utility. The more units of a good a person acquires, the lower its marginal utility and the less he or she offers for an additional unit.

If all the buyers then form an agreement to act together, we can assume that their combined demand curve remains unaltered. We can also assume that the supply curve remains unchanged, for it indicates how much all the sellers together will offer at each price. The price is based on the cost of producing each quantity, and the cost does not change after a monopsony is organized.

Under pure competition the buyer will purchase successive units of goods at any one time up to the point where the *price* is equal to marginal utility. Under monopsony the buyer will regulate his purchases in such a way that *marginal cost* is equal to marginal utility. To illustrate these propositions, consider pure competition. Suppose the going price for shoes is $10 a pair. No single buyer can influence the price, regardless of what his purchases are. Let us assume that for a particular consumer, ownership of the first pair of shoes at any one time is worth $100. A second pair is worth, say, $12 to him, a third pair is worth $10, and a fourth pair is worth $5. In this situation our consumer would buy three pairs of shoes. That is, he buys shoes up to the point where price is equal to marginal utility and both are equal to $10.

Now suppose the same consumer is contemplating buying shoes in a monopsony market. Acquiring shoes from the first through the fourth pair still has a marginal utility for him of $100, $12, $10, and $5. Assuming that the production of shoes can be increased only under conditions of increasing cost, the more shoes our consumer wishes to buy, the higher the price will be. In effect he bids up the price against himself when he increases his purchases. Suppose he can buy one pair of shoes for $6, but two pairs would cost him $9 each. The marginal cost of the second pair is $12, which is equal to the marginal utility, and it pays him to buy it. If three pairs would cost $10 each, the marginal cost of the third pair would be $12. It would not be advantageous for the consumer to buy the third pair, because adding $12 to cost is not justified when the increased utility is only $10. Thus Robinson concluded that under pure competition the buyer will purchase successive units of goods up to the point where the price equals marginal utility. Under monopsony the buyer will increase his purchases up to the point where marginal cost equals marginal utility.

It follows that with a constant supply price, when average and marginal costs are equal, the quantity purchased under monopsony will be the same as under competition. If, however, an industry is working under increasing or diminishing supply price, marginal cost to the monopsonist will not be equal to the price of the commodity; he will buy less or more than under competition.

We can illustrate the difference between average and marginal costs under conditions of rising supply price by means of this example. Suppose a buyer wishes to buy 100 pairs of shoes in a certain market, and can get them at $10 each. If she wishes to expand her purchases to 101 pairs, she may have to pay $10.05 for each pair, because the prices of raw materials and labor are being bid up, and plants are pushed beyond their lowest-cost output in order to fill the extra demand. While the average cost of 101 pairs of shoes is $10.05, the marginal cost is $15.05. This can be calculated in two ways. The total cost of 100 pairs of shoes is $1,000.00; for 101 pairs it is $1,015.05. Therefore the marginal cost—the addition to total cost—of producing the 101st pair is $15.05. Or we can figure that the cost of the 101st pair is $10.05 plus the extra 5¢ a pair on the 100 pairs in order to produce the extra one. Therefore the marginal cost curve lies above the average cost curve (which is the supply curve for the industry) when the latter is rising.

The case of increasing supply price is illustrated in Figure 7, based upon Robinson's presentation. *AC* is the average cost curve of the industry, or the supply curve. *MC* is the marginal cost curve to the industry; this is the marginal cost curve from the point of view of the monopsonist. In the absence of monopsony, *OB* units would be bought at price *BS* per unit. With monopsony, *OA* units would be bought at price *AR* per unit. Monopsony profit would be *RN* per unit, or a total of *LRNM*.

In another section of her work Robinson analyzed the productivity theory of distribution based on her theory of imperfect competition. In examining the demand curve for a factor of production, she used labor as an illustration. The *marginal physical productivity* of labor is the increment of output derived from employing an additional unit of labor with fixed expenditures for other factors. As more workers are employed this increment of output will tend to fall because of the law of diminishing returns. The *marginal revenue productivity* (Robinson called it just "marginal productivity") is the increment of value of the total output caused by employing an additional person. Under pure competition the firm can sell all it produces at the going market price; therefore marginal revenue produc-

Figure 7 Monopsony with Increasing Supply Price

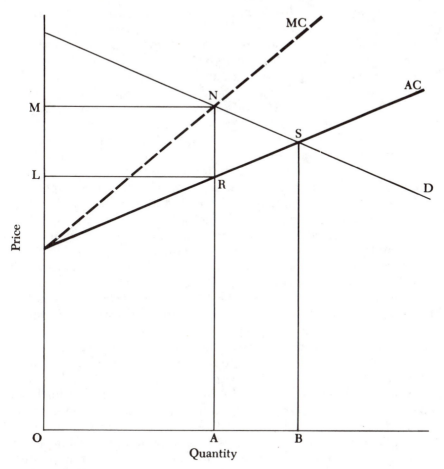

tivity is equal to the value of the marginal physical product, or marginal physical product times price. When the demand is not perfectly elastic, however, the firm has to lower the price of its goods if it wishes to increase sales; then marginal revenue productivity is less than the value of the marginal physical product.

A numerical example illustrates this relationship. Suppose 10 workers together produce 50 pairs of shoes per day, and an 11th worker would add 3 pairs to total output. Under pure competition the price is, say, $10 per pair regardless of whether 50 or 53 pairs are sold. The marginal physical productivity of the 11th worker is 3 pairs. The value of the marginal physical product is 3 × $10 = $30.

The marginal revenue productivity also is $30, which is the gross revenue added to the firm's receipts when an 11th person is employed.

Suppose that under monopolistic competition 50 pairs of shoes can be sold at $10, but to sell 53 pairs the price has to be dropped to $9.90. The marginal physical productivity remains at 3 pairs. The value of the marginal physical product is $3 \times \$9.90 = \$29.70$. The marginal revenue productivity is $24.70, the difference in total revenue between selling 50 pairs at $10 and 53 at $9.90.

Robinson then introduced the concept of gross and of net productivity. Suppose that for every extra pair of shoes produced, an extra $3 must be spent on variable inputs other than labor, such as leather, electricity, containers, and so forth. Under pure competition in the example given above, the marginal gross revenue productivity is $30, while the marginal net revenue productivity is $21. With monopolistic competition, the marginal gross revenue productivity is $24.70, and the marginal net revenue productivity is $15.70.

If wages were lower than $21 per day under pure competition, it would pay to hire the 11th worker. Under monopolistic competition, however, that worker would not be hired unless wages were below $15.70 per day, even though the net value of his or her marginal physical product is $20.70 ($29.70 minus $9.00).

Robinson therefore became involved in the touchy question of the exploitation of labor. She cited one definition of exploitation of labor as a factor of production: being employed at a price that is less than his or her marginal net revenue productivity. If the market for labor is perfect, so that each employer can hire all the labor needed at the going price, the marginal cost of labor to the individual employer is equal to its price. The employer will be impelled by self-interest to hire workers up to the point where the marginal net revenue productivity is reduced to equality with the laborer's wage. Exploitation under this definition normally does not occur.

She cited a second definition offered by A. C. Pigou, her colleague at Cambridge. Exploitation occurs when the laborer's wage is less than the marginal physical product of labor valued at its selling price. Accepting this definition, she concluded that exploitation of labor occurs both under monopsony in buying labor and under monopoly or imperfect competition in selling the products turned out by labor. To remedy exploitation under monopsony a trade union or a trade board should impose a minimum wage on the industry. Then the supply of labor to the industry becomes perfectly elastic at the imposed wage, and the marginal cost of labor is identical with the average cost. Referring to Figure 7 above, if a wage of *BS* were imposed, the monopsonist would no longer be bidding up the price of labor as he increased employment. The new supply curve would be a horizontal line going through the point *S*, and employment would increase from *OA* units to *OB*. The wage would equal the net value of the marginal physical product, and exploitation would disappear.

To eliminate exploitation under monopoly, the selling price would have to be controlled in such a way that it would equal average cost. To eliminate exploitation under imperfect competition, the most common type, markets would have to become perfect or purely competitive.

> When the market becomes perfect the firms will expand, and in the new position of equilibrium, when profits are once more normal, the firms will be of optimum size, costs will be lower, and the price of the commodity will have fallen.
>
> The removal of the imperfection of the market must therefore lower the price of the commodity. It is likely also to alter the marginal physical productivity of the number of men formerly employed in the industry, since the workers are now organised in optimum firms instead of sub-optimum firms. In the old position they were receiving less than what was then the value of their marginal physical product, and in the new position they will receive the value of their marginal physical product, but it does not follow that they will be better off in the new position than in the old, since the value of the marginal physical product may have diminished; the marginal physical product may have diminished, and the price of the commodity must have fallen.[4]

Chamberlin did not cover distribution theory in the first edition of his book, however he did so in subsequent editions. His retort to Robinson's exploitation theory was that *all* factors, not merely labor, receive less than the value of their marginal products. The Pigou-Robinson definition of exploitation applies only to pure competition, for it is impossible under other market conditions for all factors to get the value of their marginal physical products. According to their view, all factors are necessarily exploited, and it would be impossible for employers to avoid the charge of "exploitation" without going into bankruptcy.

Chamberlin raised another objection to the productivity theory of distribution as developed by Robinson:

> It has been tacitly assumed up to this point that the product added by another laborer in any firm is a net addition to social product, not offset

[4] Joan Robinson, *The Economics of Imperfect Competition* (London, 1933), pp. 284–85.

by a lessened product elsewhere in the system. This may well be true. But let us examine briefly at least one case where it is not. . . . The productivity to society of any factor or of any group of factors composing an enterprise must be considered as the total product it creates less that which its presence prevents others from creating. Let us suppose that three gasoline filling stations are adequately supplying the demands for gasoline at a particular corner at going prices when a fourth company sets itself up in business. What product does the new station add? If the outcome is simply the sharing of the available business by the four at the old prices, as it is very apt to be, it is difficult to see where there has been any appreciable addition at all. The value of the services provided by the newcomer less those no longer provided by the three others is approximately zero. To be sure, there may be some additional convenience to those for whom the new station is more advantageously located. The product then will not be zero, but it will be far less than that indicated by regarding the new firm alone. There is a further complication. Since each firm is suffering a reduced volume of sales, average unit costs are higher. It is quite possible that the profits of the first three firms were sufficient before the fourth entered so that all four can now cover their costs including minimum profits without a price adjustment. It is also possible that, faced with higher costs, they will all find it necessary to raise prices, and possible to do so with little fear of undercutting, since each has a strong interest in avoiding a price so low that he cannot cover costs when enjoying his normal share of the available business. Under these circumstances the appearance of the fourth seller has actually diminished (through higher prices) the output of the group. The physical product of the resources he employs being negative, their value at current prices would likewise be negative. Wherever price competition fails to function effectively, complications such as these arise and must be taken into account in defining the net product added by a new firm or by the marginal unit of any factor which it employs. In such cases it appears that the value of the net social marginal product of a factor may even be negative, and, in any event, that it will be far less than its marginal product to an individual firm. Clearly, the value of its net social marginal product bears no relation whatever to its marginal revenue product to the firm, and hence to its income.[5]

Two decades after her book appeared, Robinson criticized the type of economic theorizing she had helped to pioneer:

The Economics of Imperfect Competition was a scholastic book. It was directed to analysing the slogans of the text-books of twenty years ago: "price tends to equal marginal cost" and "wages equal the marginal product of labour"; and it treated of text-book questions, such as a comparison of the price and output of a commodity under conditions of mo-

[5] Chamberlin, pp. 184–85.

nopoly and of competition, demand and costs being given. The assumptions which were adequate (or which I hoped were adequate) for dealing with such questions are by no means a suitable basis for an analysis of the problems of prices, production and distribution which present themselves in reality. . . .

In principle, it is possible to set out a system of simultaneous equations showing what combination of price, outlay on production costs and outlay on selling costs would yield the best profit for a particular commodity in a particular market, taking into account the reaction upon costs and sales of other commodities produced by the same firm. Even if he had the data, the business executive would need an electric, not a human, brain to work out from the equations the correct policy in time to put it into effect. And the data are necessarily extremely vague, since the consequences of a given policy cannot be isolated in ever-changing markets. The recent development of advertising of advertisement is a witness to the difficulty which manufacturers have in knowing the consequences of advertisement, for if they knew its effects there would be no scope for persuading them that it is greater than they think. In reality, evidently, an individual demand curve (for a particular product produced by a particular firm) is a mere smudge, to which it is vain to attribute elegant geometrical properties. . . .

In my opinion, the greater weakness of *The Economics of Imperfect Competition* is one which it shares with the class of economic theory to which it belongs—the failure to deal with time. It is only in a metaphorical sense that price, rate of output, wage-rate or what not can move in the plane depicted in a price-quantity diagram. Any movement must take place through time, and the position at any moment of time depends upon what it has been in the past. The point is not merely that any adjustment takes a certain time to complete and that (as has always been admitted) events may occur meanwhile which alter the position, so that the equilibrium towards which the system is said to be *tending* itself moves before it can be reached. The point is that the very process of moving has an effect upon the destination of the movement, so that there is no such thing as a position of long-run equilibrium which exists independently of the course which the economy is following at a particular date.[6]

Alfred Marshall had anticipated this last objection of his illustrious pupil (see pp. 264–65), although he had considered this tendency only a minor interference with the larger movement toward an equilibrium price in a market for a single good.

In recent years Mrs. Robinson has turned away from her early

[6] Joan Robinson, "Imperfect Competition Revisited," *Economic Journal*, Vol. LXIII, No. 251 (September 1953), pp. 579, 585, 590. Reprinted with permission of the Royal Economic Society.

theories and explored other fields in an effort to develop a more dynamic and more realistic analysis of the economic world.

Bibliography

CHAMBERLIN, EDWARD H., *The Theory of Monopolistic Competition*, 5th ed. Cambridge, Mass.: Harvard University Press, 1946. [Originally published in 1933.]

ROBINSON, JOAN, *The Economics of Imperfect Competition*. London: Macmillan, 1933.

———, "Imperfect Competition Revisited." *Economic Journal*, LXIII, No. 251 (September 1953), 579–93.

SRAFFA, PIERO, "The Laws of Returns Under Competitive Conditions." *Economic Journal*, XXXVI, No. 144 (December 1926), 535–50.

17

Mathematical Economics

The term *mathematical economics* refers to those economic principles and analyses formulated and developed through mathematical symbols and methods. The use of graphs and mathematical symbols to supplement verbal explanations is common practice. Mathematical economics therefore does not constitute a separate school of economic thought but rather a distinct method. Theorists from all schools may use mathematical language to assist them in expressing in a clear and consistent way the definitions, postulates, and conclusions of a theory, though not all economic knowledge can be expressed in mathematical symbols. We shall now consider several topics relating to mathematical economics.

Econometrics

Econometrics, a branch of mathematical economics, combines theoretical, mathematical and statistical analysis. It deals with the determination by statistical and mathematical methods of concrete quantitative laws ruling economic life. With this mathematical aid we can obtain conclusions that may be used to test the validity of a theory. Input-output analysis and linear programming, discussed below, are examples of applied econometrics. The roots of the econometric approach go back hundreds of years. Sir William Petty's follower, Charles Davenant, defined "Political Arithmetick" as "the art of reasoning by figures upon things related to government." Quesnay, the French physiocrat, also did genuine econometric work.

The name "econometrics" was introduced in 1926 by the Norwegian economist and statistician Ragnar Frisch, who shared the first Nobel Prize in economics in 1969. He modeled the term on the expression "biometrics," which appeared late in the nineteenth century to denote the field of biological studies employing statistical methods. Econometrics as a separate method of studying economic life developed very rapidly just after World War I. The Econometric Society, which publishes the journal called *Econometrica,* was founded in 1930.

Econometrics developed in response to changing conditions in economic life. The rise of large corporations, among other factors, made the study of business cycles one of increasing concern both to private enterprises and to society as a whole. If, for example, a large enterprise could forecast business fluctuations with a reasonable degree of accuracy, it could to some extent insulate itself from their adverse effects. Also, only a large corporation could employ the staff required to make such forecasts. In addition, society as a whole, operating through government and through private nonprofit research organizations, was interested in forecasting business trends in order to control, ameliorate, or counteract them. Growing government intervention in the economy therefore stimulated econometric research, and national governments became the world's greatest agencies for gathering statistics.

Econometric analysis is important today in market studies for big corporations, including elasticities of demand faced by monopolistic enterprises that they try to influence. Unions, in negotiating the terms of sale of labor services, are concerned with the elasticity of demand for labor and the products labor helps produce. In contrast, the nineteenth-century world had little need for econometric research and few funds available for it. Unions were then weak, businesses were small, there was minimal government intervention, and no one individual had much market power.

With inadequate knowledge of the facts, theorists resorted to conditional "if, then" statements. Instead of describing the effects of a million dollars' worth of additional investment, they said that if the propensity to consume is of a certain magnitude, then national income will increase by a certain amount. Intricate relationships were thus set up and studied without reference to the actual magnitudes of the unknown elements involved. The work of deductive theorists was therefore frequently replete with abstract models that contained algebraic symbols representing quantities of unknown magnitudes. Economic theory had begun to lose its contact with reality, and econometrics was an attempt to reverse this trend.

Econometric analysis is especially useful today both in forecasting the future and in policy analysis. While forecasting involves a projection of likely events and consequences, policy analysis is important in analyzing the effects of government programs. With the proliferation of government in health care, education, urban problems, and a variety of other areas, the need has arisen to determine exactly what effects these programs have had on individuals and institutions. Econometric techniques provide the analytical framework for such determinations.

Program analysis has been proven to be much more accurate than the perilous art of forecasting. Forecasting has other merits, however, than mere prediction of GNP, investment, and so on. The real advantage of forecasting models is that they force economists and planners to consider the possible alternatives in an economic system, thereby preparing decision makers for all possible outcomes.

As the technology available to solve the arithmetic processes has become more sophisticated, econometric models have themselves grown in size and complexity. The University of Pennsylvania, The Brookings Institution, and the University of Michigan, to name a few, all have large models (200 or more equations) working to analyze changes in the United States economy.

The Dutch were the originators of comprehensive macro models. In 1939 Professor Jan Tinbergen began a model of the Dutch economy to be used by government planners; he was the corecipient of the first Nobel Prize in economics in 1969.

General Equilibrium

General equilibrium analysis, in contrast to Alfred Marshall's partial equilibrium analysis, considers the interrelationships among the many variables in the economy. One of the originators of this approach was the Frenchman Léon Walras (1834–1910), who lived in Lausanne, Switzerland; he was also a founding father of marginalism, having independently arrived at the basic marginalist principles in his *Elements of Pure Economics*, published in 1874.

Just as a stone dropped into a pond causes widening circles of ripples, any change in the economy causes further changes that radiate outward with gradually diminishing force. Take, for example, an increase in the price of butter. According to the partial equilibrium approach, if we assume that everything else remains unchanged, a reduced quantity of butter will be bought at the increased price, and that is an end of the matter. But let us consider a few of the further ramifications explored in general equilibrium analysis. The quantity demanded of a substitute good such as margarine will rise, and perhaps its price will rise. The quantity demanded of a complementary good such as bread may fall as butter consumption decreases, and perhaps the price of bread will fall. In a sense all goods are substitutes for each other, directly or indirectly, for they all compete for the consumer's dollar. If less is spent on butter and margarine, perhaps more will be spent on books. If the production of books is subject to decreasing costs as output expands, their prices may fall a little, thereby increasing consumer purchases still further. With these changes in the markets for consumer goods, factors of production will shift their employment. Less labor will be required in the industries producing bread and butter, and more in those producing margarine and books. Capital will also shift, and land use will change from dairy feed and pasture to soybeans and pulpwood. Meanwhile the changed cost of living will influence wage demands, which in turn will determine to what extent machinery will be substituted for labor. At this point we would probably need a high-powered microscope to detect the further changes brought about by the original disturbance.

Thus general equilibrium theory presents a framework consisting of the basic price and output interrelationships for the economy as a whole, including both commodities and factors of production. Its purpose is to demonstrate mathematically that all prices and quantities produced can adjust to mutually consistent levels. Its approach is static, for it assumes that certain basic determinants remain unchanged, such as consumer preferences, production functions, forms of competition, and factor supply schedules. Changes over time are generally excluded from the analysis.

An awareness of the interdependence of economic phenomena is important, for without it we might go astray. A person who loses a job because the industry involved is undermined by cheaper imported goods might very reasonably conclude that imports cause general unemployment; this is an example of partial equilibrium analysis that assumes that everything else remains unchanged. However, if we study the repercussions of increased imports and find that exports increase in response, then our conclusion may well be that imports do not cause a general increase in unemployment.

General equilibrium theory has contributed little, however, to our understanding of economic growth and other changes over time. Nor can the theory predict precise quantitative results of various changes and policies. In the example given above, we simply do not know enough about our economy to predict what the changed output of butter, margarine, bread, and books will be as a result of a 10 per cent increase in the price of butter. The variables are too numerous, too changeable, and too uncertain to be worked out precisely even with modern electronic computing equipment.

Prices in a market economy can be determined mathematically in a theoretical way, taking cognizance of the interrelatedness of all prices. The quantity demanded of a good varies with its price. That is, price is the independent variable, and the quantity demanded is the dependent variable. The quantity demanded of any one good, however, includes as variables the prices of all other commodities. A consumer will not decide how much of one good to buy without knowing the prices of all other goods. If there is a total of n commodities, the total demand for any one of them is determined by the prices of all of them. The aggregate demand for each commodity can be represented by $D_1, D_2 \ldots D_n$, and the prices by $p_1, p_2 \ldots p_n$. An equation can be set up for each commodity showing that demand for it is a function of all prices:

$$D_1 = F_1 \ (p_1, p_2 \ldots p_n)$$
$$D_2 = F_2 \ (p_1, p_2 \ldots p_n)$$
$$. \quad . \quad . \quad . \quad . \quad . \quad . \quad . \quad .$$
$$D_n = F_n \ (p_1, p_2 \ldots p_n)$$

In a state of equilibrium the demand for any particular commodity equals its supply. Therefore $D_1 = S_1, D_2 = S_2 \ldots D_n = S_n$. If supply is substituted for demand in the three equations above, we have:

$$S_1 = F_1 \ (p_1, p_2 \ldots p_n)$$
$$S_2 = F_2 \ (p_1, p_2 \ldots p_n)$$
$$. \quad . \quad . \quad . \quad . \quad . \quad . \quad . \quad .$$
$$S_n = F_n \ (p_1, p_2 \ldots p_n)$$

We assume that supply is given and fixed. With n commodities there are n prices that are unknowns. Since we have an equation for each commodity, there are n simultaneous equations, which are sufficient for determining the n unknown prices. As soon as all prices are known, the aggregate demand for any particular commodity can be calculated. Since the demand is satisfied at the prices so calculated, the problem of the distribution of the available commodities is solved.

Since general equilibrium concepts include many equations and thus many unknowns, the solution of such a system becomes exceedingly complex. Thus general equilibrium has been largely a theoretical tool helping us to understand the blueprint of the economic system rather than an operationally useful statistical device.

A variant of the general equilibrium approach, and one that has been useful for policy purposes, is the series of input-output tables constructed by Wassily Leontief, a Russian emigré.

Input-Output Analysis

Input-output analysis is largely the creation of the Russian-born American economist Wassily Leontief (born 1906) and is reminiscent of Quesnay's *Tableau Economique*, discussed in Chapter 3. This contribution won him the Nobel Prize in economics in 1973. Leontief originally sought to present the essence of general equilibrium theory in a simplified form suitable for empirical study. Thus input-output studies are a special form of general equilibrium analysis. This special form simplifies the presentation of production processes, for example, so that they are in linear form, thereby allowing for more direct conversion of such processes into empirical studies.

Leontief published his first input-output table in the *Review of Economics and Statistics* in August 1936. It depicted the economy of the United States in 1919 as a 46-sector system. Interest in his interindustry analysis spread as a result of World War II. The expansion of war industries created certain bottlenecks that made further growth more difficult. The increased output of airplanes, for example, required greater allocations of steel, aluminum, engines, and certain machine tools and other capital goods. Input-output analysis tried to anticipate these requirements and plan for the expansion of these basic industries.

An input-output table describes the flow of goods and services among different sectors of a given national economy and attempts to measure the relationship of a given industry to other industries in the economy. For example, to produce an additional million dollars' worth of new automobiles, the industry will have to buy $235,000 of iron and steel, $79,000 of nonferrous metals, $58,000 of chemicals, $39,000 of textiles, $32,000 of paper and allied products, $10,000 of finance and insurance services, $6,000 of telephone and telegraph services, and so on.[1]

Leontief worked out a grid that was later expanded by the federal Bureau of Labor Statistics. The input-output grid sums up statistical

---

[1] Wassily Leontief, *Input-Output Economics* (New York, 1966), pp. 71–73.

information about the economy, showing the sources, the amounts, and the destinations of materials. This reveals the relationship of each segment of the economy to every other segment. Every row in an input-output table shows the sales made by one economic sector to every other sector; every column shows what each economic sector purchased from every other sector.

A portion of the grid is reproduced in Table 5. We can see that in 1947 agriculture and fisheries sold $10.9 billion of their output to themselves (feed, seed, breeding livestock, and so forth). Another $15 billion was sold to food processors. These data provide the raw

Table 5 Input-Output Relations in the United States, 1947
(in millions of dollars)

		INDUSTRY PURCHASING					
		(1) Agriculture and fisheries	(2) Food and kindred products	(3) Nonferrous metals	(4) Iron and steel	(5) Motors and generators	(6) Motor vehicles	(7) Total
INDUSTRY PRODUCING	(1) Agriculture and fisheries	10,856	15,048	11	—	—	—	44,263
	(2) Food and kindred products	2,378	4,910	*	3	—	—	37,636
	(3) Nonferrous metals	—	—	2,599	324	366	176	6,387
	(4) Iron and steel	6	2	33	3,982	118	196	12,338
	(5) Motors and generators	—	—	—	—	317	—	1,095
	(6) Motor vehicles	111	3	*	*	—	4,401	14,265
	(7) Total	44,263	37,636	6,387	12,338	1,095	14,263	769,248

* Less than $500,000.

SOURCE: Wassily Leontief and others, *Studies in the Structure of the American Economy* (New York, Oxford University Press, 1953), p. 9. Reprinted with permission of Oxford University Press.

materials for computing how a change in one industry will affect all other industries. An expansion of the iron and steel industry, for example, will require an expansion of nonferrous metals, which in turn will mean more purchases of agricultural and iron and steel products.

This type of analysis is based on three simplifying assumptions. First, coefficients of production are assumed to be fixed; that is, constant quantities of each factor are necessary to produce a unit of output. Second, production functions are assumed to be linear, with no increasing or decreasing efficiencies as an industry expands or contracts; a certain percentage change in the output of one product entails the same percentage change in the inputs of the various factors used to produce it. Third, since input-output analysis is concerned solely with output adjustments recorded as physical quantities, it ignores changes in factor supplies, consumer demands, and prices.

These assumptions are rather unrealistic. Increases in output frequently do not require proportionate increases in input, mainly because various factors are indivisible. For example, one might increase by 5 per cent the ton-miles of freight hauled by a railroad without increasing the supply of locomotives and freight cars. The assumption of fixed production coefficients precludes the possibility of factor substitution.

Technological changes make the grid obsolete rather quickly, and it would have been a tremendous task to have revised the forty thousand entries that went into the two-hundred-industry table for 1947. With the passage of time the input-output table for a given year becomes less and less accurate in predicting the input requirements for future years. Greater accuracy can be achieved, however, by extrapolating from trends observed in the past, thereby anticipating steady technological advances. For example, this method would allow us to predict the continuing reduction in the quantity of coal required to generate one kilowatt-hour of electrical energy.

Input-output analysis would have been irrelevant in the days of atomistic competition and laissez faire, and, furthermore, the collection of data and staff required to construct such a table and apply it to the affairs of a small producer would have been too expensive to contemplate. A producer of buggies, for example, did not need to plan for his changing demand for wood and steel because he used so little. Wide business cycle fluctuations would have further vitiated the usefulness of the table. If the steel industry were producing far below its potential, for example, increased demand for steel would not have required the construction of additional steel mills.

The rise of the giant corporation and the development of a large government role in the economy have enhanced the usefulness of input-output analysis for at least four major reasons. First, the government has become a vast buyer of goods and services. Therefore both the government and its suppliers have to anticipate the effects of changes in the pattern of government buying. Second, government intervention has eliminated the most severe fluctuations in the production of goods and services, so that an expansion in the demand for final goods and services is more likely to require expanded investment in fixed capital than it did in the past. Third, the giant corporation, in anticipating a growth of sales, has to plan for an expansion in the supply of inputs. A vertically-integrated corporation can plan its own supply of some inputs. Others may indicate to their suppliers the extent to which they expect to increase their purchases of inputs. Fourth, we may be reaching a point of scarcity of some raw materials in the United States. The recent shortage of oil, for whatever reason, has forced government and private planners to evaluate the effect of such shortages on industry and consumers. Input-output tables are extremely valuable in such evaluations.

Input-output analysis is even more relevant in underdeveloped countries, where economic planning is more pervasive. In an underdeveloped country seeking economic growth, the construction of a large industry will require the expansion of supporting facilities; these are likely to be much scarcer than in rich industrial countries. Suppose a meat canning plant is erected in a poor country. This enterprise will require expansion of electricity, water supply, transport facilities, workers' housing, cafeteria facilities, medical services, production of metal for cans, and so on—facilities that are readily available in rich countries but must be carefully planned for in developing countries.

Input-output analysis is probably more useful in a socialist economy than in one based primarily on private enterprise. Total economic planning requires that the planning body allocate materials and anticipate future needs. Industries must correlate their expansion if serious bottlenecks are to be avoided. Because consumer preferences are subordinated to the overall plan, consumer whims and desires need not interfere with the pre-eminent goals for economic activity; in other words, in a completely socialized economy a sudden increase in consumer desire for automobiles will not divert steel away from, say, the machine-tool industry. A socialist economy is more likely to operate at or near full capacity on a sort of forced-draft basis. Shortages of equipment and raw materials are therefore more serious than in an economy that operates at 80 per cent of capacity.

And since it is more difficult to increase the output of steel or trucks on short notice in Soviet Russia than in the United States, they have to plan more carefully. Their current active interest in mathematical economics in general and in Leontief's grid in particular, though belated, suggests that these analytical approaches are more useful to Soviet Russia than to us.

Indifference Curves

The use of indifference curves to analyze consumer demand originated with the Englishman Francis Ysidro Edgeworth (1845–1926) and the Italian Vilfredo Pareto (1848–1923). The aim of the idea was to avoid measuring utility quantitatively. According to standard marginalist theory, if you spend $15 on a pair of shoes and 10¢ on an ice cream cone, the shoes are a hundred and fifty times as useful to you as the cone. This numerical precision is questionable. Perhaps we should compare small increments of utility at the margin. Suppose you have the choice between a $14 or a $15 pair of shoes, and you choose the latter. Then the increased satisfaction you obtain from acquiring the more expensive rather than the cheaper pair of shoes is exactly ten times the satisfaction you get from an ice cream cone. Such measurement of the magnitude of utility seems unrealistic and unsatisfactory.

The indifference curve approach avoids any quantitative measurement of marginal utility. All we require is that for any two goods a consumer be able to determine the various combinations that would yield the same total satisfaction. An indifference curve is analogous to a line on a contour map that joins all points of equal altitude. If we consider satisfaction as the third dimension of the altitude, an indifference curve joins all points that represent equal satisfaction.

One extreme case is that of two goods that are perfect substitutes for each other. Let us consider nickels and dimes, shown in Figure 8. Each of the three lines represents a separate indifference curve with a different level of satisfaction. The farther the curve is from the point of intersection of the two axes, the greater the satisfaction. A person taking the middle curve feels equally well off regardless of which combination of goods he has as indicated at any point on the curve. At the highest point he has 6 nickels and no dimes. At the lowest point he has 3 dimes and no nickels, and at point A he has 2 dimes and 2 nickels. He is indifferent or equally satisfied with any of these alternatives. The curve shows nothing, however, about the absolute amounts of satisfaction obtained.

Figure 8   Indifference Curves with Perfect Substitutes

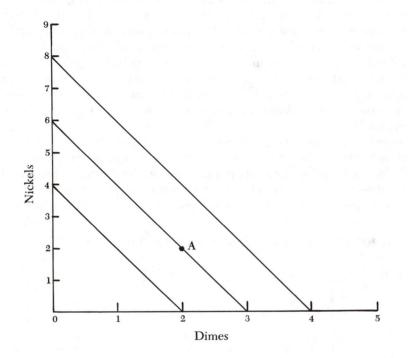

Figure 9   Indifference Curves with No Substitutability

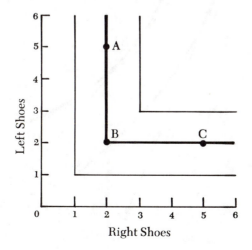

Now we shall consider the opposite case of completely non-substitutable goods, as with left and right shoes, shown in Figure 9. A person is better off as he moves from the curve closest to point zero to the middle curve. But once he decides on the middle curve, perhaps because he lacks adequate income to buy more shoes, he is equally well off with any combination of the two goods represented along that curve. At point A he has 5 left and 2 right shoes; at B he has 2 of each; and at C he has 2 left and 5 right shoes. According to our assumptions he is indifferent and equally well off with any of these combinations.

Figure 10 shows the more usual case of two products that are partial substitutes for one another. Curves 1 and 2 are indifference curves. At their upper ends they show that the person represented will give up a large quantity of potatoes to acquire a small quantity of meat and will still feel equally well off. The reason is that the for-

Figure 10　Indifference Curves with Some Substitutability

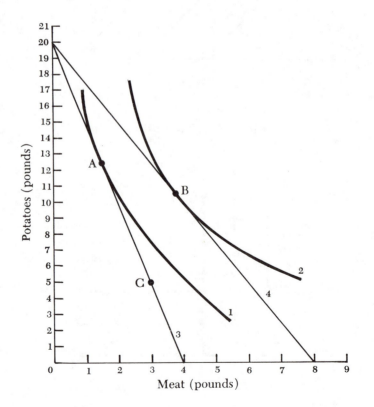

mer is abundant and the latter scarce. At the lower end of the curve, as potatoes become scarce relative to meat, he will give up fewer potatoes to acquire another pound of meat.

Line 3 in Figure 10 is a price line. Suppose the person budgets $2 a day for meat and potatoes, and the prices are 50¢ and 10¢ per pound respectively. Line 3 shows the various quantities of both commodities which can be bought for $2. At the upper end one can buy 20 pounds of potatoes and no meat; at the lower end, 4 pounds of meat and no potatoes; at point *C*, 3 pounds of meat and 5 pounds of potatoes.

We could draw countless indifference curves, and line 3 could intersect many of them. One of the curves will be tangent to line 3—in this case, curve 1. This is the curve of greatest satisfaction for the person with $2 a day to spend on meat and potatoes. Point A, with 1.5 pounds of meat and 12.5 pounds of potatoes, gives the greatest satisfaction. We have determined the quantities of each commodity the consumer will demand, given his indifference schedule, the sum he has to spend on both commodities, and their prices.

If the price of meat were cut in half, the individual could buy 8 pounds of meat with $2, and line 4 would be the new price line. He could move to a higher indifference curve, and at point *B* he would demand 3.7 pounds of meat and 10.5 pounds of potatoes. We see how the two commodities are partial substitutes for each other, and how the quantities demanded change with changing prices. We have begun, in fact, to derive a demand schedule.

While the use of indifference curves in the real world may seem to be limited, the technique of maximizing a function subject to constraints has led to a variety of uses in the business world. Linear programming, for example, is a technique that incorporates the method used in indifference analysis in order to solve problems in production, marketing, and inventory control. What is important is not whether the theory is immediately useful but whether it leads to a more precise operational concept.

Linear Programming

Linear programming was developed during and after World War II, and one of its earliest applications was to the planning activities of the United States Air Force. Linear programming is used by firms in allocating scarce resources so as to maximize the attainment of a predetermined objective. The lowest-cost diet for animals can be determined, or the cheapest way to ship goods to market, or the most profitable product mix, or the best combination of factor inputs. Costs can thereby be minimized and profits maximized. Both mathematical and geometrical techniques are used. Linear programming helps solve practical problems for businessmen that marginal analysis cannot deal with effectively.

Two elementary examples will illustrate linear programming. Suppose a man needs at least 15 grams of an iodine salt and 15 grams of an iron salt per month to stay healthy. He cannot buy either of these in a pure form, but must buy them as trademarked patent medicines. There are two available: Nostrum 12 contains 1 gram of iodine and 2 grams of iron per ounce and costs $1 per ounce. Quackstuff 31 contains 3 grams of iodine per ounce and 1 gram of iron and costs $2 per ounce. His problem is to determine what combination of the two preparations he should take to get the required medication at the lowest cost.

If he takes x ounces of Nostrum 12 and y ounces of Quackstuff 31, he will get $x + 3y$ grams of iodine and $2x + y$ grams of iron. As each element must total 15 grams, we get two equations:

$$x + 3y = 15$$
$$2x + y = 15$$

These can be plotted on a graph as straight lines. In the first equation, if $x = 0$, then $y = 5$; if $y = 0$, then $x = 15$. These two points locate a line in Figure 11. In the second equation, if $x = 0$, then $y = 15$; if $y = 0$, then $x = 7.5$. The second line can now be drawn.

The combinations of medicines lying to the left and below either line will not give the minimal requirements of iodine and iron. Point A, for example, with 2 ounces of Nostrum 12 and 10 ounces of Quackstuff 31, gives 32 grams of iodine but only 14 grams of iron. Point B, showing 9 ounces of Nostrum 12 and 1 ounce of Quackstuff 31, gives 19 grams of iron and only 12 of iodine. The proper combination of medicines will lie on or to the right of the heavy line *FEG*. Thus at point C, with 3 ounces of Nostrum 12 and 10 ounces of Quackstuff 31, more than enough iodine and iron will be obtained. Likewise at point D, with 8 ounces of each.

Which of the acceptable combinations will cost the least? Suppose we could spend $4 for the two medicines. If the whole sum were spent on Nostrum 12, 4 ounces could be bought at $1 per ounce. If it were all spent on Quackstuff 31, 2 ounces could be bought at $2 per ounce. A straight line connecting 4 on the X axis with 2 on the Y axis will show all the combinations of the two products that could be bought with $4. This is an equal-cost line. If $14 were available for

Figure 11   Linear Programming with Two Variables

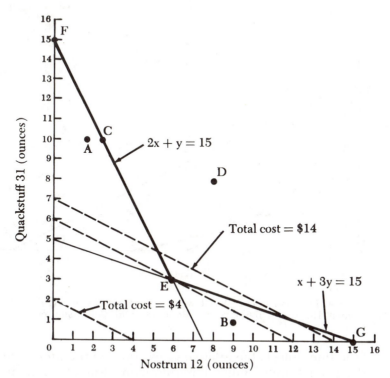

spending on the two products, the equal-cost line joins the 14 on the X axis with the 7 on the Y axis. All equal-cost lines are parallel. The lowest-cost line that will provide the required iodine and iron will go through point E where the two equation lines intersect. Twelve dollars is the lowest cost of acquiring 15 grams of each element. Three ounces of Quackstuff 31 and 6 ounces of Nostrum 12 will be bought. Any other combination will give less than the minimal dosage of medicine or will cost more than $12.

Let us examine another example of linear programming: A cattle producer wishes to fatten his steers in the most economical way. He can choose various mixtures of hay and cottonseed cake, both of which contain the four required nutrients—protein, minerals, vitamins, and carbohydrates.[2]

In Figure 12, any point on or to the right of line PP is assumed to satisfy the minimum protein requirement in the steers' ration; the

[2] This example is based on the presentation of John F. Due and Robert W. Clower, *Intermediate Economic Analysis*, 4th ed. (Homewood, Ill., 1961), pp. 471–73.

Figure 12   Linear Programming with Four Variables

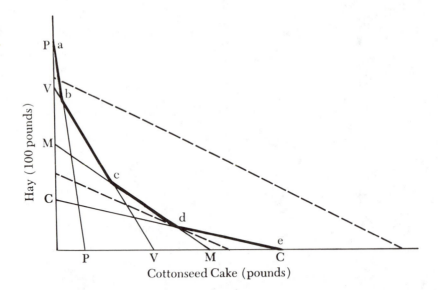

SOURCE: John F. Due and Robert W. Clower, *Intermediate Economic Analysis*, 4th ed. (Homewood, Ill., Irwin, 1961), p. 472. Reprinted with permission of Richard D. Irwin, Inc.

slope of the line reflects the relative proportions of the protein in the two feeds. The minimum mineral requirement is met by diets represented by points on or to the right of line *MM*. The minimum vitamin requirement is indicated by line *VV*, and the carbohydrate requirement by line *CC*. All points on or to the right of the heavy line *abcde* represent combinations of cottonseed cake and hay that simultaneously satisfy all four of the minimum nutritional requirements. Any point to the left of the heavy line represents a combination of feeds that fails to provide one or more of the minimum requirements.

The parallel dashed lines are equal-cost lines, with each line representing the various combinations of the two feeds that can be bought with a given outlay. The lowest-cost combination of feeds is at point *d*. If cottonseed cake were to become more expensive, the equal-cost lines would be steeper, and the lowest-cost combination might then be at *c* or *b*.

Linear programming is, then, a descendant of the indifference curve approach developed early in the twentieth century. It is still in its infancy in business policies and planning but will be more and more useful as business and government continue to expand its use.

Obviously small enterprises cannot use such sophisticated and expensive techniques, but the continuing growth of large and complex corporations has made linear programming increasingly important.

Game Theory

Game theory as applied to economic problems is based on *Theory of Games and Economic Behavior* (1944), written by the mathematician John von Neumann (1903–57) and the economist Oskar Morgenstern (born 1902). Since the theory is complex and heavily mathematical, only a few general remarks will be made here and a simple example given.

Game theory is applicable to situations analogous to games of strategy, such as chess and poker. In such situations there are conflicting interests, with each side using its ingenuity to outwit the other. In reaching decisions businessmen have to consider the probable response of others. If they are considering a cut in the price of a product, for example, it makes a world of difference whether or not other producers of similar products will also cut their prices. Some business decisions are made openly, such as publicly posted price changes, changes in advertising campaigns, and the manufacture of new products; these moves are analogous to chess, where all moves are known by both sides. Other decisions are secret, such as *sub rosa* price discounting, undertaking new research projects, and planning the invasion of new markets. Such moves are analogous to poker. If a company places a spy (such as a janitor) in its rival's business to ferret out secrets, this is like playing poker with a marked deck of cards. If businessmen join monopolistic agreements, they must still plan strategy to outwit the public and the government's "trust-busters." There is an implication in game theory that economic relations are based on economic warfare—that the gain of one party is at the expense of another. This is perhaps the logical culmination of the individualistic approach.

The underlying logic of game theory can be seen from a simplified example.[3] Among games of strategy we can distinguish between games of pure chance and games with strategic uncertainty. Shooting dice is a game of pure chance unless the dice are loaded. Whether a player wins or loses, and how much, depends only on his own

[3] Taken from Leonid Hurwicz, "Game Theory and Decisions," *Scientific American*, Vol. 192, No. 2 (February 1955), pp. 78–83. Reprinted with permission of *Scientific American*.

choices and on luck. In a game with strategic uncertainty, such as poker, an additional factor enters: What will the other fellow do?

Assume that Jones and Smith play the following game: Jones is to choose one of the three letters, *A*, *B*, or *C*. Smith is to choose one of four Roman numerals *I*, *II*, *III*, or *IV*. Each writes his choice on a slip of paper and then the choices are compared. Each player wins or loses according to the particular combination of his choice with his opponent's choice at each "turn." Winning is therefore contingent on strategic uncertainty. Payment is made according to Table 6. The figure zero means that neither pays. A positive number means that Smith pays that amount to Jones; a negative number, that Jones pays Smith. Thus if Jones picks *A* and Smith *II*, Smith pays Jones $100.

Table 6 Theory of Games

		Smith's choices			
		I	II	III	IV
Jones'	A	− 200 *	100	300	− 2 *
choices	B	0	− 1000 *	1,000	0
	C	1	2	3	4

* Jones pays Smith.

SOURCE: Leonid Hurwicz, "Game Theory and Decisions," *Scientific American*, Vol. 192, No. 2 (February 1955), p. 81. Reprinted with permission of *Scientific American*.

Let us see how Jones will make a rational choice. He will conclude that Smith will never pick *III*, for every time he does so he will lose from $3 to $1,000. Nor will he pick *IV*, because no matter which letter Jones picks, Smith is better off picking *I* rather than *IV*. If Jones picks *A*, Smith's picking *I* will give him winnings of $200, but he will win only $2 if he picks IV. If Jones picks *B*, Smith will neither win nor lose, regardless of whether he picks *I* or *IV*. If Jones picks *C*, Smith loses $1 if he picks *I*, and he loses $4 if he picks *IV*. In every case, Smith is equally well off or better off if he picks *I* rather than *IV*.

Jones therefore concludes that Smith will pick *I* or *II* every time. He may conclude that the chances are even that Smith will play either *I* or *II*. If Jones plays *A*, his expectation will be to lose $50 on each play on the average, for on two plays he will lose $100, which is $50 per play. If he plays *B*, he can expect to lose $500 per play on the average. If he plays *C*, he can expect to gain $1.50 per play. Therefore *C* is the best choice.

Suppose Jones had no idea that Smith would never choose *III* and

IV. Instead, suppose he thought the chances were even that Smith would pick any of the four Roman numerals. In that case, Jones' expectation for *A* would be

$$\frac{-200 + 100 + 300 - 2}{4} = 49.5$$

His expectation for *B* would be 0, and for *C*, 2.5. Therefore *A* would be his best choice.

If Jones is an incorrigible optimist, he will choose *B*, because it offers the opportunity for the largest payoff ($1,000). If he is a conservative man, he will always choose *C* because he must then win between $1 and $4 on each play.

From Smith's point of view, optimism will lead him to pick *II*, and pessimism will favor *I*. If Smith knows that Jones is an optimist and will pick *B*, Smith should pick *II* and collect $1,000. If, however, Jones gets wind of this reasoning by Smith, he will switch to *A* and collect $100. If both are pessimists, Jones will play *C* and Smith *I*, with Smith paying $1 to Jones. Whereupon Smith will probably quit the game and go home.

An interesting and practical application of game theory can be seen in the "soap wars."[4] In a section of the article that was called "Muddying the test waters," *Fortune* reported that soap companies test the market very carefully before launching a new brand. Market tests in the soap business usually resemble a poker game more than a scientific experiment. When player A places a new product on sale in a certain market, player B, who has a similar product in national distribution, may raise the stakes by tripling his advertising of the product in the area where player A is making his test. This confronts A with a difficult question: Does B intend to triple his *national* advertising budget if A puts his new product on sale nationally? Or is B bluffing?

A classic example of muddying the test waters was staged some years ago by the Toni Corporation, then the leading producer of home-permanent preparations. When Colgate began a market test of a rival home permanent, Toni launched a counteroffensive referred to in intracompany memoranda as "Operation Snafu." Toni already had three home permanents on the market. In cities where Colgate ran tests Toni greatly increased its advertising for all three of these

---

[4] Spencer Klaw, "The Soap Wars: A Strategic Analysis," *Fortune*, Vol. LXVII, No. 6 (June 1963), pp. 186, 191.

brands and introduced a fourth brand. The object was to scare Colgate off entirely or to make Colgate underestimate potential sales of its new product and therefore to launch it with a relatively small advertising and promotion budget. Colgate did in fact drop its plans to market its home permanent nationally.

Bibliography

CASSEL, GUSTAV, *The Theory of Social Economy,* rev. ed. tr. by S. L. Barron. New York: Harcourt Brace Jovanovich, Inc., 1932.

CHARNES, A., W. W. COOPER, and A. HENDERSON, *An Introduction to Linear Programming.* New York: Wiley, 1953.

DORFMAN, ROBERT, PAUL A. SAMUELSON, and ROBERT M. SOLOW, *Linear Programming and Economic Analysis.* New York: McGraw-Hill, 1958.

EDGEWORTH, FRANCIS YSIDRO, *Mathematical Psychics.* London: Kegan Paul, 1881.

HICKS, J. R., *Value and Capital,* 2d ed. Oxford, Eng.: Oxford University Press, 1946.

LEONTIEF, WASSILY, *Essays in Economics.* New York: Oxford University Press, 1966.

———, *Input-Output Economics.* New York: Oxford University Press, 1966.

———, *The Structure of American Economy, 1919–1939,* 2d. ed. New York: Oxford University Press, 1951.

NATIONAL BUREAU OF ECONOMIC RESEARCH, *Input-Output Analysis: An Appraisal* (Studies in Income and Wealth, Vol. XVIII). Princeton, N. J.: Princeton University Press, 1955.

NEUMANN, JOHN VON, and OSKAR MORGENSTERN, *Theory of Games and Economic Behavior,* 3d ed. Princeton, N. J.: Princeton University Press, 1953. [Originally published in 1944.]

PATINKIN, DON, *Money, Interest and Prices.* Evanston, Ill.: Row, Peterson, 1956.

WALRAS, LÉON, *Elements of Pure Economics,* tr. by William Jaffé. Homewood, Ill.: Irwin, 1954. [Originally published in 1874 and 1877.]

18

Early American Economists

American contributions to economic thought were quite modest during the colonial period and the first century of independence. The founding fathers developed a world-shaking political philosophy and a new and viable type of government; but our contributions to economics remained small until Henry George, John Bates Clark, and Thorstein Veblen won international reputations in the late nineteenth century.

Why was this so? Several factors may explain this intellectual lag. From the sixteenth century on, economic thought at first concentrated mainly on commerce and later on industry. Because America was an underdeveloped area, it did not win an important position in either field before the Civil War and therefore did not lead in theoretical analysis about them. We were accustomed to importing our economic ideas, along with our science and technology, from England. Moreover, we developed a pragmatic approach to life. With a continent to conquer, action was more important than theory. Our contempt for education and the small number of people who entered higher education hindered our development of independent, original thinking in economics. Americans were diverted from economic questions by major social and political issues that had higher priority. While the English were debating laissez faire versus government regulation, tariffs versus free trade, and the convertibility of currency into gold, we were concerned first about freedom from England, and later about slavery, Indian affairs, a homestead act, and so forth. These involved questions of economics, to be sure, and we were also concerned about purely economic issues; but a comparison of legislative debates, journals, newspapers, and contemporary books in the eighteenth and nineteenth centuries would show that the British were much more aroused over purely economic issues than were the Americans.

There were, however, interesting economic ideas appearing on the American scene. These ideas were generally more optimistic than the prevailing thought in Great Britain, for we had seemingly limitless resources with which to promote a better life. We also had less rigid class lines, so that people could get ahead more readily than they could in Europe. A society in flux is less likely to defend the status quo, and movement perpetuates hope for better things to come.

Franklin

Benjamin Franklin (1706–90) was a man of learning, wisdom, and action. Although his formal education ended when he was ten, he won world renown as a scientist, an inventor, a philosopher, a journalist and publisher, a statesman, and a diplomat. He founded a public library, a hospital, a mutual fire-insurance company, a philosophical society, a fire-fighting company, and an academy of learning (later the University of Pennsylvania). He invented an improved stove, a lightning rod, bifocal spectacles, and a popular glass harmonica. Franklin advocated crop insurance and daylight-saving time to save candles. His experiments and observations on electricity, heat and light, earthquakes, chimneys, weather, climate, botany, and medicine won the admiration of contemporary scientists everywhere. In the last years of his life he published several papers against slavery, and he served as president of the Pennsylvania Society for Promoting the Abolition of Slavery.

In 1729, at twenty-three, Franklin published a pamphlet called *The Nature and Necessity of a Paper-Currency.* In it he relied heavily on his reading, especially on Sir William Petty's work, but he showed the ability to apply others' ideas to current problems in language easily understood by his Pennsylvania readers. In taking over Petty's labor theory of value, Franklin attacked one of the key themes of mercantilism.

> By Labour may the Value of Silver be measured as well as other Things. As, Suppose one Man employed to raise Corn, while another is digging and refining Silver; at the Year's End, or at any other Period of Time, the compleat Produce of Corn, and that of Silver, are the natural Price of

each other; and if one be twenty Bushels, and the other twenty Ounces, then an Ounce of that Silver is worth the Labour of raising a Bushel of that Corn. Now if by the Discovery of some nearer, more easy or plentiful Mines, a Man may get Forty Ounces of Silver as easily as formerly he did Twenty, and the same Labour is still required to raise Twenty Bushels of Corn, then Two Ounces of Silver will be worth no more than the same Labour of raising One Bushel of Corn, and that Bushel of Corn will be as cheap as two Ounces, as it was before at one; *caeteris paribus*. Thus the Riches of a Country are to be valued by the Quantity of Labour its Inhabitants are able to purchase, and not by the Quantity of Silver and Gold they possess.[1]

In the same pamphlet, Franklin pointed out that a certain quantity of money is required to carry on a country's trade. Too much is of no advantage, and too little raises interest rates and cheapens land, both of which are bad. If interest rates are low, more money will be invested in land instead of being lent out, and rising land values will "enliven Trade." In addition, plentiful currency will raise prices and encourage agriculture, trade, shipbuilding, and handicrafts. Franklin was trying to remedy a serious colonial problem, for efforts by the colonies to import more goods and services than they could export had caused continual shortages of specie.

Franklin disapproved of the overissue of paper money because it would cause a rapid depreciation of its value. In a letter written in 1779 he deplored one aspect of the overissue of paper during the Revolutionary War. However, he could not help marveling at the expediency of paper money to meet the exigencies of war.

The Depreciation of our Money must, as you observe, greatly affect Salary Men, Widows, and Orphans. Methinks this Evil deserves the attention of the several Legislatures, and ought, if possible, to be remedied by some equitable law, particularly adapted to their Circumstances. I took all the Pains I could in Congress to prevent the Depreciation, by proposing first, that the Bills should bear Interest; this was rejected. . . . Secondly, after the first Emission, I proposed that we should stop, strike no more, but borrow on Interest those we had issued. This was not then approved of. . . . When, from the too great Quantity, they began to depreciate, we agreed to borrow on Interest; and I propos'd, that, in order to fix the Value of the Principal, the Interest should be promised in hard Dollars. This was objected to as impracticable. . . .

   The *only* Remedy now seems to be a Diminution of the Quantity by a vigourous Taxation . . . ; and the *only* Consolation under the Evil is, that the Publick Debt is proportionably diminish'd with the Depreciation; and this by a kind of imperceptible Tax. . . .

[1] Leonard W. Labaree, ed., *The Papers of Benjamin Franklin,* Vol. I (New Haven, Conn., 1959), p. 149.

This Currency, as we manage it, is a wonderful Machine. It performs its Office when we issue it; it pays and clothes Troops, and provides Victuals and Ammunition; and when we are obliged to issue a Quantity excessive, it pays itself off by Depreciation.[2]

In 1751 Franklin wrote a tract, *Observations Concerning the Increase of Mankind, Peopling of Countries, Etc.*, which was read by Adam Smith, David Hume, Turgot, and Malthus. (He later met the first three personally while in Europe.) In the tract he claimed that the easier it is to support a family, the more people will marry and the earlier in life. Therefore population grows most rapidly where the means of sustenance are most plentiful. In cities deaths exceed births because there are fewer opportunities for employment, the cost of living is greater, and luxuries are more common. Population does not increase in fully settled countries either, for wages are low and families can be supported only with difficulty. In America, with plenty of land available, population tends to at least double every twenty years. Our territory is so vast that agriculture and handicrafts will continue to expand and wages will remain high indefinitely. The demand for British manufactures will continue to grow. Not even slavery will enable us to produce manufactured goods more cheaply than the mother country can, for slave labor is more expensive than free labor for several reasons: First, high interest rates in the colonies raise the cost of slave labor. Second, insurance for the risk of the slaves' death must also be included in the cost, along with expenses for their illnesses. And, finally, slaves are not interested in doing good work since they do not benefit from it.

In a letter written in 1753 Franklin expressed the view that the poor in Protestant countries are more industrious than those in Catholic countries. To relieve the misfortunes of our fellow creatures is godlike; but to encourage laziness and folly is "against the order of God and Nature, which perhaps has appointed want and misery as the proper punishments for, and cautions against . . . idleness and extravagance." The more ample provision of relief for the poor in Catholic countries renders the people less provident and therefore retards progress.

Franklin, the product of an agricultural society, glorified agriculture. On his visits to France he met and established friendly relations with the physiocrats. In 1769 he expressed physiocratic doctrine in the following manner:

[2] Albert Henry Smyth, ed., *The Writings of Benjamin Franklin*, Vol. VII (New York, 1907), pp. 293–94.

There seem to be but three ways for a nation to acquire wealth. The first is by *war,* as the Romans did, in plundering their conquered neighbours. This is *robbery.* The second by *commerce,* which is generally *cheating.* The third by *agriculture,* the only *honest way,* wherein man receives a real increase of the seed thrown into the ground, in a kind of continual miracle, wrought by the hand of God in his favour, as a reward for his innocent life and his virtuous industry.[3]

Manufacturing was not even mentioned! In a letter written a year earlier, however, he did mention manufacturing. He wrote that "agriculture is truly *productive of new wealth;* manufacturers only change forms . . . so that riches are not *increased* by manufacturing." Yet in 1771 he approved of manufacturing because it would expand the market for agricultural produce, raise the value of land, and keep within the country money that otherwise would be exported. To Franklin the growth of manufacturing output was not an end in itself but primarily a means to promote agricultural prosperity.

In 1783 Franklin analyzed colonialism, using the West Indies, the "sugar islands," as his illustrative case. He touched upon what we now call social and private costs and benefits.

Should it be agreed and become a part of the law of nations, that the cultivators of the earth are not to be molested or interrupted in their peaceable and useful employment, the inhabitants of the sugar islands would perhaps come under the protection of such a regulation, which would be a great advantage to the nations who at present hold those islands, since the cost of sugar to the consumer in those nations consists not merely in the price he pays for it by the pound, but in the accumulated charge of all the taxes he pays in every war, to fit out fleets and maintain troops for the defence of the islands that raise the sugar, and the ships that bring it home. . . . I am persuaded, that the subjects of the Emperor of Germany, and the Empress of Russia, who have no sugar islands, consume sugar cheaper at Vienna, and Moscow, with all the charge of transporting it after its arrival in Europe, than the citizens of London or of Paris. And I sincerely believe, that if France and England were to decide, by throwing dice, which should have the whole of their sugar islands, the loser in the throw would be the gainer. The future expense of defending them would be saved; the sugars would be bought cheaper by all Europe, if the inhabitants might make it without interruption, and, whoever imported the sugar, the same revenue might be raised by duties at the customhouses of the nation that consumed it. And, on the whole, I conceive it would be better for the nations now possessing sugar colonies to give up their claim to them, let them govern themselves, and put

[3] *Ibid.,* Vol. V, p. 202.

them under the protection of all the powers of Europe as neutral countries, open to the commerce of all, the profits of the present monopolies
being by no means equivalent to the expense of maintaining them.[4]

It took the Western countries more than a century and a half to learn
Franklin's lesson that colonies are not truly profitable for the mother
country when all costs are considered.

Paine

Thomas Paine (1737–1809) was born in England to a poor Quaker
corset-maker and an Anglican mother. His education ended at thirteen, and a variety of employments followed. The last position he
held in England was in the government tax office—a job he lost after
trying to organize his fellow employees in order to improve their
working conditions. Forced to sell his possessions and threatened
with imprisonment for debt, he left England for America in 1774,
armed with a letter from Benjamin Franklin recommending him as a
clerk, assistant tutor in a school, or assistant surveyor.

In the American Revolution Paine found his *métier*. His passionate
political tracts helped defend the revolutionary cause during the
darkest days of the war with England. In 1787 he returned to England to demonstrate an iron arch bridge he had invented, which
later proved successful. Once there, however, other matters attracted
his attention. His radical speeches and publications brought the
threat of prosecution by the British government, and he sailed for
France in 1792. There he was welcomed by the Revolution, which
made him a citizen and elected him to the revolutionary National
Convention. Paine voted to convict the deposed king of treason, but
he opposed his execution. He himself was thrown into prison and
remained there for almost a year with a death sentence hanging over
him. He was finally released (after the fall of Robespierre) through
the efforts of James Monroe, American minister to France, and read-
mitted to the National Convention in 1795. In 1802 he sailed for the
United States, where he died in poverty and obscurity seven years
later.

Paine was more of a political philosopher than an economist, but
his economic views are interesting. In his *Rights of Man*, Part II
(1792), he urged disarmament, the independence of South America
in order to open her up to world trade, progressive taxation, old age
pensions, free public education for the needy, and government work

[4] *Ibid.*, Vol. IX, pp. 5–7.

for those temporarily unemployed. Commerce, he asserted, is the great civilizing force; it is the means of eliminating war, for it is cheaper to obtain commodities through commerce than through war.

Paine was one of the earliest advocates of a social security system sponsored and regulated by the government. In *Agrarian Justice* (1796) he sought to explain the widespread poverty in the most advanced nations. His argument anticipated the ideas of Henry George eighty years later.

> It is a position not to be controverted that the earth, in its natural, uncultivated state was, and ever would have continued to be, the *common property of the human race.* In that state every man would have been born to property. He would have been a joint life proprietor with the rest in the property of the soil, and in all its natural productions, vegetable and animal. . . .
>
> As it is impossible to separate the improvement made by cultivation from the earth itself, upon which that improvement is made, the idea of landed property arose from that inseparable connection; but it is nevertheless true, that it is the value of the improvement, only, and not the earth itself, that is individual property.
>
> Every proprietor, therefore, of cultivated lands, owes to the community a *ground-rent* (for I know of no better term to express the idea) for the land which he holds; and it is from this ground-rent that the fund proposed in this plan is to issue. . . .
>
> Man did not make the earth, and, though he had a natural right to *occupy* it, he had no right to *locate as his property* in perpetuity any part of it; neither did the Creator of the earth open a land-office, from whence the first title-deeds should issue.[5]

Paine acknowledged that "the fault" of private landownership is not in the present possessors but in the system, and it should be corrected over successive generations with a minimum of disturbance. This could be achieved, he thought, by a 10 per cent tax on inheritances received by direct heirs and a 100 per cent tax if there are no direct heirs. In the name of justice, not charity, the funds so raised should be distributed as follows: Every person should receive fifteen pounds on becoming twenty-one. After age fifty, every person should receive ten pounds per year for life. Blind and lame persons younger than fifty who are totally incapable of earning a livelihood should also receive ten pounds per year.

> The great mass of the poor in all countries are become an hereditary race, and it is next to impossible for them to get out of that state of them-

[5] Philip S. Foner, ed., *The Complete Writings of Thomas Paine,* Vol. I (New York, 1945), p. 611. Reprinted with permission of Citadel Press, Inc.

selves. It ought also to be observed that this mass increases in all countries that are called civilized. More persons fall annually into it than get
out of it. . . .

I have made the calculations stated in this plan, upon what is called
personal, as well as upon landed property. The reason for making it
upon land is already explained; and the reason for taking personal property into the calculation is equally well founded though on a different
principle. . . . Personal property is the *effect of society;* and it is as impossible for an individual to acquire personal property without the aid of
society, as it is for him to make land originally. . . .

All accumulation, therefore, of personal property, beyond what a
man's own hands produce, is derived to him by living in society; and he
owes on every principle of justice, of gratitude, and of civilization, a part
of that accumulation back again to society from whence the whole came.

This is putting the matter on a general principle, and perhaps it is best
to do so; for if we examine the case minutely it will be found that the accumulation of personal property is, in many instances, the effect of paying too little for the labor that produced it; the consequence of which is
that the working hand perishes in old age, and the employer abounds in
affluence.

It is, perhaps, impossible to proportion exactly the price of labor to the
profits it produces; and it will also be said, as an apology for the injustice, that were a workman to receive an increase of wages daily he
would not save it against old age, nor be much better for it in the in-
terim. Make, then, society the treasurer to guard it for him in a common
fund; for it is no reason that, because he might not make a good use of it
for himself, another should take it.[6]

Paine has received less esteem as a social and political philosopher
than he deserves because of his radical attacks on orthodox religious
doctrines. His book, *The Age of Reason* (1794–96), resulted in a continuous barrage of epithets and denunciations during the last years of
his life and after his death.

Hamilton

Alexander Hamilton (1755–1804) was a brilliant pamphleteer, statesman, financier, and promoter of American nationalism and economic
growth. Born in the British West Indies, he came to mainland
America at seventeen. He interrupted his studies at King's College
(now Columbia University) to join the colonial side when the Revolutionary War began. He distinguished himself in combat and as a
member of General Washington's staff. Hamilton was a leading partic-

[6] *Ibid.,* pp. 619–20.

ipant at the Constitutional Convention, advocating an aristocratic, strongly centralized federal government. In Washington's cabinet he became the first United States Secretary of the Treasury. In spite of his strong antagonism to Thomas Jefferson and his democratic ideas, Hamilton used his influence to have Jefferson rather than Aaron Burr, whom he heartily distrusted, elected president in 1800. And in 1804 Hamilton saw to it that Burr was defeated for the governorship of New York. Burr challenged Hamilton to a duel and killed him on the same spot where three years earlier Hamilton's eldest son, a boy of twenty, was also killed in a duel.

Hamilton was a mercantilist, but this was understandable in an underdeveloped country that could not compete effectively in manufacturing and trade with Western Europe. A laissez faire policy, it seemed, would stifle industrial growth. This did not disturb Jefferson, who favored a primarily agrarian society composed of small independent farmers. Hamilton, however, looked toward a powerful industrial-commercial-financial system, with the business interests dominating a strong central government. To achieve this, government intervention was necessary. The tremendous economic growth of the United States is a tribute to Hamilton's wisdom and foresight, just as the growth of our political democracy owes much to Jefferson.

Hamilton, in his *Report on Manufactures* submitted to the House of Representatives in 1791, had little difficulty in demolishing the physiocratic analysis. Simple agricultural labor, he said, is less productive than highly skilled industrial labor, even if nature does cooperate in agriculture; besides, nature also cooperates in manufacturing. Farm labor is only seasonally employed, while manufacturing labor "is constant and regular, extending through the year, embracing, in some instances, night as well as day." Manufacturing is not sterile or barren, for it yields a surplus in the form of profit, which is analogous to both the rent and profit in agriculture.

Hamilton enumerated seven advantages of manufacturing:

1. Increased division of labor.

2. An extension of the use of machinery.

3. Additional employment to classes of the community not ordinarily at work:

> This is the employment of persons who would otherwise be idle, and in many cases a burthen on the community, either from the bias of temper, habit, infirmity of body, or some other cause, indisposing or disqualifying them for the toils of the country. It is worthy of particular remark that, in general, women and children are rendered more useful, and the latter more early useful, by manufacturing establishments, than they

would otherwise be. Of the number of persons employed in the cotton manufactories of Great Britain, it is computed that four sevenths nearly are women and children, of whom the greatest proportion are children, and many of them of a tender age.[7]

4. The promotion of emigration from foreign countries. The government should pay the cost of emigration to this country of foreigners who would be important in promoting our industries.

5. A broadened scope for the diverse talents and abilities of people.

6. Promotion of "the spirit of enterprise."

7. Expansion of the market for farm products. The expansion of settlements in this country would expand agriculture. Foreign sales of the surplus are too uncertain, and the domestic market should be developed.

Not only do new industries face disadvantages in this country compared with more developed countries, but other countries grant bounties, premiums, and other aids to manufacturers for the production and export of their goods. Therefore if we are to compete successfully with foreigners, "it is evident that the interference and aid" of government are indispensable. To promote manufacturing Hamilton recommended high protective duties, with the revenues to be given as bounties on domestic manufactures. New inventions and discoveries should be encouraged by the government through pecuniary rewards and exclusive privileges. Hamilton favored rewarding not only discoverers and inventors but the entrepreneurs who actually introduced these inventions in business.

Good mercantilist that he was, Hamilton favored "judicious regulations for the inspection of manufactured commodities":

> This is not among the least important of the means by which the prosperity of manufactures may be promoted. It is, indeed, in many cases, one of the most essential. Contributing to prevent frauds upon consumers at home and exporters to foreign countries, to improve the quality and preserve the character of the national manufactures, it cannot fail to aid the expeditious and advantageous sale of them, and to serve as a guard against successful competition from other quarters. The reputation of the flour and lumber of some States, and of the potash of others, has been established by an attention to this point. And the like good name might be procured for those articles, wheresoever produced, by a judicious and uniform system of inspection throughout the ports of the

[7] Samuel McKee, Jr., ed., *Papers on Public Credit, Commerce and Finance by Alexander Hamilton* (New York, 1934), pp. 193–94.

United States. A like system might also be extended with advantage to other commodities.[8]

Hamilton, in his *First Report on the Public Credit* (1790) as secretary of treasury, urged that the federal government guarantee full payment on all outstanding state and federal obligations at face value to the current holders of the securities. The securities had been selling at fantastic discounts. The economic elements in his argument are interesting.

> The advantage to the public creditors, from the increased value of that part of their property which constitutes the public debt, needs no explanation. But there is a consequence of this, less obvious, though not less true, in which every other citizen is interested. It is a well-known fact, that, in countries in which the national debt is properly funded, and an object of established confidence, it answers most of the purposes of money. Transfers of stock or public debt are there equivalent to payments in specie; or, in other words, stock, in the principal transactions of business, passes current as specie. The same thing would, in all probability, happen here under the like circumstances.[9]

A sound government debt, said Hamilton, would create a capital fund that would promote trade, manufacturing, and agriculture. Interest rates would fall because the quantity of money would be increased and its circulation quickened. Land values would increase as money became more plentiful, and loans on land would be obtained more easily.

In the same report Hamilton recommended taxes and tariffs on such luxuries as wines, whiskey, tea, and coffee. To the extent that this policy would reduce imports, a favorable balance of trade would be promoted. If consumption were reduced, saving would increase.

Hamilton understood the process by which banks create credit through fractional reserve requirements. In his *Report on a National Bank* (1790) he stated that a bank augments the active, or productive, capital of a country. Gold and silver in a merchant's chest may lie idle or act merely as a means of exchange up to their own value. If the specie is deposited in a bank, however, it will become the basis of paper circulation. "Banks in good credit can circulate a far greater sum than the actual quantum of their capital in gold and silver"— perhaps two or three times as great. Though the specie is likely to be withdrawn at any moment, experience proves that "the money so

[8] *Ibid.*, pp. 244–45.
[9] *Ibid.*, p. 7.

much oftener changes proprietors than place," and if withdrawn will soon be redeposited.

Hamilton denied that the accumulation of precious metals is of overriding importance. Paper can serve as money just as well, and the intrinsic wealth of a nation should be measured not by the abundance of gold and silver it contains, but "by the quantity of the productions of its labor and industry." Hamilton had read Smith's *Wealth of Nations*. Appearing on the scene long after mercantilism had passed its zenith, Hamilton's greatness and his enthusiastic historical acclaim are largely due to his enlightened blending of mercantilist ideas with more modern ones.

Carey

Henry Charles Carey (1793–1879) was the head of the leading publishing house in the United States, inherited from his father. Much of his wealth was invested in a wide range of enterprises, including coal mines, paper mills, gas companies, and real estate. Largely self-educated, he retired from active business at forty-two in order to devote the rest of his life to his social science writings. His enormous published output, which was rambling, repetitious, and diffuse, included thirteen volumes, about three thousand pages of published tracts, and perhaps an equal quantity of newspaper articles, editorials, and correspondence on economic and political topics.

There were four major components in Carey's polemics: first, permanent protectionism (unlike Hamilton and List, Carey would not settle for temporary tariffs); second, his attempted revision of Ricardian rent theory; third, his harmony-of-interests doctrine; and fourth, his opposition to Malthusian pessimism on population. His analysis was dynamic, in marked contrast to that of most of his predecessors, contemporaries, and the first generation or two of successors in the field of economic analysis. Carey's outlook was optimistic, as befitted one who lived in a rapidly expanding country.

Early in his intellectual life, Carey had been an admirer of Adam Smith and a supporter of free trade. By 1845, however, he became an ardent protectionist. He now attributed almost all the evils in the world to international trade and felt that all virtues flow from domestic commerce. Foreign trade annihilates towns and villages, replacing them with large cities where palaces of merchant princes are surrounded by hovels. Foreign trade causes soil exhaustion, unemployment, war, and plunder. The people are impoverished while public expenditures increase. The growth of international trade enormously increases the wasteful transportation of goods, and those who control transportation dominate the farmers and the legislatures. The international division of labor limits the range of employment and compels whole populations to scratch the earth, to transport goods, or to engage in the business of trading, with production being neglected. The more people engage in transportation, the worse for society, for the transportation of goods "does least to promote development of the mind or improvement of the heart." The sailor and the wagon driver "are habitually withdrawn from the salutary influence of wives and daughters, while constantly exposed to the baneful one of the grogshop and the brothel." Business crises arise because the great distances between producers and consumers make the exchange of goods slower and more irregular. Even the danger of fires and the rising cost of fire insurance can be attributed to international trade. Self-sufficiency will develop local industry, with stone and iron taking the place of wood in building construction, thereby reducing destruction by fire.

> The loss thus resulting from the absence of power to develop the mineral treasures of the earth, and from the consequent waste of property and of labor, *is more than the total value of the merchandise received in the Union from every quarter of the world;* and yet, it is with a view to foster trade that the country pursues a policy which forbids the opening of mines, and the development of the coal and metallic ores that so much abound; and by means of which structures of every kind could be built of materials that would set at defiance the risk of fire.[10]

Carey disputed Ricardo's rent theory. Ricardo had said that as population increases, people go from better soil to poorer, and rent is based on differentials in productivity measured at the margin. Carey said that the sequence is reversed: As population grows and society progresses, people go from poorer soil to better, and therefore rents fall. The first cultivators, having neither axe nor spade, cannot fell the large trees on the best soil, nor drain the swamps of the lowlands. They are forced to seek out the higher lands, which have relatively little timber and vegetation because the soil is thin. Perhaps the fear of wild beasts, savages, and noxious fevers also keeps early humans on the hillside, away from the dense forests. As population increases and tools are acquired and improved, people move into the more fertile lowlands.

[10] H. C. Carey, *Principles of Social Science* (Philadelphia, Pa., 1888), Vol. II, pp. 247–48. [Originally published in 1858.]

The doctrine of Mr. Ricardo is that of increasing dispersion and weakness; whereas under the real laws of nature there is a tendency toward a constant increase of that power of association and combination to which alone man is indebted for the ability to subjugate the more productive soils. As he descends the hills and meets his neighbor man, efforts are combined, employments are divided, individual faculties are stimulated into action, property becomes more and more divided, equality grows, commerce becomes enlarged, and person and property become more secure; and every step in this direction is but preparation for futher progress.[11]

The differences between Carey's analysis and Ricardo's can be explained by their different points of view and basic assumptions. Ricardo assumed static conditions, with technology remaining constant. He analyzed land under cultivation only at a given point in time. This historical order of settlement was of no consequence to his theory. If the fertile lowlands could not be worked by primitive people, they were *economically* submarginal, even though they were chemically richer. Ricardo assumed that population increases while technology remains constant; as a result, rents rise and landlords grow wealthier at the expense of the rest of society. Carey arrived at an opposite position because he looked at the matter historically. People's mastery over natural forces has increased both the supply of land available for cultivation and the average yield per acre. Society thus grows richer as the growth in farm output exceeds the growth in population. Ricardo's principle of diminishing returns to labor and capital applied to land is correct as a static law. Nevertheless, Carey's principle of historically increasing returns to labor and capital in agriculture has stood the test of time in the more economically advanced countries. Yet even under Carey's scheme, there is a differential return on different grades of land at any one time; he did not overthrow Ricardian rent theory.

There has been both a clash and a harmony of interests among different groups of people, said Carey. The strong have always tried to trample the weak, and the latter have combined to limit the power of their oppressors. The feudal landowners, the lords, the tax collectors, and the slaveowners all advanced their own interests at the expense of their fellow men. In modern times, those who stand between the producers and consumers—lawyers, traders, brokers, shippers— profit unduly through their activities and impede the progress of society. Carey's suspicion of "middlemen" reflects his agrarianism.

Nevertheless, said Carey, the permanent interests of all classes of people are the same, although their temporary interests may appear

[11] *Ibid.*, Vol. I, p. 138.

to differ. Individuals and nations, blinded by the idea of immediate profit and grandeur, pursue these ends to the exclusion of the common good. In the long run everybody stands to gain as society grows wealthier and more productive.

The workers and the capitalists, said Carey, have common interests. Assume that a worker using an axe cuts more wood in a day than he can in a month without it. Suppose the capitalist who lends the worker the axe charges him three-fourths of his product for its use; the worker will still be better off than previously, notwithstanding the large proportion claimed by the capitalist as profit. In reality labor's percentage of the total output tends to increase while the capitalist's percentage decreases. Yet both receive increasing *quantities,* and both profit from improvements. The landlord, like any other capitalist, also receives a constantly decreasing proportion of the product of labor but a constantly increasing quantity because of improvements in cultivation.

> Such is the great law governing the distribution of labor's products. Of all recorded in the book of science, it is perhaps the most beautiful—being, as it is, that one, in virtue of which there is established a perfect harmony of real and true interests among the various classes of mankind. Still further, it establishes the fact, that, however great may have been the oppressions of the many at the hands of the few—however large the accumulations resulting from the exercise of the power of appropriation—however striking the existing distinctions among men—all that is required for establishing, everywhere, perfect equality before the law, and for promoting equality in social condition generally, is the pursuit of a system tending to establish in the highest degree the power of association and the development of individuality—that system being found in the observance of perfect respect for the rights of others—thus securing the maintenance of peace, and promoting the growth of wealth and population, both abroad and at home. The more rapid the increase of man's control over nature, the greater must be the tendency towards the establishment of power to direct himself—wealth and power travelling, thus, together.[12]

The harmony of classes will lead to a harmony of nations, with the love of peace becoming diffused throughout the earth.

Carey viewed population trends optimistically. He opposed Malthus on several grounds. First, the Lord directed human beings to be fruitful and multiply, and surely He does not give false advice. "Is war required to correct an error of the Creator?" asked Carey. Second, as population increases, people's cooperation and mastery of nature will improve, thereby solving the food problem. Third, plants

[12] *Ibid.,* Vol. III, pp. 113–14.

and the lower animals, which provide the necessities of life for humanity, can increase much more rapidly than humans. Fourth, as people become more intellectual, their sexual activity and reproduction rate will decline. Fifth, as people's numbers increase, the lower animals tend to diminish; this keeps the carbon dioxide in the atmosphere in correct balance. Increased vegetation decomposes more carbon dioxide given off by animals and people and liberates more of the oxygen required by human beings. The Divine Plan works harmoniously.

George

Henry George (1839–97) has inspired generations of fervid admirers and followers throughout the world. He was one of ten children of a clerk in the Philadelphia customhouse. He was largely self-educated, having quit school at fourteen to become an errand boy. His restlessness, quick temper, and radical political and economic ideas prevented him from ever holding a job for very long; at times when George was unemployed there was actual hunger in his household. At nineteen he left Philadelphia for San Francisco. He became a seaman, a prospector for gold, a farm hand, a printer, a newspaper reporter, an editor and publisher, a state inspector of gas meters, and a lecturer. Early in his career he was suggested as a candidate for the newly created chair of economics at the University of California. He was invited to lecture at Berkeley but, characteristically, he destroyed his chances of appointment by attacking orthodox economics and by criticizing university education as impractical and useless.

George observed the speculative land craze in San Francisco in 1868, on the eve of the first transcontinental railroad's completion. As people poured into California, land values rose phenomenally. Generous land grants were given to railroad companies throughout the West. Frequently railroads were promoted not to earn operating profits, but rather to profit from the sale of securities and the acquisition of state and federal land as well as cash subsidies and other benefits. Political corruption smoothed the way for the railroad promoters, the monopolists, and the profiteers. The great progress throughout the West coincided with the impoverishment and degradation of large numbers of people.

Out of this background came George's indignant and zealous *Progress and Poverty* in 1879. He could not find a publisher until he paid for making the plates himself. When D. Appleton and Company finally accepted the book at virtually no risk to itself, it did not even take the trouble to secure foreign copyrights. A paperback edition issued in 1881 outsold the popular novels of the day. In the United States and Great Britain the work ran serially in the newspapers. The book sold over two million copies in the United States, and it was translated and published in thirteen foreign languages. The book was especially popular in Great Britain, where antilandlord sentiments had been growing. The Fabian socialist movement received impetus from this work, and both Sidney Webb and G. B. Shaw acknowledged the Fabian debt to the promoter of radical land reform who was clearly opposed to socialism. John A. Hobson said in 1897 that George had exercised a more directly formative and educative influence over British radicalism since 1882 than any other man.

George ran for mayor of New York City in 1886 on a reform ticket. He wrote a platform favoring taxation of land values, abolition of other taxes, municipal ownership of railroads and the telegraph, and a reformed ballot system. George ran second in a three-way race, ahead of the young Republican candidate, Theodore Roosevelt. It was widely believed that the election was stolen from George by the Democrats. In 1897 he again ran for mayor of New York City on a third party ticket, despite his doctor's orders to the contrary. On the Thursday before the election he spoke at four meetings and died that night. His son ran for mayor in his place to enable 20,000 supporters to vote in memory of Henry George.

The idea of taxing all economic rent was based on Ricardian analysis. Nevertheless Ricardo opposed such a tax on the ground that it is unjust to tax only one class of people, many of whom have bought land with savings realized from years of toil. George's proposal also resembles the French physiocratic recommendation that only economic rent be taxed. But the differences between the two are notable. The physiocrats believed that only land rent should be taxed because that represents the only true source of wealth, the economic surplus of society; any other tax would be shifted to rent. Therefore, recognizing what they thought was inevitable, they advocated direct rather than indirect taxes. Nor did they propose to tax away all economic rent and leave nothing for the landowners; they did not wish to undermine private property. George, by contrast, considered land rent an unearned income that should be taxed away completely. Moreover, he considered it an income that grows as society progresses and that impoverishes all other classes. Yet he never regarded agriculture as the sole source of wealth. In essence, the physiocrats were agrarians, whereas George's theory reflected the rapid expansion of capitalistic industry.

George stated that labor and capital receive wages and interest; the amount they earn depends on what they could have produced jointly on rent-free land or the least productive land used. This idea inspired J. B. Clark's general law of distribution—that the earnings of any factor of production depend on the marginal productivity of that factor. George summarized his analysis of distribution as follows:

> As Produce = Rent + Wages + Interest,
> Therefore, Produce − Rent = Wages + Interest.
>
> Thus wages and interest do not depend upon the produce of labor and capital, but upon what is left after rent is taken out; or, upon the produce which they could obtain without paying rent—that is, from the poorest land in use. And hence, no matter what be the increase in productive power, if the increase in rent keeps pace with it, neither wages nor interest can increase.
>
> The moment this simple relation is recognized, a flood of light streams in upon what was before inexplicable, and seemingly discordant facts range themselves under an obvious law. The increase of rent which goes on in progressive countries is at once seen to be the key which explains why wages and interest fail to increase with increase of productive power. For the wealth produced in every community is divided into two parts by what may be called the rent line, which is fixed by the margin of cultivation, or the return which labor and capital could obtain from such natural opportunities as are free to them without the payment of rent. From the part of the produce below this line wages and interest must be paid. All that is above goes to the owners of land. Thus, where the value of land is low, there may be a small production of wealth and yet a high rate of wages and interest, as we see in new countries. And, where the value of land is high, there may be a very large production of wealth, and yet a low rate of wages and interest, as we see in old countries. And, where productive power increases, as it is increasing in all progressive countries, wages and interest will be affected, not by the increase, but by the manner in which rent is affected. If the value of land increases proportionately, all the increased production will be swallowed up by rent, and wages and interest will remain as before. If the value of land increases in greater ratio than productive power, rent will swallow up even more than the increase; and while the produce of labor and capital will be much larger, wages and interest will fall. It is only when the value of land fails to increase as rapidly as productive power, that wages and interest can increase with the increase of productive power. All this is exemplified in actual fact.[13]

The worker and the capitalist, said George, have common interests, and both have interests that are antagonistic to those of the

[13] Henry George, *Progress and Poverty* (New York, 1942), pp. 171–72. [Originally published in 1879.]

landowners. Wages tend to be minimal because rents increase even faster than society's productive power. Profits and enterprise also are thwarted by rising rents.

> Take . . . some hard-headed business man, who has no theories, but knows how to make money. Say to him: "Here is a little village; in ten years it will be a great city—in ten years the railroad will have taken the place of the stage coach, the electric light of the candle; it will abound with all the machinery and improvements that so enormously multiply the effective power of labor. Will, in ten years, interest be any higher?"
>
> He will tell you, "No!"
>
> "Will the wages of common labor be any higher; will it be easier for a man who has nothing but his labor to make an independent living?"
>
> He will tell you, "No; the wages of common labor will not be any higher; on the contrary, all the chances are that they will be lower; it will not be easier for the mere laborer to make an independent living; the chances are that it will be harder."
>
> "What, then, will be higher?"
>
> "Rent; the value of land. Go, get yourself a piece of ground, and hold possession."
>
> And if, under such circumstances, you take his advice, you need do nothing more. You may sit down and smoke your pipe; you may lie around like the lazzaroni of Naples or the leperos of Mexico; you may go up in a balloon, or down a hole in the ground; and without doing one stroke of work, without adding one iota to the wealth of the community, in ten years you will be rich! In the new city you may have a luxurious mansion; but among its public buildings will be an almshouse.[14]

George was opposed to socialistic solutions. He argued that even the mildest of them, a graduated income tax, is objectionable because it represents excessive government regulation, breeds corruption, and lessens the incentive to accumulate wealth. Instead, all economic rent derived from land and other natural resources should be taxed. Technically the land would not be confiscated, for the present owners could retain their titles. In essence, however, land would be nationalized without compensation, and it would be rented to the highest bidders. Society creates rising land values, and the unearned increment of land values should belong to it, he said. The owners of land must lose their claims to its income regardless of whether they obtained the land recently or in the distant past, perhaps through inheritance. To George, all economic rent effectively constituted robbery of those who paid the rent, and, he argued, robbery is unjustified even if the right to rob was recently purchased out

[14] *Ibid.*, pp. 293–94.

of one's frugal accumulation of savings. Even landowners would gain when justice, love, peace, and plenty triumphed. The present land-owners should, however, retain their titles to the improvements on the land, such as buildings, and these should be tax free. They would continue to use the land on which their improvements stand, merely paying the government the annual value of the use of the land. Just as two people may own a ship without sawing her in half, just as a railroad may be divided into a hundred thousand shares and yet run as if it were the property of a single owner, so all society may own a piece of land without taking it away from the one who uses and improves it. Land would not lie idle as it does now when speculators hold it for higher prices. No other taxes would be required—hence the idea of a "single tax" on the economic rent of land.

> The present method of taxation operates upon exchange like artificial deserts and mountains; it costs more to get goods through a custom house than it does to carry them around the world. It operates upon energy, and industry, and skill, and thrift, like a fine upon those quali-ties. If I have worked harder and built myself a good house while you have been contented to live in a hovel, the tax-gatherer now comes an-nually to make me pay a penalty for my energy and industry, by taxing me more than you. If I have saved while you wasted, I am mulct, while you are exempt. If a man build a ship we make him pay for his temerity, as though he had done an injury to the state; if a railroad be opened, down comes the tax-collector upon it, as though it were a public nui-sance; if a manufactory be erected we levy upon it an annual sum which would go far toward making a handsome profit. We say we want capital, but if any one accumulate it, or bring it among us, we charge him for it as though we were giving him a privilege. We punish with a tax the man who covers barren fields with ripening grain, we fine him who puts up machinery, and him who drains a swamp. How heavily these taxes bur-den production only those realize who have attempted to follow our sys-tem of taxation through its ramifications, for, as I have before said, the heaviest part of taxation is that which falls in increased prices. But mani-festly these taxes are in their nature akin to the Egyptian Pasha's tax upon date-trees. If they do not cause the trees to be cut down, they at least discourage the planting.[15]

George denied the validity of the law of diminishing returns. Plants and animals multiply much more rapidly than human beings do; therefore there should be no shortage of food. Both jayhawks and people eat chickens, but the more jayhawks the fewer chickens, while the more people the more chickens there will be. People con-

---

[15] *Ibid.*, p. 434.

trol and increase their own food supply. Since matter cannot be created or destroyed, life does not use up the forces that maintain life. "The earth could maintain a thousand billions of people as easily as a thousand millions." With every increase in population, the new mouths to feed come with hands to work, and the efficiency of production grows. It is obvious that wealth grows with population, not merely in the aggregate, but also on a per capita basis. Even if growing numbers of people require that poorer soil be worked, that is more than overcome by the growing efficiency of large numbers. Twenty people working together will, where nature is stingy, produce more than twenty times the wealth that one person can produce where nature is bountiful.

Figure 13 illustrates both the Malthusian pessimism based on the law of diminishing returns and George's optimism based on improved technology. Land is subject to diminishing returns as it is worked more intensively through the investment of more labor and capital per acre. In any one year, if technology is kept constant, the more labor and capital we invest per acre, the larger the total output but the smaller the average output per unit of labor and capital invested. But with technological improvement over a period of time, the average output per unit of labor and capital tends to increase. That is how we can feed a growing population better than in the past. George was perceptive in predicting this trend.

Figure 13   Diminishing Returns and Improved Technology

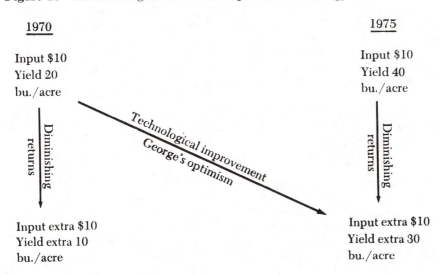

<u>1970</u>

Input $10
Yield 20
bu./acre

Diminishing returns

Technological improvement
George's optimism

Input extra $10
Yield extra 10
bu./acre

<u>1975</u>

Input $10
Yield 40
bu./acre

Diminishing returns

Input extra $10
Yield extra 30
bu./acre

Alfred Marshall delivered three lectures on *Progress and Poverty* in 1883. One of his arguments against the 100 per cent tax on rent was that it would ruin numberless poor widows and others who have invested their small wealth in land; society would be convulsed, with a danger of civil war; capital and business ability might be driven out of the country. If these things happened, then the English worker, instead of being the best paid and the heartiest in Europe, might become almost the worst paid and the weakest. A year after the Marshall lectures, George spoke in Glasgow, on February 18, 1884. His speech, titled "Scotland and Scotsmen," was brilliant, and the audience received it with the greatest enthusiasm. During the question period, a man asked about the widows and orphans who receive interest on bonds secured by land. George's reply to that question may be considered a reply to Alfred Marshall:

> Do not be deluded by this widow and orphan business. That is a matter that is always put to the front. When men talked about abolishing slavery in my country, the cry was raised about the widow and the orphan. It was said, "Here is a poor widow woman who has only two or three slaves to live upon; would you take them away?" It reminds me of the story of the little girl who was taken to see a picture of Daniel in the lions' den. She began to cry very bitterly, and her mother said, "Do not cry, do not cry; God will take care that no harm will befall him." To which she replied, "I ain't crying for him, but for the poor little lion in the back—he is so little I am afraid he won't get any." I propose to take care of the widows and the orphans. As I told those people in London whom I addressed recently, every widow, from the highest to the lowest, could be cared for. There need be no charity or degradation; every one of them could have an equal pension. It will only take twenty million pounds to give every widow in the three kingdoms a pension of £100. And in the state of society which would ensue from breaking up land monopoly, no one need fear that the helpless ones he left behind would come to want. This is not the case now.

Friedrich Engels, a founder along with Karl Marx of the modern communist movement, published a book in 1844 called *The Condition of the Working Class in England.* In a preface to the American edition of 1887 he wrote an evaluation of Henry George:

> It seems to me that the Henry George platform, in its present shape, is too narrow to form the basis for anything but a local movement, or at best for a short-lived phase of the general movement. To Henry George, the expropriation of the mass of the people from the land is the great and universal cause of the splitting up of the people into Rich and Poor. Now this is not quite correct historically. In Asiatic and classical antiq-

uity, the predominant form of class oppression was slavery, that is to say, not so much the expropriation of the masses from the land as the appropriation of their persons. . . . In the middle ages, it was not the expropriation of the people *from,* but on the contrary, their appropriation to the land which became the source of feudal oppression. The peasant retained his land, but was attached to it as a serf or villein, and made liable to tribute to the lord in labor and in produce. It was only at the dawn of modern times, toward the end of the fifteenth century, that the expropriation of the peasantry on a large scale laid the foundation for the modern class of wage-workers who possess nothing but their labour-power and can live only by the selling of that labour-power to others. But if the expropriation from the land brought this class into existence, it was the development of capitalist production, of modern industry and agriculture on a large scale, which perpetuated it, increased it, and shaped it into a distinct class with distinct interests and a distinct historical mission. . . . According to Marx, the cause of the present antagonism of the classes and of the social degradation of the working class is their expropriation from *all* means of production, in which the land is of course included.

If Henry George declares land-monopolization to be the sole cause of poverty and misery, he naturally finds the remedy in the resumption of the land by society at large. Now, the Socialists of the school of Marx, too, demand the resumption, by society, of the land, and not only of the land but all other means of production likewise. But even if we leave these out of the question, there is another difference. What is to be done with the land? Modern Socialists, as represented by Marx, demand that it should be held and worked in common and for common account, and the same with all other means of social production, mines, railways, factories, etc.; Henry George would confine himself to letting it out to individuals as at present, merely regulating its distribution and applying the rents for public, instead of, as at present, for private purposes. What the Socialists demand, implies a total revolution of the whole system of social production; what Henry George demands, leaves the present mode of social production untouched, and has, in fact, been anticipated by the extreme section of Ricardian bourgeois economists who, too, demanded the confiscation of the rent of land by the State.[16]

Recent refutations of George's single-tax proposal have included the idea that, with the growth of government expenditures, a single tax would no longer adequately supply the required revenue. In 1973 total rental payments in the personal-income account of the United States amounted to 25 billion dollars, or only 2.4 per cent of national income and 6.5 per cent of all local, state, and federal taxes.

[16] Friedrich Engels, *The Condition of the Working Class in England,* translated and edited by W. O. Henderson and W. H. Chaloner (New York, 1958), pp. 355–56.

This evidence that economic rent is a minor portion of the nation's revenue is not conclusive. In national-income accounting, rent includes actual payments for the rental of real property and the imputed rental value of owner-occupied dwellings with depreciation, taxes, and interest deducted; most of these rental payments should be excluded if we are to determine the economic rent of land. On the other hand, much economic rent is not included in national-income statistics. If an industrial firm, a railroad, a mining company, or an agricultural enterprise owns the land over or under which it operates, the economic rent of land appears as part of the enterprise's profits, or as interest on the debt secured in part by the land, or as income of unincorporated enterprise, as is the case with most farmers. As economic rent rises, land values rise proportionately; yet this capital gain does not appear in national-income calculations and neither may rent. These increases in economic rent and in the capitalized value of the land can be quite impressive. To take one extreme example, the land under Number One Wall Street, New York City, has sold for $700 a square foot,[17] or $30.5 million an acre.

According to the *Statistical Abstract of the United States,* in 1900 all the privately held land in the United States, excluding subsoil wealth, was worth about $27 billion. If we assume that land has generated a 6 per cent return on its value, the single tax would have produced about $1.6 billion of revenue each year. This is exactly what all levels of government—federal, state, and local—were spending per year. The "single tax" would have worked even as late as 1900.

In 1968 the privately held land (excluding Hawaii and Alaska) was worth something like $571 billion. At 6 per cent return, this means that all levels of government would have had $34 billion to spend in 1968. The federal government actually spent $166 billion that year, and state and local governments spent $116 billion, bringing the total to $282 billion. Apparently the tax on economic rent would have generated only 12 per cent of government requirements.

In fairness to George it must be granted that he would not admit this simple-minded comparison of single tax revenues and current expenditures as valid. He believed that his fundamental reform would unleash productivity and growth, thereby increasing government revenues and decreasing expenses. Production would increase, poverty would disappear, wages would rise, full employment would be attained, prices of goods would fall, and so on. With a world at

[17] *The New York Times Magazine,* May 7, 1961, p. 42.

peace, military spending could be eliminated and the federal government would have saved $81 billion out of the $166 billion it had spent in 1968. George hoped that his reform would enable us to eliminate welfare expenditures, police, prisons, customs houses, most tax collectors, and so on. Rising wealth and reduced poverty would generate increased government revenues from the tax on rent, and reduced expenditures.

It is very doubtful whether George's panacea would solve most of the problems of poverty and the maldistribution of income. The private ownership of capital is a more powerful cause than the private ownership of land in explaining the uneven distribution of income in industrial societies.

Bibliography

CAREY, H. C., *Principles of Social Science*. 3 vols. Philadelphia, Pa.: Lippincott, 1888. [Originally published in 1858.]

DE MILLE, ANNA GEORGE, *Henry George: Citizen of the World*. Chapel Hill, N. C.: University of North Carolina Press, 1950.

DORFMAN, JOSEPH, *The Economic Mind in American Civilization*. 5 vols. New York: Viking, 1946–59.

FONER, PHILIP S., ed., *The Complete Writings of Thomas Paine*. 2 vols. New York: Citadel, 1945.

FRANKLIN, BENJAMIN, *The Papers of Benjamin Franklin*, ed. by Leonard W. Labaree. 17 vols. New Haven, Conn.: Yale University Press, 1959–72.

————, *The Writings of Benjamin Franklin*, ed. by Albert Henry Smyth. 10 vols. New York: Macmillan, 1907.

GEORGE, HENRY, *Progress and Poverty*. New York: Robert Schalkenbach Foundation, 1942. [Originally published in 1879.]

GEORGE, HENRY, JR., *The Life of Henry George*. New York: Robert Schalkenbach Foundation, 1960. [Originally published in 1900.]

KAPLAN, A. D. H., *Henry Charles Carey: A Study in American Economic Thought* (Johns Hopkins University Studies in Historical and Political Science, Series XLIX, No. 4). Baltimore, Md.: Johns Hopkins Press, 1931.

MCKEE, SAMUEL, JR., ed., *Papers on Credit, Commerce and Finance by Alexander Hamilton*. New York: Columbia University Press, 1934.

OSER, JACOB, *Henry George*. New York: Twayne, 1974.

19

The Institutionalist School: Thorstein Veblen

The institutionalist school, which represents an outstanding American contribution to economic thought, began approximately in 1900. By then its founder, Thorstein Veblen, had published his first book as well as many articles and book reviews. The three great figures in this school were Veblen, who critically dissected orthodox thinking and provided the theoretical approach of institutional economics; Wesley C. Mitchell, who stimulated inductive research with his own statistical studies; and John R. Commons, who helped persuade the nation of the need for reform through government legislation, and who actually helped draft many social and labor laws.

Overview of the Institutionalist School

The Social Background of the School

In the period between the Civil War and World War I the achievements of American capitalism were impressive. Rapid growth made ours the biggest and most powerful industrial system in the world. The rise in the levels of living of the lowest income strata, however, did not keep pace with the rise in national income. The improvements in living conditions of most wage earners fell far short of their aspirations and of the possibilities opened by the rise in national income. Hours of labor were long; housing was inadequate; security in times of sickness, unemployment, and old age was negligible; higher education was inaccessible for most workers' children; job security was virtually nonexistent; health and safety regulations were inadequate; frequently the employers organized company towns and dominated the workers, even in their personal lives; heavy immigration tended to undermine wage rates; taxation was regressive; usury was widespread; and recurring depressions were devastating to those who lost their jobs.

The age of monopoly may be said to have begun in the 1870's, and this movement accelerated around the turn of the century, giving a preponderance of economic and political power to big business. Conservative voices predominated in the schools, in the press, in the pulpits, and in the government. The state and federal governments, which proclaimed laissez faire with respect to the workers' interests, were quick to use the police and militia against labor in industrial disputes. They were also generous in establishing tariff protection for business and in granting large subsidies to railroads. Political corruption and chicanery were common. Because of passivity, indifference, and conservatism in high places, the Interstate Commerce Act of 1887 and the Sherman Antitrust Act of 1890 were not enforced, and governmental policies allowed the wasteful exploitation of natural resources.

The American political and economic environment of the late nineteenth century made economists increasingly dissatisfied with orthodox marginalist doctrines. Besides the socialists, there were a few "respectable" or semi-respectable academic economists who disagreed with the postulates, analyses, and conclusions of the dominant school. The assumptions of the marginalists appeared more and more unrealistic, and the defense of laissez faire and the status quo as producing the best of all possible worlds seemed untenable. There was increasing concern about monopoly, poverty, depression, and waste. The operation of modern capitalism was not conforming to the predictions based on traditional economic theorizing. The movement for social control and reform was gathering momentum, and it was in this milieu that institutional economics grew.

At the time two major methods for achieving social change were recognized. The first was to reorganize society along socialist lines. This raised the possibilities of a sharpening class struggle, militant unionism, and a revolutionary orientation toward existing society. The second method was to achieve social change through social reform—that is, to ameliorate conditions through government intervention in the economy. The object was to save capitalism, not to overthrow it, by improving conditions for the masses. Although Veblen was critical of social movements, he favored a radical reconstruction of society. Nevertheless the institutionalist school he founded reflected the reformist approach. The changes wrought by the New Deal in the 1930's were greatly influenced by institutionalism.

The influence of the German historical school on American institutionalism is quite visible. Most of the founders of the American Economic Association were familiar with and friendly toward the German movement and its methodology. Some of Thorstein Veblen's illustrious teachers had studied in Germany. John Bates Clark, who taught and encouraged Veblen at Carleton College, was one of these. Although Clark's marginalist theory had nothing in common with German historicism, he also formulated a creed of Christian socialism, a program of reform that had much in common with German mildly reformist thinking. Veblen was impressed with the lectures of George S. Morris at Johns Hopkins; Morris was the teacher of John Dewey and one of the Hegelians trained in the German universities. Richard T. Ely of Johns Hopkins taught and worked with both Veblen and John R. Commons; Ely had studied under some of the leading historical economists in Germany, and he became an ardent believer in the superiority of the inductive method of research over the deductive method. We should note, however, that despite certain similarities in methodology between the German historical school and American institutionalism, the latter was not nationalistic, and it was more liberal and democratic in its outlook.

The Essence of the Institutionalist School

There are eight key ideas of this school:

1. The economy must be studied as a whole, rather than examining small parts as separate entities isolated from the whole. A complex organism cannot be understood if each segment is treated as if it were unrelated to the larger entity. Economic activity is not merely the sum of the activities of persons motivated individually and mechanically by the desire for the maximum monetary gain. In economic activity there are also patterns of collective action that are greater than the sum of the parts. A union, for example, develops a character, an ideology, and a method of operation of its own; its features cannot be deduced from a study of the individual members who belong to it. Similarly, a business cartel functions quite differently from individual corporations that are in a competitive situation.

Even the concept of economic activity is too narrow in the institutionalists' view. Economics, they assert, is tied in with politics, sociology, psychology, law, custom, ideology, tradition, and other areas of human belief and experience. If we want to explain the underdevelopment of a country, we should look at more than the level of capital accumulation, the size and skill of the labor force, the state of technology, and other economic factors. We also have to look at such noneconomic factors as people's willingness to submit to the discipline of factory work; their desire and ability to change drastically their customary way of life; their hunger for more income; and even whether they are willing to change their religious practices and, for example, to work during times when traditionally religious ceremonies are scheduled. Institutional economics deals with social processes, social relationships, and society in all its facets.

2. This school emphasized the role of institutions in economic life. An institution is not merely an organization or establishment for the promotion of a particular objective, like a school, a prison, a union, or a federal reserve bank. It is also an organized pattern of group behavior, well-established and accepted as a fundamental part of a culture. It includes customs, social habits, laws, modes of thinking, and ways of living. Slavery and a belief in slavery were institutions. Other examples are the beliefs in laissez faire, or unionism, or a government social security system. Going out on New Year's Eve to raise a din and clatter is an institution. So are Communist ideology in the Soviet Union and anti-Communism in the United States. Economic life, said the institutionalists, is regulated by economic institutions, not by economic laws. Group social behavior and the thought patterns that influence it are more germane to economic analysis than is the individualism emphasized in marginalist theory. The institutionalists were especially interested in analyzing and reforming the institutions of credit, monopoly, absentee ownership, labor-management relations, social security, and the distribution of income. They advocated economic planning and the mitigation of the swings of the business cycle.

3. The Darwinian, evolutionary approach should be used in economic analysis, because society and its institutions are constantly changing. Instead of equilibrium, there is motion. The institutionalists disagreed with the static viewpoint that sought to discover eternal economic truths without regard for differences of time and place, without concern for changes that were occurring constantly. Instead of asking "What is?" the institutionalists asked "How did we get here, and where are we going?" The evolution and functioning of economic institutions should be the central theme in economics. This approach requires a knowledge not only of economics but also of history, cultural anthropology, political science, sociology, philosophy, psychology, and social psychology.

4. The institutionalists rejected the prevailing idea of normal equilibrium. Instead they emphasized the principle of circular causation, or cumulative changes that may be either salutary or harmful in seeking economic and social goals. Maladjustments in economic life are not departures from normal equilibrium but are themselves normal. Before World War II the outstanding maladjustment was the business slump. Then the problems of economic development became the center of attention. Now we have largely turned away from that area in our concern over inflation. The institutionalists are convinced that collective controls through government are necessary to continually correct and overcome deficiencies and maladjustments in economic life.

The conflict between the concept of normal equilibrium and that of circular causation was discussed in Chapter 4 in regard to David Hume, and it will be discussed in Chapter 23 in regard to Ragnar Nurkse and Gunnar Myrdal. Myrdal is one of the leading institutional economists today, but the discussion about him is contained in the chapter on economic development because he has spent much of his life working in that area and has made enormous contributions to it.

5. Instead of the harmony of interests that most of their contemporaries and predecessors deduced from their theories, the institutionalists recognized serious clashes of interests. People, to be sure, are cooperative, collective creatures. They organize themselves into groups for the members' mutual self-interest, which becomes the common interest of the group. There are, however, clashes of interests between groups, such as big business against small business, consumers against producers, farmers against urban dwellers, employers against workers, importers against domestic producers, the makers of goods against the makers of money. Here again a representative and impartial government must reconcile or override clashing interests for the common good and for the efficient working of the economic system.

6. The institutionalists espoused liberal, democratic reforms in order to bring about the more equitable distribution of wealth and income. They denied that market prices are adequate indices of individual and social welfare and that unregulated markets lead to the efficient allocation of resources and the best distribution of income. Institutionalists were concerned with social costs and social benefits, a topic considered under the discussion of Arthur Cecil Pigou in Chapter 21. The fact that Pigou was a marginalist rather than an institutionalist suggests a significant link between the two schools of

thought. The institutionalists invariably condemned laissez faire and ·
favored a larger role for government in economic and social affairs.

7. This school favored the inductive rather than the deductive
approach. A call went forth for more fact-finding, more statistical
studies, and a closer examination of the actual workings of the system. Abstract theorizing—especially that of the marginalists—was
condemned as unrealistic and sterile.

8. The institutionalists repudiated the pleasure-pain psychology.
They reached out instead for a better psychology, and some of them
incorporated Freudian and behaviorist ideas into their thinking.

What Groups of People Did the Institutionalist School Serve or Seek to Serve?

This school represented middle-class desire for reform in an era of
growing big business and banker capitalism. It represented the
needs and interests of agrarian, small business, and labor groups.
Government workers, reformers, humanitarians, leaders of consumers' organizations, and union members were attracted to the institutionalist ideas, which they hoped might alter the orientation of
private business enterprise in favor of the common good.

How Was the Institutionalist School Valid, Useful, or Correct in Its Time?

The institutionalists retarded the development of a rigid orthodoxy
in economic thinking. Many of their criticisms of orthodox theory
were valid and helped to revise that type of theory to make it more
tenable. The institutional stress on looking at the economy as a
whole as part of an evolutionary process and in an institutional setting still has validity. For example, the wages of railroad workers
depend more on the development of craft unionism and the procedures of government regulations than they do on the marginal productivity of labor. Again, the widespread interest in national economic growth and development since World War II is a vindication
of institutionalist ideas.

The institutionalists roused belated but deep and lasting concern
over business cycles and monopolies. They promoted a reform movement that remains powerful today. Modest steps toward national
economic planning for limited objectives such as conservation and
full employment are in line with institutionalist thought. In a world
where knowledge is increasingly fragmented and compartmentalized, they urged closer integration of the social sciences. Their
emphasis on inductive studies reduced the gap between eco-

nomic theory and practice. It became popular in government circles, among private non-profit research organizations, in business and labor organizations, and among individuals who toil in the field to reap their harvests of statistical data. The National Bureau of Economic Research, founded by Wesley C. Mitchell and others in 1920 and guided by him for many years, is a monument to the institutionalist method.

How Did the Institutionalist School Outlive Its Usefulness?

To a considerable extent, the school completed its task when its method and viewpoint became part of the common property of many, if not most, economists. With the greatly expanded interest in problems of economic development, there has been new emphasis on the influence of the institutional environment on economic relationships. By their very nature, problems of economic development are dynamic and evolutionary. The growth of statistical and empirical work is a vindication of institutionalist ideas. The appearance of Keynesian analysis, however, with its aggregative approach and its prescriptions for stabilizing the economy, seemed to supersede institutionalism.

Now that reforms and controls have made considerable headway, it has become difficult to reach agreement on what further reforms should be undertaken, and in what order of priority. In 1900 the abuses of unrestricted capitalism and the neglect of social problems were so shockingly visible that reformers could reach some working agreements concerning the changes necessary to ameliorate conditions. Today, especially with legal protection for unionism, social insurance, built-in stabilizers, and governmental responsibility for full employment, people disagree far more about whether further changes are needed and about the direction such changes should take. The small but vocal and growing radical movements that seek drastic solutions to today's social problems are looking far beyond the reforms promoted by the institutionalists. The leadership for social change has passed, perhaps temporarily, to other hands.

Yet the institutional school has not altogether outlived its usefulness. It provides a valuable antidote to some of the weaknesses of standard theory—weaknesses that are as apparent today as they were a half century ago. Keynesian cycle and stabilization theory uses a static rather than a dynamic methodology. And the strong mathematical trend in economic theorizing tends to ignore the institutional determinants of economic behavior. Mathematics is very useful for the rigorous handling of complicated relationships, but it leads to a mechanistic view of the economy, in which stable relationships are given far more importance than the changes that occur in economic and social institutions and in the economic process as a whole.

R. A. Gordon, Professor of Economics at the University of California, said:

> It is clear . . . that what passes for orthodox economics is today more institutional than it was before, say, the Great Depression. . . . In an important sense, however, the central core of economic theory is about as "noninstitutional" as it was in Veblen's day. Samuelson's *Foundations* or Hicks's *Value and Capital* is developed in much more of an institutional vacuum than was Marshall's *Principles*. Theoretically inclined economists, with some exceptions, do not take kindly to the study of institutional arrangements or institutional development. Despite some of the new developments in the theory of the firm and of market behavior, micro theory is still concerned primarily with the kind of "equilibrium economics" which Veblen so severely criticized.[1]

An indication that the institutional school is viable can be seen in the fact that it has both a formal organization and a journal. The Association for Evolutionary Economics was founded in 1965 by John S. Gambs. Clarence E. Ayres became its first president and Gambs its second. This organization holds annual meetings and publishes the *Journal of Economic Issues*. The nine hundred members of the Association and the fifteen hundred subscriptions to the *Journal* testify to the relevance of institutionalism today.

We shall now turn to Thorstein Veblen, the brooding, enigmatic genius who is considered to be the founder of the institutionalist school.

Veblen

Thorstein Bunde Veblen (1857–1929), the son of Norwegian immigrants, was born on a frontier farm in Wisconsin and raised in rural Minnesota. His undergraduate college education was acquired at Carleton College, where he was a student of J. B. Clark. His graduate work was done at Johns Hopkins, where he failed to obtain a scholarship, and at Yale, where he received a doctorate in philosophy. No academic position was available to him, however, largely because he held agnostic views at a time when a divinity degree was considered a desirable prerequisite for teaching philosophy.

---

[1] Joseph Dorfman and others, *Institutional Economics: Veblen, Commons, and Mitchell Reconsidered* (Berkeley and Los Angeles, Calif, 1963), pp. 136–37.

Veblen received fellowships at Cornell and at the University of Chicago for postdoctoral work. He became the editor of the *Journal of Political Economy* at Chicago. He was an instructor in economics there from the ages thirty-nine to forty-three; he held this post at a time when many of his classmates were becoming full professors, heads of departments, and later college presidents. Veblen never reached the rank of full professor, despite his eleven books and his lasting world reputation. Even his books were not overwhelming successes during his lifetime, and he had to subsidize the publication of several of them himself.

Because of his marital troubles, his indifference to most of his students, his involvements with women, and his poor teaching techniques, he had to move from college to college. After Chicago, he taught at Stanford, the University of Missouri, and the New School for Social Research. In 1918 he worked briefly for the Food Administration in Washington, D. C., and he served as an editor of the journal *The Dial*. A former student aided him financially in his later years. He died in August 1929, a few months before the great stock market crash and the beginning of the depression he had been predicting.

Veblen was a bitter, skeptical, pessimistic, and lonely man. His books, though written somewhat ponderously and obscurely, are replete with wit, wisdom, and sardonic attacks on middle-class virtues. For example, he wrote about the middle class, which lends its conservative, affected, snobbish tone to periodical literature. In a footnote in *The Theory of Business Enterprise* he defined snobbery with a deft twist of his rapier wit:

> "Snobbery" is here used without disrespect, as a convenient term to denote the element of strain involved in the quest of gentility on the part of persons whose accustomed social standing is less high or less authentic than their aspirations.[2]

Veblen's first and most popular book was *The Theory of the Leisure Class*, published in 1899. It was this book that introduced such terms as "leisure class," "pecuniary emulation," and "conspicuous consumption." Veblen held that the leisure class is engaged in the predatory seizure of goods without working for them. Those who accumulate wealth do so not merely to take care of their physical wants, or even their spiritual, aesthetic, and intellectual wants. Rather, they wish to consume in a way that displays their wealth, for a show of wealth indicates power, prestige, honor, and success in our

[2] Thorstein Veblen, *The Theory of Business Enterprise* (New York, 1904), p. 388.

pecuniary culture. In order to be reputable, such consumption must be wasteful. Poorer people must work in order to subsist, but even their pattern of spending includes an element of wasteful conspicuous consumption. Their outlook on life is imposed by the dominant leisure class.

Women are especially useful in displaying the wealth and importance that men possess. Attired in clothing and shoes that prevent them from doing useful labor, women advertise that they are supported by men. Wearing expensive finery, they indicate that the men to whom they belong are reputably wealthy. Hampered by long fingernails, cumbersome hair styles, delicate skin, or bound and distorted feet, they give constant evidence that they are leisure-class women kept by leisure-class men.

The high gloss of a gentleman's hat or of a patent-leather shoe, said Veblen, has no more intrinsic beauty than a similarly high gloss on a threadbare sleeve. Flowers that are difficult to grow and therefore expensive are not necessarily more beautiful than those that grow wild or with little care. For cropping lawns, pastures, and parks, cows are more useful than deer, but the latter are preferred because they are more expensive, less functional, and not vulgarly lucrative. This argument inspired Henry L. Mencken to write: "Has the genial professor, pondering his great problems, ever taken a walk in the country? And has he, in the course of that walk, ever crossed a pasture inhabited by a cow? And has he, in making that crossing, ever passed astern of the cow herself? And has he, thus passing astern, ever stepped carelessly and—."

One can amuse oneself with many modern evidences of conspicuous consumption. To cite but one example, expensive picture windows in living rooms typically face the street, for that is where they can be seen. Yet the view across the street may be of other houses with other picture windows staring back, or of a cemetery, a dump, or a junk yard. The rear of the house is not favored with an expanse of glass, even if the view is magnificent, because the public would not be aware of the lavish expenditure.

Members of the leisure class must avoid useful, productive work. They must indulge only in wasteful or useless tasks if they are to remain reputable.

> These occupations are government, war, sports, and devout observances. Persons unduly given to difficult theoretical niceties may hold that these occupations are still incidentally and indirectly "productive"; but it is to be noted as decisive of the question in hand that the ordinary and ostensible motive of the leisure class in engaging in these occupations is as-

suredly not an increase of wealth by productive effort. At this as at any other cultural stage, government and war are, at least in part, carried on for the pecuniary gain of those who engage in them; but it is gain obtained by the honourable method of seizure and conversion. These occupations are of the nature of predatory, not of productive, employment.[3]

Force and fraud are present today, Veblen said, as they were among barbarian peoples. We find them in modern warfare, in business, and in sports and games.

Strategy or cunning is an element invariably present in games, as also in warlike pursuits and in the chase. In all of these employments strategy tends to develop into finesse and chicane. Chicane, falsehood, browbeating, hold a well-secured place in the method of procedure of any athletic contest and in games generally. The habitual employment of an umpire, and the minute technical regulations governing the limits and details of permissible fraud and strategic advantage, sufficiently attest the fact that fraudulent practices and attempts to overreach one's opponent are not adventitious features of the game. In the nature of the case habituation to sports should conduce to a fuller development of the aptitude for fraud; and the prevalence in the community of that predatory temperament which inclines men to sports connotes a prevalence of sharp practice and callous disregard of the interests of others.[4]

In the same book Veblen asserted that the evolution of social structure has been a process of natural selection of institutions. Progress can be attributed to the survival of the fittest habits of thought and to the enforced adaptation of individuals to a changing environment. Institutions must change with changing circumstances. The development of these institutions represents the development of society. Unfortunately there is a conflict between current beliefs and current requirements because of a cultural lag in the process of change.

The situation of to-day shapes the institutions of tomorrow through a selective, coercive process, by acting upon men's habitual view of things, and so altering or fortifying a point of view or a mental attitude handed down from the past. The institutions—that is to say the habits of thought—under the guidance of which men live are in this way received from an earlier time. . . . Institutions are products of the past process, are adapted to past circumstances, and are therefore never in full accord with the requirements of the present. . . . At the same time, men's present habits of thought tend to persist indefinitely, except as circum-

[3] Thorstein Veblen, *The Theory of the Leisure Class* (New York, 1934), p. 40. [Originally published in 1899.]
[4] *Ibid.*, pp. 273–74.

stances enforce a change. These institutions which have so been handed down, these habits of thought, points of view, mental attitudes and aptitudes, or what not, are therefore themselves a conservative factor. This is the factor of social inertia, psychological inertia, conservatism. . . . The evolution of society is substantially a process of mental adaptation on the part of individuals under the stress of circumstances which will no longer tolerate habits of thought formed under and conforming to a different set of circumstances in the past.[5]

A portion or class of society that is sheltered from environmental forces will adapt its views more slowly to the altered general situation and will therefore retard the process of social change. The wealthy leisure class is in just such a sheltered position with respect to economic forces that make for change and readjustment. The characteristic attitude of this class is indicated in the maxim that "Whatever is, is right." But the law of natural selection, as applied to human institutions asserts that "Whatever is, is wrong." That is, current institutions are wrong to some extent, from the evolutionary standpoint, because they do not change quickly enough to be in tune with the times.

Veblen attacked marginalist economics and the classical school from which it sprang, declaring John Bates Clark's system static and his "dynamics" essentially a deranged static condition. Veblen saw Clark's system as based on the pre-evolutionary view of normality and natural law—a view that prevents awareness of cumulative change. The hedonism of the dominant economic school would have

> a gang of Aleutian Islanders slushing about in the wrack and surf with rakes and magical incantations for the capture of shell-fish . . . to be engaged on a feat of hedonistic equilibration in rent, wages, and interest. And that is all there is to it. Indeed, for economic theory of this kind, that is all there is to any economic situation. The hedonistic magnitudes vary from one situation to another, but, except for variations in the arithmetical details of the hedonistic balance, all situations are, in point of economic theory, substantially alike.[6]

Hedonism presupposes rational, intelligent people who act quickly and smoothly according to their anticipation of pleasure or pain. They are clearsighted and farsighted.

> The hedonistic conception of man is that of a lightning calculator of pleasures and pains, who oscillates like a homogeneous globule of de-

[5] *Ibid.*, pp. 190–92.
[6] Thorstein Veblen, *The Place of Science in Modern Civilization and Other Essays* (New York, 1919), p. 193.

sire of happiness under the impulse of stimuli that shift him about the area, but leave him intact. He has neither antecedent nor consequent. He is an isolated, definitive human datum, in stable equilibrium except for the buffets of the impinging forces that displace him in one direction or another. Self-imposed in elemental space, he spins symmetrically about his own spiritual axis until the parallelogram of forces bears down upon him, whereupon he follows the line of the resultant. When the force of the impact is spent, he comes to rest, a self-contained globule of desire as before. Spiritually, the hedonistic man is not a prime mover. He is not the seat of a process of living, except in the sense that he is subject to a series of permutations enforced upon him by circumstances external and alien to him.[7]

Since hedonism has come to rule economics, said Veblen, the science has been in the main a theory of distribution of ownership and income. Consistent with the spirit of hedonism, this theory has centered about a doctrine of price.

The normal economic community, upon which theoretical interest has converged, is a business community, which centers about the market, and whose scheme of life is a scheme of profit and loss. Even when some considerable attention is ostensibly devoted to theories of consumption and production, in these systems of doctrine the theories are constructed in terms of ownership, price, and acquisition, and so reduce themselves in substance to doctrines of distributive acquisition.[8]

Veblen in effect accused the marginalists of supporting the present scheme of the distribution of wealth and income. Standard theory, he thought, is not truly a theory of anything, but merely folklore or theology used to justify private property and property incomes. Business economics has been developed to defend the business community, and the questions it asks and seeks to answer are not relevant to the population as a whole. Veblen was concerned with social economics instead of the business economics of price, profit, and ownership.

It is interesting to note that Veblen attacked the concept of perfect competition, which then dominated standard economic theory. He recognized that most businessmen had some monopolistic control over the prices they charged and that they used advertising to strengthen their market positions. This analysis, published in 1904, foreshadowed the rise of the theory of monopolistic or imperfect competition in 1933. Here, indeed, is an example of a cultural lag, for Veblen's contribution was largely ignored at the time. The marginalists later used the theory of monopolistic competition to explain the

[7] *Ibid.*, pp. 73–74.
[8] *Ibid.*, p. 183.

allocation of resources in a static situation. Veblen used the historical, evolutionary approach to show the long-run consequences for capitalism of such monopolistic practices.

The broad principle which guides producers and merchants, large and small, in fixing the prices at which they offer their wares and services is what is known in the language of the railroads as 'charging what the traffic will bear.' When a given enterprise has a strict monopoly of the supply of a given article or of a given class of services this principle applies in the unqualified form in which it has been understood among those who discuss railway charges. But where the monopoly is less strict, where there are competitors, there the competition that has to be met is one of the factors to be taken account of in determining what the traffic will bear; competition may even become the most serious factor in the case if the enterprise in question has little or none of the character of a monopoly. But it is very doubtful if there are any successful business ventures within the range of the modern industries from which the monopoly element is wholly absent. They are, at any rate, few and not of great magnitude. And the endeavor of all such enterprises that look to a permanent continuance of their business is to establish as much of a monopoly as may be. Such a monopoly position may be a legally established one, or one due to location or the control of natural resources, or it may be a monopoly of a less definite character resting on custom and prestige (good-will). This latter class of monopolies are not commonly classed as such; although in character and degree the advantage which they give is very much the same as that due to a differential advantage in location or in the command of resources. The end sought by the systematic advertising of the larger business concerns is such a monopoly of custom and prestige. This form of monopoly is sometimes of great value, and is frequently sold under the name of good-will, trademarks, brands, etc. Instances are known where such monopolies of custom, prestige, prejudice, have been sold at prices running up into the millions.

The great end of consistent advertising is to establish such differential monopolies resting on popular conviction. And the advertiser is successful in this endeavor to establish a profitable popular conviction, somewhat in proportion as he correctly apprehends the manner in which a popular conviction on any given topic is built up.[9]

So much for Veblen's attack on standard theory. What did he offer in its place? He believed that work is not generally irksome, or the survival of the human race would be jeopardized. Human beings' greatest triumph over the other species in the struggle for survival has been their superior ability to control the forces of environment.

[9] Thorstein Veblen, *The Theory of Business Enterprise* (New York, 1904), pp. 53–55.

It is not their proclivity for effort but for achievement that really matters. When not harassed by overwork, people have not an aversion to work, but an instinct for workmanship that conduces to the material well-being of the race and its biological success. People inherently want to do work and to do it well. They deprecate waste. Allied with the equally important instinct for parenthood, the instinct for workmanship impels the current generation to improve life for posterity. Basically we try to avoid greed and indolence, we educate and train our children, we improve technology, and we conserve our resources—all because of our instinct for workmanship and our wish to provide for our descendants. This instinct conflicts with the conventional antipathy to useful effort, but it is the dominant force, especially among the great mass of artisans, farmers, and technological experts.

Small-scale handicraft production and trade have gradually given way to large-scale capitalistic enterprises. Formerly the market was narrow and business was managed with a view to earning a livelihood. The modern industrial system has as its dominant features the machine process and investment for profit. The growth of markets and investments has created new opportunities for shrewd manipulation. As the captains of industry enlarge their domain, their interests diverge more and more from those of the rest of the community. Instead of being interested in the production of goods, they are concerned primarily with maximizing profits. While the two objectives may coincide, the production of goods is merely the means to profit; and when the two goals conflict, the former is sacrificed to the latter. If necessary, coalitions of big businessmen, holding companies, and other types of monopolies are organized to restrict output and raise prices. When making money takes precedence over making goods, the instinct for workmanship is thwarted because it comes to be rated in terms of salesmanship. The absentee owners, who are in control, hamper the increased output of goods that would otherwise occur. Their manipulations prevent prices from falling. They force workers and capital into the more competitive sectors of the economy, thus worsening the situation there. They profit from disturbances in the system that may hinder output. If the economy is unstable, the opportunities for profit increase. The shrewd operator can make money as a bull during the upswing of business and as a bear during the downswing. Progress is hampered by big business, which is more interested in the vendibility of goods than in their serviceability for the needs of society. Those interested in problems of price rather than in production include business enterprisers and their assistants—salesmen, accountants, advertisers, and so forth.

Here is how Veblen expressed the contradiction and conflict between making goods and making money:

Business is a pursuit of profits, and profits are to be had from profitable sales, and profitable sales can be made only if prices are maintained at a profitable level, and prices can be maintained only if the volume of marketable output is kept within reasonable limits; so that the paramount consideration in such business as has to do with the staple industries is a reasonable limitation of the output. "Reasonable" means "what the traffic will bear"; that is to say, "what will yield the largest net return." . . .

The business man's place in the economy of nature is to "make money," not to produce goods. The production of goods is a mechanical process, incidental to the making of money; whereas the making of money is a pecuniary operation, carried on by bargain and sale, not by mechanical appliances and powers. . . . The highest achievement in business is the nearest approach to getting something for nothing. What any given business concern gains must come out of the total output of productive industry, of course; and to that extent any given business concern has an interest in the continued production of goods. But the less any given business concern can contrive to give for what it gets, the more profitable its own traffic will be. Business success means "getting the best of the bargain."

The common good, so far as it is a question of material welfare, is evidently best served by an unhampered working of the industrial system at its full capacity, without interruption or dislocation. But it is equally evident that the owner or manager of any given concern or section of this industrial system may be in a position to gain something for himself at the cost of the rest by obstructing, retarding or dislocating this working system at some critical point in such a way as will enable him to get the best of the bargain in his dealings with the rest. This appears constantly in the altogether usual, and altogether legitimate, practice of holding out for a better price. So also in the scarcely less usual, and no less legitimate, practice of withholding needed ground or right of way, or needed materials or information, from a business rival. . . . Sabotage of this kind is indispensable to any large success in industrial business.

But it is also evident that the private gain which the business concerns come in for by this management entails a loss on the rest of the community, and that the loss suffered by the rest of the community is necessarily larger than the total gains which these manoeuvres bring to the business concerns; inasmuch as the friction, obstruction and retardation of the moving equilibrium of production involved in this businesslike sabotage necessarily entails a disproportionate curtailment of output.[10]

---

[10] Thorstein Veblen, *The Vested Interests and the Common Man* (New York, 1946), pp. 91–94. [Originally published in 1919.]

Veblen believed that the importance of the entrepreneur as a bearer of risks is negligible. Most of the risks now associated with investment and production could easily be eliminated with no reduction of the national income. Risks are associated with the promotion of corporate consolidations, with sales and advertising campaigns, with the establishment of new brand names, with the exploitation of patents and franchises, and with the attempt to capitalize business goodwill. These activities are superb for making money, but they and the risks associated with them can be dispensed with in the production of goods. There are very few real risks involved in meeting the basic living requirements of the working population. The only risks technicians cannot overcome with a high degree of success are those associated with climate, weather, and natural catastrophes. As these hazards are not a matter of individual responsibility, they could be taken care of by the community out of the net surplus product of industry. Then no private risk-taking function would require remuneration.

Credit has a special role to play in modern business, according to Veblen. Borrowing money can increase profits as long as the current rate of business earnings exceeds the rate of interest. Under competitive conditions, what is profitable for one businessman to undertake becomes compulsory for all competitors. Those who take advantage of the opportunities afforded by credit are in a position to undersell those who do not. The recourse to credit therefore becomes widespread and typical. The competitive earning capacity of an enterprise comes to rest on the basis of the initial capital plus such borrowed funds as this capital will support. As aggregate earnings are only slightly larger than they might have been without credit, the rate of profit on the total amount invested tends to fall. The competitive use of credit in extending business operations gives a business concern a differential advantage against other competitors but the expansion of credit has no aggregate effect on earnings or on total industrial output. In fact, aggregate net profits from industry are reduced by the amount of interest that has to be paid to creditors outside the industrial process.

Why does the expansion of credit have no effect on total earnings or on industrial output? Is it not true that borrowed funds represent property? Won't this property be converted to productive use by drawing into the industrial process, directly or indirectly, the material items of wealth that these funds represent? No, replied Veblen. While loans may be covered by property held by the lender, the property may be otherwise engaged. Real estate may support loans even though it cannot be converted to industrial use. Loans that are backed by corporate stock and industrial plants duplicate material items that are already a part of the industrial process. Credit created by banks has little real wealth behind it; credit therefore has only a pecuniary (business) existence and not a material (industrial) one. It represents only fictitious industrial equipment.

Veblen neglected the fact that in our private-enterprise economy, bank credit enables a businessman to mobilize a supply of labor from among those who are unemployed, underemployed, or self-employed (such as artisans and farmers). The drawing of labor into large industrial establishments increases the total output. Likewise, credit permits the mobilization of raw materials and capital equipment and the expansion of their supply. It widens the markets and thereby stimulates greater production. Veblen's strictures on credit would be valid only if the supplies of the factors of production and final products were inelastic and therefore could not be readily expanded.

It would be unfair to Veblen, however, to criticize the inadequacies of his theory for a private-enterprise economy. He did not accept that frame of reference, and he looked at our society as a detached observer. In his analysis of credit, he probably meant that credit is not essential to economic life. Primitive societies certainly functioned without it. A modern technological society could dispense with credit if it were organized as some sort of industrial republic run by engineers or as a socialist society. From this vantage point credit adds nothing to the functioning of an industrial society. In fact, credit detracts from it to the extent that it opens the way to financial manipulation, speculation, increased costs, and greater profit.

Veblen's views on credit led him directly into his business-cycle theory. The extension of credit enables competing businessmen to bid up the prices of the material capital goods used in industry. As their dollar value increases, these goods serve as collateral for the further extension of credit. The extension of loans on collateral such as shares of stock or real property has a cumulative character. Credit expands even more with the organization of monopolies, for the costs of the reorganization and the promoters' profits are capitalized in the securities issued. The expected increase in the profits of the monopolies and the imputed goodwill of the new corporations also are capitalized.

This cumulative extension of credit rests on a shaky foundation. Sooner or later a discrepancy will arise between the money value of the collateral and the capitalized value of the property computed on expected earnings. In other words, the rise in earnings does not keep pace with the inflation of the nominal capital (capital plus loans). When this discrepancy becomes obvious, a period of liquidation begins. Along with liquidation, the industrial crisis is accompanied by credit cancellations, high discount rates, falling prices, forced sales, shrinkage of capitalization, and reduced output. The creditors take over business properties, thereby further consolidating owner-ship and control into fewer hands.

Workers benefit during prosperity not through higher rates of pay but through fuller employment. As the general price level rises, the increased cost of living reduces real rates of wages. Slowly money wages rise in response to increasing prices of goods, and this helps bring prosperity to an end, for profit margins shrink and capital val-ues fall.

> Business is the quest of profits, and an inhibition of this quest must touch the seat of its vital motives. Industrial depression means that the business men engaged do not see their way to derive a satisfactory gain from letting the industrial process go forward on the lines and in the vol-ume for which the material equipment of industry is designed. It is not worth their while, and it might even work them pecuniary harm.[11]

Veblen thought that the discrepancy between capitalization and earning capacity is chronic so long as no extraneous circumstances enter temporarily to set aside the trend of business affairs. Therefore chronic depression, more or less pronounced, is normal under the fully developed regime of machine industry. Depressions are tempo-rarily overcome, however, by speculative increases of prices, new discoveries of precious metals, and credit expansion. The deliberate promotion of monopoly can restore the profitability of business by restricting output and raising prices, thereby bringing the accepted capitalization into line with the actual earning capacity. If successful, the monopoly will neutralize the cheapening of goods and services effected by current industrial progress.

The decline of profits and chronic depression can be remedied by an increase in the wasteful and unproductive consumption of goods as well as through monopoly. But private wasteful expenditure on a scale adequate to offset the surplus productivity of modern industry is nearly out of the question:

> Private initiative cannot carry the waste of goods and services to nearly the point required by the business situation. Private waste is no doubt large, but business principles, leading to saving and shrewd investment,

[11] Thorstein Veblen, *The Theory of Business Enterprise* (New York, 1904), pp. 213–14.

are too ingrained in the habits of modern men to admit an effective retardation of the rate of saving. Something more to the point can be done, and indeed is being done, by the civilized governments in the way of effectual waste. Armaments, public edifices, courtly and diplomatic establishments, and the like, are almost altogether wasteful, so far as bears on the present question. They have the additional advantage that the public securities which represent this waste serve as attractive investment securities for private savings, at the same time that, taken in the aggregate, the savings so invested are purely fictitious savings and therefore do not act to lower profits or prices. Expenditures met by taxation are less expedient for this purpose; although indirect taxes have the peculiar advantage of keeping up the prices of the goods on which they are imposed, and thereby act directly toward the desired end. The waste of time and effort that goes into military service, as well as the employment of the courtly, diplomatic, and ecclesiastical personnel, counts effectually in the same direction. But however extraordinary this public waste of substance latterly has been, it is apparently altogether inadequate to offset the surplus productivity of the machine industry, particularly when this productivity is seconded by the great facility which the modern business organization affords for the accumulation of savings in relatively few hands. There is also the drawback that the waste of time involved in military service reduces the purchasing power of the classes that are drawn into the service, and so reduces the amount of wasteful consumption which these classes might otherwise accomplish.[12]

There is conflict, then, between industry, which produces goods, and business, which produces profit; between making goods and making money; between the instinct for workmanship and pecuniary considerations; between the community at large and the absentee owners, the captains of industry; between the need for stability and the extension of credit; between the buyers, who want more goods at lower prices, and the monopolists, who offer fewer goods at higher prices; between the need for social change and the conservatism of people's patterns of thought and action; between meeting the basic needs of people, which is possible, and the desire for conspicuous consumption, which must leave the demand for goods unfulfilled as long as everyone tries to exceed others in wasteful consumption. This disharmony of interest is also revealed in the relations between workers and employers. Recurring unemployment or half-employment is due to considerations of price.

From the like competitive considerations of price, and of gain in terms of price, it has come about that the interests of the employer are not at one with those of the workmen. . . . On the one hand the workmen

[12] *Ibid.*, pp. 255–57.

have no whole-hearted interest in the efficiency of the work done, but rather in what can be got for it in terms of price; on the other hand the employer has none but a humanitarian—said to be quite secondary—interest in the well being, or even in the continued efficiency, of the workmen. From which follow, on the one hand inhibitory trades-union rules, strikes, lockouts, and the like disturbances of the industrial process, and on the other hand an exploitation of the human raw material of industry that has at times taken quite an untoward scope and direction, in the way of over-work, under-pay, unsafe and unwholesome conditions, and so forth.[13]

What is the solution to the difficulties raised by modern large-scale business enterprise? Veblen was simultaneously critical of and friendly toward socialism, but he was definitely not a socialist himself. He attacked Marx's labor theory of value as being at best tautological and at worst an unproven playful mystification. He denied the socialist claim that the rich are becoming richer and the poor poorer. The existing system, he said, has not made the workers poorer as measured absolutely; but it does tend to make them relatively poorer in terms of comparative economic importance. Modern society intensifies emulation and jealousy, which lead to unrest and make for socialism. With the abolition of private property, human nature will find nobler and socially more serviceable activities than emulating one another. At present, thought Veblen in 1892, we waste half our labor in abstaining from useful work and in conspicuous waste.

Veblen thought that the engineers would make the social revolution and operate industry for the common good. They are the ones to object to ownership, finance, sabotage, credit, and unearned income because they interfere with technological efficiency and progress. Engineers are the best representatives of the community at large, for capital and labor, bargaining over prices, have become a loose-knit vested interest that seeks its own benefit to the detriment of society. The outcome has been businesslike concession and compromise between them. The two sides play a game of chance and skill, with the industrial system becoming a victim of interference on both sides. Yet the material welfare of the community at large, and more specifically of the workers, depends on the smooth working of the industrial system without interference. This the engineers can achieve. They promote the community's material welfare and provide free income for the nonproductive classes. Unlike the owners and workers, they are not motivated by self-interest. Because the technicians are

[13] Thorstein Veblen, *Imperial Germany and the Industrial Revolution* (New York, 1915), p. 120.

more homogeneous and unified than the workers, they are the natural leaders, the officers of the line, the men with a spirit of tangible performance and the most highly developed instinct of workmanship. Veblen asserted that a soviet of technicians could solve the nation's problems, but that the chances of it are remote. At present the technical men are docile and harmless, generally well fed, and rather placidly content with the "full dinner-pail" allowed them by the vested interests.

The overview at the beginning of this chapter discussed the reforming aspect of institutionalism. This outlook definitely does not hold for Veblen. He did not base his hopes on the amelioration of conditions under capitalism; in fact, he was so fundamentally opposed to this system that he hoped to see it superseded entirely. The idea that the engineers would make the social revolution was perhaps a fleeting thought for him. Toward the end of his life he looked quite favorably at the Soviet Russian experiment. Because he died in 1929, Veblen knew nothing of the excesses of Stalinism that were to develop in the mid-1930's. Basically, however, he remained a pessimist, taking a dim view of human nature and the future prospect for humanity.

In the following chapter we shall consider two institutionalists who were reformers in varying degrees. John R. Commons was the archetypal reformer. Wesley C. Mitchell seemed to favor reforms, although his preoccupation with a maze of statistical studies led him to underemphasize the importance of reforms.

Bibliography

DORFMAN, JOSEPH, *Thorstein Veblen and His America*. New York: Viking, 1934.

———, and others, *Institutional Economics: Veblen, Commons, and Mitchell Reconsidered*. Berkeley and Los Angeles, Calif.: University of California Press, 1963.

DOWD, DOUGLAS F., *Thorstein Veblen*. New York: Twayne, 1964.

———, ed., *Thorstein Veblen: A Critical Reappraisal*. Ithaca, N. Y.: Cornell University Press, 1958.

GAMBS, JOHN S., *Beyond Supply and Demand*. New York: Columbia University Press, 1946.

GRUCHY, ALLAN G., *Contemporary Economic Thought. The Contribution of Neo-Institutional Economics*. Clifton, N. J.: Augustus M. Kelley, 1972.

———, *Modern Economic Thought: The American Contribution*. New York: Prentice-Hall, 1947.

VEBLEN, THORSTEIN, *Absentee Ownership and Business Enterprise in Recent Times*. New York: Viking, 1954. [Originally published in 1923.]

————, *The Engineers and the Price System*. New York: Viking, 1947. [Originally published in 1921.]

————, *Essays in Our Changing Order*. New York: Viking, 1934.

————, *Imperial Germany and the Industrial Revolution*. New York: Macmillan, 1915.

————, *The Instinct of Workmanship*. New York: Huebsch, 1918. [Originally published in 1914.]

————, *The Place of Science in Modern Civilization and Other Essays*. New York: Huebsch, 1919.

————, *The Theory of Business Enterprise*. New York: Scribner's, 1904.

————, *The Theory of the Leisure Class*. New York: Random House, Modern Library edition, 1934. [Originally published in 1899.]

————, *The Vested Interests and the Common Man*. New York: Viking, 1946. [Originally published in 1919.]

————, *What Veblen Taught*, ed. by Wesley C. Mitchell. New York: Viking, 1936.

20

The Institutionalist School:
Commons and Mitchell

Commons

John Rogers Commons (1862–1945) was a student of economic institutions in action. In fact he took his college classes to visit prisons, charitable organizations, mental hospitals, law courts, union halls, factories, and legislative chambers. These excursions exemplified his approach, for he sought to integrate the social sciences—ethics, sociology, psychology, political science, history, and jurisprudence—with the study of economics. Commons also became a great reformer, a forerunner of the New Dealers. He advocated an increasing role for government in adjudicating among the conflicting interests of many different groups. Instead of a harmony of interests, he detected a clash of interests that had to be curbed in order for society to function in an orderly manner.

Commons was born in Ohio during the Civil War. His parents practiced their antislavery views by helping to run an underground railway for the escape of black slaves to Canada. His father was an impoverished newspaper publisher who taught his sons the printing trade, and his mother ran a boarding house to help support the family. Commons graduated from Oberlin College at twenty-six, earning his way as a typesetter in a printing office and losing time because he suffered several nervous breakdowns. He was an ardent labor unionist, and after reading Henry George's *Progress and Poverty* in his freshman year, he became a "single-taxer." His record as an undergraduate was poor, but he was permitted to graduate because his illness was an extenuating circumstance and because his professors recognized his insatiable curiosity and persistence.

Commons did two years of graduate work at Johns Hopkins University, but he never earned his Ph.D. because he failed a history examination. He then taught a year at Wesleyan University, but his contract was not renewed. After that he found employment at Oberlin, at Indiana University, and at Syracuse University. When Commons was interviewed by Chancellor James R. Day of Syracuse in the spring of 1895, he decided to tell the whole truth: He labeled himself as a socialist, a single-taxer, a free-silverite, a greenbacker, a municipal-ownerist, and a member of the Congregational Church. The chancellor replied that he did not care what Commons was as long as he was not an "obnoxious socialist." In his autobiography called *Myself*, Commons, with whimsical exaggeration, wrote: "That settled it. I mistakenly thought I was not of the obnoxious kind."

At Syracuse Commons occupied the chair in sociology established by Mr. Huyler, the candy manufacturer. "I taught ethnology, anthropology, criminology, charity organization, taxation, political economy, municipal government, and other things, all under the name of sociology." His career at Syracuse foundered when, without prior consultation, he was announced as one of the speakers at a mass meeting of all the churches protesting Sunday baseball. Chancellor Day was the chairman and principal speaker at the meeting. After he had hurriedly investigated the problem, Commons in his speech opposed professional baseball with admission fees on Sunday. But he defended the right of the workers to play ball on Sunday in view of their having to work six full days a week. Despite threats of irate parents to withdraw their children from Syracuse unless Commons were dismissed, Chancellor Day defended his right to dissent. However, it became more difficult for Syracuse to solicit funds successfully because of the baseball episode, and a year or so later the Board of Trustees abolished the Huyler chair in sociology instead of dismissing Commons. Thus, after four years at Syracuse, he was once again without a job. He drew some inferences from this experience:

It was not religion, it was capitalism, that governed Christian colleges. Afterwards I sought the fundamental reason, and included it in my historical development of Institutional Economics. The older economists based their definitions of wealth on *holding* something useful for one's own use and exchange. I distinguished a double meaning. The other meaning was, *withholding* from others what they need but do not own. . . . It made possible a distinction of Wealth from Assets which I began to think economists and laity had failed to distinguish. . . .

I figured that a "chair" in political economy was not physically pulled out from under you, it was economically pulled out by withholding the funds. This was such a customary, legal, and quiet way of doing it, under the institution of private property, that everybody, including economists, took it as a part of the Natural Order not needing investigation. At least, I knew, after 1899 at Syracuse, that holding and withholding were not the same, and that the latter was more important. It was the foundation of assets. It converted Chancellor Day from defiance of Protestants to leg-pulling of Plutocrats.[1]

During the following five years Commons received subsidies and salaries from various sources to engage in research. In 1900 he began publishing the first monthly index of wholesale prices. The index was terminated, along with Commons' salary, in September 1900 when it started to rise, to the chagrin of the wealthy Democratic bimetallist who financed the venture. Commons' employer disliked this indication of McKinley prosperity. It may well have been Commons' deep alienation during this period of joblessness that led him to consider "unemployment the bitterest foe of the capitalist system."

Commons studied immigration for the federal Industrial Commission. He worked for the National Civic Federation, which sought to conciliate labor disputes through collective bargaining and trade agreements. In 1904 he went to the University of Wisconsin, where he remained until retirement. As an advisor to Governor Robert M. La Follette, he drafted Wisconsin's civil service law and a bill providing for state regulation of public utilities. In 1911 he wrote the draft of a law providing for workmen's compensation and accident prevention. In 1921 he developed the idea that the employer should be financially responsible for unemployment; this was enacted into law in Wisconsin in 1932. To end the "loan shark" evil, he helped get a Small Loans Act passed, limiting interest to 3.5 per cent per month. He was the author of Wisconsin's minimum wage law for women and its improved child labor law; he also advocated a program of health insurance, not established in his time. Commons pioneered in writing labor history, in promoting labor conciliation, and in advocating social legislation.

Commons, like other institutionalists, made the conflict of interests, not the harmony of interests, the starting point of his economics. Each school of economics, he said, arose out of a conflict of interests; yet each rejected the conflict from which it sprang. Economic conflicts, which lead to political and military conflicts, originate in scar-

[1] John R. Commons, *Myself* (New York, 1934), pp. 58–59.

city. Economic classes develop from similarities of interest in obtaining and retaining ownership of shares of the world's limited supply of wealth. Commons felt that Marx had erred in two respects: first, in maintaining that there are merely two classes, and, second, in failing to identify the major class conflict. Commons held that the major clash of interests occurred between producers and consumers of wealth. These two groups could be broken up into many conflicting subclasses, such as buyers versus sellers, borrowers versus lenders, farmers versus laborers, and capitalists versus landowners. These subclasses in turn could be broken down into wheat farmers, livestock farmers, bankers, manufacturers, merchants, skilled and unskilled laborers, mine owners, railway owners, and so on. Economic classes organize for concerted action according to shared economic interests. This results in collective action within groups and conflicts among groups. Out of these conflicts arise a workable harmony of interests, or a stalemate, or an untenable impasse that requires the strong arm of still another collective action—practical politics and war—to bring not harmony but order out of conflict. Besides conflict, there exist mutual dependency and a desire for orderly and stable relations. Since social phenomena embody the contradictory elements of conflict, dependence, and order, they cannot be analyzed and settled once and forever; instead they are recurring problems that must be continually dealt with.

The transaction between individuals is the key problem in economics and in jurisprudence. A transaction is surrounded by rules of conduct that give rise to rights, duties, liberties, private property, governments, and associations. These are the reciprocal promises and threats, express or implied, that govern man's relations with man. Every transaction is a meeting of wills involving a transfer of commodities and a determination of their prices.

> The transaction is two or more wills giving, taking, persuading, coercing, defrauding, commanding, obeying, competing, governing, in a world of scarcity, mechanism and rules of conduct. The court deals with the will-in-action. Like the modern physicist or chemist, its ultimate unit is not an atom but an electron, always in motion—not an individual but two or more individuals in action. It never catches them except in motion. Their motion is a transaction.
>
> A transaction occurs at a point of time. But transactions flow one into another over a period of time, and this flow is a process. The courts have fully developed the notion of this process in the concept of a "going concern," which they have taken over from the customs of business, and which is none other than a technological process of production and con-

sumption of physical things and a business process of buying and selling, borrowing and lending, commanding and obeying, according to shop rules or working rules or laws of the land. The physical process may be named a "going plant," the business process a "going business," and the two constitute a "going concern" made up of action and reaction with nature's forces and transactions between human beings according to accepted rules.[2]

Commons discerned three types of transactions: bargaining, rationing, and managerial. A *bargaining transaction* is the negotiation between individuals of approximately equal status over the purchase and sale of property. Because each party to the transaction has other alternatives neither is coerced. A *rationing transaction* also transfers ownership or amends property rights, but it is based on an authoritative rather than a voluntary relationship. Examples are governments, which allocate tax burdens; trade unions, which set the wage rates for individual workers; and corporations, which budget their departments and divisions. A *managerial transaction* is also authoritative, as when a company manager or foreman commands the services of the workers.

Commons thought that all three types of transactions coexist in any society, but that the combinations change with time and place. In this country economic factors such as the rise of large corporations enlarged the sphere of rationing and managerial transactions and reduced the scope of bargaining transactions—a substitution of authority for discretion. In other countries political developments such as the rise of Communism and Fascism led to a similar result by enhancing command and obedience relationships.

Veblen defined an institution as a widely prevalent habit of thought; Commons defined it as collective action in control of individual action. The weakness of the individual has driven him to combine into corporations and unions. Governments have granted sovereign powers and immunities to these associations. The state itself, however, interferes with supply and demand through its power to declare and conduct war, levy taxes, police the nation, and coin money. The state encourages or protects certain businesses and occupations rather than others; it restrains certain activities deemed detrimental to the whole; it induces individuals and associations to act in one direction rather than another.

Collective action means more than mere "control" of individual action. It means liberation and expansion of individual action; thus, collective

[2] John R. Commons, *Legal Foundations of Capitalism* (New York, 1924), pp. 7–8.

action is literally the means to liberty. The only way in which "liberty" can be obtained is by imposing duties on others who might interfere with the activity of the "liberated" individual. The American people obtained liberty for the slaves by imposing duties on the slaveowners.[3]

Commons attached great importance to the meaning of property. Before 1890 the Supreme Court was concerned with corporeal property. Afterwards the Court added the concept of intangible property. Commons interpreted this concept to mean the right to fix prices by withholding from others what they need but do not own. Court decisions involving reasonable value were concerned with intangible property and the conflicts of interest it engendered.

Veblen, said Commons, was introducing the same idea of intangible property into economics at the time that he was. Both men became known as institutional economists.

> But the difference was that Veblen obtained his case material from the testimony of financial magnates before the United States Industrial Commission of 1900, so that his notion of intangible property ended in the Marxian extortion and exploitation. But my sources were my participation in collective action, in drafting bills, and my necessary study, during these participations, of the decisions of the Supreme Court covering the period; so that my notion of intangible property ends in the common-law notion of reasonable value.
>
> On analyzing this notion, not only in Supreme Court cases but also in collective bargaining, labor arbitration and commercial arbitration cases, I discovered that, of course, the decisions of these tribunals began with conflict of interests, then took into account the evident idea of dependence of conflicting interests on each other; then reached a decision by the highest authority, the Supreme Court or the labor and commercial arbitration courts, endeavoring to bring—not harmony of interests—but order out of the conflict of interests, known by the Court as "due process of law." [4]

Commons contrasted the social and the individual points of view. The social concept of *wealth* depends on use values and on abundance. The individual concept of *assets* depends on scarcity value and is measured by prices. Capitalism refers to the double process of creating use value for others and restricting its supply so as to create scarcity value. Hence capitalism requires two units of measurement, the man-hour and the dollar. The first measures the quantity of use value created; the second measures its scarcity value. Man-hours

---

[3] John R. Commons, *The Economics of Collective Action* (New York, 1950), pp. 34–35. Reprinted with permission of The Macmillan Company (New York).
[4] John R. Commons, *Institutional Economics* (New York, 1934), p. 4.

measure wealth and represent a producing society, whereas dollars measure assets and represent an acquisitive society.

> Man's power over nature is productivity, measured by man-hours. His output is augmentation of wealth (use-value). Man's power over others is measured by dollars (scarcity-value). It is the quantity of production relative to the quantity wanted, and restriction of output is augmentation of prices, values, and assets.
>
> It was this confusion of production with productivity that permitted the economists to abandon Ricardo's man-power and substitute the dollar as the measure of efficiency. This confused producing-power with bargaining power. To buy at low prices and sell at high prices became a definition of efficiency, whereas it is a definition of bargaining power. The latter consists in taking advantage of the relative scarcities or abundance of labor and commodities on the markets. The former consists in taking advantage of the relative powers of man over nature's forces on the farm and in the factory.[5]

At a time when labor unions were less widely accepted than today, Commons defended them as a means of expressing the collective will of workers in bargaining with employers. Collective bargaining allows individual wills to meet and become a part of the collective will. Although government intervention in the economy was generally deplored in his time, Commons suggested that the state had expanded its powers to curb the abuses of the economic power flowing from the accumulation of private property. The state, he thought, exists as an impartial force to rectify the imbalances of power. The worker has a property right in his job, and the courts should protect it, just as they protect the businessman's right to a profit.

Commons and Samuel Gompers, long-time president of the American Federation of Labor, knew and admired each other. Both viewed intellectuals in the trade union movement with suspicion. Both believed that by frequently leading the unions into the labyrinth of politics, the intellectuals neglected the immediate issues of wages and working conditions. (Intellectuals are often frustrated and amazed when workers fail to share their enthusiasm for long-range reforms.) Commons and Gompers especially disagreed with radical intellectuals who believed that the labor movement should work toward overthrowing the capitalist system. Accepting capitalism, they opposed radical changes in the system, whether violent or peaceful. They believed in a step-by-step evolutionary process to avoid a host of unforeseeable troubles. As each stage of progress becomes rooted in successful experience, the basis for the next step is created.

[5] *Ibid.*, 285–86.

Despite Commons' gradualist approach to trade unionism, his views on this and other issues actually won him denunciations of his radical tendencies. Today, however, many of his ideas on social reform are generally accepted and are compatible with the prevailing new orthodoxy.

Mitchell

Wesley Clair Mitchell (1874–1948), Veblen's most brilliant student, was the youngest of the three towering figures of the institutionalist school. Veblen was the great iconoclast who attacked with savage glee what he considered the absurdities of orthodox theory that defended the status quo; he gave institutionalism a philosophy and a theory. Commons was the great social reformer who relied on government intervention, under the rule of law, to harmonize and compromise conflicting group interests; he made institutionalism a crusade for social reform. Mitchell was the great researcher whose most notable work centered on an analysis of business fluctuations; he gave institutionalism its empirical bent. It is possible that Mitchell immersed himself in statistical studies in order to avoid an open clash with the orthodox economic theorists. He was too gentle and discreet to strike at the roots of marginalism with the ferocity of a Veblen, but he did criticize its unrealistic abstractions and its methodology. He felt that Veblen had progressed far beyond contemporary economists because of his more adequate view of human nature and his broader understanding of cultural processes. Yet Veblen relied too much on speculations that were not verified empirically. Mitchell believed that his statistical studies would provide a firmer foundation for Veblen's pioneer work.

Mitchell was born in Rushville, Illinois. His father, a Union soldier in the Civil War, was a country doctor who suffered all his life from a badly injured leg. Despite the family's financial difficulties his mother insisted that Wesley go to college, and in 1892 he entered the first class of the newly organized University of Chicago. Later, as a graduate student, he spent a winter studying in Germany on a fellowship, but he was not impressed with the state of economic science there. In 1899 he received his Ph.D. *summa cum laude* from Chicago. He took a position in the Census Office in Washington, then he taught and did research at the University of Chicago, the University of California, Columbia University, and the New School for Social Research. During the latter part of his life he also did consultation work in Washington. In 1915 he wrote a monograph for the

Bureau of Labor Statistics called *The Making and Use of Index Numbers,* which has remained a classic over the years. In addition to his studies of business cycles and index numbers, he analyzed the functioning of a money economy, and he directed the National Bureau of Economic Research in launching one of the first comprehensive studies of the amount and distribution of national income.

Economics, said Mitchell, has always been a science of human behavior, even in the hands of those who defined it as a science of wealth. The future of economics, he contended, lies in moving toward more research and less theorizing. In an undergraduate article published in the *Journal of Political Economy* in 1896, he wrote, "Deductive reasoning is proverbially likely to lead the inquirer astray, unless its results are checked and corrected by inductive investigation."

Mitchell was a social reformer who never campaigned for immediate action to remedy a specific ill. Instead he advocated the scientific investigation of human behavior in order to promote an understanding of social problems and their interactions. Only after society is thoroughly understood can it be reformed intelligently.

> I hope that economics will become a science that explains how men behave in getting their livings. I hope it will deal with living men in the actual world of constant change. I want propositions that can be tested for conformity to fact. I want such tests made. In short, I hope we shall develop a science of economics that has such a definite application to actual behavior that it will be a safe guide in efforts to improve economic organization. . . . Perhaps, and perhaps is all we can say, if we can come to a clearer understanding of how we behave, we can learn how to condition men so that their energies will go less into making one another miserable.[6]

The National Bureau of Economic Research, which Mitchell founded in 1920 and directed for twenty-five years, is perhaps the greatest monument to his method. In almost half a century it has published a vast bulk of statistical analyses and like an iceberg has revealed merely a small part of the total data it has amassed. But it has come up with surprisingly little theory and even less in the way of proposed reforms.

Mitchell endorsed both theorizing and factual investigations, with special emphasis on the latter.

> Many of the special investigators feel that they get comparatively little help from theory. Indeed not a few of them are disdainful of what they

---

[6] Quoted in Lucy Sprague Mitchell, *Two Lives* (New York, 1953), pp. 292, 349.

call "theoretical speculations." On the other hand, many of the people who are specially interested in what is called economic theory feel that there is great danger that economics is disintegrating, that it is losing its unity as a science and is running off into the sands of a widely dispersed factual investigation which may serve certain practical purposes but has comparatively little scientific significance.

It would seem that a conception of economics is needed which will be broad enough not merely to embrace all the various types of theoretical economics but also to include the infinite range of factual investigations into special subjects. If it is to be any good, it should be a framework which shows how every item that it includes bears upon the problem as a whole. It should show how any investigation of an economic order that a man may undertake makes its contribution, how it fits in with what other investigators are doing.

Such a framework is gradually emerging not only from the labors of the theorists of different brands but also from the work of many economic specialists. If the theorist can think of economics as a science which deals with economic behavior and get the implication of that phrase he will at last be on the high road to satisfy the need for a framework. . . .

Economics will develop most fruitfully in the future upon the quantitative side. The economists of today stand the best chances of improving upon the work of their predecessors if they rely more and more upon the most accurate statistical recording of observations. That process of developing quantitative analysis in economics is likely to mean a considerable change, at least in the form in which we set many problems. For the problems of economics have in part been formulated primarily by men who were using an introspective type of method; and they were formulated in ways which are open to attack by that kind of method. If the theorist changes his method from the introspective to the objective type, if he tries to rely so far as possible upon the analysis of mass observation, then in many cases he must reformulate the problem before he gets it in shape for attack.[7]

Scientific discoveries, said Mitchell, have revolutionized the arts of production, but the methods of distributing what is produced have changed relatively little. Yet the two processes of producing and distributing wealth are interdependent in a society whose members make their living mainly by creating and spending money incomes. Economic theorists have concentrated mostly on the production of wealth, which focuses attention on industrial activities for making and using goods. The approach through distribution analyzes busi-

[7] Wesley C. Mitchell, *Types of Economic Theory from Mercantilism to Institutionalism*, Vol. II, ed. by Joseph Dorfman. (New York, 1969), pp. 749, 761.

ness efforts directed at getting and spending money. To understand economic activities, we need both approaches.

Our most grievous economic problem arises from the recurring imbalance between production and distribution. When imbalances occur, markets are glutted with unsold goods, and people and machines are unemployed. Furthermore, many enterprises remain backward in their use of equipment and methods; few are huge enough to fully exploit our technological knowledge. We therefore produce less than we might with the same effort even during periods of prosperity.

> Our industrial system is still like an army made up of many companies, each commanded by an independent captain who plans his own campaign on the basis of agreements he reaches with other captains. Only in great emergencies do we mobilize our industries under the direction of a general staff. Our reasons for putting up with such a rudimentary organization are doubtless sound; but they are based upon lack of knowledge. We do not know how to combine full use of our engineering skill with our reliance upon competition to protect the consumer from exploitation. . . .
>
> There is no difficulty in explaining the lag of the social behind the natural sciences. To win understanding of human behavior is far harder than to discover regularities in the behavior of inorganic matter or the simpler forms of life. Not only is man a vastly more complex being than the materials with which the natural sciences deal, and consequently more variable in his responses to given situations, but he is also less susceptible to experimental control by an investigator. . . .
>
> I venture to urge a practical conclusion concerning social policy. If our inability to employ our other resources to the best advantage is due largely to maladjustments among economic processes, and if economics is now applying methods that enable it to deal with actual conditions, then enlightened citizens and public men should do all they can to promote economic research.[8]

The frequent recurrence of economic crises and depressions, said Mitchell in 1935, is evidence that the automatic functioning of our business system is defective. Our difficulties have increased because of the widening of markets, the growth of combinations, the increasing importance of semidurable goods that people can stop buying when times are bad, the movement of farm people to the cities, and the increasing dependence of farmers on markets instead of being as

---

[8] Wesley C. Mitchell, "Economic Resources in Economic Theory," *Studies in Economics and Industrial Relations* (Philadelphia, 1941), pp. 12–13, 16.

self-sufficient as they once were. Business planning has not been able to counteract the growth of factors that make business cycles more serious.

> Coordination within an enterprise is the result of careful planning by experts; coordination among independent enterprises cannot be said to be planned at all; rather is it the unplanned result of natural selection in a struggle for business survival. Coordination within an enterprise has a definite aim—the making of profits; coordination among independent enterprises is limited by the conflicting aims of the several units. Coordination within an enterprise is maintained by a single authority possessed of power to carry its plans into effect; coordination among independent enterprises depends on many different authorities which have no power to enforce a common program, except so far as one can persuade or coerce others. As a result of these conditions, coordination within an enterprise is characterized by economy of effort; coordination among independent enterprises by waste.
>
> In detail, then, economic activity is planned and directed with skill; but in the large there is neither general plan nor central direction. The charge that "capitalistic production is planless" therefore contains both an important element of truth and a large element of error. Apart from the transient programs of economic mobilization adopted under stress of war, civilized nations have not yet developed systematic plans for the sustenance of their populations; they continue to rely on the badly coordinated efforts of private initiative.[9]

The task, then, is to promote careful social or national planning to overcome the worst features of business fluctuations while preserving economic liberty and increasing security. Mitchell's reliance on national planning to ameliorate the human condition was based partly on his pragmatic psychology. He believed that the relations between economics and psychology should be more carefully investigated. He rejected the hedonistic preconceptions of classical and neoclassical economics. Instincts did not interest him as they did Veblen because they are not subject to scientific measurement. Human nature as a whole can be analyzed by introducing the subject of social psychology, which can be studied through statistical and historical analysis. We must study social institutions, such as legal and business systems, that influence economic conduct. Human behavior and intelligence are largely social products. To the extent that social institutions represent past achievements of human intelligence, they provide a basis of rationality for individual behavior.

[9] Wesley C. Mitchell, *Business Cycles: The Problem and Its Setting* (New York, 1927), p. 172. Reprinted with permission of the National Bureau of Economic Research, Inc.

These views led to Mitchell's optimism about social reform. In the long run human nature is not a barrier to change. Major problems can be solved with intelligence and understanding, for human nature changes as our way of life improves.

Mitchell defended social planning, denying that it was un-American. Our national history, he said, has been a history of planning, sometimes successful, sometimes not. The United States Constitution embodied a plan for governing a country. Hamilton had a plan for economic recovery, and from 1917 to 1918 we planned economic mobilization to win the war. The greatest difficulty in social planning has been to agree on what we wish to accomplish. In fact, disunity over goals creates the most fundamental obstacle to planning in a democratic community, for unanimity of social aims is attained only on rare occasions.

A second difficulty in planning derives from the interdependence of social processes. Piecemeal planning, detail by detail, often brings unplanned and unwanted results, as illustrated by the establishment of Prohibition which encouraged rum-running and the rise of rich law-breaking syndicates. Wise social planning must consider both direct and indirect effects of social action.

Certain results cannot be attained by individual action. Thus, said Mitchell, national planning is inevitable. The question is, will it be fragmentary and unsound or systematic and technically thorough?

Mitchell's greatest contribution was in the study of business fluctuations. He called his theory of business cycles a "working hypothesis" because it was tentative and subject to revision in the light of additional evidence. Continuous change was more relevant than equilibrium. His ideas were always checked against observations from real life. Business-cycle theory in his hands approached a tested explanation of experience instead of an exercise in logic. The more intensively Mitchell sought the facts to explain fluctuations, the more his explanation broadened into a theory of how our economic system works. Instead of seeking a single decisive cause of the cycle as earlier students of fluctuations had done, he explored the conditions that collectively produce the cyclical movements of the business system. If his ideas seem commonplace now, it is because they have become so widely accepted.

Mitchell's study of business cycles led to four major conclusions. First, business fluctuations arise in a money economy. Second, business cycles are not merely fluctuations in aggregate activity but fluctuations that are widely diffused throughout the economy. Third, the ebb and flow of activity depends on the prospects of profits, except in

times of crisis when the rush toward solvency and the desire to minimize losses temporarily become the driving forces of business enterprise. Fourth, fluctuations are not minor or accidental disruptions
of equilibrium, but are systematically generated by the economy itself. Permeating Mitchell's entire work is the evolutionary and dynamic approach. Thus, as each phase of the cycle evolves into its
successor, the economy itself gradually undergoes cumulative
changes. Therefore, Mitchell believed, the economists of each generation will probably have to recast the theory of business cycles that
they learned in their youth.

Crises and depressions have been described as a disease of capitalism. Mitchell preferred to view them as arising in a society where
economic activities are carried on mainly by making and spending
money. This is characteristic of capitalism, of course; but from the
viewpoint of the business-cycle analyst, capitalism also stresses other
features of less importance, such as how the means of production are
owned.

> It is not until the uses of money have reached an advanced stage in a
> country that its economic vicissitudes take on the character of business
> cycles.
>
> This remark does not mean that the economic life of communities
> with simpler organization is free from crises, or from alternations of good
> and bad times. On the contrary, life seems to have been more precari-
> ous, economic fortune more fluctuating, in a medieval town than in a
> modern city. But until a large part of a population is living by getting
> and spending money incomes, producing wares on a considerable scale
> for wide markets, using credit devices, organizing in business en-
> terprises with relatively few employers and many employees, the eco-
> nomic fluctuations which occur do not have the characteristics of busi-
> ness cycles.[10]

Business fluctuations are widely diffused throughout the economy
because enterprises are so interdependent. Business firms are bound
to each other by industrial, commercial, and financial ties, so none
can prosper or decline without affecting others. The growth of credit
has enhanced financial interdependence. The spread of the corporate
business organization, with all its interlocking relationships, organ-
izes many nominally independent enterprises into communities of
interest. These bonds are also channels through which the quicken-
ing or slackening of activity in one part of the economy can spread to
other parts.

[10] *Ibid.*, p. 75.

Profits, said Mitchell, are the clue to business fluctuations. A business enterprise can serve the community by making goods only if it makes a profit in the long run. The subordination of service to moneymaking is not grounded in the mercenary motives of businessmen, but is a necessary result of a money economy. A public-spirited businessman who disregards profits will be put out of business. Only government and philanthropic organizations can provide services without profit.

Anticipated profits are more significant than past profits or losses, for business looks forward more than it looks backward. The prospect of future profits plays the decisive role in determining the direction of business expansion. Investment reaches its highest point at that stage of the cycle at which the anticipated profits are most attractive. Therefore an account of economic fluctuations in a business economy must deal primarily with the pecuniary aspects of economic activity.

According to Mitchell, cycles arise from forces within the economy, with each phase of the cycle generating the next:

> An incipient revival of activity, for example, develops into full prosperity, prosperity gradually breeds a crisis, the crisis merges into depression, depression becomes deeper for a while, but ultimately engenders a fresh revival of activity, which is the beginning of another cycle. A theory of business cycles must therefore be a descriptive analysis of the cumulative changes by which one set of business conditions transforms itself into another set.[11]

Mitchell chose as his starting point that stage of the cycle in which activity begins to quicken after a period of depression. Once started, a revival of activity spreads rapidly over all or a large part of the economy through interconnecting enterprises. Rising wages and higher profits stimulate both consumption and investment demand. Inventories, which have been depleted during slack times, are replenished by retailers and wholesalers. An epidemic of optimism starts and spreads, thereby producing conditions that both justify and intensify it. In the later stages of a revival, prices begin to rise. Anticipations of further price increases stimulate orders for goods. Credit expands as business conditions improve. Profits increase too because wage and overhead costs lag behind rising prices. New investment in capital goods rises.

This, then, is the cumulative upward movement of revival. But

[11] Wesley C. Mitchell, *Business Cycles and Their Causes* (Berkeley, Calif., 1941), p. ix. [Originally published in 1913.]

why does it culminate in a crisis? Why does prosperity breed depression?

Among the stresses that accumulate within the system during prosperity is the slow but sure increase in the costs of doing business. Overhead costs begin to rise as new capital is invested when the cost of capital goods is rising. New companies building new plants incur high costs in attempting to establish themselves, and sticky costs like rent and interest rise. Less efficient plants and machines, less capable management, and less efficient workers are employed during prosperity, thereby bidding up the prices of materials, labor, and so on. By adding to the supply of goods sent to market, marginal firms make it more difficult to advance selling prices to offset rising costs. Labor costs rise, not only because less capable workers are employed, but because wages begin to catch up with rising prices. During prosperity the rising demand for goods increases the need for overtime labor, which is more expensive and less productive than normal labor. Labor discipline and productivity decrease because workers are less fearful of losing their jobs than in bad times. Waste in production increases as businessmen grow careless, overoptimistic, and overly busy.

Rising production costs encroach on profits, especially since the prices of finished goods cannot be easily raised in the later stages of prosperity. The expansion of productive capacity, which promoted the growth of prosperity during its earlier period, adds to the supply of goods and increases the difficulty of raising selling prices. Buyers ultimately resist rising prices because they cannot or will not continually pay more for goods. Certain prices fail to rise in line with costs because of public regulation, contracts, and custom. An actual or even a prospective decline of profits in a few important industries suffices to create financial difficulties in all industries.

The longer prosperity lasts, the more severe these stresses become, and they inevitably lead to crisis and depression. The pyramiding of credit ends when creditors become apprehensive. At the crisis point demands are made on debtors to reduce or pay their debts in full. Vast liquidation occurs, with prices falling as goods are thrown on the market in desperate attempts to avoid bankruptcy. The expectation of falling prices further reduces the demand for goods and thereby makes this expectation come true. Since certain costs are sticky on the downward side just as they are with upward price movements, falling prices squeeze profit margins even more. Gloom spreads, investment spending declines, inventories are reduced, unemployment grows, consumer income and expenditure decline, and the economy sinks into a depression.

Given enough time a depression generates within itself the forces that produce prosperity. Businessmen cut waste and costs to the bone. Ultimately, wages, interest, rent, and other sticky costs fall to the point where they are in line with prices of goods. Labor costs also fall because overtime is eliminated, inefficient workers are discharged, and employed workers are driven to greater efforts by the fear of unemployment. Inefficient firms, plants, and machines are allowed to stand idle, thereby tending to reduce overhead costs. Though unit overhead costs tend to increase because of the declining volume of sales, sharp competition may force businessmen to price their goods at less than full overhead costs. Reorganization through bankruptcy or the scaling down of debts, interest, or rent will further reduce overhead costs. Even those businesses that never pass through the hands of receivers have their inflated capital values lowered, thereby justifying a smaller capital charge in fixing selling prices.

As the depression drags on, capital goods wear out and grow obsolete. Prices for new capital goods having fallen, the competitive struggle induces investment in new, more efficient, lower-cost machines that can be financed at low depression rates of interest. If it is at all possible, consumers must ultimately replace durable and semidurable goods that have worn out. Population continues to increase, thereby increasing the demand for all kinds of consumption goods. Inventories, which have been reduced to the barest minimum during depression, must be rebuilt as business expands. Optimism spreads, and the economy is once again on a cumulative upswing.

Mitchell's study of business cycles was a superb contribution to economic analysis. Of course, the changing economic environment has made some of his observations obsolete. For example, prices no longer fall during depressions or recessions, partly because depressions are no longer permitted to develop as catastrophically as in his day. Bankruptcies are less important now in wiping out inflated capital values and thereby restoring the profitability of business. Yet even as Mitchell's work grows increasingly antiquated, it confirms his prognosis that the economy gradually and continually changes its character. Although some of his work is superseded, he laid the foundations that made further progress possible.

Bibliography

BURNS, ARTHUR F., ed., *Wesley Clair Mitchell: The Economic Scientist.* New York: National Bureau of Economic Research, 1952.

COMMONS, JOHN R., *The Economics of Collective Action.* New York: Macmillan, 1950.

————, *Institutional Economics.* New York: Macmillan, 1934.

————, *Legal Foundations of Capitalism.* New York: Macmillan, 1924.

————, *Myself.* New York: Macmillan, 1934.

HARTER, LAFAYETTE G., *John R. Commons. His Assault on Laissez Faire.* Corvallis, Oreg.: Oregon State University Press, 1962.

MITCHELL, LUCY SPRAGUE, *Two Lives.* New York: Simon and Schuster, 1953.

MITCHELL, WESLEY C., *The Backward Art of Spending Money and Other Essays.* New York: Kelley, 1950. [Originally published 1912–36.]

————, *Business Cycles: The Problem and Its Setting.* New York: National Bureau of Economic Research, 1927.

————, *Business Cycles and Their Causes.* Berkeley, Calif.: University of California Press, 1941. [Originally published in 1913.]

————, "Economic Resources in Economic Theory," *Studies in Economics and Industrial Relations.* Philadelphia, Pa.: University of Pennsylvania Press, 1941.

————, *Types of Economic Theory from Mercantilism to Institutionalism,* 2 vols., ed. by Joseph Dorfman. New York: Augustus M. Kelley, 1967 and 1969.

————, *What Happens During Business Cycles.* New York: National Bureau of Economic Research, 1951.

21

Welfare Economics and Social Control

Welfare economics is not a distinct and unified system of ideas. It is rather a stream of thought that interests economists of different schools as well as those of no school. Thinkers as diverse as John A. Hobson, who advocated fundamental reforms, and A. C. Pigou, leading neoclassicist of his day, contributed to welfare economics. J. Maurice Clark, who was an institutionalist with roots in neoclassicism, included in his wide range of interests the problems of government intervention in the economy to promote the good of society; he too may therefore be called a welfare economist—or at least an economist concerned with the social control of enterprise.

Welfare economics raises questions about how well the economy functions, how satisfactory the society's system of distribution is, what can be done about improving total well-being, and the degree to which society must nullify the results of laissez faire in order to promote welfare.

Conservatives have deprecated the trend toward welfare economics and social control as exemplified by the programs of President Roosevelt's New Deal in the 1930's. They have accused the liberals of undermining the free-enterprise system. Do-gooders, say conservatives, try to promote the well-being of the masses by deciding what is best for them. Increasing government regulation and an ever-rising burden of taxation are weakening the flexibility and adaptability of the economy. The welfare state, because of the increased security it offers the individual regardless of his or her own efforts or abilities, is destroying ambition, energy, and willingness to do an honest day's work. As incentives to work, save, and invest are weakened, the faltering economy requires ever more government intervention, which would never have been necessary if we had not started down the road toward the welfare state. It is only through the quest for profit and the unequal distribution of income that maximum growth is possible; as the size of the income pie grows, everybody benefits.

Conservative economists have been especially unhappy about the moderate redistribution of income from the rich to the poor that occurred in this country under the New Deal and in Great Britain under the Labour Party governments. They have disavowed any possibility of interpersonal comparisons of utility. How can we be sure that a dollar transferred from a rich person to a beggar will add more to the beggar's joy than it will detract from the rich person's? Perhaps the rich person is a more efficient "pleasure machine" than the beggar. The thing to do is to add to the income and utility enjoyed by the beggar without deducting anything from the rich person. Besides, too-vigorous efforts toward redistribution will kill the ability to accumulate wealth through saving and will kill incentives to invest whatever wealth has been accumulated; therefore egalitarian sentiments, if implemented, may reduce total welfare by reducing total income. Above all, conservative economists have tried to perfect a purely scientific economics from which all judgments of moral value are excluded.

Liberal welfare economists, on the other hand, have argued that the welfare state is a state that looks after the welfare of its people. (All contestants in this debate claim, of course, that their policies will maximize welfare.) Value judgments must enter into policy-making decisions. Most liberals agree that laissez faire does not produce the best possible results, and that some government intervention is necessary to ameliorate conditions. There is disagreement among liberals as to how much government activity is required, for it is at the point of change that the greatest controversies occur. They all oppose, however, the conservative economists' argument that redistribution cannot demonstrably improve total welfare because we cannot compare utilities between different people. Liberal reformers argue that by shifting a dollar of wealth or income from a rich person to a poor person, we increase total welfare even though we cannot determine by exactly how much. We can speak about colder or warmer temperatures without looking at a thermometer; in the same approximate manner we can say that a dollar is more useful to a poor person than a rich one. The reformers also deplore the basically futile desire to increase the well-being of the poor without reducing that of the rich. They argue that almost every measure that helps some people hurts others: full employment adversely affects the dealers in bankrupt stocks and secondhand clothes; subsidized public housing for the poor hurts the economic interests of the owners of slum housing.

We should recognize that even those economists who object to welfare economics and claim to deal with economic principles and problems with the utmost objectivity also make certain ethical or value assumptions. Whether they are aware of it or not, whether their ideas of good and bad are stated explicitly or lurk in the background, even the most impartial economists work with value judgments. Typical value judgments are the following: price stability is good; rising national income is desirable; the allocation of resources through competition and consumer choice gives the best results; productivity is the most ethical basis for rewards; increased productivity is to be welcomed. Not all people in our society, and not all societies, would agree with preferences that are taken for granted by most of us.

There is not, therefore, a vast difference between welfare economists and their opponents insofar as both presume certain bases for the good life. The differences between them appear in the degree to which value judgments are openly recognized and approved and in the degree of reliance placed on individualism and laissez faire as opposed to collective, social controls over the production, distribution, and consumption of wealth.

If we identify economic growth with welfare, we have to assume a harmony of individual and social goals. If someone becomes better off because of rising income, for example, and no one is worse off, total welfare has increased. But suppose an individual's situation has an external effect on others, a social influence. Suppose as you become richer, others turn green with envy and feel themselves to be poorer in comparison with you. In that case your increased income has made those around you worse off, even though their incomes have remained unchanged. In other words, an individual's satisfaction does not depend only on his or her own consumption; it will depend also on the level and kind of other people's consumption.

In its simplest version, the fundamental idea of welfare economics is that any change that makes someone better off without making anyone else worse off is a desirable change from the point of view of society's welfare. A more sophisticated version is that any change is desirable from the point of view of total social welfare under the following condition: if those who benefit from the change can compensate those who lose from the change and still be better off them-selves. This welfare standard aims to avoid moral judgments. But many problems must be judged in terms of moral concepts rather than dollar values by themselves. How can one quantify in monetary terms the cost of poverty, sickness, early death, the destruction of our environment, urban blight, and so on? We have to make certain deci-sions about our social goals, about the kind of world we wish to live in, even if we cannot precisely weigh all the costs and benefits to every individual in our society. This does not deny, of course, that certain sacrifices must be borne; it would be rather extreme to say that we must never cut down a tree, pave a new road, or build an ad-ditional factory or power plant. Society must continually judge be-tween what is desirable and necessary, and what is undesirable and superfluous, in view of overall considerations. We do have to com-pare total social and private costs and benefits in choosing among al-ternatives, but the costs and benefits may not be in precise monetary quantities.

We turn now to Hobson, a pioneer in welfare economics, who of-fered a moderately radical approach to problems of human welfare.

Hobson

John Atkinson Hobson (1858–1940), the son of a middle-class family, studied the classics at Oxford. After graduation he taught the classics and gave university extension lectures in English literature. His in-terests soon shifted to economic subjects, and he began to develop heretical ideas through his association with the businessman and mountain-climber A. F. Mummery (killed in the Himalayas in 1895). Because of ideas then considered radical, Hobson lost his position as an extension lecturer at London University. Although excluded from academic life, he was extremely active not only as a writer of 53 books but also as a journalist and popular lecturer. One of his major themes was the interdependence of politics, economics, and ethics. A journal article he wrote on imperialism induced the editor of the Manchester *Guardian* to send him to South Africa on a study that eventually led to his writing three books, the most famous of which was *Imperialism.* He was a pacifist during World War I. Hobson was an admirer of Veblen, and he tried to interest publishers in a British edition of Veblen's *The Theory of Business Enterprise.* He wrote a book about Veblen in 1936.

Hobson's unorthodox ideas were scorned by English academic economists. In 1913 J. M. Keynes, in reviewing one of his books,

wrote, "One comes to a new book by Mr. Hobson with mixed feelings, in hope of stimulating ideas and of some fruitful criticisms of
orthodoxy from an independent and individual standpoint, but ex-
pectant also of much sophistry, misunderstanding, and perverse
thought." In the 1930's Keynes reversed his original opinion of Hobson. In 1932 he corresponded with the seventy-four-year-old reformer to reconcile their views. In *The General Theory of Employment, Interest and Money* (1936), Keynes wrote respectfully of
Hobson's "criticisms and intuitions."

Hobson was one of those rare social reformers who used economic
theory as a foundation for his proposals. He rejected the classical and
neoclassical ideas that pure competition is the typical market situation, that a harmony of interests prevails, and that laissez faire is the
best policy. In place of these ideas he developed an analysis that led
to a program of reform, largely through government intervention,
which can be considered welfare economics.

We shall examine three major strands of Hobson's thought. First,
in the 1880's he developed the idea that underconsumption and
oversaving lead to overinvestment—a concept that won him Keynes's
acclaim. Second, he believed that the inability to keep the economy
fully employed leads to imperialism; for this he was praised by
Lenin, who said that although Hobson was a bourgeois social reformer and a pacifist, he gave an excellent and comprehensive description of imperialism. Third, he advocated greater equality of income both for ethical reasons and to increase consumption spending;
to achieve the goal the government must play a major role.

The central problem of our society, said Hobson, is the recurring
unemployment of labor, capital, and land. As early as 1889 he and
Mummery argued against the classical doctrine that the more thrifty
a nation is, the more wealthy it becomes. On the contrary, they said,
an increase of capital requires a subsequent increase in the consumption of the commodities that will be produced by that capital. If
people wish to save more now they must be willing to consume more
in the near future. If they persist in saving now and in attempting to
invest their saving without adequately increasing their consumption
in the near future, the actual formation of new capital will be limited.

> Our purpose is to show . . . that an undue exercise of the habit of saving
> is possible, and that such undue exercise impoverishes the Community,
> throws labourers out of work, drives down wages, and spreads that
> gloom and prostration through the commercial world which is known as
> Depression in Trade; that, in short, the effective love of money is the
> root of all economic evil. . . .

We are thus brought to the conclusion that the basis on which all economic teaching since Adam Smith has stood, viz., that the quantity annually produced is determined by the aggregates of Natural Agents, Capital, and Labour available, is erroneous, and that, on the contrary, the quantity produced, while it can never exceed the limits imposed by these aggregates, may be, and actually is, reduced far below this maximum by the check that undue saving and the consequent accumulation of over-supply exerts on production; *i.e.*, that in the normal state of modern industrial Communities, consumption limits production and not production consumption. . . .

Reaching our main conclusion, that the undue saving of individuals impoverishes the Community, simultaneously lowering Rent, Profit, or Interest and Wages, we contradict the generally accepted dogmas that the saving of the individual must always and necessarily enrich the Community, that the individual seeking his own advantage necessarily works for that of the Community, and that wages can only rise at the expense of profit, or profit at the expense of wages, or both at the expense of rent.[1]

Why is there too much saving and not enough consumption? To answer this question Hobson developed a theory of the proper distribution of income that was quite different from that of his contemporaries. Part of the income received by labor is for maintenance, or subsistence, which enables workers to renew their strength from day to day and to raise families to replenish the labor supply. Additional wages provide for growth in the economy, for payments above the bare maintenance level enable more children to survive infancy, and people do more work because they are healthier, better educated, and more energetic. If wages cover more than maintenance (costs of subsistence) and the productive surplus (costs of growth), the remainder will be an unproductive surplus, or an unearned increment that does not increase output. Thus too high wages are unproductive because they do not call forth a greater supply of labor.

Capital likewise has two corresponding costs. The maintenance cost provides for the replacement of worn-out capital. To induce growth, both profit and interest are required to bring about saving that will be invested. If interest and profit are above the level required for the maintenance and healthy growth of capital, the surplus payments are unproductive, an unearned increment.

For land, the necessary payment covers all the costs of man's efforts and expenditures to maintain and improve its productivity. Genuine economic rent is in its entirety an unproductive surplus.

[1] A. F. Mummery and J. A. Hobson, *The Physiology of Industry* (New York, 1956), pp. iv, vi, viii. [Originally published in 1889.]

According to Hobson, labor typically gets its subsistence costs, but not the full costs of growth. In other words, higher wages generally increase the efficiency and productivity of labor. There is too much saving and not enough consumption because of the failures of competition among businessmen to work effectively toward raising wages and lowering property incomes. Because their incomes are too high, they save too much. They are motivated not only by the desire to consume now or in the future but by the urge to save and invest— to accumulate wealth—as well. This accumulation of wealth is possible only if the demand for consumer goods increases. To some extent this will occur, and then saving is socially useful. There is always some appropriate rate of saving that will increase the productive power of society proportionately with the increased effective market demand for consumption. The result is growth associated with full employment. If, however, the rate of saving is too high, unemployment then rises. If the rate of saving is too low, productive power is wasted, and the future is sacrificed to the present.

Oversaving and underconsumption create business cycles. During prosperity prices are high; capital investment is high, facilitated by the expansion of bank credit; and the productive power of society grows more rapidly than consumption. The first symptom of a coming depression is a weakening of prices, and as a consequence, profit margins are diminished. The repayment of loans and the meeting of bills become less certain, while the value of securities held as collateral shrinks. Pessimism spreads, banks curtail credit; bankruptcies spread, and financial houses may crash. Suspicion changes to panic as depositors and investors seek to withdraw their funds.

Hobson disputed the view that the financial collapse is due to the psychological aberrations of men. Collapse is based on the imbalance that arises in industry. And what reverses the downward trend? The decline in individual savings as incomes fall eventually brings about a new balance between consumption and saving.

> The whole financial system is based upon actual industry: reflects, anticipates, and frequently exaggerates its forces and tendencies. Depressions, with their accompanying unemployment, must therefore be traced through their operations in the delicate mechanism of finance to the failure of consumption to keep full pace with the increase of productive power so as to furnish a full and equable employment for this power. . . .
>
> Take the case of an economic community of a progressive type with an income of twenty units, spending seventeen, and saving three for regular investment in new productive capital, which finds full, regular em-

ployment in meeting the growing demand for commodities. Now suppose, owing to some change in distribution of incomes, some return to simplicity of living or some increased appreciation of future as compared with present satisfactions, spending is reduced to sixteen, saving raised to four, what must happen? The increased savings cannot take shape in productive capital, for, as the increase of current and prospective consumption of commodities is reduced, a smaller amount of new productive capital can be put into operation, and any attempt to put into operation as much as before must speedily be checked by the obvious glut. Instead of three units of saving taking shape in productive capital, there is now only room for two and a half. But owing to increased saving four are available. What happens to the extra one and a half? There will be some hoarding, i.e. some lingering of loanable funds in hands of financiers, from slowness in finding any sort of investment.

Let us say that this disposes of half a unit—an excessive estimate. What becomes of the remaining one?

In order to answer this question, we must look to the effect of the diminished spending of the saving classes upon the general income from industry. Since there is a reduced demand both for commodities and for new capital goods, there will be a shrinkage of money income and real income among all industrial classes. Those among these classes whose income is reduced very low will be disposed to part with any property, land, houses, factories, etc., they may possess, in order to keep living and to pay their way. This means that a large amount of such properties will at such a time become a new field of investment for the savings which cannot take shape in new productive capital. The surplus unit of saving will find this form of investment, consisting in the acquisition of productive capital already existing and belonging to classes impoverished by the very increase of saving which has glutted the investment market. Saved by the saving class, it will be spent by the non-saving class. From the standpoint of the community it represents no saving at all, but simply a transfer of spending from one class to another. But the class which gets it only maintains its former spending, while the class which parts with it has reduced its total spending. So there remains as a net effect of the operation a reduction of total demand for commodities and new forms of capital. This means reduced employment for capital and labour, diminished rate of production, and shrinkage of the general real income. This is the condition known as depression. Why does it not continue indefinitely and grow ever worse? Because from the very beginning of the maladjustment between spending and saving a process of readjustment gradually comes into play. Directly a shrinkage in demand for commodities and new productive capital occurs, the lessened rate of production begins to reduce all incomes, including those of the saving class. Aggregate income no longer stands at twenty, but falls to eighteen, or even seventeen. The saving class who were trying to save four out of a total twenty, leaving sixteen for spending, are not willing to save four or even three out of an aggregate income reduced to eighteen or seventeen. Their permanent standard of comfort stands in the way. When the shrinkage of production and of income has gone far enough, not merely is the actual amount of saving reduced, but the *proportion* of saving to spending is brought back towards the normal rate which preceded the attempt to oversave, or even below that rate.[2]

In the above excerpt we see that Hobson had a clear, if rudimentary, idea of the multiplier, of equilibrium at less than full employment, and of a rising propensity to consume and a falling propensity to save as income falls.

Hobson's analysis of oversaving and underconsumption led to his theory of imperialism. An abundance of goods that cannot be sold at home can be unloaded in the colonies. Surplus savings that cannot be invested at home because of inadequate consumption can be invested in the colonies. The industrial and financial magnates persuade their governments to acquire colonies through immense public expenditures, which in themselves further add to the profits of the industrialists and financiers. Yet if income is distributed properly, the home market is capable of indefinite expansion, and the drive to exploit colonies becomes unnecessary.

> Every improvement of methods of production, every concentration of ownership and control, seems to accentuate the tendency. As one nation after another enters the machine economy and adopts advanced industrial methods, it becomes more difficult for its manufacturers, merchants, and financiers to dispose profitably of their economic resources, and they are tempted more and more to use their Governments in order to secure for their particular use some distant undeveloped country by annexation and protection.
>
> The process, we may be told, is inevitable, and so it seems upon a superficial inspection. Everywhere appear excessive powers of production, excessive capital in search of investment. It is admitted by all business men that the growth of the powers of production in their country exceeds the growth in consumption, that more goods can be produced than can be sold at a profit, and that more capital exists than can find remunerative investment.
>
> It is this economic condition of affairs that forms the taproot of Imperialism. If the consuming public in this country raised its standard of consumption to keep pace with every rise of productive powers, there could be no excess of goods or capital clamorous to use Imperialism in order to find markets. . . .
>
> The fallacy of the supposed inevitability of imperial expansion as a necessary outlet for progressive industry is now manifest. It is not indus-

[2] J. A. Hobson, *The Industrial System*, 2d ed. (New York, 1910), pp. 301–03.

trial progress that demands the opening up of new markets and areas of investment, but mal-distribution of consuming power which prevents the absorption of commodities and capital within the country. The over-saving which is the economic root of Imperialism is found by analysis to consist of rents, monopoly profits, and other unearned or excessive elements of income, which, not being earned by labour of head or hand, have no legitimate *raison d'être*. . . .

Many have carried their analysis so far as to realise the absurdity of spending half our financial resources in fighting to secure foreign markets at times when hungry mouths, ill-clad backs, ill-furnished houses indicate countless unsatisfied material wants among our own population.[3]

In his autobiography, *Confessions of an Economic Heretic* (1938), Hobson granted that in writing about the economic basis for imperialism he had presented an excessively simple case for the economic determination of history. He said that at the time he had not yet acquired the proper perspective on the interaction among economics, politics, and ethics.

What is the remedy for oversaving, underconsumption, depression, and imperialism? A redistribution of income toward greater equality is required to reduce the proportion of saving to consumption spending. The bulk of the saving is done by the wealthy, because "the proportion of saving is generally in direct ratio to the sizes of incomes, the richest saving the largest percentage of their income, the poorest the smallest." Would redistribution check industrial progress by unduly restricting the quantity of saving and investment? Not at all. The increased demand resulting from the readjustment of income would stimulate industry, promote full and more stable employment, and increase the demand for goods. As a result, the absolute quantity of saving would be as large as before, although it would be smaller in relation to income.

One way to redistribute income is through labor union action to raise wages, pensions, and other benefits in order to provide a higher standard of living for wage earners. As workers' incomes rise within certain limits, they become more productive and efficient, and total consumption spending increases. Their incomes should not rise, however, beyond the point at which their productivity no longer increases. Then the state should step in and appropriate the remaining surplus for public services. If, however, an industry does not

[3] J. A. Hobson, *Imperialism*, 3d ed. (London, 1938), pp. 80–81, 85–86. [Originally published in 1902.] Reprinted with permission of The Macmillan Company (New York) and George Allen & Unwin Ltd.

produce a surplus return above the competitive level of profits, labor cannot and should not press for higher wages and shorter hours except insofar as these increase the efficiency of labor. Yet surplus incomes are widely diffused in modern industrial societies, and therefore unions are necessary and useful in diverting rents, excessive interest and profit, and other "unearned" income into wages.

The labor movement, Hobson said, has historically been at best a clumsy and an unreliable instrument for redistributing income, especially since the unskilled workers get the least while the highly skilled and well-organized get the most. Much more effective is reliance on the state to achieve a more equitable and more socially advantageous distribution of wealth. Such public intervention takes three main forms: government regulation of industry, government operation of industry, and taxation to raise revenue for public consumption.

Government regulation includes all legal powers to control private industry, thereby diverting surplus income into wages or other expenses to improve conditions for the workers, such as minimum wage enactments, workmen's compensation laws, limited hours of labor, improved sanitation, and so forth.

Government operation of industry is suitable where monopolies develop, or where public convenience requires it. There is a growing tendency for the state to assume ownership and control of transportation, communication, mineral resources, banking, insurance, water, gas, and electricity. Since these are industries in which large surplus profits are typical, their socialization makes these profits available to society. This kind of socialism would still leave wide areas in the economy under private enterprise, so that individual initiative would have many opportunities to serve society. Socialism cannot maintain liberty of research and personal freedom of creative expression, because human nature is too acquisitive and self-assertive. Therefore routine, unskilled industries form the right sphere for socialism, and the skilled industries for private enterprise. No wonder Hobson, in spite of his sympathies with the Labour Party, did not feel "at home in a body governed by trade union members and their finance, and intellectually led by full-blooded Socialists."

When the private sector generates too high incomes, the state should tax away the surplus. The largest and therefore the most objectionable incomes are derived from economic rent of land, and from excessive interest and profits that occur mainly when competition gives way to monopoly. This kind of taxation would strike at the root of depression and imperialism. The money received by the state should be used to provide such necessary social services as health and education. In bad times it could be used to pay for public works. The very fact that public works that are noncompetitive with private enterprise increase total employment shows that the government is taking up funds that otherwise would not be spent; taxation of surpluses cures the disease of oversaving.

Hobson amplified his system of welfare economics with a criticism of orthodox theorists in their valuation of cost and utility in terms of money. He preferred a valuation of industry in terms of human effort and satisfaction. The standard of human well-being should replace the monetary standard of wealth. A dollar's worth of cheap gin or hand-made lace sweated out of peasant women at the cost of their eyesight should not be given the same weight as a dollar's worth of good prose or wholesome bread. A day of labor in a factory costs much more in terms of human sacrifice than does a day of pleasurable artistic creation. The human cost of saving arises only for people of small incomes; there is no sacrifice involved in saving by the rich. We should be concerned, he said, with the human interpretation or valuation of industry by asking two questions about the goods we produce: What are the net human costs involved in their production? What are the net human utilities involved in their consumption? Society should distribute the costs of production according to the ability of individuals to bear these costs, and it should distribute the goods produced among consumers according to their capacity to derive utility from them. Human costs would thereby be minimized and utilities maximized. This is an interesting contrast to Bentham and his followers, who believed that all consumption represents utility and all work disutility.

Hobson's position is now at last secure in the history of economic thought. As a pioneer welfare economist he lived to see some of his ideas on the causes and remedies for depressions embodied in the Keynesian system, although in a much more sophisticated way.

Pigou

Arthur Cecil Pigou (1877–1959) succeeded Marshall in the chair of political economy at Cambridge University in 1908 and held this position until his retirement in 1943. He was the leading neoclassical economist after the death of his predecessor, and like Marshall, Pigou expressed humanitarian impulses toward the poor, hoping that economic science would lead to social improvement. In his own cautious way, Pigou was willing to go further than Marshall in allowing a role for the government in ameliorating certain undesirable features of society.

Pigou hoped to provide the theoretical basis for statesmen to enact measures that promoted welfare. As an economist he was concerned with *economic* welfare, defined as "that part of social welfare that can be brought directly or indirectly into relation with the measuring-rod of money."

Basing himself on Jevons' and Marshall's principle that the marginal utility of money diminishes as more is acquired, Pigou asserted that greater equality of incomes under certain conditions could increase economic welfare.

> Any transference of income from a relatively rich man to a relatively poor man of similar temperament, since it enables more intense wants to be satisfied at the expense of less intense wants, must increase the aggregate sum of satisfaction. The old "law of diminishing utility" thus leads securely to the proposition: Any cause which increases the absolute share of real income in the hands of the poor, provided that it does not lead to a contraction in the size of the national dividend from any point of view, will, in general, increase economic welfare.[4]

Pigou's most significant deviation from orthodox theory lay in his abandoning the idea that what is good for the individual is necessarily good for society—that total welfare is simply the sum of the welfare of all individuals. He distinguished between social and private marginal costs and benefits. The private marginal cost of a commodity or service is the expense the producer incurs in making one more unit; the social marginal cost is the expense or damage to society as the consequence of producing that unit of product. Private marginal benefit is measured by the selling price of the commodity; social marginal benefit is the total benefit society gets from the production of an added unit.

These distinctions are significant because costs may be thrown upon people who are not directly concerned, so that social costs may be greater than private costs; in such a situation the private marginal net product is greater than the social marginal net product. For example, sparks from railway engines may do damage to surrounding woods without their owners being compensated for the damage. Similarly, an entrepreneur building a factory in a residential district destroys much of the value of other people's property. The increased sale of intoxicating beverages is profitable to the distiller and the

---

[4] A. C. Pigou, *The Economics of Welfare*, 4th ed. (London, 1932), p. 89. [Originally published in 1920.]

brewer, for instance, but increased social costs are incurred when more policemen and prisons become necessary. If the excessive work of women in factories injures the health and well-being of their children, private employers will still reap the benefits of cheap labor while society has to bear the burden of increased welfare costs.

There are opposite cases, said Pigou, in which some benefits of private actions will spill over to society's benefit, but the person who renders the benefit is not compensated for it; then the social marginal net product exceeds the private marginal net product. For example, the expansion of one firm in an industry may give rise to external economies in the industry as a whole that will reduce the costs of production of other firms. Private investment in afforestation will benefit surrounding property owners. Preventing smoke from pouring out of factory chimneys will benefit the community at large much more than it will benefit the factory owner. Scientific research is generally of greater value to society than to the researcher and inventor, although the patent laws aim at bringing private and social marginal net products closer together.

The above examples can occur even under conditions of "simple competition." Even before Chamberlin and Robinson published their works in 1933, Pigou recognized in monopolistic competition another source of divergence between social and private net products.

> Where conditions of monopolistic competition—competition, that is to say, between several sellers each producing a considerable proportion of the aggregate output—are present, the way is opened up for a new kind of investment. This consists in competitive advertisement directed to the sole purpose of transferring the demand for a given commodity from one source of supply to another. There is, indeed, little opportunity for this as regards goods of a kind whose quality is uniform and, as with salt, lumber or grain, can be easily tested; but, where quality cannot be easily tested, and especially where goods are sold in small quantities, which can readily be put into distinctive packages for the use of retail customers, there is plenty of opportunity.[5]

Some advertising, Pigou believed, fulfills a social purpose by being informative. Much of it, however, is strictly competitive, and its social net product is therefore zero or negative.

In general, industries whose private costs are too low become too large; industries whose private profits are too small may remain smaller than is desirable for the public good. Thus we may have too

---

[5] *Ibid.*, p. 196.

much investment and employment in sweatshop industries and too little in schools and hospitals. Pigou showed that the success of a business or the outcome of competition is not necessarily to the advantage of society.

One problem of society arises, said Pigou, because of people's attitude toward the future. We prefer present rather than future satisfactions of equal magnitude because our telescopic faculty is defective; we therefore see future pleasures on a diminished scale. This bias contributes to a far-reaching economic disharmony, for people distribute their resources between the present, the near future, and the remote future on the basis of a somewhat irrational preference. As a consequence, efforts directed toward the remote future are sacrificed for those directed to the near future, while these in turn are skimped on to enhance present consumption. The creation of new capital is checked, and people are encouraged to use up existing capital to such a degree that larger future advantages are sacrificed for smaller present ones. Natural resources are consumed more quickly and more wastefully because satisfactions are underrated.

Pigou concluded that economic welfare is diminished by government intervention that strengthens the tendency of people to devote too much of their resources to present use and too little to future use. We should thus avoid any tax on saving, including property taxes, death duties, and progressive income taxes, if we wish to maximize economic welfare. Heavy taxes on consumption are preferable because they encourage saving, but such taxes have the disadvantage of hurting low-income people the most.

Pigou thus reached a conclusion about saving diametrically opposed to that of Hobson. Imbued with the orthodox idea that economies tend toward full employment, Pigou wanted to increase saving in order to promote economic growth. Believing that all income is automatically spent on consumption or investment, he was not concerned with Hobson's problem of excessive saving. Pigou did make some important contributions to the analysis of business fluctuations, but they were omitted from his discussion of the welfare implications of saving and consuming.

In general, said Pigou, industrialists are interested only in the private net product of their operations. If private and social net products happen to coincide, the free play of self-interest (so far as it is not hampered by ignorance) will tend to maximize economic welfare. Wherever the two net products do not coincide—and that occurs frequently—government intervention can increase welfare. Alcoholic drinks and competitive advertising may legitimately be taxed; building and zoning laws may be enacted; public subsidies to research may be granted; laws against false weights and measures, the adulteration of foods, and fraudulent promotions may be enforced; and conservation measures may be passed. The task of government is to equalize private marginal net cost and social marginal net cost by subsidies, taxes, or legal regulation.

Pigou insisted that interpersonal comparisons of satisfactions *can* properly be made if we are concerned with people of the same background raised in the same environment. In this sense he was more of a reformer than those "purely scientific" economists who fastidiously abjure value judgments and proclaim the impossibility of comparing satisfactions among different people.

Clark

John Maurice Clark (1884–1963), the son of John Bates Clark, was educated at Amherst College and Columbia University and ultimately occupied the position of professor of economics at Columbia from which his father had retired. In 1952 Clark followed Wesley C. Mitchell as the second recipient of the Walker Medal, awarded at intervals of at least five years by the American Economic Association to the most distinguished living American economist.

His intellectual heritage came from many people, including his father, Veblen, Hobson, and Pigou. Clark started with static theory, the point at which his father had left off and became a leading exponent of realistic, dynamic economics. He worked toward a fusion of neoclassical and institutional economics and was an important precursor of the Keynesian system. He was one of several leading economists who developed the idea of countercyclical fiscal policy before Keynes wrote his *General Theory.*

In 1917 Clark published his famous article on the "acceleration principle." The idea that he developed at this early date became one of the foundations of modern business cycle theory. He argued that fluctuations in the output and prices of capital goods are much greater than those for the consumer goods they produce. Even if the demand for consumer goods continues to grow, a change in the rate of growth will be transmitted back with intensified force or acceleration to the capital-goods sector. Here is the example Clark used to illustrate this principle.

Suppose a certain industry produces a consumer good, and its annual output is designated by the index number 100. A certain amount of fixed capital (buildings and machinery) is required to produce that output, and we shall designate that by 100. To maintain and replace that amount of fixed capital, Clark assumed that we need 5 goods produced each year. Under stable conditions, therefore, the consumer-good industry produces 100 and the capital-good industry produces 5.

Now assume that there is a 10 percent increase in the demand for the consumer good. The fixed capital will also have to go from 100 to 110. (He excluded such possibilities as working the existing plants overtime.) The industry producing the capital good will have to expand from 5 to 15. A 10 percent increase (100 to 110) in the demand for the final product generated a 200 percent increase (5 to 15) in the demand for the capital used in producing that product. This is the principle of acceleration.

Assume, said Clark, that this rate of increase of 10 percent of the original demand continues for 5 years. By then the demand for the consumer good is 150 per year. The fixed capital required to produce that output will also be 150. The 5 percent for maintenance and replacement will be 7.5 per year. The annual growth of the consumer-good industry will require new capital of 10 per year; therefore the output of the capital-good industry expands to 17.5.

Now suppose that at the end of 5 years the growth in the demand for the consumer good ceases, and the demand remains stationary at 150. The industry producing fixed capital has to produce 7.5 for maintenance and replacement. As it has been producing 17.5, four-sevenths of its capacity must remain idle. A cessation of growth in the demand for the final good thus led to a sharp decline in the demand for the capital good.

> This is a serious condition for any industry in the real world. It might well be serious enough to produce a panic if any considerable number of industries were in the same condition at the same time. And yet something like it is a normal effect, an inevitable effect, of changes in consumers' demands in a highly capitalistic industrial system.
>
> Thus the law of demand for intermediate products states that the demand depends, not only on the demand for the final product, but on the manner in which that demand is fluctuating.[6]

In 1923 Clark published a classic titled *Studies in the Economics of Overhead Costs*. Three years later he published the first edition of

[6] John M. Clark, "Business Acceleration and the Law of Demand," *The Journal of Political Economy*, Vol. XXV, No. 3 (March 1917), pp. 217–35. Reprinted in The American Economic Association, *Readings in Business Cycle Theory*. Philadelphia: Blakiston, 1944, p. 240.

his *Social Control of Business.* The National Bureau of Economic Research issued his *Strategic Factors in Business Cycles* in 1934.

Clark defined social control as any instance when the "individual is forced or persuaded to act in the interest of any group of which he is a member rather than in his own personal interest." The necessity for social control was woven into his "social economics," which sought to interpret and improve the functioning of a pluralistic economy embracing coexistence among government enterprises, government-controlled industries, large private corporate enterprises, and small-scale businesses.

Clark held that businessmen are generally responsible individuals, but unless they seek to serve their own interests in the narrowest sense, competition will drive them to the wall. Even if nineteen businessmen want to follow ethical practices and fair dealing, they may be prevented from doing so by a twentieth competitor who is unscrupulous. Therefore Clark's system of social economics requires social control to serve the general welfare. As early as 1916 he wrote:

By comparison with the scope of responsibility as it has been conceived and presented here the laissez-faire economics may well be characterized as the economics of irresponsibility, and the business system of free contract is also a system of irresponsibility when judged by the same standard. Of static theory we must simply say that while it does not deny social responsibilities it does to a large extent ignore them. . . .

Meanwhile the demand for control has grown with amazing speed, and in every direction experiments are being tried. This should properly be regarded as a recognition of special kinds of responsibility which the business economics leaves out of account and which the machinery of free contract furnishes no way of bringing home to the proper persons. But instead, this regulation is looked on by too many as a phase of the old irresponsible struggle, merely translated from the field of business into the field of politics. It is under suspicion as being mere irresponsible class legislation, and unfortunately the suspicion has some justification.

Hence employers often feel either contemptuous or deeply injured when laws begin to interfere with customary business practices, and when investigating committees ask prying questions which imply a demand for a righteousness that shall exceed the righteousness of the scribes and Pharisees. Business men with this point of view oppose the growth of public control with a resistance that is now adroit and now stubborn but nearly always powerful. The economics of control is at war with the economics of irresponsibility. . . .

To the extent that each of us is a factor in economic evolution, be it only that his presence adds one member to the population, he shares in all the increasing difficulties which economic evolution brings with it. He cannot do anything so far-reaching as building a house without affecting other people's property interests for better or for worse. Unless he affects them for the better he is pretty sure to affect them for the worse. And unless he leaves society stronger in its power to master the manifold troubles of modern industry he will leave it relatively weaker by just so much as those troubles have grown in size and complexity. Modern industry gives a new meaning to the text, "He that is not with me is against me," and is constantly showing new ways in which, whether we like it or not, we are our brothers' keepers.[7]

Clark contrasted the social and individual points of view by showing that what is a variable cost for the firm is an overhead cost for society. Labor is the outstanding example. An employer can lay off workers and thereby save a large part of the production costs, while reducing output. Yet workers have to be fed, housed, and clothed even during bad times; their costs of maintenance cannot be avoided when they are unemployed.

> For the nation as a whole, its labor power is a fixed asset and any failure to utilize it is just as definite a loss as failure to utilize a mechanical plant. It pays, socially, to utilize labor so long as it produces anything toward its own necessary upkeep, which must be met somehow in the long run. Thus social cost-accounting shows a gain from employing labor in a slack season, even if the product will not pay regular day wages to the laborers: social accounting shows a gain where private accounting would show a loss.[8]

If wages could be converted into an overhead cost for the employer, said Clark, production would become more regularized. A guaranteed annual wage might accomplish this.

Raw materials, like labor, are a variable cost for the purchasers but an overhead cost for their original producers and therefore for society as a whole. Producers of raw materials invest funds in their enterprises and must themselves be maintained through good and bad times. The cattle raiser, for example, must pay interest on his mortgage; meet his property-tax payments; allow for maintenance and depreciation on his buildings, machinery, and livestock; and maintain himself and his family. These are all overhead costs, yet the cost of live cattle becomes a variable cost to the packing house that buys them. This shifting of costs distorts economic calculations in

[7] J. Maurice Clark, "The Changing Basis of Economic Responsibility," *Journal of Political Economy*, Vol. xxiv, No. 3 (March 1916), pp. 218, 219, 224.
[8] J. Maurice Clark, *Studies in the Economics of Overhead Costs* (Chicago, 1923), p. 350.

deciding whether or not it is economically worthwhile to produce goods. Every producer has an incentive to maintain production, but the strength of his incentive is measured by his own overhead costs, not by the total overhead costs involved in the whole process.

Clark felt that no single measure, agency, or group can be held responsible for the whole task of seeking solutions to our economic problems. We require a coordinated effort by many agencies, including government, banking, insurance, industry, and labor. The individual firm should plan steadier production, producing goods for inventory in slow times, in order to help fill the depression hollow of the business-cycle curve. The peak of the curve could be lopped off by requiring the employer to bear some responsibility for the overhead cost of temporary labor he might hire; this would encourage him to handle his peak demand with his normal labor supply if possible, instead of adding temporary help. In addition, broad social and governmental programs, including public works, should be used to promote stability.

In a recent book Clark conceded that in spite of the many social controls that have been enacted, "the existing system is far from perfect on the score of efficiency." Yet collectivism, he said, does not offer the complete answer. Though collectivist dictatorship of the Russian type can be ruthlessly efficient, it may sacrifice the higher and more creative forms of efficiency. Democratic collectivism would also sacrifice efficiency and technical progress, perhaps as much as or more than our present system. Worst of all, even democratic collectivism would reduce personal liberty, because a central administrative authority would have ultimate power over the livelihood of every citizen. Our present system creates difficulties for radical nonconformists, but the problem would become more serious if there were in effect only one employer. On the other hand, said Clark, this argument against collectivism should not be taken as a brief for preserving the existing system.

> Existing systems are not preserved unchanged, no matter what we decide about them. They change of themselves, if they are not altered by outside forces; and our present system is not exempt from this law. No single form of existing business liberty is sacred. But this argument is a brief for continuing to struggle onward with a system embodying the principle of liberty, economic as well as personal, in spite of the difficulties. This does not offer a quick cure of basic evils. It offers rather a prospect of generations of effort, with patience, persistence, and tolerance, to strike a sane balance between liberty and control, and to reduce our worst evils to tolerable proportions by a process of adjustment, using

voluntary means to the utmost of their capacity, the whole being subject to free discussion, not directed by arbitrary fiat and suppression of dissent.

It is conceivable that at some point in such a process we might achieve enough co-ordination to reduce unemployment to minor proportions and to maintain stability in other respects without making everyone an employee of the state. At that point it would make little difference whether we called the system "socialistic" or not. "Socialism" of such a sort, reached by such a process, could still leave room for true personal liberty: it could still be democratic. But this can only be attained by a process that does not go too fast for business to adjust itself without catastrophic breakdown or violent revolution. If such a process is to continue, we must avoid committing ourselves to the experiment that would mean the end of free experimentation.[9]

As a social philosopher, Clark was willing to consider and express value judgments, provocative as this attitude may have been. Opinions about how to promote humanity's well-being have been expressed freely by economists from before Adam Smith's time to the present day. Those economists who insist on an austere and Olympian disassociation from social objectives in effect endorse the status quo. One cannot write tax laws or pass on school budgets without some concept of the social welfare and how to promote it. Nor can a person readily separate scientific economic analysis from value judgments on what is good and bad, better and worse. The economist who spells out predilections and preferences can be just as rigorously scientific as the economist who eschews ideas about maximizing welfare. Clark, like Hobson and Pigou, was willing to consider social policy that aimed at maximizing welfare.

Bibliography

CLARK, J. MAURICE, *Alternative to Serfdom*. New York: Knopf, 1948.
———, *Economic Institutions and Human Welfare*. New York: Knopf, 1957.
———, *Preface to Social Economics*. New York: Farrar and Rinehart, 1936.
———, *Social Control of Business*, 2d ed. New York: McGraw-Hill, 1939. [Originally published in 1926.]
———, *Studies in the Economics of Overhead Costs*. Chicago: University of Chicago Press, 1923.
HOBSON, J. A., *Confessions of an Economic Heretic*. London: Allen and Unwin, 1938.

[9] J. Maurice Clark, *Economic Institutions and Human Welfare* (New York, 1957), pp. 100–01.

HOBSON, J. A., *The Economics of Unemployment,* 2d ed. New York: Macmillan, 1931.

———, *Imperialism,* 3d ed. London: Allen and Unwin, 1938. [Originally published in 1902.]

———, *The Industrial System,* 2d ed. New York: Scribner's, 1910.

———, *The Problem of the Unemployed.* London: Methuen, 1896.

———, *Wealth and Life.* London: Macmillan, 1930.

———, *Work and Wealth.* New York: Macmillan, 1914.

HOMAN, PAUL T., *Contemporary Economic Thought.* New York: Harper, 1928.

KAPP, K. WILLIAM, *The Social Costs of Private Enterprise.* Cambridge, Mass.: Harvard University Press, 1950.

LITTLE, I. M. D., *A Critique of Welfare Economics,* 2d ed. London: Oxford University Press, 1957.

MUMMERY, A. F., and HOBSON, J. A., *The Physiology of Industry.* New York: Kelley and Millman, 1956. [Originally published in 1889.]

PIGOU, A. C., *The Economics of Welfare,* 4th ed. London: Macmillan, 1932. [Originally published in 1920.]

22

The Keynesian School

The Keynesian system of ideas represents the most recent great school of economic thought. It arose out of the neoclassical, or marginalist, school, and Keynes himself was steeped in the Marshallian tradition. Although Keynes sharply criticized certain aspects of neoclassical economics, which he lumped together with Ricardian doctrines under the heading of "classical" economics, he used many of its postulates and methods. His system was based on a subjective, psychological approach, and it was permeated with marginalist concepts, including static equilibrium economics. Keynes disassociated himself from attacks on the neoclassical theory of value and distribution.

John Maynard Keynes (1883–1946) was the son of eminently intellectual parents, both of whom survived him. His father was John Neville Keynes, outstanding logician and political economist. His mother, who was interested in public affairs and social work, was a justice of the peace, an alderman, and mayor of Cambridge. Among Keynes's teachers at Cambridge were Marshall and Pigou, both of whom recognized his brilliance. At twenty-eight, Keynes became editor of the *Economic Journal*. He also managed the investments of its publisher, the Royal Economic Society, with unusual success. King's College of Cambridge University likewise made phenomenal profits under Keynes's financial guidance. His own considerable fortune of a half a million pounds was accumulated mainly through dealings in

foreign currencies and commodities. He was in fact one of the speculators about whom he wrote:

> Speculators may do no harm as bubbles on a steady stream of enterprise.
> But the position is serious when enterprise becomes the bubble on a
> whirlpool of speculation. When the capital development of a country
> becomes a by-product of the activities of a casino, the job is likely to be
> ill-done. The measure of success attained by Wall Street, regarded as an
> institution of which the proper social purpose is to direct new invest-
> ment into the most profitable channels in terms of future yield, cannot
> be claimed as one of the outstanding triumphs of *laissez-faire* capital-
> ism—which is not surprising, if I am right in thinking that the best
> brains of Wall Street have been in fact directed towards a different ob-
> ject.[1]

Keynes was an important figure both in the world of practical affairs and in academic life. He was chairman of the board of a life insurance company, he served as director of other companies, and he
was a member of the governing body of the Bank of England. In addition to being a financier, he was a high government official, the author of many scholarly theoretical works, a journalist, a connoisseur
and supporter of the arts, and a teacher at Cambridge University. He
was a leading member of the "Bloomsbury group," named after the
section of London where the sisters Vanessa Bell and Virginia Woolf
had their homes. This circle of brilliant artists, writers, critics, intellectuals, and conversationalists, which functioned from 1907 to 1930,
also included Leonard Woolf, Clive Bell, Lytton Strachey, E. M. For-
ster, and other notables. Keynes was the principal representative of
the British Treasury at the peace conference after World War I, with
power to speak for the chancellor of the exchequer. His experiences
at the Paris negotiations and his strong opposition to the peace settlement forced upon Germany led him to resign his official position in
1919 and write his polemical *The Economic Consequences of the
Peace*. In 1940 he rejoined the Treasury to guide Britain through the
difficulties of war finance. He was his country's chief negotiator in
organizing the International Monetary Fund and the International
Bank for Reconstruction and Development, and in obtaining the
United States postwar loan to Britain. He became a baron in 1942,
and to those of his friends who criticized his accepting the title, his
joking defense was "I had to do it in order to get servants."

After a brief overview of the Keynesian school, we will examine
some of its major ideas in greater detail.

[1] John Maynard Keynes, *The General Theory of Employment, Interest and Money*
(New York, 1936), p. 159.

Overview of the Keynesian School

The Social Background of the School

Keynes's ideas grew out of the anxieties induced by the Great Depression of the 1930's, the worst the Western world had ever known. Yet the roots of his ideas can be traced back to before 1929. The work of many economists (including that of Mitchell and his associates in the National Bureau of Economic Research) was within the framework of aggregative economics, or macroeconomics, rather than the microeconomics of the neoclassical school. This was also the approach adopted by Keynes. World War I and the economic controls that were adopted required an overall view of the economy. The growth of large-scale industrial production and trade made the economy more susceptible to statistical measurement and control, thereby making the inductive, aggregative approach more feasible than in the past. In fact, this approach became increasingly necessary as the public became more eager for the government to deal actively with unemployment.

Keynesian thinking also had its roots in the spreading anxiety about secular stagnation. Somehow the mature private-enterprise economies of the Western world seemed less vigorous after World War I than before. The rate of population growth was declining; most of the world had already been colonized, and there seemed to be no room for further geographic expansion; production seemed to be outrunning consumption as incomes and savings rose; there were no new inventions like the steam engine, the railroad, electricity, and the automobile to stimulate new and vast capital investments; even the new methods and developments seemed as likely as not to save capital, thereby reducing investment expenditures; the decline of vigorous price competition reduced the rate of replacement of old machinery with new and better machines; as capital investment increased and depreciation allowances grew larger, the economy was dragged downward when the accumulated depreciation funds were not spent quickly enough. These observations about secular stagnation, which became particularly important after 1929, were based in part on the works of Marx, Hobson, Veblen and others and in part on actual observations and historical studies.

After the great depression erupted in 1929, many economists in the United States advocated policies that later would be called Keynesian. It is interesting to note that these policies were presented before the publication of *The General Theory of Employment, Interest and Money*. Leading figures both within and outside of the economics profession were urging public works programs, deficit budgets for the federal government, and the easing of credit by the Federal Reserve System. Many economists were aware of the multiplier effect that deficit spending should have on total spending and income. Some theorized that as the national income increases, consumer expenditures increase less rapidly than total income, and savings increase more rapidly. Wages were recognized as a source of demand for goods as well as a cost of production, and cutting wages was frequently opposed as providing no real remedy for unemployment; this was the macroeconomic approach. These ideas were arrived at independently of Keynes and were widely discussed in the United States.

The Essence of the Keynesian School

The major principles of Keynesian economics will be discussed later in this chapter under three headings. First, the immediate determinants of income and employment will be explored. Keynes assumed that there is a high correlation between national income and the level of employment. This is of course not necessarily true. Large investments in labor-saving capital, for example, can cause real national output and income to rise more rapidly than employment. It is even possible for the two variables to move in opposite directions. Keynes, however, was concerned mainly with the short run; he defended this emphasis with the quip, "In the long run we are all dead." In the short run we can neglect technological change; we can then agree that the level of income determines the level of employment, and the two variables can be used interchangeably.

The immediate determinants of income and employment are consumption and investment spending. Every dollar spent on final goods and services, either for consumption or investment, becomes income. If we include the government in this cycle, taxation represents a deduction from the income stream and therefore a potential deduction from consumption and investment spending, and government spending constitutes an addition to total spending.

The second set of components in the Keynesian system are the ultimate determinants of income and employment, or the determinants of consumption and investment spending. Keynes assumed that the level of consumption is determined by the size of income. That is, consumption spending is a given proportion of income at each level of income, and this proportion falls as income rises. This concept, called the "consumption function," means that at any income level people tend to spend a certain fixed proportion of income on consumption. Is it circular reasoning to argue that income depends in part on consumption spending and that the level of consumption spending depends on income? Not at all. The propensity to consume is a schedule, a whole series of values at different levels of income, and Keynes assumed that it is independent and stable in the short run. The level of consumption varies with income; income varies because the inducement to invest changes.

Investment spending is determined by the rate of interest and the "marginal efficiency of capital," or the expected rate of return over cost on new investments. The rate of interest depends on liquidity preference and the quantity of money. The marginal efficiency of capital depends on the expectation of future profits and on the supply price of capital assets. The three basic psychological influences on income and employment are therefore the propensity to consume, the desire for liquid assets, and the expected rate of profit from new investments. The propensity to consume is most stable, thought Keynes, and therefore does not cause fluctuations; the expected rate of profit is the least stable and one of the greatest causes of depressions.

Keynes's third main thesis was that laissez faire is obsolete and that the government should intervene actively to promote full employment by forcing down the rate of interest, thereby stimulating investment; by increasing government deficit spending; and by redistributing income in order to raise the expenditures on consumption.

As early as 1926 Keynes published a little book attacking laissez faire, his hope being that by regulating capitalism it could be preserved. He accused orthodox economics of ignoring the cost of the ruthless struggle that brings the most successful profit-makers to the top by bankrupting the less efficient. The giraffes with the longest necks starve out those whose necks are shorter.

> If we have the welfare of the giraffes at heart, we must not overlook the sufferings of the shorter necks who are starved out, or the sweet leaves which fall to the ground and are trampled underfoot in the struggle, or the overfeeding of the long-necked ones, or the evil look of anxiety or struggling greediness which overcasts the mild faces of the herd. . . .
>
> The important thing for Government is not to do things which individuals are doing already, and to do them a little better or a little worse; but to do those things which at present are not done at all.[2]

[2] John Maynard Keynes, *The End of Laissez-Faire* (London, 1926), pp. 33–34, 46–47.

The evils of our time, Keynes went on to say, are the fruits of risk, uncertainty, and ignorance. Big business is often a lottery in which some individuals are able to take advantage of ignorance and uncertainty. The consequences are great inequalities of wealth, unemployment, disappointment of reasonable business expectations, and impairment of efficiency and production.

> Yet the cure lies outside the operations of individuals; it may even be to the interest of individuals to aggravate the disease. I believe that the cure for these things is partly to be sought in the deliberate control of the currency and of credit by a central institution, and partly in the collection and dissemination on a great scale of data relating to the business situation. . . . These measures would involve Society in exercising directive intelligence through some appropriate organ of action over many of the inner intricacies of private business, yet it would leave private initiative and enterprise unhindered. . . .
>
> Devotees of Capitalism are often unduly conservative, and reject reforms in its technique, which might really strengthen and preserve it, for fear that they may prove to be first steps away from Capitalism itself. . . . For my part, I think that Capitalism, wisely managed, can probably be made more efficient for attaining economic ends than any alternative system yet in sight, but that in itself it is in many ways extremely objectionable. Our problem is to work out a social organisation which shall be as efficient as possible without offending our notions of a satisfactory way of life.[3]

Keynes did not depart from these views during the remaining two decades of his life.

What Groups of People Did the Keynesian School Serve or Seek to Serve?

The great success of Keynesian economics came partly because it offered something for almost everybody and because it rationalized what was already being done out of necessity. Society as a whole gains from full or fuller employment, and those individuals or groups who lose because of it can easily be ignored. Although labor sometimes objected to specific Keynesian proposals, it strongly approved of Keynes's larger goals, especially because counterdepression measures are always very much to labor's liking. Businessmen benefited from government contracts and government stimuli to get the economy out of deep depression. Bankers, when they had huge excess reserves in the 1930's, found a vast and profitable area for investment in government bonds, and government controls gave the banking

[3] *Ibid.*, pp. 47–48, 52–53.

system liquidity, security, and stability. Reformers and intellectuals enjoyed vastly increased employment in the government service, and they could pursue with crusading zeal the mild, safe, and sane reforms that grew out of Keynesian thinking. Farmers too came to rely heavily on government subsidies and regulations. In fact their spokesmen had put forth a crude theory of the multiplier long before it was incorporated into the Keynesian system. In defending government intervention in order to raise farmers' incomes, they claimed that each dollar received by the farmer generated a seven-dollar increase in national income through the respending of the farmer's increased receipts.

How Was the Keynesian School Valid, Useful, or Correct in Its Time?

The Keynesian approach is immensely useful even to those who do not accept the Keynesian remedies for depression. It encouraged the further development of national income accounting, and it stimulated a vast and fruitful effort at inductive studies of the real world. The methodology is applicable to inflation as well as to depression, to international economics as well as to a closed national economy, to war and to peace, to public finance, and to business-cycle studies. Keynes demolished the classical and marginalist assumption that a private-enterprise system tends to be self-adjusting at full employment.

Keynes was not the first to discover that a rise in income in the short run brings a slower rise in consumption. But he was the first to integrate this principle with other relevant ideas to formulate a general theory of income and employment. He also joined the long line of dissident economists who denied Say's principle that supply creates its own demand. On the contrary, said Keynes, all the costs of production (which become income to the owners of factors of production) are not necessarily spent in the aggregate on purchasing the product. Nor will abstention from consumption spending necessarily increase investment.

The fruitfulness of Keynes's ideas can be illustrated by the light they cast on a problem that puzzled the great authority on international trade, Harvard professor Frank W. Taussig. He developed the idea, based on the quantity theory of money, that gold movements lead to equilibrium in international trade by influencing prices and money wages. An inflow of gold into a country causes prices and money wages to rise, thereby stimulating imports, reducing exports, and causing the flow of gold to be reversed. An outflow of gold causes prices and money wages to fall, thereby reducing imports, increasing exports and reversing the outflow of gold. Yet Taussig was amazed at

> the closeness and rapidity with which the varying balance of payments has found its expression in the varying balance of trade. The actual merchandise movements seem to have been adjusted to the shifting balance of payments with surprising exactness and speed. The process which our theory contemplates—the initial flow of specie when there is a burst of loans; the fall of prices in the lending country, rise in the borrowing country; the eventual increased movement of merchandise out of the one and into the other—all this can hardly be expected to take place smoothly and quickly. Yet no signs of disturbance are to be observed such as the theoretic analysis previses; and some recurring phenomena are of a kind not contemplated by theory at all. . . . It must be confessed that here we have phenomena not fully understood.[4]

Keynes's *The General Theory of Employment, Interest and Money* stimulated the development of a new balance-of-payments theory by Mrs. Joan Robinson and others—a theory that solved Taussig's uncertainties by partly superseding and partly supplementing the old price specie-flow mechanism. If country A increases its imports from country B, its income and employment fall while B's rise. When a country's income rises it imports more, and when income falls it imports less. Therefore falling incomes in A will curtail imports from B, and rising incomes in B will increase imports from A. The imbalance in trade will be partly or completely self-correcting, even without gold movements.

Apparently there is some truth to the stagnationists' thesis that a mature private-enterprise economy will not be as buoyant and viable as a youthful one—unless something is done about it. Keynes thus geared economic theory to policy-making. World wars, worldwide depressions, and the growing complications of modern economic life undermined laissez faire. Demands that something be done about fluctuations grew more insistent, and Keynes provided both a program and a theoretical justification for it.

The neoclassical idea that reductions in money wages will overcome a depression can be questioned from the humanitarian or welfare point of view, for there are alternative ways to seek that end. More important, this step makes for bad economics, according to Keynes. He held that a single firm can increase sales and employment through wage cuts, for the demand for its product will remain

---

[4] F. W. Taussig, *International Trade* (New York, 1927), p. 239.

unaffected. A whole economy, however, cannot easily increase sales by cutting wages (assuming it is isolated from international trade), for wages are a source of demand for goods as well as a cost of production. If wages begin to fall, people expect them to fall still further; this causes a postponement of investment spending, thereby making the depression worse. If falling wages result in falling prices, this again worsens matters, because the real burden of debts increases, thereby transferring wealth from the entrepreneur to the *rentier*. In addition, profit margins become smaller, thus choking off new investments. As wage cuts hurt wage earners and help employers, the propensity to consume is diminished. An outstandingly practical man, Keynes also objected to wage cuts because they would touch off labor troubles. He was quite successful in converting people to the idea that wage policy should be divorced from counterdepression policy; there are better ways to seek full employment.

Keynes was a leading advocate of and negotiator for international financial cooperation during and after World War II. In this crusade he sacrificed his health and shortened his life, for his strenuous activities hastened a fatal heart attack. He repudiated the old laissez-faire gold standard system; in the 1930's, in the spirit of nationalism, he argued that a country, through protectionism, could insulate itself from the rest of the world by unilaterally pursuing its own full-employment policies. Yet even in 1936 he expressed the belief that if nations learned to provide themselves with full employment through their domestic policies, and if population growth were limited, an international harmony of interests might prevail. The struggle over export markets could then be replaced by an unimpeded exchange of goods and international lending under conditions of mutual advantage. Keynes lived to see these aspirations realized in part through the financial organizations of the United Nations that he helped to create.

How Did the Keynesian School Outlive Its Usefulness?

Schools of economic thought will undoubtedly arise and attempt to deal with both old and new problems in a new theoretical framework. However, no system of ideas has yet appeared to challenge the dominant Keynesian school. This school has therefore not outlived its usefulness, but we can nevertheless point out certain weaknesses in its ideas.

The short-run, static thinking of Keynes and some of his followers led them to exaggerate the trend toward secular stagnation. They assumed a stable consumption function. If it were always true that the higher the income the smaller the percentage spent on consumption, the historical rise in income levels would enormously multiply our difficulties in the long run. The Keynesian analysis of consumption is apparently true for the short run. At any moment in time poorer people spend a larger proportion of their incomes on consumption than wealthier people. Historically, however, as national and per capita incomes have risen, the percentage spent on consumption has remained fairly stable. We learn to live up to our rising incomes as new products are developed and new desires are created. We have to spend more on consumption to keep up with or exceed our neighbors if they too are spending more. Yet there is some validity to the stagnation thesis, for even though the *percentages* consumed and saved out of disposable income tend to remain stable in the long run as income rises, the *amount* of saving out of income grows and may not be invested easily.

Static thinking led to excessive pessimism about declining investment opportunities and falling rates of profit. Keynes, like many economists before him, thought that the profitability of new investment would decline as the most profitable projects were undertaken first, leaving only less attractive projects for later exploitation.

> Ancient Egypt was doubly fortunate, and doubtless owed to this its fabled wealth, in that it possessed *two* activities, namely, pyramid-building as well as the search for the precious metals, the fruits of which, since they could not serve the needs of man by being consumed, did not stale with abundance. The Middle Ages built cathedrals and sang dirges. Two pyramids, two masses for the dead, are twice as good as one; but not so two railways from London to York.[5]

The stagnationists underestimated the possibilities of technological change and the new capital investments it would stimulate.

Keynes was narrowly provincial with respect to both space and time. He seemed to think that unemployment might have become a problem in ancient Egypt and in the middle ages had it not been for the building of pyramids and cathedrals. His analysis of mercantilism strongly implied that the problems of 1636 were the same as those of 1936: "There has been a chronic tendency throughout human history for the propensity to save to be stronger than the inducement to invest." He thought that throughout history the weakness of the inducement to invest had been the key to the economic problem. Keynes, like Ricardo, uncritically assumed that the spirit of capitalism had dominated the subsistence agricultural economies of the

---

[5] Keynes, *The General Theory of Employment, Interest and Money*, p. 131.

past; and that, even though these were not basically money-using economies, they calculated profit, loss, investment, and so forth, as we do.

Keynes and many of his followers were also provincial in believing that their economics was applicable to all countries. The doctrines of excessive saving and inadequate consumption spending do not apply to underdeveloped areas, where inadequate saving is one factor limiting the growth of investment and income. In poor countries the major symptom of economic malaise is not involuntary but disguised unemployment. Keynes ridiculed the Victorian virtues of abstinence and thriftiness, but in fact this bias against saving would be harmful in nonindustrialized countries.

In his concern with short-run problems Keynes denied the importance of economic growth in industrialized countries—a problem that has since become more significant. He thought that if the propensity to consume is raised sufficiently,

> full employment can be reached with a rate of accumulation little greater than at present. In this event a scheme for the higher taxation of large incomes and inheritances might be open to the objection that it would lead to full employment with a rate of accumulation which was reduced considerably below the current level. I must not be supposed to deny the possibility, or even the probability, of this outcome. For in such matters it is rash to predict how the average man will react to a changed environment. If, however, it should prove easy to secure an approximation to full employment with a rate of accumulation not much greater than at present, an outstanding problem will at least have been solved. And it would remain for separate decision on what scale and by what means it is right and reasonable to call on the living generation to restrict their consumption, so as to establish, in course of time, a state of full investment for their successors.[6]

The Keynesians were too willing to accept slow, steady inflation to stimulate the economy. Their assumption was that certain sticky costs like property taxes, public utility charges, and fees of lawyers and accountants rise more slowly than general prices, thereby increasing profit margins and stimulating investment. The time lag between buying raw materials and selling finished products also increases profits if prices are rising. Investment in durable goods is speeded up if the higher future costs of these goods are anticipated. Keynes believed that while workers strongly resist reductions in money wages, they do not fight cuts in real wages through rising

[6] *Ibid.*, p. 377.

prices. Since wages are also sticky, rising prices thus quicken economic activity.

The Keynesian inflationary remedy has lost its charm. Since World War II this idea has been increasingly repudiated for many reasons. Wage costs are no longer sticky when unions keep up with and anticipate rising prices in presenting their wage demands. The cry against inflation has become a cry against high government budgets, high taxes, welfare spending, and the redistribution of income through government fiscal policy. A continuing inflation that is anticipated and discounted becomes dangerous; government and corporate bonds become more difficult to sell, and interest rates rise. An inflation in one country that exceeds that of the rest of the world makes it more difficult to export goods, and imports increase. Finally, anti-inflation policies win support among the millions of people whose wealth and income are impaired through rising prices.

The Keynesian school can also be criticized for too readily accepting wasteful government deficit spending. Keynes, to be sure, preferred that the state finance useful rather than useless projects. But he recognized that the business community might condemn useful public works if they competed with private enterprise; in such a situation wasteful spending was preferable to serviceable projects and was much better than doing nothing at all.

When involuntary unemployment exists, the marginal disutility of labour is necessarily less than the utility of the marginal product. Indeed it may be much less. For a man who has been long unemployed some measure of labour, instead of involving disutility, may have a positive utility. If this is accepted, the above reasoning shows how "wasteful" loan expenditure may nevertheless enrich the community on balance. Pyramid-building, earthquakes, even wars may serve to increase wealth, if the education of our statesmen on the principles of the classical economics stands in the way of anything better.

It is curious how common sense, wriggling for an escape from absurd conclusions, has been apt to reach a preference for *wholly* "wasteful" forms of loan expenditure rather than for *partly* wasteful forms, which, because they are not wholly wasteful, tend to be judged on strict "business" principles. For example, unemployment relief financed by loans is more readily accepted than the financing of improvements at a charge below the current rate of interest; whilst the form of digging holes in the ground known as gold-mining, which not only adds nothing whatever to the real wealth of the world but involves the disutility of labour, is the most acceptable of all solutions.

If the Treasury were to fill old bottles with banknotes, bury them at suitable depths in disused coal-mines which are then filled up to the surface with town rubbish, and leave it to private enterprise on well-tried principles of *laissez-faire* to dig the notes up again (the right to do so being obtained, of course, by tendering for leases of the note-bearing territory), there need be no more unemployment and, with the help of the repercussions, the real income of the community, and its capital wealth also, would probably become a good deal greater than it actually is. It would, indeed, be more sensible to build houses and the like; but if there are political and practical difficulties in the way of this, the above would be better than nothing.[7]

Of course, if increased government deficit spending scares off private investment, the effect of government spending is weakened or nullified.

Keynes was sympathetic toward private wasteful consumption spending as well as public waste. He defended Bernard Mandeville's *The Fable of the Bees: or, Private Vices, Publick Benefits* (1705), which told of the appalling plight of a prosperous community that suddenly abandoned luxurious living and amusements in the interests of saving. Professor Calvin B. Hoover of Duke University reported Keynes's whimsey on this matter in a Washington hotel:

> While I was preparing to share dinner with Keynes in his hotel suite in Washington in 1934, he genially ridiculed my niceness in selecting a towel from the rack so as not to muss the others. He made a sweep with his arm and knocked two or three on the floor. "I am convinced," he said, jokingly, "that I am more useful to the economy of the U.S.A. by stimulating employment through mussing up these towels than you are by your carefulness in avoiding waste." [8]

Finally, one can dispute Keynes's assumption that employment is a function of income. A billion dollars spent on highly sophisticated space or military technology will generate the same income on the first round of spending as the same amount spent on the construction of housing. Yet the latter will generate far more employment than the former. The Keynesian lack of concern about the kind and quality of spending ignores important welfare considerations and overlooks important employment effects. Keynes demonstrated his awareness that spending on some commodities generates more employment than an equal amount spent on other commodities, for he called his assumption that changes in employment depend solely on changes in aggregate effective demand only a "first approximation." But he and

[7] *Ibid.*, pp. 128–29.
[8] Calvin B. Hoover, "Keynes and the Economic System," *Journal of Political Economy*, Vol. LVI, No. 5 (October 1948), p. 397.

his followers based too much of their analysis and policy recommendations on that first approximation.

Immediate Determinants of Income and Employment

If we ignore the government for the moment, the immediate determinants of income and employment are consumption and investment spending. Every dollar spent on final goods and services, whether for consumption or investment, generates a dollar of income. If we designate C for consumption, I for investment, and Y for income, then

$$Y = C + I$$

Saving is the difference between income and consumption. If we consider taxation, we must then say that saving equals disposable income minus consumption. If we let S stand for saving, then

$$S = Y - C$$

Solving the two equations, we get

$$S = I$$

Aggregate savings and investment are equal at all times, but they are not always in equilibrium. Changes in the level of income, however, bring saving and investment into a stable balance. The concept of equality between saving and investment proved somewhat puzzling when Keynes first published it in 1936. In fact, in his *Treatise on Money* (1930), he assumed that inequality between saving and investment is likely because these acts are carried out by different people, and this inequality causes changes in the level of income and employment.

We might well ask how saving and investment are necessarily equal at all times. If you save fifty dollars and keep it as cash in your wallet, where is the increased investment to match it? Let us assume that you normally spend your weekly income on consumption, but you now suddenly decide to withhold the fifty dollars. Retailers who stocked goods in anticipation of selling them to you suddenly find that their sales have declined and their investment in inventories has increased. Your increased saving of fifty dollars has simultaneously and involuntarily increased retailers' investments by the same amount. Now that their sales have declined, however, they need smaller inventories. They curtail their orders from the manufacturers, people are laid off, and aggregate income and saving fall. Your increased saving is ultimately offset by the reduced saving of other people.

Let us look at another hypothetical case to illustrate the instantaneous equality between saving and investment. Suppose an entrepreneur increases her investment through the creation of bank credit at a time when some unemployment exists in the economy. Where is the increased saving to match the increased investment? The employer hires a worker to produce capital goods. When she pays her employee a hundred dollars on Friday afternoon, the hundred-dollar investment is matched by the hundred dollars of saving in the worker's pocket, for income can be considered saved as long as it is not spent on consumption. If the worker spends a dollar at a tavern on the way home, the tavernkeeper's investment in beer has declined by that amount, and the total new investment and saving now stand at ninety-nine dollars. As inventories are replaced and increased because of rising business, incomes rise and saving rises to match the increased investment originating in the expansion of bank credit.

If the banks expand credit when the economy is already at full employment, they generate inflation. From society's point of view, inflation will curtail consumption by people with fixed income; reduced consumption means increased saving, which will equal the increased investment. Who are the individuals who increase their saving as inflation develops? Those who gain from rising prices, such as debtors, farmers, and entrepreneurs.

We will now introduce the government, thereby disturbing the equality between saving and investment. Let G stand for government spending, and T for taxes. Income is generated by consumption, investment and government spending. Therefore

$$Y = C + I + G$$

Saving is what is left of income after consumption expenditures and tax payments are deducted. Therefore

$$S = Y - C - T$$

As a consequence,

$$S + T = I + G$$
$$S = I + (G - T)$$

If government spending is larger than tax receipts, the government has a budget deficit and $(G - T)$ is positive. Therefore

$$S = I + \text{government deficit}$$

If government spending is smaller than tax receipts, the government has a surplus and $(G-T)$ is negative. Then

$$S = I - \text{government surplus}$$

What do these equations mean? We can illustrate them with two examples. Suppose people save two billion dollars. One billion is used for private investment, and the other billion goes into government bonds to finance deficit spending.

$$S \text{ (2 billion)} = I \text{ (1 billion)} + \text{government deficit (1 billion)}$$

Suppose now that the government runs a surplus of one billion dollars and pays off its bondholders. This sum can now be invested.

$$S \text{ (1 billion)} = I \text{ (2 billion)} - \text{government surplus (1 billion)}$$

Keynes assumed that consumption spending depends on income, rising as income rises but not as much, and falling as income falls but again not as much. Variations in investment spending cause variations in income, which are reinforced by the induced changes in consumption. If investment falls, income falls, saving falls, and saving equals investment at a lower level of income and employment. Rising investment results in higher income, consumption, and saving. Full employment, said Keynes, is only a special case. The general and more typical case is that of underemployment equilibrium.

When consumption and investment spending are inadequate to maintain full employment, the government should be ready to add to the income stream through spending financed by budget deficits. The government should be the spender of last resort.

Ultimate Determinants of Income and Employment

Keynes borrowed the theory of the multiplier from R. F. Kahn, his Cambridge colleague, and incorporated it into his general theory. The multiplier measures the effect on income of a change in spending. If we assume with Keynes that the propensity to consume is fixed at each level of income, we must look to autonomous changes in investment or government spending to explain changes in the level of income, and the multiplier indicates the effect of these changes in spending on income. Let us assume that the marginal propensity to consume at the current level of income is 75 per cent. That is, if people receive an added dollar of income, they will spend an extra seventy-five cents on consumption. An added dollar of investment spending will immediately raise income by a dollar. When three-fourths of that is spent on consumption (with twenty-five cents being saved), income goes up another seventy-five cents. Seventy-five per cent of that additional income will in turn be spent on consumption, and 25 per cent will be saved. Given enough time, income will increase by four dollars, consumption will go up three dollars, and saving will rise by one dollar. When the original dollar injected into the income stream is entirely withdrawn through saving, the effect of the injection will be completely dissipated.

The size of the multiplier is the reciprocal of the marginal propensity to save. If the marginal propensity to consume is three-fourths, the marginal propensity to save is one-fourth, and the multiplier is four. If the marginal propensity to consume is 60 per cent or three-fifths, the marginal propensity to save is two-fifths, resulting in a multiplier of two and a half.

One of the two major determinants of investment, Keynes said, is the marginal efficiency of capital. When a man buys a capital asset, he purchases the right to a series of prospective net returns during the life of the asset. A second element to consider is the supply price or the replacement cost of the asset. Keynes defined the marginal efficiency of capital as equal to that rate of discount which makes the present value of the series of *expected* returns just equal to the supply price of the capital asset. For example, if the present cost of a capital asset is fifty-five hundred dollars, and it is expected to yield an annual return of a thousand dollars for six years, with the assets worth nothing at the end of that time, the marginal efficiency of capital is 2½ per cent. A thousand dollars per year for six years discounted to the present would be worth fifty-five hundred dollars. Alternatively, fifty-five hundred dollars invested at 2½ per cent would yield a return of a thousand dollars each year for six years. The marginal efficiency of capital is really its marginal productivity as a percentage of the original cost of the capital goods, computed over the life of the capital investment and discounted for uncertainty as well as for futurity. Or it is the expected rate of profit of a new investment, not deducting depreciation or explicit and implicit interest costs.

Investments will continue to the point at which the marginal efficiency of capital is equal to the rate of interest. In the above example, the investment would not be undertaken if the rate of interest were 3 per cent, but it would if the rate of interest were 2 per cent.

The marginal efficiency of capital is of course highly variable; it fluctuates with every change in people's expectations of future profits from present investment. If there is increased investment in any given type of capital, said Keynes, the marginal efficiency of capital will tend to fall for two reasons. First, expected profits decline as more and more investments compete with each other. Second, the supply price of capital goods will rise as more is demanded. In the long run, Keynes thought, the first cause is the more significant. The overriding problem lies in the fact that the richer a society grows, the more it saves and the more difficult it becomes to maintain full employment. A private-enterprise economy may have difficulty maintaining adequate investment unless the rate of interest is low enough. If the marginal efficiency of capital is falling more rapidly than the rate of interest because investors are pessimistic, a decline in the rate of interest will not increase investment.

In affirming a long-run tendency for the rate of profit to fall, Keynes had come to the same conclusion (but in some cases for different reasons) as Smith, Ricardo, Mill, Marx, the marginalists, and Veblen.

The second major determinant of the level of investment, in addition to the marginal efficiency of capital, is the rate of interest. Keynes disagreed with economists who thought that the rate of interest produced a balance between the demand for saving to be used in new investment and the supply of saving. The rate of interest, he said, cannot be a reward for saving or waiting as such. If a man hoards his savings in cash, he earns no interest. Nor is saving influenced significantly by the rate of interest; it depends much more on the level of income. The rate of interest is a reward for sacrificing liquidity and thus depends on liquidity preference and the quantity of money (currency plus demand deposits). A given interest rate is that price which equilibrates the individual's desire to hold wealth in cash with the available quantity of cash in the system.

Liquidity preference depends on three motives for holding money and on the reluctance to part with it except insofar as the rate of interest acts as an effective inducement. First, there is the transaction motive, the need for cash to pay for current purchases for consumption and business needs. Second, there is the precautionary motive, the desire to keep some cash on hand for unforeseen emergencies. Third, there is the speculative motive, the desire to hold cash while waiting for interest rates to rise or stock and bond prices to fall or the general price level to fall. Liquidity allows the businessman to quickly seize investment opportunities as they come along.

The quantity of money depends on central bank policy, which can increase or decrease the money supply through changes in open-market operations, reserve requirements, and the rediscount rate. An increase in the quantity of money lowers the rate of interest, unless the public's liquidity preference is increasing more than the quantity of money. A lower rate of interest does not reduce saving, as the classical and neoclassical economists thought. Instead, it tends to stimulate investment, thereby increasing income and saving.

The independent variables that determine saving and investment are the propensity to consume, the schedule of the marginal efficiency of capital, and the rate of interest. These determinants are independent in the sense that their values cannot be inferred from one another. Consumption and investment spending determine not the rate of interest but the aggregate volume of employment. Decreased consumption, other things being equal, will not increase investment; it will increase unemployment.

Government Policy to Promote Full Employment

The Keynesian school relied on a large government role to stabilize the economy at a full employment level. For example, the government should stimulate private investment during a depression by forcing down the rate of interest, which could be accomplished through a central bank policy. But there are limits to how low interest rates can fall. Keynes quoted the nineteenth-century English economist, Walter Bagehot, who said, "John Bull can stand many things, but he cannot stand 2 per cent." How can the rates of interest be forced down toward zero and even a negative figure? He drew on the German monetary reformer, Silvio Gesell, for an answer—stamped money. Money should incur carrying costs just like other stocks of barren goods. A paper currency note would retain its legal-tender quality by having a stamp affixed to it every month. If the cost were a half-cent on the dollar per month, the carrying cost of currency would be 6 per cent per year. In that case a person might be eager to lend it out at minus 4 per cent, and an investor would be willing to push investments to the point at which the marginal efficiency of capital would be minus 4 per cent. Keynes recognized that this system would generate a flight from currency, so checking accounts would have to be taxed in the same manner. But the public could find many substitutes for money, such as promissory notes, foreign money, jewelry, and precious metals.

The important point is that instead of allowing laissez faire conditions to determine interest rates the government should take action to force rates downward in order to overcome inadequate investment. If the rate of interest were forced down to zero, we could make capital goods so abundant that the marginal efficiency of capital would be zero. This would mean the "euthanasia of the rentier," the coupon clipper, the receiver of interest. The capitalist could no longer exploit the scarcity value of capital, and the most objectionable traits of capitalism would be eliminated. A person could still accumulate income to spend at a later date, but the income would not grow. There would still be room for private risk-taking, for active entrepreneurship, for earning profit. Only interest would disappear. Keynes's sympathies lay with the active entrepreneurs, the industrial capitalists, not with the finance capitalists, the speculators, and the passive receivers of interest.

Keynes was not sanguine about the feasibility of a lower rate of interest. Stamped money presents difficulties and is thus not likely to be adopted. He was skeptical too of a strictly monetary policy to influence the rate of interest. The rate of interest will not fall far enough, he said, and the marginal efficiency of capital is too inconsistent and unstable to govern the rate of interest.

Interest charges are probably less important than Keynes thought in determining the level of investment. Except for very large long-term projects like railroads, power plants, and apartment houses, interest represents only a small part of total costs. Bankers and businessmen generally do not consider the level of interest rates a significant determinant of investment. Interest rates do have some influence, but the *availability* of credit, which can be influenced by open-market operations and reserve requirements, has more influence on borrowing than the *cost* of credit.

A second and more effective way to overcome depression is for the government to undertake enough deficit spending to bring about full employment. In effect, current investment spending would be socialized. To Keynes this meant that the state would decide on the aggregate amount of investment. Ownership of capital could still be private, but the government would determine what the returns to the owners should be. Economic life as a whole need not be socialized because the existing system does not seriously misemploy the factors of production that are in use. The state should determine the volume, but not the direction, of employment.

The government should also stimulate the economy by redistributing income, thereby increasing the propensity to consume. Higher taxes on the rich and lower interest rates would help, said Keynes, although he did not emphasize this method of solving the problem of inadequate demand. In 1936 he considered the expansion of investment to be much more important than the expansion of consumption.

In later years, however, he seems to have changed his mind. Professor Calvin B. Hoover, in the article referred to above, reported that Keynes stated in a conversation with him in 1942 or 1943 that after the war the "answer will lie in consumption." It would be necessary and desirable to take action to increase the consumption of the lower-income groups rather than to depend on maintaining full employment through measures to expand investment.

Keynes's great contribution was to adapt economics to the changing institutional structure of modern society. He successfully related academic economics to the economics of government. His ideas have allowed his contemporaries and successors to integrate the analytical and statistical approaches to economics. In Keynesian economics his followers found a new liberalism on which to pin their hopes for reform. The Keynesian school has provided one of the most important alternatives to Marxism.

The "Stockholm School"

The "Stockholm school," based on Knut Wicksell's analysis of the cumulative process, studied aggregative economic processes in a manner similar to Keynes. For years the English economists were unaware of the developments in Sweden, though the Swedish economists paralleled and in some important points anticipated the Keynesians. Gunnar Myrdal (who will be discussed in the following chapter) chided Keynes for his "unnecessary originality." In 1931, as a result of the worldwide depression, the Swedish government asked its leading economists to analyze different policies to combat unemployment. To do so, economists had to solve certain theoretical problems. How can output and investment expand from a depressed state when savings are very small? When investment expands without savers deciding to save more, in what sense does investment exceed saving? Investment ultimately requires saving; where does this saving come from?

Professor Myrdal in 1933 published an analysis that now seems to sharpen the Keynesian concepts that were to appear three years later. Myrdal drew a distinction between forward-looking income, saving, and investment, which he called *ex ante*, and the backward-looking categories, or *ex post*. Thus, *ex ante* investment is planned investment for a future period based on *ex ante*, or planned, income. *Ex ante* saving is also based on expected future income and consumption. *Ex post* saving, investment, and income have been realized in some past period and thus can be examined in the statistical record.

To explain fluctuations, an *ex ante* analysis is required. One must examine expectations and plans for the future. While future expectations and plans are to some extent based on present or past experiences and conditions, there is no mechanical straight-line connection between the two.

Because planned saving and planned investment are generally undertaken by different people, the two variables are unlikely to coincide except by accident. Discrepancies between them represent disequilibria in the economy that force changes toward a new equilibrium. The result is that income shifts to the level at which *ex post* saving and investment are equal. Thus, if planned saving exceeds planned investment, income will fall until planned saving and investment are equal. If planned investment exceeds planned saving, perhaps through the expansion of bank credit, income will rise until planned saving and investment are equal. Equality of *ex ante* saving and investment produces equilibrium that normally manifests itself as an absence of gains or losses in saving and investment *ex post*. Actually, it is possible for planned saving and investment to be equal and still set off an expansion. For example, a widely held belief that income is due to expand might lead to planned saving and investment that is larger than realized saving and investment in the past.

Suppose because of optimistic anticipations investors decide to increase their investments in an economy that has some unemployment. Savers have not decided to save more than formerly. Total sales will rise, more goods will be produced, aggregate income will rise, and people will save more money. At the end of the period, realized incomes will exceed expected incomes, and realized savings will exceed planned savings. It is possible also for realized investment in this example to be less than planned investment. If people save less than the amount required to bring about equality between saving and investment, they will cause inventories of goods to be reduced, thereby reducing realized investment from the planned level.

When Keynes in his *Treatise on Money* (1930) wrote that the inequality between saving and investment causes changes in the level of income and employment, he meant *ex ante*. When, in *The General Theory of Employment, Interest and Money* (1936), he wrote about the equality of these two categories, he meant *ex post*. In his discussion of expectations and the fluctuation of income, however, he did weave *ex ante* considerations into his theory.

Kuznets

Simon S. Kuznets (born 1901) migrated in his youth from Russia to the United States. He was educated at Columbia University, where he was a student of Wesley C. Mitchell. The two men held in common the belief that only through careful measurement and quantitative analysis could economics be transformed from a set of conflicting ideologies into a science. Kuznets taught at the University of Pennsylvania, Johns Hopkins, and Harvard. He also served on the staff of the National Bureau of Economic Research and as an adviser to the United States government. He is responsible more than anyone else for the development of national income accounting and was rewarded for his contributions with the Nobel Prize in economics in 1971, the third year that the prize was given in economics. He was the second American economist to be honored in this way.

In an essay published in 1949, Kuznets criticized some of the national income concepts that grew out of his own pioneering work in that field. To what extent, he asked, is money a true measure of economic welfare? This involves questions both of time and space. If our per capita income is n times what it was two hundred years ago, does this growth really reflect our increased well-being? Similarly, do income differences between the United States and China accurately measure the extent of economic welfare in the two countries?

National income, said Kuznets, is used to measure economic wealth. But, he said, national income is an imperfect gauge because two factors create discrepancies between national income figures and the true level of economic wealth. First, nonmarket activities are excluded from national income figures, which makes economic wealth appear to be lower than it really is. For example, housewives' services are not included in national income, nor are commodities produced by amateur gardeners, photographers, cabinet makers, and other people who practice such hobbies, however unskillfully. In past years the value of housewives' services has been estimated at one-quarter of the national income in the United States.

The second discrepancy has the reverse effect: The inclusion of what Kuznets called "occupational expenses"—those that do not contribute to consumer satisfaction—inflates national income figures, thus making our economic wealth appear to be greater than it really is.

> Do all goods flowing to individuals and households really represent final products in the sense of being sources of satisfaction to consumers as consumers? If a person must use trolleys and buses to go to work, buy banking services because he is a member of the money economy, pay union dues, live in a city—not for any personal satisfaction but as a condition of earning his living—should these services be counted as a positive return to him from the economic system? This is the problem of what may be called "occupational expenses," although the term is unnecessarily narrow since it may cover even such items as the executive's big automobile or expensive membership in various clubs which may be considered indispensable prerequisites of his occupational status rather than freely made personal choices. That such occupational expenses are hardly in the nature of minutiae may be illustrated by a tentative calculation made in attempting a comparison of per capita income in the United States and China and purifying the former for what may be called inflated costs of urban civilization: the inflation in question amounted to from 20 to 30 percent of all consumers' outlay in 1929 as estimated by the Department of Commerce.[9]

To supplement what Kuznets said about occupational costs of our way of life, we may add that commuters travel over one hundred and seventy billion passenger miles annually. The costs of commuting fares and of automobile mileage exceed $12 billion per year. This hardly represents an addition to consumer satisfaction, yet these expenditures appear as consumption in the national income accounts. Similarly, nearly twenty billion checks were written in 1967. It cost the banks, the account holders, and the Federal Reserve System $3.7 billion to put these checks through some twenty different operations and to issue monthly statements. These expenditures also appear in the national income as production of final goods and services.

Kuznets asserted that the omission of nonmarket activities from national income and the inclusion of occupational expenses in it may partly offset each other. But in studies of economic progress over time, these two discrepancies exacerbate each other instead. Both give an upward bias to national income over time because with urbanization nonmarket activities shrink while occupational costs increase. Economic welfare over time therefore does not keep full pace with national income.

These same biases affect comparisons of national income between

---

[9] Simon Kuznets, *Economic Change* (New York, 1953), pp. 195–96.

urban industrialized countries and agricultural underdeveloped countries. Kuznets observed that "even with adjustments for differences in price levels, the current measures often yield the absurd result of a per capita income in underdeveloped countries, such as India or China, which *in terms of U.S. equivalents* amounts to $20 to $40 per year." If these average incomes persisted over many years, most people would starve to death. Obviously, concluded Kuznets, estimates for nonindustrialized countries underestimate nonmarket items, while those for the industrialized countries overestimate occupational expenses and the costs of urban civilization.

Government expenditures on goods and services are also a component of national income. These, said Kuznets, have an even greater bearing than the items considered above on the question of national income as a measure of welfare. How much government spending is an overhead cost of maintaining the social fabric—a precondition for net product—rather than the net product itself? To what extent does government activity represent net final product? The general trend in current national income estimation is to classify all government activities that involve commodities and services (but not transfer payments) as yielding final products. Kuznets dissented from this view. He objected to treating the expenditure of *n* billions on armaments as equivalent in welfare results to *n* billions spent on food, clothing, and other means of providing for people's welfare. Even the costs of wars themselves, argued Kuznets, are related to the character of our social institutions. Thus an overwhelming proportion of government expenditures is an overhead cost of maintaining our social institutions rather than a net return. He recommended instead that national income accounting gauge the net positive contribution of the economy to certain ultimate social goals.

As a consequence, government activity gives an upward bias to estimates of economic progress if they are based on comparisons of annual figures for widely separated years. The same bias favors urban industrialized societies in comparisons with nonurban nonindustrialized countries.

Finally, we have to consider the capital component of national income. In measuring increases of capital stock, which is part of national income, we have to estimate depreciation. All we can do is project past rates of depreciation into the future. Because little capital actually wears out physically we have to estimate the rate of obsolescence, and such projections can easily prove wrong. Nor do we compute the depletion of our natural resources in calculating national income. Conversely, the growth of knowledge and technology adds to our welfare, sometimes by finding substitutes for depleted natural resources.

The father of national income accounting concluded that he did not suggest that national income as a measure of economic welfare be discarded, but rather that national income concepts be developed further and handled more carefully, and that the data necessary to do so be collected.

Bibliography

DAVIS, J. RONNIE, *The New Economics and the Old Economists*. Ames, Iowa: The Iowa State University Press, 1971.

DILLARD, DUDLEY, *The Economics of John Maynard Keynes*. New York: Prentice-Hall, 1948.

HANSEN, ALVIN H., *A Guide to Keynes*. New York: McGraw-Hill, 1953.

HARRIS, SEYMOUR E., ed., *The New Economics*. New York: Knopf, 1948.

HARROD, R. F., *The Life of John Maynard Keynes*. New York: Harcourt Brace Jovanovich, 1951.

HELLER, WALTER W., *New Dimensions of Political Economy*. Cambridge, Mass.: Harvard University Press, 1966.

KEYNES, JOHN MAYNARD, *The End of Laissez-Faire*. London: Hogarth, 1926.

———, *Essays in Persuasion*. London: Macmillan, 1933.

———, *The General Theory of Employment, Interest and Money*. New York: Harcourt Brace Jovanovich, 1936.

———, *How to Pay for the War*. New York: Harcourt Brace Jovanovich, 1940.

———, *A Treatise on Money*. 2 vols. London: Macmillan, 1930.

KUZNETS, SIMON, *Economic Change*. New York: W. W. Norton, 1953.

———, *Modern Economic Growth: Rate, Structure and Spread*. New Haven: Yale University Press, 1966.

———, *National Income and Its Composition, 1919–1938*. New York: National Bureau of Economic Research, 1941.

———, *Population, Capital and Growth*. New York: W. W. Norton, 1973.

———, *Postwar Economic Growth*. Cambridge, Mass.: Harvard University Press, 1964.

TERBORGH, GEORGE, *The Bogey of Economic Maturity*. Chicago: Machinery and Allied Products Institute, 1945.

23

Modern Theories of Economic Development and Growth

No school of economic thought has a monopoly on concern over economic development and growth: adherents of several schools and eclectics alike have occupied themselves with these matters. Especially since World War II, economic growth has inspired a vast outpouring of active scholarship on the subject.

Although the terms "economic development" and "economic growth" are used interchangeably, there is a distinction between them. Economic growth may be defined as increasing total output, which can occur with no increased efficiency or rising levels of living. Growth can result from increased population; increased capital investments; longer hours of work; or a larger proportion of the population working, as when women, young people, and old people enter the labor force instead of remaining at home, at school, or in retirement. If the total hours worked in a society double but total output goes up only 50 per cent, there is growth even though efficiency has declined. Growth may even be associated with falling levels of living if population grows faster than output, or if capital investments grow faster than increases in output.

Economic development may be defined as rising output per hour of labor with no reduction in employment. The last qualification is important. It is possible to raise output per hour by cutting production. The least efficient factories and machines are idled; the least efficient workers are laid off; and employed workers, fearful for their jobs, can be speeded up. Even if all units of labor and capital were of equal quality, reducing the number of workers while keeping capital investment constant would increase output per hour because of the law of diminishing marginal productivity. Reductions in employment that lead to increasing output per hour do not lead to economic development.

Economic development therefore implies improvement or increasing efficiency. It is generally but not necessarily associated with economic growth and rising levels of living. We might have growing output per hour with the increase going into investment; then the level of living would not rise immediately, although it might later on. With increasing productivity, people might prefer increased leisure instead of increased income. Thus, if productivity doubled while workers chose to cut their weekly labor hours by half, there would be economic development but no growth and no rising real income unless we consider leisure part of income.

There are a number of significant reasons why interest in economic development and growth has burgeoned during the last several decades. First, economic growth is associated with growing military power; a country that produces ten million tons of steel is potentially stronger than one that produces two million, though certainly not five times stronger and perhaps less efficient. Second, Western Europe and the United States seem to have overcome the worst excesses of business depressions through moderately successful stabilization policies. The emphasis has thus shifted to policies promoting growth. Third, the world is watching the economic race between the United States and Soviet Russia to see which can grow and develop more rapidly and thereby capture world attention; the rapid rate of growth of the Communist countries, as well as private-enterprise countries like Japan, has been disturbingly impressive to the Western world. Fourth, most of the poor countries, many of them colonies before World War II, are now politically free and have decided to promote growth and development. Once called "backward" or "underdeveloped," these new nations are now called "developing" or "emerging," which recognizes their aspirations and shows the respect they have won. Fifth, the West and the Communists are fighting for leadership of and alliance with the poor countries, and the latter are watching closely to learn which approach best suits their needs. Sixth, the idea that government should actively promote growth and development has become pervasive; people are generally no longer content to accomplish these objectives through laissez faire policies. Finally, the export of capital to underdeveloped areas through private investment stimulates fuller employment in the industrialized countries.

This chapter examines four types of analysis of economic growth and development. Some theories, such as that of Schumpeter, seek to explain economic change without prescribing remedies or urging detailed policies. Others hope to influence policy toward more rational and faster progress.

Schumpeter: The Decay of Capitalism

Joseph Alois Schumpeter (1883–1950), the son of a cloth manufacturer, was born in the Austrian province of Moravia (now Czechoslovakia) and educated in law and economics at the University of Vienna. He practiced law for several years, taught political economy, and in 1913 and 1914 was exchange professor at Columbia University. It was at this time that he and Wesley C. Mitchell began their long friendship. During World War I Schumpeter made no secret of his pacifist, pro-British, anti-German sentiments. He served briefly as Minister of Finance of the Austrian Republic in 1919. In 1921 he became president of a highly respected private banking house in Vienna. When the bank collapsed in 1924 after the great inflation in Germany, he returned to the academic world and accepted a professorship at the University of Bonn in Germany. From 1932 until his death he taught at Harvard, and he served as president of the American Economic Association, the first foreign-born economist to attain this distinction. His encyclopedic *History of Economic Analysis*, edited after his death by his wife, is a monument to his gigantic scholarly achievements.

Two major intellectual influences in Schumpeter's life were Léon Walras and Karl Marx. From Walras Schumpeter derived his emphasis on the interdependence of economic quantities. Schumpeter had a strong aversion to Marx and all he stood for, but he admired Marx's understanding of the process of economic change. Schumpeter was deeply devoted to the institutions of capitalism, and he viewed with alarm the forces engendered by the very success of capitalism, for he felt that they would destroy the system. He agreed with Marx that capitalism was doomed, although for different reasons and with profound regret.

Schumpeter constructed a theoretical system to explain both business cycles and the theory of capitalist economic development. The key process in economic change is the introduction of innovations, and the central innovator is the entrepreneur. Innovation is defined as changes in the methods of supplying commodities, such as introducing new goods or new methods of production; opening new markets, conquering new sources of supply of raw material or semi-manufactured goods; or carrying out a new organization of industry, such as creating a monopoly or breaking one up. Innovation is much more than invention. Invention is not innovation if it is still-born—that is, if it is not used. An invention becomes an innovation only when it is applied to industrial processes.

The entrepreneur is the person who carries out new combinations and who introduces innovations. Not all heads of firms or managers or industrialists are entrepreneurs, for they may be running a business without trying new ideas or new ways of doing things. Nor are the entrepreneurs risk-takers. That function is left to the shareholders, who are typically capitalists but not entrepreneurs. Entrepreneurs may have only temporary connections with individual firms as financiers or promoters. But they are always pioneers in introducing new products, new processes, and new forms of business organization or in penetrating new markets. They are men with exceptional abilities who seize opportunities that others are oblivious to or who create opportunities through their own daring and imagination.

Without innovation, economic life would reach static equilibrium, and its circular flow would follow essentially the same channels year after year. Profit and interest would disappear, and the accumulation of wealth would cease. The entrepreneur, seeking profit through innovation, transforms this static situation into the dynamic process of economic development. He interrupts the circular flow and diverts labor and land to investment. Because savings generated by the circular flow are inadequate, he relies on credit to provide the means for his enterprise. The resulting economic development arises from within the economic system itself, rather than being imposed from outside.

Innovations do not occur continuously, but appear in clusters. The activities of the most enterprising and venturesome entrepreneurs create a favorable climate in which others can follow. Credit expands, prices and incomes rise, and prosperity prevails. But not forever. The economic boom generates conditions unfavorable to its continued progress. Rising prices deter investment, and the competition of new products with old ones causes business losses. When businessmen repay their debts, the deflationary process is intensified, and depression replaces prosperity. Business fluctuations therefore represent the process of adaptation to innovation. The system tends toward equilibrium, except that innovations always disrupt that tendency. The process that generates economic development also generates fluctuations, and every depression represents a struggle toward a new equilibrium.

Can capitalism survive? asked Schumpeter. No, was his reply. Capitalist society has for some time been in a state of decay. But he disagreed with most economists about the precise nature of that decay. He rejected the Ricardian law of diminishing returns and the Malthusian population principle, both of which were supposed to thwart progress. He also denied Marx's contention that economic contradictions would produce successively more severe crises. He rejected the Keynesian stagnation thesis on several counts: Opportunities for great innovations have not been exhausted; the tendency of innovations to become capital saving has not been demonstrated convincingly; although the process of opening up new countries has been completed, other opportunities may well replace these; and, finally, the falling birth rate may become economically significant in the future, but it cannot explain the events of the 1930's. His diagnosis of capitalism's fundamental sickness came closest to that of Sombart, discussed in Chapter 11.

Schumpeter wrote that if the capitalist system were to follow the pattern of growth it established in the sixty years preceding 1928, we could achieve the objectives of social reformers without significant interference with the capitalist process. But this is not likely. The economic and social foundations of capitalism are beginning to crumble because of (1) the obsolescence of the entrepreneurial function, (2) the destruction of protective political strata, and (3) the destruction of the institutional framework of capitalist society.

The entrepreneurial function is growing obsolete. Innovation is being reduced to routine. Technological progress is increasingly becoming the business of teams of trained specialists who turn out what is required and make it work in predictable ways. Economic progress is becoming depersonalized and automatized. Bureau and committee work replaces individual action. The entrepreneur no longer has the opportunity to fling himself into the fray; he is becoming just another office worker, one not always difficult to replace.

> To sum up this part of our argument: if capitalist evolution—"progress"—either ceases or becomes completely automatic, the economic basis of the industrial bourgeoisie will be reduced eventually to wages such as are paid for current administrative work excepting remnants of quasi-rents and monopoloid gains that may be expected to linger on for some time. Since capitalist enterprise, by its very achievements, tends to automatize progress, we conclude that it tends to make

itself superfluous—to break to pieces under the pressure of its own success. The perfectly bureaucratized giant industrial unit not only ousts the small or medium-sized firm and "expropriates" its owners, but in the end it also ousts the entrepreneur and expropriates the bourgeoisie as a class which in the process stands to lose not only its income but also what is infinitely more important, its function. The true pacemakers of socialism were not the intellectuals or agitators who preached it but the Vanderbilts, Carnegies and Rockefellers. This result may not in every respect be to the taste of Marxian socialists, still less to the taste of socialists of a more popular (Marx would have said, vulgar) description. But so far as prognosis goes, it does not differ from theirs.[1]

The destruction of the political strata that have offered the strongest defense of capitalist society also spells the self-destruction of the system. Schumpeter agreed with Marx that big business destroys small and medium-sized firms. In democratic politics, this process weakens the political position of the industrial bourgeoisie, for numerous small businessmen are more powerful politically than a few salaried executives and large shareholders.

The capitalist process, by substituting a mere parcel of shares for the walls of and the machines in a factory, takes the life out of the idea of property. It loosens the grip that once was so strong—the grip in the sense of the legal right and the actual ability to do as one pleases with one's own; the grip also in the sense that the holder of the title loses the will to fight, economically, physically, politically, for "his" factory and his control over it, to die if necessary on its steps. And this evaporation of what we may term the material substance of property—its visible and touchable reality—affects not only the attitude of holders but also that of the workmen and of the public in general. Dematerialized, defunctionalized and absentee ownership does not impress and call forth moral allegiance as the vital form of property did. Eventually there will be *nobody* left who really cares to stand for it—nobody within and nobody without the precincts of the big concerns.[2]

Farmers, another group that strongly defends capitalism, are declining as a percentage of the population.

Capitalism, said Schumpeter, even creates, educates, and subsidizes an intellectual group with a vested interest in social unrest. Intellectuals do not have direct responsibility for practical affairs; they are outsiders looking in, yet they wield the power of the spoken and written word. Their main chance of asserting themselves is their

[1] Joseph A. Schumpeter, *Capitalism, Socialism, and Democracy,* 3d ed. (New York, 1950), p. 134. Reprinted with permission of Harper & Row, Publishers.
[2] *Ibid.,* p. 142.

actual or potential nuisance value. Freedom of public discussion involves freedom to nibble at the foundations of capitalist society, and
the intellectual group cannot help nibbling because it lives on criticism. College graduates who are incapable of professional work and
object to manual occupations swell the ranks of the discontented,
and they develop hostility toward the capitalist order in rationalizing
their own inadequacies. Intellectuals have also invaded the labor
movement and radicalized it in order to win favor among the very
people who are naturally suspicious of them.

The third reason for the crumbling foundations of capitalism, according to Schumpeter, lies in the destruction of the institutional
framework of capitalist society. The chief merit of the stagnationist
argument is its recognition of the undeniable truth that unlike other
economic systems, the capitalist system is geared to incessant economic change. Capitalism implies recurrent industrial revolutions,
which are the main sources of profit and interest for entrepreneurs
and capitalists. The valid core of the stagnationist analysis hinges on
the inadequacy of profit expectations as the root of insufficient investment and employment. These economic problems were generated by the anticapitalist policies adopted in most European countries since World War I and in the United States since 1933—policies
that increased the unemployment figures of the 1930's beyond what
they need have been. These policies include taxation that is so high
and progressive that it prevents private accumulation; counterdepression public expenditure; labor legislation that shifts questions
of wages, hours, and factory discipline to the political sphere; and
strict regulation of the behavior of big business under the threat of
prosecution.

> Under these conditions, public income generation will automatically
> become permanent, quite irrespective of the factors stressed by the
> theories framed to prove its necessity from causes inherent in the sav-
> ing-investment process of capitalist society. Such a system will no doubt
> still be called capitalism. But it is capitalism in the oxygen tent—kept
> alive by artificial devices and paralyzed in all those functions that pro-
> duced the successes of the past. The question why it should be kept
> alive at all is therefore bound to be put before long.[3]

Nonpublic banking and finance will no longer have a role to play
in an economic world completely dependent on government financing that is itself entirely independent of private voluntary saving.

[3] Joseph A. Schumpeter, *Essays*, ed. by Richard V. Clemence (Reading, Mass., 1951),
p. 180.

Government spending as a permanent policy will develop into government planning of investment. International trade and investment will be cut off from its old background of commercial calculation and come to be managed by political considerations. This will be "guided capitalism," which will shade off into "state capitalism" as some measures of nationalization are adopted. Schumpeter defined state capitalism as government ownership and management of selected industrial sectors, complete government control in the labor and capital market, and government initiative in domestic and foreign enterprise. It is a matter of taste whether this is called socialism or not, he said. Such a state will suffer from friction and inefficiency, which could be eliminated by returning to pure capitalism or advancing resolutely to full socialism. On the other hand, Schumpeter thought that state capitalism might conserve many human values that would perish in the alternative systems.

An interesting contrast to the views of Schumpeter are the modern Marxist views of Paul Baran. Baran disputed Schumpeter's major thesis on the importance of the entrepreneur and ascribed instead primary importance in development to the struggle between economic classes.

Baran: The Marxist Analysis

Paul Alexander Baran (1909–64) was born in Russia but received Polish citizenship as a child when he and his family moved to Poland and then to Germany soon after World War I. He studied economics, history, and sociology in the Soviet Union, in France, and in Germany, receiving his Ph.D. at Berlin University. In May 1933 he left Germany, arriving in the United States in 1939 where he continued his studies at Harvard and the Brookings Institution. After serving with the government during World War II, he joined the research staff of the Federal Reserve Bank of New York. Later he became a professor of economics at Stanford University.

Baran, an ardent advocate of Marxian socialism, felt obliged to explain the brutalities of the Stalin regime as revealed by Khruschev in 1956. The preface of his book contained his answer to the widespread characterization of Soviet Russia's system as "totalitarian socialism" in contrast to Great Britain's or Sweden's "democratic socialism."

> It is not *socialism* that can be fairly charged with the misdeeds of Stalin and his puppets—it is the *political system* that evolved from the drive to develop at breakneck speed a backward country threatened by foreign

aggression and in face of internal resistance. The emergence of such a political system under the unique circumstances prevailing in Russia after Hitler's seizure of power and in the countries of Eastern and Southeastern Europe during the frightening years of the cold war does not "prove" that socialism is inherently a system of terror and repression. What it does mean—and this is a historical lesson of paramount importance—is that socialism in backward and underdeveloped countries has a powerful tendency to become a backward and underdeveloped socialism. What has happened in the Soviet Union and the socialist countries of Eastern Europe confirms the fundamental Marxian proposition that it is the degree of maturity of society's productive resources that determines "the general character of social, political and intellectual life." It casts no reflection on the fundamental rationality, desirability, and potentialities of a socialist transformation in the West. Indeed, it accentuates its desperate urgency. For a socialist society in the advanced countries would not be compelled to engage in "forced marches" towards industrialization, or bound to withdraw from popular consumption large parts of miserably low incomes, or constrained to devote to military purposes significant shares of small aggregate outputs. Such a socialist society would not only attack head-on the waste, irrationality, and cultural and moral degradation of the West, it would also throw its weight into helping to solve the entire problem of want, disease, and starvation in the underdeveloped parts of the world. Socialism in the West, once firmly established, would destroy for all time the bases and the need for any reappearance of the political and social repression that marked the early stages of socialism in the East.[4]

Economic development, said Baran, depends on the class struggle. Society has to be transformed, and as always, certain classes and groups obstruct change while others advance it. Today we have proof that an economy based on comprehensive economic planning can function and grow without the benefits of private enterprise. The dominant interests in the advanced capitalist countries are inimical to economic development in the poor countries because the latter are indispensable as the hinterlands of capitalism, supplying it with raw materials, profits, and investment outlets.

In addition to the interrelated political problems of class struggle and imperialism, the underdeveloped countries must consider the problem of economic surplus. A country's *actual* economic surplus is identical with current saving or accumulation; it is the difference between society's actual current output and its actual current consumption. A country's *potential* economic surplus is the difference between the output that could be produced in a given natural and

---

[4] Paul A. Baran, *The Political Economy of Growth*, (New York, 1957), p. viii. Reprinted with permission of the Monthly Review Press.

technological environment and what might be regarded as essential consumption. The actual surplus is less than the potential because of (1) excess consumption by the rich and middle classes; (2) output lost to society because of unproductive workers (advertisers, tax-evasion specialists, makers of armaments, and so forth); (3) output lost because of the irrational and wasteful organization of the existing productive apparatus; and (4) output lost because of unemployment caused by the anarchy of capitalist production and the lack of effective demand.

Potential economic surplus can become *planned* economic surplus in a comprehensive socialist economy. A socialist community, guided by reason and science, can use its resources to expand investment and production most efficiently, while at the same time pursuing a scientific policy of conservation of human and natural resources. The guiding force is not profit maximization, but a rational plan reflecting society's preferred balance of current and future consumption.

According to Baran, the rate and direction of economic development in a country at a given time depend on the size of the economic surplus and how it is used. The surpluses drawn from countries such as India by the dominant powers could have gone far in promoting economic development if they had been invested in the countries that produced them. The present problems in the poor countries are that the actual economic surpluses are much smaller than the potential surpluses, and much of the surplus is wasted in lavish consumption rather than being used to promote development. This surplus, while small in *absolute* terms, is a large *share* of total output—as large as, if not larger than, in advanced capitalist countries. It must be invested under government planning for maximum impact.

Baran offered several observations on problems of economic development in the underdeveloped areas. A land reform that merely breaks up large estates is inadvisable because it will simply increase the peasantry's consumption and because small inefficient holdings will keep production down; large-scale farming is required. The increase of Western assets in the underdeveloped part of the world is only partly due to capital exports in the strict sense of the term; it is primarily the result of the reinvestment abroad of some of the economic surplus secured abroad. Businesses are established by foreign corporations in poor countries to facilitate exploitation by foreign merchant capitalism. A group of native merchants emerges within the orbit of foreign capital, and it uses its influence to perpetuate the status quo. Native industrialists and feudal landowners also oppose change, and thus foreign exploitation is continued while popular movements for social and national liberation are suppressed—at least temporarily. But ultimately the property of foreign and domestic capitalists and landowners must be expropriated. Economic development will then proceed simultaneously through industrialization and the improvement of agriculture.

Some people attribute underdevelopment at least partly to the lack of entrepreneurial talent. Baran was not impressed with this argument. Marxism denies the crucial role of the entrepreneur, the symbol of capitalist exploitation.

> The trouble with the theory centering on this "central figure" is, however, that it either boils down to a tautology, or that its contents are simply fallacious. If it is to be given the former, more merciful interpretation, the doctrine is reducible to the finding that in the absence of industrial capitalism there are no industrial capitalists, and vice versa— which is indubitably a correct proposition but also one that is singularly unexciting. For in all parts of the world and at all times in history there have been ambitious, ruthless, and enterprising men who had an opportunity and were willing to "innovate," to move to the fore, to seize power, and to exercise authority. Yet at some times and places this elite supplied the headmen of tribes, at others it provided knights, courtiers, and ecclesiastical dignitaries, while in a certain phase of the historical process it produced merchant-princes, adventurers, explorers, and pioneers of science. Finally, during the latest period of historical development—in the age of modern capitalism—it has given rise to the capitalist entrepreneur organizing industrial production or mastering the art of finance so as to be able to bring under his control vast concentrations of capital. It should be obvious that what the theorist of entrepreneurship has to explain is not the sudden appearance of men of genius—such men have been with us since the beginning of time!—but the fact that these men in a certain historical constellation have turned their "genius" to the accumulation of capital, and that they found the best way to accomplish this end to be investment in industrial enterprises. Failing to do this and invoking instead a *deus ex machina* is not unlike "explaining" squalor by the existence of poverty, and renders the theory of the strategic importance of the entrepreneur entirely worthless.[5]

Baran's dictum that "the establishment of a socialist planned economy is an . . . indispensable condition for the attainment of economic and social progress in underdeveloped countries" is believed by many in those countries. It remains to be seen whether such ideas will be challenged effectively by noncommunist ideologies.

[5] *Ibid.*, pp. 235–36.

Baran's precondition of a socialist planned economy was not entirely disputed by Ragnar Nurkse, our next important economist. Nurkse placed great emphasis on economic planning, although not necessarily accompanied by a socialist political system.

Nurkse: Balanced Development

Ragnar Nurkse (1907–59) was born in Estonia. In the early 1930's his family emigrated to Canada, and he studied at Edinburgh University and the University of Vienna. As an employee of the League of Nations, he published some distinguished studies in international economics. After World War II he accepted a professorship at Columbia University and remained there until his untimely death in Geneva while on leave of absence.

Nurkse gave renewed emphasis to external economies: the more investments made, the more viable each undertaking becomes. Therefore the underdeveloped areas require progress on a broad front, with simultaneous expansion of industries that support each other and increase the chances of success. The great difficulty is that the poverty of countries has limited their capital formation.

Why do countries remain poor? asked Nurkse. Because of the vicious circle of poverty, was his reply.

> The "vicious circle of poverty" . . . implies, of course, a circular constellation of forces tending to act and react upon one another in such a way as to keep a poor country in a state of poverty. Particular instances of such circular constellations are not difficult to imagine. For example, a poor man may not have enough to eat; being under-nourished, his health may be weak; being physically weak, his working capacity may be low, which means that he is poor, which in turn means that he will not have enough to eat; and so on. A situation of this sort, applying to a country as a whole, can be summed up in the trite proposition: "a country is poor because it is poor."
>
> The most important circular relationships of this kind are those that afflict the problem of capital formation in economically underdeveloped countries. The problem of economic development is largely, though by no means entirely, a problem of capital accumulation. The so-called underdeveloped areas, as compared with the advanced, are under-equipped with capital in relation to their population and natural resources.
>
> There are two sides to the problem of real capital formation: there is a demand side and a supply side. The demand for capital is governed by the incentives to *invest*; the supply of capital is governed by the ability and willingness to *save*. In underdeveloped countries, a circular rela-

tionship exists on both sides of the problem. On the supply side, we have the small capacity to save, resulting from the low level of real income. But the low real income is a reflection of low productivity, which in its turn is due largely to the lack of capital. The lack of capital is a result of the small capacity to save, and so the circle is complete.

On the demand side, the inducement to invest may be low, because of the small buying power of the people, which is due to their small real income, which in turn is due to low productivity. The low level of productivity, however, is a result of the small amount of capital used in production, which in its turn is caused, to some extent, by the low inducement to invest. . . .

It may be surprising to hear that there can be anything wrong on the demand side of the problem of capital formation in underdeveloped countries. Can there be any deficiency in the demand for capital? Are not underdeveloped areas, almost by definition, greatly in need of capital for the efficient use of their labour and for the exploitation of their natural resources? Is not the demand for capital, in most of these areas, tremendous? It may well be; and yet, in terms of private business incentives to adopt roundabout or capitalistic methods in the productive process, there may be a difficulty, arising from the small size of the domestic market in the early stages of a country's development.

The inducement to invest is limited by the size of the market. . . . In a country, for instance, where the great majority of people are too poor to wear leather shoes, setting up a modern shoe factory may be a doubtful proposition; the market for shoes may be too small. Many articles that are in common use in the United States can be sold in an underdeveloped country in such limited quantities, that a machine, working only a few days or weeks can produce enough for a whole year's consumption, and would have to stand idle the rest of the time. In such circumstances the economic incentive to install capital equipment may be lacking. . . .

The size of the market, in the last analysis, is determined by the general level of productivity. In an all-inclusive view, capacity to buy not only depends on, but is actually defined by, capacity to produce. . . . For any individual entrepreneur, the use of capital is inhibited, to start with, by the small size of the market.[6]

Nurkse argued that if poor countries are to advance, they must rely increasingly on industrialization instead of primarily on the production and export of raw materials. The nonindustrial countries, he said, are almost all in the low-income class, and they trade very little among themselves. The rich industrial countries show vigorous advances in real income per capita, yet they are not transmitting their

[6] Ragnar Nurkse, *Some Aspects of Capital Accumulation in Underdeveloped Countries* (Cairo, 1952), pp. 1–3. Reprinted with permission of National Bank of Egypt.

own rate of growth to the rest of the world through a proportional increase in the demand for primary products. There are six major reasons for this: (1) In the advanced economies, industrial production is shifting from "light" to "heavy" industries (such as engineering and chemicals) and therefore requires fewer raw materials relative to finished output. (2) As services become increasingly important in the richer countries, their raw-material demand lags behind the rise in their national product. (3) The income elasticity of consumer demand for many agricultural commodities tends to be low. (4) Agricultural protectionism tends to reduce the imports of primary products into industrial countries. (5) Substantial economies have been achieved in the industrial uses of natural materials through such developments as electrolytic tin-plating and systematic recovery and reprocessing of metals. (6) The industrial countries have increasingly tended to displace natural raw materials with synthetics.

As a consequence of these forces at work from 1904–13 to 1944–50 the manufacturing production of the United States increased more than three times as fast as the consumption of raw materials in our economy. Traditional international trade theory, said Nurkse, is of questionable relevance in explaining the increasing discrepancies in income levels between manufacturing and raw-materials-producing countries.

If primary production for export does not offer attractive opportunities for expansion, the alternative is industrialization. There can be two types of industrialization: that which aims at producing manufactured goods for export to the industrial countries and that which caters mainly to domestic markets in the underdeveloped countries. The second type generally requires a complementary advance in domestic agriculture, while the first does not. Neither type demands the abandonment or contraction of exports of the raw materials that a country is naturally adapted to produce.

Nurkse thought that production of manufactured goods for export to the industrial countries offers little hope of success. Therefore underdeveloped areas should expand the home market for finished goods. However, the size of the market depends on the volume of production. The difficulty is that the impoverished farm population cannot buy the manufactured goods offered for sale because of their own low productivity and incomes. Nor can the local economy supply the food required to sustain the new industrial workers. Therefore industrial development for domestic markets requires a simultaneous rise of agricultural productivity on the home front.

The same principle applies within the manufacturing sphere. By itself a single industry cannot create sufficient demand for its own output, because people working in new industries will not wish to spend all their income on their own products.

> Just as it is possible for manufacturing as a whole to fail if peasants can produce no marketable surplus and are too poor to buy anything from factories, so it is possible for a single branch of manufacturing to fail for lack of support from other sectors in industry as well as agriculture; that is, for lack of markets. To be sure, an expansion of one industry will have effects on income and expenditure tending to induce other industries also to expand. But if the others are only passive receivers of the external stimulus their expansion may be slow and uncertain. And their slowness and passiveness will in turn slow down and discourage the industry that first started expanding. In short, while it is true that the active sectors will tend to pull the passive ones forward (and this is what some advocates of "unbalanced growth" have in mind), it is equally true that the passive sectors will tend to hold the active ones back. Would it not be better if every sector were in some measure "active" in the sense of advancing spontaneously, imbued with some expansive élan of its own instead of waiting for signals from others? Price incentives and restraints would then be needed merely to keep each sector's rate of advance in line with the community's pattern of demand. The principle of balanced expansion can be looked upon as a means of accelerating the overall rate of output growth.[7]

There are limits to the diversification of output. The need to maintain an efficient plant size is an important practical consideration that often limits the diversification of industry in any single country. Therefore manufacturing for home markets in the less developed countries must also include production for export to one another's markets. This is particularly important for countries with small purchasing power, which have much to gain from customs unions among underdeveloped nations.

Economic progress, said Nurkse, is not spontaneous or automatic. On the contrary, forces within the system tend to anchor it to a given level. Once the vicious circle of stagnation is broken, however, the circular relationships tend to make for cumulative advance. The synchronized investment of capital in a wide range of industries will enlarge the market for all of them, even though each industry considered separately would appear to be unattractive for investment. Most industries catering to mass consumption are complementary in the sense that they provide markets for each other. The social marginal

[7] Ragnar Nurkse, *Patterns of Trade and Development* (Stockholm, 1959), p. 43.

productivity of capital is in essence higher than its private marginal productivity.

In underdeveloped countries, Nurkse believed, the forces that would defeat the grip of economic stagnation must be deliberately organized through some central direction or collective enterprise. In this his analysis was similar to Baran's. He disagreed, however, on whether the organizing mechanism should be public or private. The actual investing could be undertaken by private enterprise, although the state might enforce compulsory saving and then coordinate investment. The deficiency of demand arises only in the private sector of the economy. For the economy as a whole there is of course no deficiency in the demand for capital. Therefore most underdeveloped countries will need a combination of private and government action in saving and investment. Each country must work out its own combination according to its particular needs and opportunities.

For the impoverished emerging countries today, balanced growth provides one possible path toward economic progress. The difficulty is that this approach requires large amounts of capital that the poor countries have difficulty in acquiring. Another alternative that Nurkse neglected is promoting growth through import substitution; if a country already is importing manufactured goods, it can undertake their production at home without requiring balanced growth.

Nurkse's analysis of development problems and prescription for change is similar in tone to that of Gunnar Myrdal, a great economist and sociologist, who was corecipient of the Nobel Prize in economics in 1974.

Myrdal: National Economic Planning

Gunnar Myrdal (born 1898) was educated in law and economics in his native Sweden and pursued advanced studies in England, France, Germany, and the United States from 1925 to 1930. An active leader of the Swedish Social Democratic Party, he was a senator and a minister of commerce, and he served in other party and government posts. After World War II he was executive secretary of the United Nations Economic Commission for Europe.

During a long and fruitful life Myrdal has been a prodigious worker and a prolific writer. He has probed such diverse fields as economic theory, American race relations, economic development in Asia, and programs and policies of the United Nations. He reported one of his introspective moments with sardonic humor:

I am well aware that I am often considered almost not a part of the profession of establishment economists. . . . I am even referred to as a sociologist. And by that, economists usually do not mean anything flattering.[8]

Myrdal's discussion of the problems of the poor countries has three major themes: First, there is a widening gap between the rich and the poor countries. Second, standard economic theory is inadequate to explain or help narrow the gap. Third, the governments of the poor countries must play a large role in promoting economic development.

The economic upper class of rich nations, said Myrdal, is growing richer with a momentum that slackens only during occasional short periods, while the underdeveloped countries are moving forward very slowly or not at all. The widening gap between the two groups can be explained by "the principle of circular and cumulative causation." Myrdal endorsed Nurkse's analysis, cited above, of the vicious circle of poverty and added that a reciprocal relationship of less poverty, more food, improved health, and higher working capacity would sustain a cumulative process upward instead of downward.

A widening of markets often strengthens in the first instance the rich and progressive countries whose manufacturing industries have the lead and are already fortified by the surrounding external economies, while the underdeveloped countries are in continuous danger of seeing even what they have of industry and, in particular, small-scale industry and handicrafts priced out by cheap imports from the industrial countries, if they do not protect them. . . .

The main positive effect of international trade on the underdeveloped countries was in fact to promote the production of primary products; and such production, employing mostly unskilled labor, has come to constitute the bulk of their exports. In these lines, however, they often meet inelastic demands in the export market, often also a demand trend which is not rising very rapidly, and excessive price fluctuations. When, furthermore, population is rapidly rising while the larger part of it lives at, or near, the subsistence level—which means that there is no scarcity of unskilled labor—any technological improvement in their export production tends to transfer the advantages from the cheapening of production to the importing countries. Since the demand is often inelastic, the market will not be greatly enlarged.

The advice—and assistance—which the poorer countries receive from the richer is, even nowadays, often directed toward increasing their

[8] Gunnar Myrdal, *Against the Stream. Critical Essays on Economics.* (New York, 1973), p. 14.

production of primary goods for export. The advice is certainly given in good faith, and it may even be rational from the short-term point of view of one underdeveloped country seen in isolation. . . .

Nor can capital movements be relied upon to counteract international inequalities. In the circumstances described, capital will, on the whole, shun the underdeveloped countries, particularly as the advanced countries themselves are rapidly developing further and can offer to owners of capital both good profits and security.[9]

Myrdal's second major theme is that orthodox economic theory cannot explain or reverse the growing gap between rich and poor countries. The doctrine that all people aspire toward economic equality is the universal idea that links the Western philosophies of conservatives and radicals, liberals and socialists alike. Orthodox economic theorists tried to avoid the equality doctrine and developed certain predilections as antidotes to this dangerous thought. From John Stuart Mill on, a leading device for evading this issue was to draw a sharp line of demarcation between the sphere of production (including exchange) and the sphere of distribution. Since natural laws were supposed to reign in the sphere of production, policy based on the equality doctrine was restricted to distribution. To avoid exploring this issue economists have for more than a hundred years directed their analysis almost entirely toward production and exchange while expressing doubts about or ignoring the need for reforms in the distribution of income and wealth.

A number of ideas were developed by orthodox economists to evade the equality doctrine. One was the notion of the harmony of interests, which is "a comforting thought for those who have drawn a lucky number in life's lottery." A second predilection was laissez-faire government. A third was the free-trade doctrine, which loses its validity because of the unrealistic nature of its basic assumptions, such as free competition; this idea provides bad advice for underdeveloped countries, for example, telling them to avoid tampering with international trade and payments. A fourth concept of orthodox economic doctrines is that the economy tends toward stable equilibrium; this, said Myrdal, is much further from the truth than the idea of circular causation and cumulative processes.

Much standard theory is a rationalization of the dominant interests of the industrial countries, said Myrdal. In general, economic theory has not been concerned with the problems of underdeveloped coun-

---

[9] Gunnar Myrdal, *Rich Lands and Poor* (New York, 1957), pp. 52–53. Reprinted with permission of Harper & Row, Publishers.

tries; they should therefore remold this theory to fit their own problems and interests.

Myrdal discussed another problem of the poor countries, developing another criticism of standard theory (including the Keynesian doctrines), and pointing to another task of governments that mean to promote economic development. This idea concerns the distribution of income within a country. Conventional theory concludes that consumption detracts from saving and investment; that substantial improvements in levels of living must be postponed for some time in order to permit capital accumulation and higher productivity and levels of living in the future; and that the unequal distribution of income promotes saving because rich people save a larger percentage of their income than poor people do. Therefore a partial conflict occurs, at least in the short run, between higher consumption and higher production. These ideas, said Myrdal, are true in the rich countries because greater consumption will not promote greater production. Most people are far enough above the minimum of subsistence so that increased consumption, while perhaps desirable for its own sake, will not enable the consumers to work harder and better.

In the poor countries, however, improved levels of living are a precondition for higher labor input and efficiency.

> In the underdeveloped countries of South Asia, levels of living are so low as seriously to impair health, vigor, and attitudes toward work. Consequently, increases in most types of consumption represent *at the same time* 'investment,' as they have an immediate and direct effect on productivity. In this situation the identity between investment and the stock of physical assets, changes in which correspond *ex post* to the magnitude of current savings, is not satisfactory. Savings and the 'investment' logically associated therewith should be more broadly defined to include all those expenditures having a positive impact on productivity; and some of them, as we mentioned, are at the same time consumption. This is one reason for doubting the usefulness for South Asia of Western-type economic models, which stress the relationships among output, employment, savings, and investment.[10]

Therefore, said Myrdal, governments in the poor countries should promote a more equal distribution of income in order to increase output; this they have generally failed to do. In fact, he asserted, economic inequality seems to have been increasing in recent times in most of the underdeveloped world.

Myrdal's third major idea was that the governments of underde-

[10] Gunnar Myrdal, *Asian Drama. An Inquiry Into the Poverty of Nations*, Vol. I (New York, 1968), p. 530.

veloped countries should play a large role in promoting progress, especially through economic planning:

> Economists now generally endorse the opinion that the underdeveloped countries need much more planning and state intervention if, under very much more difficult conditions than the now-developed countries ever faced, they are to have any chance of engendering economic development. Statesmen and officials from the rich and progressive Western countries have also been led to take the same stand on those other countries' behalf when the matter has been up for discussion and resolution-making in international organizations—although it is very apparent that they often had their fingers crossed when swearing on that strange bible. . . .
>
> As economic development cannot be expected to come by itself, planning becomes a precondition for development, not, as in the Western countries, a later consequence of development and all the other changes which accompanied it. The underdeveloped countries are thus compelled to undertake what in the light of the history of the Western world appears as a shortcut.
>
> All this follows as a consequence of the fact that planning is being applied at an earlier stage of development, and of the further fact that their conditions for development are so much worse that this seems rationally motivated. It is also a part of the logic of the underdeveloped countries' situation that their programmatic planning should be comprehensive and complete, not pragmatic and piecemeal as in the Western countries. In principle and in theoretical approach, planning anticipates public policies. It does not grow out of the necessity to coordinate such policies as have already been initiated.[11]

Every national development plan must determine the total amount of investment and the proportion of the capital to be allocated for each major sphere of the economy. It must spell out the specific inducements and controls needed to realize these directives. The government must help to raise the share of the national income that is withheld from consumption and devoted to investment. The national plan should also include a vigorous policy aimed at controlling population growth. Planning should reflect the long-term needs of the community as a whole rather than the financial welfare of individual enterprises.

If an underdeveloped country is to speed up its rate of progress, its government will find it essential to intervene in many phases of economic life. Foreign trade must be controlled, if only to use foreign

[11] Gunnar Myrdal, *Beyond the Welfare State* (New Haven, Conn., 1960), pp. 14–15, 122–23.

exchange for the most urgent requirements to stimulate growth. The import of less necessary goods should be restricted, and exports might be subsidized. Some workers may have to be offered higher wages in order to attract them to jobs in the essential sectors as required by the overall plan, thereby further straining the foreign exchange situation. Infant industries will have to be protected, preferably within regional common markets of underdeveloped countries. The government will find it necessary to own and operate enterprises, such as railroads, highways, irrigation projects, port facilities, and the like, that are essential to growth but are usually not profitable. Because of the great risks for private investors in underdeveloped countries, the capital returns frequently must be so high as to be socially intolerable; therefore intergovernmental and World Bank loans are desirable, and these too require government intervention. The state must also act vigorously to achieve land reform, not only to raise productivity in agriculture but, more important, to shatter "the foundations of the state class structure of a stagnating society" as well. In many cases foreign-owned natural resources in an underdeveloped country will be nationalized. Once an upward cumulative process is begun through widespread government controls, however, the scope for private enterprise will be enlarged rather than restricted.

Why should economic planning be so much more essential to the poor countries today than it was when today's industrial nations began their economic development? Myrdal gave these answers: First, a strong impetus is required to end the stagnation of the poor countries, for this thrust does not occur spontaneously—or at least not rapidly enough when it does take place. The poor countries suffer far greater handicaps than today's rich countries did at a comparable stage of development. Second, people in the poor countries are demanding *rapid* development. Third, the rate of population growth in the underdeveloped countries is high and accelerating quickly, tending to lower per capita incomes, levels of living, and productivity. Fourth, international flow of private capital has diminished. Nowadays the larger part of capital inflow required for development has to be negotiated with other governments or with intergovernmental organizations. Fifth, the prospects for strong demand from abroad for the products of the emerging countries is bleak, whereas the Western countries were aided in their early industrialization by a rising demand for exports. Therefore exports must now be increased by systematic government action. Sixth, governments will have to rely heavily on import substitution as a stimulus to industry.

All these reasons for state intervention, and consequently for state planning, are present in any economy, but they are, of course, much more important in an underdeveloped country bent on rapid economic development. To the list must be added: the relative lack of entrepreneurial talent and training in the private sector; the disinclination of most of those who are wealthy to risk their funds in productive investment and their preference for speculation, quick profit, and conspicuous consumption and investment; and, finally, the tendency in underdeveloped countries for any large-scale enterprises to acquire an extraordinary degree of monopoly or oligopoly. For these reasons, . . . the state will either find cause to make the industrial starts itself or else to regulate and control the entrepreneurial activities in order to obtain the most rapid development in the desired directions.[12]

Myrdal ended by envisioning a greater harmony of interests:

As long as the peoples living in the underdeveloped world were subdued and quiet their grievances could be kept away from the attention of the peoples in the richer countries by opportunistic ignorance. A new phase of the age-old struggle for greater equality—a phase in which the struggle finally encompasses the entire globe—has now begun with the Great Awakening.

I have already observed that from one point of view the Great Awakening is nothing else than the victorious spread to the peoples in the underdeveloped countries of the richer nations' inherited ideal of equality of opportunity. Those nations have themselves been sowing the seed of world revolution. . . .

In the setting of Western civilization the poorer countries, once they succeed in breaking through the barriers of opportunistic ignorance, will have, as already in earlier time the poorer regions and the lower social classes within the now-richer countries, a support in the egalitarian ideal which has an emotional and moral basis in people's feelings for what is right and wrong. Whether this support will be forthcoming so soon, and be so strong, that—in analogy to what has actually happened within the richer countries themselves—the world revolution can be canalized into a process of gradual and peaceful change is a momentous question to which the future will give the solemn answer.

Such a process toward a "welfare world," where on a world scale the principle of equality of opportunity as between nations, racial and religious groups, and individuals increasingly became realized, would, like the earlier parallel development toward the national "welfare state" in the richer countries, regularly turn out to be a paying proposition also to those who are initially better off. As in the nations so in the world at large, this process would be a precondition for raising levels of production generally and not only for promoting social justice.[13]

[12] *Ibid.*, Vol. II, pp. 717–18.
[13] Myrdal, *Rich Lands and Poor*, pp. 127–28.

Myrdal has become more pessimistic in recent years as a result of stagnation and growing inequality in the poor countries, and in reaction to the Vietnam War. He has argued that in the system of colonialism before World War II the colonial powers allied themselves with the privileged groups within the colonies; they did this in the name of "law and order" to preserve the economic and social *status quo*. A similar mechanism has been operating after the liquidation of colonialism that justifies the use of the term "neo-colonialism." The rich western countries are supporting conservative regimes in the newly independent countries that preserve the reactionary system of power inherited from colonial times. The operation of this mechanism was strengthened by the cold war.

Economic aid from the rich to the poor countries was on a very modest scale. Around 1950 the foreign aid budget of the United States suddenly grew. But "the main motivation was less a desire to meet the development needs of underdeveloped countries than it was the intensified cold war." [14] The American aid program served the political, strategic, and military interests of the United States as those interests were seen by the American government and largely by the American people. Our claim that we were trying to help the poor countries was insincere and hypocritical, according to Myrdal. Finally, our foreign aid program became a casualty of the Vietnam War.

Myrdal appealed to the broader, more humanitarian elements in the United States to provide aid to the poor countries in larger amounts and without ulterior motives. "Only by appealing to peoples' moral feelings will it be possible to create the popular basis for increasing aid to underdeveloped countries as substantially as is needed." [15]

Bibliography

BARAN, PAUL A., *The Political Economy of Growth*. New York: Monthly Review Press, 1957.

HOSELITZ, BERT F., ed. *Theories of Economic Growth*. Glencoe, Ill.: Free Press, 1960.

MYRDAL, GUNNAR, *Against the Stream. Critical Essays on Economics*. New York: Pantheon, 1973.

———, *Asian Drama. An Inquiry Into the Poverty of Nations*, 3 vols. New York: The Twentieth Century Fund, 1968.

[14] Myrdal, *The Challenge of World Poverty* (New York, 1970), p. 343.
[15] *Ibid.*, p. 368.

————, *Beyond the Welfare State*. New Haven, Conn.: Yale University Press, 1960.

————, *The Challenge of World Poverty*. New York: Pantheon, 1970.

————, *An International Economy*. New York: Harper, 1956.

————, *Rich Lands and Poor*. New York: Harper, 1957.

NURKSE, RAGNAR, *Patterns of Trade and Development*. Stockholm: Almqvist and Wiksell, 1959.

————, *Problems of Capital Formation in Underdeveloped Countries*. New York: Oxford University Press, 1953.

————, *Some Aspects of Capital Accumulation in Underdeveloped Countries*. Cairo: National Bank of Egypt, 1952.

OSER, JACOB, *Promoting Economic Development, with Illustrations from Kenya*. Evanston, Ill.: Northwestern University Press, 1967.

SCHUMPETER, JOSEPH A., *Capitalism, Socialism, and Democracy*, 3d ed. New York: Harper, 1950.

————, *Essays*, ed. by Richard V. Clemence. Reading, Mass.: Addison-Wesley, 1951.

————, *The Theory of Economic Development*, tr. by Redvers Opie. New York: Oxford University Press, 1961. [Originally published in 1911.]

24

Post-Keynesian Economics

Since the publication of Keynes's monumental work in 1936, most economists have lined up strongly as Keynesians in their approach to problems of the nation's economy. Even where the disagreements with Keynesian economics have been deep and seemingly irreparable, the approach if not the prescription has been that advocated by Keynes. As in the case of any pioneering work, scholars of the succeeding generation spend their time adding to, verifying, or amending the structure proposed by it.

The Keynesian revolution brought a profound change in the way we perceive economic problems. Instead of looking at supply (Say's law) as providing the impetus for economic activity, we now look to the presence or lack of aggregate demand.

Thus in most recent years we have looked to the Keynesian solution to macroeconomic problems. We seek to alter the amount of aggregate demand in the system in order to turn our economy away from recessions and inflations toward a path that, we hope, will bring us long-run growth without price inflation.

Has the Keynesian prescription for a sagging or run-away economy proven to be correct? Can we "fine tune" our economy to banish forever the ogres of recession and inflation? The evidence is mixed.

The first attempt at "fine tuning" the economy using the Keynesian tools was the tax cut of 1964. The cut was proposed initially in 1962 by the economic advisors of President Kennedy. They maintained, in classic Keynesian terms, that an economy that was underutilizing its resources should be assisted by an injection of increased aggregate demand, in this case in the form of increased consumer purchasing power. After much debate the tax cut was approved and did lead to increased economic activity at that crucial time.

The economy proceeded in the middle 1960's to produce goods and services at record highs. Employment was high, and job opportunities were opening up at a record level. No doubt government spending on both the Vietnam War and domestic social programs, added to the siphoning of manpower into the war, provided the primary impetus for the upsurge. Unfortunately the healthy state of the economy did not last.

Beginning in 1965 it was apparent that serious price inflation was beginning to erode the otherwise high marks the economy had so far achieved. The inflationary pressures were not only high but persistent. The simple Keynesian remedy in such a case is to reduce aggregate demand and thereby cool off the inflationary pressures. This was tried in 1969 but to no avail. Indeed, we seemed to be developing an economy that had high unemployment and serious price inflation at the same time. Why was this happening? Were our Keynesian tools inadequate during inflationary times? Three explanations have been advanced.

The first explanation is that the simple Keynesian remedy is useful only if we have a "demand pull" inflation. We have a demand pull inflation when there is excess purchasing power in the economy; thus the solution is to decrease purchasing power. However, if the inflation is due to a lack of resources necessary for production, called a "cost push" inflation, then other remedies are needed. These other remedies include taking measures to reduce the prices of raw materials, retraining and relocating workers, and reducing the cost of borrowing money for investment through monetary policy. Lower interest rates act both to reduce the cost of doing business and to stimulate investment, which can increase the supply of goods to meet the increased demand.

The second explanation for persistent inflation with unemployment involves the role of government. Since the time of Keynes, the government has become increasingly involved in economic affairs. Some of these activities have clearly promoted inflation. Among them are restricting imports by tariffs and quotas; keeping artificially high prices on agricultural products by price supports and output restriction; permitting or promoting the growth of monopolistic enterprises; allowing exorbitant increases in public utility charges; supporting high-cost, inefficient firms that supply armaments for the military program. Indeed, the government's military spending has a built-in inflationary impact.

The third explanation centers on the fact that the structure of American business has become increasingly concentrated. The number of firms in the largest industries is so small that, many economists believe, there is no effective price competition among these industrial giants. Thus the large firms may raise prices almost at will, the argument states, and dictate to the consumers the prices they must pay for their products. Under such conditions it is not surprising that the large firms pass on price increases to the public. Indeed there is no market control to compel them to do otherwise.

All three explanations of the inflation problem have the ring of truth about them. Certainly our Keynesian tools have not produced a desirable solution to the dilemma of persistent inflation and simultaneous unemployment. Perhaps the solution lies in the study of how the giants in our economy make decisions on price and output. One spokesman for such a view is John Kenneth Galbraith.

Galbraith

John Kenneth Galbraith (born 1908 in Canada) studied at the universities of Toronto and California. His experience has included the post of chief economist for the American Farm Bureau Federation; high positions with the United States government during World War II; membership on the board of editors of *Fortune* magazine; ambassador to India during the administration of President John F. Kennedy; professor of economics at Harvard University; and chairman of the Americans for Democratic Action. Galbraith is also a novelist and an expert on Far Eastern art.

The Affluent Society

Galbraith is a critic of "conventional wisdom" and static thinking. His evolutionary approach explores changing conditions and examines the need to change our ideas to fit new situations. He is an articulate and witty reformer, whose work is highly readable.

> No one will think this an angry book. Some may think it lacking in that beguiling modesty which is so much in fashion in social comment. The reader will soon discover that I think very little of certain of the central ideas of economics. But I do think a great deal of the men who originated these ideas. The shortcomings of economics are not original error but uncorrected obsolescence. The obsolescence has occurred because what is convenient has become sacrosanct. Anyone who attacks such

ideas must seem to be a trifle self-confident and even aggressive. Yet I trust that judgments will not be too hasty. The man who makes his entry by leaning against an infirm door gets an unjustified reputation for violence. Something is to be attributed to the poor state of the door.[1]

Galbraith argued that the economic attitudes of our society are rooted in the poverty and inequality of the past. Our new affluence has brought a declining interest in the inequality of wealth and income, but this decline cannot be explained by the triumph of equality. Inequality has faded as an issue because it is not growing worse; because full employment and the upward pressure on wages have increased well-being at the bottom of the income scale; and because envy and emulation are directed only at one's nearby neighbors, and not against the distant rich. In addition, unions and government have curbed the enormous power of the large corporations, while the professional managers have taken away from the man of wealth much of the power he once had within the corporation in running his business.

In the conventional wisdom of conservatives, said Galbraith, the modern search for security is regularly billed as the greatest single threat to economic progress. Yet the large corporation has been the leader in the retreat from risk. Businessmen, farmers, workers, old people—all seek economic security. This trend does not jeopardize efficiency and economic progress. In fact, a high level of economic security is essential for maximum production, and a high level of production is indispensable for economic security. But security is far more important than maximum production. The elimination of major depressions, for example, is more significant than the featherbedding and goldbricking that go on today at all levels and in all occupations.

According to Galbraith the doctrine of diminishing marginal utility states that under conditions of increasing affluence the importance of production decreases. With increasing per capita real income, people are able to satisfy additional wants that are less and less urgent.

In emphasizing production, conventional wisdom holds that private production adds to the national well-being, whereas public services are a burden even if they are necessary. Automobiles are therefore more important than roads. The expansion of telephone services and the curtailment of postal services are both approved of. Vacuum cleaners in the home are more acceptable than street cleaners, resulting in clean homes and dirty streets. Because they are privately pro-

[1] John Kenneth Galbraith, *The Affluent Society* (Boston, 1958), p. 4.

duced, alcohol, comic books, and mouthwashes are more acceptable than schools, courts, and municipal swimming pools.

Galbraith made a strong plea for less private and more public spending and felt that the balance between the two could best be corrected with sales taxes. He advocated breaking the nexus between production and income security by instituting adequate unemployment compensation that approaches the level of the weekly wage. Poverty pockets in our society can be overcome by guaranteeing each family a minimum income. A rich society can afford this expenditure, which in turn ensures that the misfortunes of parents are not inflicted on their children. To eliminate poverty efficiently we should invest more than proportionately in the children of poor communities, especially in providing high-quality schools, strong health services, and adequate nutrition.

The New Industrial State

In *The New Industrial State* Galbraith argued that investments have become very large, and the period of planning between the decision to produce a good and the actual production of it has become very long. This time lag prevents the corporation from being able to base its planning decisions on market conditions at the time of production, which cannot be foreseen. Thus the company seeks to minimize or get rid of market influences. The market must be replaced by an authoritative determination of prices and the amounts to be sold or bought at these prices. There are three ways of doing this. First, the market can be superseded by vertical integration. The planning unit takes over the source of supply or the outlet, and internal decisions replace market decisions. Second, the market can be controlled by sellers or buyers, but for this a corporation must be suitably large. General Motors, for example, can influence the prices charged by its suppliers and fix the prices of its own goods. The amount sold is controlled by advertising, the sales organization, and the size of the corporation. "And since General Motors produces some half of all the automobiles, its designs do not reflect the current mode, but *are* [italics added] the current mode. The proper shape of an automobile, for most people, will be what the automobile majors decree the current shape to be."

The third way to minimize or get rid of market influences is through contracts between the parties to buy and sell. Large firms write reliable contracts, but the long-term contracts of small firms or farmers are not very reliable. Death, accident, drought, and other unforeseen contingencies may invalidate the agreements of small units. Large firms are thus necessary for economic planning to replace market forces, and for such planning, the bigger the corporation the better. The size of General Motors, for example, permits it to design the optimum size for an automobile plant and to afford many such plants. Its size is conducive not only to technological efficiency but to planning in order to control supply and demand, provide capital, and minimize risk. "The size of General Motors is in the service not of monopoly or the economies of scale but of planning."

The entrepreneur no longer leads the firm. If today's capitalist is represented by the stockholder, then he has been separated from all effective power, for the modern corporation disenfranchises its stockholders. The capitalist's place has been taken by the "technostructure," the collective organization of executives, managers, engineers, scientists, product planners, market researchers, sales executives, and so forth—all those who participate in and contribute information to group decisions. The technostructure does not try to maximize profits for the owners. It pursues other goals: growth of the firm, technological change for its own sake, enough secure earnings to pay dividends and supply savings for reinvestment, a progressive rise in the rate of dividends, and a minimal risk of loss.

The technostructure has devised means of controlling, or at least greatly influencing, the wants of consumers. The control of management of demand is in itself a vast and rapidly growing industry whose purpose is to ensure that people buy what is produced at the prices set by the producers. Orthodox economics holds that the initiative lies with the consumer, who buys goods and services in the market in response to personal desires or demands imposed on him by his environment. In Galbraith's "revised sequence" producers decide what shall be produced and then mold consumers' taste so that they buy these products.

> Mass communication was not necessary when the wants of the masses were anchored primarily in physical need. The masses could not then be persuaded as to their spending—this went for basic foods and shelter. The wants of a well-to-do minority could be managed. But since this minority was generally literate, or sought to seem so, it could be reached selectively by newspapers and magazines, the circulation of which was confined to the literate community. With mass affluence, and therewith the possibility of mass management of demand, these media no longer served.
>
> Technology, once again, solved the problems that it created. Coincidentally with rising mass incomes came first radio and then television.

These, in their capacity to hold effortless interest and their accessibility over the entire cultural spectrum, and their independence of any educational qualification, were admirably suited to mass persuasion. Radio and more especially television have, in consequence, become the prime instruments for the management of consumer demand. There is an insistent tendency among solemn social scientists to think of any institution which features rhymed and singing commercials, intense and lachrymose voices urging highly improbable enjoyments, caricatures of the human esophagus in normal or impaired operation, and which hints implausibly at opportunities for antiseptic seduction, as inherently trivial. This is a great mistake. The industrial system is profoundly dependent on commercial television and could not exist in its present form without it. Economists who eschew discussion of its economic significance, or dismiss it as a wicked waste, are protecting their reputation and that of their subject for Calvinist austerity. But they are not adding to their reputation for relevance.[2]

The technostructure comes to rely heavily on the government. Future sales cannot be planned in the face of wide swings in business activity; therefore high government spending and stabilization policies both serve the objectives of the large corporation. And it is the modern corporate leadership that most strongly supports Keynesian policies to maintain and stabilize total demand. The technostructure also relies on the state to give massive support to higher education and scientific research and to stabilize wages and prices. "National defense, support to research and technological development, such collateral needs of industrial growth as highways and air traffic management are not neglected. Nor is education." The industrial system, however, downgrades government spending not closely related to the system's needs. It is not interested in care of the ill, the aged, and the physically or mentally infirm, nor is it concerned with health services, the provision of parks and recreation areas, the removal of rubbish, and many other services. These public expenditures are therefore starved.

What remedies did Galbraith suggest for the social problems that remain under the new conditions? He assumed no natural superiority either for the market or for government planning. In some areas market responses still serve. In others the market must give way to comprehensive planning of demand and supply. Planning is particularly needed for urban and interurban transit, urban land and housing development, the conservation of natural resources, the develop-

[2] John Kenneth Galbraith, *The New Industrial State* (Boston, 1967), pp. 207–08. Reprinted with permission of Houghton Mifflin Company.

ment of outdoor recreation, and the preservation of forests in the eastern United States. He urged that individuals have the option of lower annual pay with several months paid vacation. He also argued that the college community should retain paramount authority for the education it provides and the research it undertakes, so that the needs of the industrial system become secondary to the cultivation of general understanding and perception. The student who excels in poetry or painting and the one who serves the industrial system directly should have equal chances for scholarships and jobs. The educational and scientific estate should assert itself through political and social action.

Economics and the Public Purpose

Galbraith again challenged the "conventional wisdom" in his widely-read and controversial book *Economics and the Public Purpose.* This book descended from two of his earlier volumes—*The Affluent Society* and *The New Industrial State.* The earlier works dealt with a part of the economic system—mainly the world of the great corporations. His latest book presents the whole system, including the world of small business; this includes "the farmer, repairman, retailer, small manufacturer, plumber, television repairman, service station operator, medical practitioner, artist, actress, photographer and pornographer," [3] and they provide half of all goods and services not provided by the state.

Galbraith said that the depression of the 1930's induced us to accept state intervention to stabilize the economy as advocated by Keynes. The major tools to offset undesirable fluctuations were fiscal and monetary policies. But no one can tell what effect tighter or easier money policies will have. The intense discussions that surround central bank policy hide the uncertainty about its effects. In addition, the Keynesian model is similar to the neoclassical model in that both work through the market and rely on the market to attain stability and full employment. Monetary policy anticipates the appropriate responses of businessmen to achieve the desired ends.

The economy, according to Galbraith, can be divided into two sectors that he called the planning system and the market system. The planning system includes the thousand largest corporations in the areas of manufacturing, merchandising, transportation, power, and finance. The market system includes about twelve million smaller firms and includes farmers. The planning system does not conform to

[3] John Kenneth Galbraith, *Economics and the Public Purpose* (Boston, 1973), p. IX.

the neoclassical model of how a firm operates, but the market system does. The planning system dominates its environment while the market system is subordinate to it. The differences between the two systems can be seen in internal versus external sources of financing new investment, in control over prices, in the level of profits, in the degree of monopoly, in influencing the behavior of the customers, and in influencing the government. Even when it comes to innovation, Galbraith disagreed with other economists in stating that it is the big corporations and not the small firms that bring the new ideas into use.

Organized labor, said Galbraith, contributes to the political power of the giant corporations of the planning system. Once there was sharp conflict between labor and capital over the division of income; this in turn was reflected in political and legislative conflict. This conflict has been greatly diminished because the big corporations can now concede wage and other demands to the unions and pass the costs along in higher prices. The unions no longer regard management as the class enemy. Both gain from a high rate of growth, from government spending on large defense budgets, from the subsidized development of technology, and from aid to ailing corporations such as Lockheed Aircraft Corporation.

The market system of small-scale operations is broadly stable; while downward fluctuations in output and employment or upward movements in prices do occur, they are self-limiting and eventually self-correcting. The planning system of big business, in the absence of government intervention, is inherently unstable; recessions and inflations are cumulative rather than self-limiting, and they are especially damaging to the market system.

The cause of recession is the inadequate demand for goods and services. The problem here is primarily the danger that saving will not be spent on investment or offset by someone else's consumption spending. In the market system the degree of such a deficiency in demand is limited. The firms are numerous and small, and income is widely distributed in rather small amounts. The propensity to consume from this income is high. If a recession occurs, prices fall but the self-employed entrepreneurs continue working with smaller incomes. Falling prices result in increased sales while falling incomes reduce saving; both tendencies limit the declines in output and employment.

The planning system, however, does not contain corrective mechanisms. Corporate saving or undistributed profit is not available for consumption spending. Intentions to save can easily exceed intentions to invest. Prices are subject to corporate control and do not fall, and the wages of unionized workers cannot be reduced. As a consequence, when demand falls there is no compensating effect of added sales from lower prices. Nor would lower wages be offset by increased employment. The entire impact of reduced demand is on output and employment.

According to Galbraith, the instability of the planning system has a powerfully adverse effect on the market system. When demand in the planning system falls, the small businessmen, farmers, and workers suffer.

The Keynesian Revolution was based on the recognition that the modern economy was subject to depressions that were neither self-limiting nor self-correcting. But after the Second World War the Keynesian Revolution was absorbed by the planning system. Thereafter government policy was based on the needs of the planning system; this was especially true of spending on military and industrial development.

Although the market system can suffer from inflation, this problem is not inherent in the system, and it can be remedied. The individual producer does not have control over prices. The causes of inflation are bank lending in excess of saving or government spending in excess of taxes; both can be remedied. Unions either do not exist in the market system, or their wage demands will typically be resisted by employers who do not have the power to pass along the burden of higher wages in the form of higher prices to the purchasers of goods and services. In contrast, the planning system passes on higher wages in the form of higher prices. Rising wages and prices become chronic in the sector of corporate giants.

Keynesian economics, said Galbraith, emphasized the importance of the downward spiral of income and employment but not the upward spiral of prices. The state could offset the deficiency of demand, in essence boosting the market and thereby propping up the system. Thus the market remained as in the textbooks, with the firm subordinate to the market. "The neoclassical ideas escaped fundamental damage. So viewed, the Keynesian Revolution was a small revolution. Economists, like others, much prefer small revolutions to larger ones." [4]

The planning system, according to Galbraith, is hardly damaged by the orthodox methods of attacking inflation. There are three ways to reduce demand and thereby curb inflation: to reduce public expendi-

[4] *Ibid.*, p. 189.

tures, to reduce private expenditures from borrowed funds, and to raise taxes.

The public expenditures that serve the needs of the large corporations cannot be reduced much because, Galbraith said with irony, "you cannot gamble with the nation's security." If public expenditures are to be curtailed, it will be mostly those for welfare, housing, urban services, education, and so on.

The second way to reduce demand is by raising interest rates. The planning system relies much more on its own retained earnings than on borrowed funds, and therefore it is not affected much by high interest rates. In contrast, the heavy borrowers are the farmers, small retailers, small dealers, home builders, and states, cities, and school districts. These are the ones who feel the full force of increasing interest rates.

The third way to restrict demand is through higher taxes. The planning system, having control over its prices, can pass higher taxes along to the public. The market system cannot do that, and it is the person who runs the small business who must pay.

What does Galbraith recommend to overcome these discrepancies and inequities between the planning and the market systems? He proposed that the antitrust laws should be abandoned because they do not work and also because the planning system is more efficient than the market system. He opposed the regulation of public utilities because the regulatory agencies frequently become the instruments or the puppets of the industries they are supposed to regulate. Assuming that the state can be freed from the control of the planning system, he advocated seven lines of public action to reform the economic system.

First, power should be equalized by enhancement of the power of the market system and reduction of that of the planning system. Galbraith approved of agricultural price-fixing, and he recommended similar price and production regulation throughout the market system. He defended other support to small businessmen, support to collective bargaining, minimum-wage laws, a guaranteed minimum income, international commodity agreements, and even some protective tariffs. Small businessmen should be allowed to combine to stabilize prices and output. Strong unions should be encouraged in the market system, for the employees in that sector are in the weakest position. The minimum wage should be raised and extended to cover more workers. The large multinational corporation protects itself against the special hazards of international trade by concentrating production in the lowest-cost countries; the firm in the market system is vulnerable and may have to be protected by international agreements stabilizing prices and production, and possibly by the cautious use of tariffs.

Galbraith's second proposal to reform the economic system was to equalize competence between the two systems. Certain functions such as housing, surface transportation, health services, artistic and cultural services, do not lend themselves to organization by the planning system; nor are they provided competently by the market system. They have to be supported by social action, which Galbraith called socialism. The new socialism searches, not for sectors of power in the economy, but for sectors of weakness. Nationalization of enterprises would be appropriate in areas of exceptional strength, such as the public utilities and the giant firms producing weapons and aerospace hardware.

Third, the inherent tendency toward inequality of income between the planning and market systems should be offset by measures to enhance equality of return. The most urgent problem of the modern economy is not the production of goods but the distribution of income. The inequality of return will have to be corrected by the raising of prices in the market system in relation to those of the planning system. There will also have to be a guaranteed income as a matter of right for those who cannot find employment. Progressive income taxes should be used as a powerful instrument for promoting equality.

Fourth, the planning system should be prevented from polluting and otherwise damaging the environment. The market system also pollutes, and public money will have to be spent to clean up the dirt of both sectors. In addition, public planning will have to regulate private enterprise to coordinate it with public goals so that processes and products that pollute and destroy will be limited or banned.

Fifth, public expenditures should be controlled so that they serve public purposes rather than the planning system. We have to change our views. Why, asked Galbraith, should the government be more eager to help Lockheed than to buy pictures for the National Gallery? Why are farm subsidies more wasteful than those for airlines? Why do we reduce aid to the poor and increase defense expenditures? While the federal government serves primarily the planning system, state and local governments serve the public at large. Therefore two remedies are required. First, public functions should be transferred from the cities and states to the federal government, where funds are more ample. Second, the federal government should distribute more of its revenues to the states and cities.

Sixth, the inflationary and deflationary tendencies of the planning system must be eliminated. These must not, as in the past, be a source of added power for the planning system and a detriment to the market system. Orthodox fiscal and monetary policies have not served the public well. Taxes become less progressive, and we have the wrong kind of public spending that worsens the distribution of income. We need strongly progressive taxes, including progressive corporate income taxes. Loopholes should be closed. If demand in the private sector is deficient, public expenditure should be increased; this is especially necessary because there is a higher need for public, as opposed to private, consumption. We should favor low rather than high interest rates to help borrowers rather than lenders. Inflation should be curbed by imposing wage and price controls in the planning system, with wages being permitted to rise in step with average gains in productivity in the planning system.

Seventh and finally, we have to adopt measures to insure the interindustry coordination of which the planning system is incapable. By public action we should return freight and people to the railroads rather than to road transport. We should avoid promoting the excessive use of electricity by reducing our unnecessary electrical gadgets and by designing buildings that do not require air conditioning. Public support is necessary to develop new energy supplies or to subsidize unprofitable sources of energy.

Galbraith concluded *Economics and the Public Purpose* with a final criticism of Keynes. He cited Keynes's statement that economics would eventually become unimportant, ranking in social significance with dentistry. But Keynes did not see that, with economic development, power would pass from the consumer to the producer. As a consequence, he did not see the increasing divergence between the objectives of the planning sector and the needs of the public. Therefore development becomes unequal, the distribution of income becomes more unequal, the environment is threatened, the consumer is victimized, and inflation becomes unmanageable by Keynesian remedies.

Galbraith, certainly, is a controversial figure. He has been attacked both from the right and the left of the political spectrum. He has shaken up the economics profession, and his ideas will undoubtedly have a long-run impact on economic thinking and the formation of public policies.

While Galbraith has contributed an enormous amount to our understanding of power relationships, his Cambridge neighbor at the Massachusetts Institute of Technology, Paul Samuelson, has developed to a high degree what we know of modern mathematical economic theory.

Samuelson

When Paul Anthony Samuelson in 1970 was announced as the first American economist to be awarded the Nobel Prize, few economists were surprised at the selection. Not only has he been known to countless professionals in the field but his textbook, *Economics,* has been the largest selling book in the discipline. He is perhaps the best known of American economists, both to his fellow economists and the public at large.

Samuelson was born in Chicago in 1915, the son of Polish immigrants. His father was a pharmacist. After receiving his B.A. from the University of Chicago, Samuelson proceeded to Harvard where he enrolled in the graduate program in economics.

At Harvard Samuelson was caught up in the beginnings of the Keynesian revolution; one of his professors was the chief American interpreter of Keynes, Alvin Hansen. Already a brilliant mathematics student, Samuelson decided early to apply mathematics to the body of economic theory then described by him as "an Augean stable full of inherited contradictions, overlaps and fallacies." The result of his early efforts was his doctoral dissertation, *The Foundations of Economic Analysis,* later published by Harvard University Press.

Upon receiving his doctorate, Samuelson began searching for a university to continue his research and teaching. Surprisingly to all who knew the young scholar, Harvard did not appoint him to a post even though he had received the 1941 David A. Wells prize for outstanding work by a graduate student. Undaunted, Samuelson applied for and was appointed to a position at the neighboring Massachusetts Institute of Technology. M.I.T. had long had a reputation for engineering and science excellence but no parallel reputation in economics. Samuelson was soon to change that.

Continuing his research on economic theory, Samuelson published *Economics* in 1948. It proved to be innovative in teaching elementary economics. Since its first printing (it is now in its ninth edition) *Economics* has proven to be the masterwork in explaining the rigors of economics to beginning students. It has sold more than two million copies and has been translated into many languages. While his textbook has taught millions, his work in advanced economic theory has had a narrower audience.

Beginning with his work in *The Foundations of Economic Analy-*

sis, Samuelson has used mathematics to explain and expand the works of Walras, Quesnay, and the earlier equilibrium theorists. He is not an empiricist; indeed he still calls himself a generalist interested in expanding theory rather than testing it. Two of his major contributions to economic theory, the theory of comparative statics and the theory of revealed preference, are perhaps most widely known among economists.

Comparative Statics

Economic theory is based on the idea of equilibrium. Given a set of forces, as in supply and demand models, there will be achieved a state from which there is no tendency to move away. This equilibrium position will remain as long as no external forces disturb it. If, however, some force such as a change in consumer income upsets the equilibrium of supply and demand, then the system will enter another state of equilibrium. All of this is not new, but it is the basis for Samuelson's contributions.

The position of the first equilibrium is called a static position. It is static because the forces are fixed in time, that is, the prices and quantities are known and the other variables are assumed to be constant. As soon as these assumptions are relaxed and the variables are allowed to change, we have what is called a dynamic situation.

The classical and neoclassical scholars were all familiar with the static analysis and even, in the case of Walras, did some beginning theorizing on dynamic models. It was left to Samuelson, however, to formalize the comparative statics approach.

The comparative statics method compares two states of equilibrium *without considering the path of adjustment*. It is literally a simple comparison of two static equilibrium positions. While such an approach allows one to make inferences about the path of adjustment and the forces causing such an adjustment, it is not precise except at the beginning and end of such adjustments.

Thus if incomes and tastes change, one can expect the demand curve to shift until the intersections of the supply and demand curves produce a new price and quantity equilibrium. What happened in the intervening period between positions we do not know.

Samuelson was well aware in 1947, when he formulated such an approach, that the important part of the problem was left out—knowledge of the path of adjustment. He knew also that the empirical techniques and computer technology would have to catch up to the theory before one could know, with any precision, the economics of the adjustment path.

In addition to developing a method of solving equilibrium problems, Samuelson also sharpened the theory of consumer welfare. His famous theory of revealed preference helped solve a dilemma for micro theorists.

Revealed Preference

In Chapters 12 and 14 we saw an analysis of the theory of demand based on marginal utility. A number of economists criticized the theory because, among other things, it did not generate operationally useful concepts. Because marginal utility analysis depended on the measurement of utility, it could scarcely be classified as empirically useful. In response to this problem Samuelson developed his theory of revealed preference.

In an early paper on revealed preference that Samuelson wrote when he was 23, he considered two problems: First, how do we know which goods consumers will choose when given a choice; and second, does an index number adequately reveal the preferences of individuals?

Simply stated, Samuelson's theory avoided the measurement of utility by concentrating entirely on the actual purchases or *revealed preferences* of consumers. He also showed that previous economists had concentrated almost exclusively on the statistical problems of index numbers without considering their economic meaning. His theory showed that there will be always some uncertainty even in an ideal index number and thus considerable uncertainty in other measures of economic welfare.

Samuelson's refinements of theory have not merely been advances for economists in the realm of abstract theorizing; they were also applicable to practical problems. Indeed he participated in the policy debate over the tax cut of 1964.

Policy on the New Frontier

While developing theory for professionals, Samuelson has also conducted a public debate with Milton Friedman of the University of Chicago principally in the pages of *Newsweek* magazine.

Samuelson and Friedman disagree primarily on the importance of money and the efficacy of monetary policy in controlling fluctuations in the economy. Friedman contends that the chief ingredient in the policy variables used to raise or lower national income is the supply of money. Samuelson disagrees.

Samuelson leans toward the "constructive" use of fiscal policy (taxing and spending) in controlling the economy. He has long advocated that government take an active role in the economy to promote economic growth with stable prices. In addition to his public debate with Professor Friedman, Samuelson was one of President Kennedy's early advisors. Although he declined the offer to be the chairman of the Council of Economic Advisors, Samuelson remained an unofficial advisor of Kennedy. Indeed he was one of the architects of the 1964 tax cut.

When inflation began to become a serious problem in the late 1960's, Samuelson advocated a tax increase to stem the inflationary trend.

The public and private writings of Samuelson have had an enormous effect on both the economics profession and the public at large. His present interests are in the applicability of maxima and minima solutions to, among other areas, the problems of underdeveloped countries. This was the subject of his Nobel Prize address. One of the fruitful results of his work and a source of new ideas has been the turnpike theorem. This is a proof, using maxima techniques, that underdeveloped countries should "catch a ride" on the fastest growing sector of their economic and social systems using this fast-moving sector as the impetus. This concept was developed in opposition to the idea of balanced growth, discussed in connection with Nurkse in the previous chapter.

Samuelson's interest in the application of analytical tools to problems of development is not surprising. He believes that the solutions to economic problems, once developed, generate increasing applications.

While Samuelson has been known to many, Kenneth Arrow, Nobel Prize winner in 1972, is hardly known to anyone outside the profession. His work, however, has had a remarkable effect on economic theory.

Kenneth Arrow

The history of economic thought shows a remarkable variety of thinkers. Some have been moral theorists, others political and social activists, still others developers and refiners of existing theory. It remains for a few, however, to straddle the area between economic theory and social philosophy. Such a theorist is Kenneth Arrow.

Kenneth Arrow was born in 1921. He completed his undergraduate work at City College of New York and proceeded to do his graduate work at Columbia University. His doctoral work was distinguished. Upon receiving his doctorate in 1949 he accepted a position at Stanford University, where he was to transform the Economics Department into one of world-wide reputation.

Arrow not only displayed a rare talent for mathematics and statistics, but he also had an insight into new areas where such talents could be used. His dissertation, *Social Choice and Individual Values,* became a classic in welfare economics. In this famous work he evaluated various criteria of social welfare and suggested inconsistencies in many of the previously held ideas.

The implications for economic policy in Arrow's work are many. He said that we have to rethink our decision-making process in order to avoid the more obvious pitfalls. Perfect democracy is impossible and we have to settle for second or third best.

Working at Stanford, Arrow continued his inquiry into the tenets of welfare economics. How do we know if society is better off as a result of a policy choice? What is the logic of collective choice by members of a community with individual preferences? Is perfect democracy possible? What adjustments must be made if there exists no possible way of maintaining a perfect democracy? These questions constituted the core of his first finished work, *Social Choice and Individual Values.*

Social Choice, a Dilemma

We know from our earliest years that capitalist democracies have two methods of social choice; economic decisions are made in the marketplace and political decisions by the process of voting. In other societies decisions may be made by force, by tradition, or by rigorous social or religious codes.

In capitalist democracies, we have been told, the results of our numerous individual decisions constitute the will of the majority either to buy a product or to elect a candidate. What is this mechanism, Arrow asked, that translates individual tastes to a "pattern of social decision-making"? [5] The problem is one of the "paradox of voting."

Suppose there is a community, Arrow states, that consists of three voters, and the community has three choices to make: to disarm, to wage a cold war, or to wage a hot war. According to welfare theory the community will arrange the order of the three alternatives according to its preferences and then, if possible, choose the alternative that stands highest on the list. This means that voters will state that they prefer alternative A to B, and so on. The collective preference scale may then be established using the majority rule. If the majority preferred A to B then A would be the logical choice.

[5] Kenneth J. Arrow, *Social Choice and Individual Values* (New Haven, 1951), p. 2.

Arrow suggested that we let A, B, and C be the alternatives, and 1, 2, and 3 the voters. Suppose 1 prefers A to B and B to C (implying a preference of A over C); voter number 2 chooses B rather than C and C rather than A (implying a preference of B over A); and number 3 chooses C rather than A and A rather than B (and therefore preferring C to B). A majority therefore prefers A to B, for this is the choice of voters 1 and 3. A majority also prefers B to C, for this is the choice of voters 1 and 2. Our conclusion is that the community prefers A to B and B to C, and therefore A to C. Is our conclusion correct? Reexamine the information above and you will see that, in fact, a majority of the voters (2 and 3) preferred C to A. The method just given therefore fails, according to Arrow, to rationally order the voter preferences.

The problem outlined above may be extended to problems of welfare economics. The problem of achieving a "social maximum" from the desires of individuals is exactly the same dilemma as given above. However "rational" we believe the voting process and whatever other assumptions we include (for example, that each vote counts), there are some inherent contradictions as soon as one steps away from the simple two-choice voting system.

Arrow's major contributions have been in challenging the assumptions upon which political and economic systems of thought have been based. Since the eighteenth century, philosophers and political theorists have been grappling with the idea of the perfectibility of human institutions. Kenneth Arrow is their successor.

Bibliography

ARROW, KENNETH J., *Social Choice and Individual Values*. New Haven: Yale University Press, 1951.

———, *The Limits of Organization*. New York: W. W. Norton, 1974.

GALBRAITH, JOHN KENNETH, *The Affluent Society*. Boston: Houghton Mifflin, 1958.

———, *American Capitalism. The Concept of Countervailing Power*, 2d ed. Boston: Houghton Mifflin, 1956.

———, *Economics and the Public Purpose*. Boston: Houghton Mifflin, 1973.

———, *The New Industrial State*. Boston: Houghton Mifflin, 1967.

GAMBS, JOHN S., *John Kenneth Galbraith*. New York: Twayne, 1975.

SAMUELSON, PAUL A., *The Foundations of Economic Analysis*. New York: Atheneum, 1970.

SWEEZY, PAUL M., "Galbraith's Utopia," *The New York Review of Books*, Vol. XX, No. 18, November 15, 1973, pp. 3–6. Reprinted in *Monthly Review*, Vol. 25, No. 6, November 1973, pp. 1–11.

25

Economic History in Perspective

A Time Scale of Economic Doctrines

Figure 14 (pp. 494–95) illustrates the evolution of various schools and streams of economic thought. Each rectangle represents a major school or approach. The names within each rectangle are economists who were most important or most typical in developing that school or area. The names immediately above the rectangle are forerunners of the school; the names directly below are followers who revised or further developed the ideas of a given group.

A solid line linking two rectangles shows that the later group was generally friendly to the group from which it grew or that it superseded. A dashed line shows that the later group was antagonistic to or rose in opposition to the earlier group. Thus the physiocrats were completely antipathetic to the mercantilists, while Adam Smith and the classical school were friendly toward the physiocrats. The marginalist school showed a sharp break with the classical school from which it sprang, while Keynes in turn rejected some of the major ideas of marginalism. Therefore dashed lines appear in that sequence, although it could be argued that the similarities in both cases were greater than the differences. Certainly, however, the marginalists had closer and friendlier relations with the mathematical economists than with the welfare economists. Therefore the line is solid in the first case and dashed in the second.

The Impact of Three Scientific Revolutions
on Economics

Revolutions in science, technology, philosophy, economics, politics, culture, and other branches of human knowledge and behavior were taking place even before we discovered how to ignite and maintain those little fires that gave people many advantages over other living creatures. These revolutions will continue, hopefully, despite our recent discovery of how to ignite nuclear fires that can easily incinerate all life on earth. Invariably a revolution in one area of knowledge became diffused into other areas and had a pervasive impact far beyond its point of origin.

Three significant revolutions in scientific thought were generated by Newton, Darwin, and Einstein. These men were influenced by the times in which they lived and in turn had an enormous influence on their times. The impact of their thought was felt far beyond their own specialized sciences. By touching briefly on the relationship between these three scientific revolutions and economic and social thought, we shall in effect be reviewing in broad terms the history of economic thought from the eighteenth century on.

Isaac Newton (1642–1727) made many significant discoveries in mathematics and physics. His most famous formulation was his law of gravitation: The attractive force between any two bodies in the universe varies proportionally as the product of the masses of the two, and inversely as the square of the distance between them. This law explains, among other things, the motions of the planets. At one time the idea had prevailed that bodies had souls and tendencies that made them strive toward their natural places, so that apples had to fall down and smoke had to rise.

The revolution in seventeenth-century thought had three major aspects. First, Newton and others relied heavily on experimental evidence. His contemporaries and predecessors generally believed in innate knowledge derived from reason alone without reliance on experience. Second, Newton popularized the already existing idea that the universe is governed by natural laws. He himself was deeply religious, believing that gravitational phenomena are due to the direct will of God. Yet his critics charged that he virtually abolished God from the universe by reducing it to a self-acting machine, though God remained the original creator of the universe. The third aspect of Newton's system was a static view of the universe. Space, time, and matter are independent of each other. Nothing changes

Figure 14 A Time Scale of Economic Doctrines

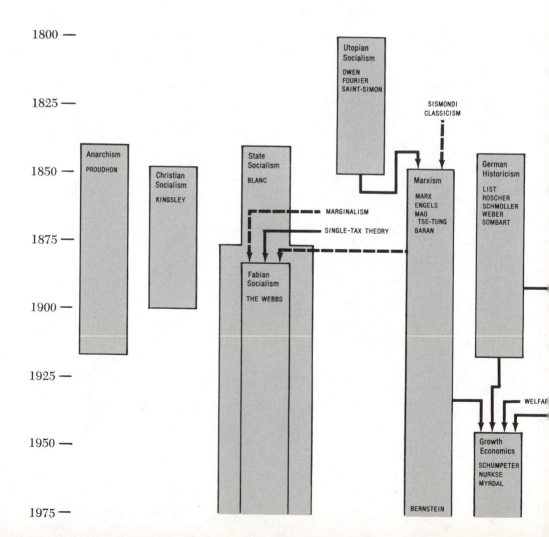

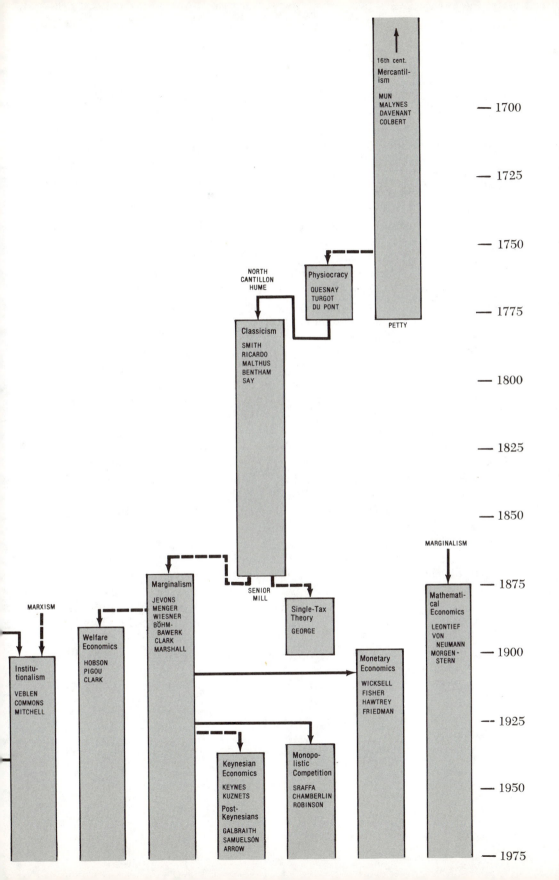

16th cent.
Mercantil-
ism

MUN
MALYNES
DAVENANT
COLBERT

— 1700

— 1725

— 1750

NORTH
CANTILLON
HUME

Physiocracy

QUESNAY
TURGOT
DU PONT

— 1775

PETTY

Classicism

SMITH
RICARDO
MALTHUS
BENTHAM
SAY

— 1800

— 1825

— 1850

MARGINALISM

— 1875

Marginalism

JEVONS
MENGER
WIESNER
BÖHM-
BAWERK
CLARK
MARSHALL

SENIOR
MILL

Single-Tax
Theory

GEORGE

Mathemati-
cal
Economics

LEONTIEF
VON
NEUMANN
MORGEN-
STERN

MARXISM

Welfare
Economics

HOBSON
PIGOU
CLARK

Monetary
Economics

WICKSELL
FISHER
HAWTREY
FRIEDMAN

— 1900

Institu-
tionalism

VEBLEN
COMMONS
MITCHELL

-- 1925

Keynesian
Economics

KEYNES
KUZNETS

Post-
Keynesians

GALBRAITH
SAMUELSON
ARROW

Monopo-
listic
Competition

SRAFFA
CHAMBERLIN
ROBINSON

— 1950

— 1975

over time: The motion and relationships in the universe continue in endless repetition.

Newton's impact on economic thinking can be seen in ideas of the classical school. The rising businessmen required a new set of ideas to help dislodge the lingering feudal institutions and the restrictive controls of mercantilism that had now become unnecessary. For them Newtonian science furnished a nature fully as effective as the earlier will of God. If the Divine Will had created a mechanism that worked harmoniously and automatically without further interference, then laissez faire was the highest wisdom in social affairs. Natural laws would guide the economic system and the actions of people. These ideas were revolutionary in their time. No longer would people unquestioningly accept ancient truths such as the immorality of interest, the virtue of charity, and the requirement that people be satisfied with their inherited station in life. Society would be best served if people were free to follow the natural law of self-interest. Newtonian thinking in classical economics provided an ideology that justified property incomes. As natural law is best left unobstructed, and as private thrift and prudence contribute to the good of society, then rent, interest, and profit are necessary and just rewards for the ownership and productive use of wealth.

Charles Robert Darwin (1809–82) was inspired by one economist while he in turn inspired others. He told how, while reading Malthus on population, it suddenly occurred to him that in the struggle for existence that he had everywhere observed favorable variations tend to be preserved and unfavorable ones to be destroyed. The result is the formation of new species. Darwin claimed to have applied the doctrine of Malthus to the whole animal and vegetable kingdoms.

Darwin's key ideas were the struggle for existence, natural selection based on individual differences, the survival of the fittest, and the evolution of species. These concepts influenced some, but by no means all, of the streams and schools of economic thought. Two strands of economic thought can be directly related to the Darwinian revolution: the evolutionary approach to economics and social Darwinism. The evolutionary approach was incorporated in the thinking of Marxism (see Chapters 9 and 10), the German historical school (see Chapter 11), and the institutional school (see Chapter 19). Outstanding social Darwinists were the English philosopher Herbert Spencer and the American economist and sociologist William Graham Sumner.

The social Darwinists applied only one aspect of Darwin's ideas to human affairs: They emphasized not evolution but the struggle for existence and the survival of the fittest. They argued that the pressure of subsistence on population has a beneficent effect on the progress of the human race, for it places a premium on skill, intelligence, self-control, and the power to adapt through technological innovation. Unrestricted competition and the struggle for existence enable the best people to survive. The poor, the sick, the uneducated, and the hungry are inferior beings, and therefore they should not blame society or the more affluent classes for their unhappy condition. If their situation is ameliorated through social action, less fit people will survive and reproduce themselves, and the race will degenerate. In international affairs, the struggle for colonies and spheres of influence was depicted as the more fit races surviving in competition against inferior peoples.

Social Darwinism virtually ended by World War I, though some of its ideas linger on. The world struggle was no longer between the "superior" Westerners and "inferior" indigenous people in the underdeveloped areas. Instead, the war was fought among Western societies themselves. Social Darwinism had justified militarism, and there was a revulsion against militarism after World War I. Some people pointed out that war killed the most fit and was therefore dysgenic instead of eugenic. Finally, social Darwinism was killed by the poor, the "unfit," who found themselves fit enough to insist upon and win certain improvements in their condition.

It is interesting to note that the social Darwinists came to the same conclusion as the classical economists who based themselves on Newton—that laissez faire is the best policy. One must not interfere with natural processes. The social laws derived from Newton were based on the natural order as illustrated by the solar system. The social Darwinists based their social laws on the natural order as developed through biology. Both ideas accepted the environment as given and not to be manipulated or changed; both ideas were suitable for those who had no basic grievance against the existing order.

The marginalist school, which arose almost simultaneously with Darwinism, remained impervious to Darwinian thinking. Its basic orientation was Newtonian. It was static in its thinking and it expressed economic laws that it considered universally applicable. Without interference by government, natural law would ensure the best of all possible worlds.

Albert Einstein (1879–1955) triggered a third great revolution in human thought. His theory of relativity, first presented to the world in 1905, has interesting implications for the social sciences. Yet it is doubtful if his influence in the social sciences is as great as Newton's and Darwin's influence has proved to be. First, Einstein's theory may not yet have had time to spread its full influence. Second, with the explosion of knowledge, learning has become more and more specialized and compartmentalized; people are less familiar than in earlier times with what is going on in disciplines other than their own. Third, the social sciences to some extent have developed a relativistic approach of their own independently of Einstein. Let us thus examine parallel developments in physics and in the social sciences that show certain common methodologies and patterns of thought.

In Einstein's theory of relativity one finds that what is "true" for an observer within one system may not be true for an observer in another system if the two systems are moving relative to one another. Imagine one observer in a train (a moving system) and another observer outside (a stationary system). From the exact middle of the train, two light rays are flashed at the same instant forward and back. For both observers the light rays travel from their source at identical speeds (approximately 186,000 miles per second), because the velocity of light is constant throughout the universe and is not affected either by the motion of its source or the motion of the receiver. Will the light rays strike the front and rear walls of the train simultaneously? From the point of view of the observer within the train the two events will be simultaneous. From the point of the observer on the ground they will not be simultaneous. Even though both rays of light travel at the same speed, the front wall of the train is moving away from the light, and the rear wall is moving toward the light. Therefore the light ray will strike the rear wall first. What is true for the observer in one system is not true for the observer in another.

Take another example of relativity. Imagine a freely falling elevator. The passengers in the elevator are in one system. Observers on the outside are in a different system. Suppose we drill two holes in opposite walls of the elevator at exactly the same height. We place a flashlight in one hole and shine the light toward the other while the elevator is falling. As the passengers see it, the light from the flashlight will travel in a straight line at constant speed, and it will strike the opposite hole.

The outside observer sees the elevator falling because the gravitational field operates on it without any impediments. He sees the light ray coming from the flashlight in one wall and reaching the hole in the opposite wall. But during the infinitesimal interval of time that it takes the light ray to travel from one wall of the elevator to the other, the outside observer sees the entire elevator move down. The light appears to leave the elevator through the hole, but at a lower level than its source. The light ray, instead of traveling in a straight line, is curved in the gravitational field. The truth from the point of view of observers in one system is not true for observers of another system.

In the social sciences, the independent development of a relativistic outlook is illustrated by such useful clichés as "frame of reference," "value system," and "point of view." Anthropologists have probably led other social scientists in this respect. What would we think of a man who ate the flesh of his dead father? Would we not regard such an act as bestial and revolting? The anthropologist Bronislaw Malinowski reported that the Melanesians of New Guinea followed such practices with some of their dead. They may have felt as much aversion toward doing it as we would, for they were filled with extreme repugnance and dread and usually suffered violent fits of vomiting. Moreover, in recent times they were severely penalized by the white government when caught performing such acts. Yet to the Melanesians of New Guinea, eating the flesh of the dead was a sacred duty, for it represented a supreme act of reverence, love, devotion, and self-sacrifice. The act is disgusting or noble, depending on one's point of view.

This relativistic point of view can be applied to ethics. Imagine a small union struggling to gain a toe-hold in a company, operating in secret because its members face reprisals if their membership is discovered. Suppose that the membership secretary of the union is secretly employed by the company to turn over to it union membership lists and campaign plans. Is he a traitor, a scab, a rat? Or is he a trustworthy employee of the company, a loyal member of one big family that is striving to exclude the disruptive influence of outside agitators?

Imagine another case. A millionaire's butler overhears plans for the grand strategy to smash a union. He rushes to the union officials to warn them, and they are able to forestall the scheme. Is the butler a traitor, a rat, a snake? Or is he a loyal son of the working class, a hero, a paragon of virtue? Perhaps right and wrong depend on one's frame of reference.

This relativistic approach has been applied to economics, and it should guide economic thinking more than it does. Will digging holes in the ground, which Keynes advocated, enrich or impoverish us? That depends on the alternatives. If the alternative is unemployment, digging holes will enrich us. If the alternative is doing useful work, digging holes will tend to impoverish us.

The revolution associated with Einstein (although he did not agree with all of it) has also encouraged economists to think in dynamic, probabilistic frames of reference. The old static system envisioned change occurring in definable patterns; the new mathematical economic systems have opened up a range of possible outcomes of events, each associated with a probability statement. The most frequent use of this approach is in the newly developed models of oligopoly markets. The analysis is called game theory.

There are certain dangers in the doctrine of cultural relativism, or "situation ethics," or "the new morality." Accepting the customs and mores of any society without critical judgment leads to a conformity that tends to stifle necessary or desirable changes. Are we to accept as quaint such social customs as the slaughter of Indians in America to take their land, or the radicals in Indonesia to eliminate them from political life, or the Jews in Nazi Germany, among other reasons, to execute the Nazi racist ideology? Does cultural relativism abjure all value judgments? Obviously it cannot.

Cultural relativism can help us understand other cultures. Also, by providing a broad humanistic framework and some knowledge of the necessary and inevitable, it allows us to judge human conduct. For example, an aboriginal Australian woman who once had to travel far to find food and water could not carry more than one child. A second child born before its younger sibling was able to walk long distances and had to be sent back to the spirit world to await a more suitable time to be born again. This we can accept. But in today's affluent United States or Australia, the murder of a child for lack of food would be criminal not only on the part of the murderer but on the part of a society that would permit such an unnecessary tragedy to occur.

Why Study Economics and Its History?

This book has examined a minute segment of intellectual and social history over the last four hundred years. Students who have struggled over this difficult terrain may well ask, "Was it worth the effort? Why study economic theory? Why study its history?"

Many answers come to mind. Two major reasons, other than the personal advantages that might be gained, justify the study of economic theory. First, we gain understanding of how an economy works, what makes it hang together and function. Second, given the economic goals that a society chooses, theory can help us reach these goals. We can make faster progress—however we define "progress"—through a knowledge of theory.

Why study the history of economic thought? Such a study above all gives us perspective and understanding of our past, of changing ideas and problems, of our direction of movement. Our study seems to confirm our initial idea that theory arises out of society's needs and problems. We can appreciate the fact that no group has a monopoly on the truth, and many groups have contributed to the richness and diversity of our intellectual, cultural, and material inheritance. A study of the evolution of economic thought and the changing social background associated with it can illuminate changes in other areas of concern to us, such as politics, art, literature, music, philosophy, and science. There is, of course, a reciprocal relationship here, so that a better understanding of the latter areas of knowledge can help explain changing economic ideas.

The vast growth of our statistical knowledge can provide a closer check on irresponsible generalizations. Hopefully we will make fewer errors in the future than in the past in guiding our economies. Yet there remains a vast *terra incognita* of unsolved problems and unanswered questions. Much progress remains to be achieved.

Unfortunately the accumulation of knowledge and understanding does not necessarily lead to a better world; change is not necessarily progress. We cannot agree on a definitive statement of what constitutes a better world or how progress should be defined. Even a perfect understanding of economic phenomena would leave us deeply divided. Suppose we all understand and agree that the operation of the gold standard will result in stable foreign exchange rates provided that money prices and wage rates are flexible. This means that the gold standard will not function well where unions, being powerful, prevent wages and prices from falling when the exchange rate requires that they should. This analytical statement can be interpreted either as an argument against unions or as an argument against the gold standard. Even if all people were perfectly well informed on economic theory, disagreements and conflicts would continue because of different ideas about what is good and what is bad, which goals should be adopted and which rejected, and what the priority of each goal should be.

Even if we agree on goals for the economy, we will disagree on their relative importance. Suppose everybody agrees that all people should have adequate diets. We may also want people to have incentives to do good work, and the two goals may be incompatible to some extent; we must then decide which should have the higher priority. Similarly, while we can all agree on the desirability of adequate diets, the vegetarian would say that avoiding the slaughter of animals should take an even higher priority, while the cannibal might argue that he is merely implementing what we all agree is a worthy aim—a well-fed people.

In certain combinations of circumstances, the desperately evil qualities of people rise to the surface. It is to be hoped that as our understanding grows, as our constructive cooperation with nature and our mastery over social problems increases, as the material well-being of the people rises, as our appreciation of the cultural, aesthetic, and intellectual facets of life enlarges, we shall become more civilized, more humane, and more considerate and understanding of our fellow inhabitants on this planet. If an understanding of economic theories and problems of the past and present contributes a modicum to achieving these goals, it will have been worth the effort.

Bibliography

BECKER, CARL L., *The Heavenly City of the Eighteenth-Century Philosophers*. New Haven, Conn.: Yale University Press, 1932.

DARWIN, CHARLES, *On the Origin of Species by Means of Natural Selection*. 1859.

HOFSTADTER, RICHARD, *Social Darwinism in American Thought*, 1860–1915. Philadelphia, Pa.: University of Pennsylvania Press, 1944.

INFELD, LEOPOLD, *Albert Einstein*. New York: Scribner's, 1950.

MALINOWSKI, BRONISLAW, *Magic, Science and Religion and Other Essays*. Glencoe, Ill.: Free Press, 1948.

SULLIVAN, J. W. N., *Isaac Newton, 1642–1727*. New York: Macmillan, 1938.

Index